NEURAL PLASTICITY AND MEMORY

FROM GENES TO BRAIN IMAGING

FRONTIERS IN NEUROSCIENCE

Series Editors
Sidney A. Simon, Ph.D.
Miguel A.L. Nicolelis, M.D., Ph.D.

Published Titles

Apoptosis in Neurobiology
Yusuf A. Hannun, M.D., Professor of Biomedical Research and Chairman/Department of Biochemistry and Molecular Biology, Medical University of South Carolina
Rose-Mary Boustany, M.D., tenured Associate Professor of Pediatrics and Neurobiology, Duke University Medical Center

Methods for Neural Ensemble Recordings
Miguel A.L. Nicolelis, M.D., Ph.D., Professor of Neurobiology and Biomedical Engineering, Duke University Medical Center

Methods of Behavioral Analysis in Neuroscience
Jerry J. Buccafusco, Ph.D., Alzheimer's Research Center, Professor of Pharmacology and Toxicology, Professor of Psychiatry and Health Behavior, Medical College of Georgia

Neural Prostheses for Restoration of Sensory and Motor Function
John K. Chapin, Ph.D., Professor of Physiology and Pharmacology, State University of New York Health Science Center
Karen A. Moxon, Ph.D., Assistant Professor/School of Biomedical Engineering, Science, and Health Systems, Drexel University

Computational Neuroscience: Realistic Modeling for Experimentalists
Eric DeSchutter, M.D., Ph.D., Professor/Department of Medicine, University of Antwerp

Methods in Pain Research
Lawrence Kruger, Ph.D., Professor of Neurobiology (Emeritus), UCLA School of Medicine and Brain Research Institute

Motor Neurobiology of the Spinal Cord
Timothy C. Cope, Ph.D., Professor of Physiology, Emory University School of Medicine

Nicotinic Receptors in the Nervous System
Edward D. Levin, Ph.D., Associate Professor/Department of Psychiatry and Pharmacology and Molecular Cancer Biology and Department of Psychiatry and Behavioral Sciences, Duke University School of Medicine

Methods in Genomic Neuroscience
Helmin R. Chin, Ph.D., Genetics Research Branch, NIMH, NIH
Steven O. Moldin, Ph.D, Genetics Research Branch, NIMH, NIH

Methods in Chemosensory Research
Sidney A. Simon, Ph.D., Professor of Neurobiology, Biomedical Engineering, and Anesthesiology, Duke University
Miguel A.L. Nicolelis, M.D., Ph.D., Professor of Neurobiology and Biomedical Engineering, Duke University

The Somatosensory System: Deciphering the Brain's Own Body Image
Randall J. Nelson, Ph.D., Professor of Anatomy and Neurobiology, University of Tennessee Health Sciences Center

The Superior Colliculus: New Approaches for Studying Sensorimotor Integration
William C. Hall, Ph.D., Department of Neuroscience, Duke University
Adonis Moschovakis, Ph.D., Institute of Applied and Computational Mathematics

New Concepts in Cerebral Ischemia
Rick C. S. Lin, Ph.D., Professor of Anatomy, University of Mississippi Medical Center

DNA Arrays: Technologies and Experimental Strategies
Elena Grigorenko, Ph.D., Technology Development Group, Millennium Pharmaceuticals

Methods for Alcohol-Related Neuroscience Research
Yuan Liu, Ph.D., National Institute of Neurological Disorders and Stroke, National Institutes of Health
David M. Lovinger, Ph.D., Laboratory of Integrative Neuroscience, NIAAA

***In Vivo* Optical Imaging of Brain Function**
Ron Frostig, Ph.D., Associate Professor/Department of Psychobiology, University of California, Irvine

Primate Audition: Behavior and Neurobiology
Asif A. Ghazanfar, Ph.D., Primate Cognitive Neuroscience Lab, Harvard University

Methods in Drug Abuse Research: Cellular and Circuit Level Analyses
Dr. Barry D. Waterhouse, Ph.D., MCP-Hahnemann University

Functional and Neural Mechanisms of Interval Timing
Warren H. Meck, Ph.D., Professor of Psychology, Duke University

Biomedical Imaging in Experimental Neuroscience
Nick Van Bruggen, Ph.D., Department of Neuroscience Genentech, Inc.
Timothy P.L. Roberts, Ph.D., Associate Professor, University of Toronto

The Primate Visual System
John H. Kaas, Department of Psychology, Vanderbilt University
Christine Collins, Department of Psychology, Vanderbilt University

Neurosteroid Effects in the Central Nervous System
Sheryl S. Smith, Ph.D., Department of Physiology, SUNY Health Science Center

Modern Neurosurgery: Clinical Translation of Neuroscience Advances
Dennis A. Turner, Department of Surgery, Division of Neurosurgery, Duke University Medical Center

Sleep: Circuits and Functions
Pierre-Hervé Luoou, Université Claude Bernard Lyon I

Methods in Insect Sensory Neuroscience
Thomas A. Christensen, Arizona Research Laboratories, Division of Neurobiology, University of Arizona

Motor Cortex in Voluntary Movements
Alexa Riehle, INCM-CNRS
Eilon Vaadia, The Hebrew University

Neural Plasticity in Adult Somatic Sensory-Motor Systems
Ford F. Ebner, Vanderbilt University

Advances in Vagal Afferent Neurobiology
Bradley J. Undem, Johns Hopkins Asthma Center
Daniel Weinreich, University of Maryland, Baltimore

The Dynamic Synapse: Molecular Methods in Ionotropic Receptor Biology
Josef T. Kittler, University College
Stephen J. Moss, University of Pennsylvania

Animal Models of Cognitive Impairment
Edward D. Levin, Duke University Medical Center
Jerry J. Buccafusco, Medical College of Georgia

The Role of the Nucleus of the Solitary Tract in Gustatory Processing
Robert M. Bradley, University of Michigan

Brain Aging: Models, Methods, and Mechanisms
David R. Riddle, Wake Forest University

Neural Plasticity and Memory: From Genes to Brain Imaging
Frederico Bermudez-Rattoni, National University of Mexico

NEURAL PLASTICITY AND MEMORY
FROM GENES TO BRAIN IMAGING

Federico Bermúdez-Rattoni
Universidad Nacional Autónoma de México

CRC Press
Taylor & Francis Group
Boca Raton London New York

CRC Press is an imprint of the
Taylor & Francis Group, an **informa** business

CRC Press
Taylor & Francis Group
6000 Broken Sound Parkway NW, Suite 300
Boca Raton, FL 33487-2742

First issued in paperback 2019

ISBN-13: 978-0-8493-9070-8 (hbk)
ISBN-13: 978-0-367-38922-2 (pbk)

Library of Congress Cataloging-in-Publication Data

Neural plasticity and memory : from genes to brain imaging / [editor] Federico Bermudez-Rattoni.
p. ; cm. -- (Frontiers in neuroscience)
"A CRC title."
Includes bibliographical references and index.
ISBN-13: 978-0-8493-9070-8 (alk. paper)
ISBN-10: 0-8493-9070-2 (alk. paper)
1. Memory--Physiological aspects. 2. Neuroplasticity. 3. Neurobiology. I. Bermúdez-Rattoni, Federico. II. Series: Frontiers in neuroscience (Boca Raton, Fla.)
[DNLM: 1. Memory--physiology. 2. Neuronal Plasticity--physiology. WL 102 N49345 2007]

QP406.N4813 2007
612.8'23312--dc22 2006032885

Visit the Taylor & Francis Web site at
http://www.taylorandfrancis.com

and the CRC Press Web site at
http://www.crcpress.com

Contents

Series Preface

Our goal in creating the Frontiers in Neuroscience Series is to present the insights of experts on emerging fields and theoretical concepts that are, or will be, at the vanguard of Neuroscience. Books in the series cover topics ranging from genetics, ion channels, apoptosis, electrodes, neural ensemble recordings in behaving animals and even robotics. The series also covers new and exciting multidisciplinary areas of brain research, such as computational neuroscience and neuroengineering, and describes breakthroughs in classical fields like behavioral neuroscience. We want these books to be the books every neuroscientist will use in order to get acquainted with new ideas and frontiers in brain research. These books can be given to graduate students and postdoctoral fellows when they are looking for guidance to start a new line of research.

Each book is edited by an expert and consists of chapters written by the leaders in a particular field. Books are richly illustrated and contain comprehensive bibliographies. Chapters provide substantial background material relevant to the particular subject. We hope that as the volumes become available the effort put in by us, the publisher, the book editors, and individual authors will contribute to the further development of brain research. The extent that we achieve this goal will be determined by the utility of these books.

Preface

The major goal of this book is to create a comprehensive multidisciplinary review and in-depth, up-to-date analysis of the study of the neurobiology of memory. The world's leading specialists share some of their scientific experience in the field, covering a wide range of topics relating how molecular, genetic, behavioral, and brain imaging techniques have been used to investigate the ways by which cellular and brain circuits may be modified by experience.

The opening chapter by James L. McGaugh, one of the leading researchers in the field of memory consolidation and brain plasticity, offers an interesting introduction to the main issues. McGaugh gives us a historical overview of the field of memory consolidation, formally initiated 100 years ago, and its enormous expansion during the last three decades. His chapter emphasizes the methodological and conceptual problems inherent to the study at different levels of analysis, from the cellular mechanisms to the systems interactions for the representation of long-lasting memories.

Subsequent chapters contain interesting reviews of the putative genetic and molecular mechanisms of cell plasticity. Several authors elaborate on how experience may induce gene and protein expression and describe the role of experience in synaptic plasticity underlying memory formation. Specifically, the authors reveal how cell circuitry is modified and modulated by electrical activity or exposure to novel spatial environments. Martha L. Escobar and Brian Derrick review work on the synaptic communication elements described as susceptible to be modified by activity and experience. In particular, they give us a journey through up-to-date studies on one of the more exciting and heuristic models of brain plasticity, long-term potentiation (LTP) and its reverse counterpart, long-term depression (LTD). In addition, they put forward important questions regarding the hypothesis that these models may be related to brain plasticity underlying memory formation. Similarly, Victor Ramirez-Amaya summarizes recent research examining gene and protein expression in brain circuits. With up-to-date techniques, he proposes the steps by which a particular ensemble of neurons becomes interconnected with others after spatial experience and how these interconnected ensembles may stand for spatial memory representations in the hippocampus.

In the following chapters, several investigators address the question of how putative modifications of brain circuits and synaptic elements through experience can become relatively permanent and hence improve brain function. A major discovery made in recent decades was the seminal finding regarding brain modification after experience by Mark R. Rosenzweig. His chapter relates a historical approach to functional, biochemical, and structural transformations in some brain areas after exposure to enriched environments during animal development. Similarly, the chapter by Jerome L. Rekart, Matthew R. Holahan, and Aryeh Routtenberg reviews how brain modifications occur in both developing animals and in adult animals in relatively short periods after spatial learning. In particular, they explore how axonal sprouting and dendrite spine modification of adult animals are induced in certain areas of the hippocampus during spatial memory formation.

The following section includes interdisciplinary reviews focusing on how nerve cell circuitry, molecular expression, neurotransmitter release, and electrical activity are modified during the acquisition and consolidation of long-term memory. In "Electrophysiological Representation of Taste Memory," Takashi Yamamoto and Yasunobu Yasoshima examine ongoing research on cellular changes in specific brain areas induced by experience. In particular, they use a model known as conditioned taste aversion — one of the most useful and effective methods for enabling animals to remember tastes. They review electrical changes in several brain areas after taste-illness experiences; specifically, they analyze how cortical and amygdalar cells change their responses to tastes after aversive experiences. In the same area, Maria Isabel Miranda reviews the literature related to the release of several neurotransmitters as measured with state-of-the-art methodologies such as *in vivo* microdialysis during different stages of memory formation, i.e., acquisition, consolidation, and retrieval. Her chapter explains how differential releases of various neurotransmitters and molecules help us to better understand and eventually modify memory formation and retrieval.

Subsequent chapters deal with receptor activation and deactivation via different neurotransmitters that enable the intracellular activation of second messengers during memory formation. The chapters by Milagros Gallo and Roberto A. Prado-Alcalá and co-workers deal with brain inactivation at different stages of memory formation. In particular, Gallo tracks down the development of methodologies to analyze brain functions and memory formation such as reversible pharmacological inactivation, protein synthesis blockers, and genetic inactivation techniques. Prado-Alcalá and co-workers describe pharmacological approaches for the better understanding of the underlying mechanisms of aversively motivated memory formation and introduce the hypothesis that it is possible to protect the brain against the effects of amnesic drugs by enhancing learning experiences.

Interestingly, Iván Izquierdo and co-workers challenge the hypothesis that short-term and long-term memories are serial events leading to memory consolidation as previously proposed. Instead they suggest that short- and long-term memories are parallel events. This proposal is based on recent findings in which intracerebral administration of different agonists and antagonists of several neurotransmitters produce disruptive effects on short- but not on long-term memory in the same animals. In addition, they support this hypothesis with data showing differential susceptibilities of LTM and STM to extinction and novel experiences.

The chapter by Rodriguez-Ortiz and Bermúdez-Rattoni summarizes recent research examining the new and hot topic of post-retrieval memory consolidation, the so-called reconsolidation process. The reconsolidation hypothesis suggests that consolidated memory returns to a labile state similar to recently acquired memory each time it is retrieved and is susceptible to disruption by the same treatments or drugs that disrupt memory consolidation. Their chapter reviews and challenges the reconsolidation hypothesis by proposing that retrieved memory can be modified as part of a mechanism for incorporating updated information into previously consolidated long-term memory.

Chapters in the last section of the book summarize current research on the modulation and regulation of the formation and consolidation of memory by different neurotransmitters and stress hormones. In her chapter, Carmen Sandi proposes that the memory dysfunctions observed after stress and aging may be related. She provides interesting evidence that some of the neural mechanisms of memory disability from stress are similar to the neural mechanisms found in memory impairments from aging. The chapter by Christa K. McIntyre and Benno Roozendaal analyzes current research on the effects that systemic and central stress hormones have on the formation and consolidation of lingering memories and their possible therapeutic use for post-traumatic stress syndrome in humans.

At the end of this section, human research on memory formation is analyzed under the framework of immune system responses and brain communication; the methods by which brain sexual differences during emotional memory formation are studied via brain imaging techniques are also discussed.

For some time it has been known that stress and/or depression induce immune response deficits to diverse immunological challenges. In this regard, Gustavo Pacheco-López and Manfred Schedlowski unveil interesting aspects of the so-called neuro-immune associative learning. Their chapter reviews a number of experiments showing how animals and humans are able to associate immune responses with specific stimulus (environments, tastes) and modify their immune responses for longer periods.

A number of studies ranging from laboratory animals to humans indicate that endogenous stress hormones and the amygdala interact to modulate memory consolidation for emotional events. Within this framework, Larry Cahill explores brain activity modifications during memory formation with the use of newly and highly sophisticated methods of brain imaging in humans, namely positron emission tomography (PET) and functional magnetic resonance (FMR). In his chapter, he analyzes several lines of investigation leading to the conclusion that males and females do not process emotional memories in the same way in particular brain areas like the amygdala. He clarifies that sexual differences are very important and should be taken into account when exploring the neurobiology of emotional memory formation and eventually improve treatments for related clinical disorders.

I would like to thank Dr. James McGaugh and Dr. Roberto A. Prado-Alcalá for their valuable comments and ideas and Israela Balderas, Vanesa Cruz, and B.A. Yahan for reviewing certain chapters. I also want to thank Dr. Sid Simon and Dr. Miguel Nicolelis, editors of the Frontiers in Neuroscience series and Barbara E. Norwitz and Jill Jurgensen of Taylor & Francis Group for their support.

Editor

Federico Bermúdez-Rattoni studied medicine at the Universidad Nacional Autónoma de México (UNAM) in Mexico City and earned a Ph.D. from the University of California at Los Angeles. After obtaining his Ph.D., he established his laboratory in the Department of Neuroscience of the Instituto de Fisiología Celular at UNAM in Mexico City. Since his student days, he has worked on the molecular mechanisms involved in memory formation and neural plasticity.

During his career, Dr. Bermúdez-Rattoni has written nearly 100 papers and 3 books about his specialty. He has been invited to present about 80 speeches at symposiums and magisterial conferences around the world and has organized several international symposiums and courses related to his specialty. His laboratory has hosted graduate students, postdoctoral fellows, and visiting scientists from many countries.

For his outstanding contributions to his field, he has been elected a fellow of the John Simon Guggenheim Foundation of New York City and received the National University Prize and the Syntex Prize for medical research. He serves as chair of the Department of Neuroscience and is currently the vice president of the Mexican Society for Neurosciences and a visiting fellow of the Center for the Neurobiology of Learning and Memory at the University of California, Irvine.

Contributors

Federico Bermúdez-Rattoni
Instituto de Fisiologia Celular
Universidad Nacional Autónoma de Mexico
Mexico City, Mexico

Lia R.M. Bevilaqua
Center for Memory Research
Biomedical Research Institute
Pontifical Catholic University
Porto Alegre, Brazil
and
Memory Research Laboratory
Institute for Cell Biology and Neuroscience
University of Buenos Aires
Buenos Aires, Argentina

Larry Cahill
Center for the Neurobiology of Learning and Memory
Department of Neurology and Behavior
University of California
Irvine, California

Martín Cammarota
Center for Memory Research
Biomedical Research Institute
Pontifical Catholic University
Porto Alegre, Brazil
and
Memory Research Laboratory
Institute for Cell Biology and Neuroscience
University of Buenos Aires
Buenos Aires, Argentina

Brian Derrick
Department of Biology
University of Texas
San Antonio, Texas

Arnulfo Díaz-Trujillo
Instituto de Neurobiologia
Universidad Nacional Autónoma de México
Querétaro, Mexico

Harald Engler
Institute for Behavioral Sciences
Psychology and Behavioral Immunobiology
ETH Zurich
Zurich, Switzerland

Martha L. Escobar
División de Investigación y Estudios de Posgrado
Facultad de Psicologia
Universidad Nacional Autónoma de México
Mexico City, Mexico

Milagros Gallo
Institute of Neurosciences
Department of Experimental Psychology and Physiology of Behavior
University of Granada
Granada, Spain

María Eugenia Garín-Aguilar
Facultad de Estudios Superiores Iztacala
Tlalnepantla, Mexico

Matthew R. Holahan
Department of Psychology
Northwestern University
Evanston, Illinois

Iván Izquierdo
Center for Memory Research
Biomedical Research Institute
Pontifical Catholic University
Porto Alegre, Brazil
and
Memory Research Laboratory
Institute for Cell Biology and Neuroscience
University of Buenos Aires
Buenos Aires, Argentina

James L. McCaugh
Center for the Neurobiology of Learning and Memory
Department of Neurobiology and Behavior
University of California
Irvine, California

Christa K. McIntyre
School of Behavioral and Brain Sciences
University of Texas
Dallas, Texas

Jorge H. Medina
Center for Memory Research
Biomedical Research Institute
Pontifical Catholic University
Porto Alegre, Brazil
and
Memory Research Laboratory
Institute for Cell Biology and Neuroscience
University of Buenos Aires
Buenos Aires, Argentina

Maria Isabel Miranda
Instituto de Neurobiologia
Universidad Nacional Autónoma de México
Querétaro, Mexico

Maj-Britt Niemi
Institute for Behavioral Sciences
Psychology and Behavioral Immunobiology
ETH Zurich
Zurich, Switzerland

Gustavo Pacheco-López
Institute for Behavioral Sciences
Psychology and Behavioral Immunobiology
ETH Zurich
Zurich, Switzerland
and
CINVESTAV
Department of Physiology, Biophysics and Neurosciences
Mexico City, Mexico

Roberto A. Prado-Alcalá
Instituto de Neurobiologia
Universidad Nacional Autónoma de México
Querétaro, Mexico

Gina L. Quírarte
Instituto de Neurobiologia
Universidad Nacional Autónoma de México
Querétaro, Mexico

César Quiroz
Instituto de Neurobiologia
Universidad Nacional Autónoma de México
Querétaro, Mexico

Victor Ramirez-Amaya
Instituto de Neurobiologia
Universidad Nacional Autónoma de México
Querétaro, Mexico

Jerome L. Rekart
Department of Psychology
Northwestern University
Evanston, Illinois
and
McGovern Institute for Brain Research
Massachusetts Institute of Technology
Cambridge, Massachusetts

Selva Rivas-Arancibia
Facultad de Medicine
Universidad Nacional Autónoma de México
Querétaro, Mexico

Carlos J. Rodriguez-Ortiz
Instituto de Fisiologia Celular
Universidad Nacional Autónoma de Mexico
Mexico City, Mexico

Benno Roozendaal
Center for the Neurobiology of Learning and Memory
University of California
Irvine, California

Mark R. Rosenzweig
Department of Psychology
University of California
Berkeley, California

Aryeh Routtenberg
Department of Psychology
and
Departments of Neurobiology and Physiology
Neuroscience Institute
Northwestern University
Evanston, Illinois

Rigoberto Salado-Castillo
Universidad de Panamá
Panama City, Panama

Carmen Sandi
Laboratory of Behavioral Genetics
Brain–Mind Institute
Swiss Federal Institute of Technology
Lausanne, Switzerland

Manfred Schedlowski
Institute for Behavioral Sciences
Psychology and Behavioral Immunobiology
ETH Zurich
Zurich, Switzerland

Takashi Yamamoto
Department of Behavior Physiology
Graduate School of Human Sciences
Osaka University
Osaka, Japan

Yasunobu Yasoshima
Department of Molecular Genetics
Institute of Biomedical Sciences
Fukushima Medical University School of Medicine
Fukushima, Japan

1 Searching for Memory in the Brain: Confronting the Collusion of Cells and Systems

James L. McGaugh

CONTENTS

How are memories made? How and where are they maintained? How are they retrieved and how do they initiate and control behavior? These questions have been asked for many centuries; the Egyptians, Greeks and Romans all offered suggested answers, both fanciful and wrong. The emergence of empirical scientific physiological inquiry in the 18th and 19th centuries created the understanding and acceptance that memory is the province of the brain, rather than the heart or other bodily organs. Memory was then firmly placed in the tissues of the brain and not in the ventricles — a previously popular notion. That previous idea was guided then, as ours are now, by facts and metaphors created by current technology. After all, before the 18th century a great deal was known about the functioning of fluids, but cells had not yet been discovered and studies of electrophysiology had not even been imagined.

1.1 ONE HUNDRED AND FIFTY YEARS OF CONTROVERSY

At the beginning of the 19th century, Franz Joseph Gall offered the then novel idea that different brain regions were responsible for different psychological functions including memory. As his colleague Spurzheim wrote, "It is certainly impossible to deny the mutual influence and dependence of the different organs; and, in fact none can insist upon this truth more than we [i.e., Gall and Spurzheim] do. There is, however, a great difference between the correct assertion, that the different organs exert a mutual influence upon each other, and the incorrect one, that each part does not exert its particular function."[1]

Although this conclusion may seem quite reasonable from our current perspectives, it was in the 19th century greeted with scientific skepticism and even ridicule. The knowledge, concepts, and technology required for investigating Gall's hypothesis were not yet available. Techniques for investigating brain functioning were not yet developed. Psychology as an empirically based science of human and animal behavior did not emerge until much later in the 19th century. Thus, the psychological functions to be attributed to specific brain regions were not derived from inquiry or systematic theory but, rather from lists of psychological personality traits and common sense attributes such as imagination, pride, affection, secretiveness, faith, destructiveness, conscience, love of offspring, wit, language, and superficial knowledge.

Pierre Flourens[2] subsequently used his newly developed technique of experimental ablation of brain tissue to mount a vigorous attack against Gall's ideas. In experiments with chickens and pigeons, he investigated the effects of brain ablations on the abilities of the animals to eat, walk, hear, see, or fly — functions quite observable and quite different from those of interest to Gall. In partial agreement with Gall he concluded that the brain does consist of some different and distinct organs; the cerebellum is the locus of locomotor coordination and the cerebrum is the seat of intelligence. However, importantly, in sharp disagreement with Gall he concluded[3] that, "Indeed, not only do all … the intellectual facilities reside exclusively in [the cerebrum], but they all reside there *coextensively*, and without any one being separable from the others" [italics mine].

Despite Broca's finding[4] of a small cortical area that is critical for speech as well as the conclusions of Fritsch and Hitzig[5] and Ferrier[6] based on their pioneering electrical stimulation and ablation studies, that different cortical regions are responsible for sensory and motor functions, Flouren's idea that all cognitive functions reside co-extensively in the brain continued to influence thinking well into the 20th century.

A second salvo against localizationalist views was initiated by S.I. Franz[7] whose findings based on cortical ablation of rat cortex suggested that learned habits are not located in any specific region of the cortex. In support of Flouren's views, Franz wrote, "… mental processes are not due to the independent activities of individual parts of the brain, but to the activities of the brain as a whole. …We have no facts which at present will enable us to locate the mental processes in the brain any better than they were located fifty years ago" [page 328].

For the next several decades Karl Lashley, who had worked with Franz, used the cortical ablation technique in his classic studies of cortical functioning in learning and, as is well known, found that the lesion-induced impairment was related to the size of the lesion and not its locus.[8,9] Lashley's research on brain functioning and memory was dominant during the first half of the 20th century and during that time the view that different brain regions may have different roles in learning and memory gained few supporters. In summarizing the status of research on brain and memory in the *Handbook of Experimental Psychology* in 1951, Clifford Morgan[10] concluded, "Why there is a correlation with mass, but not the locus of the lesion, is a vexing problem. ... Here let us simply note that there is no simple localization of memories in different parts of the brain" [page 784]. That conclusion ended an era.

1.2 THE GREAT DEBATE: WHAT IS LEARNED? KNOWLEDGE OR RESPONSES?

For almost a century and a half between Gall's proposals and Lashley's conclusions, little was learned about brain processes underlying learning and memory. Although there remained little doubt that memories are, at least in part, the products of cortical functioning, research at the middle of the 20th century provided few clear clues as to how the brain creates, maintains, and uses memories. Progress was made, however, in understanding learning and memory at a conceptual level. Although experimental studies of memory were in their infancy in the late 19th century, William James[11] managed to contribute rich insights: he offered the distinction between *primary* (recent) memory and *memory proper* or long-term memory, and by discussing memory and habits in widely separated chapters anticipated the distinction between procedural and cognitive learning and memory honored in current research and theory.[12,13]

The experimental studies of human memory launched by Herman Ebbinghaus[14] and Müller and Pilzecker,[15] as well as studies of animal learning pioneered by Pavlov[16,17] and Thorndike[18] at the turn of the century firmly established that learning and memory are subject to experimental inquiry.

For several decades, research stimulated by findings of Pavlovian and instrumental conditioning was, except for that of Lashley, largely devoid of inquiry about underlying brain processes. The great debate between Clark Hull[19] and Edward Tolman[20] that dominated animal (i.e., rat) research on learning from 1920 to 1950 centered on the issue of whether all learning was based on the acquisition of habits[19] *or* knowledge.[20] They did not base their theories on physiological hypotheses; both explicitly rejected the idea that understanding neurobiological mechanisms was required in order to provide an account of learning. As Tolman[20] put it, "A rat running a maze; a cat getting out of a puzzle box ... a psychologist reciting nonsense syllables ... these are the behaviors. ... And it must be noted that in mentioning no one of them have we referred to or, we blush to confess it, what were the exact muscles and glands, sensory nerves and motor nerves involved" [page 8].

Hull[19] suggested that in attempting to understand behavior it is helpful to "... consider the behaving organism as a completely self-maintaining robot, constructed of material as unlike ourselves as may be (and) to consider the various problems in behavior dynamics that must be solved" [page 27]. Clearly, Hull and Tolman were searching for rules that guide behavior, not mechanisms. Neither proposed any ideas about the involvement of the brain.

Experimental investigation of their hypotheses engaged the efforts of a great many disciples and other researchers for several decades in a battle that yielded no clear victory. In place-versus-response experiments commonly used as the "battlefield" for this conflict, rats were rewarded with food in one alley of a T-maze (starting from the south). To test whether the learning consisted of a turning response or, alternatively, knowledge of the location of the food, the starting arm of the T-maze was moved to the other (north) side of the alley. When tested, the animals would, thus have to make turning responses different from those used during training in order to enter the arm where they had been rewarded with food. In many experiments the rats demonstrated place learning, that is, they made turning responses different from the one acquired during training in order to go to the place where food had been located, but in other studies, they appeared to have learned responses. Although it became clear from studies such as these that rats can learn by acquiring knowledge of their environments and outcomes of their behavior, it also seemed clear that animals can acquire motor habits, as William James's writings implied and Hull insisted. Toward the end of this great debate, Tolman ultimately acknowledged that there is more than one kind of learning.[21] His conclusion was clearly prescient, as research in the subsequent decade revealed.

1.3 BRAIN SYSTEMS AND FORMS OF MEMORY

Events in 1949 signaled a new era in research on brain substrates of learning and memory. Hebb's book, *The Organization of Behavior*,[22] offered novel ideas that attempted to provide an understanding of how brain cells might cooperate to provide a basis for learning in a manner generally consistent with the evidence of functional equipotentiality suggested by his mentor, Lashley. Hebb proposed the idea (based on findings of Lorente de Nó[23]) that distributed assemblies of neurons in the brain activated by stimulation engage in reverberatory firing and provide a basis for recent memory. With repeated or sustained activation the cell assemblies stabilize and provide a basis for lasting memory. A key assumption required for Hebb's "dual-trace" hypothesis is that some change is required at junctions between neurons in order to provide the stabilization.

The process he proposed to account for that induced stability is now well-known as the Hebb hypothesis[22]; it states, "When an axon of cell A is near enough to excite a cell B and repeatedly or persistently takes part in its firing it, some growth process or metabolic change takes place in one or both cells such that A's efficiency, as one of the cells firing B, is increased" [page 62]. Initially, the main influence of Hebb's hypothesis was conceptual. It provided a way of thinking about how cells might participate in the creation of memories. Although Hebb's dual-trace hypothesis may have been the more original and important idea, his hypothesis accounting for stabilization clearly had, as discussed below, greater influence on research investigating neural mechanisms of memory.

For researchers interested in the neurobiology of memory in the early 1950s, Hebb's writings helped fill a void created by Lashley's failed quest for a locus of memory. The perseveration–consolidation hypothesis Müller and Pilzecker[15] proposed a half century earlier failed to generate much inquiry. Perhaps at least in part because of recognition that the consolidation hypothesis was very much like Hebb's dual-trace hypothesis, it gained increased attention after the publication of Hebb's book, but, by coincidence, another important influence appeared in 1949.

Carl Duncan published a seminal paper reporting that electroconvulsive shock stimulation applied to rats after they were trained induced retrograde amnesia.[24] The findings of this study and a great many subsequent studies using other kinds of treatments administered posttraining provided strong evidence that initially fragile memory traces stabilize or consolidate over time, as suggested by Müller and Pilzecker[15] and Hebb.[22,25] Such findings also stimulated studies investigating the neurobiological conditions that modulate (enhance as well as impair) memory consolidation[26] as well as mechanisms essential for such consolidation.

The search for the locus of memory traces was, of course, not abandoned when Lashley quit his quest, but rather was joined, as noted above, by efforts to understand how memories are formed as well as efforts to understand the participation of brain regions other than the cerebral cortex in creating and maintaining memories. In subsequent decades Richard Thompson's extensive research using brain ablation and many other techniques including electrophysiological recording of neuronal activity to investigate the involvement of the cerebellum in motor learning revealed that the interpositus nucleus deep within the cerebellum is a critical site of neuroplasticity mediating the learning of a discrete motor response, eyelid conditioning.[27] These more recent findings clearly served to indicate that, at the very least, the cerebral cortex does not have the sole responsibility for learning and memory. Moreover, the findings fit well with growing evidence that the systems engaged in learning and memory depend on the kind of information acquired.

Besides contributing the dual-trace hypothesis and the "Hebb synapse" Hebb made an additional crucially important contribution to research on memory: He suggested that his graduate student, Brenda Milner, conduct neuropsychological testing of patients of the neurosurgeon W.B. Scoville who were treated with bilateral medial temporal lobe surgery. Her studies, especially those based on patient H.M.,[28] revealed the remarkable and now well-known findings summarized in virtually every behavioral neuroscience textbook. Although the lesions resulted in blocked or significantly attenuated ability to form new explicit (declarative) memories they left William James's primary (recent) memory and memory proper (remote) intact. Additionally, and importantly, the learning of perceptual motor skills was unaffected. Subsequent studies determined that this type of amnesic syndrome is common to other patients who have medial temporal lobe damage.[29]

The findings of the selective effects of medial temporal lobe lesions on some aspects of memory but not others provided important new insights into memory and significantly changed the kinds of questions asked in subsequent research on memory.

Milner's findings provided a new target for investigations of brain regions and memory: the medial temporal lobe — especially the hippocampus. Initially, most animal experiments used only the technique (lesions of the medial temporal lobe) without applying the key information Milner's study revealed. Clearly, her findings suggested that some kinds of learning would be affected whereas others would not. That lesson was slowly learned. More than two decades later, Mortimer Mishkin published the first evidence of H.M.-like symptoms in monkeys with medial temporal lobe lesions.[30]

With renewed (or delayed) insight, research on medial temporal lobe involvement in memory focused on the effects of brain lesions on the learning of explicit and declarative information rather than on the learning of whatever kind of arbitrary task the specific experimenters typically favored. Experiments using rats found that hippocampal lesions impaired their ability to learn to swim to a specific location in a pool of water[31] and to remember the location of recently rewarded and non-rewarded alleys of a maze.[32] Such studies led to a growing acceptance of the idea that the hippocampus is involved in the learning of some kinds of information, especially those concerning contextual cues and the relationships among cues.[33]

What about the learning of perceptual–motor responses and habits, that do not seem to require contextual or relational learning? Studies investigating this issue found that lesions of the striatum impair such learning without affecting the learning of tasks impaired by disruption of hippocampal functioning.[34,35] Such findings provide an explanation of why the place-versus-response experiments provided evidence for both the Hull and Tolman theories. Inactivation of the hippocampus (with lidocaine) prior to testing prevented the expression of place learning acquired early in T-maze training. The inactivation of the caudate nucleus prior to testing prevented the expression of response learning acquired later in training.[36] The findings of such double-dissociation experiments provided compelling evidence of functional dissociation of brain regions mediating different forms of memory.

1.4 BRAIN SYSTEMS AND MEMORY FUNCTIONS

Milner's research findings reported soon after the middle of the 20th century triggered a new era of research on brain and memory in which experiments investigated the functions of brain systems in different forms of learning and memory. It became clear that the important issue of the locus of memory traces that dominated Lashley's research is but one of many that needed to be addressed in attempting to understand brain processes enabling memory. The finding that medial temporal lesions did not destroy either immediate or remote memories clearly indicated that the hippocampus and adjacent regions are not loci of very recent or long-term memory. That finding also suggested the novel and important idea that the medial temporal region is critically involved in the formation of new lasting memory located in other brain areas, with the cortex generally considered as a most likely site.[37–40]

Studies of the effects of selective brain lesions also suggested that the amygdala, another structure in the medial temporal region, is involved in learning induced by emotional arousal.[41] Extensive evidence suggests that the lateral nucleus of the amygdala is critically involved in such learning and may be a locus of neuroplasticity mediating the learning of associations of discrete cues with aversive stimulation.[42,43] Extensive evidence also indicates that activation of the basolateral complex of the amygdala (BLA) modulates the consolidation of different aspects or forms of memory processed in other brain regions.[44]

The findings also provide strong evidence that the BLA plays a key role in drug and hormone influences on memory consolidation. Duncan's paper (1949) reporting that posttraining ECS treatments induced retrograde amnesia stimulated investigations of the effects of posttraining drug administration on memory consolidation.[26,45] Many drugs including those acting on the GABAergic, opioid peptidergic, and noradrenergic systems are now known to enhance or impair consolidation.[46–48] Posttraining administration of epinephrine and corticosterone, the adrenal stress hormones normally released by emotion-arousing stimulation, also enhanced memory consolidation.[49] Lesions of the BLA or infusions of β-adrenoceptor antagonists into the BLA blocked drug and stress hormone influences on memory, and norepinephrine (NE) infused into the BLA posttraining enhanced retention.[50,51] Moreover, findings of experiments using inhibitory avoidance training indicate that such training induces the release of NE within the amygdala and that the increase in NE release induced by the training correlates highly with subsequent retention of the training.[52]

Several kinds of evidence support the hypothesis that activity of the BLA modulates memory consolidation by influencing the activity of other brain regions engaged in processing newly acquired memory.[53] First, drugs infused posttraining into the BLA enhanced memory assessed in a wide variety of training exercises known or thought to be mediated by different brain systems. These included spatial tasks and response tasks as well as fear conditioning and object recognition learning that were known or thought to be mediated by different brain systems.[51,54,55] Second, lesions of the stria terminalis, a major amygdala pathway, block the memory modulating effects of drugs administered systemically or intra-amygdally.[56–58] Third, lesions of the BLA or -adrenoceptor antagonists infused into the BLA prevented the memory modulatory effects of drugs infused posttraining into many other brain regions including the hippocampus, entorhinal cortex, rostral anterior cingulate cortex, and insular cortex.[59–62]

In the present context, the importance of such findings is that the BLA plays an important role in memory by serving to modulate the consolidation of long-term memory. Many other brain regions are also suggested as playing important roles of various kinds in memory, although, as with the BLA, they serve other functions as well.

The BLA has reciprocal connections with many brain regions including the medial prefrontal cortex and nucleus basalis, as well as the hippocampus. Thus, activation of the BLA also influences the functioning of these other systems involved in processing memory. The medial prefrontal cortex is known to be involved in working memory as well as the extinction of learned responses.[63–69] The acetylcholine supplied by activation of the nucleus basalis is critically important for cortical functioning such as that studied in the learning of the significance of auditory and taste and nociceptive information.[70–72]

Brain imaging techniques, especially positron emission tomography (PET) and functional magnetic resonance imagining (fMRI) techniques developed and refined in recent decades, have enabled investigation of brain systems activated by different forms and aspects of learning including the encoding and retrieval of different kinds of information. Studies using PET imaging as well as fMRI have found that the amygdala is activated by emotionally arousing information and that the degree of activation correlates very highly with subsequent memory of the arousing information.[73,74] Furthermore, the findings indicate that emotional arousal-induced activation of the amygdala is correlated with increases in hippocampal activity.[75,76] These findings are highly consistent with findings of the animals studies discussed above. Recent findings have also revealed that the amygdala and hippocampus interact with the cortex during the retrieval of emotionally arousing information.[77–79] Thus, brain imaging studies have provided significant additional evidence that the amygdala interacts with other brain regions in influencing memory.

1.5 CELLS AND SYSTEMS

The word *collusion* as used in the title of this chapter refers to its definition as a "secret understanding" or "playing together." As was fully recognized by Hebb, a major problem in the neurobiology of memory is discovering how the activation of neurons in the brain leads to the formation of knowledge and actions. How, that is, do cells collude with brain systems to produce memories that enable changes in behavior? Experience-induced changes in neuronal firing could, he proposed, provide a starting point for an explanation.

Another major discovery in recent decades was the seminal finding by Bliss and Lomo[80] that brief activation of hippocampal cells induced a change in the connectivity of existing synaptic connections with other cells — a finding now well-known as long-term potentiation (LTP). Various forms of LTP and the reverse effect, long-term depression (LTD) have been the subjects of extensive investigations for several decades. The quest of such research is to find synaptic mechanisms mediating the creation of Hebb synapses that may provide cellular bases for memory.

Progress in understanding molecular genetics has led to the development of new methods for investigating cellular processes mediating such neuroplasticity. However, creating memory involves more than changing synaptic connections. Sets of neurons must become interconnected with other sets of neurons to create organized systems that serve to represent memory. Although memory is no doubt based on experience-induced neuronal changes, the consequences of the changes must also depend on the functions of the brain system of which they are a part. Collusion of cells and systems is required.

Within a system, the firing of some cells is no doubt involved in inducing synaptic changes enabling memory. The activity of other cells that project to other brain regions can act to modify the functioning in those distal regions. For example, the firing of cells in the BLA of a cat is increased greatly by a single foot shock and the increased firing lasts at least 2 hours.[81] Such increased firing may serve to modulate memory processing in efferent brain regions including the entorhinal cortex and hippocampus.[82,83] In support of this view, electrophysiological studies have reported that noradrenergic stimulation of the BLA enhances the induction of long-term potentiation LTP in the hippocampus and that disruption of the BLA with lesions or a β-adrenoceptor antagonist blocks the induction of such LTP.[84,85] Other recent findings indicate that noradrenergic stimulation of the BLA that enhances memory consolidation also increases dorsal hippocampal levels of activity-regulated cytoskeletal Arc protein,[86] an immediate-early gene implicated in hippocampal synaptic plasticity and memory consolidation processes.[87] Additionally, inactivation of the BLA with infusions of lidocaine impairs memory consolidation and decreases

Arc protein levels in the dorsal hippocampus.[86] Clearly, the BLA is a major player in the collusion of cells and brain systems involved in memory consolidation.

1.6 TWO CENTURIES OF PROGRESS IN RESEARCH ON BRAIN AND MEMORY

As noted earlier in this chapter, a little over a century ago Franz[7] concluded that, "We have no facts which at present will enable us to locate the mental processes in the brain any better than they were located 50 years ago." Clearly many discoveries of the past century, especially in the last few decades, now suggest a very different conclusion. Many different brain regions are involved in different aspects and forms of memory. Also, Gall was proven at least partially correct in conclusions drawn almost two centuries ago. Although he was wrong about the kinds of cognitive functions represented in the brain, he was correct in his assertion that the systems of the brain very clearly interact and that each has specific responsibilities.[88] Discovering the different roles of brain systems is one of the major outcomes of research on memory in the past two centuries as well as one of the most important areas for future research.

REFERENCES

1. Spurzheim, J.G. *The Physiognomical System of Dr. Gall and Spurzheim.* Baldqan, Cradock and Joy, London, 1815.
2. Flourens, P. Reserches experimentales sur les proprietes et les functions du system nerveux dans les animaux vertebras, 2nd ed. J.B. Balliere, Paris, 1842.
3. Flourens, P. *Psychologie Comparee*, 2nd ed. Garnier Freres, Paris, 1864.
4. Broca, P. Sur le siège de las faculté du langage articulé. *Bull. Soc. Anthropol.*, 6, 337, 1861.
5. Fritsch, G. and Hitzig, E. Über die elektrische Erregbarkeit des Grosshirns. *Archiv. Für Anatomie und Physiologie*, 1870, 300–332; in von Bonin, G., Ed., *Some Papers on the Cerebral Cortex* (translated as *On the Electrical Excitability of the Cerebrum*), Charles C Thomas, Springfield, IL, 1960.
6. Ferrier, D. *The Functions of the Brain*, 2nd ed. Smith, Elder, London, 1886.
7. Franz, S.I. New phrenology. *Science*, 35, 321, 1912.
8. Lashley, K.S. *Brain Mechanisms and Intelligence.* University of Chicago Press, Chicago, 1929.
9. Lashley, K.S. In search of the engram. *Symp. Soc. Exp. Biol.,* 4, 454, 1950.
10. Morgan, C.T. The psychophysiology of learning. *Handbook of Experimental Psychology.* John Wiley & Sons, New York, 1951, pp. 758–788.
11. James, W. *Principles of Psychology.* Henry Holt, New York, 1890.
12. Packard, M.G. and Knowlton, B.J. Learning and memory functions of the basal ganglia. *Annu. Rev. Neurosci.,* 25, 563, 2002.
13. Poldrack, R.A. and Packard, M.G. Competition among multiple memory systems: converging evidence from animal and human brain studies. *Neuropsychologia*, 41, 145, 2003.
14. Ebbinghaus, H. *Über das Gedächtnis.* Drucker & Humblat, Leipzig, 1885.

15. Müeller, G.E. and Pilzecker, A. Experimentalle beitrage zur lehre vom gedachtnis. *Z. Psychol.*, 1, 1, 1900.
16. Pavlov, I.P. The physiology of digestion, in *Nobel Lectures: Physiology or Medicine, 1901–1921*. Elsevier, New York, 1967.
17. Pavlov, I.P. *Conditioned Reflexes*. Oxford University Press, London, 1927.
18. Thorndike, E.L. Animal intelligence: an experimental study of the associative processes in animals. *Psychol. Rev.,* Monogr. Suppl. 2, No. 8, 1898.
19. Hull, C.L. *Principles of Behavior.* Appleton-Century-Crofts, New York, 1943.
20. Tolman, E.C. *Purposive Behavior in Animals and Men.* Century, New York, 1932.
21. Tolman, E.C. There is more than one kind of learning. *Psychol. Rev.*, 144, 1949.
22. Hebb, D.O. *The Organization of Behavior.* John Wiley & Sons, New York, 1949.
23. Lorento de Nó, R. Analysis of the acitivity of chains of neurons. *J. Neurophysiol.*, 1, 207, 1938.
24. Duncan, C.P. The retroactive effect of electroshock on learning. *J. Comp. Physiolog. Psychol.,* 42, 32, 1949.
25. McGaugh, J.L. and Herz, M.J. *Memory Consolidation.* Albion, San Francisco, 1972.
26. McGaugh, J.L. Time-dependent processes in memory storage. *Science*, 153, 1351, 1966.
27. Thompson, R.F. In search of memory traces. *Annu. Rev. Neurosci.*, 56, 1, 2005.
28. Scoville, W.B. and Milner, B. Loss of recent memory after bilateral hippocampal lesions. *J. Neurol. Neurosurg. Psychiatr.*, 20, 11, 1957.
29. Squire, L.R., Stark, C.E. and Clark, R.E. The medial temporal lobe. *Annu. Rev. Neurosci.*, 27, 279, 2004.
30. Mishkin, M. Memory in monkeys severely impaired by combined but not by separate removal of amygdala and hippocampus. *Nature*, 273, 297, 1978.
31. Morris, R.G., Garrud, P., Rawlins, J.N., and O'Keefe, J. Place navigation impaired in rats with hippocampal lesions. *Nature*, 297, 681, 1982.
32. Olton, D.S., Mazes, maps, and memory. *Am. Psychol.*, 34, 583, 1979.
33. Eichenbaum, H. How does the brain organize memories? *Science,* 277, 330, 1997.
34. Packard, M.G., Hirsh, R., and White, N.M. Differential effects of fornix and caudate nucleus lesions on two radial maze tasks: evidence for multiple memory systems. *J. Neurosci.*, 9, 1465, 1989.
35. White, N.M. and McDonald, R.J. Multiple parallel memory systems in the brain of the rat. *Neurobiol. Learn. Mem.*, 77, 125, 2002.
36. Packard, M.G. and McGaugh, J.L. Inactivation of hippocampus or caudate nucleus with lidocaine differentially affects expression of place and response learning. *Neurobiol. Learn. Mem.*, 65, 65, 1996.
37. Squire, L.R. and Alvarez, P. Retrograde amnesia and memory consolidation: a neurobiological perspective. *Curr. Opin. Neurobiol.*, 5, 169, 1995.
38. Tyler, T.J. and DiScenna, P. The hippocampal memory indexing theory. *Behav. Neurosci.*, 100, 147, 1986.
39. McClelland, B.L., McNaughton, J.L., and O'Reilly, R.C. Why there are complementary learning systems in the hippocampus and neocortex: Insights from the successes and failures of connectionist models of learning and memory. *Psychol. Rev.*, 102, 419, 1995.
40. Buchel, C., Morris, J., Dolan, R.J., and Friston, K.J. Brain systems mediating aversive conditioning: an event-related fMRI study. *Neuron*, 20, 947, 1998.
41. Weiskrantz L. Behavioral changes associated with ablation of the amygdaloid complex in monkeys. *J. Comp. Physiol. Psychol.*, 49, 381, 1956.
42. LeDoux, J.E. Emotion circuits in the brain. *Annu. Rev. Neurosci.*, 23, 255, 2000.

43. Davis, M. The role of the amygdala in conditioned and unconditioned fear and anxiety, in Aggleton, J.P., Ed., *The Amygdala*, Oxford University Press, Oxford, 2000.
44. McGaugh, J.L. Memory consolidation and the amygdala: a systems perspective. *TINS*, 25, 456, 2002.
45. McGaugh, J.L. and Petrinovich, L.F. Effects of drugs on learning and memory. *Int. Rev. Neurobiol.*, 8, 13, 1965.
46. McGaugh, J.L., Introini-Collison, I.B., Cahill, L., Kim, M., and Liang, K.C. Involvement of the amygdala in neuromodulatory influences on memory storage, in Aggleton, J.P., Ed., *The Amygdala*, John Wiley & Sons, New York, 1992, pp. 431–451.
47. McGaugh, J.L. et al. Involvement of the amygdala in the regulation of memory storage, in McGaugh, J.L. et al., Eds., *Plasticity in the Central Nervous System: Learning and Memory*, Lawrence Erlbaum Associates, Hillsdale, NJ, 1995, pp. 17–40.
48. McGaugh, J.L. and Cahill, L. Emotion and memory: central and peripheral contributions, in Davidson, R.J. et al., Eds., *Handbook of Affective Science*, Oxford University Press, Oxford, 2002, pp. 93–116.
49. McGaugh, J.L. and Roozendaal, B. Role of adrenal stress hormones in forming lasting memories in the brain. *Curr. Opin. Neurobiol.*, 12, 205, 2002.
50. Hatfield, T. and McGaugh, J.L. Norepinephrine infused into the basolateral amygdala posttraining enhances retention in a spatial water maze task. *Neurobiol. Learn. Mem.*, 71, 232, 1999.
51. LaLumiere, R.T., Buen, T.V., and McGaugh, J.L. Posttraining intra-basolateral amygdala infusions of norepinephrine enhance consolidation of memory for contextual fear conditioning. *J. Neurosci.*, 23, 6754, 2003.
52. McIntyre, C.K., Hatfield, T. and McGaugh, J.L. Amygdala norepinephrine levels after training predict inhibitory avoidance retention performance in rats. *Eur. J. Neurosci.*, 16, 1223, 2002.
53. McGaugh, J.L. The amygdala modulates the consolidation of memories of emotionally arousing experiences. *Annu. Rev. Neurosci.*, 27, 1, 2004.
54. Hatfield, T. and McGaugh, J.L. Norepinephrine infused into the basolateral amygdala posttraining enhances retention in a spatial water maze task. *Neurobiol. Learn. Mem.*, 71, 232, 1999.
55. Roozendaal, B., Okuda, S., Van der Zee, E.A., and McGaugh, J.L. Glucocorticoid enhancement of memory requires arousal-induced noradrenergic activation in the basolateral amygdala. *Proc. Natl. Acad. Sci. USA*, 103, 6741, 2006.
56. Introini-Collison, I.B., Arai, Y., and McGaugh, J.L. Stria terminalis lesions attenuate effects of posttraining oxotremorine and atropine on retention. *Psychobiology*, 17, 397, 1989.
57. Liang, K.C., McGaugh, J.L. and Yao, H.-Y. Involvement of amygdala pathways in the influence of posttraining amygdala norepinephrine and peripheral epinephrine on memory storage. *Brain Res.*, 508, 225, 1990.
58. Roozendaal, B. and McGaugh, J.L. The memory-modulatory effects of glucocorticoids depend on an intact stria terminalis. *Brain Res.*, 709, 243, 1996.
59. Roozendaal, B. and McGaugh, J.L. Basolateral amygdala lesions block the memory-enhancing effect of glucocorticoid administration in the dorsal hippocampus of rats. *Eur. J. Neurosci.*, 9, 76, 1997.
60. Roozendaal, B., Nguyen, B.T., Power, A., and McGaugh, J.L. Basolateral amygdala noradrenergic influence enables enhancement of memory consolidation induced by hippocampal glucocorticoid receptor activation. *Proc. Natl. Acad. Sci. USA*, 96, 11642, 1999.

61. Roesler, R., Roozendaal, B., and McGaugh, J.L. Basolateral amygdala lesions block the memory-enhancing effect of 8-Br-cAMP infused into the entorhinal cortex of rats after training. *Eur. J. Neurosci.*, 15, 905, 2002.
62. Miranda, M.I. and McGaugh, J.L. Enhancement of inhibitory avoidance and conditioned taste aversion memory with insular cortex infusions of 8-Br-cAMP: involvement of the basolateral amygdala. *Learn. Mem.*, 11, 312, 2004.
63. Fuster, J.M. *Memory in the Cerebral Cortex: An Empirical Approach to the Neural Networks in the Human and Nonhuman Primate*. MIT Press, Cambridge, MA, 1995.
64. Fuster, J.M. Distributed memory for both short and long term. *Neurobiol. Learn. Mem.*, 70, 268, 1998.
65. Hikosaka, O., Miyashita, K., Miyachi, S., Sakai, K., and Lu, X. Differential roles of the frontal cortex, basal ganglia and cerebellum in visuomotor sequence learning. *Neurobiol. Learn. Mem.*, 70, 137, 1998.
66. Roozendaal, B, Okuda, S., de Quervain, D.J.F., and McGaugh, J.L. Glucocorticoids interact with emotion-induced noradrenergic activation in influencing different memory functions. *Neuroscience*, 138, 901, 2006.
67. Arnsten, A.F. and Li, B.M. Neurobiology of executive functions: catecholamine influences on prefrontal cortical functions. *Biol. Psychiatr.*, 57, 1377, 2005.
68. Quirk, G.J., Garcia, R., and Gonzalez-Lima, F. Prefrontal mechanisms in extinction of conditioned fear. *Biol. Psychiatr.*, 60, 337, 2006
69. Milad, M.R. and Quirk, G.J. Neurons in medial prefrontal cortex signal memory for fear extinction. *Nature*, 420, 70, 2002.
70. Weinberger, N.M. The nucleus basalis and memory codes auditory cortical plasticity and the induction of specific, associative behavioral memory. *Neurobiol. Learn. Mem.*, 80, 268, 2003.
71. Bermudez-Rattoni, F., Okuda, S., Roozendaal, B., and McGaugh, J.L. Insular cortex is involved in consolidation of object recognition memory. *Learn. Mem.*, 12, 447, 2005.
72. Malin, E. and McGaugh, J.L. Differential involvement of the hippocampus, anterior cingulate cortex and basolateral amygdala in memory for context and footshock. *Proc. Natl. Acad. Sci. USA*, 103, 1959, 2006.
73. Cahill L. et al. Amygdala activity at encoding correlated with long-term, free recall of emotional information. *Proc. Natl. Acad. Sci. USA*, 93, 8016, 1996.
74. Canli T., Zhao Z., Brewer J., Gabrieli J.D., and Cahill L. Event-related activation in the human amygdala associates with later memory for individual emotional experience. *J. Neurosci.,* 20, RC99, 2000.
75. Kilpatrick L. and Cahill L. Amygdala modulation of parahippocampal and frontal regions during emotionally influenced memory storage. *NeuroImage,* 20, 2091, 2003.
76. LaBar, K.S. and Cabezz, R. Cognitive neuroscience of emotional memory. *Nat. Rev. Neurosci,.* 7, 54, 2006.
77. Smith, A.P., Stephan. K.E., Rugg, M.D., and Dolan, R.J. Task and content modulate amygdala-hippocampal connectivity in emotional retrieval. *Neuron*, 49, 631, 2006.
78. Greenberg, D.L. et al. Co-activation of the amygdala hippocampus and inferior frontal gyrus during autobiographical memory retrieval. *Neuropsychologia*, 43, 659, 2005.
79. Dolcos, F., LaBar, K.S., and Cabeza, R. Remembering one year later: role of the amygdala and the medial temporal lobe memory system in retrieving emotional memories. *Proc. Natl. Acad. Sci. USA*, 102, 2626, 2005.
80. Bliss, T.V.P. and Lomo, T. Long-lasting potentiation of synaptic transmission in the dentate gyrus of the anaesthetized rabbit following stimulation of the perforant path. *J. Physiol.,* 232, 331, 1973.

81. Pelletier, J.G., Likhtik, E., Filali, M., and Paré, D. Lasting increases in basolateral amygdala activity after emotional arousal: implications for facilitated consolidation of emotional memories. *Learn. Mem.*, 12, 96, 2005.
82. Paré, D., Collins, D.R., and Pelletier, J.G. Amygdala oscillations and the consolidation of emotional memories. *TICS*, 6, 306, 2002.
83. Pelletier, J.G. and Paré, D. Role of amygdala oscillations in the consolidation of emotional memories. *Biol. Psychiatr.*, 55, 559, 2004.
84. Ikegaya, Y, Saito, H., and Abe, K., Requirement of basolateral amygdala neuron activity for the induction of long-term potentiation in the dentate gyrus in vivo. *Brain Res.*, 671, 351, 1995.
85. Ikegaya, Y, Nakanishi, K., Saito, H., and Abe, K., Amygdala beta-noradrenergic influence on hippocampal long-term potentiation in vivo. *Neuroreport*, 8, 3143, 1997.
86. McIntyre, C.K. et al. Memory-influencing intra-basolateral amygdala drug infusions modulate expression of Arc protein in the hippocampus. *Proc. Natl. Acad. Sci. USA.*, 102, 10718, 2005.
87. Guzowski, J.F. et al. Inhibition of activity-dependent arc protein expression in the rat hippocampus impairs the maintenance of long-term potentiation and consolidation of long-term memory. *J. Neurosci.*, 20, 3993, 2000.
88. Gold, P.E. Coordination of multiple memory systems. *Neurobiol. Learn. Mem.*, 82, 230, 2004.

2 Long-Term Potentiation and Depression as Putative Mechanisms for Memory Formation

Martha L. Escobar and Brian Derrick

CONTENTS

2.1 INTRODUCTION

Experience-dependent changes in behavior are thought to derive from lasting changes in synaptic strength and neuronal excitability. This chapter attempts an overview of the mechanisms underlying induction and maintenance of long-lasting activity-dependent synaptic modifications as at least one of the key mechanisms by which experiences modify neural circuit behavior. We consider the important yet complex regulation of long-term potentiation and depression by prior synaptic activity as well as the influence of some neurotrophins as regulators of synaptic efficacy crucial issues concerning the contribution of long-lasting forms of synaptic modification to learning and memory.

2.2 LONG-LASTING FORMS OF SYNAPTIC MODIFICATION: METHODOLOGICAL APPROACH

2.2.1 LONG-TERM POTENTIATION (LTP)

Tim Bliss and Terje Lomo[1,2] first reported the phenomenon of long-term potentiation (LTP), an increase in synaptic efficacy following synaptic activity, over 30 years ago. Since then, LTP has generated enormous interest as a potential mechanism of memory, primarily because it exhibits numerous properties expected of a synaptic associative memory mechanism, such as rapid induction, synapse specificity, associative interactions, persistence, and dependence on correlated synaptic activity. Given these important features, LTP remains only a model of the synaptic and cellular events that may underlie memory formation. Although LTP-like phenomena are appealing as models of the synaptic changes in learning and memory, one question crucial to this research is the contribution of LTP to learning and memory. While this issue has been the subject of numerous behavioral studies since LTP was discovered, more recent studies combining advanced methodologies offer new avenues and compelling data that offer the potential for defining the role of LTP in hippocampal function, learning, and memory.

Many features of LTP as a phenomenon make it a compelling candidate for the synaptic processes underlying neural information storage. First, LTP is induced rapidly. Soon after its induction (which usually involves postsynaptic depolarization induced by high frequency stimulation of a sufficient number of afferents), LTP appears within minutes. In some situations, the actual development of LTP is obscured by short-term potentiation (STP), an exponentially decaying increase in synaptic strength that appears to involve NMDA receptors as well,[3] but decays within 5 to 20 min (Figure 2.1). Prior evaluations of STP and LTP determined the onset of LTP by subtracting STP. Hanse and Gustafsson[4] suggest that it develops incrementally, reaching asymptotic levels by approximately 5 to 20 sec, depending upon the synapse studied.

LTP is not always rapidly expressed and can show incremental growth over a period of 10 to 20 min. The precise reasons why such incremental LTP is observed in some cases and not others is unknown.

Our experience is that the methodology used to induce LTP can determine initial LTP magnitude. For example, rapid LTP induction is seen with direct stimulation of afferents in both commissural and perforant path inputs to the CA3 region. However, a slowly developing, incremental LTP often is observed when LTP is induced in an associative manner by pairing weak commissural or perforant path trains with a strong tetanus to a convergent CA3 afferent system.[5] Thus, while LTP develops relatively rapidly, it can take some time to develop fully. In line with these observations, the emergence of both *place cells* in the CA1 region and the appearance of *place field expansion*, a gradual increase in the place field that reflects earlier firing of place cells with experience, also occur over a duration of 5 to 10 min. This is a crucial point because these processes are thought to involve associative synaptic changes and possibly LTP.[6,7]

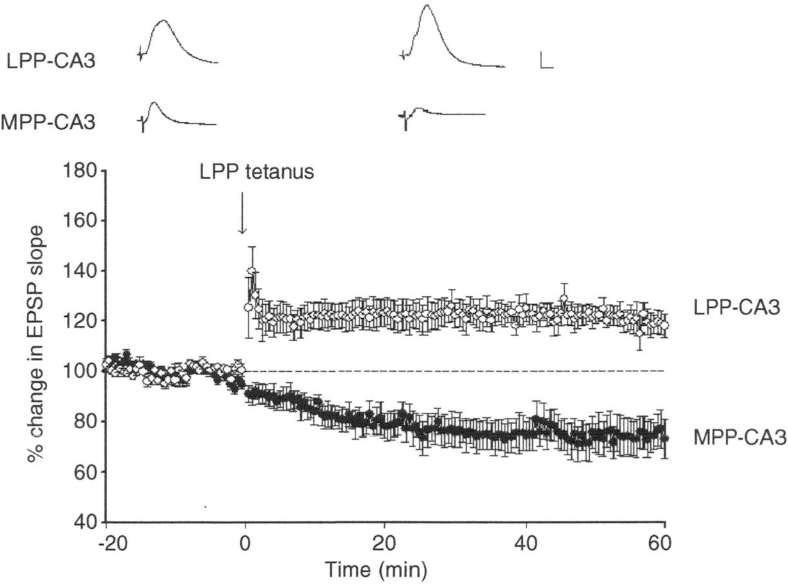

FIGURE 2.1 LTP and heterosynaptic LTD in the dentate gyrus. Point plot representing magnitude of extracellular synaptic responses (slope of field EPSP, mV/ms) in awake behaving rats evoked once every minute. High frequency stimulation of the lateral perforant pathway (arrow) induces STP and LTP of lateral perforant path dentate field synaptic responses (○). By contrast, synaptic responses evoked in the medial perforant pathway (●) not stimulated at high frequencies displayed heterosynaptic LTD induced by high-frequency stimulation of the lateral perforant path.

It should be noted that STP is not necessary for LTP to develop, and LTP is often observed even in the absence of STP. Our own experience is that STP is a phenomenon that, like rapidly induced LTP, is seen *in vivo* only following rather extended intense trains. For example, STP is observed following 0.5- to 1-sec bursts of 400 Hz, whereas STP is rarely observed in perforant path projections with brief bursts of stimulation given at 200 msec intervals that mimic theta rhythm (or so-called theta burst stimulation.[8]). Thus it remains to be determined whether STP reflects a process that can normally occur with endogenous patterns of synaptic activity, and, if so, whether it has any role in learning or memory.

Another feature is that LTP is associative. If high frequency stimulation of one set of afferents induces LTP, individual active synapses can also be recruited to express LTP — provided that the synapse is coactive within a delimited window. Associativity can be derived from the requirements for activation of the NMDA receptor (specifically, both glutamate and postsynaptic depolarization essential for relieving the magnesium block of the NMDA channel).

The property of associativity can be derived directly from and is essentially identical to the property of cooperativity,[9] indicating that LTP has a threshold and a threshold number of afferents must be active to induce LTP. That LTP can be induced in "cooperating" synapses is indicative that associativity is an inherent property of this phenomenon. While it has been suggested that the term *associativity* refers to cooperative LTP involving distinct sets of afferents, it should be noted that this first demonstration of cooperativity used two distinct afferent systems to the dentate gyrus: the medial and lateral perforant pathways.[9] However, because interactions among a critical number of afferent fibers may underlie this effect, it is probable that the cooperativity term was chosen out of prudence since the associativity term as envisaged by Hebb tacitly implies a post-synaptic integration of presynaptic activity at the postsynaptic element — something that cannot be ruled out in the cooperativity effect. Perhaps a more realistic and convincing demonstration of associativity is provided by studies showing that the pairing of low frequency afferent activity with induced postsynaptic depolarization also induces LTP.[10]

Input specificity is a crucial property of virtually all forms of LTP and refers to the fact that LTP is synapse-specific and restricted only to synapses of activated afferents (Figure 2.1). This is in contrast to the nonassociative phenomena such as sensitization in which specificity of stimuli (or afferent input) is absent and a more general facilitation of responses is observed in other afferent inputs. Obviously, input specificity is an important feature given that information storage capacity is increased when plasticity can be regulated at individual synapses.

Another feature of LTP is that it is remarkably persistent. Prior to its discovery, the only activity-dependent electrophysiological change that came close to LTP in duration was post-tetanic potentiation (PTP) a primarily presynaptic phenomenon lasting from seconds to minutes. By contrast, LTP in the hippocampal formation can persist from hours to weeks or months, depending upon the stimulation parameters.

In intact animals, LTP is decremental and usually decays within 1 to 2 weeks.[11] While this is certainly too brief a period for the storage of long-term memory, several points should be made with respect to LTP longevity. First, LTP in the hippocampus need not be permanent. Current findings support the view that, as is suspected in humans, the hippocampus has a time-delimited role in memory; persistent long-term memory is gradually consolidated in neocortical areas.[12] In this view, memories formed by the hippocampus are transferred to and consolidated in the neocortex, possibly during slow wave or REM sleep states.[13,14] This usually occurs within 2 weeks in rats, as indicated by both lesion and imaging data.[15] Thus, if the hippocampus indeed serves as a temporary repository of information, LTP may not last long simply because it may not need to. In fact, any long-term retention of information within the hippocampus beyond the usual several weeks may even be detrimental to hippocampal-based memory, resulting in interference with previously stored patterns of synaptic activity.

How long then can LTP last? It is reported that LTP decay is an active process mediated by NMDA receptors, and blocking these receptors can prevent LTP decay.[16] Although it is not known for certain, many forms of long-term depression (LTD) — which, like LTP is a long-term change in synaptic strength — reduces synaptic strength. Like LTP, LTD usually requires the activation of NMDA receptors. Thus LTD may mediate LTP decay. However, because LTP decay is an active process that requires NMDA receptor activation (and possibly the induction of LTD), LTP is theoretically, permanent and may last as long as the synapse itself, provided that it is not erased by subsequent synaptic activity and NMDAR activation.

2.2.2 Long-Term Depression (LTD)

LTP is particularly noteworthy in that its induction follows the rule of pre- and postsynaptic associativity as formalized by Donald Hebb.[17] However, a mechanism serving to increase synaptic strength cannot operate alone; otherwise the strength of synapses could only increase, eventually reaching a point of saturation. Other mechanisms that permit either the reversal or the inverse of LTP are likely to be necessary. Such a phenomenon is observed at the same synapses that display LTP and is termed long-term depression (LTD). LTD was noted in early studies, although its possible role in information storage was only suggested.[18] As it became apparent that any device that serves as a temporary repository for information must have some way to decrease synaptic strength, LTD became a focus of many studies in the 1990s.[19]

In contrast to LTP, distinct forms of LTD were noted early on in these studies, as evidenced by the distinct mechanisms of their induction. Homosynaptic LTD is used to describe LTD that follows synaptic activity and typically is induced by repetitive low frequency (0.5 to 5 Hz) stimulation. In most synapses, homosynaptic LTD is, like LTP, input-specific, dependent upon NMDA receptor activation,[20] associative,[21,22] and also requires calcium, although the levels of calcium influx necessary for LTD induction appear to be lower than those for LTP. This may reflect the modulation of phosphatases associated with LTD induction by calcium, which require much smaller changes in calcium concentration.

LTD also is observed when either synaptic activity or LTP occurs at neighboring synapses. This form of LTD is referred to as *heterosynaptic* in that it is observed at synapses that are not potentiated (and even are inactive). Heterosynaptic LTD is usually most evident in the perforant path projections to the dentate, where induction of LTP in one set of afferents (such as the medial perforant path) can induce heterosynaptic LTD of responses evoked by a separate inactive set of afferents (the lateral perforant path), and vice versa (Figure 2.1). Here, LTD induction appears sensitive to both NMDA receptors and the voltage-dependent calcium channels,[23,24] suggesting that low levels of calcium necessary for LTD may be provided by VDCCs activated in response to NMDA receptors, perhaps via distinct NMDA receptors at distinct extrasynaptic locations (such as the NR2B variant of the NMDA receptor or similar receptors on dendrites or the spine base and neck).[25]

In addition, a distinct form of LTD in the CA1 involving metabotropic glutamate receptors, specifically Group I metabotropic receptors in addition to NMDA receptors, has been reported.[26] This type of LTD is seen with application of mGluR1/5 agonists and is blocked by mGluR1/5 antagonists. Likewise, in the mossy fiber pathway, one form of LTD appears to depend on postsynaptic factors, including postsynaptic calcium,[27–30] whereas another form appears to depend on the activation of presynaptic metabotropic glutamate receptors.[31]

The diversity of types or forms of LTD induction mechanisms may reflect distinct roles for these forms of plasticity in hippocampal function and memory. As noted earlier, utilizing a mechanism that serves to increase synaptic strength would be expected to be accompanied by other mechanisms that reverse LTP or weaken synapses; otherwise interference would follow the progressive saturation of synaptic plasticity. As graceful degradation rather than catastrophic interference appears to be characteristic of many neural systems,[32] this serves as another indicator that synaptic potentiation within the hippocampus is tightly regulated and likely utilizes an activity-dependent mechanism that serves to weaken synaptic strength.

Thus LTD may play a role in reversing LTP (also referred to as depotentiation). However, LTD may also play a role in normalizing synaptic strength (synaptic scaling; see below), a factor that would ensure that the net excitatory input to a neuron is maintained. This is thought to be a crucial aspect of neuronal homeostasis: maintaining the dynamic range of neuronal output. Thus LTP induced in a set of synapses on a neuron may result in a concomitant, and equivalent "net" decrease in the strength of other inactive synapses on the same neuron. LTD also may play a role in sparse coding,[33] ensuring that only the most active synapses increase in strength in response to a given input. Other less active synapses are depressed, preserving the sparse encoding essential for distributed memory systems that employ the Hebb rule. In this view, heterosynaptic LTD and homosynaptic LTD may contribute to both synaptic scaling and sparse encoding.[34]

2.3 LTP AND LTD: TRIGGERING, EXPRESSION, AND MAINTENANCE MECHANISMS

While LTP is often equated with memory, it is nothing but a model. In this case, LTP is thought to reflect an artificially induced manifestation of the cellular processes that occur during normal synaptic transmission and that normally underlie the synaptic changes that mediate memory. As such, it is often criticized on methodological grounds, but often for the wrong reasons. For example, it is noted that LTP is often induced using massive stimulation of a single afferent system, an event that is decidedly nonphysiological and unlikely to occur in anything but pathological states. However, LTP need not be induced this way; simply pairing low frequency afferent activity with postsynaptic depolarization or cell firing is sufficient to induce LTP.[35] Massive afferent stimulation usually is employed as a method to induce LTP or LTD, merely to achieve levels of postsynaptic depolarization necessary to activate NMDA receptors. As noted with the studies of cooperativity, a critical number of fibers must be activated to induce LTP.[9] It has been estimated that in order to reach the LTP experimentally, a sufficient number of afferent inputs must be activated. Experimentally, it appears that this threshold is close to the stimulation intensity necessary to bring granule cells near their thresholds for firing, as indicated by the evocation of a "population spike" in field recordings.[9] Extrapolating from this, it is likely that the postsynaptic depolarization necessary for eliciting LTP is near the cell threshold for eliciting an action potential. The fact that actively firing principal cells are frequently observed in behaving animals shows that the levels of post-synaptic depolarization necessary for NMDA receptor activation and LTP induction likely occur quite frequently during normal hippocampal operation. Thus it is likely that LTP is not a rare event and is likely to occur during normal hippocampal functioning.

An astonishing amount of effort has been put forth in an attempt to delineate the molecular mechanisms of LTP induction and expression. However, any delineation of processes must be tempered by the knowledge that LTP has a variety of forms, and any single molecular cascade is unlikely to reflect the diversity of processes mediating LTP, even among synaptic populations in the hippocampus. Roughly, a general scheme for LTP induction can be described for the factors that are important for LTP induction. These include an increase in postsynaptic depolarization[36] and an increase in postsynaptic calcium.[37] This is usually provided by the NMDA glutamate receptor, although postsynaptic calcium appears to be critical for LTP induction even at synapses that display LTP not mediated by NMDAR activation.[38,39] The subsequent activation of a number of kinases including calcium–calmodulin kinase II (CamKII), MAP kinase and ERK, PKA and PKC are also implicated in LTP development, although it should be noted that over 100 molecules have been implicated in the processes collectively described as LTP.[40]

The roles of these kinases are twofold, with the first possibility remaining that rapid effects are due to direct actions of kinases and phosphorylation of AMPA subunits[41] that may affect channel properties directly or may be essential for AMPA subunit trafficking.[42]

The second role is phosphorylation of transcription factors, such as CREB.[43] Subsequent protein synthesis initiated by these transcription factors is thought to result in the synthesis of mRNA and proteins at the soma and the eventual targeting of these molecules to the potentiated synapse. It should be noted that an extensive amount of protein synthesis occurs locally within dendritic regions shortly after LTP induction. Although it is possible that these locally translated proteins participate directly in enhancing synaptic strength, they may serve as synaptic "tags"[44] necessary for targeting somatically synthesized proteins to potentiated synapses.

Is LTP a singular phenomenon? Although the LTP term often is used collectively to describe any increase in synaptic strength, it has become clear that LTP can be expressed at many synapses in the nervous system following high frequency synaptic activity. While many forms of LTP involve NMDA receptors, this is not always the case.[45] Furthermore, the cellular mechanisms implicated in LTP induction differ even among synapses within the hippocampal formation. For example, the expression of the immediate early genes (IEG) Arc, Homer, and Zif268 (*egr-1*) is observed with LTP induction in the dentate, but is not observed following LTP induction at Schaffer-CA1 synapses.[46] It thus appears that LTP may actually be a collection of synaptic phenomena that, while appearing similar in phenomenology, utilize distinct mechanisms of induction and possibly expression in different synaptic populations.

Many now refer to distinct forms of LTP. Likewise, LTD displays distinct forms that can be expressed at many different synapses by a variety of receptor mechanisms.[38] The assignment of forms of LTP must be distinguished from temporal phases of LTP. Following NMDAR activation and LTP induction, the initial or early phase of LTP (E-LTP) requires the activation of NMDARs, but decays relatively rapidly. The later (> 3 hr) phases of LTP (L-LTP) are dependent upon protein synthesis.[47–49]

Thus NMDAR-dependent LTP appears to be expressed via a concatenation of processes that mediate LTP maintenance.

The assignment of forms of LTP has been rooted in the different mechanisms of induction and the particular synapse under study. Thus it is not too speculative to suggest that these distinct forms of LTP induction also involve distinct molecular mechanisms of expression and maintenance. Conversely, it is also possible that the various forms of LTP induction seen in the hippocampal formation may simply reflect differences only among induction mechanisms and yet share common downstream maintenance mechanisms. In this case, the distinct mechanisms of LTP induction may serve distinct functions by defining the precise synaptic conditions necessary to induce LTP in a particular synaptic system. For example, sustained, protein synthesis-dependent LTP observed at mossy fiber synapses appears to require high frequency mossy fiber activity in order to provide postsynaptic depolarization,[50] postsynaptic calcium,[51] and the release of opioid peptide co-transmitters.[52]

As peptide co-transmitters often require repetitive presynaptic activity for their release from dense core vesicles, LTP at this synapse appears to display a strict requirement for high frequency mossy fiber activity.[52] As bursting in granule cells is also a rare and highly regulated event,[53] this novel induction requirement may serve to impose tight constraints on plasticity in this sparse synaptic system. It is easy to imagine that such constraints may be necessary to maintain sparse activity among mossy fiber input lines, given that one principal function of the mossy fibers is thought to be the encoding of sparse orthogonal representations in the CA3 region.[54,55]

That LTP involves multiple effector systems, kinases, and genes leads to important questions: are each of these kinases essential for establishing or maintaining the increase in synaptic strength? Or do some of these factors regulate other aspects of LTP such as its persistence? Or do some processes mediate metaplastic effects that regulate LTP or LTD thresholds following prior activity?[56] All these questions along with the view that LTP may involve a number of distinct induction and expression mechanisms indicate that the mechanisms of LTP are not only complex, but are unlikely to be delineated into a single sequential molecular process. Methodological issues also complicate analysis of LTP because the techniques used to induce LTP (namely high frequency afferent activation) are also likely to induce other processes and other effector systems unrelated to LTP expression. For example, LTP can be induced in the mossy fibers following high frequency stimulation. However, this same stimulation also induces mossy fiber synaptogenesis[57] and increases granule cell neurogenesis.[58] In such cases, analysis of the kinases and genes expressed presents a number of difficulties. Which genes generated by stimulation are essential for LTP as opposed to neurogenesis or synaptogenesis? Is mossy fiber synaptogenesis a distinct process, or is it perhaps the end point of mossy fiber LTP? It appears that the concomitant characterization of other synaptic processes altered with high frequency activity will be essential to dissect the myriad cellular processes induced by activity necessary for the induction and expression of LTP.

Further work will no doubt elaborate on the differences in the molecular machinery underlying LTP induction and expression, and make us reconsider classification of LTP based only upon only induction mechanisms. It should be noted that the majority of studies addressing LTP expression and maintenance have looked at time points under 3 hours. Because this is the time period prior to protein synthesis that is essential for sustained LTP,[47–49] it is entirely possible that the mechanisms underlying LTP expression and maintenance after 3 hours and even after several days, may be completely different. Thus, not only may the mechanisms of LTP maintenance differ among the various forms of LTP induction, but LTP at a given synapse may involve a concatenation of numerous maintenance processes over time that may change as LTP persists from hours to days.

It is also premature to assign LTP forms based on the specific synaptic population under study. Distinct forms of LTP expression can be observed at a given synapse, depending on induction variables such as the high frequency stimulation used or the behavioral state of the animal during LTP induction. In the former case, it is reported that high frequency stimulation that mimics the natural theta rhythm produces a "nondecremental" form of LTP at Schaffer-CA1 synapses,[8] possibly by inducing multiple forms of LTP.[59–61] In the latter case, the temporal characteristic of LTP can depend on behavioral state of the animal when LTP is induced. While LTP in perforant path–dentate synapses typically persists for 5 to 7 days following a single session of stimulation,[11] the duration of LTP is extended to about 2 weeks if dentate LTP is induced while the animal is actively engaged in learning (such as during the initial exploration of a novel environment.[62])

The mechanisms underlying this effect remain to be elucidated, although it appears that monoamines likely play a role in this facilitating LTP longevity.[63,64] In both cases, when LTP is induced with theta bursts or induced in novel environments, it displays a distinct extended time course. This tacitly implies that distinct molecular mechanisms (or the modulation of a common molecular mechanism) mediate LTP maintenance when induced in these conditions. Not only do different synapses display different forms of LTP, depending on behavioral state or means of induction, but a given synapse may display distinct forms of LTP, depending upon the behavioral conditions during induction. The present challenge is to determine necessary mechanisms common to the different forms of LTP and the possible functional roles of distinct forms of LTP induction or maintenance normally occurring in the normal operation of the hippocampal formation in learning and memory.

2.4 PERSISTENT SYNAPTIC PLASTICITY: METAPLASTIC POINT OF VIEW

The most remarkable property of synapses lies in their capacity to modify the efficiency with which they transmit information from one neuron to another. This property, known as synaptic plasticity, is the basis of information storage in the brain. It enables us to store and use vast amounts of information in the form of learned behaviors and conscious memories.

Synaptic plasticity can be modulated, sometimes dramatically, by prior synaptic activity; this property is named metaplasticity.[56] It is induced by synaptic or cellular activity, but it is not necessarily expressed as a change in the efficacy of normal synaptic transmission. Instead, it is manifest as a change in the ability to induce subsequent synaptic plasticity, such as long-term potentiation or depression. Thus, metaplasticity is a higher order form of synaptic plasticity.

Another mechanism that could help maintain relatively constant activity levels is if neurons increased the strength of all excitatory connections in response to a prolonged drop in firing rates and *vice versa.* Such bidirectional plasticity of synaptic currents has recently been demonstrated in cultured cortical and spinal networks and occurs through a scaling up or down of the strength of all of a neuron's excitatory inputs. This form of plasticity has been termed synaptic scaling.[65]

Classical Hebbian plasticities (such as LTP and LTD) that are rapid and synapse-specific coexist with other long-lasting modifications of synapses (such as metaplasticity and synaptic scaling) that work over longer time scales and are crucial for maintaining and orchestrating neuronal network function. Metaplasticity and synaptic scaling are parts of the homeostatic plasticity mechanisms that stabilize neuronal activity. Bienenstock, Cooper, and Munro put forth one proposal (the BCM theory) to account for such homeostatic regulation in their model of visual cortical receptive field plasticity during development.[66] They suggested that the "modification threshold" or Θ m (level of post-synaptic response below which gives LTD and above which gives LTP) is dynamically regulated by the average level of post-synaptic activity (Figure 2.2).

For example, if visual cortical neurons suffer prolonged reductions in their activity because of visual deprivation, then the modification threshold would be correspondingly reduced. This adaptive response allows the preservation of a broad range of LTP and LTD responses despite treatments that restrict the firing repertoires

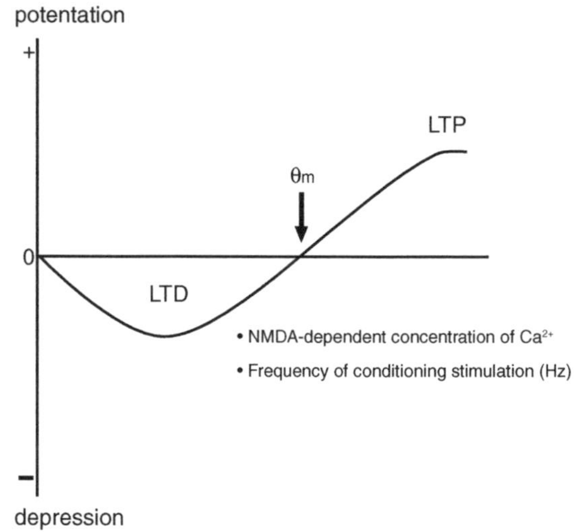

FIGURE 2.2 Bidirectional modification of synaptic plasticity as predicted by BCM theory. NMDA-dependent concentration of Ca^{2+} or frequencies of conditioning stimulation represent experimental approaches through which the function can be reached. (Modified from Abraham, W. and Bear, M., *Trends Neurosci.*, 19, 126, 1996.) Θm = modification threshold.

of those neurons. A converse process involving an elevated modification threshold occurs if a neuron's level of activity is increased over a prolonged period.

It is now widely accepted that the trafficking of AMPA-type glutamate receptors mediates rapid synaptic modification in the classic Hebbian forms of plasticity, LTP and LTD. Several other cellular and molecular changes have been implicated in synaptic homeostasis but one common feature of many forms of homeostatic plasticity is an alteration in the number or complement of NMDA-type glutamate receptors. A series of new studies has revealed that NMDA receptors cycle rapidly into and out of synapses and that regulated trafficking of NMDA receptors working cumulatively and over longer time scales can effectively modify the number and composition (NR2A/NR2B subunit ratio) of synaptic NMDA receptors as demonstrated in the visual cortex by Quinlan et al.[67] and Philpot et al.[68] Thus, an emerging concept is that activity-dependent alterations in NMDA receptor trafficking contribute to homeostatic plasticity at central glutamatergic synapses (Figure 2.3).

Experience-dependent regulation of synaptic strength has long been hypothesized to be the physiological basis of learning and memory. Accordingly, an increase in synaptic strength accompanies learning *in vivo* as demonstrated by Rogan et al. in the amygdala[69] and persists in brain slices *ex vivo* as shown by the observations of McKernan and Shinnick-Gallagher in the same pathway[70] and by Rioult-Pedotti et al. in the motor cortex.[71] Learning-induced potentiation of synaptic strength is also accompanied by an increase in the threshold for further synaptic enhancements.

These dual changes in synaptic function are thought to initiate and maintain the memory encoded by experience. In this regard, studies of the insular cortex (IC), a region of the temporal cortex implicated in acquisition and retention of conditioned taste aversion (CTA), demonstrated that induction of LTP in the basolateral amygdaloid nucleus (BLa)-IC projection previous to CTA training enhances the retention of this task.[72] We recently showed that CTA training prevents the subsequent induction of LTP in the BLa-IC projection for at least 120 hours (unpublished data). These findings provide evidence that CTA training produces a change in the ability to induce subsequent synaptic plasticity on the BLa-IC pathway, supporting the notion that the mechanisms responsible for behaviorally induced synaptic changes are similar to those underlying electrically induced LTP. Accordingly, the activity history of a given neuron influences its future responses to synaptic input.

2.5 ROLE OF ACTIVITY-DEPENDENT SYNAPTIC PLASTICITY IN BRAIN FUNCTION

While NMDAR-dependent LTP and LTD in the CA1 region of the hippocampus remain the most extensively studied and therefore prototypic forms of synaptic plasticity, it is now clear that additional forms of LTP and LTD may share some, but certainly not all, of the properties and mechanisms of NMDAR-dependent LTP and LTD. Therefore, when discussing LTP and LTD, it is necessary to define at which specific synapses these phenomena are being studied, at what time point during development, and how they are triggered. Indeed, it may be most useful to conceptualize LTP and LTD as a general class of cellular/synaptic phenomena.[73]

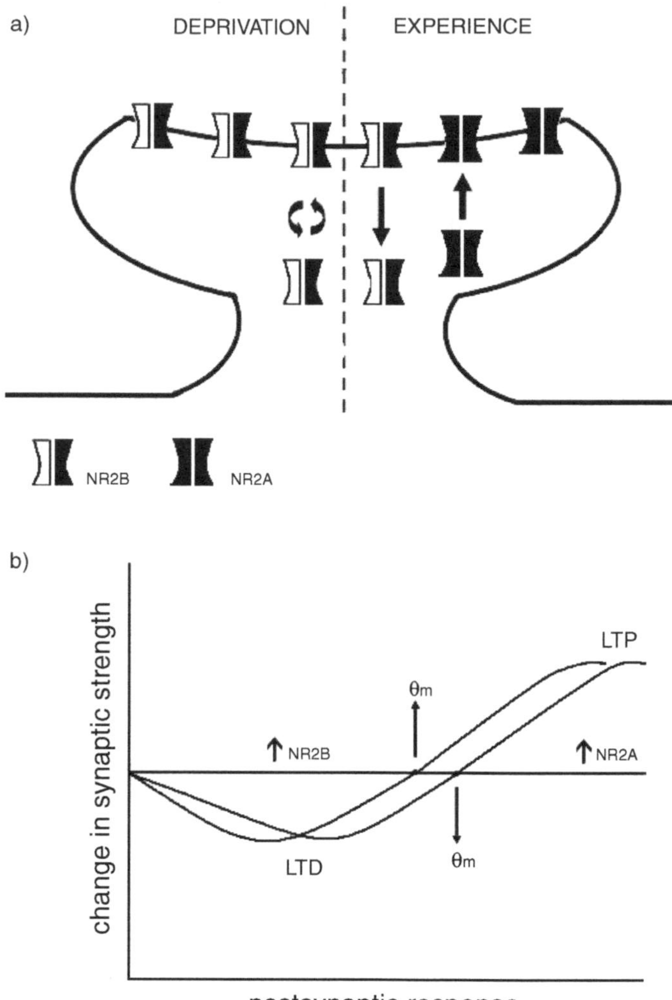

FIGURE 2.3 Experience-dependent changes in NMDA receptor subunit composition may underlie the sliding synaptic modification threshold. (a) Dynamic trafficking of NMDA receptor composition. (b) Model relating NMDA receptor subunit switch to changes in synaptic plasticity thresholds. Activity below the modification threshold (Θm) results in synaptic weakening (LTD); activity above Θm leads to synaptic potentiation (LTP). The Θm crossover point is dynamic and can be shifted by changes in the NR2A: NR2B ratio. (Modified from Philpot, B.D. et al., *Neuron*, 29, 157, 2001.)

LTP and LTD are experimental phenomena that can be used to demonstrate the repertoire of long-lasting modifications of which individual synapses are capable. Given the ubiquity of various forms of LTP and LTD at excitatory synapses throughout the brain, it seems virtually certain that the brain takes advantage of neuronal capability to express long-lasting activity-dependent synaptic modifications as at least one of the key mechanisms by which experiences modify neural circuit behavior. Largely through correlational studies involving genetic and pharmacological manipulations, it is possible to begin to establish that *in vivo* experiences generate synaptic modifications analogous to LTP and LTD and these modifications are required for the behavioral or cognitive plasticity generated by the experience.

As mentioned above, the BCM theory suggests that the depression of deprived-eye inputs in visual cortex is specifically triggered by presynaptic activity when it fails to consistently correlate with a strong evoked postsynaptic response. Indeed the BCM theory was the motivation behind the ultimately successful search for homosynaptic LTD in the hippocampus and visual cortex. The idea that depression of responses in visual cortex is actually caused by activity in the deprived eye was tested experimentally by Rittenhouse et al.[74] Additional evidence that the mechanisms of LTD underlie sensory deprivation has come from studies of the somatosensory[75,76] and visual cortices.[77]

Naturally occurring response potentiation can also be observed in the sensory cortex. For example, chronic recordings from adult mouse visual cortex have shown that closing one eye enables a gradual experience-dependent enhancement of the responses to stimulation of the other eye. The effect persists for many days after opening the deprived eye and fails to occur in mice with reduced expression of NMDA receptors in the superficial layers of the visual cortex.[78]

It has become apparent that the neural mechanisms underlying adaptive forms of learning and memory likely also play a critical role in the pathophysiology of addiction.[79,80] In this regard, it has been found that administration of single doses of several classes of drugs of abuse caused significant increases in synaptic strength at excitatory synapses on mesolimbic dopaminergic cells that are critical for mediating several forms of long-lasting, drug-induced behavioral plasticity. These increases share mechanisms with LTP, involving for example the up-regulation of AMPA receptors.[81,82] Additionally, drugs of abuse can also modify the triggering of LTP and LTD of the mesolimbic system. Thus, long-lasting synaptic plasticity is thought to be a principal mechanism by which functional properties of the nervous system are expressed.

2.6 SUBSTRATES OF LTP AND LTD: STRUCTURAL PLASTICITY

Since LTP and LTD appear to play a role in plasticity in a variety of behaviors and structures, what are the consequences of this in the induction of LTP and LTD and the cascade of numerous kinases thought to be involved? Studies over the past 10 years have attempted to address the locus of LTP and focused on the locus of change (pre- or postsynaptic). It is generally accepted that postsynaptic mechanisms are essential for LTP induction, and the primary putative mechanisms that serve to maintain increased synaptic responses also involve the postsynaptic element.

Evidence currently implicates postsynaptic mechanisms in LTP induction and expression. In addition, even though many of the effects revealed by quantal analysis suggest presynaptic changes, considerable evidence indicates that these apparent presynaptic changes reflect a postsynaptic recruitment of "silent" synapses. Silent synapses possess only NMDA receptors, possibly the NR2B heteromers that have sustained calcium conductance. It is thought that the activation of NMDA receptors by activity and ambient glutamate, presumably provided heterosynaptically by active neighboring synapses, may initiate the translocation of calmodulin kinases to postsynaptic density, allowing for the assembly of functional receptors and the conversion of silent synapses to functional synapses that express both NMDA and AMPA glutamate receptors.[83] Currently, the trafficking of subunits and alterations of AMPA and NMDAR receptor stoichiometry at existing functional synapses will turn out to be one of the most compelling and comprehensive of the current models of LTP expression.[84,85]

While silent synapses may explain the apparent presynaptic effects seen with quantal analysis, the abundance of more recent data suggesting presynaptic changes[86–90] cannot be ignored. The most parsimonious view is that changes take place both pre- and postsynaptically. Such a view is prudent since most studies of the mechanisms of LTP maintenance and expression have been restricted to the earliest time points in LTP expression (usually within 1 hour after its induction). As noted above, it is quite possible that the later protein synthesis-dependent phases that maintain LTP for days and weeks may use entirely different mechanism for later LTP expression, including presynaptic mechanisms.

One mechanism that appears crucial for both LTP and LTD expression involves AMPA receptors — multimeric ionotropic receptors that serve as the principal receptors mediating fast excitatory synaptic transmission at glutamatergic responses. Currently, the primary candidate mechanism for the increases and decreases is seen with LTP and LTD is thought to involve trafficking of AMPA subunits and the formation and alteration of AMPA glutamate receptors. These multimeric ionotropic receptors are the principal receptors that mediate fast glutamatergic responses. Of particular interest are the GluR1 and GluR2 subunits of this receptor that appear to be regulated in several ways. Also crucial is the activation of the type II calcium–calmodulin kinase (CamKII), a kinase that requires both calcium and calmodulin. A process thought important in both these mechanisms is a translocation of CaMKII to postsynaptic density[91,92] that can dramatically alter both its activity and its regulation by both calcium and calmodulin.

The mechanism of LTP expression that has received the most interest is AMPA receptor trafficking, an idea that likely originated with the discovery of subunit trafficking following the activation of silent synapses. It has been shown that after LTP, AMPA subunits are inserted or move laterally into the PSD immediately following LTP induction.[93] Conversely, these receptors are internalized via endocytosis with LTD.[94] In this process, it appears that both GluR1 and GluR2 subunits are transported with LTP induction, whereas GluR2 trafficking may occur alone during normal processes of synaptic homeostasis.[85] [85]. It is of historical note that in 1983 Gary Lynch and Michel Baudry presented a "new and specific" hypothesis of LTP, suggesting that LTP was a postsynaptic phenomenon involving the expression of new receptors into the postsynaptic density. This hypothesis was not only prescient, but notable in that Lynch and Baudry based their molecular hypothesis on established cellular mechanisms that had not been considered in terms of synaptic function.[95]

A crucial component of this process appears to be CaMKII binding to the PSD via interaction with the NR2B NMDA receptor subunit that can "lock" CamKII in an active conformation.[91] In this way, CamKII is in an ideal position to phosphorylate existing AMPA subunits. Alternatively, the CaMKII molecule may be part of a more extensive scaffolding device attached to the NR2B subunit that promotes translocation of AMPA subunits into synaptic regions and the PSD.[96] Although both subunit phosphorylation and receptor trafficking mechanisms are viable candidates for mechanisms that underlie LTP and LTD, perhaps these two mechanisms, AMPA phosphorylation and AMPA insertion, represent two mechanisms or forms of LTP within a heterogeneous synaptic population and reflect potentiation for extant and silent synapses, respectively. Another alternative is that such phosphorylation works in tandem with CaMKII to allow rapid insertion or removal of phosphorylated subunits.[97]

In addition to AMPA subunits and receptors, another aspect of trafficking is the insertion of NMDA receptors following LTP induction. While such an effect may play a crucial role in increasing synaptic efficacy, it is possible that the dynamic modification of NMDA receptors may play other roles in inducing or maintaining plasticity. For instance, alterations of NMDARs may mediate metaplastic effects (see above) that allow the alteration of LTP or LTD thresholds in response to recent synaptic activity.[98]

2.7 NEUROTROPHINS AND SYNAPTIC PLASTICITY

Neurotrophins constitute a family of structurally related proteins that includes nerve growth factor (NGF), brain-derived neurotrophic factor (BDNF), neurotrophin-3 (NT-3), and neurotrophin 4/5 (NT-4/5) identified in the mammalian brain. The signaling and biological functions of these molecules are mediated primarily by the Trk receptor tyrosine kinases. NGF binds to TrkA; BDNF and NT-4/5 to TrkB; and NT-3 to TrkC (Figure 2.4).

Neurotrophins play diverse roles in regulating neuronal structure, function, and survival during development and into adulthood. One unexpected facet of neurotrophin actions was elucidated in the early 1990s, when Lohof et al.[99] discovered that exogenously applied BDNF and NT-3 enhanced synaptic efficacy at the *Xenopus* neuromuscular junction. Since then, experiments from many laboratories have demonstrated that neurotrophins indeed play important roles in synaptic development and plasticity.

Recent studies suggest that one of the neurotrophins, BDNF, plays a critical role in long-term synaptic plasticity in the adult brain. BDNF acutely enhances glutamatergic synaptic transmission and increases phosphorylation of the NR2B subunit of the NMDA receptor in postsynaptic densities isolated from cortex and hippocampus. NMDA receptor-dependent long-term potentiation is associated with the up-regulation of BDNF and its TrkB receptor in the hippocampus of awake freely moving rats, as well as in hippocampal slices. In BDNF knockout mice, LTP is

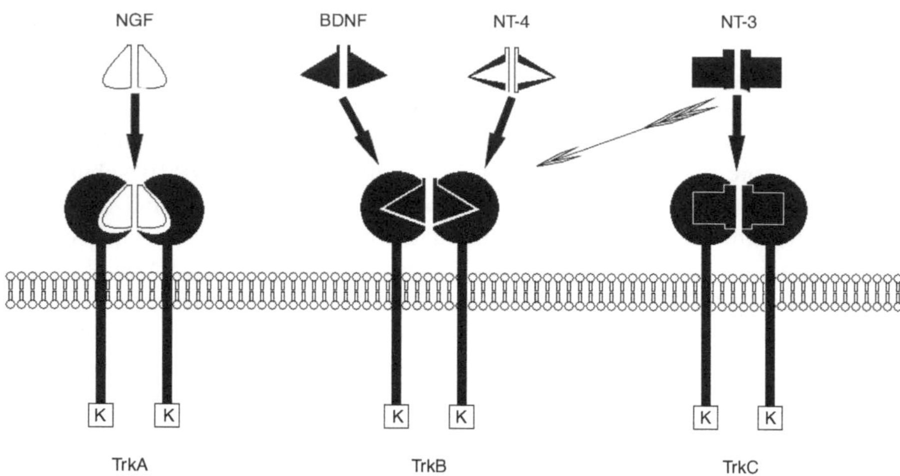

FIGURE 2.4 Neurotrophins and their ligand binding preferences for each member of the TrK receptor family.

markedly impaired, but the changes are restored by either adenovirus-mediated transfection or by the bath application of BDNF.

Moreover, the application of exogenous BDNF to slices enhances electrically induced LTP in rodent hippocampus. In a series of studies using bath perfusion of BDNF onto hippocampal slices, Schuman and colleagues demonstrated long-lasting enhancement of transmission at Schaffer collateral-CA1 synapses.[100] Furthermore, using intrahippocampal infusions of BDNF in intact rats revealed a robust long-lasting potentiation at perforant path–granule cell synapses in the dentate gyrus.[101] Thus, a combination of genetic and pharmacological approaches has revealed multiple and distinct contributions of BDNF signaling to LTP.

These actions may be classified as permissive or instructive.[102] Permissive refers to effects of BDNF that make synapses capable of LTP in the first place, but which are not causally involved in generating LTP. In contrast, instructive refers to BDNF signaling that is initiated in response to HFS and causally involved in the development of LTP. Recent findings suggest that BDNF is a key protein synthesis product needed to carry on the necessary functions for long-lasting modification of hippocampal synapses[103] and drives the formation of stable protein synthesis-dependent LTP, a process referred to as synaptic consolidation.[102]

BDNF and its TrkB high affinity receptor are also abundantly expressed in neurons of the neocortex of the mammalian brain. BDNF also influences the development of patterned connections and the growth and complexity of dendrites in the cerebral cortex. Electrophysiological recordings made in slices of visual cortex have implicated BDNF in synaptic plasticity during the critical period for the formation of ocular dominance columns.[104] BDNF participates in the activity-dependent scaling of cortical synaptic strengths and adjusts the relative balance of cortical excitation and inhibition. BDNF enhances the magnitude of LTP induced by tetanic stimulation in visual cortex and also induces long-lasting potentiation of synaptic transmission in the visual cortices of young rats.[105]

It is considered that memory process involves short- and long-term changes in synaptic communication, including alterations in electrical properties and structural modifications. Since BDNF significantly modulates both forms of synaptic changes, it may play an important role in learning and memory. In this regard, it has been demonstrated that spatial learning is associated with an increase in BDNF mRNA levels in the hippocampus. Furthermore, the expression of its TrkB receptor in the hippocampus was selectively increased in response to spatial learning. Tokuyama et al.[106] recently reported that BDNF mRNA is up-regulated in the inferior temporal cortex during the formation of visual pair association memory in monkeys. Previous studies of one of the authors demonstrated that acute intracortical microinfusion of BDNF in anesthetized adult rats induced a lasting potentiation of synaptic efficacy in the insular cortex, an area that has been implicated in the acquisition and storage of different aversive learning tasks.[107] Moreover, as mentioned above, we showed that induction of LTP in the Bla-IC projection previous to CTA training enhanced the retention of this task.[72] In a similar manner, recently we showed that acute intracortical microinfusion of BDNF (in a concentration capable of inducing a lasting potentiation of synaptic efficacy in the insular cortex) enhanced the retention of CTA.[108]

Although the signaling pathways of BDNF/TrkB activation in learning and memory formation remain to be determined, modulation of NMDA and non-NMDA receptor functions and the expression of synaptic proteins required for exocytosis may be implicated. The mitogen-activated protein kinase (MAPK) signaling pathway appears to be involved in pre- and postsynaptic BDNF actions.[109] Studies of Minichielo et al.[110] provide genetic evidence that TrkB mediates hippocampal plasticity via recruitment of phospholipase C (PLC) and by subsequent phosphorylation of CAMKIV (calcium–calmodulin-dependent kinase IV) and CREB (cAMP response element-binding protein). Recent experimental evidence indicates that BDNF/TrkB signaling converges on MAPK pathways through the activation of extracellular-regulated kinase (ERK) to enhance excitatory synaptic transmission *in vivo* as well as hippocampal-dependent learning in behaving animals[111] (Figure 2.5).

Taken together, this evidence suggests that BDNF and other neurotrophins may represent a class of neuromodulators that regulate activity-dependent synaptic efficacy.

2.8 EXPERIENCE-DEPENDENT MODIFICATIONS: IS LTP INVOLVED IN LEARNING AND MEMORY?

Although most research into LTP and LTD focused on the cellular and molecular mechanisms surrounding its expression, these questions tacitly assume LTP is involved with learning. However, the cellular mechanisms underlying the induction and expression of LTP and LTD may be entirely moot if these phenomena are not involved in information storage in any appreciable way. Thus, principal among the

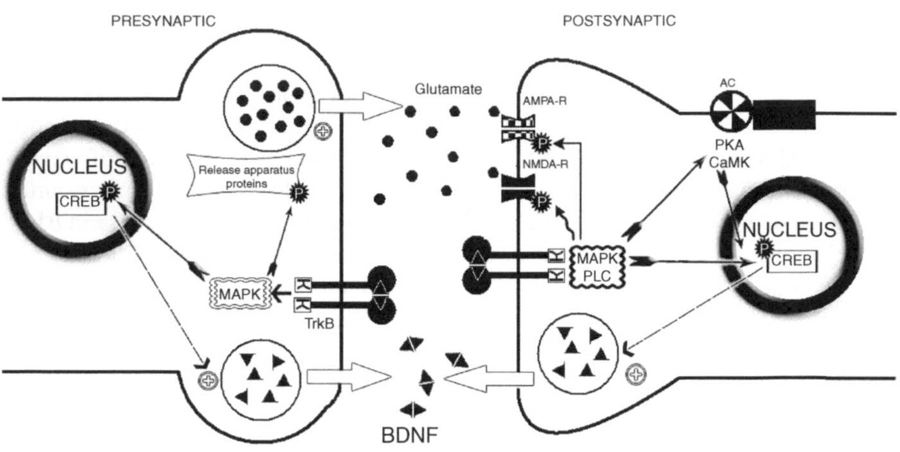

FIGURE 2.5 Signaling pathways of BDNF/TrkB activation in learning and memory. Activity increases BDNF expression and release from pre- and postsynaptic sites. BDNF binds to TrkB receptors located on presynaptic axons, leading to its auto-phosphorylation and activation of the signal transduction MAPK pathway, facilitating neurotransmitter release. BDNF also binds to postsynaptic TrkB, leading to the activation of AMPA and NMDA receptors through the activation of the MAPK and PLC pathways that lead the subsequent phosphorylation of PKA, CAMK, and CREB. (Modified from Yamada, K. et al., *Life Sci.,* 70, 735, 2002.)

many issues that surround LTP is whether LTP contributes to learning and memory. A definitive demonstration is lacking, and no one has yet seen a synapse display LTP with learning or a loss of synaptic LTP with forgetting. Clearly, such a demonstration presents technical difficulties we have yet to overcome. However, the convergence of confirmatory studies undertaken in the last 20 years supplies compelling evidence for the view that LTP is involved in learning and memory.

Morris and McNaughton[55] proposed three crucial experimental findings that are necessary to establish LTP as a memory mechanism. First, blocking LTP induction should impair acquisition without impairing retention of previously encoded information. Second, if LTP serves as a mechanism of encoding, saturating LTP should impair acquisition of new memories. Third, the selective erasure of LTP should disrupt the retention of established memories, but not impair acquisition of new information.

The first postulate suggests that blocking LTP induction should impair acquisition without impairing retention of previously encoded information. The pioneering work by Morris and colleagues[112,113] using NMDA antagonists has remained one of the most solid collections of studies implicating LTP in learning. In sum, it appears that both LTP induction and spatial learning are impaired by NMDAR antagonists (here AP-5). Importantly, dose response analysis of antagonist effects shows that AP-5 is effective in attenuating memory, but only at concentrations that also effectively block LTP.[113]

While numerous studies offer support for the dual effects of NMDAR antagonists in LTP and learning, it is appropriately noted in these studies that the simple fact that a drug blocks both LTP and learning does not denote causality; thus one cannot yet conclude that blocking LTP blocks learning. There always remains the possibility that treatments may exert effects on a third unknown variable crucial for learning, but separate from LTP, that also may be altered by NMDAR antagonists.

The disruption of other synaptic processes by the drug may also impair learning. The possibility that emerges is that theta rhythm, a 5- to 12-Hz frequency oscillation considered crucial for mnemonic hippocampal functions, may be a confound because a number of studies indicate that theta rhythm (specifically, type 2 theta, which is thought to reflect activity within the CA3-CA3 system)[114] is attenuated by systemic administration of NMDAR antagonists.[115,116] Because blocking theta rhythm (for instance, with scopolamine, a muscarine antagonist) impairs learning, there remains the possibility that some of the effects of NMDAR antagonists on behavioral measures of learning may arise from alterations in theta rhythm rather than LTP.

Transgene knockouts have provided useful techniques for assessing the contributions of various proteins to LTP. Deletion of a number of genes including genes for NR1 NMDA receptors,[117] the alpha isoforms of CamKII[118] and CREB,[43] support the view that these proteins are necessary for the full expression of LTP.

While a number of reviews dealt with the various genetic manipulations and their effects on LTP and learning, several studies of note are based on methodologies using several levels of analyses. In one study, Silva and colleagues demonstrated an attenuation of both LTP and learning following a point mutation of the auto-phosphorylation site of CamKII.[119] Crucially, the normal phosphorylating ability of CamKII appears unaltered. As previous accounts have suggested important roles for CamKII auto-phosphorylation in LTP, a sustained CamKII functioning could serve to maintain LTP by maintaining CamKII in an active state long after synaptic activation. In addition, it is proposed that the formation of CamKII assemblies and "hyperphosphorylation" of this assembly at their auto-phosphorylation sites may be a mechanism that serves in AMPA subunit trafficking to insert AMPA receptor subunits to the post-synaptic density.[96]

While the deletion of the NR1 subunit would certainly be expected to impair LTP, a novel methodology employing these same knockouts is presented by Nakazawa[120] and remains an excellent example of combining genetic, electrophysiological, and behavioral methodologies to address LTP and its contribution to learning from an information–theoretic view.

The NR1 subunit was "conditionally deleted" in the CA3 region, a region with extensive recurrent connections that is thought to operate as an autoassociative device. Such devices are of interest in that they can perform pattern completion, that is, an entire stored pattern is recalled from only a subset of the original pattern. LTP among CA3 connections was impaired, as would be expected. However, the investigators went one step further and trained the animals on a spatial maze task that relied on extra-maze cues. Tests of recall involved removing some of the extra-maze cues. While animals with the normal complements of NMDA NR1 subunits showed only minor deficits, animals with NR1 knockouts in the CA3 region showed significant impairment in recalling the maze when these cues were removed. Together these data indicate that NR1 subunit deletions impaired LTP and learning and also that plasticity among the recurrent CA3 synapses prevented recall with a subset of patterns — evidence that firmly supports the view that the CA3 recurrent system performs its hypothesized autoassociative function.

The second postulate is that saturating LTP should both disrupt previously encoded memories and also impair acquisition of new memories. The first study to address this postulate[121] reported that repeated stimulation of the perforant path saturated dentate LTP. Over the time LTP was saturated, deficits were observed in spatial memory tasks. Importantly, following the decay of LTP, these same animals were then able to acquire the task. However, initial attempts to replicate this study using the same methodology met with little success. This is likely due to procedural details.

While LTP was saturated by stimulation of perforant path fibers at one site in the study of Castro et al., stimulation with a single electrode in the angular bundle, a substantial tract containing virtually all of the perforant path fibers that project to the hippocampal formation, is unlikely to activate all perforant path inputs to the dentate.[122] As the dentate and hippocampal formation are particularly resilient to damage,[123] a characteristic of distributed memory systems, the remaining unstimulated fibers and synapses within the angular bundle likely were sufficient to sustain spatial learning. Subsequent studies modified the methodology and used multiple stimulating electrodes that afforded a near-complete stimulation of the angular bundle. This, combined with lesions of the contralateral hippocampus, provided positive results confirming the prediction that saturation of LTP impairs the acquisition of a spatial task.[124]

The third crucial experiment is that the selective erasure of LTP should disrupt the retention of established memories, but not impair acquisition of new memories. However, the technical knowledge of selectively erasing LTP is not yet available. Nevertheless, the inverse of this prediction is that enhancing LTP persistence should also enhance the persistence of memory. One study[16] first showed that CPP, an NMDA antagonist, blocks the decay of perforant path–dentate LTP induction in behaving animals when administered 1 hour after LTP induction and daily thereafter for 6 days. Thus, sustained blockade of NMDARs prevented the decay of LTP over a 1-week period.

This is significant in that it indicates that LTP decay is an active process mediated by NMDA receptors. This finding tacitly suggests that, at least theoretically, not only is LTP permanent, but that the decay of LTP in the dentate is an active process, suggesting it is important for the normal operation of the dentate gyrus, possibly operating to prevent interference of newly acquired information with older accrued synaptic changes in the dentate. Because NMDAR antagonists block LTP decay and LTP is thought to manifest physical changes that constitute memory, it would be predicted that sustaining LTP also would sustain memory. This appears to be the case; animals trained to criteria on an eight-arm radial maze were then returned to their home cages for 1 week, during which they received either CPP daily at a dose effective in blocking LTP decay or the water vehicle. Following this 1-week period, the animals were then returned to the radial maze. During the first session, animals that received the vehicle only showed significantly more errors than animals that received CPP. Importantly, the performance of the CPP-treated animals in terms of maze errors was identical to scores observed on the last day of training to criterion 1 week earlier. Thus sustaining LTP also sustains memory, although it remains to be determined which synaptic populations affected by CPP were crucial for preserving the spatial memory, as systemic administration of CPP was used.

As more sophisticated techniques of analyzing hippocampal operation evolve, new opportunities to address the role of LTP in learning will arise as well. This is the case with hippocampal place cells. Simultaneous with the discovery of LTP was the discovery of hippocampal place cells, principal cells of the hippocampus (pyramidal cells, granule cells) that fire in complex bursts in particular regions of an environment.[125] While place cells were in the process of being characterized about the same time as LTP was first touted as a possible mnemonic device, only recently have there been any successful attempts to link place cells with LTP. This may be due in part to the absence of data indicating the dynamic aspects of place cells. Early in their discovery, it was believed that place fields were "hard wired" due to their rapid emergence. However, subsequent studies using high density recording revealed in the mid 1990s that place cells show dynamic changes with experience, suggesting they can be plastic in their firing features.[126] Subsequently, a number of studies attempting to link LTP with place cells emerged. Some studies attempted to determine whether treatments that impair LTP also impair the characteristics of place cells and their place fields. For instance, knockouts and transgenic point mutations of a number of proteins thought crucial for LTP (such as NMDA receptor NR1 subunits, CamKII, CREB, and GluR2) were consistent in their effects in that they did not prevent place field formation, although they appeared to disrupt selectivity of place cells, producing irregular and diffuse fields, even though these same treatments reduced LTP expression.[127]

If place fields depend upon information embedded within the synapses of hippocampal networks due to LTP, then it would be expected that a disruption of established plasticity using LTP would similarly disrupt established place fields. In studies in the spirit of the LTP saturation experiments, Buzsaki and colleagues[128] induced LTP following the establishment of place fields in an environment. LTP was induced by stimulation of the ventral hippocampal commissure (which contains primarily commissural fibers from CA3 that project to both CA3 and CA1). Subsequent analysis of place fields revealed that after tetanization, re-exposure to the environment led to remapping. Importantly, LTP was measured at various electrode sites and revealed various degrees of LTP at different sites following stimulation. It was observed that place fields were more likely to be altered in regions showing larger degrees of LTP. This experiment is a variation of one of the hypotheses of Morris and McNaughton[55] indicating that saturating LTP should disrupt previously encoded memories. These results offer compelling evidence that LTP is involved with the dynamic behaviors of place cells.

A curious finding in this study was that once LTP decayed, the alterations in place cell responses disappeared as well. This is in stark contrast to the endogenously formed place fields that, once established, remain stable indefinitely, even with subsequent learning. The reasons for this discrepancy are unknown, but several possible explanations exist. First, LTP in this study was induced using standard bursts of 200 Hz. While that level is sufficient for LTP induction, a number of studies noted that induction by theta bursts produced a more sustained LTP,[8] possibly by inducing multiple forms of LTP.[59,60]

Second, certain behavioral states and neuromodulators are crucial for the formation of both stable LTP and stable place fields. For instance, the presence of essential neuromodulators (such as dopamine, norepinephrine, and serotonin) associated with attention or arousal may be crucial for the normal stabilization of place field firing. Such factors may not only serve a permissive role in plasticity; their absence may preserve stability such that stable synaptic strengths (and place fields) predominate unless subsequent synaptic plasticity occurs in the presence of specific neuromodulatory signals. Such an effect would suggest plasticity and stability states regulated by neuromodulators and behavioral states and may reflect a partial solution to the stability–plasticity dilemma. In support of this view, we have reported that when LTP is induced while animals explore novel cages, both LTP magnitude and longevity are increased dramatically.[62] Thus, had LTP been induced in an aroused condition or in a novel environment, sustained LTP and sustained place fields might have been observed.

Of particular relevance to learning are the studies investigating the phenomenon of place cell remapping. Normally, place cells fire within circumscribed regions; cell activity remains stable and the cells retain their place specificity with repeated exposures to the same environment. This selective activity will persist, even with removal of a subset of cues. However, if the environment is changed beyond a threshold or an animal is placed in an unfamiliar environment, the most common result is a complete remapping of cells within that environment, frequently in a pattern that bears no resemblance to the original distribution of place fields.

Obviously, the remapping effect suggests rapid plastic interactions among principal cells that map features of the altered or new environment and as such would be expected to involve LTP. However, the results here are somewhat confounding. In a study by Kentros et al.,[7] the effects of CPP, an NMDA antagonist, on the remapping of place fields was addressed. Normally, remapping occurs when animals are then placed in a novel environment. These remapped place fields in both environments are stable among the distinct environments for days, and do not interfere with each other.

Would blocking LTP also block remapping? This was addressed by administering CPP and exposing an animal to a novel environment. As noted above, CPP had no effect on established place fields. However, the surprising result is that CPP did not alter initial remapping; in fact, this new remapped state persisted for 90 min after exposure. Clearly memory occurred in the presence of an NMDAR antagonist. However CPP did eliminate this stability of the newly formed map 24 hours later, such that reintroduction to the same novel environment 1 day later resulted in another distinct remapping of the environment. Thus NMDARs appear necessary for the long-term stability of place fields. A similar effect is seen with protein synthesis inhibitors that specifically block establishment of the late phase of LTP.[47–49] Here, as in the studies with NMDAR antagonists, anisomycin, a protein synthesis inhibitor, similarly blocked the long-term stability of place fields.

These studies suggest NMDARs and protein synthesis are necessary for the long-term stability of remapped place fields, a finding that fits with the view that L-LTP, which is mediated by NMDARs and protein synthesis, is involved in sustaining newly generated place fields. However, the most interesting aspect of this study is that NMDARs, and, presumably, LTP, apparently are not involved in the rapid experience-dependent formation of such fields. This is a peculiar result, given that remapping involves conditions in which LTP would be an ideal mechanism (specifically, rapid, associative and activity-dependent induction that usually precedes the later protein synthesis-dependent L-LTP). While these studies suggest the importance of LTP, particularly late or L-LTP, in long-term stability of place fields, the more important finding is that LTP, or more accurately, NMDARs, appear not to be involved in the rapid formation of place cell representations.

What plastic process, then, may underlie initial rapid remapping? If CPP blocks long-term stability (and presumably, L-LTP), how could L-LTP be involved in this later stability in the absence of the initial E-LTP? One possible explanation is that E-LTP is indeed involved in this process, although NMDAR blockade may not alter its induction. As an example, mossy fiber CA3 LTP and its presumed role in encoding offer a plausible framework to explain these results. A common theme in models of hippocampal function is that the CA3 region serves an autoassociative function by virtue of its extensive recurrent (CA3-CA3) excitatory connections. The view first formalized by Marr[54] that autoassociative processes are performed by the CA3 region remains a feature of most models of hippocampal function.[55,129]

These recurrent connections constitute the majority of excitatory inputs to CA3 pyramidal cells and can display Hebbian LTP.[52] Representations within the CA3 autoassociative system is thought to involve the formation of attractor states (or ensembles of active recurrently connected CA3 cells) as a result of plastic changes among CA3-CA3 synapses. Importantly, the formation of CA3 attractors is thought to occur via LTP of CA3-CA3 synapses by the coincident activity of the dentate mossy fiber projection, whose synapses are thought to act as powerful "detonator synapses."[54,55,130] The concurrent activation of CA3 pyramidal cells by detonator synapses is thought to mediate associative LTP induction of only those CA3-CA3 synapses that immediately preceded mossy fiber activity. Thus mossy fibers serve to establish a sparse ensemble of co-active CA3-CA3 cells thought to reflect a hippocampal "representation" within the CA3 region.

In the above context, how can the lack of an effect of NMDAR antagonists on remapping be explained? First, it should be noted that mossy fiber LTP was one of the first to be deemed a distinct form of LTP due to its independence from NMDARs and its unusual time course *in vivo*.[45,131] Second, our studies demonstrate an unusual property of associative LTP. If LTP is induced in a synaptic population in an associative manner, in this case by pairing weak synaptic activation of one pathway with a more intense activation of a separate set of converging afferents, LTP is observed in both pathways. However, the induction of LTP in the weak or "associated" pathway appears to be sensitive only to manipulations that block LTP induction in the other more intense, associating pathway used to induce LTP.

For example, NMDA receptor antagonists such as CPP normally block LTP induction in medial perforant path projections to the CA3 region. By contrast, projections arising from the lateral perforant path are unaffected by these antagonists.[132,133] However, if LTP is induced in lateral perforant path-CA3 synapses by the strong coactivation of the NMDAR-dependent medial perforant path, NMDAR antagonists effectively block LTP in both pathways. Conversely, if LTP is induced in this NMDAR-dependent medial pathway by strong activation of the NMDAR-independent lateral perforant pathway, CPP has no effect on associative LTP at medial perforant path synapses and LTP is observed in both lateral and medial perforant path-CA3 synaptic populations.

Extrapolation of this feature of associative LTP with current models assigning a detonator (or associating) function to mossy fiber synapses suggests the possibility that rapid encoding does indeed involve NMDAR-dependent LTP. However, during encoding, as NMDAR-dependent LTP among CA3-CA3 recurrents is thought to be induced in an associative manner via activation of the NMDAR-independent mossy fiber detonator synapses, it is possible that rapid remapping is unaffected by the NMDAR antagonist simply because associative LTP may have been induced by the coactivation of the mossy fiber detonators. Because the mossy fiber synapses display LTP that is insensitive to NMDAR antagonists, NMDAR antagonists may have had no effect on CA3-CA3 LTP or initial remapping due to the associative induction of NMDAR-dependent LTP by the stronger NMDAR-independent mossy fiber pathway.

Taken together, evidence for the role of LTP in establishing place fields is supportive; however, it is likely that a more definitive role for LTP in establishing place cells fields will emerge as details of place cell dynamics are revealed. Other than remapping, plastic processes associated with place cells and their fields are apparently quite subtle. Studies addressing such subtle changes in place cell dynamics have emerged; in particular, place cells can display dynamic changes with experience. In particular, if a rat runs along a linear trajectory that sequentially fires cells A, B, and C, repeated experiences with this trajectory result in an asymmetric "expansion" of the place field in the opposite direction of the animal's trajectory. Thus, over time, the activity of cell B slowly shifts in the direction of A, such that place cell B fires closer to the A place field earlier in the trajectory.[7] Because this phenomenon experience-dependent, it is not unreasonable to assume associative plastic processes may underlie its development. In addition, the closer association of sequences of cells would be expected with associative experience-dependent plastic changes, making LTP a likely candidate.

The phenomenon of asymmetric place field expansion also fits with the features of LTP seen experimentally. One aspect of LTP seen in addition to an increase in the amplitude of synaptic responses is a reduction in the latency of the population spike. Cells fire earlier at potentiated synapses after LTP induction, presumably due to the increases in synaptic strength. Thus asymmetric place field expansion and the earlier firing of recently activated cells within a sequence may be consequences of the reduced latency to cell discharge that normally follows LTP induction.

The property of asymmetric expansion fits well with the view that an associative process underlies this phenomenon. Subsequent studies revealed that in contrast to remapping, systemic administration of NMDAR antagonists blocks the asymmetric expansion of place fields.[134] Again, as noted for LTP, caution must be used when interpreting the effects of NMDAR antagonists and possible confounds because they appear to alter theta rhythm.[115,116] As place cell firing is tightly coupled to theta rhythm even within a place field, it is entirely possible that the temporal aspects place cell activity and their plastic coupling may depend on the integrity of theta during learning.

This progress is illustrative of an important heuristic approach to linking LTP with memory; many of the negative findings observed in studies linking LTP with behavioral learning arise primarily as a result of our rudimentary understanding of subtleties in the processes of LTP (such as the finding that the induction of associative LTP is determined exclusively by the receptor mechanisms of the stronger coactive pathway). Likewise, studies attempting to link LTP and place field formation are hindered by our lack of understanding of both the mechanics of LTP and the role of place cells in memory and their dynamic changes with experience. Future studies that integrate newly discovered features of place cell dynamics (Guzowski et al.[135]) with behavioral manipulations clearly serve as avenues that will contribute to our knowledge of LTP and our understanding of hippocampal function in general.

OUTSTANDING QUESTIONS AND NEW DIRECTIONS

By elucidating the underlying mechanisms of LTP and LTD, it seems possible to reconstruct some of the subcellular events triggered by experience and deprivation to alter neuronal function. It is also likely that more information about LTP and hippocampal function in general, will follow the studies of place cell dynamics and their plastic properties, particularly during remapping. The coming years will bring further understanding of the factors regulating the induction, maintenance, and distribution of long-lasting synaptic modifications and their contributions to normal adaptive behavior.

ACKNOWLEDGMENTS

The authors thank D. Castillo and A. Gómez-Palacio Shjetnan for their help during the preparation of the figures. Part of the work was supported by PAPIIT IN213503 (M.L.E.), NIH/NINDS and NIH/NIGMS (B.E.D.).

REFERENCES

1. Bliss, T.V.P. and Lomo, T. Long-lasting potentiation of synaptic transmission in the dentate area of the anaesthetized rabbit following stimulation of the perforant path. *J. Physiol.,* 232, 331, 1973.
2. Bliss, T. and Gardner-Medwin, A. Long-lasting potentiation of synaptic transmission in the dentate area of the unanesthetized rabbit following stimulation of the perforant path. *J. Physiol.,* 232, 357, 1973.
3. Xie, X., Barrionuevo, G., and Berger, T.W. Differential expression of short-term potentiation by AMPA and NMDA receptors in dentate gyrus. *Learn. Mem.*, 3, 115, 1996.

4. Hanse, E. and Gustafsson, B. Onset and stabilization of NMDA receptor-dependent hippocampal long-term potentiation. *Neurosci. Res.* 20, 15, 1994.
5. Martinez, C.O., Do, V.H., and Derrick, B.E. Associative LTP among afferents to the CA3 region *in vivo. Brain Res.* 94, 86, 2002.
6. Mehta, M.R., Barnes, C.A., and McNaughton B.L. Experience-dependent asymmetric expansion of hippocampal place fields. *Proc. Natl. Acad. Sci. USA,* 94, 8918, 1997.
7. Kentros, C., Hargreaves, E., Hawkins, R.D., Kandel, E.R., Shapiro, M., and Muller R.V. Abolition of long-term stability of new hippocampal place cell maps by NMDA receptor blockade. *Science*, 280, 2121, 1998.
8. Staubli, U. and Lynch, G. Stable hippocampal long-term potentiation elicited by "theta" pattern stimulation. *Brain Res.,* 435, 227, 1987.
9. McNaughton, B.L., Douglas, R.M., and Goddard, D.V. Synaptic enhancement in fascia dentata: cooperativity among coactive afferents. *Brain Res.*, 157, 277, 1978.
10. Gustafsson, B., Wigstrom, H., Abraham, W.C., and Huang, Y.Y. Long-term potentiation in the hippocampus using depolarizing current pulses as the conditioning stimulus to single volley synaptic potentials. *J. Neurosci.*, 7, 774, 1987.
11. Barnes, C.A. Memory deficits associated with senescence: a neurophysiological and behavioral study in the rat. *J. Comp. Physiol. Psychol.,* 93, 74, 1979.
12. Squire, L.R. *Memory and the Brain.* Oxford University Press, New York, 1987.
13. Wilson, M.A. and McNaughton, B.L. Reactivation of hippocampal ensemble memories during sleep. *Science*, 265, 676, 1994.
14. Cartwright, R.D. The role of sleep in changing our minds: a psychologist's discussion of papers on memory reactivation and consolidation in sleep. *Learn. Mem.*, 11, 660, 2004.
15. Bontempi, B., Laurent-Demir, C., Destrade, C., and Jaffard, R. Time-dependent reorganization of brain circuitry underlying long-term memory storage. *Nature*, 400, 671, 1999.
16. Villarreal, D., Do, V., Haddad, E., and Derrick, B.E. NMDA antagonists sustain LTP and spatial memory: evidence for active processes underlying LTP decay. *Nat. Neurosci.,* 5, 48, 2002.
17. Hebb, D.O. *The Organization of Behavior.* John Wiley & Sons, New York, 1949.
18. Barrionuevo, G., Schottler, F., Lynch, G. The effects of repetitive low frequency stimulation on control and "potentiated" synaptic responses in the hippocampus. *Life Sci.*, 27, 2385, 1980.
19. Bear, M.F. Homosynaptic long-term depression: a mechanism for memory? *Proc. Natl. Acad. Sci. USA*, 96, 9457, 1999.
20. Mulkey, R.M., Herron, C.E., and Malenka, R.C. An essential role for protein phosphatases in hippocampal long-term depression. *Science*, 261, 1051, 1993.
21. Christie, B.R. and Abraham, W.C. Priming of associative long-term depression in the dentate gyrus by theta frequency synaptic activity. *Neuron*, 9, 79, 1992.
22. Debanne, D. and Thompson, S.M. Associative long-term depression in the hippocampus *in vitro. Hippocampus,* 6, 9, 1996.
23. Wickens, J.R. and Abraham, W.C. Involvement of L-type calcium channels in heterosynaptic long-term depression in the hippocampus. *Neurosci. Lett.* 130, 128, 1991.
24. Normann, C., Peckys, D., Schulze, C.H., Walden, J., Jonas, P., and Bischofberger, J. Associative long-term depression in the hippocampus is dependent on postsynaptic N-type Ca^{2+} channels. *J. Neurosci.*, 15, 8290, 2000.
25. Massey, P.V. et al. Differential roles of NR2A and NR2B-containing NMDA receptors in cortical long-term potentiation and long-term depression. *J. Neurosci.* 24, 7821, 2004.

26. Moult, P.R. et al. Tyrosine phosphatases regulate AMPA receptor trafficking during metabotropic glutamate receptor-mediated long-term depression. *J. Neurosci.*, 26, 2544, 2006.
27. Wang, J., Yeckel, M.F., Johnston, D., and Zucker, R.S. Photolysis of postsynaptic caged Ca^{2+} can potentiate and depress mossy fiber synaptic responses in rat hippocampal CA3 pyramidal neurons. *J. Neurophysiol.*, 91, 1596, 2004.
28. Lei S. et al. Depolarization-induced long-term depression at hippocampal mossy fiber-CA3 pyramidal neuron synapses. *J. Neurosci.*, 23, 9786, 2003.
29. Domenici, M.R., Berretta, N., and Cherubini, E. Two distinct forms of long-term depression coexist at the mossy fiber-CA3 synapse in the hippocampus during development. *Proc. Natl. Acad. Sci. USA*, 95, 8310, 1998.
30. Derrick, B.E. and Martinez, J.L., Jr. Associative bidirectional modifications at the hippocampal mossy fibre CA3 synapse. *Nature*, 381, 429, 1996.
31. Kobayashi, K., Manabe, T., and Takahashi, T. Presynaptic long-term depression at the hippocampal mossy fiber CA3 synapse. *Science,* 273, 648, 1996.
32. Brown, G.D., Dalloz, P., and Hulme, C. Mathematical and connectionist models of human memory: a comparison. *Memory,* 3, 113, 1995.
33. Skaggs, W.E. and McNaughton, B.L. Computational approaches to hippocampal function. *Curr. Opin. Neurobiol.,* 2, 209, 1992.
34. Morris, R.G.M. Computational neuroscience: modeling the brain, in *Parallel Distributed Processing Implications for Psychology and Neurobiology,* Morris, R.G.M., Ed., Oxford University Press, New York, 1989, p. 203.
35. Gustafsson, B. and Wigstrom, H. Long-term potentiation in the hippocampal CA1 region: its induction and early temporal development. *Progr. Brain Res.*, 83, 223, 1990.
36. Malinow, R. and Miller, J.P. Postsynaptic hyperpolarization during conditioning reversibly blocks long-term potentiation. *Nature*, 320, 529, 1986.
37. Lynch, G., Larson, J., Kelso, S., Barrionuevo, G., and Schottler, F. Intracellular injections of EGTA block induction of hippocampal long-term potentiation. *Nature*, 305, 719, 1983.
38. Johnston, D., Williams, S., Jaffe, D., and Gray, R. NMDA receptor-independent long-term potentiation. *Annu. Rev. Physiol.*, 54, 489, 1992.
39. Yeckel, M.F., Kapur, A., and Johnston., D., Multiple forms of LTP in hippocampal CA3 neurons use a common postsynaptic mechanism. *Nat. Neurosci.*, 2, 625, 1999.
40. Sanes, J.R. and Lichtman, J.W. Can molecules explain long-term potentiation? *Nat. Neurosci.*, 2, 597, 1999.
41. Derkach, V., Barria, A., and Soderling TR. Ca^{2+}/calmodulin kinase II enhances channel conductance of alpha-amino-3-hydroxy-5-methyl-4-isoxazolepropionate type glutamate receptors. *Proc. Natl. Acad. Sci. USA*, 96, 3269, 1999.
42. Oh, M.C. et al. Extrasynaptic membrane trafficking regulated by GluR1 serine 845 phosphorylation primes AMPA receptors for long-term potentiation. *J. Biol. Chem.*, 281, 752, 2006.
43. Bourtchuladze, R. et al. Deficient long-term memory in mice with a targeted mutation of the cAMP-responsive element-binding protein. *Cell,* 79, 59, 1994.
44. Frey, U. and Morris, R.G. Synaptic tagging: implications for late maintenance of hippocampal long-term potentiation. *Trends Neurosci.*, 385, 533, 1998.
45. Harris, E.W. and Cotman, C.W. Long-term potentiation of guinea pig mossy fiber responses is not blocked by N-methyl D-aspartate antagonists. *Neurosci. Lett.,* 70, 132, 1986.

46. French, P.J. et al. Subfield-specific immediate early gene expression associated with hippocampal long-term potentiation *in vivo*, *Eur. J. Neurosci.*, 13, 968, 2001.
47. Stanton, P.K. and Sarvey, J.M. Rapid spine delivery and redistribution of AMPA receptors after synaptic NMDA receptor activation: blockade of long-term potentiation in rat hippocampal CA1 region by inhibitors of protein synthesis. *J. Neurosci.*, 4, 3080, 1984.
48. Krug, M., Lossner, B.. and Ott, T. Anisomycin blocks the late phase of long-term potentiation in the dentate gyrus of freely moving rats. *Brain Res. Bull.*, 13, 39, 1984.
49. Otani, S., Marshall, C.J., Tate, W.P., Goddard, G.V., and Abraham, W.C. Maintenance of long-term potentiation in rat dentate gyrus requires protein synthesis but not messenger RNA synthesis immediately post-tetanization. *Neuroscience,* 28, 519, 1989.
50. Jaffe, D. and Johnston, D. Induction of long-term potentiation at hippocampal mossy fibers follow a Hebbian rule. *J. Neurophys.,* 64, 948, 1990.
51. Williams, S. and Johnston, D. Long-term potentiation of hippocampal mossy fiber synapses is blocked by postsynaptic injection of calcium chelators. *Neuron*, 3, 583, 1989.
52. Derrick, B.E. and Martinez, J.L., Jr. Opioid receptor activation is one factor underlying the frequency dependence of mossy fiber LTP induction. *J. Neurosci.*, 14, 4359, 1994.
53. Jung, M.W. and McNaughton, B.L. Spatial selectivity of unit activity in the hippocampal granular layer. *Hippocampus*, 3, 165, 1993.
54. Marr, D. Simple memory: a theory for archicorticortex. *Proc. R. Soc. London B,* 262, 23, 1971.
55. Morris, R.G.M. and McNaughton, B.L. Memory storage in a distributed model of hippocampal formation. *Trends Neurosci.*, 10, 408, 1987.
56. Abraham, W. and Bear, M. Metaplasticity: plasticity of synaptic plasticity. *Trends Neurosci*, 19, 126, 1996.
57. Escobar, M., Barea-Rodriguez, E.J., Derrick, B.E., and Martinez, J.L., Jr. Mossy fiber synaptogenesis is induced by high frequency stimulation of mossy fibers. *Brain Res.*, 751, 330, 1997.
58. Derrick, B.E.,York, A., and Martinez, J.L., Jr. Increases in granule cell neurogenesis following stimulation that induces mossy fiber LTP. *Brain Res.*, 857, 800, 2000.
59. Morgan, S.L. and Teyler, T.J. Electrical stimuli patterned after the theta-rhythm induce multiple forms of LTP. *J. Neurophysiol.*, 86, 1289, 2001.
60. Raymond, C.R. and Redman S.J. Different calcium sources are narrowly tuned to the induction of different forms of LTP. *J. Neurophysiol.*, 88, 249, 2002.
61. Hoffman, D.A., Sprengel, R., and Sakmann, B. Molecular dissection of hippocampal theta-burst pairing potentiation. *Proc. Natl. Acad. Sci. USA,* 99, 7740, 2002.
62. Davis, C.D., Jones, F.L., and Derrick, B.E. Novel environments enhance the induction and maintenance of long-term potentiation in the dentate gyrus. *J. Neurosci.*, 24, 6497, 2004.
63. Li, S., Cullen, W.K., Anwyl, R., and Rowan, M.J. Dopamine-dependent facilitation of LTP induction in hippocampal CA1 by exposure to spatial novelty. *Nat. Neurosci.*, 6, 526, 2003.
64. Straube, T., Korz, V., Balschun, D., and Frey, J.U. Requirement of beta-adrenergic receptor activation and protein synthesis for LTP-reinforcement by novelty in rat dentate gyrus. *J. Physiol.*, 552, 953, 2003.

65. Turrigiano, G.G., Leslie, K.R., Desai, N.S., Ruterford, L.C., and Nelson, S.B. Activity dependent scaling of quantal amplitude in neocortical neurons. *Nature*, 391, 892, 1998.
66. Bienenstock, E.L., Cooper, L.N., and Munro, P.W. Theory for the development of neuron selectivity: orientation specificity and binocular interaction in visual cortex. *J. Neurosci.*, 2, 32, 1982.
67. Quinlan, E.M., Olstein, D.H., and Bear, M.F. Bidirectional, experience-dependent regulation of N-methyl-D-aspartate receptor subunit composition in the rat visual cortex during postnatal development. *Proc. Natl. Acad. Sci. USA*, 96, 876, 1999.
68. Philpot, B.D., Sekhar, A.K., Shouval, H.Z.. and Bear, M.F. Visual experience and deprivation bidirectionally modify the composition and function of NMDA receptors in visual cortex. *Neuron*, 29, 157, 2001.
69. Rogan, M.T., Staubli, U.V., and LeDoux, J.E. Fear conditioning induces associative long-term potentiation in the amygdala. *Nature,* 390, 604, 1997.
70. McKernan, M.G. and Shinnick-Gallagher, P. Fear conditioning induces a lasting potentiation of synaptic currents *in vitro*. *Nature*, 390, 607, 1997.
71. Rioult-Pedotti, M.S., Friedman, D., Hess, G., and Donoghue, J.P., Strengthening of horizontal cortical connections following skill learning. *Nat. Neurosci.*, 1, 230, 1998.
72. Escobar, M.L. and Bermúdez-Rattoni, F. Long-term potentiation in the insular cortex enhances conditioned taste aversion retention. *Brain Res.*, 852, 208, 2000.
73. Malenka, R.C. and Bear, M. LTP and LTD: an embarrassment of riches. *Neuron*, 44, 5, 2004.
74. Rittenhouse, C.D., Shouval, H.Z., Paradiso, M.A., and Bear, M.F. Monocular deprivation induces homosynaptic long-term depression in visual cortex. *Nature*, 397, 347, 1999.
75. Allen, C.B., Celikel, T., and Feldman, D.E. Long-term depression induced by sensory deprivation during cortical map plasticity *in vivo*. *Nat. Neurosci.*, 6, 291, 2003.
76. Celikel, T., Szostak, V.A., and Feldman, D.E. Modulation of spike timing by sensory deprivation during induction of cortical map plasticity. *Nat. Neurosci.*, 7, 534, 2004.
77. Heynen, A.J. et al. Molecular mechanisms for loss of visual cortical responsiveness following brief monocular deprivation. *Nat. Neurosci.*, 6, 854, 2003.
78. Sawtell, N.B., Huber, K.M., Roder, J.C., and Bear, M.F. Induction of NMDA receptor-dependent long-term depression in visual cortex does not require metabotropic glutamate receptors. *J. Neurophysiol.*, 82, 3594, 1999.
79. Hyman, S.E. and Malenka, R.C. Addiction and the brain: the neurobiology of compulsion and its persistence. *Nat. Rev. Neurosci.*, 2, 695, 2001.
80. Kelley, A.E. Memory and addiction: Shared neural circuitry and molecular mechanisms. *Neuron*, 44, 161, 2004.
81. Ungless, M.A., Whistier, J.L., Malenka, R.C., and Bonci, A. Single cocaine exposure *in vivo* induces long-term potentiation in dopamine neurons. *Nature*, 411, 583, 2001.
82. Faleiro, L.J., Jones, S., and Kauer, J.A. Rapad synaptic plasticity of glutamatergic synapses on dopamine neurons in the ventral tegmental area in response to acute amphetamine injection. *Neuropsychopharmacology,* 29, 2115, 2004.
83. Liao, D., Hessler, N.A., and Malinow, R. Activation of post-synaptically silent synapses during pairing-induced LTP in CA1 region of hippocampal slice. *Nature*, 375, 400, 1995.
84. Malinow, R. and Malenka, R.C. AMPA receptor trafficking and synaptic plasticity. *Annu. Rev. Neurosci.*, 25, 103, 2002.
85. Collingridge, G.L., Isaac, J.T.R., and Wang, Y.T. Receptor trafficking and synaptic plasticity. *Nat. Rev. Neurosci.*, 5, 952, 2004.

86. Emptage, N.J., Reid, C.A., Fine, A., and Bliss, T.V. Optical quantal analysis reveals a presynaptic component of LTP at hippocampal Schaffer-associational synapses. *Neuron*, 38, 797, 2003.
87. Choi, S., Klingauf, J., and Tsien, R.W. Fusion pore modulation as a presynaptic mechanism contributing to expression of long-term potentiation. *Philos. Trans. R. Soc. London B,* 358, 695, 2003.
88. Zakharenko, S.S. et al. Presynaptic BDNF required for a presynaptic but not post-synaptic component of LTP at hippocampal CA1-CA3 synapses. *Neuron*, 39, 975, 2003.
89. Lauri, S.E. et al. Functional maturation of CA1 synapses involves activity-dependent loss of tonic kainate receptor-mediated inhibition of glutamate release. *Neuron*, 50, 415, 2006.
90. Schulz, P.E., Cook, E.P., and Johnston, D. Changes in paired-pulse facilitation suggest presynaptic involvement in long-term potentiation. *J. Neurosci.*, 14, 5325, 1994.
91. Bayer, K.U., De Koninck, P., Leonard, A.S., Hell, J.W., and Schulman, H. Interaction with the NMDA receptor locks CaMKII in an active conformation. *Nature*, 411, 801, 2001.
92. Leonard, A.S. et al. Regulation of calcium/calmodulin-dependent protein kinase II docking to N-methyl-D-aspartate receptors by calcium/calmodulin and alpha-actinin. *J. Biol. Chem.*, 277, 48441, 2002.
93. Si, S.H. et al. Phosphorylation of the AMPA receptor GluR1 subunit is required for synaptic plasticity and retention of spatial memory. *Science*, 284, 1755, 1999.
94. Luthi, A. et al. Hippocampal LTD expression involves a pool of AMPARs regulated by the NSF-GluR2 interaction. *Neuron,* 24, 389, 1999.
95. Lynch, G. and Baudry, M. The biochemistry of memory: a new and specific hypothesis. *Science*, 224, 1057, 1984.
96. Lisman, J.E. and McIntyre, C.C. Synaptic plasticity: a molecular memory switch. *Curr. Biol.*, 11, 788, 2001.
97. Boehm, J. and Malinow, R. AMPA receptor phosphorylation during synaptic plasticity. *Biochem. Soc. Trans.*, 33, 1354, 2005.
98. Perez-Otaño, I. and Ehlers, M.D. Homeostatic plasticity and NMDA receptor trafficking. *Trends Neurosci.,* 28, 229, 2002.
99. Lohof, A.M., Ip, N.Y., and Poo, M.M. Potentiation of developing neuromuscular synapses by the neurotrophins NT-3 and BDNF. *Nature,* 363, 350, 1993.
100. Kang, H. and Schuman, E.M. Long-lasting neurotrophin-induced enhancement of synaptic transmission in the adult hippocampus. *Science*, 267, 1658, 1995.
101. Ying, S.W. et al. Brain-derived neurotrophic factor induces long-term potentiation in intact adult hippocampus: requirement for ERK activation coupled to CREB and upregulation of Arc synthesis. *J. Neurosci.*, 22, 1532, 2002.
102. Bramham, C.R. and Messaoudi, E. BDNF function in adult synaptic plasticity: the synaptic consolidation hypothesis. *Progr. Neurobiol.*, 76, 99, 2005.
103. Pang, P.T. et al. Cleavage of proBDNF by tPA/plasmin is essential for long-term hippocampal plasticity. *Science*, 306, 487, 2004.
104. McAllister, A.K., Katz, L.C., and Lo, D.C. Neurotrophins and synaptic plasticity. *Annu. Rev. Neurosci.*, 22, 295, 1999.
105. Jiang, B. et al. Brain-derived neurotrophic factor induces long-lasting potentiation of synaptic transmission in visual cortex in vivo in young rats, but not in the adult. *Eur. J. Neurosci.*, 14, 1219, 2001.

106. Tokuyama, W., Okuno, H., Hashimoto, T., Li, Y.X., and Miyashita, Y. BDNF upregulation during declarative memory formation in monkey inferior temporal cortex. *Nat. Neurosci.*, 3, 1134, 2000.
107. Escobar, M.L., Figueroa-Guzmán, Y., and Gómez-Palacio Schjetnan, A. *In vivo* insular cortex LTP induced by brain-derived neurotrophic factor. *Brain Res.*, 991, 274, 2003.
108. Castillo, V., Figueroa-Guzmán, Y., and Escobar, M.L. Brain-derived neurotrophic factor enhances conditioned taste aversion retention. *Brain Res.,* 1067, 250, 2006.
109. Yamada, K., Mizuno, M., and Nabeshima, T. Role for brain-derived neurotrophic factor in learning and memory. *Life Sci.*, 70, 735, 2002.
110. Minichiello, L. et al. Mechanism of Trk-mediated hippocampal long-term potentiation. *Neuron*, 36, 121, 2002.
111. Tyler, W.J., Alonso, M., Bramham, C.R., and Pozzo-Miller, L.D. From acquisition to consolidation: on the role of brain-derived neurotrophic factor signaling in hippocampal-dependent learning. *Learn. Mem.* 9, 224, 2002.
112. Morris, R.G., Anderson, E., Lynch, G.S., and Baudry, M. Selective impairment of learning and blockade of long-term potentiation by an N-methyl-D-aspartate receptor antagonist AP5. *Nature*, 319, 774, 1986.
113. Davis, S., Butcher, S.P., and Morris, R.G. The NMDA receptor antagonist D-2-amino-5-phosphonopentanoate (D-AP5) impairs spatial learning and LTP *in vivo* at intracerebral concentrations comparable to those that block LTP *in vitro*. *J. Neurosci.*, 12, 21, 1992.
114. Buzsaki, G. Theta oscillations in the hippocampus. *Neuron*, 33, 325, 2002.
115. Pitkanen, M., Sirvio, J., Ylinen, A., Koivisto, E., and Riekkinen, P., Sr. Effects of NMDA receptor modulation on hippocampal type 2 theta activity in rats. *Gen. Pharmacol.*, 26, 1065, 1995.
116. Leung, L.W. and Desborough, K.A. APV, an N-methyl-D-aspartate receptor antagonist, blocks the hippocampal theta rhythm in behaving rats. *Brain Res.*, 463, 148, 1988.
117. Tsien, J.Z., Huerta, P.T., and Tonegawa, S. The essential role of hippocampal CA1 NMDA receptor-dependent synaptic plasticity in spatial memory. *Cell*, 87, 1327, 1996.
118. Hinds, H.L., Tonegawa, S., and Malinow, R. CA1 long-term potentiation is diminished but present in hippocampal slices from alpha-CaMKII mutant mice. *Learn. Mem.*, 5, 344, 1998.
119. Giese, K.P., Fedorov, N.B., Filipkowski, R.K., and Silva, A.J. Auto-phosphorylation at Thr286 of the alpha calcium-calmodulin kinase II in LTP and learning. *Science*, 279, 870, 1998.
120. Nakazawa, K. et al. Requirement for hippocampal CA3 NMDA receptors in associative memory recall. *Science*. 297, 211, 2002.
121. Castro, C.A., Silbert, L.H., McNaughton, B.L., and Barnes, C.A. Recovery of spatial learning deficits after decay of electrically induced synaptic enhancement in the hippocampus. *Nature*, 342, 545, 1989.
122. Barnes, C.A. et al. LTP saturation and spatial learning disruption: effects of task variables and saturation levels. *J. Neurosci.*, 14, 5793, 1994.
123. McNaughton, B.L., Barnes, C.A., Meltzer, J., and Sutherland, R.J. Hippocampal granule cells are necessary for normal spatial learning but not for spatially selective pyramidal cell discharge. *Exp. Brain Res.*, 76, 485, 1989.
124. Moser, E.I., Krobert, K.A., Moser, M.B., and Morris, R.G. Impaired spatial learning after saturation of long-term potentiation. *Science*, 281, 2038, 1998.

125. O'Keefe, J. and Nadel, L. *The Hippocampus as a Cognitive Map.* Oxford University Press, New York, 1978.
126. Wilson, M.A. and McNaughton, B.L. Dynamics of the hippocampal ensemble code for space. *Science,* 261,1055, 1993.
127. Jeffery, K.J. et al. A proposed architecture for the neural representation of spatial context. *Neurosci. Biobehav. Rev.,* 28, 201, 2004.
128. Dragoi, G., Harris, K.D., and Buzsaki, G. Place representation within hippocampal networks is modified by long-term potentiation. *Neuron,* 39, 843, 2003.
129. Treves, A. and Rolls, E.T. Computational analysis of the role of the hippocampus in memory. *Hippocampus*, 4, 374, 1994.
130. Henze, D.A., Wittner, L., and Buzsaki, G. Single granule cells reliably discharge targets in the hippocampal CA3 network *in vivo. Nat. Neurosci.*, 5, 790, 2002.
131. Derrick, B.E. and Martinez, J.L., Jr. A unique opioid peptide-dependent form of long-term potentiation is found in the CA3 region of the rat hippocampus. *Adv. Biosci.,* 75, 213, 1989.
132. Do, V., Martinez, C.O., Martinez, J.L.M., and Derrick, B.E. Long-term potentiation in direct perforant path projections to hippocampal area CA3 *in vivo. J. Neurophys.*, 87, 669, 2002.
133. Kosub, K.A., Do, V.H., and Derrick, B.E. NMDA receptor antagonists block heterosynaptic long-term depression (LTD) but not long-term potentiation (UP) in the CA3 region following lateral perforant path stimulation. *Neurosci. Lett.*, 374, 29, 2005.
134. Ekstrom, A.D., Meltzer, J., McNaughton, B.L., and Barnes C.A. NMDA receptor antagonism blocks experience-dependent expansion of hippocampal "place fields." *Neuron*, 31, 631, 2001.
135. Guzowski, J.F., Knierim, J.J., and Moser, E.I. Ensemble dynamics of hippocampal regions CA3 and CA1. *Neuron*, 44, 581, 2005.

3 Molecular Mechanisms of Synaptic Plasticity Underlying Long-Term Memory Formation

Victor Ramirez-Amaya

CONTENTS

3.1 INTRODUCTION

Learning a new behavior and acquiring information from the environment require that specific patterns of neural activity induced by experience are maintained through plasticity in specific neural networks.[1] The persistence of the acquired information depends on how long the plastic changes are preserved. It is believed that persistent forms of synaptic plasticity, including structural synaptic plasticity among others, occur in specific neuronal ensembles, in order to maintain the information in long-term memory.

Neural activity leads to a series of molecular events such as the activation of certain neurotransmitter and kinase systems, Ca2+ influx, induction of gene expression, translation and regulation of proteins, and many others that are essential to establish the plastic changes underlying long-term memory. In this chapter I will review some of the molecular events that are relevant for the persistent forms of synaptic plasticity.

3.2 EARLY SIGNALS

Throughout the process of memory consolidation, structural changes may be driven by the initial activation of one or several neurotransmitter receptors. Probably the most important excitatory neurotransmitter system for cognitive-related plasticity is the glutamatergic system. Its involvement in persistent forms of synaptic plasticity is well accepted.[2,3] During development, dendritic spines are highly motile and it has been observed that stimulation of either α-amino-5-hydroxy-3-methyl-4-isoxazole propionic acid (AMPA) or N-methyl d-aspartate (NMDA) receptors inhibit this motility.[4]

By the use of time-lapse imaging of fluorescent glutamate receptor subunits, Washburne and colleagues[5] demonstrated that NMDA and AMPA receptor subunits are present in motile filopodia before and during synaptogenesis and the activation of this glutamatergic receptors inhibits their motility.[6] This suggests that glutamatergic transmission is important for stabilizing synaptic contacts and also that the formation of new synapses may depend on glutamatergic-related activity.

Consistent with this interpretation, in the adult brain LTP induction alters the structure of synapses[7] and inhibition of LTP with an NMDA receptor antagonist, D(-)-2-amino-5-phosphonovaleric acid (AP5), prevents this structural change.[9] Behavioral studies show similar results; for example, water maze overtraining induces changes in the distribution of mossy fiber boutons in the CA3 region of the hippocampus[10] and these changes are blocked by pre-treating animals with the NMDA receptor antagonist MK801.[11]

Increased spine density in the hippocampus is observed 24 h after trace eyeblink conditioning, and again, NMDA receptor antagonists block these changes.[12] This supports the idea that glutamatergic transmission may be an important first step in the mechanisms underlying structural synaptic plasticity.

Another interesting feature of glutamatergic transmission that may be of importance for the persistence forms of memory is that the number of AMPA and NMDA receptor molecules in the postsynaptic membrane is a function of the activity history of the synapse.[13–16] The regulation of glutamate receptor density in the postsynaptic membrane has been implicated in a special form of synaptic plasticity known as synaptic scaling.[17–19] This is a homeostatic regulation, in which the strength of the synaptic inputs across the dendrite are modulated, while preserving their relative weights. This mechanism homeostatically adjust the postsynaptic dendrite to recent changes in the efficiency of the synapse, and it is required to stabilize the plastic changes in the neural network.[17,20-22] In this way, the mechanisms that regulate the endocytosis, aggregation, and trafficking of glutamate receptors in the postsynaptic membrane is involved in this persistent form of synaptic plasticity and consequently in long-term memory.

Studies of LTP using inhibitory avoidance tasks, the Morris water maze, and conditioned taste aversion indicate that the progress of memory formation requires early involvement of NMDA, AMPA, and metabotropic glutamate receptors that may be regulated by cholinergic and GABA-ergic transmission.[23]

An interaction of cholinergic and glutamate receptors has been postulated. Their activity converges, as demonstrated by studies of the multiple signal transduction pathways mediated by these receptors.[24,25] It is possible that different signal transduction cascades of fast (glutamatergic) and modulatory (cholinergic) neurotransmissions are both necessary for long-term synaptic plasticity and may converge in a given neuron.[26] Moreover, it has been suggested that this convergent signaling may promote morphological changes in such neurons.[27] This led to the hypothesis of a cholinergic regulation of long-term synaptic plasticity, suggesting that cholinoceptive cells can undergo changes in their dendritic structures as a result of ACh receptor activation by inducing the degradation of MAP-2 structures.[27] It is suggested that such structural changes may occur during memory consolidation and may be responsible for long-term memory storage. Recently, it has been demonstrated that cholinergic receptors mediate NGF-induced excitatory synaptogenesis,[28] supporting the idea that ACh can be related with molecular signals leading to morphological plasticity.

Postnatal lesions of the nucleus basalis magnocellularis in rats that produce robust cholinergic deafferentations in the cortex alter the differentiation of cortical neurons and synaptic connectivity that persist into maturity and contribute to altered cognitive behavior.[29] In the honey bee brain, it has been observed that treatment with pilocarpine, a muscarinic agonist, induced an increase in the volume of the neuropil similar to that observed after foraging behavioral experience.[30] This represents some of the most direct evidence of a possible role of ACh in structural synaptic plasticity.

Other neurotransmitter systems may also contribute to triggering or modulating persistent forms of synaptic plasticity.[31] It is possible that synergistic actions between various systems may be required to trigger long-lasting synaptic changes. Nevertheless, these initial signals may converge in certain common cellular events such as the influx of calcium and the activation of the kinase–phosphatase system among others.

2.3 CA^{2+} AND ITS TRANSDUCER

After the activation of neurotransmitter receptors, several downstream signals are triggered. Probably the most prominent signal for synaptic plasticity is calcium which has the ability to interact with the actin cytoskeletons of dendrites and through this interaction regulates structural synaptic plasticity (for review, see Oertner and Matus[32]). However, after synaptic activation, the influx of calcium ions (Ca^{2+}) into cells through ligand- and voltage-gated calcium channels or from internal reservoirs results in a complex set of transitory and oscillatory signals. This complex signal requires a molecular device to transform it into a more stable and perdurable message. Such a device should be capable of activating the intracellular cascades involved in the stabilization of synaptic plasticity.

The Ca^{2+}/calmodulin-dependent protein kinase II (CaMKII) is a ubiquitous and broad specificity Ser/Thr protein kinase highly enriched in the central nervous system. This enzyme is highly concentrated in the post-synaptic density and is considered an important Ca^{2+} detector in the postsynaptic region.[33] The unique regulatory properties of CaMKII make it an ideal interpreter of the diversity of Ca^{2+} signals. Evidence has shown that CaMKII can interpret messages coded in the amplitude and duration of individual Ca^{2+} spikes and translate them into distinct amounts of long-lasting Ca^{2+}-independent activity.[34]

In a nonactivated state, CaMKII is auto-inhibited, but when it interacts with Ca^{2+}/CaM complexes, the blockade is released. After activation, CaMKII phosphorylates other proteins but also displays an important autophosphorylation activity.

When CaMKII is autophosphorylated, the dissociation rate with CaM decreases; the enzyme is able to remain active even after CaM has dissociated from it. Thus, autophosphorylation generates a constitutive active form of CaMKII able to translate a transient Ca^{2+} signal into a persistent and independent one (for review, see Cammaroto et al.[35]). The ability of CaMKII to maintain phosphorylation activity for a prolonged period through autophosphorylation[36] represents an important way to sustain signaling and may have great relevance for the consolidation of long-term synaptic plasticity.

Interestingly, CaMKII mRNA is located in the dendrites and accumulates in their active regions.[37,38] It is well-known that polyribosomal complexes are selectively localized beneath postsynaptic sites in dendrites,[39,40] and their activation can be regulated by glutamatergic activity.[41] The translation of CaMKII mRNA in dendrites is regulated by synaptic activity[37,38] and depends on NMDA receptor activation.[42]

The active form of CaMKII is found in the postsynaptic density[43] where it interacts with different molecules important for the structures and functions of the postsynapses. The molecules include PSD-95,[44] densin-180,[45,46] F-actin,[47] and particularly the NMDA glutamate receptor.

After CaMKII is activated in the postsynaptic density, it interacts with NMDA glutamate receptors.[48] This interaction is very important because it increases CaMKII autophosphorylation and its ability to become hyperphosphorylated.[49] For this reason, CaMKII–NMDA interaction has several consequences important for synaptic plasticity. It increases the affinity of CaMKII and the NMDA receptor subunit NR2B, making this interaction to last longer.[49] It will enhance AMPA receptor conductance by phosphorylating AMPA receptors.[50] Hyperphosphorylation can also increase the period of activation by saturating local phosphatase molecules, preventing dephosphorylation.[51] Finally, hyperphosphorylation of CaMKII may increase the interactions between NMDA and AMPA receptors.[51] The interactions may induce the insertion of AMPA receptors into synaptic sites that already contain NMDA receptors.[52]

These functional properties of CaMKII are highly relevant for the proposal that CaMKII may work as a memory switch, in which CaMKII activity changes between a transitory to a stable state depending on the interaction between CaMKII and the NMDA receptor.[33] Recent evidence has shown that this may indeed be the most prominent feature of CaMKII.[53] After stimulation CaMKII transiently translocates to the synapses where it binds the NMDA receptor at its substrate binding S-site; in this condition CaMKII activity is Ca2+/CaM-dependent, but after prolonged stimulation a persistent interaction between CaMKII and the NMDA receptor can be formed where NR2B binds at the T286-binding site, keeping the autoregulatory domain displaced and enabling Ca2+/CaM independent kinase activity.

Together, this evidence supports a crucial role of CaMKII in the persistent forms of synaptic plasticity. In agreement, induction of LTP in the CA1 region of the hippocampus is known to rapidly increase the synthesis and accumulation of CaMKII[54] and also induces its autophosphorylation activity.[55,56] Administration of Ca^{2+}/CaM in the postsynapse induces synaptic potentiation and the maintenance of this potentiation depends on the activity of CaMKII.[57] Also, the induction of LTP causes the redistribution of GluR1 from intracellular pools into dendritic spines.[58] This redistribution may be important for the stability of LTP and can be mimicked by the activation of CaMKII.[52] It is noteworthy that local translation of CaMKII protein is required for late-phase LTP,[59] which further emphasizes the central role of CaMKII in long-term synaptic plasticity.

One of the ways synaptic plasticity may persist is through structural synaptic changes. Evidence has shown that CaMKII participates in structural synaptic plasticity. The induction of LTP along with sensory stimulation promotes rapid growth of dendritic filopodia and the formation of dendritic spines and new synapses.[8,9,60] In a remarkable work using hippocampal organotypic slice cultures,[61] the intracellular administration of the autophosphorylated form of CaMKII reproduced the effects of LTP by inducing filopodia growth and spine formation. The inhibition of phosphatases (which activates CaMKII) and the application of CaM in neurons produced the same effect. Consistent with these results, blocking CaMKII activity prevented LTP, filopodia growth, and spine formation.[61] Moreover, CaMKIIβ (but not CaMKIIα) has strong morphogenic activity and regulates dendritic growth, filopodia extension, and synapse formation in cell cultures.[62] Also, CaMKII mediates the effect of integrin in structural synaptic plasticity.[63] *In vivo* studies confirm that CaMKII is involved in structural synaptic plasticity. In drosophila larvae, CaMKII regulates dendritic structure by increasing the formation of dendritic filopodia.[64]

CaMKII participation in structural synaptic plasticity is consistent with the idea that it plays an important role in persistent forms of synaptic plasticity and consequently most be important for long-term memory. Mutant flies expressing an inducible CaMKII inhibitor peptide presented serious learning deficits.[65] Mice expressing a constitutively active form of CaMKII independent of Ca^{2+} presented impairments of spatial and fear-motivated tasks.[37]

Training in the Morris water maze task induces the activation of CaMKII in the hippocampus; interestingly, retention performance of this spatial memory task positively correlates with levels of CaMKII activity.[66] Frankland and colleagues[67] showed that although heterozygous mutations of CaMKII exhibited normal memory retention for contextual fear and water maze tasks 1 to 3 days after training, the animals were amnesic when tested 10 to 50 days after training, suggesting that long-term (and not short-term) memory depends on CaMKII. These data indicate that CaMKII is an important molecule whose activity can be related to persistent forms of synaptic plasticity and may play a prominent role in long-term memory formation. However, CaMKII and other molecules directly activated by second messengers such as Ca^{2+} may interact with recently transcribed genes and their protein products.

3.4 IMMEDIATE EARLY GENES

It is well accepted that long-term memory formation requires the rapid synthesis of mRNAs and their translation in proteins. Several immediately early genes (IEGs) have been identified and they include two kind of immediate early genes, the factors that regulate the transcription of other genes such as *c-fos*, *c-jun*, *zif268*, and *Egr-3*, and the so called effector IEGs such as *Arc*, *Narp*, *Homer*, *Cox-2*, and *Rheb*[68] that act directly upon cells to promote different effects including plastic changes.

The *c-fos*, *c-jun*, and *zif268* transcription regulators IEGs are considered good candidates for the initial steps of learning inducing long-term synaptic plasticity.[69]

This is because their regulatory functions are believed to trigger cascades of activity-dependent neuronal gene expression that can lead to plastic events in neurons that may be critical for memory consolidation.[69] Importantly, the patterns of activity that induce LTP can be the same as those that induce some (but not all) immediate early genes.[70] Note that *zif268* expression in the hippocampus is triggered by the same pattern of activity that induces LTP.[70] This indicates that the thresholds of synaptic activation inducing the expression of some transcription regulator genes in particular regions can be closely linked to synaptic plasticity. What is also important in the study of long-term synaptic plasticity is that these genes, like *c-fos*, are strongly induced in the hippocampus by experimental models of epilepsy.[71] This manipulation is known to produce structural changes such as mossy fiber sprouting in the hippocampus.[72]

Kleim and colleagues[73] found evidence suggesting that the expression of the immediate early gene *c-fos* preludes the morphological changes in the cortex associated with motor skill learning. Mice with *c-fos* null mutations lacked the ability to present mossy fiber sprouting as result of kindling.[74] These data suggest that c-fos may be able to trigger the expression of other genes related to structural plasticity and one of such genes can be *BDNF*.[75] Its role in long-term synaptic plasticity will be addressed below.

Particularly interesting for the persistent forms of synaptic plasticity are the effector IEGs like *Arc*, *Homer*, and *Narp*. *Arc* (activity-regulated cytoskeleton associated protein, also called *Arg 3.1*) was identified in the hippocampus and cortex.[76,77] It is induced after strong cellular activity and presents a high homology to α-spectrin, and co-precipitaltes with F-actin, both of which are important cytosketetal proteins. Interestingly, the sequence of Arc presents sites for CaMKII and PKC phosphorylation.[76] The expression of *Arc* is rapidly induced by cellular activity and depends on NMDA glutamate-receptor activation.[76] Trophic factors such as nerve growth factor (NGF) and epidermal growth factor can also induce its expression.[76]

In hippocampal and cortical cells, expression of the Arc IEG is observed *after* spatial behavioral experience.[78] Importantly, in these regions, the proportion of cells that present electrophysiological activity characteristic of place cell firing[79,80] during spatial exploration are the same ones that show *Arc* expression after the same behavioral conditions.[78] In different species and using different behaviors, the expression of *Arc* is observed in the regions relevant to the correspondent behavior.[81–84]

One of the most interesting features of *Arc* is that its mRNA travels very rapidly throughout the dendrites[85,86] (~300 μm/hr) and the speed appears independent of protein synthesis. In addition, the traffic for *Arc* mRNA through the dendrites is selectively seen in the activated regions of the dendrite,[86] that is, LTP stimulation of the lateral entorhinal cortex produced a band of labeling for *Arc* mRNA in the outer molecular layer; while stimulation of the commissural projection produced a band of labeling in the inner molecular layer.[86,87] This selective localization of Arc mRNA is followed by accumulation of Arc protein in the same activated laminae. Moreover, the selective location of *Arc* mRNA in the activated laminae is dependent on NMDA, but not on AMPA receptor activation or protein synthesis.[39,87]

Administering antisense oligonucleotides against *Arc* mRNA in the hippocampus negatively affected LTP maintenance and consolidation of the water maze task.[88] BDNF-induced LTP depends on the translation of Arc protein.[89] Recently, with the use of an *Arc* knock-out mice these observations were confirm and important additional information was added.[90] Arc knock-out mice showed normal short-term memory but clearly impaired longterm memory for several different learning tasks.[90] Also, not only LTP maintenance was impaired but also LTD.[90] These data demonstrate that the effector IEG *Arc* is important for long-lasting synaptic plasticity and memory formation.

The dynamics of *Arc* expression have introduced us to a fascinating world of orchestrated molecular events that may regulate and fine-tune the long-lasting synaptic changes that allow memory to persist. Since *Arc* expression is dependent on neural activity, the detection of *Arc* can be used to identify individual cells activated after a particular behavior. This strategy allowed the development of a new imaging method known as compartmental analysis of temporal activity using fluorescence *in situ* hybridization (catFISH).[78] When neural activity is observed with catFISH, recent *Arc* transcription is detected in the nucleus as two foci of transcription; 20 to 30 min after the initiation of *Arc* mRNA transcription, *Arc* is translocated into the cytoplasm and observed surrounding the nuclei of cells.[78] This allows us to distinguish between cells activated by recent behavior (those with *Arc* mRNA in the nucleus) and those activated by a behavioral event that occurred 30 min earlier (when *Arc* mRNA in the cytoplasm was detected). This method was used to identify groups of cells that responded to two behavioral events separated by 20- to 30-min intervals and has the power to identify brain regions that discriminate the subtle differences among behavioral conditions.[91–93]

The proportion of cells that showed electrophysiological activity after exploration is ~35% in the CA1 region of the hippocampus, and the same proportion of cells expressed *Arc* mRNA under the same behavioral conditions.[78,94] In the CA3 region, the proportion of cells showing both electrophysiological activity and Arc expression was ~20%[94,95]; the proportion in the cortex was 50%.[94,96] This indicates a close correspondence between behaviorally induced neuronal spiking and *Arc* mRNA expression in regions where neuronal firing patterns are associated with behavioral experience. This also shows that the detection of *Arc* mRNA is a reliable method to identify cells that were activated during periods of behavioral activity.

Because a high proportion of cells express *Arc* in response to behavioral exploration, the role of *Arc* in synaptic plasticity may represent a serious problem for the system if all those cells underwent synaptic plasticity and became parts of a neural ensemble that will represent the acquired information. If so, the system should rapidly saturate, limiting the amount of memory stored. The theory suggests that the ensembles of cells that store information in long-term memory may use a sparse code to be more efficient and avoid system saturation.[97,98]

Some mRNAs located in dendritic compartments are regulated at the translation level by synaptic activity; translation of *Arc* mRNA in particular is known to be regulated at the dendritic level.[99] For this reason we thought it was possible that the translation of *Arc* mRNA into protein could be regulated throughout the whole cellular structure, limiting the number of cells expressing Arc protein after behavioral exploration. If that were the case, we would be able to identify the selected group of cells that will become part of the plastic neural network responsible for maintaining the information in long-term memory.

With this in mind, we performed an experiment to characterize the time course of Arc protein expression.[100] Animals explored a square open box for 5 min; after varying intervals, the animals explored the same space for a second 5-min exploration. Eight different intervals were used: 30, 60, 120, 180, 240, 360, 480, and 1440 min. Two groups of animals were used as controls; the animals in one group remained undisturbed in their home cages and were sacrificed at different times throughout the day matching the sacrifice times of the other groups (Caged). The second control group explored only once and was sacrificed immediately after the first exploration (5 min). The rest of the animals were sacrificed immediately after the second exploration. The tissue sections were processed for Arc protein fluorescent immunohistochemistry, *Arc* mRNA FISH, and a combination of both methods to identify both Arc protein and *Arc* mRNA in the same tissue.

The first observation was that the percentages of cells that show *Arc* mRNA in the nucleus 5 min after exploration matches express the proportion of cells that presented Arc protein 60 min after exploration (Figure 3.1). These results indicate that it is not through translational regulation of Arc that the system limits the number of plastic cells involved in information storage.

Surprisingly, we found an off-line reactivation (this is an activation without further stimulation) of Arc in the CA regions and the parietal cortex 8 hours after exploration. This off-line reactivation involved only 50% of the originally activated cells. More than 80% of the cells that showed protein expression at 480 and 1440 minutes also responded to the second exploration by expressing *Arc* mRNA (see Figure 3.2). We interpret this as a highly specific off-line reactivation of Arc expression in a subset of the originally activated cells. The role of this reactivation is not yet clear, but it is interesting that the proportion of cells that reactivated represented only 50% of the originally activated ensemble. Although 12% of cells in CA3 and 25% in the parietal cortex comprise too a large number of cells to be considered a sparse code, this could be part of a dynamic process that reduces the number of cells involved in a long-lasting representation.

Similarly, in a recent, astonishing study using a powerful method that visualized the expression of Arc-GFP (by inserting the green fluorescent protein after the *Arc* promotor) in the living mouse brain,[101] Wang and colleagues made the observation that after repeated daily stimulation with a visual stimulus of one specific orientation, the size of the Arc-GFP-expressing ensemble in the visual cortex gradually decresed.[101] Those cells responding to one orientation the first day that responded again the next day were more likely to respond to the same stimulus on the next consecutive days; similarly, the cells that first responded to such stimuli but did not respond the next day were less likely to respond on subsequent days. This can be interpreted as evidence that the cells that kept firing together on several consecutive days had a higher probability of continuing to fire together. The lack of Arc protein does not affect this progressive decrease in the size of the activated neural ensemble, but it does significantly increase the number of activated neurons. This suggests that Arc is required to maintain a finely tuned neural network, an idea supported by other

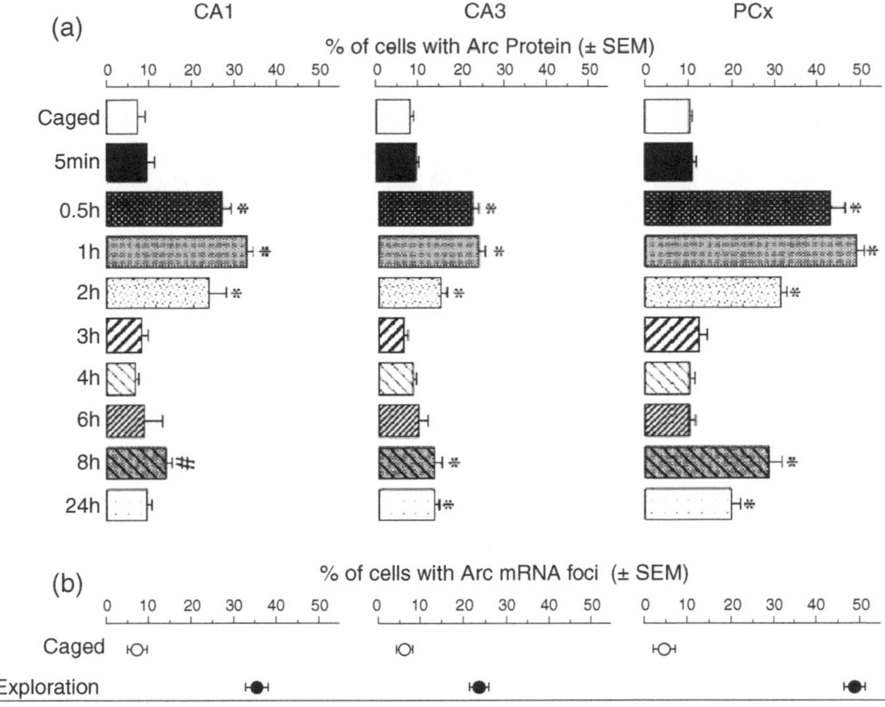

FIGURE 3.1 Kinctics of exploration-induced Arc protein expression in CA1, CA3, and PCx. **A.** Percentage of total cells showing Arc protein (induced by first exploration) in CA1, CA3, and PCx at all time points studied. All groups were exposed twice to the same environment, except for the caged and 5-min control groups. Caged: n = 10; 5 min, 1, 2, and 4 hours; n = 8; 0.5, 3, 6, 8, and 24 hours; n = 6. * $p= 0.0014$ relative to controls. # $p = 0.04$ (not statistically significant after correction for multiple comparisons). **B.** Percentage of total cells with Arc mRNA foci (induced by second exploration) in CA1, CA3, and PCx for caged control (open circles) and exploration (filled circles) groups. * $p = 0.001$ compared with controls. Cytoplasmic Arc mRNA is not shown in these regions because the Arc mRNA signal decreases to baseline after 30 min. (Taken with copyright permission from Ramirez-Amaya[100])

observations made in this important work, in which they found that orientation selectivity, measured by either Arc-GFP expression or electrophysiological activity, was impaired with the lack of Arc.[101] These data suggest that also during on-line reactivation the number of plastic cells decrease which strengths the idea that this possible selection process may be a mechanism through which the system fine-tunes the neural representation that will be stored in long-term memory.

However, in response to exploration, sparse codes were observed in the dentate gyrus at all times. In this region, a very small group of cells (only ~2%) responded to exploration.[100,102,103] Interestingly, the dynamics of Arc expression were also different from those found in the CA and cortical regions. In the dentate gyrus *Arc* mRNA and protein are observed in the cytoplasm 30 minutes after exploration, and they continue to be present for at least 8 hours.[100]

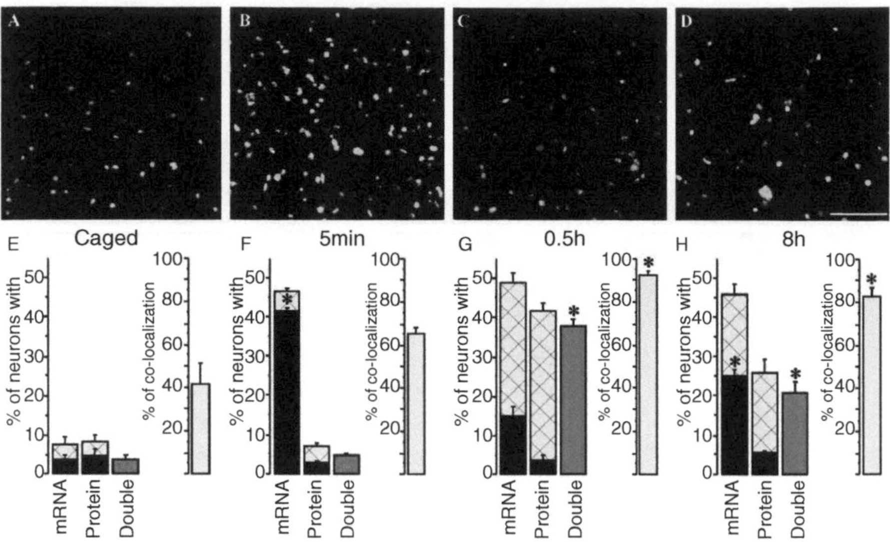

FIGURE 3.2 (See color insert following page 202.) Arc protein is expressed in the same neurons that express Arc mRNA. **A through D.** Example confocal images from parietal cortex (nuclei shown in green) taken from a caged control animal. **A.** Animal killed 5 min after single exploration session. **B.** Animal given two exploration sessions separated by 0.5 hour (**C**) or 8 hours (**D**). The latter two time points correspond to the first appearance of Arc protein in the first and second waves of protein expression, respectively. Arc mRNA intranuclear foci are shown in red, Arc protein is shown in purple, and the colocalization of Arc mRNA and protein is shown in pink (25× magnification; scale bar = 100 μm). **E through H.** Quantification of proportions of neurons containing Arc mRNA foci only (red), Arc cytoplasmic protein only (blue), and double-stained neurons with Arc mRNA and protein (green) for caged, 5-min, 0.5-, and 8-hour conditions. To reflect the total proportions of neurons that expressed Arc mRNA and protein, the double category is added to each of the mRNA and protein counts indicated by the cross-hatched bars. For each group, the total number of cells that expressed Arc protein and mRNA was also determined (yellow histogram on right reflects co-localization). Compared with caged controls, the 5-min and 8-hour groups showed significantly increased numbers of Arc mRNAexpressing cells (* $p = 0.05$; ** $p = 0.01$ with Bonferroni correction). Neither the mRNA nor protein alone was significantly different from caged controls for the 0.5-hour group, but the double-stained population was significantly increased from controls (** $p = 0.01$); for the 8-hour group, the double-labeled cells were also significantly different from controls (** $p = 0.01$). The proportions of neurons that showed co-localization of Arc mRNA and protein were statistically greater than caged controls only in the 0.5- and 8-hour groups (yellow bars). The results (data not shown) from the 3-, 4-, and 6-hour groups were similar to those from the 5-min group shown. Those from the 1-hour group (data not shown) were similar to those from the 0.5-hour group shown. Those from the 24-hour group (data not shown) were similar to those from the 8-hour group shown. Note that co-localization is close to chance levels in the caged control animals, whereas it is well above chance (80%) in the 0.5-, 1-, 8-, and 24-hour groups. (Taken with copyright permission from Ramirez-Amaya[100])

Preliminary data suggest that this sustained presence of Arc depends on sustained transcription of this gene, which apparently does not occur with other IEGs, and also appear to be exclusive of the dentate gyrus granule cells since pyramidal cells has not shown evidence of sustain *Arc* transcription. These suggest that while in the CAs and cortical regions, off-line reactivation of *Arc* expression may be an important component of the neural network required to accomplish the plastic changes related to long-term memory formation, in the dentate gyrus, a sustained transcription of *Arc* may perform the plastic job.

A recent group of highly relevant papers from Dr Paul Worley's and other's laboratories had shown what exactly the role of Arc protein in synaptic plasticity can be. Chowdhury's and colleagues work[104] show that Arc regulates the trafficking of glutamate AMPA receptors by interacting with dynamin 2 and endophilin 3. This highly specific interaction of Arc with the above mentioned molecules modulates the endocytosis of AMPA glutamate receptors.[104] This mechanism allows Arc to mediate synaptic scaling by regulating the density of AMPA GluR2 receptors in the membrane[105] which consequently specifically modulates AMPA mediated synaptic currents.[106] This suggests that synaptic scaling is one important mechanism by which Arc modulates the stabilization of synaptic plasticity and long-term memory consolidation.[88–90]

Also, an important link between Arc and CaMKII exists. We were interested in studying the cell types that are able to express *Arc*. We found that only neurons (and not glia) are able to express *Arc* after behavioral stimulation or after maximal electrical stimulation. Interestingly, all the cells that express Arc under both stimulation conditions were also CaMKII-positive cells. In regions such as the hippocampus and cortex; they are considered excitatory principal cells. However, the principal cells in the striatum are GAD65/67-positive and interestingly they were also CaMKII-positive and *Arc*-expressing cells after exploration.[104] This suggests an important interaction between two plasticity-related molecules such as Arc and CaMKII.

Preliminary observations using fluorescence resonance energy transfer in culture neurons indicated that Arc and CaMKII proteins interact only in the dendrites.[108] This interaction may have important implications for plasticity in local dendrites. In agreement, it has been shown that Arc interaction with CaMKII in neuroblastoma cells can promote neurite outgrowth,[109] suggesting that this interaction may induce structural plasticity in dendritic compartments. If it occurs in adult mammalian neurons, this interaction between Arc and CaMKII may be associated with structural synaptic plasticity and could explain the actions of other important plastic related molecules such as the trophic factors that have also been shown to induce Arc expression.[76]

3.5 TROPHIC FACTORS

Neurotrophins are regulatory factors known to be involved in cell development, survival, and repair. One of their most interesting features is their role in neural plasticity. The neurotrophin family includes nerve growth factor (NGF), brain-derived neurotrophic factor (BDNF), neurotrophins 3 and 4 (NT3 and NT4), and two other members recently were found in fish NT6 and NT7.[107] Each neurotrophin has been shown to promote neurite outgrowth by responsive neurons via *in vitro* or *in vivo* studies.[111]

BDNF is known to regulate the development of connections[112] and the complexities and sizes of dendrites[113] in the cerebral cortex. The involvement of BDNF in synaptic plasticity has been suggested for a long time and is known to regulate glutamatergic activity by increasing NMDA receptor phosphorylation.[114] During development, BDNF regulates neuronal proliferation, neuronal migration, axon path finding, dendritic growth, synapse formation, and maintenance of the synaptic contact.[115] Interestingly, BDNF can be of great importance for learning-induced structural plasticity, particularly because its important role in spatial memory formation has been shown.[116] Animals that underwent Morris Water maze training increased the expression of both BDNF mRNA and the BNDF receptor TrkB in the hippocampus.[116-118] This expression is observed only after several days of training, but not before.[117] That is, when animals were trained for 1, 3, or 6 days, reaching an asymptotic level of performance at day 6, an increase in BDNF mRNA expression, measured by in situ hybridization, was observed only in animals trained for 3 and 6 days but not in the animals trained for 1 day.[117] This interesting result resembles our previous observations[10,11] in which animals over-trained for 4 to 5 days in the Morris water maze task showed an increase in the density of mossy fiber boutons in the stratum oriens of the CA3 hippocampal region.[11] The coincidences of BDNF expression after water maze training and our observation regarding mossy fiber sprouting are remarkable and suggest that BDNF could be part of the molecular mechanisms that underlie spatial learning-induced structural plasticity in the hippocampus. Accordingly, it has been demonstrated that blockade of BDNF mRNA or its protein product[119] produced spatial memory impairments.[116]

The features of BDNF make it a prominent regulator of the persistent forms of synaptic plasticity. However, it does not act alone and interacts with other molecules mentioned above. For example, it has been observed that BDNF induces the synthesis of Arc in synaptoneurosomes.[120] BDNF induction of LTP depends on Arc protein translation.[121] These data suggest an important role of Arc in BDNF-induced synaptic plasticity.

An interaction between BDNF and CaMKII has also been observed. In cultured neurons using a GFP reporter of CaMKII, BDNF induced the translation of CaMKII in dendritic spines.[122] Based on these data, Braham and Messaudi suggested that CaMKII, Arc, and BDNF may interact in dendrites to mediate long-term synaptic plasticity. They proposed that Arc should have a mechanism to consolidate its plastic effect in dendrites.

We obtained evidence that Arc may achieve this in two ways: (1) via the off-line reactivation of Arc in which the ensemble of cells is reduced progressively and (2) the sustained transcription of Arc — a reaction that apparently occurs only in dentate gyrus granule cells. Both mechanisms may interact with CaMKII, Ca^{2+} influx, and other events triggered by NMDA receptor activation that, when occurring at the time of TrKb activation by BDNF, may promote the stable plastic changes underlying memory formation.

3.6 CONCLUSIONS

The evidence review in this chapter show that the interactions between glutamate-receptor activation, CaMKII autophosphorylation activity, Arc-expression and BDNF activation of TrKb receptors are some of the cellular events associated with persistent forms of synaptic plasticity, such as synaptic scaling and structural synaptic changes.

After a behavioral situation that promote long-term memory formation, glutamatergic transmission can stimulate NMDA receptor activation and trigger Ca2+ influx into the cell, which generates a complex signal. This signal, in turn, can be translated through CaMKII which by switching between a transitory to a long-term activation that may promote long-lasting effects. Ca2+ along with other molecules such as MAPK, can regulate the expression of *Arc123*. After the induction of *Arc* expression, its mRNA will travel to the activated regions of dendrites where it can be locally translated. The dynamics of *Arc* expression can maintain the presence of Arc for prolonged periods of time.[100] The activation of TrKb receptors by BDNF will only happen after a prolonged period of training[118] and when this activation converges with NMDA-receptor activation, it will enhance CaMKII activity. When these events coincide with the presence of Arc in dendrites, the interaction can promote long-term synaptic plasticity.

Although it is well accepted that synaptic plasticity in specific group of cells determines the stabilization of the cell assemblies that will maintain the patterns of neural activity that represent an episode, we have not yet identify the individual neurons that constitute this neural ensembles. Our current methods and new technical developments will allow us to identify precisely the individual neurons that are part of the long-term representing ensemble by identifying which neurons activate plastic related molecules and in which of them this molecules act as a molecular long-term memory switch, as suggested for CaMKII. We believe that the immediate early gene *Arc* is another crucial candidate for the long-term neural ensembles, because *Arc* is important for synaptic plasticity and its dynamics has shown an apparent selection process. We now need to completely characterize the decrease in the size of the Arc-expressing ensemble during off-line or on-line reactivation, in order to identify reliably these possible selected groups of cells, in which persistent forms of synaptic plasticity may occur. These include structural synaptic changes, such as changes in the structural features of the existing dendrites, increased density and distribution of spines, and the generation and stabilization of new synaptic contacts; also, the cells that belong to the plastic cell assemblies will be subjected to synaptic scaling of AMPA receptors and/or other persistent forms of synaptic plasticity. By characterizing the persistent forms of synaptic plasticity in the selected groups of cells we will be able to identify the plastic neural networks underlying long-term memory formation.

REFERENCES

1. Hebb, D.O. *The Organization of Behavior.* John Wiley & Sons, New York, 1949.
2. Dudai, Y. Molecular bases of long term memories: a question of persistence. *Curr. Opin. Neurobiol.*, 12, 211, 2002.
3. Lamprecht, R. and LeDoux, J. Structural plasticity and memory. *Nat. Rev. Neurosci.*, 5, 45, 2004.
4. Fischer, M., Kaech, S., Wagner, UY., Brinkhaus, H., and Matus, A.M. Glutamate receptors regulate actin-based plasticity in dendritic spines. *Nat. Neurosci.*, 3, 887, 2000
5. Washbourne, P., Bennett, J.E., and McAllister, A.K. Rapid recruitment of NMDA receptor transport packets to nascent synapses. *Nat. Neurosci.*, 5, 751, 2002.
6. Chang, S. and DeCamilli, P. Glutamate regulates actin-based motility in axonal filopodia. *Nat. Neurosci.*, 4, 787, 2001.
7. Desmond, N.L. and Levy, W.B. Synaptic correlates of associative potentiation and depression: an ultrastructural study in the hippocampus. *Brain Res.*, 265, 21, 1983.
8. Escobar, M.L., Barea-Rodriguez, E.J., Derrick, B.E., Reyes. J.A. and Martinez, J.L. Jr. Opioid receptor modulation of mossy fiber synaptogenesis: independence from long term potentiation. *Brain Res.*, 751, 330, 1997.
9. Toni, N., Buchs, P.A., Nikonenko, I., Bron, C.R., and Muller, D. LTP promotes formation of multiple spine synapses between a single axon terminal and a dendrite. *Nature*, 402, 421, 1999.
10. Ramirez-Amaya, V., Escobar, M.L., Chao, V., and Bermudez-Rattoni, F. Synaptogenesis of mossy fibers induced by spatial water maze overtraining. *Hippocampus*, 9, 631, 1999.
11. Ramirez-Amaya. V., Balderas, I., Sandoval, J., Escobar, M.L. and Bermudez-Rattoni, F. Spatial long-term memory is related to mossy fiber synaptogenesis. *J. Neurosci.*, 21, 7340, 2001.
12. Leuner, B., Falduto, J., and Shors, T.J. Associative memory formation increases the observation of dendritic spines in the hippocampus. *J. Neurosci.*, 23, 659, 2003.
13. Lüscher, C. et al. Role of AMPA receptor cycling in synaptic transmission and plasticity. *Neuron*, 24, 649, 1999.
14. Shi, S.H. et al. Rapid spine delivery and redistribution of AMPA receptors after synaptic NMDA receptor activation. *Science*, 284, 1811, 1999.
15. Lan, J.Y. et al. Activation of metabotropic glutamate receptor 1 accelerates NMDA receptor trafficking. *J. Neurosci.*, 21, 6058, 2001.
16. Crump, F.T., Dillman, K.S., and Craig, A.M. cAMP-dependent protein kinase mediates activity regulated synaptic targeting of NMDA receptors. *J. Neurosci.*, 21, 5079, 2001.
17. Perez-Otano, I. and Ehlers, M.D. Homeostatic plasticity and NMDA receptor trafficking. *Trends Neurosci.*, 28, 229, 2005.
18. Wierenga, C.J., Ibata, K., and Turrigiano, G.G. Postsynaptic expression of homeostatic plasticity at neocortical synapses. *J. Neurosci.*, 16, 2895, 2005.
19. Andrasfalvy, B.K. and Magee, J.C. Distance-dependent increase in AMPA receptor number in the dendrites of adult hippocampal CA1 pyramidal neurons. *J. Neurosci.*, 21, 9151, 2001.
20. Turrigiano, G.G., Leslie, K.R., Desai, N.S., Rutherford, L.C., and Nelson, S.B. Activity-dependent scaling of quantal amplitude in neocortical neurons. *Nature*, 391, 892, 1998.

21. Abbott, L.F. and Nelson, S.B. Synaptic plasticity: taming the beast. *Nat. Neurosci.*, 3 (Suppl.), 1178, 2000.
22. London, L. and Segev, I. Synaptic scaling *in vitro* and *in vivo*. *Nat. Neurosci.*, 4, 853, 2001.
23. Izquierdo, I., Medina, J.H., Vianna, M.R., Isquierdo, L.A., and Barros, D.M. Separate mechanisms for short- and long-term memory. *Behav. Brain Res.*, 103, 1, 1999.
24. Ferreira, G., Gutierrez, R., DeLaCruz, V., and Bermudez-Rattoni, F. Differential involvement of cortical muscarinic and NMDA receptors in short- and long-term taste aversion memory. *Eur. J. Neurosci.*, 16, 1139, 2002.
25. Woolf, N.J. A structural basis for memory storage in mammals. *Progr. Neurobiol.*, 55, 59, 1998.
26. Rosenblum, K. Futter, M., Jones, M., Hulme, E.C., and Bliss, T.V. ERKI/II regulation by the muscarinic acetylcholine receptors in neurons. *J. Neurosci.*, 20, 977, 2000.
27. Woolf, N.J. Critical role of cholinergic basal forebrain neurons in morphological change and memory encoding: a hypothesis. *Neurobiol. Learn. Mem.*, 66, 258, 1996.
28. Woodin, M.A., Munno, D.W., and Syed, N.I. Trophic factor-induced excitatory synaptogenesis involves post-synaptic modulation of nicotinic acetylcholine receptors. *J. Neurosci.*, 22, 505, 2002.
29. Hohmann, C.F. A morphogenetic role for acetylcholine in mouse cerebral neocortex. *Neurosci. Biobehav. Rev.*, 27, 351, 2003.
30. Ismail, N., Robinson, G.E., and Fahrbach, S.E. Stimulation of muscarinic receptors mimics experience-dependent plasticity in the honey bee brain. *Proc. Natl. Acad. Sci. USA*, 103, 207, 2006.
31. Imai, H., Mutsumi-Matsukawa, M., and Okado, N. Lamina-selective changes in the density of synapses following perturbation of monoamines and acetylcholine in the rat medial prefrontal cortex. *Brain Res.*, 1012, 138, 2004.
32. Oertner, T.G. and Matus, A. Calcium regulation of actin dynamics in dendritic spines. *Cell Calcium*, 37, 477, 2005.
33. Lisman, J.E. and McIntyre, C.C. Synaptic plasticity: a molecular memory switch. *Curr. Biol.*, 11, R788, 2001.
34. DeKoninck, P. and Schulman, H. Sensitivity of CaM kinase II to the frequency of Ca2C oscillations. *Science*, 279, 227, 1998.
35. Cammarota, M. et al. Participation of CaMKII in neuronal plasticity and memory formation. *Cell. Mol. Neurobiol.*, 22, 259, 2002.
36. Lisman, J., Schulman, H., and Cline, H. The molecular basis of CaMKII function in synaptic and behavioural memory. *Nat. Rev. Neurosci.*, 3, 175, 2002.
37. Mayford, M. et al. Control of memory formation through regulated expression of a CaMKII transgene. *Science*, 174, 1678, 1996.
38. Steward, O. and Halpain, S. Lamina-specific synaptic activation causes domain-specific alterations in dendritic immunostaining for MAP2 and CAM kinase II. *J. Neurosci.*, 19, 7834, 1999.
39. Steward, O. and Worley, P. Localization of mRNAs at synaptic sites on dendrites. *Results Probl. Cell. Differ.*, 34, 1, 2001.
40. Steward, O. and Schuman, E.M. Protein synthesis at synaptic sites on dendrites. *Annu. Rev. Neurosci.*, 24, 299, 2001.
41. Greenough, W.T. et al. Synaptic regulation of protein synthesis and the fragile X protein. *Proc. Natl. Acad. Sci. USA*, 98, 7101, 2001.
42. Scheetz, A.J., Nairn, A.C., and Constantine-Paton, M. MDA receptor-mediated control of protein synthesis at developing synapses. *Nat. Neurosci.*, 3, 211, 2000.

43. Yoshimura, Y., Nomura, T., and Yamauchi, T. Purification and characterization of active fragment of Ca^{2+}/calmodulin-dependent protein kinase II from the postsynaptic density in the rat forebrain. *J. Biochem. (Tokyo)*, 119, 268, 1996.
44. Yoshimura, Y., Aoi, C., and Yamauchi, T. Investigation of protein substrates of Ca2C/calmodulin-dependent protein kinase II translocated to the postsynaptic density. *Brain Res. Mol. Brain Res.*, 81, 118, 2000.
45. Strack, S., Robison, A., Bass, M., and Colbran, R. Association of calcium/calmodulin-dependent kinase II with developmentally regulated splice variants of the postsynaptic density protein densin-180. *J. Biol. Chem.*, 275, 25061, 2000.
46. Walikonis, R., Oguni, A., Khorosheva, E., Jeng, C., Asuncion, F. and Kennedy, M. Densin-180 forms a ternary complex with the (alpha)-subunit of Ca2+/calmodulin-dependent protein kinase II and (alpha)-actinin. *J. Neurosci.*, 21,423, 2001.
47. Allison, D., Chervin, A., Gelfand, V., and Craig, A. Post-synaptic scaffolds of excitatory and inhibitory synapses in hippocampal neurons: maintenance of core components independent of actin filaments and microtubules. *J. Neurosci.*, 20, 4545, 2000.
48. Gardoni, F. et al. Calcium/calmodulin-dependent protein kinase II is associated with NR2A/B subunits of NMDA receptor in postsynaptic densities. *J. Neurochem.*, 71, 1733, 1998.
49. Bayer, K.U., DeKoninck, P., Leonard, A.S., Hell, J.W., and Schulman, H. Interaction with the NMDA receptor locks CaMKII in active conformation. *Nature*, 411, 801, 2001.
50. Derkach, V., Barria, A., and Soderling, T.R. Ca^{2+}/calmodulin kinase II enhances channel conductance of alpha-amino-3-hydroxy-5-methyl-4-isoxazolepropionate type glutamate receptors. *Proc. Natl. Acad. Sci. USA*, 96, 3269, 1999.
51. Lisman, J.E. and Zhabotinsky, A.M. Model of synaptic memory: a CaMKII/PP1 switch that potentiates transmission by organizing an AMPA receptor anchoring assembly. *Neuron*, 31, 191, 2001.
52. Hayachi Y. et al. Driving AMPA receptors into synapses by LTP and CaMKII: requirement for GluR1 and PDZ domain interaction. *Science*, 287, 2262, 2000.
53. Bayer, K.U. et al. Transition from reversible to persistent binding of CaMKII to post-synaptic sites and NR2B. *J. Neurosci.*, 26, 1164, 2006.
54. Ouyang, Y., Rosenstein, A., Kreiman, G., Schuman, E., and Kennedy, M. Tetanic stimulation leads to increased accumulation of Ca2C/calmodulin-dependent protein kinase II via dendritic protein synthesis in hippocampal neurons. *J. Neurosci.*, 19, 7823, 1999.
55. Fukunaga, K., Stoppini, L., Miyamoto, E., and Muller, D. Long-term potentiation is associated with increased activity of Ca2C/calmodulin-dependent protein kinase II. *J. Biol. Chem.*, 268, 7863, 1993.
56. Fukunaga, K., Muller, D., and Miyamoto, E. Increased phosphorylation of Ca2C/calmodulin-dependent protein kinase II and its endogenous substrates in the induction of long term potentiation. *J. Biol. Chem.*, 270, 6119, 1995.
57. Wang, J.H. and Kelly, P.T. Postsynaptic injection of CA^{2+}/CaM induces synaptic potentiation requiring CaMKII and PKC activity. *Neuron*, 15, 443, 1995.
58. Shi, S. et al. Rapid spine delivery and redistribution of AMPA receptors after synaptic NMDA receptor activation. *Science*, 284, 1811, 1999.
59. Miller, S. et al. Disruption of dendritic translation of CaMKII-alpha impairs stabilization of synaptic plasticity and memory consolidation. *Neuron*, 36, 507, 2002.
60. Engert, F. and Bonhoeffer, T. Dendritic spine changes associated with hippocampal long-term synaptic plasticity. *Nature*, 399, 66, 1999.

61. Jourdain, P., Fukunaga, K., and Muller, D. Calcium/calmodulin-dependent protein kinase II contributes to activity-dependent filopodia growth and spine formation. *J. Neurosci.*, 23, 10645, 2003.
62. Fink, C.C. et al. Selective regulation of neurite extension and synapse formation by the beta but not the alpha isoform of CaMKII. *Neuron*, 39, 283, 2003..
63. Shi, Y. and Ethell, I.M. Integrins control dendritic spine plasticity in hippocampal neurons through NMDA receptor and Ca^{2+}/calmodulin-dependent protein kinase II-mediated actin reorganization. *J. Neurosci.*, 26, 1813, 2006.
64. Andersen, R., Li, Y., Resseguie, M., and Brenman, J.E. Calcium/calmodulin-dependent protein kinase II alters structural plasticity and cytoskeletal dynamics in Drosophila. *J. Neurosci.*, 25, 8878, 2005.
65. Griffith, L. et al. Inhibition of calcium/calmodulin-dependent protein kinase in Drosophila disrupts behavioral plasticity. *Neuron*, 10, 501, 1993.
66. Tan, S. and Liang, K. Spatial learning alters hippocampal calcium/calmodulin-dependent protein kinase II activity in rats. *Brain Res.*, 711, 234, 1996.
67. Frankland, P., O'Brien, C., Ohno, M., Kirkwood, A., and Silva, A. Alpha CaMKII-dependent plasticity in the cortex is required for permanent memory. *Nature*, 411, 309, 2001.
68. Lanahan, A. and Worley, P. Immediate early genes and synaptic function. *Neurobiol. Learn. Mem.*, 70, 37, 1998.
69. Abraham, W.C., Dragunow, M., and Tate, W.P. Role of immediate early genes in the stabilization of long-term potentiation. *Mol. Neurobiol.*, 5, 297, 1991.
70. Worley, P.F. et al. Thresholds for synaptic activation of transcription factors in hippocampus: correlation with long-term enhancement. *J. Neurosci.*, 13, 4776, 1993.
71. Dragunow, M., Yamada, N., Bilkey, D.K., and Lawlor, P. Induction of immediate early gene proteins in dentate granule cells and somatostatin interneurons after hippocampal seizures. *Brain Res. Mol. Brain Res.*, 13, 119, 1992.
72. Epsztein, J., Represa, A., Jorquera, I., Ben-Ari, Y., and Crepel, V. Recurrent mossy fibers establish aberrant kainate receptor-operated synapses on granule cells from epileptic rats. *J. Neurosci.*, 25, 8229, 2005.
73. Kleim, J.A., Lussnig, E., Schwarz, E.R., Comery, T.A., and Greenough, W.T. Synaptogenesis and Fos expression in the motor cortex of the adult rat after motor skill learning. *J. Neurosci.*, 16, 4529, 1996.
74. Watanabe, Y. et al. Null mutation of c-fos impairs structural and functional plasticities in the kindling model of epilepsy. *J. Neurosci.*, 16, 3827, 1996.
75. Dong, M., Wu, Y., Fan, Y., Xu, M., and Zhang, J. c-fos modulates brain-derived neurotrophic factor mRNA expression in mouse hippocampal CA3 and dentate gyrus neurons. *Neurosci. Lett.*, 400, 177, 2006; epub, March 13, 2006.
76. Lyford, G.L. et al. Arc, a growth factor and activity-regulated gene, encodes a novel cytoskeleton-associated protein that is enriched in neuronal dendrites. *Neuron*, 14, 433, 1995.
77. Link, W. et al. Somatodendritic expression of an immediate early gene is regulated by synaptic activity. *Proc. Natl. Acad. Sci. USA*, 92, 5734, 1995.
78. Guzowski, J.F., McNaughton, B.L., Barnes, C.A., and Worley, P.F. Environment-specific expression of the immediate early gene Arc in hippocampal neuronal ensembles. *Nat. Neurosci.*, 2, 1120, 1999.
79. O'Keefe, J. Place units in the hippocampus of the freely moving rat. *Exp. Neurol.*, 51, 78, 1976.
80. O'Keefe, J. and Nadel, L. *The Hippocampus as a Cognitive Map*, Clarendon Press, Oxford, 1978.

81. Leitner, S., Voigt, C., Metzdorf, R., and Catchpole, C.K. Immediate early gene (ZENK, Arc) expression in the auditory forebrain of female canaries varies in response to male song quality. *J. Neurobiol.*, 64, 275, 2005.
82. Ons, S., Marti, O., and Armario, A. Stress-induced activation of the immediate early gene Arc (activity-regulated cytoskeleton-associated protein) is restricted to telencephalic areas in the rat brain: relationship to c-fos mRNA. *J. Neurochem.*, 89, 1111, 2004.
83. Ostrander, M.M. et al. Environmental context and drug history modulate amphetamine-induced c-fos mRNA expression in the basal ganglia, central extended amygdala, and associated limbic forebrain. *Neuroscience*, 120, 551, 2003.
84. Kelly, M.P. and Deadwyler, S.A. Experience-dependent regulation of the immediate early gene arc differs across brain regions. *J. Neurosci.*, 23, 6443, 2003.
85. Wallace, C.S., Lyford, G.L., Worley, P.F., and Steward, O. Differential intracellular sorting of immediate early gene mRNAs depends on signals in the mRNA sequence. *J. Neurosci.*, 18, 26, 1998.
86. Steward, O., Wallace, C.S., Lyford, G.L., and Worley, P.F. Synaptic activation causes the mRNA for the IEG Arc to localize selectively near activated post-synaptic sites on dendrites. *Neuron*, 21, 741, 1998.
87. Steward, O. and Worley, P.F. Selective targeting of newly synthesized Arc mRNA to active synapses requires NMDA receptor activation. *Neuron*, 30, 227, 2001.
88. Guzowski, J.F. et al. Inhibition of activity-dependent arc protein expression in the rat hippocampus impairs the maintenance of long-term potentiation and the consolidation of long term memory. *J. Neurosci.*, 20, 3993, 2000.
89. Braham, C.R. and Messaoudi, E. BDNF function in adult synaptic plasticity: the synaptic consolidation hypothesis. *Progr. Neurobiol.*, 76, 99, 2005.
90. Plath, N., Ohana, O., Dammermann, B., Errington, M.L., Schmitz, D., Gross, C., Mao, X., Engelsberg, A., Mahlke, C., Welzl, H., Kobalz, U., Stawrakakis, A., Fernandez, E., Waltereit, R., Bick-Sander, A., Therstappen, E., Cooke, S.F., Blanquet, V., Wurst, W., Salmen, B., Bosl, MR., Lipp, H.P., Grant, S.G., Bliss, T.V., Wolfer, D.P. and Kuhl, D. Arc/Arg3.1 is essential for the consolidation of synaptic plasticity and memories. *Neuron.*, 52,437, 2006.
91. Vazdarjanova, A. and Guzowski, J.F. Differences in hippocampal neuronal population responses to modifications of an environmental context: evidence for distinct, yet complementary, functions of CA3 and CA1 ensembles. *J. Neurosci.*, 24, 6489, 2004.
92. Burke, S.N. et al. Differential encoding of behavior and spatial context in deep and superficial layers of the neocortex. *Neuron*, 45, 667, 2005.
93. Petrovich, G.D., Holland, P.C., and Gallagher, M. Amygdalar and prefrontal pathways to the lateral hypothalamus are activated by a learned cue that stimulates eating. *J. Neurosci.*, 25, 8295, 2005.
94. Vazdarjanova, A., McNaughton, B.L., Barnes, C.A., Worley, P.F., and Guzowski, J.F. Experience-dependent coincident expression of the effector immediate early genes arc and Homer-1a in hippocampal and neocortical neuronal networks. *J. Neurosci.*, 22, 10067, 2002.
95. Leutgeb, S., Leutgeb, J.K., Treves, A., Moser, M.B., and Moser, E.I. Distinct ensemble codes in hippocampal areas CA3 and CA1. *Science*, 305, 1295, 2004; epub, July 22, 2004.
96. McNaughton, B.L. et al. Cortical representation of motion during unrestrained spatial navigation in the rat. *Cerebr. Cortex*, 4, 27, 1994.
97. McNaughton, B.L. et al. Deciphering the hippocampal polyglot: the hippocampus as a path integration system. *J. Exp. Biol.*, 199, 173, 1996.

98. Sakurai, Y. How do cell assemblies encode information in the brain? *Neurosci. Biobehav. Rev.*, 23, 785, 1999.
99. Dong, E. et al. A reelin–integrin receptor interaction regulates Arc mRNA translation in synaptoneurosomes. *Proc. Natl. Acad. Sci. USA*, 100, 5479, 2003.
100. Ramirez-Amaya V. et al. Spatial exploration-induced Arc mRNA and protein expression: evidence for selective, network specific reactivation. *J. Neurosci.*, 25, 1761, 2005.
101. Wang, K.H. et al. *In vivo* two-photon imaging reveals a role of arc in enhancing orientation specificity in visual cortex. *Cell*, 126, 389, 2006.
102. Rosi, S. et al. Neuroinflammation alters the hippocampal pattern of behaviorally induced Arc expression. *J. Neurosci.*, 25, 723, 2005.
103. Chawla, M.K. et al. Sparse environmentally selective expression of Arc RNA in the upper blade of the rodent fascia dentata by brief spatial experience. *Hippocampus*, 15, 579, 2005.
104. Chowdhury, S., Shepherd, J.D., Okuno, H., Lyford, G., Petralia, R.S., Plath, N., Kuhl. D., Huganir, R.L. and Worley, P.F. Arc/Arg3.1 interacts with the endocytic machinery to regulate AMPA receptor trafficking. *Neuron.*, 52,445, 2006.
105. Shepherd, J.D., Rumbaugh, G., Wu, J., Chowdhury, S., Plath, N., Kuhl, D., Huganir, R.L. and Worley, P.F. Arc/Arg3.1 Mediates Homeostatic Synaptic Scaling of AMPA Receptors. *Neuron.*, 52,475, 2006.
106. Rial-Verde, E.M., Lee-Osbourne, J., Worley, P.F., Malinow, R. and Cline, H.T. Increased expressionof the immediate-early gene arc/arg3.1 reduces AMPA receptor-mediated synaptic transmission. *Neuron.*, 52,461, 2006.
107. Vazdarjanova, A. et al. Spatial exploration induces ARC, a plasticity-related immediate early gene, only in calcium/calmodulin-dependent protein kinase II positive principal excitatory and inhibitory neurons of the rat forebrain. *J. Comp. Neurol.*, 498, 317, 2006.
108. Okuno, H., Chowdhury, S., Worley, P. and Bito, H. Interaction between Arc and CaM Kinase II in dendrites monitored by fluorescence resonance energy transfer. *Soc. Neurosci. Abstracts*, 164,16, 2004.
109. Donai, H. et al. Interaction of Arc with CaM kinase II and stimulation of neurite extension by Arc in neuroblastoma cells expressing CaM kinase II. *Neurosci. Res.*, 47, 399, 2003.
110. McAllister, A.K. Neurotrophins and cortical development. *Results Probl. Cell Differ.*, 39, 89, 2002.
111. Frade, J.M., Bovolenta, P., and Rodriguez-Tebar, A. Neurotrophins and other growth factors in the generation of retinal neurons. *Microsc. Res. Tech.*, 45, 243, 1999.
112. Horch, H.W. Local effects of BDNF on dendritic growth. *Rev. Neurosci.*, 15,117, 2004.
113. McAllister, A.K., Lo, D.C., and Katz, L.C. Neurotrophins regulate dendritic growth in developing visual cortex. *Neuron*, 15, 791, 1995.
114. Slack, S.E., Pezet, S., McMahon, S.B., Thompson, S.W., and Malcangio, M. Brain-derived neurotrophic factor induces NMDA receptor subunit I phosphorylation via ERK and PKC in the rat spinal cord. *Eur. J. Neurosci.*, 20, 1769, 2004.
115. Thomas, K. and Davies, A. Neurotrophins: a ticket to ride for BDNF. *Curr. Biol.*, 15, R262, 2005.
116. Mizuno, M., Yamada, K., Olariu, A., Nawa, H., and Nabeshima, T. Involvement of brain-derived neurotrophic factor in spatial memory formation and maintenance in a radial arm maze test in rats. *J. Neurosci.*, 20, 7116, 2000.

117. Kesslak, J.P. et al. Learning up-regulates brain-derived neurotrophic factor messenger ribonucleic acid: a mechanism to facilitate encoding and circuit maintenance? *Behav. Neurosci.*, 112, 1012, 1998.
118. Gomez-Pinilla, F., So, V., and Kesslak, J.P. Spatial learning induces neurotrophin receptor and synapsin I in the hippocampus. *Brain Res.*, 904, 13, 2001.
119. Mu, J.S., Li, W.P., Yao, Z.B., and Zhou, X.F. Deprivation of endogenous brain-derived neurotrophic factor results in impairment of spatial learning and memory in adult rats. *Brain Res.*, 835, 269, 1999.
120. Yin, Y., Edelman, G.M., and Vanderklish, P.W. The brain-derived neurotrophic factor enhances synthesis of Arc in synaptoneurosomes. *Proc. Natl. Acad. Sci. USA*, 99, 2368, 2002; epub, February 12, 2002.
121. Braham, C.R. and Messaoudi, E. BDNF function in adult synaptic plasticity: the synaptic consolidation hypothesis. *Progr. Neurobiol.*, 76, 125, 2005.
122. Aakalu, G., Smith, W.B., Nguyen, N., Jiang, C., and Schuman, E.M. Dynamic visualization of local protein synthesis in hippocampal neurons. *Neuron*, 30, 489, 2001.

4 Modification of Brain Circuits through Experience

Mark R. Rosenzweig

CONTENTS

4.1 BRAIN PLASTICITY DISCOVERED THROUGH SERENDIPITY

Although my colleagues and I were the first to demonstrate brain plasticity and modification of brain circuits through experience, this was not the original purpose of our work. Instead, we were looking for neural bases of the individual differences in problem-solving behavior exhibited by rats. As this research progressed, we discovered brain plasticity through serendipity.

To go back to the start, soon after I arrived at the University of California at Berkeley in 1951, my colleague David Krech asked me to consider with him what might be neural bases of the individual differences in tests of problem-solving behavior he had been finding among rats of inbred strains. As a "rat runner" of long standing, Krech had been impressed by sizeable individual differences of problem-solving abilities among rats of the same strain, sex, and age. I suggested that we might investigate whether individual differences in cortical acetylcholine metabolism correlated with individual differences in problem-solving ability. Krech turned to his friend Melvin Calvin, head of the campus Laboratory of Chemical Biodynamics, and Calvin agreed to encourage the younger chemists in his laboratory to collaborate with us if the project interested them. In the fall of 1953, I met three chemists for lunch in the faculty club and explained our project. One of them, Edward L. Bennett, decided that it might be interesting to collaborate with psychologists for a few months, and thus began a fruitful collaboration that lasted for more than 40 years. We also benefitted from the continued interest and support of Professor Calvin.

4.1.1 The Field in the 1950s

Brief consideration of the state of the field in the 1950s provides some context for our research. It may also help explain the skeptical initial reaction to our discoveries. In the 1950s pessimism about being able to discover the neural bases of learning and memory prevailed. For example, Karl S. Lashley, in a highly critical review in 1950, surveyed the literature on possible synaptic changes as a result of training and concluded that there was no solid evidence to support any of the growth theories. Specifically, Lashley offered these criticisms: (1) neural cell growth appears to be too slow to account for the rapidity with which some learning takes place (we will return to this point later) and (2) because Lashley was unable to localize the memory trace, he held that there was no warrant to look for localized changes.

I witnessed the vehemence of this opinion at a small informal lunch in New York in 1950 during a meeting of the Association for Research in Nervous and Mental Diseases. When someone asked Lashley his opinion of Donald Hebb's recently published book, *The Organization of Behavior*, Lashley stated sharply that the ideas in the book were garbled versions of his own ideas that Hebb had misunderstood.

Edwin G. Boring, the historian of psychology with whom I studied in the late 1940s, testified to the lack of progress on this problem[1] in the 1950 edition of his history of experimental psychology:

> Where or how does the brain store memories? That is the great mystery … The physiology of memory has been so baffling a problem that most psychologists in facing it have gone positivistic, being content with hypothesizing intervening variables or with empty correlations (p. 670).
>
> In general, it seems safe to say that progress in this field is held back, not by lack of interest, ability, or industry, but by the absence of some one of the other essentials for scientific progress. Knowledge of the nature of the nerve impulse waited on the discovery of electric currents and galvanometers of several kinds. Knowledge of psychoacoustics seemed to get nowhere until electronics developed. The truth about how the brain functions may eventually yield to a technique that comes from some new field remote from either physiology or psychology. Genius waits on insight, but insight may wait on the discovery of new concrete factual knowledge (p. 688).

A few years later, Hans-Lukas Teuber stated in his 1955 *Annual Review of Psychology* chapter on physiological psychology[2] that:

> The absence of any convincing physiological correlate of learning is the greatest gap in physiological psychology. Apparently, the best we can do with learning is to prevent it from occurring, by intercurrent stimulation through implanted electrodes …, by cerebral ablation …, or by depriving otherwise intact organisms, early in life, of normal sensory influx (p. 267).

In fact, some major advances were already beginning to occur in research on the neural mechanisms of learning and memory. Some of these resulted from applications of recently developed techniques such as single cell electrophysiological recording, electron microscopy, and use of new neurochemical methods. Another major influence encouraging research on neural mechanisms of learning and memory was Donald O. Hebb's monograph, *The Organization of Behavior*.[3] I had the opportunity to become familiar early with the book and Hebb's thinking when I was a graduate student because Hebb used a mimeographed version of the book in a graduate seminar he gave at Harvard in the summer of 1947 — 2 years before the book was published in 1949.

Hebb was more positive about possible synaptic changes in learning than his mentor Lashley. Hebb noted some evidence for neural changes and did not let the absence of conclusive evidence deter him from reviving hypotheses about the conditions that could lead to formation of new synaptic junctions and underlie memory. In essence, Hebb's hypothesis of synaptic changes underlying learning resembled William James's formulation[4] of 1890: "When two elementary brain-processes have been active together or in immediate succession, one of them, on recurring, tends to propagate its excitement into the other" (p. 566). This, in turn, resembled the still earlier formulation[5] of associationist philosopher Alexander Bain: "For every act of memory, every exercise of bodily aptitude, every habit, recollection, train of ideas, there is a specific grouping or coordination of sensations and movements, by virtue of specific growths in the cell junctions" (p. 91).

Hebb's dual trace hypothesis — that a labile short-term memory trace may be followed by a stable long-term trace — also resembled the 1900 consolidation–perseveration hypothesis of Müller and Pilzecker.[6] Much current neuroscience research concerns properties of what are now known as Hebbian synapses. Hebb was somewhat amused that his name was connected to this resurrected hypothesis rather than to concepts he considered original.[7]

Still, a decade after Hebb had revived these long-standing hypotheses, the postulate of use-dependent neural plasticity had not yet been demonstrated experimentally. This was to change in the early 1960s when our group announced that both formal training and informal experience in varied environments led to chemical[8] and anatomical plasticity of the brain.[9] Soon after came the reports of Hubel and Wiesel that occluding one eye of a kitten led to a reduction in the number of cortical neurons responding to that eye, but only if the occlusion occurred during an early critical period.[10–12]

4.1.2 Our Approach and Early Findings

The strategy of our group was stated in a symposium paper in 1955.[13] We proposed that to find "changes in the nervous system that accompany learning" a "biochemical analysis which could integrate changes over thousands of neural units might provide an entering wedge … Further analysis might then focus more narrowly on the exact sites of change" (p. 367).

We decided to use the activity of the acetylcholinesterase (AChE) enzyme as an index to acetylcholine (ACh) metabolism. We hypothesized, wrongly as it would turn out, that AChE activity of brain tissue was a stable characteristic of the individual. Relatively rapid measurement of AChE activity was feasible with a recently devised automatic titration apparatus. Our first experiments attempted to account for individual differences in behavior in Krech's hypothesis apparatus. This was a four-unit Y-maze that was unsolvable because the correct visual and spatial cues were changed on successive trials. Nevertheless, rats tended to show hypotheses, that is, they would show runs of choices in which they favored visual hypotheses (light or dark) or spatial hypotheses (right or left). Most of our subjects were two strains of rats maintained by the department: the S1 strain (descendants of rats that had been selectively bred in the 1930s for maze-bright behavior by our Berkeley colleague Robert C. Tryon) and the S3 strain (descendants of Tryon's maze-dull strain). Findings we published during the first few years of our research provided baselines for unexpected discoveries we were soon to make. Some of the main early findings were:

1. Within both the S1 and S3 strains, there are significant correlations between behavioral scores and cortical AChE activity.[14,15] This justified the original purpose of our project.
2. There are significant strain differences in cortical AChE activity, with the S1 (maze-bright) strain showing significantly higher values than the S3 rats.[16]
3. AChE activity differs significantly among regions of the cortex,[17] although previous investigators concluded that there were not significant regional differences. The lactic dehydrogenase enzyme did not show such differences, nor differences between the S1 and S3 strains, so the correlations between AChE activity and behavior could not be ascribed to general differences in cerebral metabolic level.[17] 4.Cortical AChE activity in rats increases with age until about 100 days and then declines.[18]
5. At the start of our work, we assumed from work of others that AChE would provide an index to metabolism of the ACh system, and we later obtained direct support for this, finding that brains of S1 rats showed significantly higher concentrations of ACh than did brains of S3 rats, just as the S1s showed significantly greater AChE activity.[19]

4.2 UNEXPECTED DISCOVERY OF BRAIN PLASTICITY

4.2.1 Finding Plasticity of Brain Chemistry

To try to explore further the correlations between behavior and brain chemistry, we tested different groups of rats in different spatial mazes and obtained surprising results. As I reported at a symposium in 1958,[14] there were systematic differences among the cortical AChE values of rats tested in different apparatuses.[20] We had been assuming that the brain AChE value of an animal was an independent variable, but now it appeared that the value depended in part on the experience the animal had undergone! To test further this unexpected finding, we compared animals subjected to behavioral tests with animals not subjected to testing and found the tested animals to differ significantly from the untested in cortical AChE activity.

Rather than continue the expensive process of testing animals in various mazes, we then decided to explore the results of informal learning by placing rats for prolonged periods in environments that were either more enriched or more impoverished than the standard colony (SC) housing of three rats to a cage. For the enriched condition (EC), we placed 10 to 12 rats in a large cage provided with varied stimulus objects, as students of Hebb had done.[21] We also gave this group a small amount of maze training. For the impoverished condition (IC), we placed rats in individual cages. In initial experiments of this sort, we placed littermates in the three conditions at weaning, at about 25 days of age, and kept them there for 80 days. Analysis of cortical samples at the end of the period showed significant differences among the groups. Contrary to our expectation, AChE activity per unit of tissue weight in the cerebral cortex was significantly lower in EC than in IC animals; SC activity was intermediate. In the rest of the brain, however, AChE activity was significantly highest in the ECs and lowest in the ICs.

4.2.2 A Surprising Discovery: Plasticity of Brain Anatomy

Another surprise helped us to interpret this unexpected result. After years of dividing AChE activity by tissue weight of each sample to obtain enzymatic activity per unit of tissue weight, we were astonished to realize that the tissue weights of the samples differed significantly among experimental groups! Specifically, for a cortical tissue sample of fixed surface area, the weight was greatest for EC rats and least for IC rats[9] so the anatomy as well as the chemistry of the brain was altered by experience! This effect was larger in the occipital region than in other regions of the cortex. Subsequent work showed that the increased weight of cortex in the EC rats was paralleled by increased protein in the samples.[22] Anatomical measurements of brain sections showed the cortex of EC rats to be significantly thicker than that of IC rats, by about 5%.[23] This difference was not large, but it was consistent and, because the brain shows relatively little anatomical variability, it was highly significant statistically.

We and coworkers also found that enriched experience in rats led to increased amounts of RNA[24] and increased expression of RNA in rat brains.[25] We also found that maze training caused differences not only in brain anatomy but also in cortical RNA:DNA ratios.[26]

Having found differences in the gross anatomy of the brain caused by differential experience, we then proceeded to investigate more detailed neuroanatomical features. In a review article in the *Scientific American*,[27] we described several such neuroanatomical differences induced by enriched experience in the occipital cortex:

1. The cross-sectional area of cortical pyramidal cell bodies increased significantly (by about 13%). For more on this effect, see Diamond et al.[28]
2. The number of neurons per unit of volume of occipital cortex decreased slightly with enriched experience, probably because the number of neurons remained fixed while the thickness of the cortex increased.
3. Conversely, the number of glial cells per unit of volume of cortex increased significantly (by 14%).
4. Pyramidal neurons of EC rats showed significantly more dendritic spines than those of IC rats, especially on the basal dendrites. For more detail on this effect, see Globus et al.[29]
5. The sizes of synaptic junctions increased significantly. See West and Greenough.[30]

4.2.3 Our Finding Contradicted Dogma of Fixity of Brain Weight

Our finding of changes in cortical weights with differential experience ran counter to the established dogma that brain weights are strictly fixed. Consider, for example, the following quotations from the outstanding neuroanatomist Santiago Ramón y Cajal[31] that are pertinent to our research in more than one way:

> If we are not worried about putting forth analogies, we could say that the cerebral cortex is like a garden planted with innumerable trees — the pyramidal

> cells — which, thanks to intelligent cultivation, can multiply their branches and sink their roots deeper, producing fruits and flowers of ever greater variety and quality (p. 467).

But Ramón y Cajal then considered an obvious objection to his hypothesis:

> You may well ask how the volume of the brain can remain constant if there is a greater branching and even formation of new terminals of the neurons. To meet this objection we may hypothesize either a reciprocal diminution of the cell bodies or a shrinkage of other areas of the brain whose function is not directly related to intelligence (p. 467).

To preserve the supposed fixity of brain volume, Ramón y Cajal hypothesized a diminution of cell bodies to compensate for the greater branching of neurons, but as we found, the cell bodies increase in volume with enriched experience. His other hypothesis, that other regions of the brain shrink as the cortex expands, may be supported by our finding of diminution of the noncortical parts of the brain as a consequence of enriched experience. Nevertheless, we found an overall increase in brain weight (and presumably in brain volume), overthrowing the long-standing dogma of fixity of the brain.

4.2.4 An Early Predecessor

Years after our discovery that experience can induce changes in brain anatomy, I learned that similar research had been conducted in the 18th century. In 1783, the prominent Swiss naturalist Charles Bonnet and the Piedmontese anatomist Michele Vicenzo Malacarne discussed the possibility of testing experimentally whether mental exercise could induce growth of the brain.[32] Malacarne agreed to test the hypothesis and used an experimental design that anticipated ours. He chose as subjects two littermate dogs and also pairs of birds, each pair coming from the same clutch of eggs. He gave one animal of each pair extensive training while the other received none. After a few years of this differential treatment, Malacarne sacrificed the animals and compared the brains of each pair. A brief review of the results of his experiment published in the *Journal de Physique* in Paris in 1793 (vol. 43, p. 73) reported positive findings: the trained animals had more folds in the cerebellum than did the untrained.

The prominent German physician Samuel Tomas von Soemmering probably knew of Malacarne's work when he wrote the following passage in his major 1791 book on human anatomy:

Does use change the structure of the brain? Does use and exertion of mental power gradually change the material structure of the brain, just as we see, for example, that much used muscles become stronger and that hard labor thickens the epidermis considerably? It is not improbable, although the scalpel cannot easily demonstrate this (vol. 5, p. 91).*

* In the 1800 edition, the last sentence read "It is not improbable, although anatomy has not yet demonstrated this" (p. 394).

I do not know of any attempts to replicate Malacarne's experiment in the 18th or 19th centuries. Obviously, no one thought then that brain activity implied modifying brain circuits because Malacarne wrote a century before the neural doctrine or knowledge of synaptic connections. Malacarne's work appeared too early to affect the development of knowledge about the brain.

4.2.5 Cerebral Effects of Experience Occur Rapidly and Can Be Induced Across Life Span

Originally we placed rats into the differential environments at weaning and kept them there for 80 days because we wanted to allow a good chance for effects to occur. Having found clear effects of differential experience on brain measures, we then tried varying both the age at onset and the duration of differential experience. We obtained similar cerebral effects in rats assigned for 30 days to the differential environments (EC versus IC), either as 50-day juveniles or as 105-day young adults. In one experiment, we placed rats in EC or IC at 60 days of age and sacrificed successive groups after 15, 30, 45, or 60 days in the differential environments.

The EC–IC differences in total cortical weight for the different durations were, respectively, 3.1, 6.9, 3.9, and 3.1%.[33] Thus, the effect increased over the first month in the differential environments and decreased somewhat thereafter. Walter H. Riege[34] in our laboratory assigned rats to the differential environments at 285 days of age and kept them there for periods of 30, 60, or 90 days. In these year-old rats, the EC–IC differences in cortical weights were slower to develop and were greater after 90 days than at the earlier intervals. Although the capacities for these plastic changes in the nervous system and for learning remain in older subjects, the cerebral effects of differential experience develop somewhat more slowly in older than in younger animals, and the magnitude of the effects is often smaller in the older animals. The fact that cerebral effects of differential experience occur across the entire life span marks a strong difference from the effects reported by Hubel and Wiesel that can be induced only during an early critical period.

Recent research demonstrated that differential experience produced both structural and biochemical changes in the brains of adult primates.[35] Adult male–female pairs of marmosets were assigned to new standard cages or were placed in groups in larger cages equipped with a variety of stimulus objects. A month-long stay in the more complex environment resulted in increases in dendritic spine density, dendritic length, and dendritic complexity of neurons in the hippocampus and the prefrontal cortex, and it raised the expression levels of several synaptic proteins in the same regions.

The duration of differential experience need not be long to produce significant effects. When rats spent 2 hours a day in the differential environments over a period of 30 or 54 days, they showed cerebral weight effects similar to those induced by 24-hour-a-day exposure for the same number of days.[36] Only 4 days of differential housing produced clear effects on cortical weights[37] and on dendritic branching.[38]

Ferchmin and Eterovic[39] found that four 10-min daily sessions in EC significantly altered cortical RNA concentrations.

4.3 CEREBRAL EFFECTS OF EXPERIENCE OCCUR IN ALL SPECIES TESTED

Experiments with several strains of rats showed similar effects of EC versus IC experience in both brain values and problem-solving behavior, as reviewed by Renner and Rosenzweig[40] (pp. 53–54). Similar effects on brain measures have been found in several species of mammals — mice of several strains, gerbils, two species of ground squirrels, cats, and monkeys (pp. 54–59). Further work has extended these brain effects to birds and fish and to fruitflies and spiders. The ubiquity of effects across species led neurobiologist Abdul Mohammed[41] to exclaim that these effects occur "from flies to philosophers" (p. 127).

4.3.1 Cerebral Effects Are Caused by Differential Experience — Not by Other Variables

It was possible that the unexpected cerebral effects were not the results of differential experience but of other aspects of the experimental situation, so we promptly ran a number of experiments to control for other possible causes. The results of the control experiments did not support the importance of any of the other variables, as the following examples show.

Handling — Handling rats, particularly young ones, is known to increase the weight of their adrenal glands. Since the EC rats were handled more often than SC or IC rats, perhaps cerebral differences were caused by handling or stress. In control experiments, some rats were handled for several minutes each day for either 30 or 60 days; littermates were never handled. No differences developed between the handled rats and the unhandled ones in brain weight or brain enzyme activity, although they did exhibit differences in adrenal weights. In further experiments, rats in both EC and IC were handled once a day, and the usual brain differences were found at the end of the experimental period.[42]

Stress — Stress may have been a cause of the cerebral effects we found. IC rats may have suffered from isolation stress and EC rats may have suffered from information overload. To test the possible effects of stress on brain measures, we conducted five experiments in which some rats were given intermittent unavoidable electric shocks for 12 min daily. At the same time, littermate controls were placed in similar enclosures but with no shocks and in a different room. Although the stress of shock affected body weight and adrenal weight, it had little effect on brain measures. None of the four cortical regions showed significant differences. Total cortex did weigh 2.3% less in the shocked rats ($p < 0.05$), but when allowance was made through analysis of variance for the reduction in body weight in the shocked rats, the differences shrank and became nonsignificant. Even if the absolute weights were considered, the pattern of differences over cortical areas did not parallel that of EC–IC differences. AChE activity was analyzed in only one of these experiments. It showed no significant difference between shocked and control rats for any brain region. For more on experiments on possible effects of stress on brain measures, see Rosenzweig et al.[27] and Rosenzweig and Bennett.[43]

In a later experiment, Riege and Morimoto in our laboratory subjected some rats to a daily period of stress in which they were briefly tumbled in a revolving drum or given mild electric shocks. They also kept rats in EC and IC. There was a clear double differentiation in effects. The stress was effective in producing a significant increase in the weight of the adrenal glands, but it did not cause changes in the brain measures we studied. Meanwhile, the environmental EC–IC treatment produced the usual brain effects but did not affect adrenal weights.[44]

The experiments on stress also included the variable of handling because the stressed rats were removed from their cages daily and taken to another room for the stress treatment, while the control rats remained in their cages. We concluded, therefore, that the combination of stress and handling did not give rise to the EC–IC brain effects.

Accelerated maturation — Some of the changes we found between EC and IC rats went in the same direction as changes that occur in normal maturation — greater cortical weight, greater glial/neural ratio, and fewer neurons per unit of cortical volume. Thus it seemed possible that enriched experience accelerates maturation or that impoverished experience retards it, but we found that some changes with enriched experience went in the opposite direction from what is found in normal growth. Also, as we have seen above, typical EC–IC brain effects can be induced in animals placed in differential environments as adults. Thus the EC–IC differences cannot be attributed to differences in rates of maturation of animals in the differential environments.

Differential locomotion — Rats in an EC cage are more active than those in IC, so we wanted to determine whether locomotor activity might account for the EC–IC effects. In our initial publication on EC–IC effects, we reported a control experiment in which some IC rats had free access to a running wheel while others were never allowed such access. The experimental (running wheel) rats averaged more than 100,000 revolutions during the experimental period. At the conclusion of the 80-day period, there was no significant difference in AChE measures between the experimental and control groups; the small differences found were opposite in direction from those seen in EC–IC groups.[8]

Hormonal mediation — Although stress had been ruled out as the cause of the EC–IC cerebral effects, other hormones may have mediated these effects. We therefore tested the hypothesis that the pituitary gland is essential to occurrence of these effects.[27] The pituitary was chosen not only to eliminate its secretions but also to control for effects of glands controlled by feedback relations with the pituitary: the thyroid, adrenal cortex, and gonads.

Three experiments were run, and results were analyzed only for those animals in which we could verify complete hypophysectomy at sacrifice. Although hypophysectomy stunts bodily growth and reduces brain growth somewhat, significant EC–IC differences nevertheless occurred in both the brain weights and brain chemical measures of the operated as well as in the control animals. We therefore did not pursue further experiments in the endocrine direction.

4.3.2 Skepticism Greeted Initial Reports of Brain Plasticity

Our first reports that differential experience induces measurable changes in the brain were greeted with skepticism and incredulity. The responses reminded me of an old story. A villager was accused of returning a borrowed teapot in poor condition. Vehemently he replied, "In the first place, I never borrowed it; in the second place, I returned it in perfect condition; in the third place, the teapot was already dented when I got it!" Thus, on the one hand, some critics told us that such changes could not exist. On the other, we were told that it is well-known that one can induce changes in a rat's brain just by looking at it cross-eyed. We were asked whether changes were found in all tissue of ectodermal origin, such as the thickness of the soles of the paws.

At a meeting where I reported an increase in number of synaptic contacts (dendritic spines) with experience, John C. Eccles[45] stated his firm belief that learning and memory storage involve "growth just of bigger and better synapses that are already there, not growth of new connections" (p. 97). Donald Hebb, whom I had gotten to know better when he spent the summer of 1953 as a visiting professor in Berkeley and with whom I maintained contact, cautioned me that the more important the claim, the more carefully one must test it. Beyond normal scientific caution, questions of turf may have been involved. I have the impression that neurophysiologists were reluctant to believe that psychologists and their collaborators could be the first to present evidence of changes in the brain as a result of experience.

Over the next several years, reports of replications and extension by us[22] and by others[46–48] gained acceptance for the idea that training or differential experience could produce measurable changes in the brain. Thus in 1972, neurobiologist B.G. Cragg wrote[49] that "Initial incredulity that such differences in social and psychological conditions could give rise to significant differences in brain weight, cortical thickness, and glial cell numbers seems to have been overcome by the continued series of papers from Berkeley reporting consistent results. Some independent confirmation by workers elsewhere has also been obtained" (p. 42).

4.4 ENRICHED ENVIRONMENTS AND THE BRAIN

4.4.1 Our Work Introduced Enriched Environments to Neuroscience Community

We did not invent the concept of the enriched environment, but I believe that our publications introduced the concept and the term to the neuroscience community. Our first paper with "enriched and impoverished environments" in the title appeared in 1962.[50] The first citation for "enriched environment" on the National Library of Medicine website known as PubMed was a paper from our group.[23] It was followed later the same year by a paper by Altman and Das[46] that cited four of our papers (1960 through 1964) showing effects of enriched environments on brain chemistry and brain anatomy. Our first papers reporting effects of environment on brain plasticity used the term "environmental complexity"[8,9] The next PubMed citation for enriched environment after 1964 was another paper from our group.[51] Seven citations for enriched environment appeared from 1970 through 1974. Thereafter, such citations increased exponentially, reaching 46 for 1995 through 1999 and 122 for 2000 through 2004.

Although the enriched environment term has become widely used, it has no standard definition. Some investigators avoid it, preferring instead to use "complex environment." We tried to make clear from the beginning that our enriched laboratory environment is enriched only in comparison with a standard animal colony cage. A natural environment may be much richer in learning experiences than even an enriched laboratory environment. For inbred laboratory animals, however, it is no longer clear what the natural environment is. Laboratory rats and mice have been kept for more than 100 generations in protected environments, and inbreeding has made their gene pool different from the natural one.

4.4.2 Comparing Laboratory-Enriched Environment with Natural Environment

We tried in two ways, with two different species, to determine how our enriched laboratory environment compared with the natural environment. First, we tried raising laboratory rats in a semi-natural outdoor environment at the Field Station for Research in Animal Behavior of the University of California at Berkeley. This environment consisted of a 30 × 30 foot concrete enclosure filled with dirt to a depth of 2 feet above the concrete base, with screening over the top. Food and water were provided ad lib., and a few stimulus objects were placed in the enclosure. For a diagram of this environment, see Rosenzweig et al.[27] (p. 24).

Groups of a dozen male laboratory rats thrived in the outdoor setting and, when the weather was not too wet, dug burrows, something their ancestors had not been able to do for more than 100 generations. In each of eight experiments, rats kept for 1 month in the outdoor setting showed greater cortical development than their littermates been kept in enriched laboratory cages. This indicates that even the enriched laboratory environment is indeed impoverished in comparison with a natural environment. We had hoped to test the rats from the outdoor environment to see whether their increased cortical development was accompanied by increased problem-solving ability. Unfortunately, however, in the outdoor setting the rats became too savage to handle, so we were unable to conduct behavioral tests.

In a second attempt to compare effects of laboratory and natural environments on brain development, we used Belding's ground squirrels (*Spermophilus beldingi*). This research was done in collaboration with our colleague Paul Sherman who was studying a population of the squirrels in the Sierra near Tioga Pass, California. We live-trapped pregnant ground squirrels in the Sierra and brought them to the field station in Berkeley. The young were weaned at about 30 days of age and assigned to EC and IC conditions where they were kept for 40 days. Ten male and 10 female squirrels were kept in each condition. Just before sacrifice, feral (F) juveniles of the same age were live-trapped where the pregnant ground squirrels had been obtained, and their brains were analyzed along with those of the EC and IC squirrels.

In weights of cerebral cortex, values from F and EC squirrels were equal, and both exceeded the IC squirrels significantly ([F = EC] >IC, $p < .01$). In total RNA of occipital cortex, (F = EC) >IC, p <.05. In total DNA of occipital cortex, F> (EC = IC), p <.05. In skeletal development measured by hindfoot length, F> EC> IC; F> IC, p <.01. Thus, in two of three brain measures, EC squirrels equalled F squirrels, although F exceeded EC in skeletal development.[52] A further study substantially replicated these findings.[53]

Thus, in the case of ground squirrels, the laboratory enriched environment seemed to support brain development as did the natural environment. Clearly, the differences between results of the studies with rats and ground squirrels show that this question still lacks a general resolution. Nevertheless, this has not prevented the increasing use of enriched laboratory environments.

The latter study[53] also showed plastic responses of the brain during hibernation. For this study, ground squirrels were live-trapped at about 80 days of age. Some were sacrificed for baseline values and others were placed for 5 months in EC or IC cages or in a cold room at 5°C where they hibernated. The non-hibernating squirrels continued to gain in brain and body weights during the experimental period, whereas the hibernators lost in both parameters, showing significant decreases in weights of certain brain regions (hypothalamus, caudate nucleus, and medulla), and decreases of DNA in these regions, indicating loss of cells.

4.4.3 Enriched Experience Improves Ability to Learn and Solve Problems

Hebb[3] (p. 298) reported briefly that when he allowed seven laboratory rats to explore his home for some weeks as pets of his children and then returned the rats to the laboratory, they then showed better problem-solving ability than most rats that remained in the laboratory. Moreover, although he did not present evidence for this, he stated that they maintained their superiority or even increased it during a series of problems in the Hebb-Williams maze. Hebb (pp. 298–299) concluded that "*the richer experience of the pet group during development made them better able to profit by new experience at maturity* — one of the characteristics of the 'intelligent'; human being" (italics in original). Thus the results seemed to show a permanent effect of early experience on problem-solving at maturity, and this conclusion continues to be cited.

We and others confirmed the first conclusion of Hebb's exploratory study, that is, experience in an enriched environment improves learning and problem-solving on a wide variety of tasks, although such differences have not been found invariably. The more complex the task, the more likely it is that animals with EC experience will perform better than animals from SC or IC groups[40] (pp. 46–48).

We were unable, however, to replicate Hebb's report that over a series of tests, EC rats maintained or even increased their superiority over IC rats. On the contrary, we found that IC rats tended to catch up with EC rats over a series of trials in a test; this occurred in three different tests including the Hebb-Williams maze[54] (p. 321). We did not find that early deprivation of experience caused a permanent deficit, at least for rats tested on spatial problems. Rather, the rats showed a persistent capacity to benefit from experience. Somewhat similarly, decreases in cortical weights induced by 300 days in the IC (versus EC) environment were overcome by a few weeks of training and testing in the Hebb-Williams maze.[55] Similar effects were found with beagles. Fuller[56] found restricted-experience beagles to be inferior to pets in reversal learning, but only on the first five reversals; thereafter there was no significant difference.

4.4.4 Caveat

We were careful to state that an enriched environment or specific training might not improve all types or learning or brain measures.[27] For example, we noted that Harry Harlow found that early problem-solving in monkeys may have the deleterious effect of fixating infantile behavior patterns; such monkeys may never reach the efficient adult performance they would have attained without early training.

Recent research similarly shows that enriched experience does not always increase the number of synapses in the brain region affected. Thus, an editorial comment[57] on a recent article is entitled "The brain: use it and lose it." The article[58] cited reports that long-term sensory deprivation through trimming the whiskers of young adolescent mice prevents the normal substantial loss of dendritic spines in the barrel region of primary somatosensory cortex. Allowing the whiskers to regrow after adolescence accelerates spine elimination. The authors point out that these effects are counter to the general expectation that experience increases the number of synapses. In this case, however, experience contributes to the normal sculpting of connections through selective elimination.

4.4.5 Enriched Environments as Therapy for Animals and People

Once the brain was seen to respond to environmental influences, not only in young but also in mature animals, investigators soon began testing whether environmental enrichment might aid recovery from brain disorders that have identifiable neuropathies. An intriguing report of 1964 stated that an enriched environment aided rats to recover from effects of neonatal cortical lesions.[59] We began in 1974 to replicate and extend this effect[60] and research along this line continues. One of the major questions is the extent to which experience actually improves in recovery or only in compensation for the effects of brain injury.

In people, at a minimum, behavioral techniques aid the quality of life of patients with injuries of the brain or spinal cord. Beyond this, there may be interactions between physiological and behavioral interventions. By 1976, an edited volume titled *Environments as Therapy for Brain Dysfunction*[61] treating such topics as recovery from brain injury, malnutrition, endocrinopathies, and sensory deprivation was published. Chapters considered the relevance, generalizability, and limitations of animal models for therapy, and work on these questions continues. Investigators have asked which is most effective in promoting recovery from brain injury in animals — environmental enrichment, physical exercise, or formal training? A review of research on this topic from 1990 to 2002 shows that enriched experience is the most potent of these treatments.[62]

Soon after we began publishing about the effects of differential environments on brain and behavior, people began asking us about possible applications to human behavior, all the way from child development to successful aging. Thus, in 1965, I was invited to address the Division of Child Psychology at the Convention of the American Psychological Association.[63] Many of the developmental psychologists who attended my talk expressed surprise at hearing that an enriched environment stimulates brain growth not only in infant but also in adult rats. On such occasions I was always careful to point out limitations in what we found and was cautious about extrapolations of animal research[27] (p. 28). Nevertheless, invitations to speak and write about possible applications continued to come and I accepted many of them.[52,64–71] At an international symposium on cognitive decline in old age,[72] I summarized the research as follows (p. 63):

> It's a fortunate person whose brain
> Is trained early, again and again,
> And who continues to use it
> To be sure not to lose it,
> So the brain, in old age, may not wane.

Although I did not do research on effects of environment with human subjects, I was active in an innovative program to promote higher education for disadvantaged and under-represented youth. In 1964, physicist Owen Chamberlain and I became co-chairs of the newly established Berkeley faculty Special Opportunity Scholarship Committee. Our committee obtained faculty and university financial support for an on-campus summer precollege program for promising high school students and we continued that with a year-round contact program that soon became a federal Upward Bound program. After a few years, the students who completed the preparatory program were able to secure admission to the University of California and to other universities and colleges through the committee and became the first in their families to obtain higher education. The faculty committee continues its work; it was renamed in 2005 as the Committee on Student Diversity and Academic Development. Its favorable results suggest that even at high school age, students from family backgrounds and high schools that do not predispose to postsecondary education can be prepared and encouraged to undertake successful college studies. The results also suggest that public schools are falling short of what they should accomplish.

I did in fact attempt to do research on the effectiveness of the Special Opportunity Scholarship Program. After the program had been active for a few years, I proposed to the faculty committee that we attempt to measure its effectiveness in the following way: each year we would draw up a pool of twice as many candidates as the program could accommodate and then select at random those to be accepted. Both those accepted and those not included would then be followed up over the next 6 to 10 years to determine whether the program made a difference. I was unable, however, to convince my fellow committee members that such research was appropriate, so the attempt was not made.

4.4.6 Should All Laboratory Animals Be Housed in Enriched Environments?

There is a growing movement to house all laboratory animals in enriched environments, with exceptions only for specific research purposes. Some proponents cite evidence from work such as ours that indicates that enriched experience is necessary for full growth of the nervous system and behavioral capacities. Others favor this as part of the movement to improve animal welfare.

The history of enriching environments of laboratory animals goes back at least to psychologist Robert Yerkes' work with primates in the 1910s and 1920s. Hebb, who did research at the Yerkes primate laboratory, helped to extend concept of enrichment to laboratory rodents in the 1950s. Our publications beginning in 1960 popularized use of enriched environments by showing that they contributed to full development of the brain as well as to behavioral capacities.

Providing enriched environments is not without its problems. For one thing, definitions of enrichment vary, although most attempt to foster species-specific behaviors. It is important for investigators to avoid the temptation to anthropomorphize in choosing enriched conditions. Thus, it is amusing to see photographs of enriched environments for laboratory rodents that show cages filled with brightly colored objects. While the colors may be attractive to the researchers, they do nothing for rats or mice who do not discriminate hues. There are also concerns because enriched environments are more expensive than standard housing: they take up more space and require more care.

Some investigators have expressed concerns that enriched environments may differ among laboratories and thus decrease the reproducibility of results. In a recent attempt to deal with these concerns, investigators from three laboratories performed an experiment in which they raised female mice of two inbred strains in either standardized cages or following an enrichment protocol. They then tested the mice on four common behavioral tests. The results were highly consistent, indicating that standardization among laboratories was almost as good as within laboratories.[73] The authors note that it remains to be seen whether similar results would also be obtained for male mice who may respond to enrichment with increased dominance behavior and aggression.

The growing concern about enriched environments is shown by *ILAR*, the journal of the Institute for Laboratory Animal Research, which devoted its Spring 2005 number to this topic. The 12 articles in this issue range from enriched housing for laboratory rodents to enriched housing for nonhuman primates, and from theoretical to practical concerns.

In the near future, whether to use enriched environments may no longer be a matter of choice for the individual investigator or research unit. Enriched environments are among the revisions of animal welfare standards that the Council of Europe is preparing as recommended practices for its 45 member nations, and these standards may affect practices in other countries as well. The website of the Council of Europe reported that a working party at a meeting of September 2004 completed a revision of its recommendations for protection of vertebrate animals used for experimental and other scientific purposes and submitted it for adoption. The changes proposed included not only increasing the minimum recommended cage sizes but would also require that laboratory animals be housed in enriched environments that permit the expression of normal behaviors.

Whatever the fate of regulations concerning enriched environments, the clear evidence of the importance of animal environments in determining the results of research shows the necessity of describing animal housing clearly and accurately in all reports of research.

4.4.7 Stimulant Drugs Enhance Effects of Environment on Recovery of Function

Our finding that a daily 2-hour period of exposure to EC was sufficient to produce cerebral effects allowed us to test whether stimulant drugs altered brain measures directly or only in conjunction with EC. We gave some animals low doses of methamphetamine just before putting them into EC for a daily 2-hour period; other animals received the drug at a different part of the day when they were in their individual home cages. The drug enhanced cortical weight only when the drug was active during the daily EC period.[74]

The drug–environment interaction result was even clearer with shorter daily periods of EC or in shorter-duration experiments. Effects on AChE measures were somewhat larger, but not significantly so, in the drug-EC groups. A low dose of pentobarbital sodium depressant reduced the effect of EC experience on cortical weights, but again only if the drug was active during the daily period of EC. Thus it was the combination of drug and environment that counted in determining cortical weights.

Considering this finding and research on recovery of function, we proposed testing[74] "whether the conjunction of enriched environment and an excitant drug may be even more favorable for recovery from brain damage than is either treatment alone" (p. 327). We did not follow our own suggestion, but in the last two decades others have conducted fruitful research on this topic with both animal subjects and human patients.

In an early study of this sort, Feeney, Gonzales, and Law[75] removed motor cortex unilaterally in rats and studied their behavior 24 hours later in locomotion on a narrow beam. After a single trial, subgroups received either a single daily injection of saline, a low dose of amphetamine, or a haloperidol depressant. Further tests of locomotion showed that amphetamine improved recovery while haloperidol impaired it in relation to the saline controls. Confining the animals in a small cage to prevent locomotion for 8 hours after drug administration blocked the effects of the drugs, so they were effective only in combination with behavioral practice.

Reviews of research with both animal and human subjects have shown the generality of these effects.[76–79] More recently, Walker-Batson reported that amphetamine plus intensive speech therapy aids recovery from aphasia,[80] and Walker-Batson and her colleagues reviewed neuromodulation paired with learning in rehabilitation for various deficits resulting from stroke.[81]

An obvious extension of this research would be to combine enriched experience or training with other pharmacological treatments. Hamm et al.[82] reviewed research in which traumatic head injury in rats was followed by a number of different drug treatments including agents that affected the monoamine system, the cholinergic system, the glutaminergic system, nerve growth factor, and basic fibroblast growth factor. Each agent led to some improvement, but none was as effective as exposure to an enriched environment. It will be interesting to see results of research that combine some of these pharmacological treatments with enriched experience.

In attempts to promote recovery from brain damage, some neuroscientists are transplanting fetal brain cells into the region of a brain lesion. Some investigators have studied the separate and the combined effects of enriched environment and neural transplants.[83] Under some conditions, neither the enriched experience nor the transplant alone had a beneficial effect, but the combination of the two treatments yielded a significant improvement in learning. Further work indicates that formal training of rats may be more effective than enriched environment in promoting the effects of brain cell grafts on recovery of learning ability.[84]

These results of animal research may find application in attempts to aid human patients. Perhaps the differences among clinics in success of brain cell grafts reflect, in part at least, the kinds and amounts of training and stimulation given the patients; this may interact with the skill of the neurosurgeon. The combination of brain implants with training and stimulation may become an increasingly important area of interaction between research and application in the field of plasticity of brain and behavior.

4.4.8 Recent Research Involving Enriched Environments Falls into Three Main Categories

Research for the period 2000 through 2004 that involves enriched environments falls into three main categories, two of which were pioneered by work of our group:

1. By far the most frequent category is enriched environment as therapy. This has been studied recently for many kinds of brain injury, including trauma, brain infarcts, focal ischemia, and transient global ischemia. Spinal cord injuries have also been studied. Besides injury, other studies have taken up therapy for cocaine exposure, epilepsy, prenatal stress, immune challenges, and lead poisoning. Although most of this research uses animal subjects, some is conducted with human subjects.
2. The next most frequent category is effects of enriched environments on gene expression. This was anticipated by our studies showing greater expression and variety of RNA in EC than in IC animals.
3. The third most frequent category of recent research involving enriched environments concerns effects of environmental treatments on neurogenesis. A group including Marian Diamond was the first to report that EC increased neurogenesis in the dentate gyrus of adult rats.[85]

Other groups besides ours have recently written reviews of the neurobiological effects of enriched environments and have extended the research into new directions, notably Mohammed et al.[41] see also Rampon and Tsien[86] andvan Praag et al.[87]

4.5 NEUROCHEMICAL CASCADES UNDERLIE MODIFICATION OF NEURAL CIRCUITS

4.5.1 Similar Neurochemical Cascades Underlie Different Kinds of Learning

Having found that learning or enriched experience led to plastic changes in the nervous system, Edward Bennett and I decided to try to find the mechanisms that lead to such changes. We learned early that enriched experience causes increased rates of protein synthesis and increased amounts of protein in the cortex.[22] Others later reported that imprinting increased the rates of incorporation of precursors into RNA and protein in the forebrain of the chick.[88] and, as mentioned above, we and coworkers found that enriched experience in rats led to increased amounts of RNA in rat brain. We viewed these and related findings in the light of the hypothesis perhaps first enunciated by Katz and Halstead,[89] that protein synthesis is required for memory storage.

Tests of the protein synthesis hypothesis of memory formation were initiated by Flexner and associates in the early 1960s,[90,91] but the interpretation of the findings was clouded by serious problems. The research involved administering to experimental subjects an inhibitor of protein synthesis at various times close to training (control subjects received an inactive substance) and comparing test performance of experimental and control subjects at a later time. Unfortunately, the inhibitors of protein synthesis then available for research (such as puromycin and cycloheximide) were rather toxic, which impeded experiments and complicated interpretation. Also, it appeared that inhibition of protein synthesis could prevent memory formation after weak training but not after strong training.[92]

A recently discovered protein synthesis inhibitor, anisomycin (ANI), helped to overcome these problems. Schwartz, Castelluci, and Kandel[93] reported that ANI did not prevent an electrophysiological correlate of short-term habituation or sensitization in an isolated ganglion of Aplysia, but they did not investigate whether ANI could prevent long-term effects. Then Bennett discovered that ANI administered shortly before training prevents formation of long-term memory (LTM) in rats.[94] This opened the way to resolving the main challenges to the protein synthesis hypothesis of formation of LTM.

ANI is much less toxic than other protein synthesis inhibitors and giving doses repeatedly at 2-hour intervals can prolong the duration of cerebral inhibition at amnestic levels. By varying the duration of amnestic levels of inhibition in this way, we found that the stronger the training, the longer inhibition of protein synthesis had to be maintained to prevent formation of LTM.[95,96] We also found that protein must be synthesized in the cortex soon after training if LTM is to be formed; short-term memory (STM) and intermediate-term memory (ITM) do not require protein synthesis.[94,97,98] From the time that Bennett showed the value of ANI in studying formation of LTM, this agent has been in frequent use for this purpose.

We then designed further studies to find the neurochemical processes that underlie formation of STM and LTM. Lashley's concern, mentioned above, that some kinds of memory appear to be formed too quickly to allow growth of neural connections, ignored the distinction between STM and LTM, even though William James[4] had already distinguished them (although under different names). Observing this distinction was necessary if one was to look for different mechanisms of the two kinds of memory traces that Hebb distinguished: transient, labile memory traces on the one hand and stable structural traces on the other.

4.5.2 Similar Neurochemical Cascades Occur in Different Species

Much of our work on the neurochemistry of STM and ITM was done with chicks, which have several advantages for this research. The chick system is convenient for studying the stages of memory formation because chicks can be trained rapidly in a one-trial peck-avoidance paradigm and can be tested within seconds after training or hours and days later. Large numbers of chicks can be studied in a single run, so one can compare different agents, doses, and times of administration within the same batch of subjects. Unlike invertebrate preparations, the chick system can be used to study the roles of different vertebrate brain structures and investigate questions of hemispheric asymmetry in learning and memory. The chick system also permits studies of learning and memory in intact animals. The successive neurochemical stages occur more slowly in the chick than in the rat, thus allowing them to be separated more clearly. I have stated further advantages elsewhere.[99,100]

Although some amnestic agents such as ANI diffuse readily throughout the brain, we found that others affect only a restricted volume of tissue at amnestic concentrations.[101] We employed such agents to reveal the roles of different brain structures in different stages of memory formation.[101,102]

Using the chick system, several investigators traced a cascade of neurochemical events from initial stimulation to synthesis of protein and structural changes.[100,103–105] At some if not all stages, parallel processes occur. The following is a brief description of some of the events.

The cascade is initiated when sensory stimulation activates receptor organs that stimulate afferent neurons by using various synaptic transmitter agents such as acetylcholine (ACh) and glutamate. Inhibitors of ACh synaptic activity such as scopolamine and pirenzepine can prevent STM as can inhibitors of glutamate receptors including both the NMDA and AMPA receptors. Alteration of regulation of ion channels in the neuronal membrane can inhibit STM formation, as seen in effects of lanthanum chloride on calcium channels and of ouabain on sodium and potassium channels. Inhibition of second messengers is also amnestic, for example, inhibition of adenylate cyclase by forskolin or of diacylglycerol by bradykinin.

These second messengers can activate protein kinases — enzymes that catalyze additions of phosphate molecules to proteins. We found that two kinds of protein kinases are important in formation, respectively, of ITM or LTM. Agents that inhibit calcium/calmodulin protein kinases (CaM kinases) prevent formation of ITM, whereas agents that do not inhibit CaM kinases but do inhibit protein kinase A (PKA) or protein kinase C (PKC) prevent formation of LTM.[100,106] From this research, Serrano et al.[102] in our laboratories were able to predict for a newly available inhibitor of PKC, chelerythrine, its effective amnestic dose, and how long after training it would cause memory to decline.

One-trial training leads to an increase of immediate early gene messenger RNA in the chick forebrain[107] and an increase in the density of dendritic spines.[108] Many of these effects occur only in the left hemisphere of the chick or are more prominent in the left than in the right hemisphere. Thus, learning in the chick system permits study of many steps that lead from sensory stimulation to formation of neuronal structures involved in memory.

The neurochemical cascade involved in formation of memory in the chick was soon shown to be similar to the cascade involved in long-term potentiation in the mammalian brain[109] and in the nervous systems of invertebrates.[110] DeZazzo and Tully[111] compared STM, ITM, and LTM in fruitflies, chicks, and rats. Tully and coworkers have shown that the three stages of memory in the fruitfly depend on three different genes.[112]

Many of the steps in formation of memory in the chick can also be modulated by opioids and other substances. Opioid agonists tend to impair and opioid antagonists to enhance memory formation. We found that different opioids appear to modulate formation of different stages of memory.[100,113–115]

4.5.3 Parts of Neurochemical Cascade Can Be Related to Different Stages of Memory Formation

Some of the difficulty in attempting to relate parts of the neurochemical cascade to different stages of memory formation may come from problems of defining the stages of memory in terms of their durations, as I have discussed more fully elsewhere.[116] Consider, for example, some very different notions about the duration of short-term memory. Early investigators of human STM[117,118] reported that it lasts only about 30 sec. if rehearsal is prevented.

At the other extreme, Agranoff, Davis, and Brink[119] reported that in goldfish, if formation of LTM is prevented by an inhibitor of protein synthesis, STM can last up to 3 days, although normally LTM forms within an hour after training. Kandel et al.[120] wrote that in Aplysia, "A single training trial produces short-term sensitization that lasts from minutes to hours" (p. 17) and that long-term memory is "memory that lasts more than one day" (p. 35). Rose[121] suggested that memories that persist only a few hours involve a first wave of glycoprotein synthesis in chicks, whereas true long-term memory requires a second wave of glycoprotein synthesis, occurring about 6 hours after training.

Instead of considering that STM can last several hours or even a day or more, it is useful to posit one or more ITM stages occurring between STM and LTM, as some theorists have done since the 1960s.[122,123] Gibbs and Ng[103] referred to a "labile" stage occurring between STM and LTM and later (1984) called this the intermediate stage of memory. My coworkers and I discussed mechanisms of STM, ITM, and LTM in a series of papers.[98,100,116,124]

In investigating effects of protein kinase inhibitors (PKIs) on memory formation in chicks, we reported that those agents that inhibit CaM kinase activity disrupt formation of what some workers with chicks identify as ITM (lasting from about

15 min to about 60 min posttraining); those agents that inhibit PKC, PKA, or PKG but do not inhibit CaM kinase disrupt the formation of LTM.[100,106] Other investigators prefer to refer to different phases or stages of LTM rather than use the expression ITM. Thus, studying the LTP analog to memory in slices of rat hippocampus, Huang and Kandel[125] reported findings similar to those of Rosenzweig et al.[100] and Serrano et al.[106] with regard to the roles of two classes of protein kinases. Inhibitors of CaM kinase activity disrupted what Huang and Kandel called a transient early phase of LTP (E-LTP) evoked by moderately strong stimuli and lasting from 1 hour to less than 3 hours after induction of LTP. Agents that inhibit PKA but do not inhibit CaM kinase disrupt the formation of what they called a later, more enduring phase of LTP (L-LTP) evoked by strong stimulation and lasting at least 6 to 10 hours. Weak stimuli evoke only short-term potentiation (STP), lasting only 20 to 30 min.

As mentioned above, Rose[121] suggested that in chicks a kind of LTM that lasts a few hours involves a first wave of glycoprotein synthesis, whereas "true long-term memory" requires a second wave of glycoprotein synthesis, occurring about 6 hours after training. Rather than call the memory associated with Rose's first 6-hour long wave a form of LTM, I believe it is better to designate it by a special term such as ITM and to note that there is an earlier STM lasting only a few minutes, as shown in many experiments with chicks. The findings in this area seem to support the hypothesis of at least three sequentially dependent stages of memory formation, each dependent on different neurochemical processes.

ACKNOWLEDGMENTS

It is a pleasure for me to acknowledge that in my research and publications I have benefitted from association and collaboration with many gifted and stimulating collaborators. My hearty thanks and deep appreciation go to all of them, and especially to Edward L. Bennett, Marian C. Diamond, and David Krech. My appreciation also goes to the talented students and postdoctoral fellows and skillful assistants who worked with me.

I also want to acknowledge indispensable financial support from a number of agencies and organizations: March of Dimes; Miller Institute for Basic Research in Science, University of California; National Institute of Drug Abuse; National Institutes of Health, U.S. Public Health Service; National Institute of Mental Health, U.S. Public Health Service; National Science Foundation; Office of Education; U.S. Atomic Energy Commission.

REFERENCES

1. Boring, E.G. *A History of Experimental Psychology*, 2nd ed., Appleton-Century-Crofts, New York, 1950.
2. Teuber, H.L. Physiological psychology. *Annu Rev Psychol* 6, 267, 1955.
3. Hebb, D.O. *The Organization of Behavior: A Neuropsychological Theory*. John Wiley & Sons, New York, 1949.
4. James, W. *Principles of Psychology*. Henry Holt, New York, 1890.

5. Bain. *Mind and Body: The Theories of Their Relation*. Henry S. King, London, 1872.
6. Müller, G.E. and Pilzecker, A. Experimentale Beitrage zur Lehre vom Gedächtnis (Experimental research on memory). *Zeitschrift für Psychologie* Suppl. 1, 1900.
7. Milner, P.M. The mind and Donald O. Hebb. *Sci Am* 268, 124, 1993.
8. Krech, D., Rosenzweig, M.R., and Bennett, E.L. Effects of environmental complexity and training on brain chemistry. *J Comp Physiol Psychol* 53, 509, 1960.
9. Rosenzweig, M.R. et al. Effects of environmental complexity and training on brain chemistry and anatomy: a replication and extension. *J Comp Physiol Psychol* 55, 429, 1962.
10. Wiesel, T.N. and Hubel, D.H. Single-cell responses in striate cortex of kittens deprived of vision in one eye. *J Neurophysiol* 26, 1003, 1963.
11. Wiesel, T.N. and Hubel, D.H. Comparison of the effects of unilateral and bilateral eye closure on cortical unit responses in kittens. *J Neurophysiol* 28, 1029, 1965.
12. Hubel, D.H. and Wiesel, T.N. Binocular interaction in striate cortex of kittens reared with artificial squint. *J Neurophysiol* 28, 1041, 1965.
13. Rosenzweig, M.R., Krech, D., and Bennett, E.L. in *Biological and Biochemical Bases of Behavior*, Harlow, H.F. and Woolsey, C.N., Eds. Wisconsin University Press, Madison, WI, 1958, 367.
14. Rosenzweig, M.R., Krech, D., and Bennett, E.L. in *Ciba Foundation Symposium on Neurological Basis of Behaviour*. J. & A. Churchill, London, 1958, p. 337.
15. Rosenzweig, M.R., Krech, D., and Bennett, E.L. A search for relations between brain chemistry and behavior. *Psychol Bull* 57, 476, 1960.
16. Bennett, E.L. et al. Individual, strain and age differences in cholinesterase activity of the rat brain. *J Neurochem* 3, 144, 1958.
17. Bennett, E.L. et al. Cholinesterase and lactic dehydrogenase activity in the rat brain. *J Neurochem* 3, 153, 1958.
18. Bennett, E.L., Rosenzweig, M.R., Krech, D., Ohlander, A., and Morimoto, H. Cholinesterase activity and protein content of rat brain. *J Neurochem* 6, 210, 1961.
19. Bennett, E.L. et al. Strain differences in acetylcholine concentration in the brain of the rat. *Nature* 187, 787, 1960.
20. Rosenzweig, M.R., Krech, D., and Bennett, E.L. in *Current Trends in Psychological Theory*, University of Pittsburgh Press, Pittsburgh, 1961, p. 87.
21. Forgays, D.G. and Forgays, J.W. The nature of the effect of free-environmental experience in the rat. *J Comp Physiol Psychol* 45, 322, 1952.
22. Bennett, E.L. et al. Chemical and anatomical plasticity of the brain. *Science* 146, 610, 1964.
23. Diamond, M.C., Krech, D., and Rosenzweig, M.R. Effects of an enriched environment on the histology of the rat cerebral cortex. *J Comp Neurol* 123, 111, 1964.
24. Ferchmin, P.A., Eterovic, V.A., and Caputto, R. Studies of brain weight and RNA content after short periods of exposure to environmental complexity. *Brain Res* 20, 49, 1970.
25. Grouse, L.D., Schrier, B.K., Bennett, E.L., Rosenzweig, M.R., and Nelson, P.G. Sequence diversity studies of rat brain RNA: effects of environmental complexity on rat brain RNA diversity. *J Neurochem* 30, 191, 1978.
26. Bennett, E.L. et al. Maze training alters brain weights and cortical RDA/DNA ratios. *Behav Neural Biol* 26, 1, 1979.
27. Rosenzweig, M.R., Bennett, E.L., and Diamond, M.C. Brain changes in response to experience. *Sci Amer* 226, 22, 1972.

28. Diamond, M.C., Johnson, R., Ingham, C., Rosenzweig, M.R., and Bennett, E.L. Effects of differential environments on neuronal, nuclear and perikarya dimensions in the rat cerebral cortex. *Behav Biol* 15, 107, 1975.
29. Globus, A. et al. Effects of differential experience on dendritic spine counts in rat cerebral cortex. *J Comp Physiol Psychol* 82, 175, 1973.
30. West, R.W. and Greenough, W.T. Effect of environmental complexity on cortical synapses of rats: preliminary results. *Behav Biol* 7, 279, 1972.
31. Cajal, R.S. La fine structure des centres nerveux. *Proc R Soc* 55, 444, 1894.
32. Bonnet, C. *Oeuvres d'Histoire Naturelle et de Philosophie*. S. Fauche, Neuchatel, 1779–1783.
33. Rosenzweig, M.R., Bennett, E.L., and Diamond, M.C. *Proc 75th Annu Conv Amer Psychol Assn* 1967, p. 105.
34. Riege, W.H. Environmental influences on brain and behavior of year-old rats. *Dev Psychobiol* 4, 157, 1971.
35. Kozorovitskiy, Y. et al. Experience induces structural and biochemical changes in the adult primate brain. *Proc Natl Acad Sci USA* 102, 17478, 2005.
36. Rosenzweig, M.R., Love, W., and Bennett, E.L. Effects of a few hours of enriched experience on brain chemistry and brain weights. *Physiol Behav* 3, 819, 1968.
37. Bennett, E.L., Rosenzweig, M.R., and Diamond, M.C. in *Molecular Approaches to Learning and Memory*, Academic Press, New York, 1970, p. 69.
38. Kilman, V.L. et al. Four days of differential housing alters dendritic morphology of weanling rats. *Soc Neurosci Abstr* 14, 1988.
39. Ferchmin, P.A. and Eterovic, V.A. Forty minutes of experience increase the weight and RNA content of cerebral cortex in periadolescent rats. *Dev Psychobiol* 19, 511, 1986.
40. Renner, M.J. and Rosenzweig, M.R. *Enriched and Impoverished Environments: Effects on Brain and Behavior*, Springer Verlag, New York, 1987.
41. Mohammed, A.H. et al. Environmental enrichment and the brain. *Progr Brain Res* 138, 109, 2002.
42. Rosenzweig, M.R., Bennett, E.L., and Diamond, M.C. in *Early Experience and Behavior*, Newton, G. and Levine, S., Eds., C.C. Thomas, Springfield, IL, 1968, p. 258.
43. Rosenzweig, M.R. and Bennett, E.L. in *Knowing, Thinking, and Believing*, Petrinovich, L. and McGaugh, J.L., Eds., Plenum Press, New York, 1976, p. 179.
44. Riege, W.H. and Morimoto, H. Effects of chronic stress and differential environments upon brain weights and biogenic amine levels in rats. *J Comp Physiol Psychol* 71, 396, 1970.
45. Eccles, J.C. in *The Anatomy of Memory*, Kimble, D.P., Ed., Science and Behavior Books, Palo Alto, CA, 1965.
46. Altman, J. and Das, G.D. Autoradiographic examination of the effects of enriched environment on the rate of glial multiplication in the adult rat brain. *Nature* 204, 1161, 1964.
47. Geller, E., Yuwiler, A., and Zolman, J.F. Effects of environmental complexity on constituents of brain and liver. *J Neurochem* 12, 949, 1965.
48. Greenough, W.T. and Volkmar, F.R. Pattern of dendritic branching in occipital cortex of rats reared in complex environments. *Exp Neurol* 40, 491, 1973.
49. Cragg, B.G. in *The Structure and Function of Nervous Tissue*, Bourne, G.H., Ed., Academic Press., New York, 1972, p. 2.

50. Krech, D., Rosenzweig, M.R., and Bennett, E.L. Relations between chemistry and problem-solving among rats raised in enriched and impoverished environments. *J Comp Physiol Psychol* 55, 801, 1962.
51. Diamond, M.C. et al. Increases in cortical depth and glia numbers in rats subjected to enriched environment. *J Comp Neurol* 128, 117, 1966.
52. Rosenzweig, M.R., Bennett, E.L., and Sherman, P.W. *Soc Neurosci Abstr* 1979, p. 634.
53. Rosenzweig, M.R. et al. in *Soc Neurosci Abstr* 1980, p. 635.
54. Rosenzweig, M.R. in *The Biopsychology of Development*, Tobach, E. et al., Eds., Academic Press, New York, 1971, p. 303.
55. Cummins, R.A. et al. Environmentally induced changes in the brains of elderly rats. *Nature* 243, 516, 1973.
56. Fuller, J.L. Transitory effects of experiential deprivation upon reversal learning in dogs. *Psychonom Sci* 4, 273, 1966.
57. Editor's summary: the brain: use it and lose it. *Nature* 436, 11, 2005.
58. Zuo, Y. et al. Long-term sensory deprivation prevents dendritic spine loss in primary somatosensory cortex. *Nature* 436, 261, 2005.
59. Schwartz, S. Effect of neonatal cortical lesions and early environmental factors on adult rat behavior. *J Comp Physiol Psychol* 57, 72, 1964.
60. Will, B.E. et al. Relatively brief environmental enrichment aids recovery of learning capacity and alters brain measures after postweaning brain lesions in rats. *J Comp Physiol Psychol* 91, 33, 1977.
61. Walsh, R.N. and Greenough, W.T. *Environment as Therapy for Brain Dysfunction*, Plenum Press, New York, 1976.
62. Will, B. et al. Recovery from brain injury in animals: relative efficacy of environmental enrichment, physical exercise or formal training. *Progr Neurobiol* 72, 167, 2004.
63. Rosenzweig, M.R. Environmental complexity, cerebral change, and behavior. *Am Psychol* 21, 321, 1966.
64. Rosenzweig, M.R. in *Psychopathology and Child Development,* Schopler, E. and Reichler, R.J., Eds., Plenum Press, New York, 1976, p. 33.
65. Rosenzweig, M.R. in *Development and Evolution of Brain Size: Behavioral Implications*, Hahn, M. et al., Eds., Academic Press, New York, 1979, p. 263.
66. Rosenzweig, M.R. in *Recovery of Function Following Brain Injury: Theoretical Considerations*, Bach-y-Rita, P., Ed., Hans Huber, Bern, 1980, p. 127.
67. Rosenzweig, M.R. Neural bases of intelligence and training. *J Special Ed* 15, 106, 1981.
68. Rosenzweig, M.R. in *Proc XXII Int Congr Psychol*, Leipzig, 1980, p. 200.
69. Rosenzweig, M.R. in *The Brain, Cognition and Education*, Friedman, S.L. et al., Eds., Academic Press, New York, 1986, p. 347.
70. Rosenzweig, M.R. in *The Changing Nervous System: Neurobehavioral Consequences of Early Brain Disorders*, Broman, S.H. et al., Eds., Oxford University Press, New York, 1999, p. 25.
71. Rosenzweig, M.R. Animal research on effects of experience on brain and behavior: Implications for rehabilitation. *Inf Young Childr* 15, 1, 2002.
72. Rosenzweig, M.R. and Bennett, E.L. Psychobiology of plasticity: effects of training and experience on brain and behavior. *Behav Brain Res* 78, 57, 1996.
73. Wolfer, D.P. et al. Laboratory animal welfare: cage enrichment and mouse behavior. *Nature* 432, 821, 2004.

74. Bennett, E.L., Rosenzweig, M.R., and Chang Wu, S.Y. Excitant and depressant drugs modulate effects of environment on brain weight and cholinesterases. *Psychopharmacologia* 33, 309, 1973.
75. Feeney, D.M., Gonzalez, A., and Law, W.A. Amphetamine, haloperidol, and experience interact to affect rate of recovery after motor cortex injury. *Science* 217, 855, 1982.
76. Davis, J.N. et al. in *Cerebrovascular Diseases: Fifteenth Research Conference*, Powers, W.R. et al., Eds., Raven Press, New York, 1987, p. 297.
77. Feeney, D.M. in *Brain Plasticity: Advances in Neurology*, Freund, H.J. et al., Eds., Lippincott Raven, Philadelphia, 1997, p. 383.
78. Feeney, D.M. in *Restorative Neurology: Advances in Pharmacotherapy for Recovery after Stroke*, Goldstein, L.B., Ed., Futura, Armonk, NY, 1998, p. 35.
79. Goldstein, L.B. and Hulsebosch, C.E. Amphetamine facilitates poststroke recovery. *Stroke* 30, 289, 1999.
80. Walker-Batson, D. et al. A double-blind, placebo-controlled study of the use of amphetamine in the treatment of aphasia. *Stroke* 32, 2093, 2001.
81. Walker-Batson, D. et al. Neuromodulation paired with learning dependent practice to enhance poststroke recovery? *Restor Neurol Neurosci* 22, 387, 2004.
82. Hamm, R.J. et al. in *Cerebral Reorganization of Function after Brain Damage*, Leven, H.S. et al., Eds., Oxford University Press., New York, 2000.
83. Kelche, C., Dalrymple-Alford, J.C., and Will, B. Housing conditions modulate the effects of intracerebral grafts in rats with brain lesions. *Behav Brain Res* 28, 287, 1988.
84. Kelche, C. et al. The effects of intrahippocampal grafts, training, and postoperative housing on behavioral recovery after septohippocampal damage in the rat. *Neurobiol Learn Mem* 63, 155, 1995.
85. York, A.D. et al. *Soc Neurosci Abstr*, 1989, p. 962.
86. Rampon, C. and Tsien, J.Z. Genetic analysis of learning behavior-induced structural plasticity. *Hippocampus* 10, 605, 2000.
87. van Praag, H., Kempermann, G., and Gage, F.H. Neural consequences of environmental enrichment. *Nat Rev Neurosci* 1, 191, 2000.
88. Haywood, J., Rose, S.P., and Bateson, P.P. Effects of an imprinting procedure on RNA polymerase activity in the chick brain. *Nature* 228, 373, 1970.
89. Katz, J.J. and Halstead, W.G. Protein organization and mental function. *Comp Psychol Monogr* 20, 1, 1950.
90. Flexner, J.B. et al. Inhibition of protein synthesis in brain and learning and memory following puromycin. *J Neurochem* 9, 595, 1962.
91. Flexner, J.B. et al. Loss of memory as related to inhibition of cerebral protein synthesis. *J Neurochem* 12, 535, 1965.
92. Barondes, S.H. in *Molecular Approaches to Learning and Memory*. Byrne, W.L., Ed., Academic Press, New York, 1970, p. 27.
93. Schwartz, J.H., Castellucci, V.F., and Kandel, E.R. Functioning of identified neurons and synapses in abdominal ganglion of Aplysia in absence of protein synthesis. *J Neurophysiol* 34, 939, 1971.
94. Bennett, E.L., Orme, A.E., and Hebert, M. Cerebral protein synthesis inhibition and amnesia produced by scopolamine, cycloheximide, streptovitacin A, anisomycin, and emetine in rat. *Fed Proc* 31, 838, 1972.
95. Flood, J.F., Bennett, E.L., Rosenzweig, M.R., and Orme, A.E. The influence of duration of protein synthesis inhibition on memory. *Physiol Behav* 10, 555, 1973.

96. Flood, J.F., Bennett, E.L., Orme, A.E., and Rosenzweig, M.R. Relation of memory formation to controlled amounts of brain protein synthesis. *Physiol Behav* 15, 97, 1975.
97. Mizumori, S.J., Rosenzweig, M.R., and Bennett, E.L. Long-term working memory in the rat: effects of hippocampally applied anisomycin. *Behav Neurosci* 99, 220, 1985.
98. Mizumori, S.J. et al. Investigations into the neuropharmacological basis of temporal stages of memory formation in mice trained in an active avoidance task. *Behav Brain Res* 23, 239, 1987.
99. Rosenzweig, M.R. in *Behavior as Indicator of Neuropharmacological Events: Learning and Memory*, Erinoff, L., Ed., NIDA Monographs, Washington, 1990, p. 1.
100. Rosenzweig, M.R. et al. in *Neuropsychology of Memory*, Squire, L.R. et al., Eds., Guilford, New York, 1992, p. 533.
101. Patterson, T.A. et al. Memory stages and brain asymmetry in chick learning. *Behav Neurosci* 100, 856, 1986.
102. Serrano, P.A. et al. Protein kinase C inhibitor chelerythrine disrupts memory formation in chicks. *Behav Neurosci* 109, 278, 1995.
103. Gibbs, M.E. and Ng, K.T. Psychobiology of memory: towards a model of memory formation. *Biobehav Rev* 1, 113, 1977.
104. Rose, S.P.R. *The Making of Memory*. Doubleday, New York, 1992.
105. Rose, S.P.R. in *Neuropsychology of Memory*, Squire, L.R. et al., Eds., Guilford, New York, 1992, p. 547.
106. Serrano, P.A. et al. Differential effects of protein kinase inhibitors and activators on memory formation in the 2-day-old chick. *Behav Neural Biol* 61, 60, 1994.
107. Anokhin, K.V. and Rose, S.P. Learning-induced increase of immediate early gene messenger RNA in chick forebrain. *Eur J Neurosci* 3, 162, 1991.
108. Lowndes, M. and Stewart, M.G. Dendritic spine density in the lobus parolfactorius of the domestic chick is increased 24 h after one-trial passive avoidance training. *Brain Res* 654, 129, 1994.
109. Colley, P.A. and Routtenberg, A. Long-term potentiation as synaptic dialogue. *Brain Res Brain Res Rev* 18, 115, 1993.
110. Krasne, F.B. and Glanzman, D.L. What we can learn from invertebrate learning. *Annu Rev Psychol* 46, 585, 1995.
111. DeZazzo, J. and Tully, T. Dissection of memory formation: from behavioral pharmacology to molecular genetics. *Trends Neurosci* 18, 212, 1995.
112. Tully, T. et al. A return to genetic dissection of memory in Drosophila. *Cold Spring Harb Symp Quant Biol* 61, 207, 1996.
113. Colombo, P.J. et al. Kappa opioid receptor activity modulates memory for peck-avoidance training in the 2-day-old chick. *Psychopharmacology (Berlin)* 108, 235, 1992.
114. Colombo, P.J. et al. Dynorphin(1-13) impairs memory formation for aversive and appetitive learning in chicks. *Peptides* 14, 1165, 1993.
115. Patterson, T.A. et al. Influence of opioid peptides on learning and memory processes in the chick. *Behav Neurosci* 103, 429, 1989.
116. Rosenzweig, M.R. et al. Short-term, intermediate-term, and long-term memories. *Behav Brain Res* 57, 193, 1993.
117. Brown, J. Some tests of the decay theory of immediate memory. *Q J Exp Psychol* 10, 12, 1958.
118. Peterson, L.R. and Peterson, M.J. Short-term retention of individual verbal items. *J Exp Psychol* 58, 193, 1959.

119. Agranoff, B.W., Davis, R.E. and Brink, J.J. Chemical studies on memory fixation in goldfish. *Brain Res* 1, 303, 1966.
120. Kandel, E.R., Schacher, S., Castelluci, V.F., and Goelet, P. in *Fidia Research Foundation Neuroscience Award Lectures*, Liviana Press, Padova, 1987.
121. Rose, S.P. Glycoproteins and memory formation. *Behav Brain Res* 66, 73, 1995.
122. McGaugh, J.L. Time-dependent processes in memory storage. *Science* 153, 1351, 1966.
123. McGaugh, J.L. in *Recent Advances in Learning and Memory*, 3rd ed., Bovet, D. et al., Eds., Accademia Nazionale dei Lincei, Rome, 1968.
124. Patterson, T.A. et al. Time courses of amnesia development in two areas of the chick forebrain. *Neurochem Res* 13, 643, 1988.
125. Huang, Y.Y. and Kandel, E.R. Recruitment of long-lasting and protein kinase A-dependent long-term potentiation in the CA1 region of hippocampus requires repeated tetanization. *Learn Mem* 1, 74, 1994.

5 Presynaptic Structural Plasticity and Long-Lasting Memory: Focus on Learning-Induced Redistribution of Hippocampal Mossy Fibers

Jerome L. Rekart, Matthew R. Holahan, and Aryeh Routtenberg

CONTENTS

5.1 LEARNING AND STRUCTURAL PLASTICITY

The fundamental problem of whether learning-dependent morphological malleability is related to long-lasting memory, as originally articulated by Cajal and Hebb, remains a galvanizing issue in neuroscience. In 1906, Ramon y Cajal[1] stated that "... new pathways are established through continued branching and growth of dendritic and axonal arborizations. The hypothesis that new communication pathways ... only takes place after long efforts requiring attention and reflection, as well as the reorganization of mnemonic areas" (p. 724). Hebb[2] espoused a similar view, noting that the increased efficacy of synapses was likely due to "growth or metabolic change" that would take place at the synapse "in one or both cells" (p. 62). While there is an emphasis on changes occurring at both the pre- (axonal) and post- (dendritic) synaptic components following learning in both passages, the question remains whether the data truly support these theories.

5.1.1 Postsynaptic Plasticity

Post-synaptically, dendritic spines exhibit motility and are responsive to activity, making them ideal substrates for information storage.[3,4] Rapid increases in spine density have been observed as soon as 30 minutes after induction of long-term potentiation (LTP)[5] in CA1 neurons undergoing stimulation in hippocampal slice culture.[6]

Spatial learning has also been shown to increase the density of dendritic spines in the hippocampus.[7] Training rats to find a hidden platform in a water maze, a hippocampal-dependent task,[8] increases the density of dendritic spines on the basal dendrites of CA1[7] and the surface area, volume, and number of perforated post-synaptic densities of CA3 thorny excrescences.[9]

Trace eye-blink conditioning, which like the water maze is hippocampal-dependent,[10] increases the number of multisynaptic boutons (MSBs) in the CA1 stratum radiatum.[11] Because MSBs are presynaptic terminals that form synapses with two or more post-synaptic spines,[11] an increment in the proportion of MSBs suggests the occurrence of structural modifications of existing spines. Furthermore, learning-induced structural modifications to dendritic spine synapses are not restricted to the hippocampus, but have also been observed in the cerebellum,[12–14] motor cortex,[15] amygdala,[16] striatum,[17] and olfactory bulbs[18] of trained rodents.

5.1.2 Presynaptic Plasticity

While we can cite a number of examples of postsynaptic structural plasticity (see above and Harris and Kater[19] for an earlier review and Kasai et al.[20] for a recent review), there is a paucity of examples of learning-related presynaptic structural plasticity. The current status of our knowledge of presynaptic structural plasticity is epitomized in this quote from Chklovskii et al.[21]:

> "... cortical axons maintain the capacity to grow and elaborate in the adult brain. However, axonal remodeling has only been observed in response to

prolonged (months to years) injury. In addition, such lesions are at least in some cases associated with massive subcortical changes, including transneuronal atrophy. Such pathological subcortical changes might release mechanisms of cortical rewiring that are not normally observed in the brain. Clearly, our understanding of axonal plasticity in the adult brain remains in its infancy. How plastic are axonal arbors in the adult brain and what is the spatial range of growth? Do axons grow in response to learning, or only with injury?" (p. 786).

This chapter offers affirmative answers to both the question of whether there is plasticity of axonal arbor in the adult and the issue of learning-dependent axonal growth.

5.1.2.1 Invertebrate Presynaptic Structural Plasticity

Perhaps the best examples of learning-induced structural plasticity in the invertebrate domain have been observed in the slug *Aplysia californicus*. Long-term sensitization of a gill withdrawal reflex in Aplysia increases the size and number of active zones as well as the number of vesicles per active zone.[22] This change is likely a result of incremental axonal branching and increases in the number of presynaptic boutons of trained animals.[23] Such morphological changes appear to be bidirectionally influenced by learning as long-term habituation decreases multiple indices of presynaptic structural alterations.[22,24] Thus, it is believed that changes in the total number of synapses as mediated by presynaptic remodeling underlie associative learning in Aplysia.[24] What is more, such changes can be quite rapid, due in part to post-translational modifications of the actin cytoskeleton.[25]

Are learning-induced presynaptic changes restricted to the invertebrate nervous system? In the remainder of this chapter, we will examine the best evidence for learning-induced growth of presynaptic terminals in mammals. These data come from studies examining learning-induced growth of axonal projections — the hippocampal mossy fibers.

5.1.2.2 Mammalian Presynaptic Structural Plasticity

In mammals, increased expression of a protein or gene associated with structural remodeling is often taken as evidence for presynaptic morphological changes. For instance, increased expression of SNAP-25, a protein associated with reactive synaptogenesis,[26] has been observed to change with learning and memory.[27] However, SNAP-25 is also a critical component of the vesicle release machinery, the SNARE complex,[28] and thus, functional rather than structural effects cannot be ruled out.[29] Rather than merely observing changes in protein or gene expression, another approach is to directly manipulate the levels of a presynaptic protein and examine subsequent effects on learning and memory. Unfortunately, without sufficient information regarding the biochemical and cell biological role of a given protein, this approach can yield results that are difficult to interpret.[30]

A notable exception to the "knock out first, interpret later" approach to current neurobiological research is found in the body of work examining the effects of modifying the levels of the presynaptic growth protein, GAP-43, on information processing. In addition to learning-induced increases in protein levels,[31,32] two studies using genetically-engineered mice demonstrated bidirectional regulation of memory storage by this axonal growth protein. On a radial arm maze task requiring the hippocampus, transgenic mice overexpressing GAP-43 exhibited superior learning relative to wild type littermates[33] while heterozygous GAP-43 knockout mice trained on a hippocampal-dependent aversive conditioning task exhibited impairments.[34] Coupled with the wealth of evidence for the role of GAP-43 in axonal growth both *in vivo* and *in vitro* (for review see Benowitz and Routtenberg[35]), these data can be taken as strong support for the role of presynaptic structural plasticity in learning and memory.

Despite evidence for molecular control of learning and memory by a presynaptic growth protein such as GAP-43, there remains a dearth of direct evidence linking information processing with specific cellular morphological changes. A number of reports of reactive presynaptic sprouting after lesion (Hardman et al.[36]), neurotransmitter blockade (e.g., using APV; Colonnese and Constantine-Paton[37]), and pathological insult[38] examined expression of presynaptic markers and (importantly) directly compared measurements of the number of presynaptic terminals with and without a given experimental treatment. Thus, sufficient evidence suggests that presynaptic structural plasticity may underlie nonpathological forms of activity such as learning.[39] Recently evidence has begun to accumulate that demonstrates learning-induced presynaptic structural plasticity in the mossy fiber system of the hippocampus. Before discussing the empirical support for structural plasticity of mossy fiber pathways, the anatomy of this system will be reviewed.

5.2 HIPPOCAMPAL GRANULE CELL AXON TERMINALS AND LEARNING

5.2.1 Granule Cell Mossy Fiber Anatomy

Granule cells of the dentate gyrus give rise to the mossy fiber axons[1,40] that contain the heavy metal, zinc.[41] Zincergic presynaptic mossy fiber terminals are readily identified using the Timm's staining method for heavy metals.[42] Mossy fiber boutons synapse on large thorny excrescences of CA3 pyramidal neurons[40] and on mossy fiber-associated inhibitory interneurons.[43,44] The glutamatergic mossy fibers provide excitatory input to the apical dendrites of CA3 pyramidal cells in the stratum lucidum. CA3 pyramidal cells also receive major excitatory inputs from other CA3 neurons via recurrent collaterals[45,46] and direct cortical input from layer III of the entorhinal cortex via the perforant path.[47]

Each granule cell mossy fiber makes anywhere from 10 to 18 synapses with CA3 pyramidal cells in the stratum lucidum.[48] The sparseness of the granule cell input to CA3 pyramids is highlighted when compared with the number of contacts made by a single CA3 pyramidal neuron axon that can contact 12,000 to 60,000 neighboring pyramidal neurons within the ipsilateral CA3 region.[49]

5.2.1.1 Mossy Fiber Pathways and Axonal Termination Zones

As illustrated in Figure 5.1, four separate ipsilateral mossy fiber pathways terminate on CA3 pyramidal cells: the suprapyramidal (SP) mossy fiber pathway (A in Figure 5.1), the infra-intra-pyramidal (IIP) mossy fiber pathway (B), the distal stratum oriens (dSO) pathway (C) that projects to CA3 basal dendrites. and the descending longitudinal pathway (DP) of the mossy fibers (D) that projects septo-temporally to other CA3 lamella.

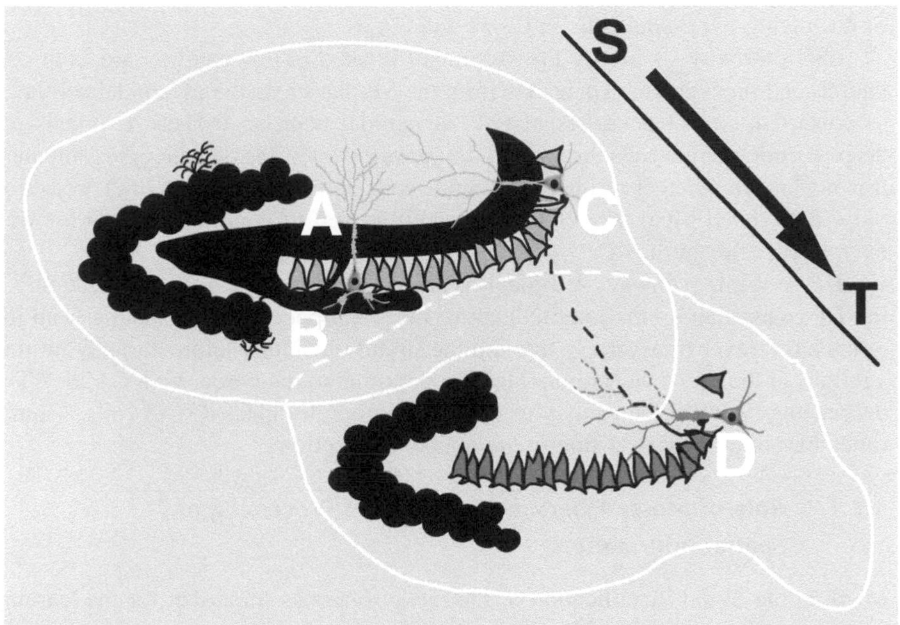

FIGURE 5.1 (See color insert following page 202.) The rat hippocampus has four mossy fiber projections to CA3 pyramidal cells. The figure shows the four mossy fiber projections from granule cells (red) to CA3 pyramidal neurons (green). Note that the basal distribution of Timm's staining used to observe mossy fiber terminals is indicated in black. (A) The suprapyramidal mossy fiber pathway projects from granule cells in both blades of the dentate gyrus to the apical dendrites of CA3 pyramids throughout the regio inferior. (B) The infra- and intrapyramidal mossy fiber pathway (IIPMF) primarily originates with granule cells from the infrapyramidal blade and extends to the basal dendrites of superficial CA3 pyramids and the apical dendrites of deep-lying CA3 pyramidal cells, proximal to the stratum oriens. As illustrated, the IIPMF is normally restricted to the proximal limb of CA3, rarely extending to or beyond the genu of CA3 superior to the fimbria. (C) Suprapyramidal mossy fibers in distal CA3, often referred to as CA3a, can extend axons into the pyramidal cell layer and innervate CA3 pyramidal neurons. This projection has a greater rostral–caudal extent within the septal hippocampus than the IIPMF that is restricted to the rostral-most regions. (D) In addition to the three largely "lamellar" projections that extend transversely to the longitudinal axis, mossy fibers from the suprapyramidal pathway can enter the distal stratum lucidum proximal to CA2 and abruptly turn temporally. This descending mossy fiber pathway then innervates CA3 pyramids from lamella situated farther temporally than the lamella of origin. S = septal. T = temporal.

SP pathway — This pathway is responsible for the majority of granule cell synapses on CA3 pyramids and is derived from granule cells located throughout both the internal (dorsal) and external (ventral) blades as well as the crest of the dentate gyrus.[48,50] SPMF boutons terminate in the stratum lucidum (SL) on the proximal (to the soma) 100 μm of CA3 pyramidal cell apical dendrites.[51] This projection innervates CA3c through CA3a pyramidal cells, terminating at the border of CA3a at the boundary with the large pyramids of CA2.[45,50]

IIP pathway — Primarily originating from granule cells of the ventral (external) blade, this pathway contacts the basal dendrites of superficial and the apical dendrites of deep-lying pyramidal cells in CA3b and CA3c.

dSO pathway — Mossy fiber terminals located in this pathway are axon collaterals and presynaptic expansions from the SP that cross the pyramidal cell layer to contact the basal dendrites of CA3 pyramidal neurons.[50] These terminals are derived from granule cells throughout the entire extent of the dentate gyrus, although it is not known whether a subset of granule cells are marked for the dSO projection only. Both the IIP and the dSO have been observed to continue to grow for well over 1 year after birth.[40]

DP — While pathways A through C are arranged in a lamellar organization,[47,52] the DP courses along the longitudinal axis of the hippocampus, traveling from the granule cell layer transversely through the stratum lucidum before abruptly turning ventrally at the tip of the stratum lucidum proximal to the border with CA2.[45,50] The descending pathway then synapses on more temporally located CA3 cells,[40] sometimes traveling as far as 2 mm in the temporal direction.[52]

5.2.1.2 Role of Mossy Fibers in Learning and Processing of Spatial Information

Much of the initial identification of the mossy fibers as important for the learning process was conducted by Dr. Hans-Peter Lipp and colleagues who focused on correlations between the basal size of the IIP and various forms of hippocampal-dependent learning.[53,54] Because hippocampal function is associated with the formation of spatial maps,[55] Lipp and colleagues investigated whether increased distribution of IIPs found in some mammals might be correlated with superior spatial learning.

Consistent with this view, the length of rat hippocampal IIP mossy fibers is positively correlated with performance on spatial navigation using the Morris water maze.[56] Similarly, differences in the distribution of the IIP pathways in various inbred strains of mice predicted performance on tests of hippocampal function.[54] For example, on two different hippocampal-dependent tasks, significant positive correlations between the extent of the IIP pathway in DBA and C57 inbred mice and task performance have been described.[57,58]

Reversible inactivation of CA3 MF-terminal fields with injections of diethyldithiocarbamate (DDC) during the acquisition phase of a hidden platform water maze task-impaired retention of the platform location as shown by a lack of a spatial preference during a probe test.[59] A similar study found that the DDC-impairing effect was selective for spatial but not nonspatial water maze tasks.[60] In a spatial object recognition task, injections of DDC into the CA3 region during the acquisition phase did not affect acquisition of the task but did impair recall of the spatially displaced object.[61] These data indicate a causal relationship between MF function and spatial information processing.

Although studies by Lipp and colleagues demonstrates the importance of the IIP to learning and memory, their work was primarily concerned with how anatomical differences conveyed by development and genetics correlate with cognitive differences and not with the plasticity of this or other mossy fiber pathways. Non-pathological structural plasticity of mossy fiber pathways was first demonstrated by Ramirez-Amaya and colleagues, who observed that training adult Wistar rats in the Morris water maze resulted in an increased distribution of Timm's-stained mossy fiber terminal fields (MFTFs) in the stratum oriens (SO) sublayer of the CA3 region of the hippocampus.[62,63] The change in Timm's staining that they reported required several days (>3) of training and persisted for at least 30 days.[63] Despite the implications of these results, both studies have remained largely overlooked. For example, no mention of these findings is made in two recent articles, one on cortical axonal remodeling[21] and the other on mossy fibers.[64] Possible reasons for the obscurity of these reports include (1) the lack of replication by independent laboratories, (2) reliance upon the Timm's stain to identify growth, (3) the implication that this growth was pathological because mossy fiber sprouting has traditionally been linked with epilepsy, and (4) lack of adequate controls to establish dependence upon hippocampal function.

Building upon the paradigm first described by Ramirez-Amaya et al.,[62,63] we subsequently found that MFTF area is indeed significantly increased in Wistar rats (WRs) trained to find a hidden platform compared to yoked swim controls that swam in the water maze for a similar amount of time but with no platform present.[65,66] Importantly, no changes in the area of MFTFs were observed in WRs trained to find a cued visible platform, which does not require the hippocampus.[8] Thus, the learning-induced presynaptic growth that we observed 7 days after the fifth day of water maze training was a direct result of learning that specifically recruited the hippocampus. The observed growth was also independent of any stress-related responses that may have resulted from exposure to the water maze. What is more, the growth process appeared to be protracted, as we did not observe significant increments in MFTF area when animals were sacrificed 2 (rather than 7) days after the fifth day of training.[65]

To confirm the presynaptic localization and mossy fiber identity of learning-specific increments in Timm's histological staining, we immunostained hippocampal tissue from hidden platform-trained rats and swim controls for Tau and ZnT3, respectively, and found corresponding increments in immunoreactivity for both proteins in the SOs of hidden platform-trained rats.[66]

We also found that another strain, Long Evans rats, learned and retained water maze tasks more rapidly than Wistar rats. To demonstrate a possible difference in mossy fiber morphology, we examined the distribution of IIP in non-trained animals and found that consistent with the findings of Lipp and others, the better-learning Long Evans strain possessed a greater basal distribution of mossy fibers. We also observed spatial learning-specific expansion of MFTFs in Long Evans rats. Interestingly, the rapidity with which Long Evans rats recalled the location of a hidden platform was reflected in their equally rapid expansion of stratum oriens MFTFs. Significant increments in learning-induced MFTF expansion were observed as soon as 24 hours after end of the fifth day of training.[66]

Thus, we have demonstrated that learning can actually induce a remodeling of the presynaptic input circuitry within a specific portion of the hippocampus. Furthermore, this phenomenon is not restricted to a particular strain of rat but is found even in animals that begin training with a prominent distribution of mossy fibers (e.g., Long Evans rats). Because mossy fibers primarily terminate in the stratum lucidum (SL in Figure 5.2c), the observed learning-induced increment in the SO likely represents increased innervation of CA3 basal dendrites by granule cell mossy fiber terminals (Figure 5.2d).

Indeed, an expansion of mossy fiber terminals on the basal dendrites of CA3 pyramids may impact learning by positively influencing future encoding by increasing the granule cell input to a given pyramidal cell. Clusters of thorny excrescences on basal dendrites of CA3 neurons are located closer (27 ± 3.1 versus 77 ± 1.9 μm) to pyramidal cell bodies than clusters on apical dendrites.[67,68] Because any MF input to basal dendrites would be substantially closer to the soma than corresponding input to apical dendrites, Gonzales et al. hypothesized, using the logic outlined in Carnevale et al.,[67] that mossy fiber–basal dendritic synapses may hold greater influence over somatic voltages than mossy fiber–apical dendritic synapses.[68] Given the sparseness of mossy fiber–CA3 coding, increasing the efficacy of individual synaptic contacts would facilitate the ability of individual groups of mossy fibers to act as "detonators"[69] and thereby enhance the encoding of spatial information.[70]

5.3 MECHANISMS OF PRESYNAPTIC STRUCTURAL PLASTICITY

Presynaptic structural plasticity, such as is observed in the learning-specific expansion of hippocampal MFTFs, can manifest in a number of different ways. One possibility is that prior to learning there are a number of presynaptic filopodia or "pioneer" terminals that continually seek out prospective postsynaptic partners. With sustained, correlated activity, as is presumed to take place with learning, extracellular signaling could then induce filopodial differentiation to mature, active terminals.[64,71]

Another possibility is the actual learning-induced growth of presynaptic terminals. This growth can take several forms. First, there is a possibility that sustained activity results in the sprouting of new presynaptic terminals that are likely to synapse with existing dendritic spines. It is interesting to note that although learning-induced synaptogenesis could result in a net increment in the number of boutons, it does not have to result in changes in the actual density of active zones.[72] Alternatively, an activity-induced remodeling of the presynaptic terminal is possible. This remodeling would not result in any changes in the number of terminals *per se* but would increase the effective number of active zones and neurotransmitter release sites. Such remodeling may be considered growth as it would require substantial cytoskeletal and intracellular remodeling.[73]

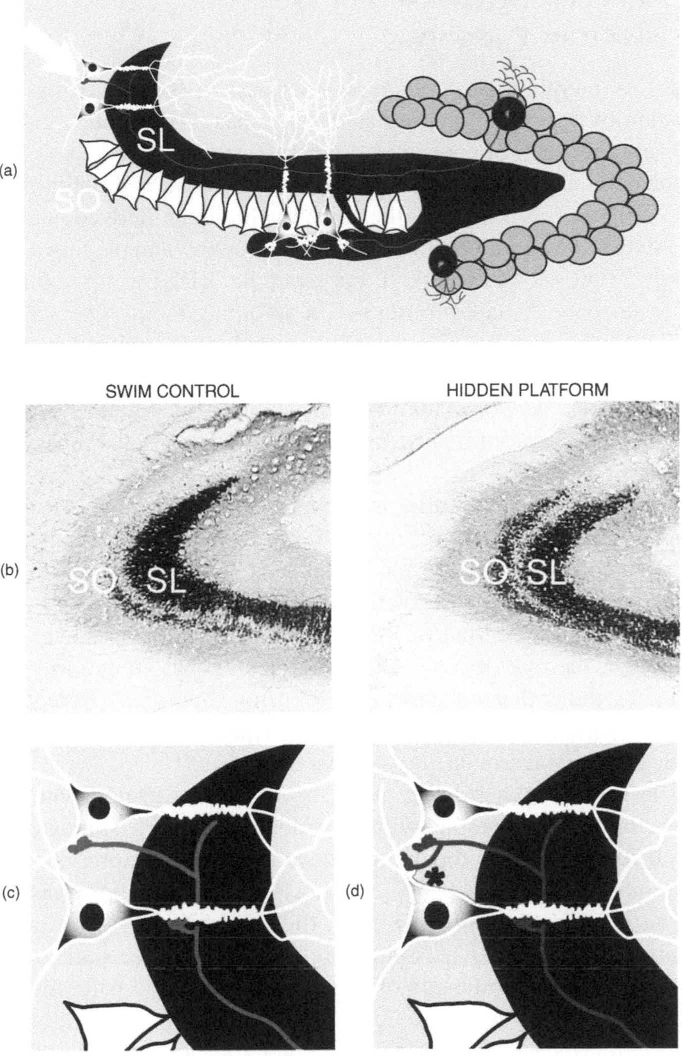

FIGURE 5.2 Learning-induced expansion of mossy fiber terminal fields. (a). Cartoon of the hippocampus, demonstrating mossy fiber pathways between dentate gyrus granule cells (black/gray circles) and CA3 pyramidal neurons (white triangles). Mossy fibers primarily terminate on the apical dendrites of CA3 cells in the stratum lucidum (SL); however, there are some (although fewer) connections on to the basal dendrites as well (SO; white arrow). (b) Hidden platform training induces a specific growth of mossy fibers in the SOs (and pyramidal cell layers) of trained rats. Representative photomicrographs demonstrate the difference in the distribution of Timm's silver precipitate (black) in the SO of a hidden platform-trained rat with respect to a swim control rat. Swim controls spent an equal amount of time in the pool as hidden rats but swam without a platform present. (c) Cartoon expansion of the area indicated by the white arrow in (a). This panel is hypothesized to reflect the distribution of mossy fibers before learning and the adjacent panel in (d) reflects the situation after learning. Note sprouting of existing SO presynaptic terminals (*).

5.3.1 Molecular Determinants of Presynaptic Structural Plasticity

The types of morphological changes discussed in the preceding section require mobilization by specific growth-related molecules. Presynaptic structural plasticity is thus likely the result of coordinated increments in trophic factors and decrements in chemorepellants. Candidate growth factors include neurotrophin-3[74] nerve growth factor.[75] Particularly attractive is the neurotrophin brain-derived neurotrophic factor (BDNF) shown to be important for axonal outgrowth[76] and playing a role in synaptic plasticity[77,78] (but see Qiao et al.[79]). For example, BDNF is up-regulated in granule cells after seizures[79,80] and is observed in sprouting mossy fibers.[79] Application of BDNF and bFGF to cultured rat dentate granule cell explants resulted in marked increases in axon number and extension.[81] Furthermore, BDNF knockout mice, unlike wild types, do not display seizure-induced mossy fiber sprouting.[82] Thus, BDNF may be necessary for structural plasticity of axons and mossy fiber terminals in particular.

As mentioned previously, the presynaptic growth protein, GAP-43, may mediate presynaptic plasticity; however, interestingly it may not do so in the mossy fiber system as it contains little or no endogenous GAP-43 in the adult.[83] Unlike the neurotrophins, GAP-43 is restricted to presynaptic processes and is probably part of membrane-associated lipid rafts[84] where it likely influences cytoskeletal dynamics.[85] However, the role of GAP-43 in neuronal axonal growth *in vivo* may be one of pathfinding rather than outgrowth or extension *per se*.[86–88] Up-regulation of GAP-43 after experimental induction of status epilepticus appears to be a critical factor in pathological supragranular mossy fiber sprouting.[89–92]

Any increment in a trophic factor is likely coordinated with a reduction in chemorepellants. For example, with KA-induced seizures, supragranular sprouting was only evident when accompanied by decrements in the expression of the chemorepellant semaphorin3A.[93] KA-induced GAP-43 up-regulation was insufficient to induce supragranular sprouting in the absence of diminished levels of semaphorin3A.[93] In fact, an accumulating body of evidence suggests that the semaphorins are critical determinants of axonal outgrowth and patterning during development of the nervous system.

Neuropilin-1 is a transmembrane receptor for the extracellular chemorepellant semaphorin 3A.[94,95] In the adult mouse, the highest expression of neuropilin-1 in the hippocampus is in mossy fiber axonal terminals.[96] Although highly expressed relative to surrounding molecular layers, neuropilin-2 expression is substantially lower in the adult. Recent evidence links reductions in semaphorin 3A expression in the rat with mossy fiber sprouting in kainate models of epilepsy.[93] In addition, neuropilin-2 knockout mice showed robust hypertrophy of the IIPMF.[97] Furthermore, 7 days after kainic acid-induced seizures, expression of sema3A mRNA in CA3 pyramids was shown to decrease by 67%.[98] Although Barnes et al. did not assess mossy fiber sprouting in their kainic acid-treated animals, such dramatic reductions in expression of a chemorepellant are temporally and regionally consistent with increments in MF staining in CA3 after KA and pilocarpine-induced seizures.[99,100]

Adhesion molecules may also transduce learning into morphological change, possibly by coordinating pre- and postsynaptic changes. The polysialylated form of the neural cell adhesion molecule (PSA-NCAM) is a marker of immature terminals that is enriched during development.[101] Following kainate administration, immunoreactivity for PSA-NCAM is enriched on the cytoplasmic membranes of axon shafts.[102] Removal of PSA from NCAM via either enzymatic degradation or genetic manipulation using NCAM-180 mice (engineered not to polysialylate NCAM) reveals an aberrant and persistent innervation of the pyramidal cell layer by granule cell mossy fibers, including a defasciculation of processes.[103]

The cadherins are adhesion molecules that are precisely and specifically upregulated in sprouting terminals, both during development and in adults.[104] Expression of the neural adhesion molecule, n-cadherin, is also increased after seizures and is believed to contribute to epileptic axonal reorganization.[105] Additionally, cadherin-9 is known to play a major role in cellular adhesion during the development of connectivity.[106]

5.4 PRESYNAPTIC DISPARITY: ANTI-BOUTONISM OR BIOLOGICAL REALITY?

Based on the literature reviewed in preceding sections, it seems worthwhile to inquire as to the reason for the strong emphasis on the role played by the postsynaptic element. It may be that presynaptic structural plasticity is a phenomenon that is specific to only a subset of axons in the mature nervous system.

Certainly the mossy fibers and their neurons of origin, dentate gyrus granule cells, can be considered a unique cellular population within the brain.[47] As one of only a few consensus neurogenic sites in the adult animal, over 9000 new neurons are produced per day in the rat dentate gyrus.[107,108] Because hippocampal-dependent learning enhances the survival of adult-derived granule cells,[109] the contribution of neurogenesis to learning-induced expansion of MFTFs must be considered. However, a comparison of the rapidity with which learning-induced presynaptic growth is observed in Long Evans rats with the time required for axonal extension of nascent granule cells[66,110] strongly suggests that synaptogenesis of existing terminals plays a part in learning-induced growth of mossy fiber terminals in the adult.

A more likely reason for the pre- versus postsynaptic disparity is that learning-induced growth of presynaptic terminals can also result in retraction of inactive or redundant terminals.[111] Indeed, a highly transient population of presynaptic terminals[64] would be congruent with theories of homeostatic plasticity,[112] suggesting that although there may be local fluctuations in the number of synapses, the total synaptic weight in a given region of the brain remains largely the same, irrespective of activity. Thus, for every increment in the number of synaptic inputs from a given cell population, there is likely a roughly equal decrement in inputs from a different source. Such mechanisms would account for the lack of quantitative data demonstrating activity-induced changes in the number of presynaptic terminals because merely measuring the number of terminals in a region of fixed neuropil would produce numbers that belie the dynamic processes taking place in living tissue.

With improved and more readily accessible application of technologies, such as 2-photon microscopy (e.g., Engert and Bonhoeffer[6]), researchers in the not-so-distant future will be able to visualize individual presynaptic terminals *in vivo* and study their real-time responses to activities. Indeed, the giant mossy fiber terminals may be the ideal systems for exploring this exciting possibility. Thus future studies may allow direct observation of actual presynaptic plasticity mechanisms and would provide insight into how they regulate learning and memory *in vivo*.[113]

REFERENCES

1. Ramon y Cajal, S. *Histology of the Nervous System.* Oxford University Press, New York, 1995.
2. Hebb, D.O. *The Organization of Behavior: A Neuropyschological Theory.* John Wiley & Sons, New York, 1949.
3. Fischer, M. et al. Rapid actin-based plasticity in dendritic spines. *Neuron,* 20, 847, 1998.
4. Sorra, K.E. and Harris, K.M. Overview on the structure, composition, function, development, and plasticity of hippocampal dendritic spines. *Hippocampus,* 10, 501, 2000.
5. Bliss, T.V. and Collingridge, G.L. A synaptic model of memory: long-term potentiation in the hippocampus. *Nature,* 361, 31, 1993.
6. Engert, F. and Bonhoeffer, T. Dendritic spine changes associated with hippocampal long-term synaptic plasticity. *Nature,* 399, 66, 1999.
7. Moser, M.B., Trommald, M., and Andersen, P. An increase in dendritic spine density on hippocampal CA1 pyramidal cells following spatial learning in adult rats suggests the formation of new synapses. *Proc. Natl. Acad. Sci. USA,* 91, 12673, 1994.
8. Morris, R.G. et al. Place navigation impaired in rats with hippocampal lesions. *Nature,* 297, 681, 1982.
9. Stewart, M.G. et al. Stress suppresses and learning induces plasticity in CA3 of rat hippocampus: a three-dimensional ultrastructural study of thorny excrescences and their postsynaptic densities. *Neuroscience,* 131, 43, 2005.
10. Moyer, J.R. Jr., Deyo, R.A., and Disterhoft, J.F. Hippocampectomy disrupts trace eye-blink conditioning in rabbits. *Behav. Neurosci.,* 104, 243, 1990.
11. Geinisman, Y. et al. Associative learning elicits the formation of multiple-synapse boutons. *J. Neurosci.,* 21, 5568, 2001.
12. Anderson, B.J., Alcantara, A.A., and Greenough, W.T. Motor-skill learning: changes in synaptic organization of the rat cerebellar cortex. *Neurobiol. Learn. Mem.,* 66, 221, 1996.
13. Kim, H.T. et al. Specific plasticity of parallel fiber/Purkinje cell spine synapses by motor skill learning. *Neuroreport,* 13, 1607, 2002.
14. Kleim, J.A. et al. Synapse formation is associated with memory storage in the cerebellum. *Proc. Natl. Acad. Sci. USA,* 99, 13228, 2002.
15. Kleim, J.A. et al. Motor learning-dependent synaptogenesis is localized to functionally reorganized motor cortex. *Neurobiol. Learn. Mem.,* 77, 63, 2002.
16. Lamprecht, R. et al. Fear conditioning drives profilin into amygdala dendritic spines, *Nat. Neurosci.,* 9, 481, 2006.
17. Robinson, T.E. et al. Cocaine self-administration alters the morphology of dendrites and dendritic spines in the nucleus accumbens and neocortex. *Synapse,* 39, 257, 2001.

18. Knafo, S., Libersat, F., and Barkai, E. Dynamics of learning-induced spine redistribution along dendrites of pyramidal neurons in rats, *Eur. J. Neurosci.,* 21, 927, 2005.
19. Harris, K.M. and Kater, S.B. Dendritic spines: cellular specializations imparting both stability and flexibility to synaptic function, *Annu. Rev. Neurosci.,* 17, 341, 1994.
20. Kasai, H. et al. Structure-stability-function relationships of dendritic spines, *Trends Neurosci.,* 26, 360, 2003.
21. Chklovskii, D.B., Mel, B.W., and Svoboda, K. Cortical rewiring and information storage. *Nature,* 431, 782, 2004.
22. Bailey, C.H. and Chen, M. Morphological basis of long-term habituation and sensitization in Aplysia, *Science,* 220, 91, 1983.
23. Bailey, C.H. and Chen, M. Long-term memory in Aplysia modulates the total number of varicosities of single identified sensory neurons, *Proc. Natl. Acad. Sci. USA,* 85, 2373, 1988.
24. Bailey, C.H. and Chen, M. Long-term sensitization in Aplysia increases the number of presynaptic contacts onto the identified gill motor neuron L7, *Proc. Natl. Acad. Sci. USA,* 85, 9356, 1988.
25. Hatada, Y. et al. Presynaptic morphological changes associated with long-term synaptic facilitation are triggered by actin polymerization at preexisting varicosities, *J. Neurosci.,* 20, 1, 2000.
26. Osen-Sand, A. et al. Inhibition of axonal growth by SNAP-25 antisense oligonucleotides *in vitro* and *in vivo*, *Nature,* 364, 445, 1993.
27. Hou, Q. et al. SNAP-25 in hippocampal CA1 region is involved in memory consolidation, *Eur. J. Neurosci.,* 20, 1593, 2004.
28. Sorensen, J.B. SNARE complexes prepare for membrane fusion. *Trends Neurosci.,* 28, 453, 2005.
29. Washbourne, P. et al. Genetic ablation of the t-SNARE SNAP-25 distinguishes mechanisms of neuroexocytosis. *Nat. Neurosci.,* 5, 19, 2002.
30. Sanes, J.R. and Lichtman, J.W. Can molecules explain long-term potentiation? *Nat. Neurosci.,* 2, 597, 1999.
31. Young, E. et al. Changes in protein kinase C (PKC) activity, isozyme translocation, and GAP-43 phosphorylation in the rat hippocampal formation after a single-trial contextual fear conditioning paradigm, *Hippocampus,* 12, 457, 2002.
32. Young, E.A. et al. Alterations in hippocampal GAP-43 phosphorylation and protein level following contextual fear conditioning, *Brain Res.,* 860, 95, 2000.
33. Routtenberg, A. et al. Enhanced learning after genetic overexpression of a brain growth protein, *Proc. Natl. Acad. Sci. USA,* 97, 7657, 2000.
34. Rekart, J.L., Meiri, K., and Routtenberg, A. Hippocampal-dependent memory is impaired in heterozygous GAP-43 knockout mice, *Hippocampus,* 15, 1, 2005.
35. Benowitz, L.I. and Routtenberg, A. GAP-43: an intrinsic determinant of neuronal development and plasticity, *Trends Neurosci.,* 20, 84, 1997.
36. Hardman, R. et al. Evidence for recovery of spatial learning following entorhinal cortex lesions in mice, *Brain Res.,* 758, 187, 1997.
37. Colonnese, M.T. and Constantine-Paton, M. Chronic NMDA receptor blockade from birth increases the sprouting capacity of ipsilateral retinocollicular axons without disrupting their early segregation, *J. Neurosci.,* 21, 1557, 2001.
38. Dancause, N. et al. Extensive cortical rewiring after brain injury, *J. Neurosci.,* 25, 10167, 2005.
39. De Paola, V. et al. Cell type-specific structural plasticity of axonal branches and boutons in the adult neocortex, *Neuron,* 49, 861, 2006.

40. Amaral, D.G. and Dent, J.A. Development of the mossy fibers of the dentate gyrus: I. A light and electron microscopic study of the mossy fibers and their expansions, *J. Comp. Neurol,*. 195, 51, 1981.
41. Wenzel, H.J. et al. Ultrastructural localization of zinc transporter-3 (ZnT-3) to synaptic vesicle membranes within mossy fiber boutons in the hippocampus of mouse and monkey, *Proc. Natl. Acad. Sci. USA,* 94, 12676, 1997.
42. Haug, F.M. Electron microscopical localization of the zinc in hippocampal mossy fibre synapses by a modified sulfide silver procedure, *Histochemie,* 8, 355, 1967.
43. Vida, I. and Frotscher, M. A hippocampal interneuron associated with the mossy fiber system, *Proc. Natl. Acad. Sci. USA,* 97, 1275, 2000.
44. Maccaferri, G., Toth, K., and McBain, C.J. Target-specific expression of presynaptic mossy fiber plasticity, *Science,* 279, 1368, 1988.
45. Lorente de No, R. Studies on the structure of the cerebral cortex II. Continuation of the study of the ammonic system, *J. Psychol. Neurol.,* 46, 113, 1934.
46. Miles, R. and Wong, R.K. Single neurones can initiate synchronized population discharge in the hippocampus, *Nature,* 306, 371, 1983.
47. Henze, D.A., Urban, N.N., and Barrionuevo, G. The multifarious hippocampal mossy fiber pathway: a review, *Neuroscience,* 98, 407, 2000.
48. Claiborne, B.J., Amaral, D.G., and Cowan, W.M. A light and electron microscopic analysis of the mossy fibers of the rat dentate gyrus, *J. Comp. Neurol.,* 246, 435, 1986.
49. Amaral, D.G., Ishizuka, N., and Claiborne, B. Neurons, numbers and the hippocampal network, *Progr. Brain Res.,* 83, 1, 1990.
50. Swanson, L.W., Wyss, J.M., and Cowan, W.M. An autoradiographic study of the organization of intrahippocampal association pathways in the rat, *J. Comp. Neurol.,* 181, 681, 1978.
51. Gaarskjaer, F.B. The development of the dentate area and the hippocampal mossy fiber projection of the rat, *J. Comp. Neurol.,* 241, 154, 1985.
52. Amaral, D.G. and Witter, M.P. The three-dimensional organization of the hippocampal formation: a review of anatomical data, *Neuroscience,* 31, 571, 1989.
53. Lipp, H.P. et al. Infrapyramidal mossy fibers and two-way avoidance learning: developmental modification of hippocampal circuitry and adult behavior of rats and mice, *J. Neurosci.,* 8, 1905, 1988.
54. Schwegler, H. and Crusio, W.E. Correlations between radial-maze learning and structural variations of septum and hippocampus in rodents, *Behav. Brain Res.,* 67, 29, 1995.
55. O'Keefe, J. and Nadel, L. *The Hippocampus as a Cognitive Map.* Clarendon, London, 1978.
56. Prior, H., Schwegler, H., and Ducker, G. Dissociation of spatial reference memory, spatial working memory, and hippocampal mossy fiber distribution in two rat strains differing in emotionality, *Behav. Brain Res.,* 87, 183, 1997.
57. Crusio, W.E., Schwegler, H., and Lipp, H.P. Radial-maze performance and structural variation of the hippocampus in mice: a correlation with mossy fibre distribution, *Brain Res.,* 425, 182, 1987.
58. Schopke, R. et al. Swimming navigation and structural variations of the infrapyramidal mossy fibers in the hippocampus of the mouse, *Hippocampus,* 1, 315, 1991.
59. Lassalle, J.M., Bataille, T., and Halley, H. Reversible inactivation of the hippocampal mossy fiber synapses in mice impairs spatial learning, but neither consolidation nor memory retrieval, in the Morris navigation task, *Neurobiol. Learn. Mem.,* 73, 243, 2000.

60. Florian, C. and Roullet, P. Hippocampal CA3-region is crucial for acquisition and memory consolidation in Morris water maze task in mice, *Behav. Brain Res.,* 154, 365, 2004.
61. Stupien, G., Florian, C., and Roullet, P. Involvement of the hippocampal CA3-region in acquisition and in memory consolidation of spatial but not in object information in mice, *Neurobiol. Learn. Mem.*, 80, 32, 2003.
62. Ramirez-Amaya, V. et al. Synaptogenesis of mossy fibers induced by spatial water maze overtraining, *Hippocampus,* 9, 631, 1999.
63. Ramirez-Amaya, V. et al. Spatial long-term memory is related to mossy fiber synaptogenesis, *J. Neurosci.,* 21, 7340, 2001.
64. De Paola, V., Arber, S., and Caroni, P. AMPA receptors regulate dynamic equilibrium of presynaptic terminals in mature hippocampal networks, *Nat. Neurosci.,* 6, 491, 2003.
65. Routtenberg, A. et al. Rat, yes; mouse, no: water maze training leads to axonal growth in the hippocampus, *Soc. Neurosci. Abstr.,* 29, 717.17, 2003.
66. Holahan, M.R. et al. Spatial learning induces presynaptic structural remodeling in the hippocampal mossy fiber system of two rat strains, *Hippocampus*, 16, 560, 2006.
67. Carnevale, N.T. et al. Comparative electrotonic analysis of three classes of rat hippocampal neurons, *J. Neurophysiol.,* 78, 703, 1997.
68. Gonzales, R.B. et al. Distribution of thorny excrescences on CA3 pyramidal neurons in the rat hippocampus, *J. Comp. Neurol.,* 430, 357, 2001.
69. McNaughton, B.L. and Morris, R.G. Hippocampal synaptic enhancement and information storage within a distributed memory system, *Trends Neurosci.,* 10, 408, 1987.
70. Jung, M.W. and McNaughton, B.L. Spatial selectivity of unit activity in the hippocampal granular layer, *Hippocampus,* 3, 165, 1993.
71. Tashiro, A. et al. Bidirectional regulation of hippocampal mossy fiber filopodial motility by kainate receptors: a two-step model of synaptogenesis, *Neuron,* 38, 773, 2003.
72. Reiff, D.F., Thiel, P.R., and Schuster, C.M. Differential regulation of active zone density during long-term strengthening of Drosophila neuromuscular junctions, *J. Neurosci.,* 22, 9399, 2002.
73. Ahmari, S.E., Buchanan, J., and Smith, S.J. Assembly of presynaptic active zones from cytoplasmic transport packets, *Nat. Neurosci.*, 3, 445, 2000.
74. Xu, B. et al. Continuous infusion of neurotrophin-3 triggers sprouting, decreases the levels of TrkA and TrkC, and inhibits epileptogenesis and activity-dependent axonal growth in adult rats, *Neuroscience,* 115, 1295, 2002.
75. Adams, B. et al. Nerve growth factor accelerates seizure development, enhances mossy fiber sprouting, and attenuates seizure-induced decreases in neuronal density in the kindling model of epilepsy, *J. Neurosci.*, 17, 5288, 1997.
76. Rabacchi, S.A. et al. BDNF and NT4/5 promote survival and neurite outgrowth of pontocerebellar mossy fiber neurons, *J. Neurobiol.,* 40, 254, 1999.
77. Scharfman, H.E. Hyperexcitability in combined entorhinal/hippocampal slices of adult rat after exposure to brain-derived neurotrophic factor, *J. Neurophysiol.,* 78, 1082, 1997.
78. Scharfman, H.E., Goodman, J.H., and Sollas, A.L. Actions of brain-derived neurotrophic factor in slices from rats with spontaneous seizures and mossy fiber sprouting in the dentate gyrus, *J. Neurosci.,* 19, 5619, 1999.
79. Qiao, X. et al. Absence of hippocampal mossy fiber sprouting in transgenic mice overexpressing brain-derived neurotrophic factor, *J. Neurosci. Res.*, 64, 268, 2001.

80. Goutan, E., Marti, E., and Ferrer, I. BDNF, and full length and truncated TrkB expression in the hippocampus of the rat following kainic acid excitotoxic damage: evidence of complex time-dependent and cell-specific responses, *Brain Res. Mol. Brain Res.,* 59, 154, 1998.
81. Lowenstein, D.H. and Arsenault, L. Dentate granule cell layer collagen explant cultures: spontaneous axonal growth and induction by brain-derived neurotrophic factor or basic fibroblast growth factor, *Neuroscience,* 74, 1197, 1996.
82. Maidya, V.A. et al. Hippocampal mossy fiber sprouting induced by chronic electroconvulsive seizures, *Neuroscience,* 89, 157, 1999.
83. Meberg, P.J. and Routtenberg, A. Selective expression of protein F1/(GAP-43) mRNA in pyramidal but not granule cells of the hippocampus, *Neuroscience,* 45, 721, 1991.
84. Arni, S. et al. Association of GAP-43 with detergent-resistant membranes requires two palmitoylated cysteine residues, *J. Biol. Chem.,* 273, 28478, 1998.
85. Laux, T. et al. GAP43, MARCKS, and CAP23 modulate PI(4,5)P(2) at plasmalemmal rafts, and regulate cell cortex actin dynamics through a common mechanism, *J. Cell. Biol.,* 149, 1455, 2000.
86. Meiri, K.F. and Burdick, D. Nerve growth factor stimulation of GAP-43 phosphorylation in intact isolated growth cones, *J. Neurosci.,* 11, 3155, 1991.
87. Strittmatter, S.M. et al. Neuronal pathfinding is abnormal in mice lacking the neuronal growth cone protein GAP-43, *Cell,* 80, 445, 1995.
88. Maier, D.L. et al. Disrupted cortical map and absence of cortical barrels in growth-associated protein (GAP)-43 knockout mice, *Proc. Natl. Acad. Sci. USA,* 96, 9397, 1999.
89. Meberg, P.J., Gall, C.M., and Routtenberg, A. Induction of F1/GAP-43 gene expression in hippocampal granule cells after seizures, *Brain Res. Mol. Brain Res.,* 17, 295, 1993.
90. McNamara, R.K. and Routtenberg, A. NMDA receptor blockade prevents kainate induction of protein F1/GAP-43 mRNA in hippocampal granule cells and subsequent mossy fiber sprouting in the rat, *Brain Res. Mol. Brain Res.,* 33, 22, 1995.
91. Cantallops, I. and Routtenberg, A. Rapid induction by kainic acid of both axonal growth and F1/GAP-43 protein in the adult rat hippocampal granule cells, *J. Comp. Neurol.,* 366, 303, 1996.
92. Bendotti, C. et al. Relationship between GAP-43 expression in the dentate gyrus and synaptic reorganization of hippocampal mossy fibres in rats treated with kainic acid, *Eur. J. Neurosci.,* 9, 93, 1997.
93. Holtmaat, A.J. et al. Transient downregulation of Sema3A mRNA in a rat model for temporal lobe epilepsy: a novel molecular event potentially contributing to mossy fiber sprouting, *Exp. Neurol.,* 182, 142, 2003.
94. He, Z. and Tessier-Lavigne, M. Neuropilin is a receptor for the axonal chemorepellent semaphorin III, *Cell,* 90, 739, 1997.
95. Kolodkin, A.L. et al. Neuropilin is a semaphorin III receptor, *Cell,* 90, 753, 1997.
96. Sahay, A. et al. Secreted semaphorins modulate synaptic transmission in the adult hippocampus, *J. Neurosci.,* 25, 3613, 2005.
97. Sahay, A. et al. Semaphorin 3F is critical for development of limbic system circuitry and is required in neurons for selective CNS axon guidance events, *J. Neurosci.,* 23, 6671, 2003.
98. Barnes, G. et al. Temporal specific patterns of semaphorin gene expression in rat brain after kainic acid-induced status epilepticus, *Hippocampus,* 13, 1, 2003.
99. Represa, A. and Ben-Ari, Y. Long-term potentiation and sprouting of mossy fibers produced by brief episodes of hyperactivity, *Epilepsy Res. Suppl.,* 7, 261, 1992.

100. Parent, J.M. et al. Dentate granule cell neurogenesis is increased by seizures and contributes to aberrant network reorganization in the adult rat hippocampus, *J. Neurosci.*, 17, 3727, 1997.
101. Seki, T. and Arai, Y. Different polysialic acid-neural cell adhesion molecule expression patterns in distinct types of mossy fiber boutons in the adult hippocampus, *J. Comp. Neurol.*, 410, 115, 1999.
102. Niquet, J. et al. NCAM immunoreactivity on mossy fibers and reactive astrocytes in the hippocampus of epileptic rats, *Brain Res.*, 626, 106, 1993.
103. Seki, T. and Rutishauser, U. Removal of polysialic acid-neural cell adhesion molecule induces aberrant mossy fiber innervation and ectopic synaptogenesis in the hippocampus, *J. Neurosci.*, 18, 3757, 1998.
104. Benson, D.L. and Tanaka, H. N-cadherin redistribution during synaptogenesis in hippocampal neurons, *J. Neurosci.*, 18, 6892, 1998.
105. Shan, W. et al. Neural (N-) cadherin, a synaptic adhesion molecule, is induced in hippocampal mossy fiber axonal sprouts by seizure, *J. Neurosci. Res.*, 69, 292, 2002.
106. Bekirov, I.H. et al. Identification and localization of multiple classic cadherins in developing rat limbic system, *Neuroscience*, 115, 213, 2002.
107. Altman, J. and Das, G.D. Autoradiographic and histological evidence of postnatal hippocampal neurogenesis in rats, *J. Comp. Neurol.*, 124, 319, 1965
108. Cameron, H.A. and McKay, R.D. Adult neurogenesis produces a large pool of new granule cells in the dentate gyrus, *J. Comp. Neurol.*, 435, 406, 2001.
109. Gould, E. et al. Learning enhances adult neurogenesis in the hippocampal formation, *Nat. Neurosci.*, 2, 260, 2001.
110. Hastings, N.B. and Gould, E. Rapid extension of axons into the CA3 region by adult-generated granule cells, *J. Comp. Neurol.*, 413, 146, 1999.
111. Rusakov, D.A. et al. Ultrastructural synaptic correlates of spatial learning in rat hippocampus, *Neuroscience*, 80, 69, 1997.
112. Turrigiano, G.G. Homeostatic plasticity in neuronal networks: the more things change, the more they stay the same, *Trends Neurosci.*, 22, 221, 1999.
113. Lichtman, J.W. and Fraser, S.E. The neuronal naturalist: watching neurons in their native habitat, *Nat. Neurosci.*, 4 Suppl., 1215, 2001.

6 Electrophysiological Representation of Taste Memory

Takashi Yamamoto and Yasunobu Yasoshima

CONTENTS

6.1 INTRODUCTION

The taste of food can be memorized after single or repetitive exposures to it, especially when the intake is associated with pleasant or unpleasant consequences to the body. The memory of taste is an important physiological function for organisms, especially for omnivorous animals to expand their repertories of edibles on the bases of their tastes. After acquiring such gustatory memories, we can anticipate the taste of food simply by looking at it. Gustatory memories enable us to generate hallucinations of tastes in the absence of peripheral gustatory inputs. Signals evoked by recalling gustatory memories as well as those from the peripheral gustatory system may play important roles in gustatory information processing.[1] One of the most convenient and effective methods that enable the animals to remember tastes is the conditioned taste aversion (CTA) paradigm. CTA is a kind of fear learning established on the basis of association of the quality of the taste of food and post-ingestional malaise.

6.2 CTA PARADIGM

When the ingestion of a food (CS) is paired with malaise (US) such as gastrointestinal disorders and nausea, CTA, an association between the taste of the CS and the US, is quickly established.[2,3] CTA is a kind of fear-based learning to avoid subsequent intake of "harmful" food by exhibiting aversive behavior to its taste. When saccharin is used as a CS, the sweet and palatable taste is treated as an aversive taste after CTA acquisition. While the taste quality itself may not change, the perceived intensity may be enhanced to facilitate detection of the harmful substance and a hedonic shift from positive to negative occurs. Neural substrates for these alterations of sensory and hedonic aspects of the CS will be elucidated mainly on the basis of electrophysiological studies in this chapter.

6.3 ENHANCED RESPONSES TO CS

Bures and his colleagues[4,5] first reported neuronal responses in the brain in response to gustatory CS after the acquisition of CTA. They found altered responses of neurons in inhibitory or excitatory directions to the CS in the ventromedial nucleus of the hypothalamus (VMH) and lateral hypothalamus (LH) in paralyzed rats[4] and neurons in the insular cortex (IC or gustatory cortex), thalamus, amygdala, and VMH at the retrieval of the CS in freely moving rats.[5]

After the elapse of two decades, Shimura et al.[6] recorded neuronal responses to taste stimuli from the pontine parabrachial nucleus (PBN) of the rat under deep urethane anesthesia. Animals were separated into two groups: a CTA group that acquired CTA to 0.1 M NaCl (CS) by paired presentation of intraperitoneal (i.p.) injection of LiCl (US), and a control group without CTA experience. Taste-responsive neurons in the CTA group showed larger responses to NaCl at concentrations below 0.1 M, but showed similar responses to 0.3 M and 0.5 M NaCl when compared with those in the control group. All the recorded neurons were located in the medial part of the PBN, which is the recipient zone for sodium taste information.[7,8] These results suggest that the aversive conditioning to NaCl modified the responsiveness of PBN neurons so that the sodium taste became more salient than before conditioning.

A further study using similar experimental procedures was performed by Tokita et al.[9] They found that the enhanced responses to the CS (0.1 M NaCl) were observed exclusively in amiloride-sensitive NaCl (ASN)-best neurons, but neither in amiloride-insensitive NaCl (AIN)-best nor any other best neurons (Figure 6.1). Electrical stimulation of the central nucleus of the amygdala (CeA), but not the IC, produced a significantly larger effect on the excitatory responses of PBN neurons in the CTA group as compared to the control group. Decerebration after CTA acquisition abolished the increased responses to the CS in ASN-best neurons. The results also suggest that descending information from the CeA could modulate CTA-related gustatory processing in the PBN and furthermore that amiloride-sensitive components of NaCl-best neurons play a critical role in the recognition of the distinctive taste of NaCl.

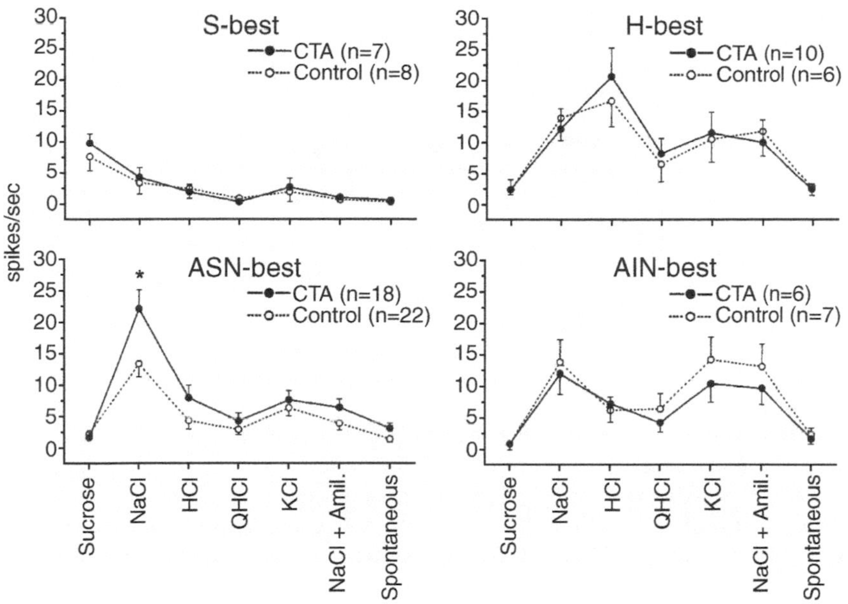

FIGURE 6.1 Comparison of mean response profiles of best-stimulus categories of PBN neurons in CTA and control rats. Taste-responsive neurons were classified into best-stimulus categories, depending on their best sensitivities to any one of the four basic stimuli represented by sucrose, NaCl, HCl, and quinine hydrochloride (QHCl) as S-best, N-best, H-best, and Q-best, respectively. N-best neurons were further classified into amiloride-sensitive and amiloride-insensitive N-best (ASN- and AIN-best) categories by application of an epithelial sodium transport blocker, amiloride. Each data point shows the mean ± SE number of spikes/sec to each of the taste stimuli shown on abscissa. Taste responses to NaCl were significantly higher (*$p < 0.01$) in the CTA group than in the control group in the ASN-best category, whereas taste responses in the AIN- and other best-stimulus categories were almost identical between the groups. (*Source:* Tokita, K. et al., *J. Neurophysiol.*, 92, 65, 2004. With permission.)

Li et al.[10] found in the hamster PBN that more sucrose-best neurons were excited than inhibited, whereas the opposite occurred for citric acid- and quinine-best neurons in response to electrical stimulation of the CeA. These findings suggest that the descending information from the CeA modulates PBN activities toward the direction that sucrose-best neurons are excited and citric acid- and quinine-best neurons are suppressed. In accordance with this suggestion, when saccharin was used as the CS in rats, Chang and Scott[11] showed that taste activity was enhanced after the acquisition of CTA in the subset of sweetener-sensitive neurons in the nucleus of the tractus solitarius which is also known to receive inputs from the CeA.[12] When nonpreferred HCl was used as the CS, PBN neuronal response to the CS decreased after conditioning.[13]

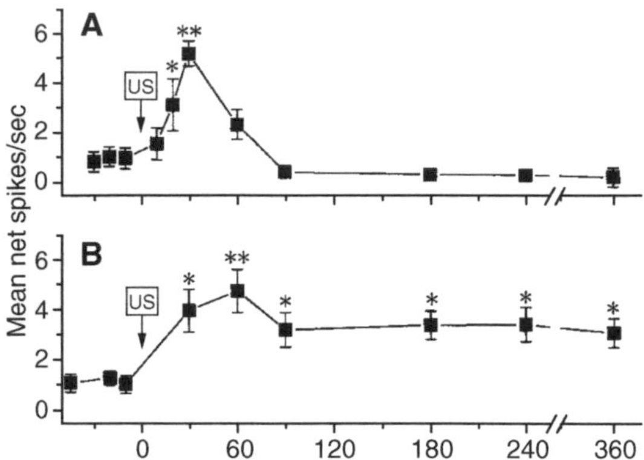

FIGURE 6.2 Time courses of excitability changes of neuronal responses to the saccharin CS after CTA in two types of neurons in the ICs of conscious rats. Each data point represents the mean ± SEM number of spikes/sec (spontaneous rate was subtracted). A. Short-term enhancement neurons (n = 8). B. Long-term enhancement neurons (n = 6). The significantly larger responses to the CS after CTA area indicated by asterisks: * p <0.05; **p <0.01. (*Source:* Yasoshima, Y. and Yamamoto, T., *Neuroscience*, 84, 1, 1998. With permission.)

Enhanced responses to the CS after CTA are also reported in rat IC neurons.[14] According to this report, 20 min and 30 min after the pairing of saccharin (CS) with an i.p. injection of LiCl (US), 29% and 100% of rats showed aversive taste responses to saccharin, respectively. When unit activities were recorded from the IC simultaneously with this behavioral test, 14 (11%) of 122 neurons showed significant enhancements of excitability in response to saccharin but not to the other taste stimuli after CTA. Eight of these 14 neurons showed short-term enhancements, and 6 neurons exhibited long-term enhancements (Figure 6.2).

6.4 ALTERATION OF RESPONSES REFLECTING HEDONIC SHIFT

When CTA is acquired, hedonics of the CS change from positive to negative or from ingestive to aversive behaviors. Electrophysiological responses of neurons recorded from the IC in awake behaving rats also change in such a way as to reflect a hedonic shift in a subset of neurons. Yamamoto et al.[15] classified taste-responsive neurons recorded from the IC into quality type (Type 1 neuron in Figure 6.3) and hedonic type (Type 2 neuron in Figure 6.3) according to the response patterns to licking of various taste stimuli. The former neurons showed enhanced responses to the CS after acquisition of CTA, and the latter exhibited alteration of the response direction, from excitatory to inhibitory or from inhibitory to excitatory, equivalent to that shown to aversive stimuli. Essentially the same types of neurons and the altered responsiveness after CTA acquisition were observed in the amygdala in conscious rats.[16,17]

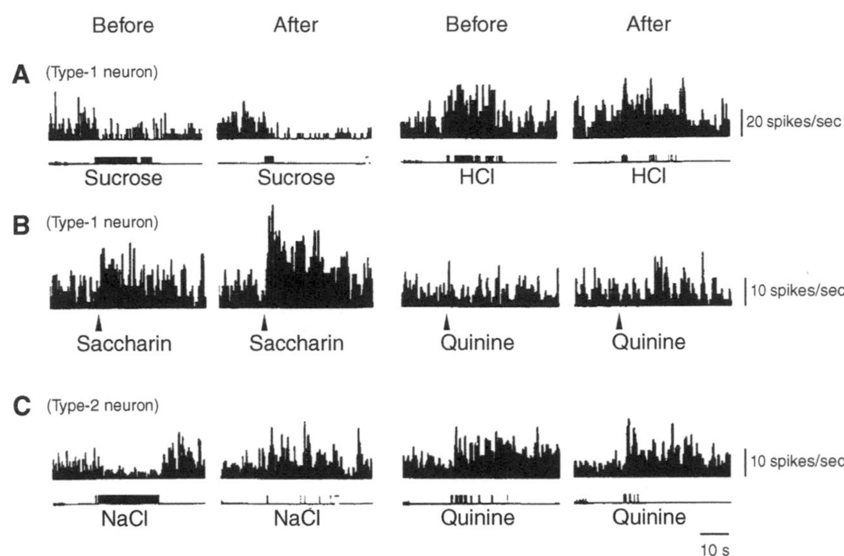

FIGURE 6.3 Responses of two type 1 (quality type) neurons (A and B) and one type 2 (hedonic type) neuron (C) in rat ICs before and after acquisition of CTA. A. Neuron showed a marked reduction of spontaneous discharge to licking of sucrose after conditioning to sucrose. B. Neuron showed a marked excitation to licking of saccharin after conditioning to sucrose. C. Neuron, which showed an inhibitory response to NaCl before conditioning, showed an excitatory response after conditioning to NaCl. Note that taste responses to stimuli other than conditioned stimuli remained unaltered after the conditioning procedure. (*Source:* Yamamoto, T. et al., *J. Neurophysiol.*, 61, 1244, 1989. With permission.)

To understand simultaneous overall activation of the brain, Yasoshima et al.[18,19] explored brain regions that were selectively activated by reexposure to the CS in conditioned rats by mapping immunoreactivity of c-*fos* expression as a marker of neuronal activation. One of their findings was that learned aversion to the CS after the acquisition of CTA is different from an innately aversive substance such as quinine in terms of brain regions activated to these stimuli. The supramammillary nucleus,[18] thalamic paraventricular nucleus,[18] extended amygdala,[19] and nucleus accumbens (NAcb)[19] were activated by retrieval of (or first reexposure to) the CS after CTA. The former two regions are suggested to be involved in the expression of anxiety and psychological stress.[20–24]

Yasoshima et al.[18] suggested that the supramammillary nucleus is activated by memory-elicited discomfort during retrieval of CTA. The extended amygdala and NAcb are involved in the reward or feeding system[25,26] where memory-based CS information from the basolateral nucleus of the amygdala (BLA) reaches the NAcb directly or via the extended amygdala.[27–29] The GABAergic neurons in the NAcb send axons to the ventral pallidum (VP) as the main output target[30] and from there, GABAergic projection to the LH arises.[31] The importance of such neural connections as the neural substrate of hedonic shift after the CTA acquisition will be described later in this chapter.

6.5 CS–US ASSOCIATION

The bases of modifications or alterations of neural responses to the CS after CTA are plastic changes of responses resulting from CS–US associations on single cells. Such neuronal plasticity may be derived from activity-dependent modification of synaptic efficacy designated long-term potentiation (LTP). LTP data underlying CTA formation is available for neurons in the IC and amygdala.

6.5.1 Insular Cortex

Several investigators dealt with possible electrophysiological and molecular mechanisms of the neuronal plasticity underlying the CTA formation. Escobar et al.[32,33] showed that LTP could be induced *in vivo* in rat IC, i.e., the LTP of field EPSPs evoked in the IC by single shocks applied to the BLA was developed by tetanic stimulation of the BLA and maintained at least 1 hour after stimulation. This LTP, mediated by NMDA receptors but not by metabotropic glutamate receptors (mGluRs) in the BLA-IC pathway, is suggested as a potential candidate for the cellular substrate of a physiological mechanism underlying the acquisition and long-term memory formation of CTA.[32,34] Moreover, phosphorylation of the NR2B subunit of NMDA receptors in the IC plays a role in CTA learning[35] and an LTP-like change in the BLA-IC connection may be involved in the retention mechanism of CTA.[36]

LTP induced by administration of brain-derived neurotrophic factor (BDNF)[37] was blocked by co-administration of K252a, an inhibitor of Trk (tropomyosin receptor kinase) receptor tyrosine kinase, into the IC.[38] These results suggest that BDNF/TrkB and related signaling pathways in the IC contribute to LTP-like synaptic plasticity underlying the acquisition and retention of CTA through extracellular signal-regulated kinase (ERK) and MAPK or ERK kinase (MEK) pathways and immediate early gene expression (c-*fos*, *egr*-1, *Arc*[39,40]) mediated by an active functional interaction between the BLA and IC. This is in line with the evidence that the BLA–IC positive interaction regulates the strength of CTA formation through NMDA receptors in the IC.[41]

6.5.2 Amygdala

The amygdala receives multimodality sensory inputs including taste and smell information. Several papers indicate that amygdalar neurons responded to taste stimuli in anesthetized rats,[42] conscious rats,[16,17,43,44] and conscious monkeys.[45,46] Reddy and Bures[47] showed in anesthetized rats that visceral stimulation by intraperitoneal injection of LiCl increased mean spontaneous activities in 13 (48%) units of 27 neurons in the BLA, but not in the sensorimotor cortex, from 2.5 spikes/sec (before) to 8.2 spikes/sec (after) with a latency 6.5 ± 1.4 min; this increase lasted 15.3 ± 2.3 min.

The time course of the change seems to correspond well with the behavioral symptoms of LiCl poisoning such as inactivation and lying on bellies. In line with this report, activity in some amygdala neurons gradually increased after LiCl injection during CTA conditioning.[16,17] Figure 6.4 shows the association of the CS and US reflected by enhanced responses to reexposed CS.

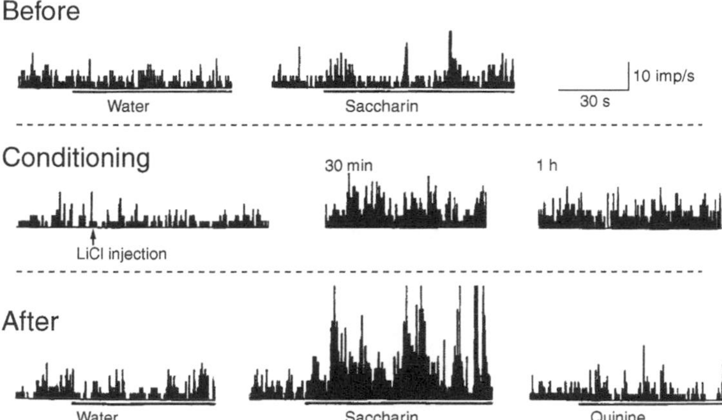

FIGURE 6.4 Pre- and poststimulus time histograms for responses of a neuron in the BLA to intra-oral infusion of taste stimuli before, during, and after acquisition of CTA to saccharin in a conscious rat. Infusion of saccharin solution (CS) was followed by an intraperitoneal injection of 0.15M LiCl (US). About 4 hours after LiCl injection, responses to saccharin were markedly enhanced, while responses to water were not changed. Innately aversive quinine did not induce any obvious responses. (*Source:* Yamamoto, T. and Fujimoto, Y., *Brain Res. Bull.*, 27, 403, 1991. With permission.)

Figure 6.5 shows the evoked potentials recorded from the amygdala in response to electrical stimulation applied to the ipsilateral sides of PBNs in Wistar rats anesthetized with urethane (Yamamoto, T., unpublished data, 1990). The recording electrodes were either glass micropipettes or glass-insulated Elgiloy wires and stimulation was performed with coaxial electrodes. Square wave electrical pulses of 50 to 100 mA were delivered at 0.2 Hz. To examine LTPs of evoked potentials, train pulses of the same intensity at 100 Hz were applied for 60 to 90 sec.

Electrical stimulation of the PBN elicited potentials in the ipsilateral amygdala with a mean latency of about 2 msec. As shown in the figure, the amplitude of the response was potentiated by tetanic stimulation of the PBN for more than 70 min. The second tetanus applied about 40 min after the first one increased the amplitude 1.7 times larger than the pre-tetanus amplitude. These results suggest that amygdalar responses through direct parabrachioamygdalar projection can be potentiated in a long-term manner by a high frequency excitation of PBNs, although it was not clear in this experiment how the gustatory and visceral zones of the PBNs[8] were electrically stimulated.

6.6 IMPORTANCE OF AMYGDALA IN CTA FORMATION

After the pioneering work by Bures and his colleagues who analyzed unit activity obtained from the amygdalas of conscious rats at the retrieval of CTA,[5] more detailed

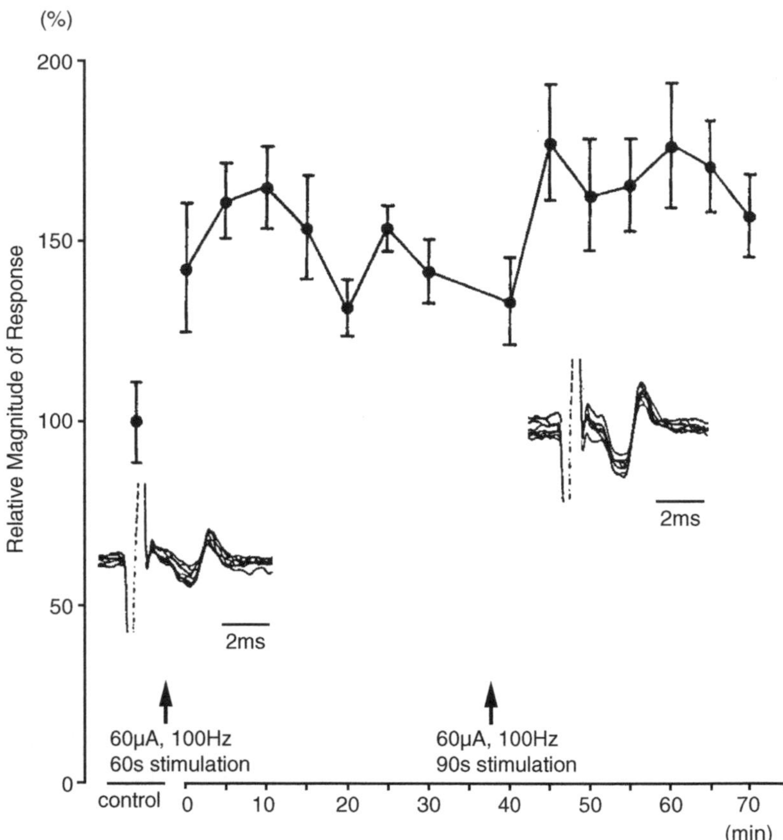

FIGURE 6.5 Long-term potentiation of evoked potentials recorded from the CeA in response to electrical stimulation of the ipsilateral PBN. Data obtained from rats anesthetized with urethane. (*Source:* Yamamoto, T. [unpublished data].)

analyses of amygdalar unit responses during voluntary drinking or intra-oral infusion of the saccharin CS after conditioning were carried out in freely behaving animals.[16,17] Although only a limited number of amygdala neurons, 9 (6.6%) of 137, showed responses to taste stimuli before conditioning, 32 (23%) of 137 responded to the CS in excitatory or inhibitory manners: 20 of the 32 were facilitatory type and 12 were inhibitory type.[17]

As shown in Figure 6.6, the facilitatory types responded to the CS in an excitatory direction after CTA conditioning and were found more frequently in the BLA (17 of 20 or 85%) than in the CeA (3 of 20 or 15%). The facilitatory type BLA neurons did not respond to the innately aversive HCl or quinine.

The BLA sends monosynaptic excitatory inputs to the VMH (satiety center)[48] and inhibitory inputs to the LH (feeding center), with long-lasting inhibitory postsynaptic potentials through the stria terminalis.[49] These anatomical connections

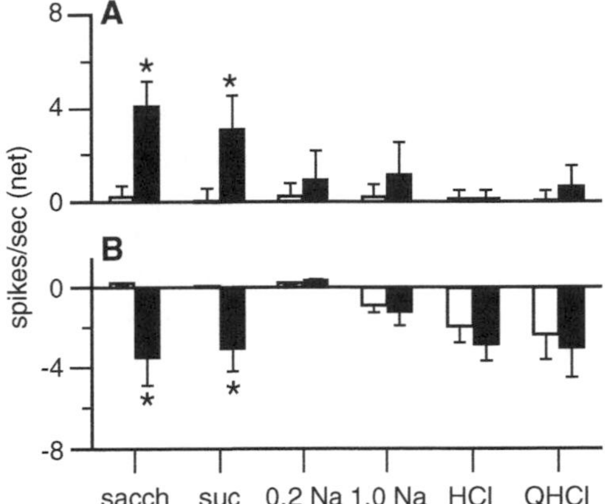

FIGURE 6.6 Two types of amygdalar neurons exhibiting facilitatory or inhibitory responses (means + SDs) to the saccharin CS after CTA in conscious rats. A. Facilitatory type; responses to saccharin (sacch) and sucrose (suc) were enhanced significantly after CTA in comparison with those before CTA. B. Inhibitory type; responses to saccharin and sucrose were inhibited significantly after CTA. 0.2Na = 0.2 M NaCl. 1.0Na = 1.0 M NaCl. QHCl = quinine hydrochloride. Open bars = responses before CTA. Solid bars = responses after CTA. *P <0.01. (*Source:* Yasoshima, Y. et al., *NeuroReport*, 6, 2424, 1995. With permission.)

suggest that the enhanced BLA response to the CS activates the VMH and inhibits the LH, resulting in the suppression of ingestion of the CS or keeping away from the CS. The idea is in line with the evidence that the electrical stimulation of the BLA arrested feeding behavior[50] and evoked epigastric sensations such as feeling about to belch or experiencing nausea.[51] The inhibitory-type units responded to the CS in the inhibitory direction and were found more frequently in the CeA (11 of 12 or 92%) than in the BLA (1 of 12 or 8%).

The functional dissociation between the BLA and CeA is also supposed by the developmental origin and anatomical connection.[52] The BLA is a cortex-like structure and its pyramidal neurons as projection neurons have close connections with multiple cortical areas. The BLA complex may play an inhibitory role in feeding behavior because lesions of the posterodorsal amygdaloid area including the BLA resulted in increases of food intake and obesity[53,54] and are also involved in the modulation of emotion[55] and in learning and memory.[52,56–58]

In the CTA paradigm, the long-lasting excitation in the vagal afferents after LiCl (US) injection[59] may induce strong impact in the amygdala, resulting in strong and persistent activation of the amygdalar neurons through glutamatergic transmission.[60] The US-induced strong input to the amygdala may cause heterosynaptic potentiation in the CS-evoked gustatory pathway reaching BLA neurons as an analogue to fear conditioning.[61] The potentiated synaptic activity in the CS pathway may be a possible candidate for the cellular substrate underlying the acquisition and long-term CTA memory that is NMDA receptor-dependent[33,62] The facilitated synaptic efficacy in the CS pathway mediated by AMPA receptors may be involved in memory retrieval.[16,17,62]

In contrast, the CeA consists of cells morphologically similar to those in the striatum; they have many connections with the limbic regions and the related brain regions for autonomic functions.[63,64] As described in the previous section, the electrical stimulation of the CeA enhanced the taste responsiveness of the pontine PBN neurons to the CS in conditioned animals,[9] suggesting that the descending pathways from the CeA to brainstem are involved in CTA formation.[65]

A number of studies have dealt with the functions of the amygdaloid subnuclei in the formation of CTA. Although the studies yielded inconsistent behavioral results, overall electrolytic or excitotoxic lesions show little, if any, involvement of the CeA in CTA,[66–70] whereas the lesions of the BLA in many cases disrupted or attenuated CTA.[69–74] The BLA may play an important role in CS–US association, and this nucleus is also suggested to be involved in the neophobia requisite for CTA formation.[75] The electrophysiological, lesion-behavioral, and immunohistochemical studies described in this chapter suggest that lesions of the CeA exert few effects on CTA because this subnucleus is involved with the enhanced responsiveness to the CS after CTA. Lesions of the BLA impair CTA because this subnucleus plays an important role in the acquisition and maintenance of hedonic shifts from positive to negative.

6.7 INVOLVEMENT OF REWARD SYSTEM

Apart from its well known role in reward-related behaviors, the reward system or NAcb–VP–LH circuitry has also been reported to be involved in the acquisition and retrieval of CTA.[76–80] NMDA receptor-mediated glutamatergic and muscarinic cholinergic transmitter systems in the NAcb play roles in CTA formation.[79–81] Especially, dopaminergic transmission in the NAcb is involved in the acquisition of CTA[76,77] and activated during its retrieval.[78]

To elucidate further the role of the VP in the expression of CTA, Inui et al.[82] examined the effects of microinjection of a $GABA_A$ receptor antagonist, bicuculline, on the intake of CS in a retrieval test. Rats drank 5 mM saccharin or 0.3 mM quinine hydrochloride as the CS, which was followed by an i.p. injection of 0.15 M LiCl. Blockade of $GABA_A$ receptors in the bilateral VP before the retention test by microinjection of bicuculline disrupted the retrieval of saccharin CTA, but not quinine CTA. Microinjection of bicuculline resulted in impaired aversive reactions, while the vehicle did not deteriorate the aversive behavior. These results suggest that conditioned aversion to palatable taste is mediated by the GABAergic neurotransmission in the VP and conditioned aversion to non-palatable taste is processed by separate system.

NAcb neurons may receive excitatory inputs from the BLA directly or indirectly in response to the CS after CTA acquisition. Since the innately aversive quinine does not activate the BLA,[19] NAcb neurons may be less excited by quinine, in accordance with recent electrophysiological results.[83] In addition to the reduction of aversion to the CS by the blockade of $GABA_A$ receptor in the VP,[82] increasing the palatability of the sweet-tasting CS by systemic or intra-BLA administration of midazolam, a benzodiazepine agonist, also impaired aversive behavior to the saccharin CS or sucrose CS after the acquisition of CTA.[84,85]

The NAcb receives inputs from the amygdala, especially from the BLA,[86,87] and is involved in appetitive and aversive behaviors,[25,26,88–90] suggesting an important role of the NAcb in CTA formation. Using the c-*fos* immunostaining technique, activation of the dorsal striatum[80], NAcb[19], and extended amygdala[19,86,91] when the sucrose CS was re-exposed to the CTA-acquired rats, while the same CS did not elicit noticeable activation in these regions before CTA.[19]

These results indicate that after CTA conditioning, activation of the NAcb to the CS is enhanced to a level enough to activate c-*fos* gene expression. The pathway from the amygdala to the NAcb and extended amygdala may be a possible route to convey the memory-based command signal to the brainstem orofacial motor centers to elicit aversive behavioral outputs, suggesting that the NAcb and extended amygdala are possible interfaces between the central memory stores (amygdala and/or IC)[2,69,92] and brainstem centers for aversive behavioral expression.[93] The idea is in line with the evidence that decerebration at the midbrain level causes severe impairment of CTA formation.[94]

6.8 SUMMARY

Electrophysiological studies indicated that enhancement of neuronal responses to reexposure to the CS occurs after acquisition of CTA in different brain regions including amygdala, IC, and PBN. This enhancement is based on the plastic changes of synaptic efficacy, possibly derived from LTP between the heterosynaptic inputs of the CS (taste) and US (visceral distress) during the acquisition period. Enhanced activity in the CeA may influence the brainstem gustatory nuclei and autonomic centers, while activity in the BLA may induce activation of the stress and fear centers, VMH to depress ingestive behavior and NAcb to depress motivation and elicit aversive behaviors. In conclusion, the enhanced activation to the CS after the acquisition of CTA originates in the CeA, and the hedonic shift originates in the BLA.

ACKNOWLEDGMENTS

The research by the authors and their collaborators was supported in part by the Grants-in-Aid for the 21st Century COE Program and a research grant (No. 17390494) from the Japan Society for the Promotion of Science.

REFERENCES

1. Kobayashi, M. et al. Functional imaging of gustatory perception and imagery: "top-down" processing of gustatory signals. *Neuroimage*, 23, 1271, 2004.
2. Garcia, J., Kimeldorf, D.J., and Koelling, R.A. Conditioned aversion to saccharin resulting from exposure to gamma radiation. *Science,* 122, 157, 1955.
3. Bures, J., Bermudez-Rattoni, F., and Yamamoto, T. *Conditioned Taste Aversion: Memory of a Special Kind.* Oxford University Press, Oxford, 1998.

4. Aleksanyan, Z.A., Buresova, O., and Bures, J. Modification of unit responses to gustatory stimuli by conditioned taste aversion in rats. *Physiol. Behav.,* 17, 173, 1976.
5. Buresova, O., Aleksanyan, Z.A., and Bures, J. Electrophysiological analysis of retrieval of conditioned taste aversion in rats: unit activity changes in critical brain regions. *Physiol. Bohemoslov.,* 28, 525, 1979.
6. Shimura, T., Tanaka, H., and Yamamoto, T. Salient responsiveness of parabrachial neurons to the conditioned stimulus after the acquisition of taste aversion learning in rats. *Neuroscience*, 81, 239, 1997.
7. Yamamoto, T. et al. c-Fos expression in the parabrachial nucleus after ingestion of sodium chloride in the rat. *NeuroReport,* 10, 1223, 1993.
8. Yamamoto, T. et al. Representation of hedonics and quality of taste stimuli in the parabrachial nucleus of the rat. *Physiol. Behav.*, 56, 1197, 1994.
9. Tokita, K. et al. Centrifugal inputs modulate taste aversion learning associated parabrachial neuronal activities. *J. Neurophysiol.*, 92, 265, 2004.
10. Li, C.S., Cho, Y.K., and Smith, D.V. Modulation of parabrachial taste neurons by electrical and chemical stimulation of the lateral hypothalamus and amygdala. *J. Neurophysiol.*, 93, 1183, 2005.
11. Chang, F.C. and Scott, T.R. Conditioned taste aversions modify neural responses in the rat nucleus tractus solitarius. *J. Neurosci.*, 4, 1850, 1984.
12. Li, C.S., Cho, Y.K., and Smith, D.V. Taste responses of neurons in the hamster solitary nucleus are modulated by the central nucleus of the amygdala. *J. Neurophysiol.*, 88, 2979, 2002.
13. Shimura, T., Tokita, K., and Yamamoto, T. Parabrachial unit activities after the acquisition of conditioned taste aversion to a nonpreferred HCl solution in rats. *Chem. Senses*, 27, 153, 2002.
14. Yasoshima, Y. and Yamamoto, T. Short-term and long-term excitability changes of the insular cortical neurons after the acquisition of taste aversion learning in behaving rats. *Neuroscience*, 84, 1, 1998.
15. Yamamoto, T. et al. Taste responses of cortical neurons in freely ingesting rats. *J. Neurophysiol.*, 61, 1244, 1989.
16. Yamamoto, T. and Fujimoto, Y. Brain mechanisms of taste aversion learning in the rat. *Brain Res. Bull.*, 27, 403, 1991.
17. Yasoshima, Y., Shimura, T., and Yamamoto, T. Single unit responses of the amygdala after conditioned taste aversion in conscious rats. *NeuroReport*, 6, 2424, 1995.
18. Yasoshima, Y., Scott, T.R., and Yamamoto, T. Involvement of the supramammillary nucleus in aversive conditioning. *Behav. Neurosci.*, 119, 1290, 2005.
19. Yasoshima, Y., Scott, T.R., and Yamamoto, T. Memory-dependent c-*fos* expression in the nucleus accumbens and extended amygdala following the expression of conditioned taste aversive behavior in the rat. *Neuroscience*, 141, 45, 2006.
20. Beck, C.H., and Fibiger, H.C. Conditioned fear-induced changes in behavior and in the expression of the immediate early gene c-fos: with and without diazepam pretreatment. *J. Neurosci.*, 15, 709, 1995.
21. Bubser, M. and Deutch, A.Y. Stress induces Fos expression in neurons of the thalamic paraventricular nucleus that innervate limbic forebrain sites. *Synapse*, 32, 13, 1999.
22. Ryabinin, A.E. et al. Alcohol selectively attenuates stress-induced c-fos expression in rat hippocampus. *J. Neurosci.,* 15, 721, 1995.
23. Spencer, S.J., Ebner, K., and Day, T.A. Thalamic paraventricular nucleus lesions facilitate central amygdala neuronal responses to acute psychological stress. *Brain Res.*, 997, 234, 2004.

24. Wirtshafter, D., Stratford, T.R., and Shim, I. Placement in a novel environment induces Fos-like immunoreactivity in supramammillary cells projecting to the hippocampus and midbrain. *Brain Res.*, 789, 331, 1998.
25. Kelley, A.E. Ventral striatal control of appetitive motivation: role in ingestive behavior and reward-related learning. *Neurosci. Biobehav. Rev.*, 27, 765, 2004.
26. Kelley, A.E. et al. Corticostriatal–hypothalamic circuitry and food motivation: integration of energy, action and reward. *Physiol. Behav.*, 86, 773, 2005.
27. Groenewegen, H.J. et al. Convergence and segregation of ventral striatal inputs and outputs. *Ann. NY Acad. Sci.*, 877, 49, 1999.
28. Shammah-Lagnado, S.J., Alheid, G.F., and Heimer, L. Afferent connections of the interstitial nucleus of the posterior limb of the anterior commissure and adjacent amygdalostriatal transition area in the rat. *Neuroscience*, 94, 1097, 1999.
29. Shammah-Lagnado, S.J., Alheid, G.F., and Heimer, L. Striatal and central extended amygdala parts of the interstitial nucleus of the posterior limb of the anterior commissure: evidence from tract-tracing techniques in the rat. *J. Comp. Neurol.*, 439, 104, 2001.
30. Zahm, D.S. et al. Evidence for the coexistence of glutamate decarboxylase and Met-enkephalin immunoreactivities in axon terminals of rat ventral pallidum. *Brain Res.*, 325, 317, 1985.
31. Groenewegen, H.J., Berendse, H.W., and Haber, S.N. Organization of the output of the ventral striatopallidal system in the rat: ventral pallidal efferents. *Neuroscience*, 57, 113, 1993.
32. Escobar, M.L., Alcocer, I., and Chao, V. The NMDA receptor antagonist CPP impairs conditioned taste aversion and insular cortex long-term potentiation *in vivo*. *Brain Res.*, 812, 246, 1998.
33. Escobar, M.L., Chao, V., and Bermudez-Rattoni, F. *In vivo* long-term potentiation in the insular cortex: NMDA receptor dependence. *Brain Res.*, 779, 314, 1998.
34. Escobar, M.L., Alcocer, I., and Bermudez-Rattoni, F. *In vivo* effects of intracortical administration of NMDA and metabotropic glutamate receptors antagonists on neocortical long-term potentiation and conditioned taste aversion. *Behav. Brain Res.*, 129, 101, 2002.
35. Rosenblum, K. et al. NMDA receptor and the tyrosine phosphorylation of its 2B subunit in taste learning in the rat insular cortex. *J. Neurosci.*, 17, 5129, 1997.
36. Escobar, M.L. and Bermudez-Rattoni, F. Long-term potentiation in the insular cortex enhances conditioned taste aversion retention. *Brain Res.*, 852, 208, 2000.
37. Castillo, D.V., Figueroa-Guzman, Y., and Escobar, M.L. Brain-derived neurotrophic factor enhances conditioned taste aversion retention. *Brain Res.*, 1067, 250, 2006.
38. Escobar, M.L., Figueroa-Guzman, Y., and Gomez-Palacio-Schjetnan, A. *In vivo* insular cortex LTP induced by brain-derived neurotrophic factor. *Brain Res.*, 991, 274, 2003.
39. Jones, M.W. et al. Molecular mechanisms of long-term potentiation in the insular cortex *in vivo*. *J. Neurosci.*, 19, RC36, 1999.
40. Yasoshima, Y. et al. Acute suppression, but not chronic genetic deficiency, of c-*fos* gene expression impairs long-term memory in aversive taste learning. *Proc. Natl. Acad. Sci. USA,* 103, 7106, 2006.
41. Ferreira, G.. et al. Basolateral amygdala glutamatergic activation enhances taste aversion through NMDA receptor activation in the insular cortex. *Eur. J. Neurosci.* 22, 2596, 2005.
42. Azuma, S., Yamamoto, T., and Kawamura, Y. Studies on gustatory responses of amygdaloid neurons in rats. *Exp. Brain Res.*, 56, 12, 1984.

43. Nishijo, H. et al. Hypothalamic and amygdalar neuronal responses to various tastant solutions during ingestive behavior in rats. *J. Nutr.*, 130 (4S Suppl.), 954S, 2000.
44. Nishijo, H. et al. Gustatory and multimodal neuronal responses in the amygdala during licking and discrimination of sensory stimuli in awake rats. *J. Neurophysiol.*, 79, 21, 1998.
45. Nishijo, H., Ono, T. and Nishino, H. Single neuron responses in amygdala of alert monkey during complex sensory stimulation with affective significance. *J. Neurosci.*, 8, 3570, 1988.
46. Scott, T.R. et al. Gustatory neural coding in the amygdala of the alert macaque monkey. *J. Neurophysiol.*, 69, 1810, 1993.
47. Reddy, M.M. and Bures, J. Unit activity changes elicited in amygdala and neocortex of anaesthetized rats by intraperitoneal injection of lithium chloride. *Neurosci. Lett.*, 22, 169, 1981.
48. Murphy, J.T., Dreifuss, J.J., and Gloor, P. Topographical differences in the responses of single hypothalamic neurons to limbic stimulation. *Am. J. Physiol.*, 214, 1443, 1968.
49. Oomura, Y., Ono, T., and Ooyama, H. Inhibitory action of the amygdala on the lateral hypothalamic area in rats. *Nature*, 228, 1108, 1970.
50. Fonberg, E. and Del Gado, J.M. Avoidance and alimentary reactions during amygdala stimulation. *J. Neurophysiol.*, 24, 651, 1961.
51. Halgren, E. Emotional neurophysiology of the amygdala within the context of human cognition, in *The Amygdala: Neurobiological Aspects of Emotion, Memory, and Mental Dysfunction*, Aggleton, J.P., Ed., John Wiley & Sons, New York, 1992, p. 191.
52. Sah, P. et al. The amygdaloid complex: anatomy and physiology. *Physiol. Rev.*, 83, 803, 2003.
53. Grundmann, S.J. et al. Combination unilateral amygdaloid and ventromedial hypothalamic lesions: evidence for a feeding pathway. *Am. J. Physiol. Regul. Integr. Comp. Physiol.*, 288, R702, 2005.
54. King, B.M. et al. Obesity-inducing amygdala lesions: examination of anterograde degeneration and retrograde transport. *Am. J. Physiol. Regul. Integr. Comp. Physiol.*, 284, R965, 2003.
55. Phelps, E.A. and LeDoux, J.E. Contributions of the amygdala to emotion processing: from animal models to human behavior. *Neuron*, 48, 175, 2005.
56. Grace, A.A. and Rosenkranz, J.A. Regulation of conditioned responses of basolateral amygdala neurons. *Physiol. Behav.*, 77, 489, 2002.
57. McGaugh, J.L. Memory: a century of consolidation. *Science*, 287, 248, 2000.
58. Rodrigues, S.M., Schafe, G.E., and LeDoux, J.E. Molecular mechanisms underlying emotional learning and memory in the lateral amygdala. *Neuron*, 44, 75, 2004.
59. Niijima, A. and Yamamoto, T. The effects of lithium chloride on the activity of the afferent nerve fibers from the abdominal visceral organs in the rat. *Brain Res. Bull.*, 35, 141, 1994.
60. Miranda, M.I., Ferreira, G., Ramirez-Lugo, L. et al. Glutamatergic activity in the amygdala signals visceral input during taste memory formation. *Proc. Natl. Acad. Sci. USA*, 99, 11417, 2002.
61. Bauer, E.P. and LeDoux, J.E. Heterosynaptic long-term potentiation of inhibitory interneurons in the lateral amygdala. *J. Neurosci.*, 24, 9507, 2004.
62. Yasoshima, Y., Morimoto, T., and Yamamoto, T. Different disruptive effects on the acquisition and expression of conditioned taste aversion by blockades of amygdalar ionotropic and metabotropic glutamatergic receptor subtypes in rats. *Brain Res.*, 869, 15, 2000.

63. Quirk, G.J. and Gehlert, D.R. Inhibition of the amygdala: key to pathological states? *Ann. NY Acad. Sci.*, 985, 263, 2003.
64. Shekhar, A. et al. The amygdala, panic disorder, and cardiovascular responses. *Ann. NY Acad. Sci.*, 985, 308, 2003.
65. Schafe, G.E. and Bernstein, I.L. Forebrain contribution to the induction of a brainstem correlate of conditioned taste aversion: I. The amygdala. *Brain Res.*, 741, 109, 1996.
66. Bermudez-Rattoni, F. and McGaugh, J.L. Insular cortex and amygdala lesions differentially affect acquisition on inhibitory avoidance and conditioned taste aversion. *Brain Res.*, 549, 165, 1991.
67. Kemble, E.D., Studelska, D.R., and Schmidt, M.K. Effects of central amygdaloid nucleus lesions on ingestion, taste reactivity, exploration and taste aversion. *Physiol. Behav.*, 22, 789, 1979.
68. Morris, R. et al. Ibotenic acid lesions of the basolateral, but not the central, amygdala interfere with conditioned taste aversion: evidence from a combined behavioral and anatomical tract-tracing investigation. *Behav. Neurosci.*, 113, 291, 1999.
69. Yamamoto, T. A neural model for taste aversion learning, in *Olfaction and Taste XI*, Kurihara, K., Suzuki, N., and Ogawa, N., Eds., Springer-Verlag, Tokyo, 1994, p. 471.
70. Yamamoto, T. et al. Conditioned taste aversion in rats with excitotoxic brain lesions. *Neurosci. Res.*, 22, 31, 1995.
71. Aggleton, J.P., Petrides, M., and Iversen, S.D. Differential effects of amygdaloid lesions on conditioned taste aversion learning by rats. *Physiol. Behav.*, 27, 397, 1981.
72. Fitzgerald, R.E. and Burton, M.J. Neophobia and conditioned taste aversion deficits in the rat produced by undercutting temporal cortex. *Physiol. Behav.*, 30, 203, 1983.
73. Rollins, B.L. et al. Effects of amygdala lesions on body weight, conditioned taste aversion, and neophobia. *Physiol. Behav.*, 72, 735, 2001.
74. Simbayi, L.C., Boakes, R.A., and Burton, M.J. Effects of basolateral amygdala lesions on taste aversions produced by lactose and lithium chloride in the rat. *Behav. Neurosci.*, 100, 455, 1986.
75. Reilly, S. and Bornovalova, M.A. Conditioned taste aversion and amygdala lesions in the rat: a critical review. *Neurosci. Biobehav. Rev.*, 29, 1067, 2005.
76. Fenu, S., Bassareo, V., and Di Chiara, G. A role for dopamine D1 receptors of the nucleus accumbens shell in conditioned taste aversion learning. *J. Neurosci.*, 21, 6897, 2001.
77. Fenu, S. and Di Chiara, G. Facilitation of conditioned taste aversion learning by systemic amphetamine: role of nucleus accumbens shell dopamine D1 receptors. *Eur. J. Neurosci.*, 18, 2025, 2003.
78. Mark, G.P., Blander, D.S., and Hoebel, B.G. A conditioned stimulus decreases extracellular dopamine in the nucleus accumbens after the development of a learned taste aversion. *Brain Res.*, 551, 308, 1991.
79. Ramírez-Lugo, L., Zavala-Vega, S., and Bemúdez-Rattoni, F. NMDA and muscarinic receptors of the nucleus accumbens have differential effects on taste memory formation. *Learn. Mem.,* 13, 45, 2006.
80. Turgeon, S.M. and Reichstein, D.A. Decreased striatal c-Fos accompanies latent inhibition in a conditioned taste aversion paradigm. *Brain Res.*, 924, 120, 2002.
81. Mark, G.P. et al. Extracellular acetylcholine is increased in the nucleus accumbens following the presentation of an aversively conditioned taste stimulus. *Brain Res.*, 688, 184, 1995.
82. Inui, T., Shimura, T., and Yamamoto, T. The role of $GABA_A$ receptors in the ventral pallidum on the retrieval of conditioned taste aversion in rats. *Neurosci. Res.*, 52, S193, 2005.

83. Roitman, M.F. Wheeler, R.A., and Carelli, R.M. Nucleus accumbens neurons are innately tuned for rewarding and aversive taste stimuli, encode their predictors, and are linked to motor output. *Neuron*, 45, 587, 2005.
84. Parker, L.A. Chlordiazepoxide enhances the palatability of lithium-, amphetamine-, and saline-paired saccharin solution. *Pharmacol. Biochem. Behav.*, 50, 345, 1995.
85. Yasoshima, Y. and Yamamoto, T. Effects of midazolam on the expression of conditioned taste aversion in rats. *Brain Res.*, 1043, 115, 2005.
86. Alheid, G.F. Extended amygdala and basal forebrain. *Ann. NY Acad. Sci.*, 985, 185, 2003.
87. Groenewegen, H.J. et al. The anatomical relationship of the prefrontal cortex with the striatopallidal system, the thalamus and the amygdala: evidence for a parallel organization. *Progr. Brain Res.*, 85, 95, 1990.
88. Berridge, K.C. Pleasures of the brain. *Brain Cogn.*, 52, 106, 2003.
89. Salamone, J.D. The involvement of nucleus accumbens dopamine in appetitive and aversive motivation. *Behav. Brain Res.*, 61, 117, 1994.
90. Salamone, J.D. et al. Beyond the reward hypothesis: alternative functions of nucleus accumbens dopamine. *Curr. Opin. Pharmacol.*, 5, 34, 2005.
91. Alheid, G..F. and Heimer, L. Theories of basal forebrain organization and the emotional motor system. *Progr. Brain Res.*, 107, 461, 1996.
92. Yamamoto, T. et al. Neural substrates for conditioned taste aversion in the rat. *Behav. Brain Res.*, 65, 123, 1994.
93. DiNardo, L.A. and Travers, J.B. Distribution of fos-like immunoreactivity in the medullary reticular formation of the rat after gustatory elicited ingestion and rejection behaviors. *J. Neurosci.*, 17, 3826, 1997.
94. Grill, H.J. and Norgren, R. Chronically decerebrate rats demonstrate satiation but not bait shyness. *Science*, 201, 267, 1978.

7 Changes in Neurotransmitter Extracellular Levels during Memory Formation

Maria Isabel Miranda

CONTENTS

7.1 INTRODUCTION

The current challenge of studying the mechanisms involving memory formation requires the possibility of capacity to analyze in the different brain regions that comprise the neuronal system and circuits underlying the different stages of memory. A timely detailed description of the dynamics of neurotransmitter release can and does provide information on the different areas of the brain, the chemical mechanisms involved, and their levels of participation during different physiological processes. Accordingly, the possibility of correlating behavior with changes in the extracellular level of neurotransmitters in CNS regions involved in information transmission and modulation is a great advantage in the study of memory formation. Also, the knowledge of the neurotransmitters released in different brain areas may result in the identification of important pharmacological targets.

In this regard, *in vivo* microdialysis is a well-established method for monitoring the extracellular levels of neurotransmitters in the CNS. This technique has been used extensively in neuroscience for almost 30 years.[1–6] Microdialysis allows online estimates of neurotransmitters in living animals and is a suitable method for monitoring the extracellular levels of neurotransmitters during local administration of pharmacological agents.[7] Different doses of a drug or a combination of agonists and antagonists can be administered in the same experiment without adding any fluid to extracellular spaces. Older alternative *in vivo* methods for the study of neurotransmitter release are the push–pull technique used in the brain,[8] spinal cord,[9] and intrathecal space.[10]

Currently, measuring the changes in neurotransmitter extracellular levels in discrete brain areas is considered an important tool for identifying the neuronal systems involved in specific memory processes. Several neurotransmitters including acetylcholine (ACh), glutamate, γ-amino-butyric acid (GABA), and catecholamines have been investigated in a variety of memory models, with considerable evidence of extracellular level variations that correlated with changes in neuronal activity during memory formation.

This chapter summarizes and discusses the results obtained from investigating changes in ACh, glutamate, GABA, dopamine, and noradrenaline release during exposure to novel stimuli and performance of several kinds of long-term memory tasks such as operant and spatial memory tasks, and during taste recognition memory.

7.2 FREE MOVING MICRODIALYSIS TECHNIQUE

The development of the microdialysis technique more than two decades ago[1,2] allowed the study of neurochemical mechanisms involved in memory to make fundamental progress by analyzing neurotransmitter release in unrestrained behaving animals. Microdialysis is a technique designed to monitor the chemistry of extracellular spaces in living tissue and allows monitoring of neurotransmitters released from practically any region of the brain, from the cortex to subcortical structures, which were previously available only with the push–pull cannula, a cumbersome and difficult technique.[11]

Microdialysis is the filtration of water-soluble substances in extracellular fluid through a dialysis membrane into a perfusion fluid that is collected and then analyzed for the substances of interest. With this technique, extracellular neurotransmitter levels and other molecules equilibrate with the solution flowing through dialysis tubings implanted in discrete brain areas. Usually microdialysis is coupled with high performance liquid chromatography (HPLC), making it possible to detect extracellular levels of many compounds, from small neurotransmitters to larger peptides.[5]

An important advantage of microdialysis is that it allows previsualization of what is happening in tissues before any chemical events are reflected in changes of systemic blood levels. The core of microdialysis is the dialysis probe designed to

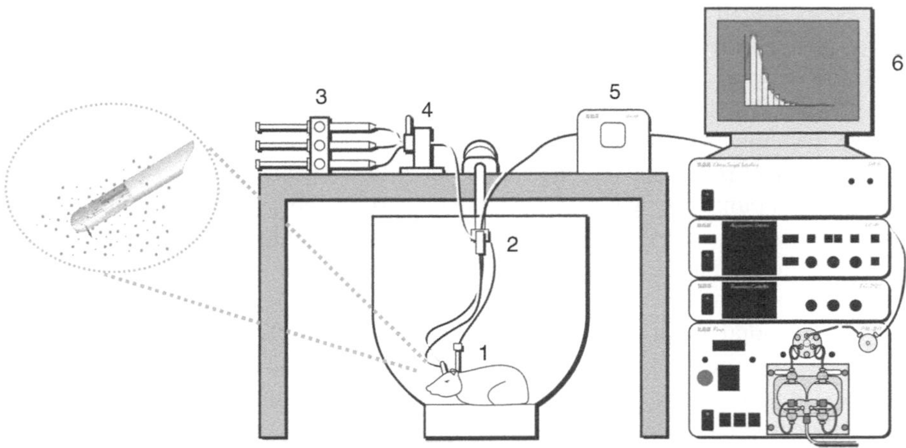

FIGURE 7.1 (See color insert following page 202.) Microdialysis system is formed by microdialysis probe (1), dual-channel microdialysis swivel, head block tether, and lever arm (2), syringe pump (3), syringe selector (4), fraction collector (5), and analysis system p.e. HPLC (6). Some researchers are working with a relative new microdialysis system based in a movement-responsive cage. The microdialysis inlet and outlet lines in this system remain intact all the way from the probe to the syringe pump or fraction collector. Animal movement is accommodated by the response of the cage to movement, >270° of rotation. Therefore, the swivel is not necessary. (Figures showing BAS equipment provided by Bioanalytical Systems, Inc.)

mimic a blood capillary. When a physiological salt solution is slowly pumped through the microdialysis probe, the solution equilibrates with the surrounding extracellular tissue fluid. After a while, it will then contain a representative proportion of the tissue fluid's molecules. Instead of inserting an analysis instrument such as a biosensor into the tissue, the microdialysate is extracted and later analyzed in the laboratory.

The body of any microdialysis system consists of a dual-channel microdialysis swivel that has a quartz-lined center and side channels to minimize dead volume and prevent neurotransmitter oxidation (Figure 7.1). Some swivels incorporate a miniature seal system for ultra-low torque and quartz lining on both the center and side channels for low dead volumes and minimal interactions with neurotransmitters. Dialysate is typically infused through one channel of the swivel, removed through the other, and then collected with a fraction collector. The head block tether and lever arm are necessary to minimize stress on microdialysis probes. The counter-balanced lever arms generally move vertically and horizontally with the animal to prevent slack in the tether. Most of the lever arms use a mass as the counterbalance, but new models use an adjustable spring that makes them lighter and more responsive. The animal can generally stay in a round container that prevents it from damaging the probes (Figure 7.1).

These containers used to be durable polycarbonate enclosures designed to house tethered rodents during short-term microdialysis and infusion experiments. Since the tank is round, tethers will not tangle as they sometimes do in shoebox-type cages. Also, animals are less likely to dislodge sensitive probes because the containers have no sharp corners. The enclosures are most frequently used with counter-balanced lever arms. Feeders, water bottles, and tops are available to enable researchers to leave the animals for longer periods.

A syringe pump delivers the smooth low flow rates required for microdialysis; to choose a pump configuration, one must determine how much programmability is required during the experiment. Generally with applications such as microdialysis that require high accuracy and low flow rates without the need for fluid withdrawal or complex protocols, an infusion-only pump is recommended.

A microdialysis probe is usually constructed as a concentric tube. The perfusion fluid enters through an inner tube; flows to its distal end; exits the tube and enters the space between the inner tube and the outer dialysis membrane, which may be of different lengths, depending on the brain region analyzed. The direction of flow is now reversed and the fluid moves toward the near end of the probe (see Figure 7.1). Dialysis (the diffusion of molecules between the extracellular and perfusion fluids) takes place at the end of the probe, in the membrane space. It is important to realize that dialysis is an exchange of molecules in both directions. The difference in concentration through the membrane governs the direction of the gradient. It is possible to collect an endogenous compound at the same time that an exogenous compound such as a drug is introduced into the tissue.

The gradient of a particular compound into the membrane depends on the difference in concentration between the perfusate and the extracellular fluid and also on the flow velocity inside the microdialysis probe. The absolute recovery (mol/time unit) of a substance from the tissue or of substances entering the tissue from the probe depends on (1) the flow rate of the perfusion fluid, (2) the length of the membrane, (3) the "cut-off" of the dialysis membrane, and (4) the diffusion coefficient of the compound through the extracellular fluid.

The initial exercise to obtain samples of sufficient concentrations for measurement must consider each of the above-mentioned variables. To obtain adequate estimates of the substances, first it would be advisable to begin with shorter membranes, for example, 1 mm, with low flows such as 1.0 to 0.1 ml/min, then quantify the behavior release as of the first fractions to thus determine the stabilization times of a given brain region. Once the initial values are established, both membrane sizes and flow velocity can be increased to optimize the sampling times in the desired region (Figure 7.2).

The large number of research experiments performed with microdialysis leads us to believe that this is an ideal technique because:

1. Multiple sampling of the brain and several regions in a living free-moving animal is possible.
2. No clean-up procedures such as extraction and homogenization of tissue are required before analysis.
3. Behavioral and pharmacology studies can span long periods (even days); activities around the brain capillaries and neuronal cells can be continuously monitored.

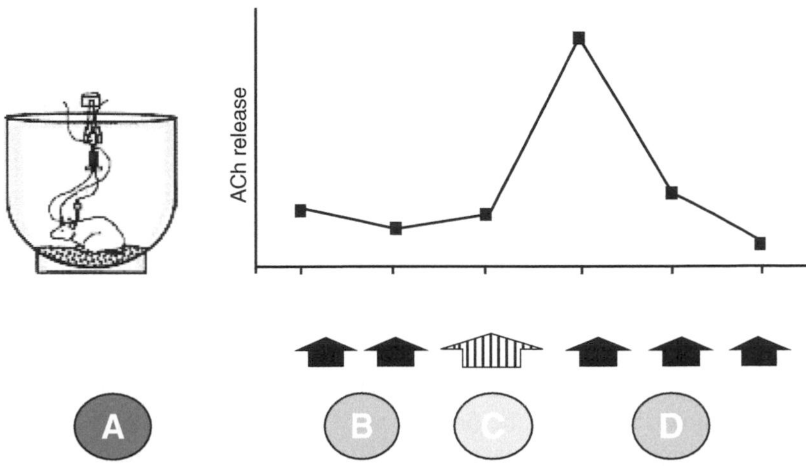

FIGURE 7.2 Example of microdialysis protocol. Stabilization times of a given brain region (A), base line sampling (B), behavioral manipulation (C), and reestablishment of base line release (D).

4. Various drugs can be administered without having to inject additional volumes, as is the case with pharmacological manipulations.
5. The concentration of drug exchanged for the dialysis probe can be estimated from that in the dialysis fluid sampled using the *in vitro* dialysis efficiency of the probe, which can be readily obtained from dialysis experiments carried out in a flask. However, this approach results in underestimation of the drug concentration in the brain interstitial fluid in most cases because the dialysis efficiency *in vivo* is different from that *in vitro*. Several researchers proposed methods to estimate the real concentration in the brain interstitial fluid.[4,12–17]

7.3 ACETYLCHOLINE RELEASE DURING MOTOR ACTIVITY, ATTENTION, AND NOVELTY

Substantial evidence indicates the important function of the cholinergic system during memory formation (for reviews see References 18 through 21). The release of acetylcholine in different brain areas appears to be involved in processes of attention,[22] detection of novelty or saliency,[23] and during the consolidation of different types of long-term memory.[24–26]

Locomotor activation associated with increases in ACh release in several brain regions also is generally involved during the tasks used to study memory formation in animals. Nonetheless, there is scarce evidence to confirm a direct correlation between motor activity and ACh release without the involvement of other components of memory formation. ACh release from the cerebral cortex, hippocampus, and striatum and locomotor activity have been demonstrated and considered measures of behavioral arousal.[27,28] Also, a direct correlation has been shown between spontaneous motility and ACh release from the striatum under conditions minimizing the effect of arousal and novelty, suggesting that drug-induced striatal ACh release may be modified by changes in levels of motor activity in free moving rats.[29] However, other research did not confirm this correlation because no significant differences were noted between the basal motor activity and the release of acetylcholine in the control subjects.[30–32]

It has been demonstrated that the same amount of motor activity is needed for the acquisition of an operant behavior, during which it has been proved that attention is required and a large increase in cortical and hippocampal ACh release occurs, as is required for recall that is not associated with an increased release and requires a low level of attention.[19,33] Pepeu and Giovannini[34] suggest that ACh release from the hippocampus and frontal cortex may have several components including motor activity, attention, arousal, anxiety, and stress. They found no correlation between ACh release and motor activity in the first exposure to a novel environment, but only in a second exposure to the same environment after 1 hour, when habituation was setting in.[34] Further evidence that ACh release and motor activity are not necessarily related is that glucose administration was followed by an increase in ACh release from the hippocampus and an improvement in spontaneous alternation in a four-arm maze, with no increase in the number of arms explored.[35]

The several complex functions associated with ACh release during memory formation, and the relationship between motor activity and ACh release may depend on the different levels of arousal and attention required at the time of the behavior task and the brain region analyzed by microdialysis. All these variables may also be the causes of the differences in existing results (for review see Reference 19).

We should not ignore the primary importance of the cholinergic system during the modulation of arousal. It has been demonstrated in the hippocampus that ACh release has a circadian variation,[27,36,37] increasing at the start of the dark period in nocturnal animals such as rats, that corresponds to the active phase. In this regard, Sei et al.[38] showed that in *clock* mutant mice, with ~2-hour delayed circadian profiles in body temperature, activity, and sleep–wake rhythm, the increase in hippocampal ACh release in the first 2 hours of the active period was suppressed. This suggests that the molecular basis of the circadian system appears to have a strong effect on hippocampal cholinergic function and is probably associated with individual temporary differences in voluntary behavior, cognition, learning and/or memory performance.[38]

Activation of the forebrain cholinergic system measured by microdialysis has been demonstrated in some tasks and conditions in which the environment requires an animal to analyze novel stimuli that may represent a threat or offer a reward. The sustained cholinergic activation demonstrated by high levels of extracellular ACh observed during the behavioral paradigms indicates that many behaviors occur within or require the facilitation provided by the cholinergic system to the operation of pertinent neuronal pathways.[39]

The evidence supports the idea that ACh may be a marker of differential participation of several neural systems during the formation and expression of learned behavior, i.e., the cholinergic system may modulate the differential participation of the brain regions required during early stages of memory formation. On the other hand, it is possible that a role in regulating the activational balance of memory systems is a consequence of ACh regulation of neural plasticity within different neural systems.[40]

In this regard, Inglis and Fibiger[41] observed that auditory, tactile, visual, and olfactory stimuli increased ACh release in the cerebral cortex and hippocampus and produced different behaviors including signs of fear in response to noise and stimulation, exploratory behavior after a visual stimulus, and sniffing and consummatory behavior after olfactory stimulation. All of the stimuli increased acetylcholine release in both the hippocampus and cortex. In the hippocampus, this increase was statistically significant with everything except the olfactory stimulus, whereas in the cortex everything but the visual stimulus resulted in significant increases.[41] Additionally, they demonstrated significant variations between the magnitudes of acetylcholine release produced by the different stimuli in the cortex; acetylcholine release elicited by tactile stimulation was greater than that produced by the other stimuli. These results could indicate that acetylcholine release is associated with a variety of behavioral responses to stimuli designed to produce arousal, and point to a role for cortical and hippocampal cholinergic mechanisms in arousal or attention. Also, under some circumstances, cortical and hippocampal acetylcholine release may be regulated differentially.[28]

The relationship between stimulation and the activation of the cholinergic system was also observed during paired tone and light stimulus. A significantly increased ACh release in the frontal cortex and hippocampus was observed when it was presented for the first time or was the conditioned stimulus of a conditioned fear paradigm. Interestingly, no increase in ACh release and behavioral response occurred if the tone and noise stimuli were presented repeatedly over an 8-day period leading to familiarization.[42]

In other series of experiments, animals placed in novel environments, either an arena with objects or different kinds of maze forms, showed significant increases in ACh release from the cerebral cortex.[34,43] These animals were left habituated for 30 min in the arena, as demonstrated by a much smaller increase in motor activity when they were placed again in the arena 60 min later; also, a significant decrease in ACh release was observed in comparison with the first exposure (Figure 7.3). The increase in ACh release from the frontal cortex and the hippocampus corroborated previous findings obtained by electrophysiological techniques that demonstrated the activation of the forebrain cholinergic neurons by spatial novelty[44] and the hippocampal theta rhythm that depends on the septo-hippocampal cholinergic pathway[45] and is present during attention[46] and exploratory activity.[47]

The results obtained indicate a close relationship between the release of ACh and novel stimuli. However, these results could be interpreted to mean that a novel environment represents a stressful condition, and the first exposure to it causes pronounced behavioral activation.[48,49] Furthermore, activation of basalocortical cholinergic afferents may promote the attentional processing that is central to the memory-related aspects of anxiety caused by threat-related stimuli and associations.[50]

A learning model that clearly demonstrates the independence of ACh release from motor activity during the presentation of a novel stimulus is taste memory

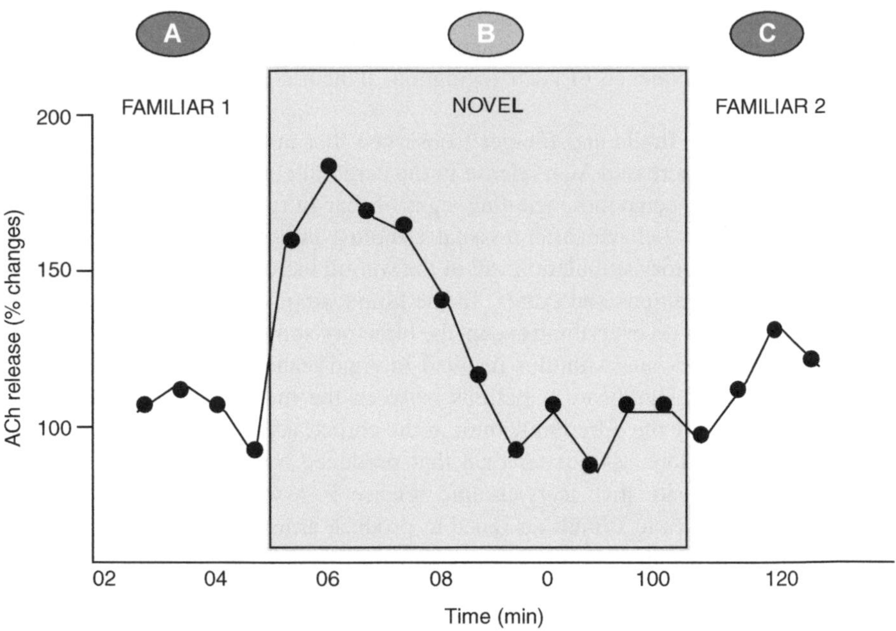

FIGURE 7.3 Animals placed in novel environments, either an arena with objects or different kinds of maze forms, showed significant increases in ACh release from the cerebral cortex. (Modified from Giovannini, M.G. et al., *Neuroscience*, 2001. 106: 43.)

recognition. With this learning model, a highly significant increase in ACh release was demonstrated in the insular cortex of rats only during the first consumptions of saccharin or quinine solutions. The ACh release observed after several presentations of the same taste stimuli decreased to similar levels as those produced by the familiar taste, indicating an inverse relationship between familiarity and cortical ACh release. These results suggest that the cholinergic system plays an important role in the identification and characterization of different kinds of taste stimuli[51] (Figure 7.4).

Nonetheless, taste novelty is not the only factor related to cholinergic activity; the manipulation of a novel object (toy) by rats significantly increased the hippocampal ACh efflux as a correlation of active manipulation of the object.[52] Similarly, a single 1-hour introduction of the novel object immediately after a training session in a radial arm maze significantly improved memory only if the animals actively manipulated the object. The data suggest that environmental enrichment during a critical period is sufficient to improve learning and memory and that this effect is probably mediated through an enhancement of hippocampal cholinergic neurotransmission.[52] It seems that the cholinergic system activates in response to external inputs when they are novel[41] but not when the stimuli are repeated, leading to habituation.[42] The evidence indicates that the forebrain cholinergic system may become activated by tasks that require the analysis of novel stimuli representing a threat or offering a reward.[53]

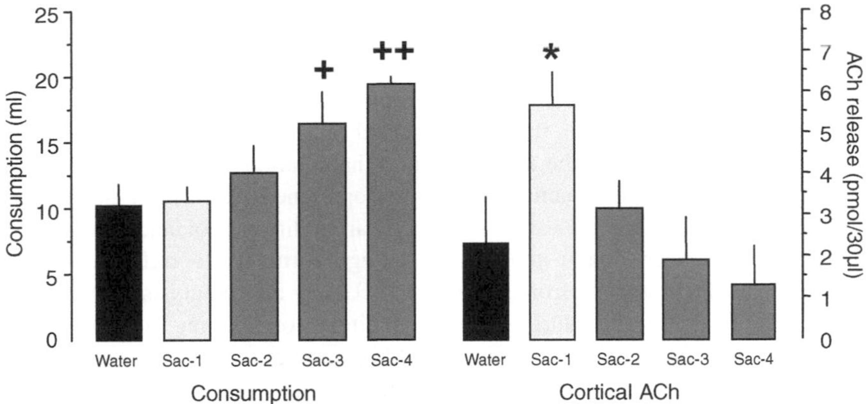

FIGURE 7.4 ACh release observed after several presentations of the same taste stimuli decreased to similar levels as those produced by the familiar taste, indicating an inverse relationship between familiarity and cortical ACh release.[51]

7.4 NOVELTY AND OTHER NEUROTRANSMITTER RELEASES

The interactions of forebrain cholinergic neurons with other neurotransmitter systems during motor activity, arousal, and novelty have not yet been unraveled. Regardless of whether the forebrain cholinergic neurons are activated by novelty, learning, or sensory and stressor stimuli, the question arises as to which neuronal circuits and neurotransmitters trigger and/or accompany this activation. Papeu and Blandina[54] found no changes in glutamate extracellular levels in the cerebral cortex or hippocampus of rats during either novel or familiar exploration.[54]

However, the same group of researchers suggested that even though cortical and hippocampal glutamatergic systems are not apparently involved in exploration of a novel environment and habituation, glutamatergic pathways modulate cortical and hippocampal cholinergic activity directly because antagonists of the *N*-methyl-D-aspartate (NMDA) receptors injected into the nucleus basalis inhibit spontaneous and stimulated ACh release[55,56] and administration of NMDA and -amino-3-hydroxy-5-methyl-4-isoxazole propionate/kainate antagonists in the medial septum inhibits handling-evoked ACh release in the hippocampus.[57] Also, glutamatergic pathways indirectly regulate the activities of GABAergic neurons impinging on cholinergic neurons in the medial septum.[58,59] The researchers argued that changes in glutamate release could be detected if the microdialysis probes were placed in the nucleus basalis or medial septum. On the other hand, the question raised the possibility of detecting changes in the small glutamate pool of neuronal origin that is only a fraction of the larger nonsynaptic glutamate pool.[34,60]

Giovannini et al.[34] also determined by microdialysis the GABA extracellular levels and revealed that cortical GABA release increased significantly only during familiar exploration, while hippocampal GABA release did not increase during exploration periods. They also found a correlation between motor activity and GABA release, but only during familiar exploration.[34] Furthermore, under similar experimental conditions, the increases in aspartate, glutamate, GABA, and ACh in the ventral hippocampus associated with exploratory activity in a novel environment tended to be much smaller in the second period of exposure to the spatial stimulus than in the first, indicating the development of habituation.[61]

Regarding novelty, the activation of the dopamine system increase in medial prefrontal cortex during the establishment of an auditory avoidance strategy in a shuttle box has been demonstrated and strategy formation correlated with high dopamine levels in the prefrontal cortex.[62,63] Using microdialysis in the medial prefrontal cortex of gerbils during aversive auditory conditioning in the shuttle box showed a transient increase of dopamine efflux correlation with the establishment of avoidance behavior. The authors hypothesized that the acquisition of a new behavioral strategy is generally accompanied by this extra prefrontal dopamine release. The subsequent formation of discrimination behavior led to a similar extra dopamine increase as found during establishment of the avoidance strategy, and the significant enhancement was observed only in rapidly relearning individuals. These results suggest that the dopamine system may be critically involved in the initial formation of associations for new behavioral strategies.[64]

7.5 LESIONS AND BLOCKADE OF CHOLINERGIC ACTIVITY DURING MEMORY FORMATION

The forebrain cholinergic system is salient for arousal, attention, learning, and memory.[18,21,65,66] Lesions of forebrain cholinergic neurons made by different neurotoxins provided important information related to the role of ACh in learning and memory and demonstrated that the decrease in ACh extracellular levels is accompanied by specific behavioral deficits.[67–69] Activation of basalocortical cholinergic afferents, revealed *in vivo* by increased cortical ACh release, is involved in the attentional processing central to memory formation.[34,65,70] Excitotoxic lesions of the nucleus basalis induced a long-lasting significant decrease in cortical ACh release both at rest and under K^+ depolarization, paralleled by disruption of a passive avoidance task,[71,72] working memory,[71,72] and conditioned taste aversion.[68] Disruption of the septo-hippocampal projections impaired choice accuracy in short-term memory[73] and resulted in deficits in T-maze performance.[74]

The use of intracerebral 192IgG-saporin is a selective procedure for the disruption of the cholinergic neurons[75] and causes an almost complete cholinergic deafferentation to the cortex and hippocampus and a significant decrease in ACh release from these structures.[76] The rat behavioral studies performed with this procedure suggested that only very extensive lesions involving >90% of cholinergic neurons resulted reliably in severely impaired performances.[77] Impairments were found in delayed matching[78] and nonmatching to position task,[79] water-maze acquisition,[80] spatial working memory,[81] and acquisition (but not retention) of object discrimination[82] and conditioned taste aversion.[83]

Despite the consistency of the above results, it remains to be clearly established whether the detectable limits of ACh using current measurement methods are capable of determining release variations after 192IgG-saporin lesions. Moreover, systematic research is required to examine the probable compensatory mechanisms arising in response to a lesion of the magnitude induced by the injections of 192IgG-saporin.

In addition to the information provided from the experiments with transitory and permanent lesions of the basal forebrain that indicate its relevant function during memory formation of varied tasks, injections of 192IgG-saporin demonstrated the participation of basal forebrain cholinergic lesions on attentional processing.[84] Most studies reported disrupted attentional processing in nucleus basalis- or medial septum-injected animals,[77,85] thus confirming the role of the cholinergic system in attention. However, a correlation was not always found between attentional effort required by task difficulties and ACh release.[86]

Several behavioral studies indicate that cholinergic projections may be required not for learning per se, but may be important for specific aspects of attention.[65] Microdialysis experiments indicate that cortical ACh increases during the performance of simple operant tasks are limited to early acquisition stages, when demands on attentional processing are high.[87] Cortical ACh release increased in rats performing a visual attentional task[88] and directly correlated with the attentional effort during an operant task designed to assess sustained attention.[89]

Recent findings in transgenic mice (TgCRND8), characterized by many β-amyloid plaques with reduced neuronal and axonal staining, white matter demyelination, glia reaction, and choline acetyltransferase immunoreactivity significantly decreased in the nucleus basalis magnocellularis demonstrated that extracellular acetylcholine levels investigated by microdialysis and M2 muscarinic receptor immunoreactivity were reduced in the cortices of TgCRND8 mice. Scopolamine administration increased cortical extracellular acetylcholine levels in control mice, but not in TgCRND8 mice. Also, a cognitive impairment was demonstrated in the step-down test. These findings demonstrate that neuronal damage and cholinergic dysfunction *in vivo* underlie the impairment in learning and memory functions in this mouse model of Alzheimer's disease.[90]

7.6 ACETYLCHOLINE AND LONG-TERM MEMORY TASKS

Cortical acetylcholine release increases (1) during acquisition but not during recall of a rewarded operant behavior,[33](2) during acquisition of operant tasks when demands on attentional processing are high,[87] (3) during conditioned taste aversion,[91] and (4) during performance of visual attentional tasks.[88] It has been also related to attentional effort.[89] Furthermore, in the hippocampus, ACh release increases during the performance of a learned spatial memory task,[35,92] and the increase is positively correlated to performance improvement during task learning,[93] showing that cholinergic neurons are modified functionally during learning and become progressively more active. Also, the initial use of a place strategy coincided with an immediate increase in hippocampus ACh release.[94] Furthermore, as rewarded spontaneous alternation testing progressed, a switch to a repetitive response strategy accompanied an increase in striatum ACh release.[40]

7.6.1 Spatial Memory

Different evidence suggests that ACh release in the hippocampus and striatum may reflect the relative participation of these systems during different kinds of learning. For example, on a T-maze, animals can successfully solve the task of finding food in one arm, using either a place strategy, repeatedly visiting a specific part of the room (e.g., west) for food reward, or a response strategy, repeatedly turning the same direction at the choice point (e.g., left) for a food reward.[95–98] Rats that expressed place strategies in the probe trial had higher ratios of hippocampus and striatum ACh release, while rats using response strategies had lower ratios[94,99] and demonstrated training-related changes in release of ACh in the hippocampus and striatum during the acquisition.[40]

The behavioral findings shown by these researchers suggest that rats changed the bases for their performance from a spatial working memory strategy to a persistent turning strategy during testing. ACh release in both hippocampus and striatum increased at the onset of testing. Increases in ACh release in the striatum began at two times above baseline during the first 5 min of testing and steadily increased, reaching six times above baseline during the final 5 min. The increase of ACh release in the striatum during testing occurred around the time the rats adopted a persistent turning strategy. In contrast, ACh release in the hippocampus increased over five times from its baseline but remained at this level until declining slightly during the last 5 min of testing. The relative changes in ACh release in the striatum and hippocampus resulted in a close negative relationship between the ratio of ACh release in the hippocampus and striatum and alternation scores.[40]

McIntyre et al.[99] demonstrated that the release of ACh in the hippocampus and striatum during acquisition of a dual-solution T-maze task is associated with differential strategy use during training in tasks that can be solved with either a place or response strategy.[99] They showed that when rats were trained in a similar dual-solution T-maze task, baseline levels of ACh release in the hippocampus and striatum predicted the strategy rats used on a probe trial 1 hour later. Other groups confirmed these data by demonstrating that changes in the amount of ACh released in the hippocampus and striatum during training coincided with changes in strategy.[94] The initial use of a place strategy coincided with an immediate increase in hippocampus ACh release. As rewarded spontaneous alternation testing progressed, a switch to a repetitive response strategy accompanied an increase in striatum ACh release.[40]

Additionally, data on the release of ACh measured in the hippocampus while rats learned and were tested on an amygdala-dependent conditioned place preference task and a hippocampus-dependent spontaneous alternation task demonstrated that ACh in the hippocampus increased when rats were tested on either task. Amygdala ACh release was positively correlated with performance on the hippocampus-dependent task. However, the magnitude of the increase in the release of hippocampal ACh was negatively correlated with good performance in the amygdala-dependent conditioned place preference task, suggesting that ACh release may reflect activation and participation of the hippocampus in learning and memory, but in a manner that can be detrimental to performance in a task dependent on another brain area. These results demonstrated a competition and interaction between the hippocampus and the amygdala through cholinergic activity.[99]

The previous evidence summarized experiments demonstrating that simultaneous monitoring of ACh release from different brain areas establishes the possibility of understanding the specific roles of certain neurotransmitters in the different brain regions and during different stages of several memory tasks. All this evidence on the release of ACh in the cortex, hippocampus, amygdala, and striatum during learning is in agreement with the evidence showing that manipulations of ACh in these brain regions regulate learning and memory.[100] Regarding the stages of memory formation, increases in the levels of ACh release in the hippocampus and striatum appear to correlate with the related participation of these structures during acquisition and consolidation. In the hippocampus, measurements of ACh release while rats learn several tasks revealed a close relationship between the magnitude of training-related increases of ACh release in the hippocampus and increased memory processing.[40]

More examples indicate that hippocampal ACh release increases during performance of other spatial tasks.[92,101] It has been shown that improvement in radial arm maze performance is positively correlated to an increase in ACh release during 12 days of task learning.[93,102] These results suggest that the learning of a spatial task modifies the functions of cholinergic neurons projecting to the hippocampus that become progressively more active. In a behavioral paradigm investigating spatial orientation during the acquisition period, exploration-associated synaptic changes were significantly correlated, and it has been suggested that variations in ACh release accompanied by alterations in muscarinic receptors density may reflect these changes.[103]

The previous evidence indicates a significant correlation between the increase in ACh release in the hippocampus and the increase in performance of spatial learning and memory functions in rats.[104,105] Also, it has been demonstrated that male rats show greater daily ACh releases in the hippocampus than female rats.[106] The authors suggest that sex differences in spatial learning and memory functions are considered to reflect the sex differences in ACh release in rats.[107]

7.6.2 Inhibitory Avoidance and Contextual Memory

The involvement of the cholinergic system both in attention and in the consolidation of new memories[100] has also been demonstrated by the enhancing or inhibitory effects of posttraining administration of cholinergic agonists[108,109] or antagonists.[110–112] Inhibitory avoidance is a form of associative learning acquired in one trial by activation of several brain structures such as the amygdala, hippocampus and various cortical regions through several sensorial stimuli including spatial and visual perceptions, pain, and fear.[113–115] Inhibitory avoidance also entails working memory since an animal may choose to avoid an aversive stimulus.[116] The inhibitory avoidance response is a learning task that depends on the activation of the cholinergic system.[108,117–121] However, a limited amount of evidence directly correlates the increased ACh release in rats with the performance of an inhibitory avoidance task.[53]

Giovannini et al.[53] investigated the involvement of the cholinergic and glutamatergic systems projecting to the medial prefrontal cortex and ventral hippocampus and the extracellular regulated kinase signal transduction pathway in the acquisition and recall of step-down inhibitory avoidance. Using microdialysis, they studied the release of acetylcholine and glutamate, and found that cholinergic, but not glutamatergic, neurons projecting to the medial prefrontal cortex and ventral hippocampus were activated during acquisition of the task, as shown by increases in cortical and hippocampal acetylcholine release. Released acetylcholine in turn activated extracellular regulated kinase in target neurons.

These authors also demonstrated that both increased acetylcholine release and extracellular regulated kinase activation were necessary for memory formation, indicating that a critical function of the learning-associated increase in acetylcholine release is to promote the activation of the extracellular regulated kinase signal transduction pathway. These results help explain the role of these systems in the encoding of inhibitory avoidance memory. In the same series of experiments, the authors found an increased release of ACh during recall, suggesting the stressful experience a rat faces when re-exposed to the same environment. In this regard, it has been shown that stress activates the forebrain cholinergic pathways.[41,42,49,122] Other data that indicate cholinergic involvement during inhibitory avoidance came from experiments related to dietary restriction of choline, inducing the reduction in the capacity to release ACh in the hippocampus, as confirmed by *in vivo* microdialysis, and impairing performance of a inhibitory avoidance task in rats.[123]

7.6.3 Acetylcholine Release Induced by Other Systems

Although the objectives of this chapter do not allow us to include all the work that has demonstrated the manipulation of the cholinergic system through pharmacological treatments or administration of agonists or antagonists of innumerable receptors, the relevance of certain systems that may have significant interactions during the formation of different long-term memory is worth pointing out. In this regard, the physiological role of synaptically released histamine has been demonstrated. In addition to affecting cholinergic transmission in the amygdala, it modulates the consolidation of fear memories.[124] Cangioli et al.[125] demonstrated that the blockade of histaminergic H3 receptors decreased the spontaneous release of ACh from the basolateral amygdalas (BLAs) of freely moving rats and impaired the retention of fear memory.[125]

Furthermore, a dopamine receptor type D_2R agonist stimulated ACh release in the ventral hippocampus during a 14-unit T-maze (Stone maze) task, indicating that D_2R in the ventral hippocampus may be involved in mnemonic function via ACh release.[126] Other studies provided evidence of a possible interaction of cholinergic and dopaminergic systems. It was reported that dopamine during mild foot-shock presentations was markedly increased by a preceding novel tone stimulus[127–130] and hippocampal ACh–dopamine interactions in mnemonic processing, as suggested by the finding that the retention of inhibitory avoidance behavior was impaired by the focal injection of a D_2R antagonist into the ventral hippocampus.[131]

Finally, we should not forget the information obtained through systemic and intrahippocampal injections of glucose that augmented the increases in the release of ACh in the hippocampus during alternation tests and also enhanced alternation scores relative to control injected rats.[35,132–134] On the other hand, it has been shown that systemic injections of morphine resulted in decreases in the release of ACh in the hippocampus and in alternation scores; glucose injections at the time of morphine treatment reversed both morphine-induced reductions in ACh release and morphine-induced impairments of alternation scores.[135,136]

This section has provided evidence of ACh activity under different behavioral and pharmacological manipulations. It is important to note that most of the reported studies required the use of inhibitors (e.g., eserine and neostigmine) of acetyl cholinesterase. The ACh degradation enzyme is usually added in the perfusion medium, because once released in the synaptic cleft, ACh diffuses, binds to pre- and postsynaptic muscarinic and nicotinic receptors and is quickly hydrolyzed by cholinesterase. Only small amounts of ACh can be detected in extracellular fluid even in the absence of cholinesterase inhibitors if cholinesterase efficiency is manipulated.[165] Scali et al.[166] found ACh levels of 5.5 ± 1.0 and 5.0 ± 1.0 fmole/μL in the cerebral cortex and hippocampus perfusates, respectively[166] in the effluent from microdialysis probes in young rats at rest.

7.7 NORADRENALINE RELEASE DURING MEMORY FORMATION

It has been clearly demonstrated that the BLA is a critical region where converging inputs from different neuronal circuitries such as noradrenergic and cholinergic are integrated and modulate the consolidation of emotional memory.[137,138] Furthermore, the BLA is implicated in emotional memory such as fear conditioning and also in acquisition (but not retention) of inhibitory avoidance-conditioned responses.[139] It has been reported that the BLA and the medial prefrontal cortex interact in influencing the performance of affectively motivated tasks such as conditioned fear.[140]

Recent findings suggest that noradrenaline release in the amygdala may be critical for regulating memory consolidation; several experimental results indicate that foot-shock and several drugs that modulate memory consolidation altered noradrenaline release in the amygdala.[137,141–143] McIntyre et al.[144] examined the relationship of noradrenaline release in the amygdala assessed after inhibitory avoidance training and 24-hour retention performance of individual animals. They found that noradrenaline levels significantly increased to pretraining baseline 30 min after training and remained elevated for 2 hours. Interestingly, for individual rats, the increases in noradrenaline levels after training correlated highly with 24-hour retention performance. These findings may indicate that the degree of activation of the noradrenergic system within the amygdala in response to a novel emotionally arousing experience predicts the extent of long-term memory for that experience.[144]

It has been suggested that improved cognitive processing is related to stimulation-induced increases of noradrenaline release in limbic brain structures. It has been demonstrated that vagal nerve stimulation improves memory, presumably by affecting activity in central nervous system structures that process recently acquired information.[142,145] Vagal nerve stimulation at an intensity and duration that improves memory also increases BLA noradrenaline release. These studies help explain how peripheral neural activity modulates limbic structures to encode and store new information into long-term memory.[142,145,146]

Tronel et al.[147] investigated the role of the noradrenergic system in the late stage of memory consolidation in the prelimbic region of the prefrontal cortex 1 hour after training of an appetitively motivated foraging task based on olfactory discrimination. They observed that the extracellular noradrenaline levels in the prelimbic region significantly increased shortly after training, with a rapid return to baseline, with another increase around the 2-hour posttraining window. Pseudo-trained rats showed smaller early levels and did not show the second wave of increase at 2 hours. These results correlated with earlier pharmacological and immunohistochemical studies suggesting a delayed role of noradrenaline in a late phase of long-term memory consolidation and the engagement of the prelimbic region during these consolidation processes.[148]

Additionally, a complex effect has been demonstrated in the frontal cortex after stimulation of the locus coeruleus in anesthetized rats. Noradrenaline inhibited spontaneous activity and at the same time facilitated evoked responses in the frontal cortex.[149] More recent *in vitro* studies showed that NE has a complex effect on GABAergic interneurons in this region.[150]

7.8 GLUTAMATE AND GABA RELEASE DURING MEMORY FORMATION

The neurotransmitter glutamate is the major excitatory transmitter of the brain and is involved in practically all aspects of cognitive function since it is the transmitter located on the cortical and hippocampal pyramidal neurons and also throughout different subcortical regions. Furthermore, glutamate and glutamate receptors are involved in long-term memory formation as well as in long-term potentiation, a process believed to underlie learning and memory.[151–153]

In relation to the evidence described above, the involvement of the forebrain cholinergic system in arousal, learning, and memory has been well established. The involvement of the interaction of forebrain cholinergic neurons with the glutamatergic system in the retrieval of aversive memory has been postulated.[154] Glutamate and GABA may be involved in the mechanisms of memory by modulating the forebrain's cholinergic pathways. Giovannini et al.[34] studied the activities of cortical and hippocampal cholinergic, GABAergic, and glutamatergic systems during novelty and habituation in rats using microdialysis during exposure to a novel environment. They observed that cortical GABA release increased significantly only during familiar exploration, while hippocampal GABA release did not increase during either exploration. No change in cortical and hippocampal glutamate release was observed. The researchers suggested that GABAergic activity may be involved in habituation.[34]

Furthermore, it has been suggested that glutamate release from the vagus nerve onto the nucleus of the solitary tract (NTS) is one mechanism by which the vagus influences memory and neural activity in limbic structures. When glutamate was infused into the NTS, it significantly enhanced memory on the retention test and this effect was attenuated by blocking noradrenergic receptors in the amygdala with propranolol (a β-adrenergic antagonist). Using *in vivo* microdialysis to determine whether foot-shock plus glutamate altered noradrenergic output in the amygdala, it was demonstrated that it caused a significant and long-lasting increase in amygdala noradrenergic concentrations. These results indicate that glutamate may be one transmitter that conveys the effects of vagal activation on brain systems involved in memory formation.[155]

The effect of glutamate receptor antagonists on taste aversion learning has also been studied in rats. The first relay where the short-term memory of a novel gustatory stimulus and the visceral malaise stimulus could be associated during taste learning takes place in the parabrachial nuclei (PBN) of the brainstem. Direct evidence indicates glutamate release in the PBN during taste aversive learning, which demonstrates that the extracellular level of glutamate rises during saccharin drinking.[156] Also, microdialysis administration of selective glutamate metabotropic receptor antagonists into the PBN disrupted the formation of CTA, but not the application of NMDA receptor antagonist.[157] Also in CTA, evidence indicates that visceral stimulus (i.p. injection of lithium chloride) induced a dramatic increase in glutamate release in the amygdala and a modest but significant release in the insular cortex.[158] Moreover, CTA can be elicited by intra-amygdalar microinjections of glutamate; consequently, when glutamate is administered just before the presentation of a weak visceral stimulus, a clear CTA is induced.

In contrast, the injection of glutamate alone or glutamate 2 hours after suboptimal US did not have any effect on the acquisition of CTA. These results demonstrate that glutamate activation of the amygdala can mimic the visceral stimulus signal during taste aversive memory formation, providing a clear indication that the amygdala conveys visceral information for this kind of memory.[91,158]

Further research examined whether glutamate release in other tasks also plays a role in memory formation. For example, female mice form olfactory memories of the pheromones of mating males during a critical period after mating. It seems that neural changes underlying this memory are located in the accessory olfactory bulb, are dependent on noradrenergic neurotransmission, and most likely involve changes at the mitral granule cell reciprocal synapses.[159] During olfactory memory, an increase has been shown in GABA levels in response to a glutamate, and the aspartate:GABA ratio was decreased following memory formation during exposure to the pheromones of the mating male.

These findings are consistent with our hypothesis that memory formation involves a long-lasting increase in the inhibition of the subset of mitral cells that respond to the mating male's pheromones. An increment was also observed in the concentrations of the excitatory transmitters glutamate and aspartate in non-mating females, suggesting that exposure to male pheromones alone, without the association of mating, causes a long-lasting decrease in the inhibitory control of the subset of mitral cells responding to these pheromones.[160]

7.9 CONCLUSIONS

This chapter provides evidence obtained via *in vivo* microdialysis techniques that demonstrates the activation of the forebrain cholinergic system and other neurotransmitters such as glutamate, noradrenaline, and dopamine in several types of learning and during several stages of memory formation. The results of innumerable studies indicate that during memory formation different regions of the brain act in coordinated fashion through different neurotransmission systems. The experiments analyzed in this chapter offer a sample of what may be achieved through the timely and direct evaluation of neurochemical activity in the brain. A clear interpretation will help explain how different processes such as motor activity, attention, and stress are interlinked during long-term memory formation.

One caveat in the interpretation of the results obtained with microdialysis is that stressor stimuli such as prolonged handling,[161,162] restraint,[163] and fear[42] strongly activate the cholinergic system. Consequently, before associating a behavioral response with variations in ACh release or any neurotransmitter, it is essential to exclude the possible interference of stressors or at least have the correct control groups to help interpret the results obtained

In addition, as in any other model for *in vivo* measurement of neurotransmitter release, microdialysis should not be based on the assumption that the extracellular concentration accurately reflects synaptic concentration (for reviews of microdialysis techniques see References 1 and 2). We must remember that extracellular concentration of a neurotransmitter is not only affected by neuronal release, but also by enzymatic metabolism, diffusion, and re-uptake. Furthermore, neurotransmitters and metabolites obtained by microdialysate may have glial origins.[164] Thus, variations in microdialysate neurotransmitter concentrations during stimulation or behavior do not necessarily reflect synaptic neuronal release.

Last but not least, to achieve neurotransmitter concentrations in dialysates, the microdialysis technique requires large quantities (around 10 to 30 μl), enough to be quantified with the respective HPLC assays. In most experiments recorded in this chapter, the collection periods were at least 5 min. The problem is that memory acquisition and behavioral responses usually occur within seconds. This time scale difference makes it very difficult to demonstrate a precise correlation between activation of cholinergic neurons and specific cognitive processes, and this currently represents the technical limit of microdialysis experiments.

Based on the data in this chapter, the development of new analysis models may eventually provide responses to questions that cannot yet be answered through microdialysis or other neurochemical measurement techniques, and will enable us to observe more closely the neurotransmitter releases in different regions of the brain during memory formation.

However, despite all these disadvantages, the microdialysis technique currently provides the best method for detailed descriptions of the dynamics of neurotransmitter release as demonstrated in this chapter, providing important information on the different areas of the brain, the chemical mechanisms involved, and their levels of participation during different stages of memory formation. Accordingly, the correlation of behavior with changes in the extracellular level of neurotransmitters in

CNS regions has provided important data related to the chemical interaction and modulation of different brain areas that form part of the circuitry of several kinds of long-term memory.

A significant and growing number of publications report microdialysis results because this technique allows for on-line estimates of neurotransmitters in living animals and is a suitable method for monitoring the extracellular levels of neurotransmitters during local administration of pharmacological agents.[7] This confirms that the microdialysis technique is an alternative real and elegant method for the *in vivo* study of neurotransmitter function in several memory systems.

REFERENCES

1. Westerink, B.H., Brain microdialysis and its application for the study of animal behaviour. *Behav Brain Res*, 1995. 70: 103.
2. Ungerstedt, U., Microdialysis: principles and applications for studies in animals and man. *J Intern Med*, 1991. 230: 365.
3. Robinson, T.J., Techniques in the behavioral and neural sciences, in *Microdialysis in the Neurosciences*, Vol. 7, Elsevier, Amsterdam, 1991.
4. Benveniste, H. Brain microdialysis. *J Neurochem*, 1989. 52: 1667.
5. Benveniste, H. and P.C. Huttemeier, Microdialysis: theory and application. *Progr Neurobiol*, 1990. 35: 195.
6. Di Chiara, G., *In vivo* brain dialysis of neurotransmitters. *Trends Pharmacol Sci*, 1990. 11: 116.
7. Hammarlund-Udenaes, M., The use of microdialysis in CNS drug delivery studies: pharmacokinetic perspectives and results with analgesics and antiepileptics. *Adv Drug Deliv Rev*, 2000. 45: 283.
8. Singewald, N. and A. Philippu, Release of neurotransmitters in the locus coeruleus. *Progr Neurobiol*, 1998. 56: 237.
9. Zachariou, V. and B.D. Goldstein, Dynorphin-(1-8) inhibits the release of substance P-like immunoreactivity in the spinal cord of rats following a noxious mechanical stimulus. *Eur J Pharmacol*, 1997. 323: 159.
10. Yaksh, T.L. and G.M. Tyce, Resting and K^+-evoked release of serotonin and norephinephrine *in vivo* from the rat and cat spinal cord. *Brain Res*, 1980. 192: 133.
11. Gaddum, J.H., The technique of superfusion. *Br J Pharmacol*, 1997. 120 (Suppl.): 82–7; discussion, 80–1.
12. Bungay, P.M., P.F. Morrison, and R.L. Dedrick, Steady-state theory for quantitative microdialysis of solutes and water *in vivo* and *in vitro*. *Life Sci*, 1990. 46: 105.
13. Jacobson, I., M. Sandberg, and A. Hamberger, Mass transfer in brain dialysis devices: a new method for the estimation of extracellular amino acids concentration. *J Neurosci Methods*, 1985. 15: 263.
14. Lerma, J. et al., *In vivo* determination of extracellular concentration of amino acids in the rat hippocampus: a method based on brain dialysis and computerized analysis. *Brain Res*, 1986. 384: 145.
15. Lonnroth, P., P.A. Jansson, and U. Smith, A microdialysis method allowing characterization of intercellular water space in humans. *Am J Physiol*, 1987. 253(2 Pt 1): E228.

16. Scheller, D. and J. Kolb, The internal reference technique in microdialysis: a practical approach to monitoring dialysis efficiency and to calculating tissue concentration from dialysate samples. *J Neurosci Methods*, 1991. 40: 31.
17. Deguchi, Y. and K. Morimoto, Application of an *in vivo* brain microdialysis technique to studies of drug transport across the blood-brain barrier. *Curr Drug Metab*, 2001. 2: 411.
18. Sarter, M., J.P. Bruno, and B. Givens, Attentional functions of cortical cholinergic inputs: what does it mean for learning and memory? *Neurobiol Learn Mem*, 2003. 80: 245.
19. Pepeu, G. and M.G. Giovannini, Changes in acetylcholine extracellular levels during cognitive processes. *Learn Mem*, 2004. 11: 21.
20. Baxter, M.G. and A.A. Chiba, Cognitive functions of the basal forebrain. *Curr Opin Neurobiol*, 1999. 9: 178.
21. Everitt, B.J. and T.W. Robbins, Central cholinergic systems and cognition. *Annu Rev Psychol*, 1997. 48: 649.
22. Marrosu, F. et al., Microdialysis measurement of cortical and hippocampal acetylcholine release during sleep–wake cycle in freely moving cats. *Brain Res*, 1995. 671: 329.
23. Baxter, M.G. et al., Impairments in conditioned stimulus processing and conditioned responding after combined selective removal of hippocampal and neocortical cholinergic input. *Behav Neurosci*, 1999. 113: 486.
24. Power, A.E., Muscarinic cholinergic contribution to memory consolidation: with attention to involvement of the basolateral amygdala. *Curr Med Chem*, 2004. 11: 987.
25. McIntyre, C.K., L.K. Marriott, and P.E. Gold, Cooperation between memory systems: acetylcholine release in the amygdala correlates positively with performance on a hippocampus-dependent task. *Behav Neurosci*, 2003. 117: 320.
26. Hasselmo, M.E., Neuromodulation: acetylcholine and memory consolidation. *Trends Cogn Sci*, 1999. 3: 351.
27. Mizuno, T. et al., Acetylcholine release in the rat hippocampus as measured by the microdialysis method correlates with motor activity and exhibits a diurnal variation. *Neuroscience*, 1991. 44: 607.
28. Fibiger, H.C., G. Damsma, and J.C. Day, Behavioral pharmacology and biochemistry of central cholinergic neurotransmission. *Adv Exp Med Biol*, 1991. 295: 399.
29. Watanabe, H., H. Shimizu, and K. Matsumoto, Acetylcholine release detected by trans-striatal dialysis in freely moving rats correlates with spontaneous motor activity. *Life Sci*, 1990. 47: 829.
30. Day, J. and H.C. Fibiger, Dopaminergic regulation of cortical acetylcholine release. *Synapse*, 1992. 12: 281.
31. Moore, H., M. Sarter, and J.P. Bruno, Age-dependent modulation of *in vivo* cortical acetylcholine release by benzodiazepine receptor ligands. *Brain Res,* 1992. 596: 17.
32. Thiel, C.M., J.P. Huston, and R.K. Schwarting, Hippocampal acetylcholine and habituation learning. *Neuroscience*, 1998. 85: 1253.
33. Orsetti, M., F. Casamenti, and G. Pepeu, Enhanced acetylcholine release in the hippocampus and cortex during acquisition of an operant behavior. *Brain Res*, 1996. 724: 89.
34. Giovannini, M.G. et al., Effects of novelty and habituation on acetylcholine, GABA, and glutamate release from the frontal cortex and hippocampus of freely moving rats. *Neuroscience*, 2001. 106: 43.
35. Ragozzino, M.E., K.E. Unick, and P.E. Gold, Hippocampal acetylcholine release during memory testing in rats: augmentation by glucose. *Proc Natl Acad Sci USA*, 1996. 93: 4693.

36. Mizuno, T., J. Arita, and F. Kimura, Spontaneous acetylcholine release in the hippocampus exhibits a diurnal variation in both young and old rats. *Neurosci Lett*, 1994. 178: 271.
37. Mitsushima, D., C. Yamanoi, and F. Kimura, Restriction of environmental space attenuates locomotor activity and hippocampal acetylcholine release in male rats. *Brain Res*, 1998. 805: 207.
38. Sei, H. et al., Increase of hippocampal acetylcholine release at the onset of dark phase is suppressed in a mutant mice model of evening-type individuals. *Neuroscience*, 2003. 117: 785.
39. Hasselmo, M.E. and J. McGaughy, High acetylcholine levels set circuit dynamics for attention and encoding and low acetylcholine levels set dynamics for consolidation. *Progr Brain Res*, 2004. 145: 207.
40. Pych, J.C. et al., Acetylcholine release in hippocampus and striatum during testing on a rewarded spontaneous alternation task. *Neurobiol Learn Mem*, 2005. 84: 93.
41. Inglis, F.M. and H.C. Fibiger, Increases in hippocampal and frontal cortical acetylcholine release associated with presentation of sensory stimuli. *Neuroscience*, 1995. 66: 81.
42. Acquas, E., C. Wilson, and H.C. Fibiger, Conditioned and unconditioned stimuli increase frontal cortical and hippocampal acetylcholine release: effects of novelty, habituation, and fear. *J Neurosci*, 1996. 16: 3089.
43. Giovannini, M.G. et al., Acetylcholine release from the frontal cortex during exploratory activity. *Brain Res*, 1998. 784: 218.
44. Gray, J.A. and N. McNaughton, Comparison between the behavioural effects of septal and hippocampal lesions: a review. *Neurosci Biobehav Rev*, 1983. 7: 119.
45. Stewart, M. and S.E. Fox, Do septal neurons pace the hippocampal theta rhythm? *Trends Neurosci*, 1990. 13: 163.
46. Green, J.D. and A.A. Arduini, Hippocampal electrical activity in arousal. *J Neurophysiol*, 1954. 17: 533.
47. Whishaw, I.Q. and C.H. Vanderwolf, Hippocampal EEG and behavior: changes in amplitude and frequency of RSA (theta rhythm) associated with spontaneous and learned movement patterns in rats and cats. *Behav Biol*, 1973. 8: 461.
48. Aloisi, A.M. et al., Effects of novelty, pain and stress on hippocampal extracellular acetylcholine levels in male rats. *Brain Res*, 1997. 748: 219.
49. Ceccarelli, I. et al., Effects of novelty and pain on behavior and hippocampal extracellular ACh levels in male and female rats. *Brain Res*, 1999. 815: 169.
50. Berntson, G.G., M. Sarter, and J.T. Cacioppo, Anxiety and cardiovascular reactivity: the basal forebrain cholinergic link. *Behav Brain Res*, 1998. 94: 225.
51. Miranda, M.I., L. Ramirez-Lugo, and F. Bermudez-Rattoni, Cortical cholinergic activity is related to the novelty of the stimulus. *Brain Res*, 2000. 882: 230.
52. Degroot, A., M.C. Wolff, and G.G. Nomikos, Acute exposure to a novel object during consolidation enhances cognition. *Neuroreport*, 2005. 16: 63.
53. Giovannini, M.G. et al., Inhibition of acetylcholine-induced activation of extracellular regulated protein kinase prevents the encoding of an inhibitory avoidance response in the rat. *Neuroscience*, 2005. 136: 15.
54. Pepeu, G. and P. Blandina, The acetylcholine, GABA, glutamate triangle in the rat forebrain. *J Physiol Paris*, 1998. 92: 351.
55. Rasmusson, D.D., Cholinergic modulation of sensory information. *Progr Brain Res*, 1993. 98: 357.

56. Giovannini, M.G. et al., Differential regulation by N-methyl-D-aspartate and non-N-methyl-D-aspartate receptors of acetylcholine release from the rat striatum *in vivo*. *Neuroscience*, 1995. 65: 409.
57. Moor, E. et al., Involvement of medial septal glutamate and GABAA receptors in behaviour-induced acetylcholine release in the hippocampus: a dual probe microdialysis study. *Brain Res*, 1998. 789: 1.
58. Giovannini, M.G. et al., Glutamatergic regulation of acetylcholine output in different brain regions: a microdialysis study in the rat. *Neurochem Int*, 1994. 25: 23.
59. Giovannini, M.G. et al., NMDA receptor antagonists decrease GABA outflow from the septum and increase acetylcholine outflow from the hippocampus: a microdialysis study. *J Neurosci*, 1994. 14: 1358.
60. Timmerman, W. and B.H. Westerink, Brain microdialysis of GABA and glutamate: what does it signify? *Synapse*, 1997. 27: 242.
61. Bianchi, L. et al., Investigation on acetylcholine, aspartate, glutamate and GABA extracellular levels from ventral hippocampus during repeated exploratory activity in the rat. *Neurochem Res*, 2003. 28: 565.
62. Stark, H., A. Bischof, and H. Scheich, Increase of extracellular dopamine in prefrontal cortex of gerbils during acquisition of the avoidance strategy in the shuttle-box. *Neurosci Lett*, 1999. 264: 77.
63. Stark, H. et al., Stages of avoidance strategy formation in gerbils are correlated with dopaminergic transmission activity. *Eur J Pharmacol*, 2000. 405: 263.
64. Stark, H. et al., Learning a new behavioral strategy in the shuttle-box increases prefrontal dopamine. *Neuroscience*, 2004. 126: 21.
65. Sarter, M. and J.P. Bruno, Cortical cholinergic inputs mediating arousal, attentional processing and dreaming: differential afferent regulation of the basal forebrain by telencephalic and brainstem afferents. *Neuroscience*, 2000. 95: 933.
66. Robbins, T.W. et al., Cognitive enhancers in theory and practice: studies of the cholinergic hypothesis of cognitive deficits in Alzheimer's disease. *Behav Brain Res*, 1997. 83: 15.
67. Ridley, R.M. et al., Further analysis of the effects of immunotoxic lesions of the basal nucleus of Meynert reveals substantial impairment on visual discrimination learning in monkeys. *Brain Res Bull*, 2005. 65: 433.
68. Miranda, M.I. and F. Bermúdez-Rattoni, Reversible inactivation of the nucleus basalis magnocellularis induces disruption of cortical acetylcholine release and acquisition, but not retrieval, of aversive memories. *Proc Natl Acad Sci USA*, 1999. 96: 6478.
69. Nieto-Escamez, F.A., F. Sanchez-Santed, and J.P. de Bruin, Cholinergic receptor blockade in prefrontal cortex and lesions of the nucleus basalis: implications for allocentric and egocentric spatial memory in rats. *Behav Brain Res*, 2002. 134: 93.
70. Arnold, H.M. et al., Differential cortical acetylcholine release in rats performing a sustained attention task versus behavioral control tasks that do not explicitly tax attention. *Neuroscience*, 2002. 114: 451.
71. Casamenti, F. et al., Morphological, biochemical and behavioural changes induced by neurotoxic and inflammatory insults to the nucleus basalis. *Int J Dev Neurosci*, 1998. 16: 705.
72. Bartolini, L., F. Casamenti, and G. Pepeu, Aniracetam restores object recognition impaired by age, scopolamine, and nucleus basalis lesions. *Pharmacol Biochem Behav*, 1996. 53: 277.
73. Flicker, C. et al., Behavioral and neurochemical effects following neurotoxic lesions of a major cholinergic input to the cerebral cortex in the rat. *Pharmacol Biochem Behav*, 1983. 18: 973.

74. Rawlins, J.N. and D.S. Olton, The septo-hippocampal system and cognitive mapping. *Behav Brain Res*, 1982. 5: 331.
75. Heckers, S. et al., Complete and selective cholinergic denervation of rat neocortex and hippocampus but not amygdala by an immunotoxin against the p75 NGF receptor. *J Neurosci*, 1994. 14: 1271.
76. Rossner, S. et al., 192IGG-saporin-induced selective lesion of cholinergic basal forebrain system: neurochemical effects on cholinergic neurotransmission in rat cerebral cortex and hippocampus. *Brain Res Bull*, 1995. 38: 371.
77. Wrenn, C.C. and R.G. Wiley, The behavioral functions of the cholinergic basal forebrain: lessons from 192 IgG-saporin. *Int J Dev Neurosci*, 1998. 16: 595.
78. Leanza, G. et al., Selective immunolesioning of the basal forebrain cholinergic system disrupts short-term memory in rats. *Eur J Neurosci*, 1996. 8: 1535.
79. McDonald, M.P., G.L. Wenk, and J.N. Crawley, Analysis of galanin and the galanin antagonist M40 on delayed non-matching-to-position performance in rats lesioned with the cholinergic immunotoxin 192 IgG-saporin. *Behav Neurosci*, 1997. 111: 552.
80. Leanza, G. et al., Selective lesioning of the basal forebrain cholinergic system by intraventricular 192 IgG-saporin: behavioural, biochemical and stereological studies in the rat. *Eur J Neurosci*, 1995. 7: 329.
81. Shen, J. et al., Differential effects of selective immunotoxic lesions of medial septal cholinergic cells on spatial working and reference memory. *Behav Neurosci*, 1996. 110: 1181.
82. Vnek, N. et al., The basal forebrain cholinergic system and object memory in the rat. *Brain Res*, 1996. 710: 265.
83. Gutierrez, H. et al., Differential effects of 192IgG-saporin and NMDA-induced lesions into the basal forebrain on cholinergic activity and taste aversion memory formation. *Brain Res*, 1999. 834: 136.
84. Stoehr, J.D. et al., The effects of selective cholinergic basal forebrain lesions and aging upon expectancy in the rat. *Neurobiol Learn Mem*, 1997. 67: 214.
85. McGaughy, J., T. Kaiser, and M. Sarter, Behavioral vigilance following infusions of 192 IgG-saporin into the basal forebrain: selectivity of the behavioral impairment and relation to cortical AChE-positive fiber density. *Behav Neurosci*, 1996. 110: 247.
86. Passetti, F. et al., Increased acetylcholine release in the rat medial prefrontal cortex during performance of a visual attentional task. *Eur J Neurosci*, 2000. 12: 3051.
87. Muir, J.L., B.J. Everitt, and T.W. Robbins, The cerebral cortex of the rat and visual attentional function: dissociable effects of mediofrontal, cingulate, anterior dorsolateral, and parietal cortex lesions on a five-choice serial reaction time task. *Cereb Cortex*, 1996. 6: 470.
88. Dalley, J.W. et al., Distinct changes in cortical acetylcholine and noradrenaline efflux during contingent and noncontingent performance of a visual attentional task. *J Neurosci*, 2001. 21: 4908.
89. Himmelheber, A.M., M. Sarter, and J.P. Bruno, Increases in cortical acetylcholine release during sustained attention performance in rats. *Brain Res Cogn Brain Res*, 2000. 9: 313.
90. Bellucci, A. et al., Cholinergic dysfunction, neuronal damage and axonal loss in TgCRND8 mice. *Neurobiol Dis*, 2006.
91. Miranda, M.I. et al., Role of cholinergic system on the construction of memories: taste memory encoding. *Neurobiol Learn Mem*, 2003. 80: 211.
92. Stancampiano, R. et al., Serotonin and acetylcholine release response in the rat hippocampus during a spatial memory task. *Neuroscience*, 1999. 89: 1135.

93. Fadda, F., S. Cocco, and R. Stancampiano, A physiological method to selectively decrease brain serotonin release. *Brain Res Brain Res Protoc*, 2000. 5: 219.
94. Chang, Q. and P.E. Gold, Switching memory systems during learning: changes in patterns of brain acetylcholine release in the hippocampus and striatum in rats. *J Neurosci*, 2003. 23: 3001.
95. Packard, M.G., Glutamate infused posttraining into the hippocampus or caudate putamen differentially strengthens place and response learning. *Proc Natl Acad Sci USA*, 1999. 96: 12881.
96. Packard, M.G. and J.L. McGaugh, Inactivation of hippocampus or caudate nucleus with lidocaine differentially affects expression of place and response learning. *Neurobiol Learn Mem*, 1996. 65: 65.
97. Restle, F., Discrimination of cues in mazes: a resolution of the place-versus-response question. *Psychol Rev*, 1957. 64: 217.
98. Tolman, E.C. and H. Gleitman, Studies in spatial learning; place and response learning under different degrees of motivation. *J Exp Psychol*, 1949. 39: 653.
99. McIntyre, C.K., L.K. Marriott, and P.E. Gold, Patterns of brain acetylcholine release predict individual differences in preferred learning strategies in rats. *Neurobiol Learn Mem*, 2003. 79: 177.
100. Power, A.E., A. Vazdarjanova, and J.L. McGaugh, Muscarinic cholinergic influences in memory consolidation. *Neurobiol Learn Mem*, 2003. 80: 178.
101. Ragozzino, M.E. and R.P. Kesner, The role of the agranular insular cortex in working memory for food reward value and allocentric space in rats. *Behav Brain Res*, 1999. 98: 103.
102. Fadda, F., F. Melis, and R. Stancampiano, Increased hippocampal acetylcholine release during a working memory task. *Eur J Pharmacol*, 1996. 307: R1.
103. Van der Zee, E.A. et al., Alterations in the immunoreactivity for muscarinic acetylcholine receptors and colocalized PKC gamma in mouse hippocampus induced by spatial discrimination learning. *Hippocampus*, 1995. 5: 349.
104. Liu, D. et al., Maternal care, hippocampal synaptogenesis and cognitive development in rats. *Nat Neurosci*, 2000. 3: 799.
105. Marriott, L.K. and D.L. Korol, Short-term estrogen treatment in ovariectomized rats augments hippocampal acetylcholine release during place learning. *Neurobiol Learn Mem*, 2003. 80: 315.
106. Masuda, J. et al., Sex and housing conditions affect the 24-h acetylcholine release profile in the hippocampus in rats. *Neuroscience*, 2005. 132: 537.
107. Takase, K. et al., Feeding with powdered diet after weaning affects sex difference in acetylcholine release in the hippocampus in rats. *Neuroscience*, 2005. 136: 593.
108. Baratti, C.M. et al., Memory facilitation with posttrial injection of oxotremorine and physostigmine in mice. *Psychopharmacology* (Berlin), 1979. 64: 85.
109. Kopf, S.R. and C.M. Baratti, Memory modulation by posttraining glucose or insulin remains evident at long retention intervals. *Neurobiol Learn Mem*, 1996. 65: 189.
110. Kopf, S.R., M.M. Boccia, and C.M. Baratti, AF-DX 116, a presynaptic muscarinic receptor antagonist, potentiates the effects of glucose and reverses the effects of insulin on memory. *Neurobiol Learn Mem*, 1998. 70: 305.
111. Rudy, J.W., Scopolamine administered before and after training impairs both contextual and auditory-cue fear conditioning. *Neurobiol Learn Mem*, 1996. 65: 73.
112. Schroeder, J.P. and M.G. Packard, Posttraining intra-basolateral amygdala scopolamine impairs food- and amphetamine-induced conditioned place preferences. *Behav Neurosci*, 2002. 116: 922.

113. Izquierdo, I., Mechanism of action of scopolamine as an amnestic. *Trends Pharmacol Sci*, 1989. 10: 175.
114. Izquierdo, I., Different forms of posttraining memory processing. *Behav Neural Biol*, 1989. 51: 171.
115. Izquierdo, I. and J.H. Medina, Memory formation: the sequence of biochemical events in the hippocampus and its connection to activity in other brain structures. *Neurobiol Learn Mem*, 1997. 68: 285.
116. Wilensky, A.E., G.E. Schafe, and J.E. LeDoux, The amygdala modulates memory consolidation of fear-motivated inhibitory avoidance learning but not classical fear conditioning. *J Neurosci*, 2000. 20: 7059.
117. Giovannini, M.G. et al., Effects of histamine H3 receptor agonists and antagonists on cognitive performance and scopolamine-induced amnesia. *Behav Brain Res*, 1999. 104: 147.
118. Izquierdo, I. et al., Differential involvement of cortical receptor mechanisms in working, short-term and long-term memory. *Behav Pharmacol*, 1998. 9: 421.
119. McGaugh, J.L. and I. Izquierdo, The contribution of pharmacology to research on the mechanisms of memory formation. *Trends Pharmacol Sci*, 2000. 21: 208.
120. Barros, D.M. et al., Bupropion and sertraline enhance retrieval of recent and remote long-term memory in rats. *Behav Pharmacol*, 2002. 13: 215.
121. Izquierdo, I. et al., Short- and long-term memory are differentially regulated by monoaminergic systems in the rat brain. *Neurobiol Learn Mem*, 1998. 69: 219.
122. Smythe, J.W. et al., The effects of intrahippocampal scopolamine infusions on anxiety in rats as measured by the black-white box test. *Brain Res Bull,* 1998. 45: 89.
123. Nakamura, A. et al., Dietary restriction of choline reduces hippocampal acetylcholine release in rats: *in vivo* microdialysis study. *Brain Res Bull*, 2001. 56: 593.
124. Passani, M.B. et al., Central histaminergic system and cognition. *Neurosci Biobehav Rev*, 2000. 24: 107.
125. Cangioli, I. et al., Activation of histaminergic H3 receptors in the rat basolateral amygdala improves expression of fear memory and enhances acetylcholine release. *Eur J Neurosci*, 2002. 16: 521.
126. Umegaki, H. et al., Involvement of dopamine D(2) receptors in complex maze learning and acetylcholine release in ventral hippocampus of rats. *Neuroscience*, 2001. 103: 27.
127. Young, A.M., M.H. Joseph, and J.A. Gray, Latent inhibition of conditioned dopamine release in rat nucleus accumbens. *Neuroscience*, 1993. 54: 5.
128. Gray, J.A. et al., Latent inhibition: the nucleus accumbens connection revisited. *Behav Brain Res*, 1997. 88: 27.
129. Young, A.M. et al., Increased extracellular dopamine in the nucleus accumbens of the rat during associative learning of neutral stimuli. *Neuroscience*, 1998. 83: 1175.
130. Young, A.M. and K.R. Rees, Dopamine release in the amygdaloid complex of the rat, studied by brain microdialysis. *Neurosci Lett*, 1998. 249: 49.
131. Fujishiro, H. et al., Dopamine D2 receptor plays a role in memory function: implications of dopamine-acetylcholine interaction in the ventral hippocampus. *Psychopharmacology* (Berlin), 2005. 182: 253.
132. Ragozzino, M.E. et al., Modulation of hippocampal acetylcholine release and spontaneous alternation scores by intrahippocampal glucose injections. *J Neurosci*, 1998. 18: 1595.
133. Gold, P.E., Role of glucose in regulating the brain and cognition. *Am J Clin Nutr*, 1995. 61: 987S.
134. Gold, P.E., J. Vogt, and J.L. Hall, Glucose effects on memory: behavioral and pharmacological characteristics. *Behav Neural Biol*, 1986. 46: 145.

135. Ragozzino, M.E., G.L. Wenk, and P.E. Gold, Glucose attenuates a morphine-induced decrease in hippocampal acetylcholine output: an *in vivo* microdialysis study in rats. *Brain Res*, 1994. 655: 77.
136. Ragozzino, M.E. and P.E. Gold, Glucose injections into the medial septum reverse the effects of intraseptal morphine infusions on hippocampal acetylcholine output and memory. *Neuroscience*, 1995. 68: 981.
137. McGaugh, J.L., C.K. McIntyre, and A.E. Power, Amygdala modulation of memory consolidation: interaction with other brain systems. *Neurobiol Learn Mem*, 2002. 78: 539.
138. Power, A.E. and J.L. McGaugh, Cholinergic activation of the basolateral amygdala regulates unlearned freezing behavior in rats. *Behav Brain Res*, 2002. 134: 307.
139. Sah, P. et al., The amygdaloid complex: anatomy and physiology. *Physiol Rev*, 2003. 83: 803.
140. Garcia, R. et al., The amygdala modulates prefrontal cortex activity relative to conditioned fear. *Nature*, 1999. 402: 294.
141. McIntyre, C.K. et al., Role of the basolateral amygdala in memory consolidation. *Ann NY Acad Sci*, 2003. 985: 273.
142. Williams, C.L. et al., Norepinephrine release in the amygdala after systemic injection of epinephrine or escapable footshock: contribution of the nucleus of the solitary tract. *Behav Neurosci*, 1998. 112: 1414.
143. Galvez, R., M.H. Mesches, and J.L. McGaugh, Norepinephrine release in the amygdala in response to footshock stimulation. *Neurobiol Learn Mem*, 1996. 66: 253.
144. McIntyre, C.K., T. Hatfield, and J.L. McGaugh, Amygdala norepinephrine levels after training predict inhibitory avoidance retention performance in rats. *Eur J Neurosci*, 2002. 16: 1223.
145. Hassert, D.L., T. Miyashita, and C.L. Williams, The effects of peripheral vagal nerve stimulation at a memory-modulating intensity on norepinephrine output in the basolateral amygdala. *Behav Neurosci*, 2004. 118: 79.
146. Clayton, E.C. and C.L. Williams, Adrenergic activation of the nucleus tractus solitarius potentiates amygdala norepinephrine release and enhances retention performance in emotionally arousing and spatial memory tasks. *Behav Brain Res*, 2000. 112: 151.
147. Tronel, S., M.G. Feenstra, and S.J. Sara, Noradrenergic action in prefrontal cortex in the late stage of memory consolidation. *Learn Mem*, 2004. 11: 453.
148. Arnsten, A.F. et al., Noradrenergic influences on prefrontal cortical cognitive function: opposing actions at postjunctional alpha 1 versus alpha 2-adrenergic receptors. *Adv Pharmacol*, 1998. 42: 764.
149. Mantz, J. et al., Differential effects of ascending neurons containing dopamine and noradrenaline in the control of spontaneous activity and of evoked responses in the rat prefrontal cortex. *Neuroscience*, 1988. 27: 517.
150. Kawaguchi, Y. and T. Shindou, Noradrenergic excitation and inhibition of GABAergic cell types in rat frontal cortex. *J Neurosci*, 1998. 18: 6963.
151. Maren, S., Synaptic mechanisms of associative memory in the amygdala. *Neuron*, 2005. 47: 783.
152. Lynch, M.A., Long-term potentiation and memory. *Physiol Rev*, 2004. 84: 87.
153. Martin, S.J., P.D. Grimwood, and R.G. Morris, Synaptic plasticity and memory: an evaluation of the hypothesis. *Annu Rev Neurosci*, 2000. 23: 649.
154. Szapiro, G. et al., Facilitation and inhibition of retrieval in two aversive tasks in rats by intrahippocampal infusion of agonists of specific glutamate metabotropic receptor subtypes. *Psychopharmacology* (Berlin), 2001. 156: 397.

155. Miyashita, T. and C.L. Williams, Glutamatergic transmission in the nucleus of the solitary tract modulates memory through influences on amygdala noradrenergic systems. *Behav Neurosci*, 2002. 116: 13.
156. Bielavska, E., I. Miksik, and J. Krivanek, Glutamate in the parabrachial nucleus of rats during conditioned taste aversion. *Brain Res*, 2000. 887: 413.
157. Vales, K., P. Zach, and E. Bielavska, Metabotropic glutamate receptor antagonists but not NMDA antagonists affect conditioned taste aversion acquisition in the parabrachial nucleus of rats. *Exp Brain Res*, 2006. 169: 50.
158. Miranda, M.I. et al., Glutamatergic activity in the amygdala signals visceral input during taste memory formation. *Proc Natl Acad Sci USA*, 2002. 99: 11417.
159. Sanchez-Andrade, G., B.M. James, and K.M. Kendrick, Neural encoding of olfactory recognition memory. *J Reprod Dev*, 2005. 51: 547.
160. Brennan, P.A., K.M. Kendrick, and E.B. Keverne, Neurotransmitter release in the accessory olfactory bulb during and after the formation of an olfactory memory in mice. *Neuroscience*, 1995. 69: 1075.
161. Nilsson, O.G. et al., Acetylcholine release in the rat hippocampus as studied by microdialysis is dependent on axonal impulse flow and increases during behavioural activation. *Neuroscience*, 1990. 36: 3258.
162. Rosenblad, C. and O.G. Nilsson, Basal forebrain grafts in the rat neocortex restore in vivo acetylcholine release and respond to behavioural activation. *Neuroscience*, 1993. 55: 353.
163. Imperato, A. et al., Changes in brain dopamine and acetylcholine release during and following stress are independent of the pituitary–adrenocortical axis. *Brain Res*, 1991. 538: 111.
164. Taylor, B.K. and A.I. Basbaum, Neurochemical characterization of extracellular serotonin in the rostral ventromedial medulla and its modulation by noxious stimuli. *J Neurochem*, 1995. 65: 578.
165. Jenden, D.J. et al., Acetylcholine turnover estimation in brain by gas chromatography-mass spectrometry. *Life Sci*, 1974. 14: 55.
166. Scali, C. et al., Effect of metrifonate on extracellular brain acetylcholine and object recognition in aged rats. *Eur J Pharmacol*, 1997. 325: 173.

8 Reversible Inactivation of Brain Circuits in Learning and Memory Research

Milagros Gallo

CONTENTS

8.1 INTRODUCTION

The field of learning and memory has benefited from reversible brain interventions since they were introduced more than four decades ago.[1,2] Progress in developing a variety of reversible inactivation procedures has led to a wide array of potent tools that now allow us to investigate different levels of learning and organization of brain memory processes. As noted in the literature,[3] the complexity and variety of processes involved in learning and memory require a complex approach to advance the understanding of the relevant neurobiological mechanisms. Although much progress has been made at the molecular and cellular levels, a complete picture will be only attained by advancing knowledge of the functional organization of learning and memory brain circuits at the system level, which it is also recognized as the most difficult approach.[4]

Limitations of the available techniques for undergoing a lesion approach in the field may contribute to the difficulties. This chapter will address the advantages and limitations of reversible inactivation techniques for research on the neural substrate of learning and memory at the system level. Thus, results of reversible manipulations aimed to explore the molecular mechanisms of learning and memory will not be considered because extensive reviews[5–9] are available on specific topics.

Since the seminal work of Bures and Buresova[10] inactivating wide brain regions to dissociate sensory and associative processes in taste aversion learning and also investigating interhemispheric transfer of memory traces, a range of procedures for temporary inactivation of discrete brain sites has been developed and applied to learning and memory research. Several reviews centering upon different learning procedures have been published in the past decade and show the value of the reversible inactivation approach for advancing knowledge in the field.[11,13,14,37] This chapter does not intend to be a comprehensive review of the knowledge gained using reversible inactivation approaches, but will show representative issues that have benefited from this approach, thus leading to a better knowledge of the brain organization of learning and memory processes at the system level. The need for careful interpretation of the behavioral results based on the specific brain changes induced by the currently available reversible inactivation techniques will be stressed.

8.2 BRAIN LESION APPROACH AND DYNAMIC NATURE OF LEARNING AND MEMORY SYSTEMS

The brain creates representations of the world based on the information received through the sensory systems. Learning depends on the plastic properties of brain circuits that are able to undergo functional reorganization to adjust the representation of the world in response to ongoing changes of relevant incoming information. Memory consists of the processes involved in the maintenance of the effects induced in the brain by the learning process. Learning systems are able to detect and modify accordingly, not only to changes in the various features of a specific stimulus, but also to changes involving the relationships among stimuli and between responses and consequences. Thus, from a conceptual view, different types of learning can be considered. Based on the variety of learning procedures and various types of memory,[15] dissociable brain circuits are responsible of different forms of memory. Therefore, as noted, memory is defined by the properties of brain circuits subserving the neural changes induced by learning experiences.[16,17]

The first step toward understanding the brain organization of learning and memory is to identify the particular brain circuit that contains the site or sites forming and retaining the memory traces induced by a specific learning experience. As plasticity is a widespread property of neurons, these sites may be located at different levels of the brain organization. In addition to the plastic brain sites, the brain circuits necessary for the basic aspects of learning include the input and output circuits that are also modified by the learning experience. This "essential memory trace circuit"[17] may be dissociated from other brain areas that may also show learning-related plastic changes but are not necessary for basic learning.

Locating the essential brain circuits subserving different forms of learning has benefited from the lesion approach. Brain lesions allow us to identify the brain sites necessary for learning and memory. Other approaches are required for unraveling the specific roles of particular brain sites in the circuit and for identifying brain areas that may be involved but are not required in a learning situation. A problem for the lesion approach is that learning and memory-related changes can only be assessed by behavioral changes. Thus, a given learning situation involves not only learning and memory processes but also sensory, performance, arousal, attentional, motivational, and emotional processes. A brain lesion disrupting any of these processes can lead to similar impaired performance in a retrieval test. Thereafter, for attributing a crucial role in memory to a specific brain site using the lesion approach, it is necessary to discard its potential involvement in other required processes. Additionally, the lack of a given lesion effect may be attributed to a recovery of function due to damage-induced brain reorganization.[18]

Nevertheless, research using permanent lesions has contributed to draw a rather complex picture of the anatomical organization of the learning and memory systems of the brain. It has been shown that different types of learning depend on dissociable distributed brain circuits formed by areas located at different brain levels. Moreover, independent learning circuits may share components as well as modulatory actions by higher-order brain circuits. Interactions among dissociable brain circuits add complexity to this general picture. Also, memory may involve additional brain sites beyond those initially modified by the learning experience.

However, this static picture does not allow us to fully understand the functional architecture of learning and memory systems. Learning and memory consist of time-dependent dynamic processes. Various successive stages of learning such as acquisition, consolidation, retention, retrieval, reactivation, and extinction may be dissociated. Even these conceptually defined stages are not unitary and include independent processes. As these processes take place successively, permanent lesions may not be able to dissociate them, even if applied at different times in a learning situation. The disruption of different processes that takes place after a lesion could equally explain memory impairment induced by permanent damage of a particular brain site. Moreover, the same brain site may have independent roles in different learning stages, which cannot be evidenced by permanent lesions.

Reversible inactivation techniques solve some of these problems, because they allow a particular brain area to be inactivated during a particular stage, being fully functional during later stages. On the one hand, depending on the behavioral procedure and type of learning studied, a reversible lesion may be able to dissociate learning from sensory and performance processes. On the other hand, the specific contribution of a particular brain site to one stage, but not to another, may be unveiled by selective disruption at a specific time window.[10] Moreover, if the same area is required to be functional at different stages, several independent roles may be envisaged. A related issue that may benefit from reversible inactivation techniques is dissociating brain circuits subserving different but temporally overlapping learning processes.[11] This is the case of retrieval and extinction, because each retrieval test represents also an extinction session. Reversible inactivation allows us to explore the independent role of a given brain site on extinction by later testing on a functionally intact brain. Similar or different outcomes of the functional inactivation in retrieval and extinction would lead to valuable hypotheses concerning the brain areas involved.

In all, reversible inactivation techniques represent valuable tools for exploring not only the temporal organization of the processes involved in learning and memory, but also the structural organization of independent but overlapping learning circuits contributing to the observed outcomes.

8.3 REVERSIBLE INACTIVATION TECHNIQUES

There are a number of procedures for reversible brain inactivation since it can block the neural function by interfering with it at different levels. The spatial and temporal parameters of inactivation depend on the technique applied, thus affecting the application to system studies of learning and memory. A variety of enzyme inhibitors have been used to dissect the molecular mechanisms of learning and memory, but reviewing these techniques is beyond the scope of this chapter.[5–9]

8.3.1 Transcranial Magnetic Stimulation

First used as a technique to measure the conduction times of motor pathways, transcranial magnetic stimulation (TMS) is a noninvasive technique that may have various applications in humans.[19–21] In addition to its application as an essay similar to the Wada test or electrical cortical stimulation in patients candidates for brain surgery, TMS may be used as a tool for creating reversible lesions. Although the action mechanisms of TMS on neuronal activity are not well understood, it may interfere with the ongoing pattern of activity with high precision timing. In single-pulse studies (duration of magnetic stimulus <1 msec) it induces neurophysiological effects lasting up to 100 msec. In repetitive TMS trains with frequencies of 1 to 25 Hz and a duration from hundreds of milliseconds to seconds, the interfering effects last throughout the stimulation and may persist at least 1 hour following magnetic stimulation in memory studies.[22]

Longer-lasting effects that may have applications in the treatment of depression are being explored.[19,20,23] It has been calculated that TMS penetrates no deeper than 2 cm from the surface of the scalp and therefore induces focal changes of brain activity only in the area of the cortex directly underneath the coil. However, studies combining TMS and neuroimaging have shown that the effect spread to adjacent areas within 5 to 10 msec and to homologous regions in the opposite hemisphere within 20 msec.[22] Cortical and subcortical distal areas that are connected with the affected area also showed changes in blood flow.[21,24]

8.3.2 Cryogenic Inactivation Techniques

Cooling a brain site at around 20°C induces a neuronal block surrounded by a concentric hyperexcitable area at 30°C at the periphery of the inactivated lesion.[25] Depending on the temperature reduction, either synaptic transmission affecting the cell bodies or axonal conduction may be blocked. Local neuronal activity and synaptic transmission, but not axonal conduction, seem to be blocked if tissue temperature is kept between 8.5 and 20°C.[60] Cryogenic techniques allow a high precision control over the inactivation onset, duration, and recovery. A complete block can be induced within a few minutes, be maintained for minutes to hours, and readily terminated in minutes. Cryogenic techniques also permit repeating the inactivation of a constant extent area several times in a 24-hour period without affecting reversibility.

Minor deterioration of the tissue has been identified only when the tissue is cooled and rewarmed more than 40 times in a 12-hour period.[27,28] The extent of the inactivation depends on the specific technique used. Inactivating deep brain structures require implanting cryotips — small devices formed by two stainless steel tubes.[26,29,30] The inner tube delivers the coolant at the tip of the probe, which is insulated or even warmed to avoid unspecific cooling of the overlying brain tissue. While the tip of a cryoprobe was kept at 4.0 to 5.0°C, the brain temperature recorded at a distance of 0.5 mm was 7.0 to 10.0°C. It raised to 21.0 to 22.0°C at a distance of 1 mm and reached 32°C at a distance of 1.5 mm.[26] The effect did not extend beyond 2.0 mm; temperature recorded at this distance was normal. The main drawbacks of cryogenic techniques are the complex technical requirements and the fact that the cooling probe is thicker than the injection cannula used for pharmacological techniques, thus inducing damage to a greater extent in the overlying brain tissue.

8.3.3 Pharmacological Techniques

Inactivating a brain site by injecting pharmacological agents can be accomplished via two main methods: (1) sodium channel blockers such as tetrodotoxin (TTX) and local anesthetics that prevent initiation and transmission of action potentials both in cell bodies and axons, and (2) agonists and antagonists of neurotransmitters that interfere with neuronal activity at the synaptic level. Both require delivering the pharmacological agent through injection cannulae connected to microsyringes driven by injection pumps.[25]

The injection cannula may be inserted in chronically implanted guiding cannulae in most behavioral studies. For deep brain areas, the microinjection procedure allows more deactivation of smaller regions than the previous techniques and damage to the overlying tissue is minimized due to the smaller diameter of the injection cannula. The possibility of permanent damage due to tissue displacement is minimized by controlling the drug volume (typically a maximum of 1 μl) and infusion rate (1 μl/60 sec has been widely used but lower rates around 1 μl/90 sec minimum are recommended). Although it is possible to apply repeated injections, the spread of the agent may be variable and mechanical damage to the overlying tissue may be enhanced due to repeated insertions of the injection cannula.[25] Moreover, in certain brain regions, the repeated administration of some agents may cause permanent damage.[28] The tissue elements inactivated and temporal parameters of the inactivation vary, depending on the agent injected.

8.3.3.1 Sodium Channel Blockers

Sodium channel blockers prevent neuronal transmission both in cell bodies and fibers passing throughout the area, inducing both local and distant effects. They may be applied for inactivating any brain region because sodium channels are present in all parts of the nervous system. Both TTX and local anesthetics have been widely used.

The spatiotemporal extent of TTX-induced inactivation has been calculated for different dosages and brain sites. Zhuravin and Bures[31] reported that 1 μl of TTX (10 ng) injected into the Edinger/Westphal nucleus blocked a spherical volume of tissue about 3 mm in diameter, with a maximum effect lasting 2 hours and decaying during the subsequent 20 hours. These results were in accordance with those obtained by Harlan et al.[32] who monitored lordosis and other reflexes following a similar dosage of TTX in female rats. Intrahypothalamic TTX injections suppressed multiunit activity completely within 6 min, and this suppression lasted at least several hours. Reduced lordotic responsiveness was evident 40 min after the injection and peaked 2 to 4 hours later; complete recovery required 12 to 24 hours.

In a later study using the same response, Rothfeld et al.[33] reported that TTX injections in the dorsal midbrain reduced responsiveness within 2 min following TTX injection and lasted up to 8 hours. Klement et al.[34] found that 5 ng/μl TTX injected in the dorsal hippocampus reduced spontaneous local field potentials within 3 min and abolished synaptic and population responses evoked by stimulation of the perforant pathway at sites 2 mm away from the TTX infusion point. The diffusion of TTX, estimated by injecting 5% India ink solution did not exceed a radius of 1.4 mm, which is in agreement with previous findings.

Local anesthetics include both amides such as lidocaine, and esters such as procaine. They have shorter induction and inactivation times than TTX due to rapid enzymatic breakdown. For lidocaine, the blockade duration may last from 15 min to 1 hour, depending on the dosage and much longer (up to 90 minutes) in fiber tracts. The usual range is 20 to 40 ng in 1 μl for single injection studies. Autoradiographic assessment in cortical tissue has shown that the maximum spread takes place within 10 to 15 min, achieving a radius of 1.5 to 2 mm.[25] Glucose uptake and metabolism monitoring has indicated hypometabolism in an extensive area of 3 mm which doubles the area where the drug level declines. Thus, reduced synaptic activity of neurons efferent from the inactivated site may explain it.

Boehnke and Rasmusson[35] compared the extent and duration of the neuronal inactivation induced by TTX (10 μM) and lidocaine (10%) delivered via microdialysis in the somatosensory cortex. Electrophysiological recordings of sensory-evoked potentials indicated that TTX induced a more complete neural blockade (60%) over a wider radius than lidocaine (2 and 1 mm, respectively). Responses recovered within

40 min at 0.5 mm after lidocaine infusion while they remained at least 2 hours after TTX infusion. Differences in metabolism, removal mechanisms, and relative binding strengths may explain these differences.[35]

8.3.3.2 Agonists and Antagonists of Neurotransmitter Receptors

The use of agonists and antagonists of neurotransmitter receptors provides useful techniques for inactivating specific brain systems and regions. The infusion of neurotransmitter receptor agonists and antagonists in a particular brain area has the advantage of temporary inactivation of the local neurons, avoiding fibers of passage.

A comparison of permanent and reversible lesions that equate neurotoxic lesions and neurotransmitter agonists and antagonists versus electrolytic lesions and lidocaine or TTX in terms of tissue affected has been established.[14] For specific brain regions such as the hippocampus, antagonists of the main excitatory transmitter receptors such as glutamate may block neuronal activity in the area. However GABA-A receptor agonists that hyperpolarize neurons, preventing action potential generation, are good choices for most brain sites because GABA-A receptors have a wide distribution in the central nervous system.

The glutamate AMPA/kainate receptor antagonist LY326225 has been applied for reversible inactivation of the hippocampus in a study that examined the extent and time course of functional inactivation. Dentate gyrus field potentials in response to perforant pathway stimulation or CA1 potentials in response to stimulation of the homotopic contralateral CA1 region were monitored. Acute infusions (1 μl; 1.5 mM) reduced 90% extracellular field potentials in 4 to 6 hours. Chronic infusions (0.375 mM) through osmotic minipumps for 7 days abruptly decreased the fast synaptic transmission that returned within 1 day of pump exhaustion.[14] The extent of the inactivation was measured with 2-DG autoradiography during and after drug infusion. The results showed that dorsal hippocampus (CA1-CA3 and dentate gyrus), but not ventral hippocampus, showed reduced glucose utilization. The reversibility of the inactivation was demonstrated by the fact that normal levels of glucose utilization were recorded after a 7-day inactivation.

The GABA-A agonist muscimol is the most common agonist in reversible inactivation studies. Unlike the short-lasting blockade induced by GABA with a duration similar to those of local anesthetics, the effects of muscimol persist for 12 to 24 hours.[25] This can be attributed to the multiple mechanisms for clearing unbound GABA from synapses and the fact that muscimol has a higher affinity and bonds more tightly to GABA-A receptors. Thus muscimol is either immediately bound to local GABA receptors or is taken up locally by glia.[25]

Drug spread measured by autoradiography and spatial extent of inactivation monitored by local glucose uptake and metabolism was similar for muscimol and lidocaine.[25] Muscimol produced a local block of neuronal firing by hyperpolarization. However, this does not preclude the induction of distal effects on remote brain areas connected with the inactivated site. Both these effects should be taken into account for an accurate interpretation of effects of muscimol injections on behavior. In order to dissociate both local and distant effects, agents such as muscimol that act at the synaptic level and those such as TTX that disrupt axonal transmission are usually applied.[17,36]

8.3.4 Protein Synthesis Blockers

Disregarding specific enzyme inhibitors that inactivate particular molecular cascades, a variety of protein synthesis blockers administered to specific brain sites have been applied to induce transient metabolic lesions. Anisomycin is the most used inhibitor of protein synthesis used in learning and memory studies, although other inhibitors such as puromycin and cycloheximide are also used. Anisomycin is considered a relatively specific inhibitor that blocks the peptidyl transferase reaction in ribosomes.[27] It has been reported that local anisomycin injections in the gustatory cortex, but not intraventricular injections, reduced protein synthesis more than 90% as assessed by injection of [^{35}S] methionine. The inhibition increased rapidly in the first 20 min and lasted for 90 min, slowly decaying in the next 240 min. The effect was localized, affecting tissue with a radius smaller than 2 mm.[37]

8.3.5 Genetic Inactivation Techniques

A similar reversible lesion approach at the system level by inactivating a particular gene in learning and memory has become possible nowadays through the development of mouse genetic manipulation techniques. The use of region-specific inducible knockouts solves some of the problems posed by conventional knockout mice and affecting all tissues and life stages.[38] By temporarily switching off a particular gene in a specific brain region of the adult mouse, ontogenesis is left undisturbed and brain circuits involved in sensory and motor processes may be spared, thus, facilitating the interpretation of the behavioral outcome.

However, this technique presented difficulties related to the mutant mice generation method, requiring at least four independent mutant mouse strains in order to generate the final knockout mice. Moreover, the temporal resolution of the inactivation may not adjust to the time scale of some learning and memory processes. Most knockouts of gene expression take hours to days after beginning the treatment with the inducer and several days of inducer withdrawal may be required for restoring the gene expression.[38] Cui et al.[39] reported that the knockout of NMDAR function in inducible, reversible, forebrain-specific NMDAR1 knockout (iFB-KO) mice occurred 5 days after feeding the animals with food containing the inducer doxycycline. This long delay is due to the time required for the previously made NMDAR to be degraded, because the inducer readily switches off the transgene expression. Thus, a new approach has been applied to generate mutant transgenic mice expressing inhibitors that compete with the natural form by inactivating a target molecule at the protein level.[38]

Josselyn et al.[40] reported a delay of 6 hours for CREB disruption after tamoxifen administration in transgenic mice that reversibly expressed a dominant negative form of CREB in the forebrain. In the absence of the inducer, the CREB repressor is inactive, but when active it competes with the endogenous CREB disrupting CREB-mediated transcription. Wang et al.[41] were able to inactivate and activate CAMKII with a high temporal resolution in a range of minutes by generating a transgenic mouse strain with a modified protein containing a silent structural mutation that creates an artificial site so that a synthesized ATP inhibitor can bind to it. According to the pharmacokinetics, the inhibitor enters the brain 3 to 5 min after i.p. injection and reaches peak brain levels at 20 min, decreasing to basal level in 45 min. A single i.p. injection of the inhibitor completely suppressed kinase activity for the following 8 to 35 min. Chronic oral intake in drinking water induced partial inhibition by 6 hours and complete suppression after 24 hours. This inhibition can be maintained without observable side effects and it is easily reversed within 2 days after withdrawal of the inhibitor.

8.3.6 Advantages and Limitations of Reversible Inactivation Techniques

Certain issues should be taken into account for the selection of the technique to be applied and the interpretation of the behavioral outcomes in learning and memory studies. First, although the particular neuronal mechanisms interfered with may be different, all the techniques mentioned share the abrupt disruption of a specific site, which induces a completely different brain state affecting also distal areas. This represents an advantage because circuit reorganization does not seem to play a relevant role in reversible lesions because no permanent damage occurs.[34] However, the altered brain state induced by the abrupt local functional inactivation may affect learning and memory. It is well-known that both retrieval and extinction are context-dependent processes, being either external or internal.

The learned response may be under the control of contextual cues present during acquisition or extinction. In state-dependent learning, the relevant contextual cue is usually a centrally acting drug such as ethanol or morphine,[42] but altered brain activity induced by epilepsy has also been proposed to play a role.[43] The absence of the drug during the test day impairs memory retrieval following pre-training administration of drugs. This impairment may be reversed by pre-test administration of a dose similar to that applied during training.

Drug-induced state-dependent learning is well documented in different species from *C. elegans*[44] to humans.[42] Thus, the absence of the CR during retrieval with an intact brain following inactivation of a given brain site during acquisition could be attributed to a state-dependent learning impairment rather than a disruption of the acquisition processes. A similar explanation may account for retrieval deficits following pretesting inactivation of a brain site that was intact during acquisition. Control groups demonstrating that a similar inactivation in different areas or different learning tasks does not induce a similar impairment are required for excluding such an effect. Additionally, the altered brain state may have aversive properties, thus being able to act as an unconditioned stimulus. This is an important issue as aversive learning protocols are widely used for studying brain memory circuits. Demonstrating no aversive properties of the brain intervention is required if the results show intact conditioned responses.[45]

The second issue is that most of the techniques mentioned require stereotaxic surgery and infusion procedures. These procedures have the great advantage of allowing access to deep brain sites but show limitations regarding both the precision of the brain intervention and behavioral consequences. In addition to the issues shared with permanent lesions, stereotaxic and infusion procedures raise specific concerns in reversible inactivation studies. On the one hand, the current development of stereotaxic procedures permits limited spatial precision in target locations that vary among subjects. In permanent lesion studies, subsequent histological analysis of the damage area overcomes this limitation. However, only the location of the injection device track can be assessed in reversible inactivation studies, unless additional staining procedures are added. In fact, most of the reversible inactivation studies aimed to monitor the extent of the deactivated area have been performed in independent groups of animals. Variability of the infusion point location is increased in pharmacological studies if repeated injections in the same animal are required, because only the guiding cannula, but not the injection cannula, remains in place during the interval between infusions.

On the other hand, microinfusion procedures are also great sources of variability. Unless the injected volume and infusion rate are carefully controlled, variability among subjects can be expected due to unnoticed occlusion of the injection cannula as it is advanced through the brain because the tubing connecting the microsyringe and the infusion device can expand slightly.[25] Additionally, unnoticed changes in the rate and the volume of the injection may induce irreversible tissue trauma that can be detected by subsequent histological analysis.

With respect to the behavioral effects of infusion procedure, the possibility that the procedure may provide contextual cues should be considered. A role for the i.p. injection cues has been proposed in other learning phenomena.[46,47] Whenever appropriate, and depending on the technique used, previous habituation to the injection procedure or applying control vehicle injections can be an appropriate control procedure.[48] A further issue is the time that infusion takes, that may exclude detecting short-lasting changes involved in learning and memory.[8] Infusion usually takes about 3 min and the drug remains in the target area for several minutes before diffusion.

Finally, a third issue concerns the reversibility of the brain inactivation that represents the advantage of the mentioned techniques. On the one hand, the choice of the inactivation technique will depend on the estimated duration of the process under study. However, the temporal parameters of the transient inactivation cannot be established precisely with most techniques. Individual variability should be also taken into account. Thus, as the temporal parameters of hidden learning and memory processes are not always well known, careful interpretation of negative results is needed. Conversely, the advantage of reversible techniques for applying within-subject designs[28] may be limited by restrictions imposed in repeating the intervention. Depending on the brain area and the particular technique applied, the risk of a decreased effect or permanent damage after repeated inactivation should be considered.

In all, a good knowledge of the brain and behavioral effects of the reversible inactivation techniques available is required for the advantages that they bring to the study of learning and memory brain systems to be most useful.

8.4 LEARNING BEHAVIORAL MODELS AND REVERSIBLE INACTIVATION TECHNIQUES

Considering that the functional brain architecture underlying memory is complex because it is formed by a variety of dissociable brain circuits that may interact, a choice strategy for applying the reversible approach reducing alternative interpretation may be to use simple learning procedures inducing robust learned responses that are not easily disrupted by nonspecific effects of transient brain inactivation. Previous knowledge of the behavioral parameters and well-defined sensory and performance pathways involved in the particular learning type will facilitate the experimental design and the interpretation of the reversible inactivation effects.

This is the case of eyeblink classical conditioning, one of the best defined procedures of learning at the behavioral and neurobiological levels, which benefits from the reversible inactivation approach. Eyeblink conditioning has the advantage of depending on brain plastic sites located outside the main sensory and motor pathways. The anatomical dissociation of these processes eliminates some of the interpretation problems using the lesion approach. However, permanent lesions cannot dissociate the specific role of a given brain site in the learning process. Instead, learning and performance deficits would lead to similar outcomes.

The use of one-trial learning procedures provides two main advantages when applying reversible inactivation techniques. First, the acquisition process is localized more precisely in time, making easier to dissociate acquisition and retrieval. Second, the use of one-trial learning protocols reduces the number of brain inactivation periods required, thus avoiding the problems related to repeated blocking in most of the inactivation techniques. Extensive research applying the reversible inactivation approach to inhibitory avoidance learning,[12,13] fear conditioning,[49–51] and taste aversion learning[10,11] has achieved fruitful results. In fact, inactivation of a critical learning brain site during the acquisition stage using one-trial learning should lead to impaired CR during a subsequent retrieval test after inactivation removal. However, no effect should appear if the inactivated site is only involved in performance.

An additional advantage is the possibility of temporally separating sensory and learning processes during acquisition such as in taste aversion learning which permits long delays in ranges of minutes or even hours between the conditioned stimulus (CS) and the unconditioned stimulus (US). Thus, inactivation of a given brain area may be applied after taste processing, leaving the brain intact again during later conditioning and retrieval test.

Taking advantage of this peculiar feature, reversible inactivation techniques have facilitated identifying an associative role of brain sites that are also relay areas in the main gustatory system such as the parabrachial area.[53–55] Nevertheless, the problem of dissociating sensory, motor, or performance factors from learning processes does not apply to reversible post-trial interventions because the brain may be intact during both acquisition and testing. In fact, studying the brain mechanism of the consolidation of the memory trace has been one of the fields that has benefited most from the use of reversible interventions.[6,9,56]

Finally, complex learning phenomena protocols may be useful behavioral tools for dissociating sensory and learning processes that overlap during acquisition or retrieval sessions. It is well-known that previous experience either with a CS or US interferes with subsequent learning. Thus, latent inhibition induced by the previous exposure to the conditioned CS and the effect of the US pre-exposure may be used as powerful tools if reversible brain inactivation during the acquisition phase results in memory impairments. As both phenomena require a previous temporally separated pre-exposure phase, disruption by reversible inactivation of the relevant brain site during this phase may disclose its sensory role.

Instead, a taste memory role for the gustatory insular cortex has been supported by Berman and Dudai[37,45] using a latent inhibition procedure. Also, negative results of inactivation during the pre-exposure phase (the inactivation conditions identical to those inducing disruption during the acquisition phase) exclude an interpretation based exclusively in sensory impairment and suggest an associative role for the area. As an example, Ballesteros et al.[53] showed that transient PBN blockade by TTX injections 30 min after LiCl exposure did not interfere with the US pre-exposure effect, showing that the pre-exposed group had reduced taste aversions. These results demonstrated that the disrupting effect of PBN inactivation during taste aversion acquisition using an identical procedure could not be attributed to impaired processing of US-aversive properties.

However, the use of reversible inactivation technique in complex learning behavioural protocols has the main limitation of requiring a higher number of animals, thus increasing cost and time requirements. The need of several control groups to demonstrate complex phenomena represents a serious pitfall of neurobiological studies[57] and may be the reason why reversible inactivation techniques are rarely applied to studies of more complex learning protocols.

8.5 DISSOCIATING INDEPENDENT LEARNING AND MEMORY PROCESSES

The reversible inactivation approach has proven especially valuable for localization of associative loci in the previously identified essential brain circuit of a given type of learning. Research on taste aversion learning and eyeblink classical conditioning may exemplify two different strategies aimed to dissociate sensory, motor and associative roles of a brain area. Additionally, research aimed to dissociate the neural circuits subserving overlapping learning processes can benefit from reversible inactivation studies. Research on the neural mechanisms of extinction may be representative of this issue.

8.5.1 Dissociating Sensory and Associative Processes during Acquisition

Due to the fact that taste aversion permits introducing a long delay between the taste CS and the LiCl injection usually applied for inducing malaise (US), reversible lesions are especially appropriate to leave intact taste processing both during acquisition and testing. This temporal dissociation has been essential for identifying an associative role of the parabrachial nuclei (PBN) in taste aversion learning because the area is the second brainstem relay in the main gustatory and visceral pathways.[52]

While total permanent lesions of the PBN interfere with autonomic functions essential for survival, partial permanent lesions may disrupt either taste or visceral processing, thus preventing a clear interpretation in terms of associative deficits.[10,11] Pioneering studies using TTX for temporary inactivation of the PBN after taste processing[54] or following the acquisition trial[55] support an associative role of the area. These interventions prevented the acquisition of conditioned taste aversions, suggesting an associative role of the area in addition to its sensory role. Moreover, a potential explanation of the results in terms of visceral processing impairment induced by pre- or post-trial PBN inactivation has been discarded. A similar dosage TTX injection after LiCl administration does not prevent visceral processing as demonstrated by efficient US pre-exposure effects on subsequent conditioning.[53]

8.5.2 Dissociating Motor and Associative Processes during Acquisition

In eyeblink classical conditioning, a variety of reversible lesion techniques such as muscimol, TTX, reversible cooling, and protein synthesis inhibitors have been combined to dissociate the specific roles of previously identified brain areas forming the basic learning circuit in acquisition and motor performance.[17] Inactivation of each brain site forming the basic circuit during acquisition would prevent the conditioned response (CR). However, inactivation during acquisition of those areas relevant for motor output should not prevent learning unless CR performance would be required.

Consistently, animals trained during inactivation of the cerebellar anterior interpositus nucleus and its afferent sites did not exhibit the CR in a later test after removal of the inactivation. No savings were seen in later training. In contrast, inactivation of the areas receiving efferent projections from the interpositus nucleus, such as the superior peduncle, red nucleus, and motor nuclei, prevented CR during training but this was evident in a later test leaving the brain intact. In fact, a complete learning reaching the asymptote was reported. These results dissociate the role of the explored brain sites in acquisition and performance and support an associative role for the interpositus nucleus in eyeblink conditioning (see alternative interpretations based on electrophysiological data[58,59]).

8.5.3 Dissociating Overlapping Learning Processes

The use of reversible inactivation during extinction tests is providing a new tool for exploring the neural substrates underlying extinction in different types of learning. The results demonstrating the possibility of dissociating anatomical and functional circuits involved in acquisition, expression, and extinction are in accordance with the current view of extinction as a form of new learning that interferes with the previous learned CR. Local injections of anisomycin into different amygdalar nuclei yielded opposite results on acquisition and extinction of conditioned taste aversion.

Injections applied 20 min before the extinction test into the basolateral (BLA) but not the central (CeA) nucleus of the amygdala impaired extinction. In contrast, the same inactivation procedure in CeA but not BLA impaired learning if applied 20 min before the conditioning session.[60] Immediate post-trial anisomycin injections in the same amygdala nuclei yielded similar results. Moreover, the same basolateral amygdala inactivation induced no effect in a behavioral protocol including intensive two-trial learning which depressed extinction.[61] A similar interference of extinction by anisomycin injections into the insular gustatory cortex before the retrieval test has been reported; an aversive effect of the transient inactivation "may be" discarded as anisomycin in the insular cortex did not induce aversions.[45] These results suggest independent neural circuits for conditioned taste aversion extinction and other acquisition, retrieval, or consolidation processes.

Consistent results have been obtained with other learning procedures such as eyeblink classical conditioning.[62] Reversible inactivation of the motor nuclei relevant for the CR by muscimol injections completely prevented extinction, which was resumed on subsequent extinction tests with an intact brain.[63] However, the inactivation of the same nuclei did not prevent acquisition of the CR. An unspecific effect of preventing RC expression on extinction can be discarded because muscimol inactivation of the red nucleus that interferes with the CR does not prevent extinction.[62]

8.6 SUMMARY

The current development of the lesion approach takes advantage of reversible brain inactivation for the study of the neural substrates of learning and memory at the system level. The advantages and limitations of the available techniques have been reviewed. Careful consideration should be given to behavioral and technical pitfalls of reversible brain inactivation in order to avoid inaccurate interpretation of the results. Some issues such as dissociating both independent processes contributing to a given learning situation and overlapping learning processes may benefit from the reversible approach.

ACKNOWLEDGMENTS

The research of the author and her collaborators was supported in part by grants BSO2002-01215 (MICYT, Spain) and SEJ2005-01344 (MEC, Spain).

REFERENCES

1. Bures, J. and Buresova, O., The use of Leao's spreading depression in the study of interhemispheric transfer of memory traces. *J. Comp. Physiol. Psychol.*, 53, 558, 1960.
2. McGaugh, J.L. et al., Facilitation of maze learning with post-trial injections of 5-7-dyphenyldiazadamantan-6-ol (1757 I.S.), *J. Comp. Physiol. Psychol.,* 55, 710, 1962.
3. Cahill, L., McGaugh, J.L., and Weinberger, N.M., The neurobiology of learning and memory: some reminders to remember, *Trends Neurosci.,* 24, 578, 2001.
4. Kandel, E.R. and Pittenger, Ch., The past, the future and the biology of memory storage, *Phil. Trans. R. Soc. Lond.* B, 2, 354, 2027, 1999.

5. Cammarota, M. et al., Retrieval and the extinction of memory, *Cell. Mol. Neurobiol.*, 25, 465, 2005.
6. Dudai. Y., Molecular bases of long-term memories: a question of persistence, *Curr. Opin. Neurobiol.*, 12, 211, 2002.
7. Izquierdo, I. and Medina, J.H., Memory formation: the sequence of biochemical events in the hippocampus and its connection to activity in other brain structures, *Neurobiol. Learn. Mem.*, 68, 285, 1997.
8. Izquierdo, L.A. et al., Molecular and pharmacological dissection of short- and long-term memory, *Cell. Mol. Neurobiol.*, 22, 269, 2002.
9. McGaugh, J.L. and Izquierdo, I., The contribution of pharmacology to research on the mechanisms of memory formation. *Trends Pharmacol. Sci.*, 21, 208, 2000.
10. Bures, J. and Buresova, O., Reversible lesions allow reinterpretation of system level studies of brain mechanisms. *Concepts Neurosci.*, 1, 69, 1990.
11. Bures, J., Reversible lesions reveal hidden stages of learning, in *Plasticity in the Central Nervous System: Learning and Memory,* McGaugh, J.L. et al., Eds., Lawrence Erlbaum, Mahway, NJ, 1995, chap. 7.
12. Lorenzini, C.G.A. et al., Analysis of mnemonic processing by means of totally reversible neural inactivation, *Brain Res. Protocol,* 1, 391, 1997.
13. Lorenzini, C.G.A. et al., Neural topography and chronology of memory consolidation: a review of functional inactivation findings, *Neurobiol. Learn. Mem.*, 71, 1, 1999.
14. Riedel, G. et al., Reversible neural inactivation reveals hippocampal participation in several memory processes, *Nat. Neurosci.*, 2, 898, 1999.
15. Squire, L., Memory systems in the brain: a brief history and current perspective, *Neurobiol. Learn. Mem.*, 82, 171, 2004.
16. Lamprecht, R. and Dudai, Y., The amygdala in conditioned taste aversion: it's there, but where, in *The Amygdala: A Functional Aanalysis*, Aggleton, J.P., Ed., Oxford University Press, Oxford, 2000, chap. 9.
17. Thompson, R.F., In search of memory traces, *Annu. Rev. Psychol.*, 56, 1, 2005.
18. Cimadevilla, J.M. et al., Inactivating one hippocampus impairs avoidance of a stable room-defined place during dissociation o0f arena cues from room cues by rotation of the arena, *Proc. Natl. Acad. Sci. USA,* 98, 3531, 2001.
19. Paus, T., Imaging the brain before, during, and after transcranial magnetic stimulation, *Neuropsychologia,* 37, 219, 1999.
20. Paus, T. and Barret, J., Transcranial magnetic stimulation (TMS) of the human frontal cortex: implications for repetitive TMS treatment of depression, *J. Psychiatr. Neurosci.,* 29, 3268, 2004.
21. Paus, T. et al., Transcranial magnetic stimulation during positron emission tomography: a new method for studying connectivity of the human cerebral cortex, *J. Neurosci.,* 17, 3178, 1997.
22. Grafman, J. and Wassermann, E., Transcranial magnetic stimulation can measure and modulate learning and memory, *Neuropsychology,* 37, 159, 1999.
23. Barret, J. et al., Mechanisms of action underlying the effect of repetitive transcranial magnetic stimulation on mood: behavioral and brain imaging studies, *Neuropsychopharmacology,* 29, 1172, 2004.
24. Paus, T. and Wolforth, M., Transcranial magnetic stimulation during PET: reaching and verifying the target site, *Hum. Brain Mapping,* 6, 399, 1998.
25. Martin, J.H. and Ghez, C., Pharmacological inactivation in the analysis of the central control of movement, *J. Neurosci. Meth.,* 86, 145, 1999.

26. Wang, Y., Lavond, D.G. and Chambers, K.C., The effects of cooling the area postrema of male rats on conditioned taste aversions induced by LiCl and apomorphine, *Behav. Brain Res.,* 82, 149, 1997.
27. Dudai., Y. and Eisenberg, M., Rites of passage of the engram: reconsolidation and the lingering consolidation hypothesis, *Neuron,* 44, 93, 2004.
28. Lomber, S.G. , The advantages and limitations of permanent or reversible deactivation techniques in the assessment of neural function, *J. Neurosci. Meth.,* 86, 109, 1999.
29. Clark, R.E., Zhang, A.A., and Lavond, D.G. , The importance of cerebellar cortex and facial nucleus in acquisition and retention of eyeblink/NM conditioning: evidence for critical unilateral regulation of the conditioned response, *Neurobiol. Learn. Mem.,* 67, 96, 1997.
30. Wikgren, J. et al., Cooling of the cerebellar interpositus nucleus abolishes somatosensory cortical learning-related activity in eyeblink conditioned rabbits, *Behav. Brain Res.,* 170, 94, 2006.
31. Zhuravin, I.A. and Bures, J., Extent of the tetrodotoxin induced blockade examined by papillary paralysis elicited by intracerebral injection of the drug, *Exp. Brain Res.,* 83, 687, 1991.
32. Harlan, R.E. et al., Estrogenic maintenance of lordotic responsiveness: requirement for hypothalamic action potentials, *Brain Res.,* 268, 67, 1983.
33. Rothfeld, J.M. et al., Reversible disruption of lordosis via midbrain infusions of procaine and tetrodotoxin, *Pharmacol. Biochem. Behav.,* 25, 857, 1986.
34. Klement, D., Pastalkova, E., and Fenton, A., Tetrodotoxin infusions in the dorsal hippocampus block non-locomotor place recognition, *Hippocampus,* 15, 460, 2005.
35. Boehnke, S.E. and Rasmusson, D.D., Time course and effective spread of lidocaine and tetrodotoxin delivered via microdialysis: an electrophysiological study in cerebral cortex, *J Neurosci. Meth.*, 105,133, 2001.
36. Nilaweera, W.U., Zenitsky, G.D., and Braha, V., Inactivation of the brachium conjunctivum prevents extinction of classically conditioned eyeblinks, *Brain Res.,* 1045, 175, 2005.
37. Rosenblum, K., Meiri, N., and Dudai, Y., Taste memory: the role of protein synthesis in gustatory cortex, *Behav. Neural Biol.,* 59, 49, 1993.
38. Nakajima, A. and Ya-Ping Tang, Genetic approaches to the molecular/neuronal mechanisms underlying learning and memory in the mouse, *J. Pharmacol. Sci.,* 99, 1, 2005.
39. Cui, Z. et al., Requirement of NMDA receptor reactivation for consolidation and storage of nondeclarative taste memory revealed by inducible NR1 knockout, *Eur. J. Neurosci.,* 22, 755, 2005.
40. Josselyn, S.A, Kida, S., and Medina, J.H., Inducible repression of CREB function disrupts amygdale-dependent memory, *Neurobiol. Learn. Mem.,* 82, 159, 2004.
41. Wang, H. et al., Inducible protein knockout reveals temporal requirement of CaMKII reactivation for memory consolidation in the brain, *Proc. Nat. Acad. Sci. USA,* 100, 4287, 2003.
42. Overton, D.A., Historical context of state dependent learning and discriminative drug effects, *Behav. Pharmacol.,* 2, 253, 1991.
43. Aldecamp, A.P. et al., Acute cognitive effects of nonconvulsive difficult-to-detect epileptic seizures and epileptiform electroencephalographic discharges, *J. Child Neurol.,* 16, 119, 2001.
44. Bettinger, J.C. and McIntire, S.L., State-dependency in C. elegans, *Genes Brain Behav.,* 3, 266, 2004.

45. Berman, D.E. and Dudai, Y., Memory extinction, learning anew, and learning the new: dissociation in the molecular machinery of learning in cortex, *Science,* 291, 2417, 2001.
46. DeBrugada, I., Gonzalez, F., and Candido, A., The role of the injection cues in the associative control of the US pre-exposure effect in flavour aversion learning, *Q. J. Exp. Psychol. B,* 56, 241, 2003.
47. DeBrugada, I., Hall, G., and Symonds, M., The US-preexposure effect in lithium-induced flavor-aversion conditioning is a consequence of blocking by injection cues, *J. Exp. Psychol. Anim. Behav. Process,* 30, 58, 2004.
48. Maviel, T. et al., Sites of neocortical reorganization critical for remote spatial memory, *Science*, 305, 96, 2004.
49. Phelps, E.A. and LeDoux, J.E., Contribution of the amygdale to emotion processing: from animal models to human behavior, *Neuron,* 48, 175, 2005.
50. Sanders, M.J., Wiltgen, B.J., and Fanselow, M.S., The place of the hippocampus in fear conditioning, *Eur. J. Pharmacol.,* 463, 217, 2003.
51. Schafe, G.E., Doyere, V., and LeDoux, J.E., Tracking the fear engram: the lateral amygdale is an essential locus of fear memory storage, *J. Neurosci.,* 25, 10010, 2005.
52. Bures, J., Bermúdez-Rattoni, F., and Yamamoto, T., *Conditioned Taste Aversion: Memory of a Special Kind.* Oxford University Press, Oxford, 1998.
53. Ballesteros, M. A. et al., Dissociation of the associative and visceral sensory components of taste aversion learning by tetrodotoxin inactivation of the parabrachial nucleus in rats, *Neurosci. Lett.,* 322, 169, 2002.
54. Ivanova, S.F. and Bures, J., Acquisition of conditioned taste aversion in rats is prevented by tetrodotoxin blockade of a small midbrain region centered around the parabrachial nuclei, *Physiol. Behav.*, 48, 543, 1990.
55. Ivanova, S.F. and Bures, J., Conditioned taste aversion is disrupted by prolonged retrograde effects on intracerebral inyections of tetrodotoxin in rats, *Behav. Neurosci.,* 104, 948, 1990.
56. Dudai. Y., The neurobiology of consolidations, or how stable is the engram? *Annu. Rev. Psychol.,* 55, 51, 2004.
57. Robbins, T.W. et al., Methods for assessing attention and stimulus control in the rat, in *Behavioural Neuroscience: A Practical Approach*, Sahgal, A., Ed., Oxford University Press, Oxford, 1993, chap. 3.
58. Delgado-Garcia, J.M. and Gruart, A., Building new motor responses: eyelid conditioning revisited, *Trends Neurosci.,* 29, 330, 2006.
59. Jimenez-Diaz, L. et al., Role of the cerebellar interpositus nucleus in the genesis and control of reflex and conditioned eyelid responses, *J. Neurosci.,* 24, 9138, 2004.
60. Bahar, A. et al., The amygdalar circuit that acquires taste aversion memory differs from the circuit that extinguishes it, *Eur. J. Neurosci.,* 17, 1527, 2003.
61. Bahar, A., Dorfman, N., and Dudai, Y., Amygdalar circuits required for either consolidation or extinction of taste aversion memory are not required for reconsolidation, *Eur. J. Neurosci.,* 19, 1115, 2004.
62. Robleto, K., Poulos, A.M., and Thompson, R.F., Brain mechanisms of extinction of the classically conditioned eyeblink response, *Learn. Mem.,* 11, 517, 2004.
63. Kruppa, D.J. and Thompson, R.F., Inhibiting the expression of a classically conditioned behavior prevents its extinction, *J. Neurosci.,* 23, 10577, 2003.

9 Enhanced Learning Protects Brain against Effects of Amnesic Treatments

Roberto A. Prado-Alcalá, Rigoberto Salado-Castillo, César Quiroz, María Eugenia Garín-Aguilar, Arnulfo Díaz-Trujillo, Selva Rivas-Arancibia, and Gina L. Quírarte

CONTENTS

9.1 INTRODUCTION

9.1.1 Brief History

The beginning of the 20th century coincided with a conceptual advancement that has guided most of the experimental research on the neurobiology of memory: the hypothesis of memory consolidation. Georg Elias Müller and his pupil Alfons Pilzecker published an ample monograph in which they reported 40 experiments carried out between 1892 and 1900, with the aim of identifying laws that govern the establishment and retrieval of memory. They devised the concept of memory consolidation and introduced it into scientific literature. The major conclusions of their work were that memory fixation requires time (consolidation) and that memory is vulnerable during the period of consolidation.[1]

The 100 years that followed Müller and Pilzecker's seminal work witnessed rapid development in the field of the neurobiology of memory.[2] The first descriptions of cerebral structures necessary for storing learned information were made with the use of physiological and pharmacological tools, coupled to behavioral and neuroanatomic techniques. Thus, it was found that lesions, electric stimulation, and reversible inactivation of a number of brain regions produce significant deficiencies of memory. The use of systemic or direct administration into the cerebral parenchyma of drugs that activate or block the action of neurotransmitter molecules indicated that specific neurotransmitter systems were involved in memory consolidation.[3–6]

Evidence that began accumulating decades ago strongly indicates that *de novo* gene expression is required to establish long-term memory.[7,8] Recently, molecular and genetic techniques have permitted the identification and characterization of genes and molecules that seem to play key roles in memory consolidation.[9] For example, numerous experiments strongly suggest that the cyclic AMP-dependent activation pathway, the cAMP response element binding proteins, and a cyclic AMP-dependent cascade of gene expression are necessary for consolidation of simple and complex forms of memory.[10–13]

In general, data obtained using the methodologies described above are consistent with one another. In other words, if a lesion of a particular cerebral structure produces a memory deficit, then the same consequence is observed after functional interference with the same structure produced by electric stimulation, pharmacologic blockade of some of its neurotransmission systems, or by other means including inhibition of protein synthesis. On the other hand, local administration of agonists or precursors of the corresponding neurotransmitters brings about improvement of memory processes. In this manner, it was possible to identify specific cerebral structures whose activities are essential for storage of particular types of memory or for storage of several types of memory.

White and McDonald[14,15] put forth an interesting proposition about multiple memory systems. In an elegant experimental series in which three versions of the eight-arm radial maze were studied, they demonstrated[14] that damage to the striatum impedes the establishment of procedural memory (habit learning), while lesions of the amygdala or hippocampus did not. On the other hand, amygdalar lesions, but not lesions of the striatum or hippocampus, caused deficiencies of emotional memory. Furthermore, hippocampal lesions interfered with spatial memory, but no interference was produced by lesions of the striatum or amygdala. In other words, they found that particular types of memory are dependent upon normal activity of particular cerebral structures.

A learning task that has been widely used to study the acquisition, consolidation, and retrieval of memory is one-trial inhibitory avoidance. The procedure used in many laboratories involves a box with two compartments (bright and dark) divided by a sliding door. The floor of the dark compartment can be electrified. The subject, usually a small rodent, is placed first in the bright compartment while the sliding door is closed. The door is then opened and if the rodent passes through the door to the dark compartment, the door is closed and the floor is electrified. After a few seconds the door is opened again and the rodent usually escapes to the bright compartment. The retention (memory) test session can be performed shortly after the training session to evaluate short-term memory and 24 hours or more after training to check the integrity of long term-memory. The test session consists of placing the rodent again in the bright compartment and measuring the time it takes the animal to cross to the dark compartment; if an animal does not cross after a predetermined maximum time, the session is ended. High latencies reflect a well established memory, while disruptions in memory are revealed as short latencies to cross to the dark side.

The types of memory studied by McDonald and White[14] are implicated in this task: (1) it has a high emotional component, (2) it is established through spatial cues, and (3) it implies the association between a particular context and a motor response. According to the proposal of McDonald and White, the striatum, amygdala, and hippocampus should be necessary for memory consolidation of this task. Indeed, this is the case.[16–21]

Despite the antecedents described above, a series of experimental studies initiated systematically in our laboratory indicate that the prevailing theory of memory consolidation does not apply to memory of relatively strong learning situations, such as those mediated by multiple learning sessions (overtraining) or by relatively high aversive stimulation (over-reinforcement). It should be kept in mind that consolidation theory postulates that memory fixation requires the passage of time (consolidation) and that memory is fragile during the period of consolidation.[1,2]

What follows is an account of data that have led us to an alternative proposal germane to the way memory consolidation occurs in situations of enhanced training. The experiments to be described do not necessarily follow a chronological order. They deal with studies of inhibitory avoidance unless stated otherwise.

9.2 PROTECTIVE EFFECT OF ENHANCED TRAINING

9.2.1 Systemic Treatments

9.2.1.1 Cholinergic System

One neurotransmission system that has received ample attention because of its probable involvement in memory processes is the cholinergic system. Although exceptions[22,23] exist, numerous studies demonstrate that systemic or intracerebral administration of acetylcholine antagonists produces significant deficiencies in a great variety of learned behaviors including inhibitory avoidance; likewise, administration of agonists or precursors of memory formation.[3,24–28]

In 1990, Durán-Arévalo, Cruz-Morales, and Prado-Alcalá[29] reported that intraperitoneal (i.p.) administration of scopolamine (a muscarinic receptor blocker) immediately after training produced the known amnesic effect when retention was tested 24 hours later. However, when other groups of rats were submitted to stronger learning experiences by increasing the intensity of foot-shock during training, scopolamine did not produce any detrimental effect on memory, as depicted in Figure 9.1.

Along these lines, Cruz-Morales et al.[30] conducted a study to determine whether the protective effect of enhanced learning against the amnesic effect of scopolamine was a gradual phenomenon or whether a certain intensity threshold had to be reached in order to observe this effect. Independent groups of rats were trained with increasing intensities of foot-shock at 0.1-mA intervals. They found that all intensities produced optimal retention scores in the control groups and a strong amnesic effect, within a range of relatively low intensities, in those treated with scopolamine. A further increment of less than 4% of the intensity that previously produced amnesia completely counteracted the effect of scopolamine. In other words, it seems that within an ample range of intensities, the cholinergic blocker produces amnesia, but when the aversive stimulation is slightly increased beyond a certain value, the cholinergic system is disengaged from the process of memory consolidation.

Later we assessed the effects of posttraining systemic scopolamine on memory with groups of rats trained with very low, medium, or high levels of foot-shock

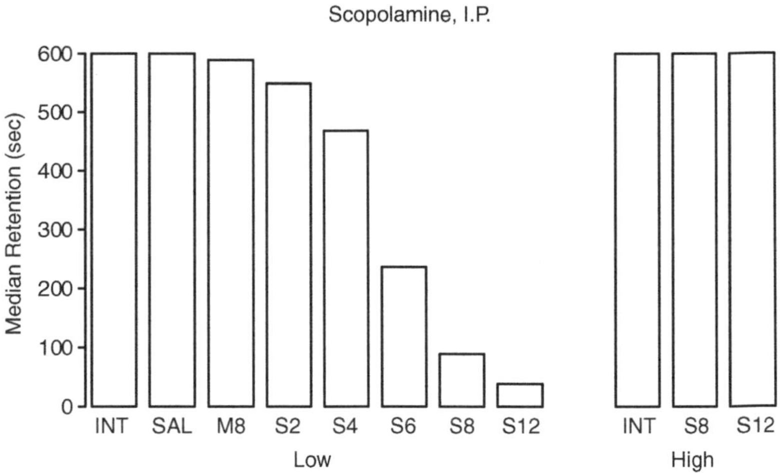

FIGURE 9.1 Median retention scores obtained 24 hours after training with low or high foot-shock intensities. INT = intact animals. The rest of the groups were injected i.p. with SAL (isotonic saline), M8 (8 mg methylscopolamine — a cholinergic blocker that does not readily cross the blood-brain barrier), S (2, 4, 6, 8, or 12 mg/kg scopolamine bromide) 5 min after training.

intensities. As expected, scopolamine produced the typical amnesic state in the animals with an intermediate level of training and no effect in animals with high levels of training. Surprisingly, animals with low degrees of training (very low foot-shock intensity) did not show memory deficits.[31]

Taken together, these data indicate that cerebral cholinergic activity is necessary for memory consolidation under conditions of intermediate levels of training, but is not required when very low magnitudes of aversive stimulation (sufficient only to produce some amount of retention) or relatively high levels of the negative reinforcer are administered. Thus, it can be concluded that enhanced learning and weak learning as well protect memory from the amnesia typically produced by anticholinergic agents. One important question was whether this phenomenon can be generalized to other neurochemical systems. As described below, the answer is positive.

9.2.1.2 Serotonergic System

Depletion and blockade of cerebral serotonin and lesions of central serotonergic pathways impede normal learning and memory, while activation of some of the 14 serotonin-receptor subtypes improves these cognitive processes.[32–39]

In a first attempt to find out whether enhanced learning counteracts the typical amnesic effects of interference with serotonergic activity, we used p-chloroamphetamine (PCA). When injected i.p., PCA produces a large depletion of cerebral serotonin associated with lesions of neurons that synthesize and of axons that contain this neurotransmitter. Rats treated with PCA were trained with relatively low or high foot-shock levels. PCA produced amnesia, regardless of the intensity of the aversive stimulation.[40]

Subsequently, Solana-Figueroa et al.[41] administered PCA to independent groups of rats trained with the same intensities of electric shocks as those in the previous study,[40] but they also included training at still higher intensities. As expected, PCA produced amnesia in the groups that had been trained with the lower intensities. No significant amnesia was found in those trained with the highest intensities, thus confirming the protective effect of enhanced training (Figure 9.2).

In line with the results described above, extended training ameliorated behavioral deficits in active avoidance that were consistently produced by peripheral depletion of noradrenaline.[42] Moreover, animals that were pretrained with as few as two sessions of active avoidance were significantly less impaired by pimozide than animals that were not pretrained.[43]

The results described above clearly indicate that enhanced training impedes the amnesic states typically observed as consequences of systemic administration of anticholinergic and antiserotonergic drugs. Nevertheless, these findings do not reveal where in the brain this protective effect occurs. To answer this question, we designed experiments in which drugs were injected into discrete zones of the brains of animals that had previously been subjected to low and high degrees of training.

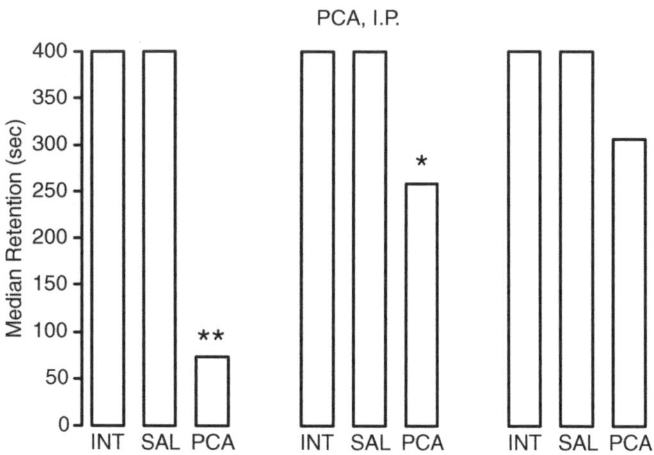

FIGURE 9.2 Median retention scores of intact (INT) rats and rats injected i.p. with isotonic saline (SAL) or p-chloramphetamine (PCA) 30 min before training with low, medium or high foot-shock intensity. * = $p < 0.02$. ** = $p < 0.0005$ versus SAL.

9.2.2 Intracerebral Treatments

9.2.2.1 Striatum

Haycock et al.[44] showed that scopolamine infusion into the striatum produced amnesia. This result was confirmed,[45] but it was also shown that the same treatment produced no changes in memory in animals that received aversive stimulation of relatively high intensities during training (Figure 9.3). A few years later, Díaz del Guante et al.[46] reported the same protective effect of enhanced training.

These results strongly suggested that the striatal cholinergic system is not required for the process of memory consolidation or retention of enhanced inhibitory avoidance training, and led to two alternative hypotheses to explain the protective effect: (1) that the participation of the striatum in memory under these conditions depends upon intrinsic neurotransmitter systems other than the cholinergic system, and (2) that the striatum is no longer necessary for consolidation. If the second hypothesis turned out to be correct, the first one would be discarded. Hence, the second hypothesis was tested experimentally.

Groups of rats were trained with relatively low or high foot-shock intensities; immediately after training, they received bilateral infusions of lidocaine, and retention of the task was tested 24 hours later. We expected to find amnesia in the low foot-shock group, and indeed this was the case. On the other hand, the high foot-shock group showed optimal retention (Figure 9.4). These results indicated that under conditions of enhanced training the striatum is not necessary for memory consolidation,[47] thus supporting the second hypothesis.

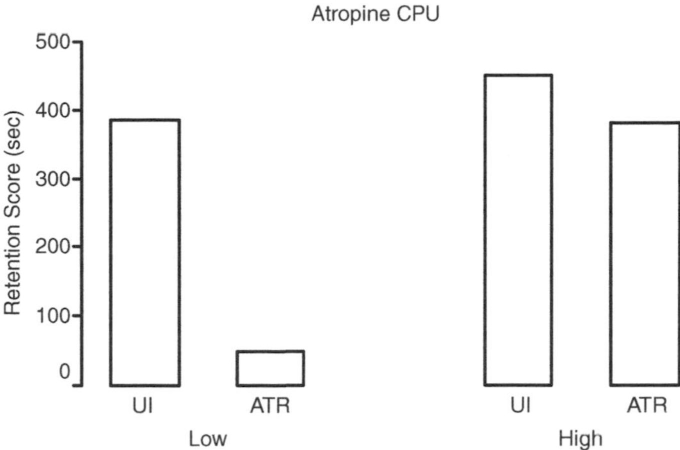

FIGURE 9.3 Retention scores of groups of rats microinjected after training into the caudate–putamen with atropine (ATR). UI = unimplanted intact group. Atropine produced amnesia only in the group trained with the lowest foot-shock intensity.

9.2.2.2 Substantia Nigra

Based on the theoretical importance of the protective effect, we decided to explore the possibility that it might also be found in other cerebral nuclei known to participate in memory. We first selected the substantia nigra because it is directly connected, functionally and anatomically, to the striatum and because it is, without doubt, involved in memory processes.[48–52]

One of the main projections of the striatum to the substantia nigra is GABAergic; for this reason Cobos-Zapiaín et al.[53] explored the effects of posttraining infusions of bicuculine or picrotoxin (GABA blockers with different modes of action) into the substantia nigra of rats given low or high levels of foot-shock. The results were not surprising: both drugs produced amnesia in the low foot-shock groups, while no significant retention deficits were observed in the high foot-shock groups (Figure 9.5).

Up to this point, the protective effect of enhanced training against memory deficits had been demonstrated in the nigrostriatal system (striatum and substantia nigra). We then decided to study the possibility that this effect might be generalized to another system. Two neuronal conglomerates of the limbic system play important roles in processing emotional information and in the integration of spatial cues: the amygdala and the hippocampus, respectively.

9.2.2.3 Amygdala

A wealth of experimental data supports the idea that the amygdala contributes to memory formation.[18,28,54] In an early study, Thatcher and Kimble[55] found that lesions

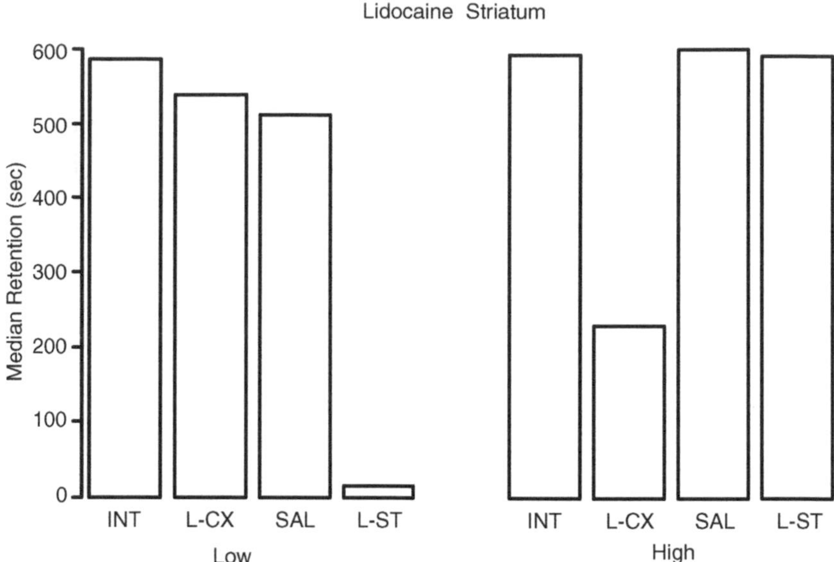

FIGURE 9.4 Median retention scores of groups of rats trained with low or high foot-shock intensities. INT = intact rats. The rest of the groups were microinjected with lidocaine into the parietal cortex (L-CX), with isotonic saline into the striatum (SAL) or with lidocaine into the striatum (L-ST). Only the L-ST group trained with low foot-shock showed a significant retention deficit.

of the amygdala produced a significant memory deficit of an avoidance task; such deficit was not found when the intensity of training was increased. About three decades later, in an important series of experiments conducted in the laboratory of J.L. McGaugh, Parent et al. demonstrated that lesions or temporary inactivation of the amygdala of rats trained on multiple-trial inhibitory avoidance or with relatively high foot-shock intensities did not show the typical amnesia obtained with lower levels of training.[56–59]

Consistent with these results are those of Salado-Castillo et al.[60] who reported that infusions of lidocaine into the amygdala, striatum, or substantia nigra immediately after training produced marked amnesic states in rats trained with a low intensity foot-shock, but they detected no effect on memory in rats trained with relatively high levels of foot-shock.

9.2.2.4 Hippocampus

The hippocampus is essential for memory consolidation of inhibitory avoidance and other types of tasks.[61–64] In a recent experiment, Martínez et al.[63] found that lesions of hippocampal fields CA1 and CA3 produced by microinjections of kainic acid caused the well-known impairment of long-term memory; however, when short-term memory was evaluated in these same animals, it remained intact. To test whether long-term memory could be saved after an enhanced training experience, Quiroz et

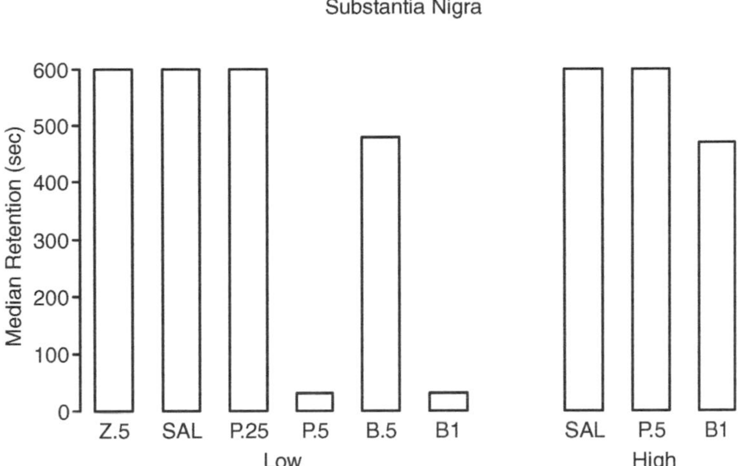

FIGURE 9.5 Median retention scores of groups of rats trained with low or high levels of foot-shock and injected with isotonic saline (SAL), 0.25 or 0.5 μg of picrotoxin (P), 0.5 or 1.0 μg of bicuculine (B) into the substantia nigra, or 0.5 μg of picrotoxin injected into the zona incerta (Z).

al.[65] induced temporary inactivation of the hippocampus, infusing tetrodotoxin immediately after training. The toxin produced amnesia when a foot-shock of low intensity was administered; in contrast, tetrodotoxin was totally ineffective in animals trained with higher foot-shocks (Figure 9.6). Data obtained from the animals submitted to high levels of training before normal activity of the amygdala or hippocampus was disrupted (via lesions or reversible inactivation) indicated that the protective effect of enhanced training also occurs in structures of the limbic system.

9.3 OVERTRAINING OF POSITIVELY REINFORCED LEARNING

The experiments described to this point are germane to the protection of memory against typical amnesic treatments and have dealt with learning and memory of an inhibitory avoidance task mediated by aversive stimulation. Can this protective effect be seen when learning is mediated by positive reinforcers?

The effects of microinjections of atropine into the caudate nuclei of cats on the retention of a positively reinforced fixed ratio-1 (FR-1) task (lever pressing reinforced with milk) was reported by Prado-Alcalá et al.[66] A few years later, it was reported for the first time that when this instrumental task was overtrained, cholinergic blockade of the caudate did not interfere with retention of the task.[67] The same protective effect was found when cholinergic activity of the striatum was blocked in rats overtrained in a spatial alternation task, reinforced with water.[68]

The next logical step was to determine whether, as in the case of inhibitory avoidance, the caudate and striatum as a whole were no longer needed for retention

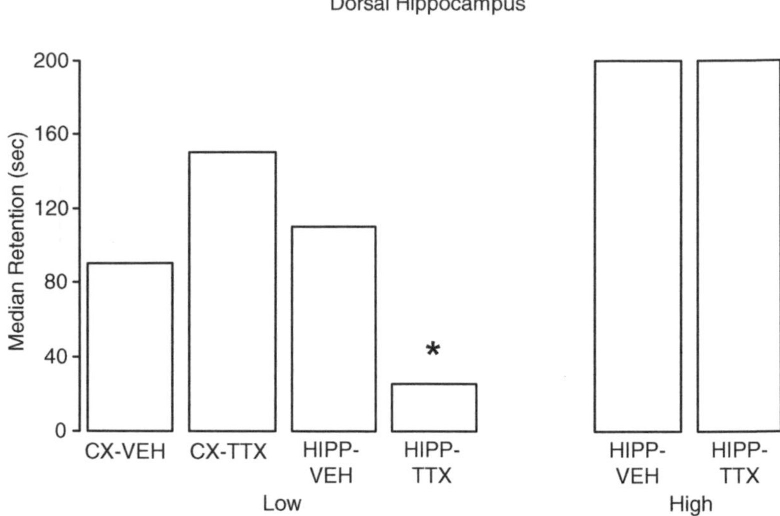

FIGURE 9.6 Retention scores of rats trained with low or high intensity of foot-shock and injected with tetrodotoxin (TTX) or vehicle solution (VEH) into the parietal cortex (CX) or dorsal hippocampus (HIPP). * = $p < 0.05$ as compared with the rest of the groups.

of overtrained tasks. To this end, both cats[69] and rats[70] were trained on an FR-1 schedule for a low, medium, or high number of sessions. After training, the memories of the animals were tested under the influence of a high concentration of potassium chloride (KCl, 3 M), infused into the caudate or striatum. The results of both experiments were equivalent: groups trained for fewer sessions showed marked amnesia; those with intermediate degrees of training showed moderate amnesia; overtrained animals showed the same performance as the control animals treated with vehicle solution (Figure 9.7).

Taken together, the experiments summarized above clearly show that the protective effect of enhanced training occurs regardless of the type of task (inhibitory avoidance, spatial alternation, FR schedule), reinforcer (negative or positive), or animal species (feline or rodent). Importantly, enhanced training protects against the amnesic effects of a number of treatments (lidocaine, tetrodotoxin, potassium chloride, permanent lesions, and drugs that interfere with the synaptic activities of acetylcholine, GABA, and serotonin). This result has been observed with systemic and intracerebral interventions. In the latter case, the effect was found after disrupting normal activities of the caudate, striatum, substantia nigra, amygdala, and hippocampus.

9.4 TWO MODELS

In 1995, two theoretical models were proposed. They involved series and parallel models of memory that aimed for parsimonious interpretations of the data related to the protective effects of enhanced training.[71] These will be briefly explained below.

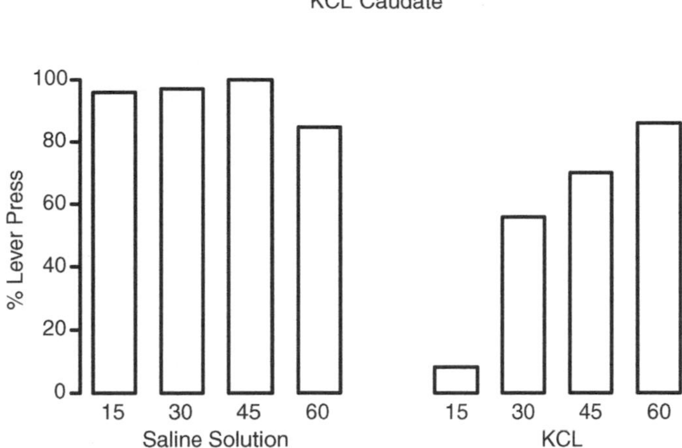

FIGURE 9.7 Effects of isotonic saline and 3 M potassium chloride (KCl) injections into the caudate nuclei of cats trained for 15, 30, 45, or 60 sessions on a FR-1 schedule, reinforced with milk. KCl produced amnesia in all groups except the overtrained group trained for 60 sessions.

Numerous examples indicate that interference with normal activity of any of a number of cerebral structures brings about deficiencies in memory consolidation or retention. The point is that a set of cerebral nuclei is essential for the establishment of memory for particular types of tasks, and that if any one of these nuclei does not function normally, the information derived from a learning situation cannot be stored in long-term memory.

We postulated that the members of this set of nuclei were functionally connected in series, that is, the neural activity derived from the learning experience must flow through all of them before reaching a hypothetical integrative "center" whose activation is necessary for consolidating memory. This flow is halted when any component of this ensemble of structures is not functional and thus consolidation is not achieved. The nature of the integrative center is far from known (it may be one particular cerebral structure, a fixed system of structures, or a number of structures involved in a probabilistic fashion).

The second model hypothesizes that in conditions of learning mediated by enhanced training (high levels of positive or negative reinforcers, a high number of trials or training sessions, or some combination of these factors), those structures that were originally connected in series undergo a functional change whereby they become functionally reconnected in parallel (additional structures may become involved in this process). Consequently, even when one or several components of this circuit are damaged or do not function normally, the neural activity produced by the learning experience will be able to continue its trajectory toward the putative integrative center, thus allowing for memory consolidation to occur. Figure 9.8 and Figure 9.9 depict these models.

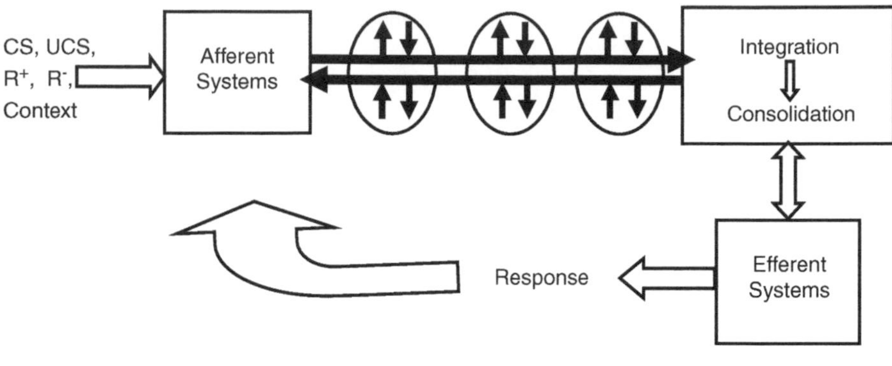

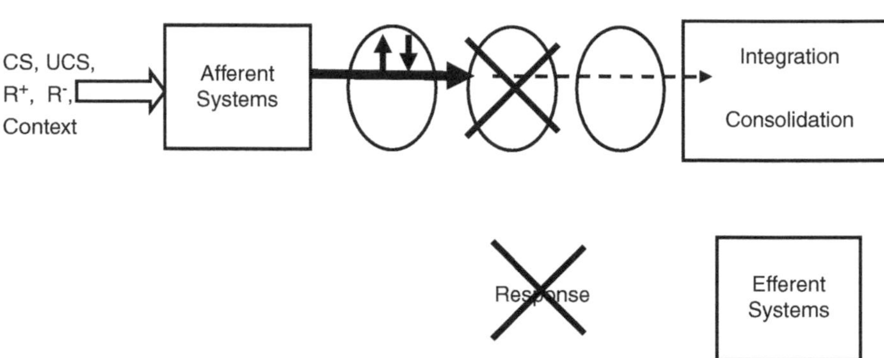

FIGURE 9.8 Model that represents the way in which, under conditions usually considered to be normal learning, interference with activity of cerebral structures produces amnesia. Information about the learning experience activates afferent sensory systems that convey neural activity to neural structures (ovals) involved in processing this information, which in turn communicate with a hypothetical integrative center necessary for consolidation of memory (upper diagram). Interference with functioning of any of these structures or connecting pathways results in consolidation deficiencies (amnesia; lower diagram). Therefore, it is reasonable to think that these structures are functionally connected in series. Arrows represent direction of flow of neural transmission. CS = conditioned stimulus. UCS = unconditioned stimulus. R^+ = positive reinforcer. R^- = negative reinforcer.

9.5 CONCLUSIONS

The vast majority of experiments dealing with the effects on memory of interference with normal activity of the brain support the century-old theory of memory consolidation because of the consistent finding that administration of a variety of treatments

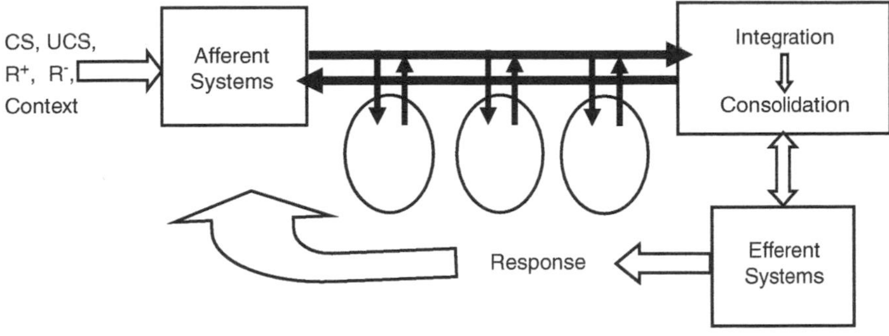

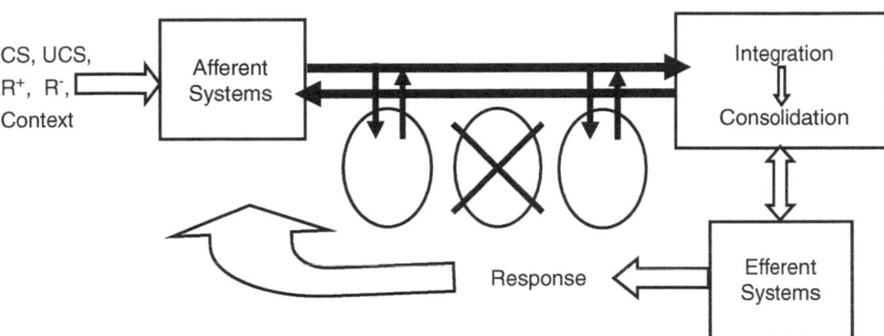

FIGURE 9.9 Model that represents the manner in which enhanced training protects memory against the amnesic effects commonly produced by treatments that interfere with activities of cerebral structures involved in memory processes. Information derived from the learning situation activates afferent systems and is relayed in the form of neural signals to those neural structures involved in processing this information (ovals); in turn, these structures communicate with a hypothetical integrative center necessary for consolidation of memory (upper diagram). Interference with functioning of any of the neural processing structures does not produce amnesia, because, as a consequence of enhanced training, there is a rearrangement whereby they become functionally connected in parallel (lower diagram). Thus, derangement of any one of these structures does not hinder consolidation because the flow of information is still able to reach the hypothetical integrative center. Arrows represent direction of flow of neural transmission.

shortly after a learning experience produces amnesia. This detrimental effect diminishes as the interval between learning and treatment increases, until the treatments become ineffective. Evidence has accumulated, however, that does not fit the consolidation theory. Treatments that produce amnesia of learning mediated by positive and negative reinforcers become innocuous when the same learning is overtrained.

This effect has been found independently of the amnesic agents used and the mode of their administration.

Based on the kind of data reviewed in this chapter, two models have been proposed to help explain the protective effect of enhanced training against amnesic treatments. More experiments are under way to test the validity of these models. If the new data are consistent with the predictions that can be derived from these models, then it will be possible to think about the brain as having at least two different ways to store learned information, depending on whether it is dealing with normal or enhanced learning.

ACKNOWLEDGMENTS

We thank Dr. Dorothy D. Pless for reviewing the manuscript and M.V.Z. Norma Serafín for technical assistance. Some experiments described in this chapter were financed by PAPIIT-DGAPA-UNAM and by CONACYT.

REFERENCES

1. Müller, G.E. and Pilzecker, A., Experimentelle beitrage zur lehre vom gedachtniss, *Zeitsch. Psychol. Erganzungs.*, 1, 1, 1900.
2. McGaugh, J.L., Memory: a century of consolidation, *Science*, 287, 248, 2000.
3. Bammer, G., Pharmacological investigations of neurotransmitter involvement in passive avoidance responding: a review and some new results, *Neurosci. Biobehav. Rev.*, 6, 247, 1982.
4. Bermúdez-Rattoni, F. and Prado-Alcalá, R.A., *Memoria: ¿En dónde está y cómo se forma?* Trillas, México, 2001, chap.1.
5. Decker, M.W. and McGaugh, J.L., The role of interactions between the cholinergic system and other neuromodulatory systems in learning and memory, *Synapse*, 7, 151, 1991.
6. Izquierdo, I. and McGaugh, J.L., Behavioral pharmacology and its contribution to the molecular basis of memory consolidation, *Behav. Pharmacol.*, 11, 517, 2000.
7. Bailey, C.H., Bartsch, D., and Kandel, E.R., Toward a molecular definition of long-term memory storage, *Proc. Natl. Acad. Sci. USA*, 93, 13445, 1996.
8. Stork, O. and Welzl, H., Memory formation and the regulation of gene expression, *Cell. Mol. Life Sci.*, 55, 575, 1999.
9. Mineur, Y.S., Crusio, W.E., and Sluyter, F., Genetic dissection of learning and memory in mice, *Neural Plast.*, 11, 217, 2004.
10. Josselyn, S.A. and Nguyen, P.V., CREB, synapses and memory disorders: past progress and future challenges, *Curr. Drug Targets CNS Neurol. Disord.*, 4, 481, 2005.
11. Alberini, C.M., Genes to remember, *J. Exp. Biol.*, 202, 2887, 1999.
12. Silva, A.J. et al., CREB and memory, *Annu. Rev. Neurosci.*, 21, 127, 1998.
13. Tischmeyer, W. and Grimm, R., Activation of immediate early genes and memory formation, *Cell. Mol. Life Sci.*, 55, 564, 1999.
14. McDonald, R.J. and White, N.M., A triple dissociation of memory systems: hippocampus, amygdala, and dorsal striatum, *Behav. Neurosci.*, 107, 3, 1993.
15. White, N.M. and McDonald, R.J., Multiple parallel memory systems in the brain of the rat, *Neurobiol. Learn. Mem.*, 77, 125, 2002.

16. Ambrogi-Lorenzini, C.G. et al., Neural topography and chronology of memory consolidation: a review of functional inactivation findings, *Neurobiol. Learn. Mem.*, 71, 1, 1999.
17. Izquierdo, I. and Medina, J.H., Role of the amygdala, hippocampus and entorhinal cortex in memory consolidation and expression, *Braz. J. Med. Biol. Res.*, 26, 573, 1993.
18. McGaugh, J.L., Memory consolidation and the amygdala: a systems perspective, *Trends Neurosci.*, 25, 456, 2002.
19. McGaugh, J.L., McIntyre, C.K., and Power, A.E., Amygdala modulation of memory consolidation: interaction with other brain systems, *Neurobiol. Learn. Mem.*, 78, 539, 2002.
20. Packard, M.G. and Knowlton, B.J., Learning and memory functions of the basal ganglia, *Annu. Rev. Neurosci.*, 25, 563, 2002.
21. Prado-Alcalá, R.A., et al., Memoria: consolidación y experiencia, in *Temas Selectos de Neurociencias III*, Velazquez-Moctezuma, J., Ed., Universidad Autónoma Metropolitana, México, 2004, p. 127.
22. Lewis, D.J. and Bregman, N.J., The cholinergic system, amnesia and memory, *Physiol. Behav.*, 8, 511, 1072.
23. Myers, B., Some effects of scopolamine on passive avoidance response in rats, *Psychopharmacologia*, 8, 111, 1965.
24. Bartus, R.T., et al., The cholinergic hypothesis: a historical overview, current perspective, and future directions, *Ann. NY Acad. Sci.*, 444, 332, 1985.
25. Fibiger, H.C., Cholinergic mechanisms in learning, memory and dementia: a review of recent evidence, *Trends Neurosci.*, 14, 220, 1991.
26. Gold, P.E., Acetylcholine modulation of neural systems involved in learning and memory, *Neurobiol. Learn. Mem.*, 80, 194, 2003.
27. Prado-Alcalá, R.A., Is cholinergic activity of the caudate nucleus involved in memory? *Life Sci.*, 37, 2135, 1985.
28. Power, A.E., Muscarinic cholinergic contribution to memory consolidation: with attention to involvement of the basolateral amygdala, *Curr. Med. Chem.*, 11, 987, 2004.
29. Duran-Arevalo, M., Cruz-Morales, S.E., and Prado-Alcalá, R.A., Is acetylcholine involved in memory consolidation of over-reinforced learning? *Brain Res. Bull.*, 24, 725, 1990.
30. Cruz-Morales, S.E. et al., A threshold for the protective effect of over-reinforced passive avoidance against scopolamine-induced amnesia, *Behav. Neural Biol.*, 57, 256, 1992.
31. Quirarte, G.L., et al., Protective effect of under-reinforcement of passive avoidance against scopolamine-induced amnesia, *Brain Res. Bull.*, 32, 521, 1993.
32. Altman, H.J. and Normile, H.J., Enhancement of the memory of a previously learned aversive habit following pretest administration of a variety of serotonergic antagonists in mice, *Psychopharmacology*, 90, 24, 1986.
33. Archer, T., Ögren, S.O., and Ross, S.B., Serotonin involvement in aversive conditioning: Reversal of the fear retention deficit by long-term p-chloroamphetamine but not p-chlorophenylalanine, *Neurosci. Lett.*, 34, 75, 1982.
34. Meneses, A., A pharmacological analysis of an associative learning task: 5-HT1 to 5-HT7 receptor subtypes function on a Pavlovian/instrumental autoshaped memory, *Learn. Mem.*, 10, 363, 2003.
35. Meneses, A., 5-HT system and cognition, *Neurosci. Biobehav. Rev.*, 23, 1111, 1999.

36. Meneses, A., et al., Expression of the 5-HT receptors in rat brain during memory consolidation, *Behav. Brain Res.*, 152, 425, 2004.
37. Ögren, S.O., Evidence for a role of brain serotonergic neurotransmission in avoidance learning, *Acta Physiol. Scand. Suppl.*, 544, 1, 1985.
38. Ögren, S.O., Analysis of the avoidance learning deficit induced by the serotonin releasing compound p-chloroamphetamine, *Brain Res. Bull.*, 16, 645, 1986.
39. Ögren, S.O., Serotonin receptor involvement in the avoidance learning deficit caused by p-chloroamphetamine-induced serotonin release, *Acta Physiol. Scand.*, 126, 449, 1986.
40. Solana-Figueroa, R., Quirarte, G.L., and Prado-Alcalá, R.A., Effects of pretraining systemic administration of p-chloroamphetamine on inhibitory avoidance trained with high and low foot-shock, *Rev. Mex. Psicol.*, 16, 211, 1999.
41. Solana-Figueroa, R., et al., Enhanced inhibitory avoidance training protects against the amnesic effect of p-chloroamphetamine, *Life Sci.*, 71, 391, 2002.
42. Oei, T.P.S. and King, M.G., Effects of extended training on rats depleted of central and/or peripheral catecholamines, *Pharmacol. Biochem. Behav.*, 9, 243, 1978.
43. Benninger, R.J., Phillips, A.G., and Fibiger, H.C., Prior training and intermittent retraining attenuate pimozide-induced avoidance deficits, *Pharmacol. Biochem. Behav.*, 18, 619, 1983.
44. Haycock, J.W. et al., Retrograde amnesia and cholinergic systems in the caudate–putamen complex and dorsal hippocampus, *Exp. Neurol.*, 41, 201, 1973.
45. Giordano, M. and Prado-Alcalá, R.A., Retrograde amnesia induced by post-trial injection of atropine into the caudate-putamen: protective effect of the negative reinforcer, *Pharmacol. Biochem. Behav.*, 24, 905, 1986.
46. Díaz del Guante, M.A. et al., Over-reinforcement protects against memory deficits induced by muscarinic blockade of the striatum, *Bol. Estud. Med. Biol.*, 38, 49, 1990.
47. Pérez-Ruíz, C. and Prado-Alcalá, R.A., Retrograde amnesia induced by lidocaine injection into the striatum: protective effect of the negative reinforcer, *Brain Res. Bull.*, 22, 599, 1989.
48. Ambrogi-Lorenzini, C.G. et al., Passive avoidance response distribution by posttraining substantia nigra functional tetrodotoxin inactivation in the rat, *Arch. Ital. Biol.*, 132, 85, 1994.
49. Da Cunha, C., et al., The lesion of the rat substantia nigra pars compacta dopaminergic neurons as a model for Parkinson's disease memory disabilities, *Cell. Mol. Neurobiol.*, 22, 227, 2002.
50. Da Cunha, C. et al., Evidence for the substantia nigra pars compacta as an essential component of a memory system independent of the hippocampal memory system, *Neurobiol. Learn. Mem.*, 79, 236, 2003.
51. Díaz del Guante, M.A. et al., Amnesia produced by pretraining infusion of serotonin into the substantia nigra, *Neuroreport*, 15, 2527, 2004.
52. Routtenberg, A. and Holzman, N., Memory disruption by electrical stimulation of substantia nigra, pars compacta, *Science*, 181, 83, 1973.
53. Cobos-Zapiaín, G.G. et al., High level of footshock during inhibitory avoidance training prevents amnesia induced by intranigral injection of GABA antagonists, *Neurobiol. Learn. Mem.*, 65, 202, 1996.
54. Rodrigues, S.M., Schafe, G.E., and LeDoux, J.E., Molecular mechanisms underlying emotional learning and memory in the lateral amygdala, *Neuron*, 44, 75, 2004.
55. Thatcher, R.W. and Kimble, D.P., Effect of amygdaloid lesions on retention of an avoidance response in overtrained and non-overtrained rats, *Psychonomic Sci.*, 6, 9, 1966.

56. Parent, M.B. and McGaugh, J.L., Posttraining infusion of lidocaine into the amygdala basolateral complex impairs retention of inhibitory avoidance training, *Brain Res.*, 661, 97, 1994.
57. Parent, M.B. et al., Spared retention of inhibitory avoidance learning after posttraining amygdala lesions, *Behav. Neurosci.*, 109, 803, 1995.
58. Parent, M.B., Tomaz, C., and McGaugh, J.L., Increased training in an aversively motivated task attenuates the memory-impairing effects of posttraining N-methyl-D-aspartate-induced amygdala lesions, *Behav. Neurosci.,* 106, 789, 1992.
59. Parent, M.B., West, M., and McGaugh, J.L., Memory of rats with amygdala lesions induced 30 days after footshock-motivated escape training reflects degree of original training, *Behav. Neurosci.*, 108, 1080, 1994.
60. Salado-Castillo, R. et al., Reversible lesions of striatum, amygdala, and substantia nigra after inhibitory avoidance: differential effects of high and low footshock intensity, *SNF 25th Annual Meeting*, San Diego, CA, 1995.
61. Izquierdo, I. et al., Neurotransmitter receptors involved in posttraining memory processing by the amygdala, medial septum, and hippocampus of the rat, *Behav. Neural Biol.*, 58, 16, 1992.
62. Lorenzini, C.A. et al., Role of dorsal hippocampus in acquisition, consolidation and retrieval of rat's passive avoidance response: a tetrodotoxin functional inactivation study, *Brain Res.*, 730, 32, 1996.
63. Martinez, I. et al., Effects of lesions of hippocampal fields CA1 and CA3 on acquisition of inhibitory avoidance, *Neuropsychobiology*, 46, 97, 2002.
64. Stubley-Weatherly, L., Harding, J.W., and Wright, J.W., Effects of discrete kainic acid-induced hippocampal lesions on spatial and contextual learning and memory in rats, *Brain Res.*, 716, 29, 1996.
65. Quiroz, C. et al., Enhanced inhibitory avoidance learning prevents the memory-impairing effects of posttraining hippocampal inactivation, *Exp. Brain Res.*, 153, 400, 2003.
66. Prado-Alcalá, R.A. et al., A possible caudate-cholinergic mechanism in two instrumental conditioned responses, *Psychopharmacologia*, 25, 339, 1972.
67. Prado-Alcalá, R.A. and Cobos-Zapiaín, G.G., Learning deficits induced by cholinergic blockade of the caudate nucleus as a function of experience, *Brain Res.*, 138, 190, 1977.
68. Prado-Alcalá, R.A. and Cobos-Zapiaín, G.G., Interference with caudate nucleus activity by potassium chloride, Evidence for a "moving" engram, *Brain Res.*, 172, 577, 1979.
69. Prado-Alcalá, R.A. et al., Cholinergic blockade of the caudate nucleus and spatial alternation performance in rats: overtraining induced protection against behavioral deficits, *Life Sci.*, 23, 889, 1978.
70. Prado-Alcalá, R.A., Kaufmann, P., and Moscona, R., Scopolamine and KCl injections into the caudate nucleus: overtraining-induced protection against deficits of learning, *Pharmacol. Biochem. Behav.*, 12, 249, 1980.
71. Prado-Alcalá, R.A., Serial and parallel processing during memory consolidation, in *Plasticity in the Central Nervous System: Learning and Memory*, McGaugh, J.L., Bermúdez-Rattoni, F., and Prado-Alcalá, R.A., Eds., Erlbaum, Mahwah, NJ, 1995, chap. 4.

10 Studies of Short-Term Avoidance Memory

Martín Cammarota, Lia R.M. Bevilaqua, Jorge H. Medina, and Iván Izquierdo

CONTENTS

10.1 SUMMARY

For almost a century it has been assumed that short-term memory (STM) is in charge of cognition while long-term memory (LTM) is consolidated over several hours. A major question is whether STM is merely a step toward LTM or a separate entity. This chapter presents experimental evidence showing that several compounds with specific molecular actions given into different memory-relevant areas of the brain after inhibitory avoidance training can effectively block or enhance STM retention without affecting or producing inverse effects on LTM consolidation. The effects of different metabolic inhibitors on working memory (WM) were also studied. In some brain regions WM is affected by receptor blockers that alter either STM or LTM; in other areas it is not affected. We also present behavioral data that further endorse the hypothesis that STM is separated from LTM: (1) STM is not susceptible to extinction while LTM can be readily extinguished and (2) STM retention is not sensitive to a novel experience 1 hour after training while LTM certainly is.

10.2 INTRODUCTION

We are all aware that, despite the fact we employ only one word to name them all, memories are not all equal. We form memories that tell us who we are, where we come from, and (hopefully) where we are going. These are called declarative memories,[1,2] and they can be either episodic (autobiographic) or semantic (general knowledge of the world). We also have memories that allow us to ride a bike or to type and format this chapter using appropriate computer software. These memories are procedural or implicit. In humans, declarative memory is related to the ability to recall or recognize people, places, and objects. It is obvious that experimental animals like rodents cannot declare anything. However, rodents can be tested about their memories for places, objects, and odors. Several studies indicate that lesions of the hippocampus and related structures interfere with long-term storage of this kind of memory. One major focus of research on declarative memory in rodents concerns the role of hippocampus in aversive and spatial memories.

This chapter deals with another classification of memory — one that is particularly valid for declarative memories — and subdivides them taking into account their durations. Therefore, we have short-term memories (STMs) that last seconds or a few minutes and long-term memories (LTMs) that we usually refer to when colloquially speaking about memory and which can persist for a lifetime.[3,4] Despite the fact that for almost a century it has been assumed that STM is in charge of cognition while LTM is slowly formed (or consolidated; see below) over several hours, this issue is still unsolved. A major question is whether STM is merely a step toward LTM or a separate entity.

In one-trial inhibitory avoidance (IA; sometimes also called passive avoidance), animals learn not to step down from a platform in order to avoid mild foot shocks.[5–16] This may be viewed as explicit memory, to the point that terms such as "declarative" or "explicit" can be applied to experiments using rodents. IA has the following characteristics:

1. Its rapid acquisition (in seconds) facilitates the analysis of the biochemical events involved in memory formation.
2. It is usually acquired in a single trial, uncontaminated by prior or further trials, rehearsals, or retrievals.
3. It depends on the integrated activity of CA1, the entorhinal cortex, and the posterior parietal cortex; it is modulated early on by the amygdala and medial septum and indirectly by stress hormones.
4. It is not an inborn or implicit learning.

IA is a form of learning that engages several sensory stimuli including spatial and visual perception, sensitivity to pain, and emotional, fear-driven components. It involves the specific repression of the natural tendencies of rats to survey a novel environment without affecting the performance of exploratory behavior while on the safe, nonaversive part of the training box. This is evidenced by the repeated approximations to the border of the safe area during testing and the display of abortive step-down (or -through, depending on the nature of the test; see below) responses. For this reason, we prefer the term *inhibitory* to *passive*.[17]

Many variants of inhibitory avoidance exist. A rodent, for example will not step through a door into a compartment where it received a foot shock. Flies will not reenter a foul-odor area and chicks will not peck bitter beads. Humans refrain from putting their fingers into electrical outlets and crossing streets without looking for traffic. Obviously, these activities represent major determinants of survival behavior throughout the animal kingdom.

This chapter deals, in particular, with STM and LTM of IA. In addition, we touchupon the possible relations of STM and LTM with working memory (WM), a nonarchival type of short-term memory that results from the recent processing of both previously stored and recently acquired information. Putative subdivisions of STM and LTM will be ignored inasmuch as they are irrelevant to the findings discussed here and we have no tangible biological basis to substantiate any such subdivision. We will therefore restrict ourselves to James McGaugh's concept of "three memory trace systems: one for immediate memory ... one for short-term memory (which develops in a few seconds or minutes and lasts for several hours); and one which consolidates slowly and is relatively permanent."[3]

Immediate memory lasting seconds or a few minutes[18] is now identified with WM[19] and indeed is often the only way to measure it. WM and the other types (STM and LTM) pertain to entirely different categories of phenomena. WM is primarily dependent on the electrical activities of neurons of the prefrontal cortex and other efferent cortical regions.[20,21] It persists only as long as this electrical activity persists; i.e., it is basically an online system. STM and LTM are, instead, systems whose main role is to preserve memory off-line for further use when required. The lingering of WM over a few seconds or minutes is accounted for by off-responses of the neurons in charge of WM. Unlike STM and LTM, WM is not an archive of individual memories but rather an administrator of cognitive events that constantly change and it can relate them to information that is already stored or may be archived.

Since WM subserves an entirely different function from STM or LTM, it makes no sense to call processes that take place between the end of WM and the consolidation of LTM "intermediate" — a term in use decades ago. Here we will use STM to designate memory that develops within a few seconds or minutes and lasts several hours while the consolidation of LTM proceeds slowly. LTM will be used to designate memories lasting 24 hours or more.

10.3 STM AND LTM: PARALLEL OR SEQUENTIAL?

In 1890, William James[22] proposed that while LTM formation is taking place, one or more STM systems are in charge. Other authors developed this concept, but a key question remained unanswered until recently: is STM only a step toward LTM or does formation of these memory types reflect separate processes? To respond to the question, it is necessary to demonstrate in the same animal that STM for a given task can be suppressed without affecting LTM.

Early attempts to disentangle STM from LTM were unsuccessful because the treatments used to block one or the other memory type were either too stressful or unspecific and therefore ended up affecting performance.[18,23] Further, most early experiments were based on the premise that memory measured 1 min or so after acquisition was expressed from STM. Now we know that it reflects WM instead. Over the years, many treatments were found to preserve STM but cancel LTM.[24,25]

These experiments were uninformative as to the questions presented above. Treatments that spared STM and blocked LTM were ambiguous as to whether these memory types were separated or sequential. Several years ago, it was found that the non-specific 5HT antagonist cyproheptadine blocked short- but not long-lasting 5HT-dependent facilitation of monosynaptic responses in the Aplysia mollusk.[26] This was the first report concerning a mechanistic separation of short- and long-lasting forms of plasticity. The results were clear but doubts remained about how good an example of memory is the facilitation of a monosynaptic response.

To extend these findings to STM and LTM of one-trial step-down inhibitory avoidance in rats, we used drugs with specific actions on definite receptors or on the intracellular signaling pathways associated with them. The LTM of IA is not established immediately after acquisition; it undergoes a protracted consolidation process that takes from 3 to 9 hours and involves a sequence of tightly knit and highly specific molecular events in the CA1 area of the hippocampus and connected subcortical and neocortical structures.[27]

There is no direct way to extricate the biochemistry of the early consolidation stages from that of STM because both occur simultaneously in the same brain regions. Lesions and genetic manipulations are particularly unsuitable for such an enterprise because both have consequences that are long-lasting or irreversible and will contaminate any memory studied after them, whether short or long. The only adequate tool to address this problem is to use drugs known to rapidly, specifically, and reversibly affect those biochemical events.

Here we show the effect on the STM and LTM of IA — and in some cases on WM as well — of drugs known to act exclusively on certain molecular targets (see Table 10.1) and affect specific steps of LTM consolidation when given into (1) the CA1 region of the dorsal hippocampus; (2) the entorhinal cortex; (3) the posterior parietal cortex; (4) the prefrontal cortex; and (5) the basolateral amygdala of rats. We did not measure STM at posttraining times shorter than 1.5 hours to avoid the possible effects of the infused drugs (or of the infusion procedure itself) on memory retrieval.

We chose to use a one-trial step-down inhibitory avoidance task in rats because its rapid acquisition facilitates the analysis of the time of occurrence of posttraining events and mainly because its pharmacology and molecular bases have been most extensively studied by our group, particularly in the CA1 and entorhinal cortex.[11,28–41] Moreover, unlike multitrial learning tasks, IA allows discrimination between the pharmacology of immediate memory (WM) and that of STM.

Three-month old Wistar male rats weighing 230 to 260 g and raised in our own facilities were used in all the experiments. They had free access to food and water and were housed four or five to a cage and kept at 21 to 23°C under a 12-hour light-and-dark cycle (lights on at 7 a.m.). To implant the rats with indwelling cannulae,

TABLE 10.1
Drugs Used to WM, STM, and LTM of IA in Rats

Drug	Action
AP5	NMDA receptor antagonist
CNQX	AMPA receptor antagonist
SC	Muscarinic receptor antagonist
Muscimol (MUS)	GABAa receptor agonist
KN62	CaMKII inhibitor
Noradrenaline (NOR)	Adrenoceptor agonist
Staurosporine (STA)	PKC inhibitor
SCH23390 (SCH)	Dopamine D1 receptor antagonist
MCGP	mGluR antagonist
SKF38393 (SKF)	Dopamine D1 receptor agonist
Timol OL (TIM)	Noradrenergic antagonist
8-OH-DPAT (DPAT)	5-HT1A receptor agonist
NAN-190 (NAN)	5-HT1A receptor antagonist
Lavendustin A (LAV)	Tyr kinase inhibitor
LY83583 (LY)	Guanylyl ciclase inhibitor
KT5823	PKG inhibitor
PD098059 (PD)	MEK1/2 inhibitor
8-BR-cAMP (8-Br)	cAMP analog
Forskolin (FOR)	Adenylyl ciclase activator
KT5720	PKA inhibitor
Picrotoxin (PIC)	Cl^- channel blocker

they were deeply anesthetized with thiopental (30 to 50 mg/Kg i.p.) and 27-gauge cannulae were stereotaxically aimed to different brain regions in accordance with coordinates taken from the atlas of Paxinos and Watson.[42] The animals were allowed to recover from surgery for at least 4 days before training commenced. IA training was performed in a 50 × 25 × 25 cm Plexiglass box with a 5 cm high, 8 cm wide, and 25 cm long platform on the left end of a series of bronze bars that formed the floor of the box.

During the training session, the animals were gently placed on the platform facing the left rear corner of the training box. When an animal stepped down and placed its four paws on the grid, it received a 2-sec, 0.5-mA scrambled footshock (US). Memory retention was evaluated twice: first at 1.5 hours after training to measure STM and again at 24 hours to measure LTM. One concern was whether testing the animals twice might alter LTM either by extinction or by a reminder effect. This was ruled out by four facts: (1) no significant differences between STM and LTM were noted in control groups; (2) all the treatments studied were found to affect LTM retention scores equally regardless of whether a preceding STM test was administered or not; (3) repeated nonreinforced testing during the first 4.5 hours after training did not lead to extinction, whereas recurred retrieval in the absence of the ensuing foot shock between 24 and 96 hours posttraining did so (Figure 10.1)[43] (4) we found no evidence of a Kamin-like effect, a non-associative inhibition of retrieval that sometimes occurs early after training that has been described for

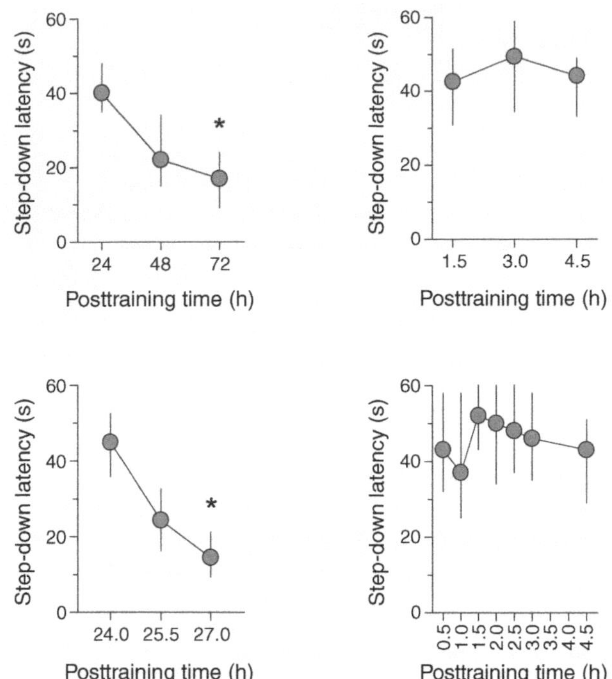

FIGURE 10.1 Animals trained in IA were submitted to three or seven nonreinforced test sessions at 24, 48, and 72 hours (A); 1.5, 3.0, and 4.5 hours (B); 24, 25.5, and 27.0 hours (C); or 0.5, 1, 1.5, 2, 2.5, 3, and 4.5 hours (D) after training. Values expressed as median ± interquartile range of step-down latency. n = 8 to 12 animals per group. * = $p < 0.005$ versus test latency 24 hours after training in Mann-Whitney U test.

animals trained using high intensity and/or repeated unconditioned stimuli in active avoidance tasks.[44,45]

10.4 ROLE OF HIPPOCAMPUS IN SHORT- AND LONG-TERM AVOIDANCE MEMORY

Table 10.2 summarizes the effects of different compounds infused into the CA1 region of the dorsal hippocampus. Several drugs, particularly glutamate and muscarinic antagonists (AP5, CNQX, MCPG, and scopolamine), PKA inhibitors (KT5720), and GABAa agonists (muscimol) blocked both STM and LTM. This suggests a link between STM and LTM at the glutamate receptor level and at the level of modulation by GABAergic and cholinergic muscarinic neurotransmission and also indicates a key role for hippocampal PKA activity immediately posttraining.

The effects of 8-Br-cAMP and forskolin agree with the latter suggestion. Some treatments had no effect on STM or on LTM (Timolol, NAN-190). Others selectively affected LTM: epinephrine improved it; KN-62, staurosporin, and KT5823 worsened

TABLE 10.2
Effects of Bilateral Infusions of Different Drugs into CA1 Region of Dorsal Hippocampus (CA1) or Entorhinal Cortex (EC) on IA STM and LTM Retention

	CA1		EC	
Drug	**STM**	**LTM**	**STM**	**LTM**
AP5	▼	▼	=	=
CNQX	▼	▼	▼	=
SC	▼	▼	=	=
MUS	▼	▼	▼	=
KN62	ND	▼	ND	ND
NOR	ND	▲	▲	▲
STA	ND	▼	▼	▼
SCH	▲	=	=	▼
MCGP	▼	▼	ND	ND
SKF	▼	▲	▼	▲
TIM	ND	ND	▼	ND
DPAT	▼	ND	▲	▼
NAN	ND	ND	▼	ND
LAV	ND	▼	ND	ND
LY	▼	▼	ND	ND
KT	ND	▼	ND	ND
PD	▼	ND	▲	▼
8-BR	▲	▲	ND	ND
FOR	▲	▲	ND	ND
KT	▼	▼	▼	▼

▼ = Impairment. ▲ = Enhancement. Equal sign = no change. ND = not determined. For doses employed, see original publications.[8,31,40,46–49] See text for additional references.

it. This suggests that in the CA1 region of the dorsal hippocampus, STM does not require CaMKII, PKC, or PKG activity. Most important, three of the compounds selectively blocked STM without affecting LTM when given into CA1, SKF38393, 8-OH-DPAT, and PD098059, while one compound, SP600125, enhanced STM but blocked LTM.

10.5 ROLE OF ENTORHINAL CORTEX IN SHORT- AND LONG-TERM AVOIDANCE MEMORY

Table 10.2 summarizes the results obtained with infusions of several of the drugs listed in Table 10.1 into the entorhinal cortex. Only two of the compounds tested blocked STM and LTM: staurosporin and KT5720. SCH23390 impaired LTM selectively. Several drugs had opposing effects on both memory types. Thus 8-OH-DPAT and PD098059 enhanced STM but blocked LTM retention while SKF38393 depressed STM but improved LTM. As is the case with other physiological functions, similar regulatory mechanisms, mainly those that regulate the Ras-MAPK pathway and brain monoamines, simultaneously exert opposite effects on different parts of the brain (see below). CNQX and muscimol blocked STM selectively.

10.6 ROLES OF OTHER CORTICAL REGIONS AND AMYGDALA IN SHORT- AND LONG-TERM AVOIDANCE MEMORY

Table 10.3 shows the effects on STM and LTM of drugs given into the posterior parietal cortex (PPC) and the anterolateral prefrontal cortex (APC). Scopolamine blocked LTM when infused into any of these areas; in the parietal cortex, in addition, it inhibited STM. CNQX and muscimol blocked STM selectively when given into the parietal cortex. Surprisingly, AP5 had no effect on either STM or LTM when given into the parietal or prefrontal cortex. None of the treatments given into the amygdala had any effect on STM; conversely, all of them affected LTM.

It is important to stress here that none of the treatments mentioned above affected in any way retention test performance when given 5 min prior to the STM test or 1.5 hours before the LTM test.

10.7 NEUROBIOLOGICAL SEPARATION OF SHORT- AND LONG-TERM AVOIDANCE MEMORY

As the results presented above show, our experiments replicated and considerably extend those of Emptage and Carew.[26] STM can be depressed without affecting LTM, and this can be brought about by several treatments acting on different

TABLE 10.3
Effects of Bilateral Infusions of Different Drugs into Posterior Parietal Cortex (PAR), Anterolateral Prefrontal Cortex (PrF), or Basolateral Amygdala (BLA) on IA STM and LTM retention

	PAR		PrF		BLA	
Drug	**STM**	**LTM**	**STM**	**LTM**	**STM**	**LTM**
AP5	=	=	=	=	=	▼
CNQX	▼	=	=	▼	=	▼
SC	▼	▼	=	▼		▼
MUS	▼	=	=	▼	ND	▼
KN62	ND	ND	ND	ND	=	▼
PIC	ND	ND	ND	ND	=	▲
NOR	ND	ND	ND	ND	=	▲
SCH	=	=	=	▼	ND	ND

▼ = Impairment. ▲ = Enhancement. Equal sign = no change. ND = not determined. For doses employed, see original publications.[46–48,50,51] See text for additional references.

receptors and cellular signaling pathways in different regions of the brain. Moreover, a number of treatments were found to have opposite effects, depending on the memory type under scrutiny. Clearly, the mechanisms dealing with formation and maintenance STM are separated from those involved in LTM consolidation.

Obviously links exist between the processes involved with STM and LTM, both at the receptor and post-receptor levels. Both STM and LTM deal with the same basic sensorimotor representation. Indeed, a variety of treatments given in different brain areas affected both similarly (see Table 10.2 and Table 10.3). Frey and Morris[52] suggested various possible mechanisms of "synaptic tagging" in order to explain the links between short- and long-term potentiation (STP and LTP, respectively) or between the early and late molecular events that determine persistence of the plastic change over long periods.

10.8 STM AND LTM ARE BEHAVIORALLY DIFFERENT

At first glance, the STM and LTM of IA exhibit identical behavioral characteristics. The same set of stimuli and behavioral actions lead to the appearance of a tendency to refrain from stepping down from a platform placed inside a training box (i.e., the animals utilize the same information as input and emit identical behavioral responses as output). It is known that other behaviors (rearing, ambulation, etc.) are not modified by IA training. Furthermore, freezing is rarely seen during test sessions. All these characteristics apply both to STM and LTM. That is why we and others call this task inhibitory rather than passive avoidance.

However, STM and LTM have two major behavioral differences. One is the apparent lack of extinction of the former (Figure 10.1), which is by all means one characteristic that should be expected from its role of STM in cognition: to maintain remembering as long as it takes for LTM to be formed.[22] Step-down latencies do not change over a series of non-reinforced test sessions carried out in same animal from 0.5 to 4.5 hours after training, i.e., for the duration of STM. In contrast, if animals are repeatedly tested at 24, 48, and 72 or 24, 25.5, and 27.5 hours posttraining when their memories are retrieved from LTM, there is extinction.

In view of the long interval between tests used in these studies (0.5 to 1.5 hours), it is clear that this difference cannot be accounted for by a massed versus distributed trial-like effect. Furthermore, it is improbable that the resistance of STM to extinction is due to short-term sensitization of motor or sensory pathways that mask formation and/or expression of the CS-no-US association during STM. The foot shock used as unconditioned stimulus is too mild to produce such an effect. Further, if it existed in this task, short-term sensitization of sensory responses should induce reinforcement by retrieval with a subsequent increase in short- and long-term retention scores, something that did not happen.

The other major behavioral difference between STM and LTM is that the former is not while the latter is indeed greatly susceptible to the amnesic effect of exposure to a novel environment. Exposure to a novel environment 1 or 2 hours posttraining, but not 6 hours posttraining or 5 min preceding it has been known for some time to hinder LTM[53–55] and has been recently found to also inhibit CA1 LTP.[56] In the case of LTM, the effect is apparently due to a resetting of the NMDA receptor and

CaMKII-dependent mechanisms involved in CA1 in the early phases of IA LTM consolidation.

10.9 BIOCHEMISTRY OF SHORT-TERM MEMORY

Several of the experiments presented above provided hints of the biochemical differences between STM and LTM, mainly in the CA1 region and in the entorhinal cortex (Table 10.2 and Table 10.3). In CA1, both STM and LTM are dependent on the integrity of AMPA, NMDA, and metabotropic glutamate receptors, and on their presumable modulation by cholinergic, muscarinic, β-adrenergic. and GABAa receptors. LTM[30,34,57] is and STM is not dependent upon PKC, PKG, and CaMKII activation.[46–48]

PKA activity evidently exerts different influences on the two memory types. The role of PKA in LTM formation involves phosphorylation of the nuclear transcription factor CREB twice: first right after training and again 3 to 6 hours posttraining.[28,35] The role of PKA in STM presumably involves other substrates inasmuch as CREB phosphorylation levels are low between those two peaks. It is tempting to suggest that some substrate of PKA may be involved in the tagging of synapses during the early phase of memory formation in CA1 during which STM runs its full course as has indeed been suggested for the early phase of LTP.[52]

The effect of PD098059 given immediately posttraining into CA1 or entorhinal cortex (Table 10.2) on STM and LTM shows an interesting mirror image. In CA1, the role of the ERK1/2 pathway would appear to be restricted largely to the up-regulation of STM. Simultaneously, in the entorhinal cortex, the activation of this pathway seems to impair STM formation and to be necessary for the formation of LTM. Studies with PD098059 and U0126 given at different times after training into these two brain regions indeed point to a role of ERK1/2 in LTM consolidation.[35,40] This pathway plays a rather complex regulatory role in plastic events. It is linked at various different levels with the PKC, CaMKII, and PKA cascades,[58,59] all of which are crucial for LTP and LTM and, depending on brain structure and posttraining time, also for STM.

With respect to the dual effect of the JNK inhibitor SP600125,[11] it is quite possible that because JNK activation up-regulates gene expression through the phosphorylation of the transcription factor c-jun at Ser 63 and 73,[60] the deleterious effect of SP600125 on LTM consolidation could probably be due to inhibition of this transcription factor. Indeed, considerable evidence indicates that c-jun activity is necessary for the consolidation of the long-term mnemonic trace associated with a variety of learning paradigms.

It is unlikely that JNK influences on gene expression are involved in STM, a form of memory that is brief in nature and probably maintained as a consequence of a transient enhancement in synaptic functionality and neurotransmitter release. In this respect, it has been reported that JNK activation is negatively correlated with the depolarization-induced release of glutamate from synaptosomes, an effect that may indicate that JNK controls the release of this neurotransmitter in some way. In fact, it has been suggested that the rapid up-regulation of the JNK pathway induced

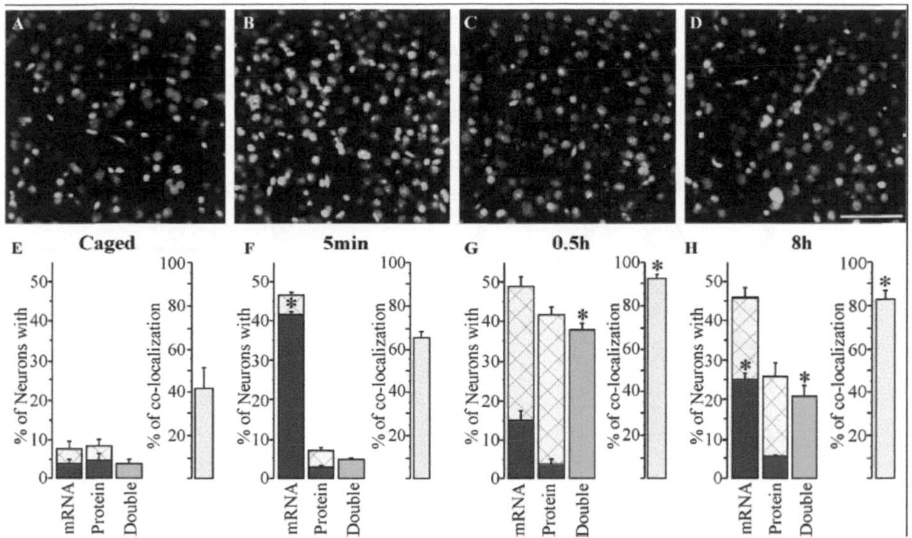

FIGURE 3.2 (See Figure caption on page 56.)

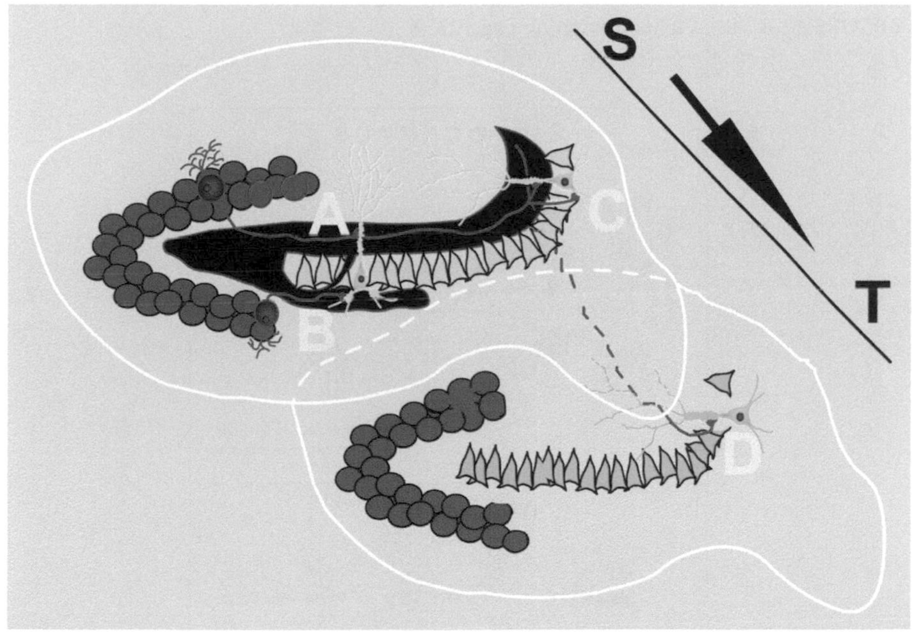

FIGURE 5.1 (See Figure caption on page 99.)

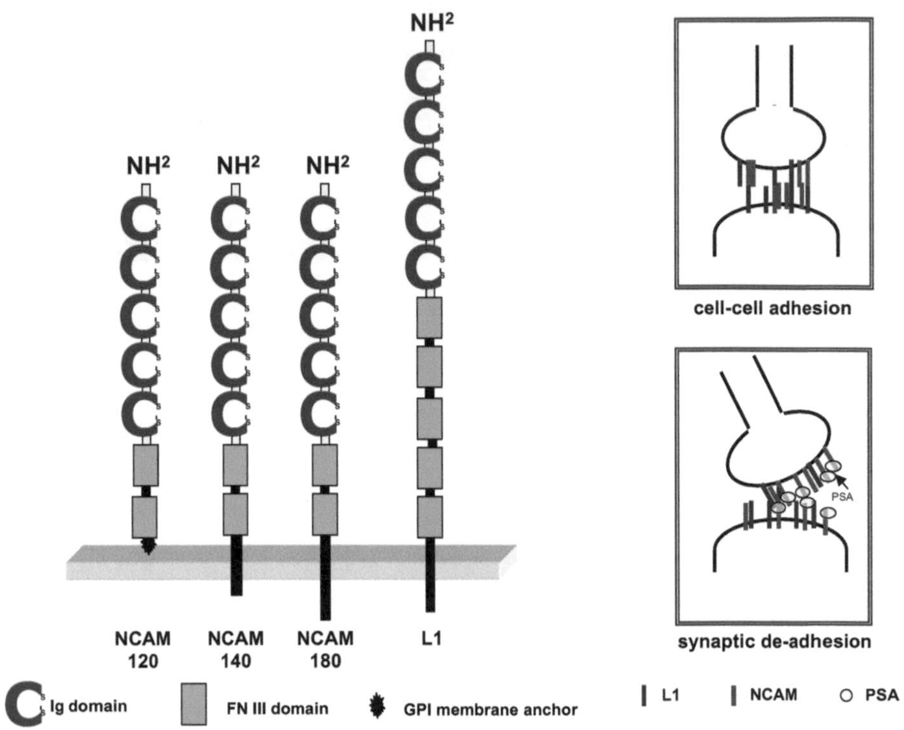

FIGURE 12.4 (See Figure caption on page 235.)

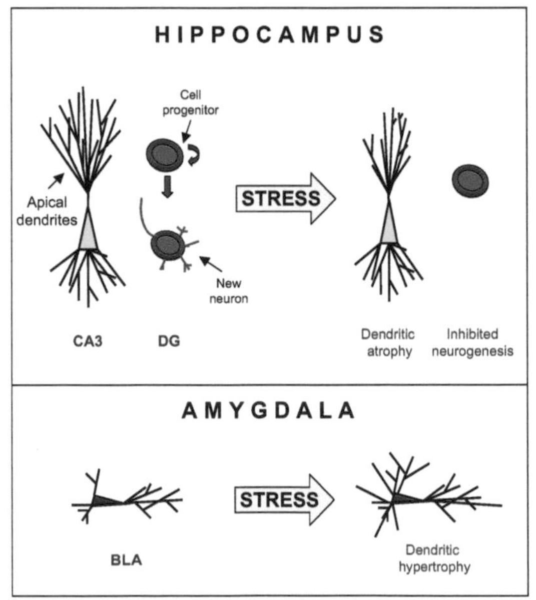

FIGURE 12.6 (See Figure caption on page 240.)

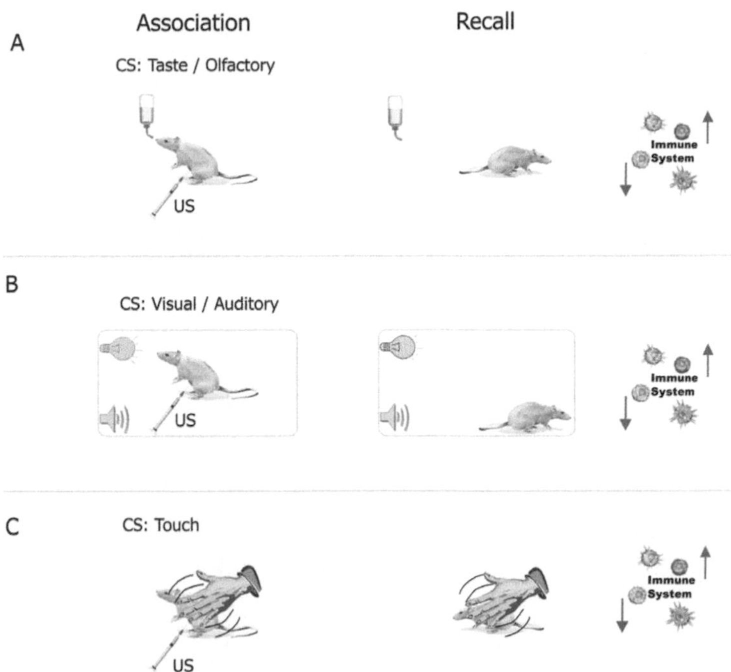

FIGURE 14.1 (See Figure caption on page 289.)

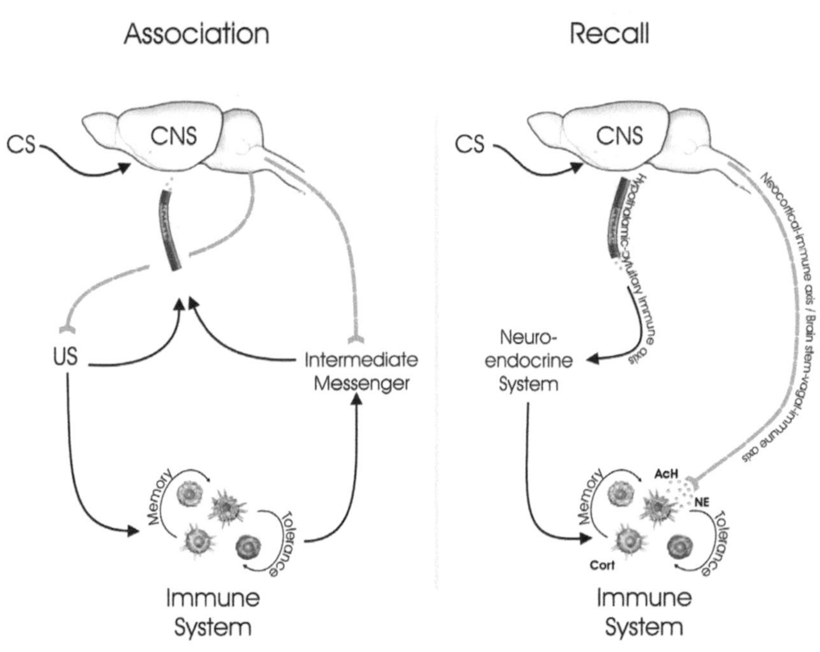

FIGURE 14.3 (See Figure caption on page 292.)

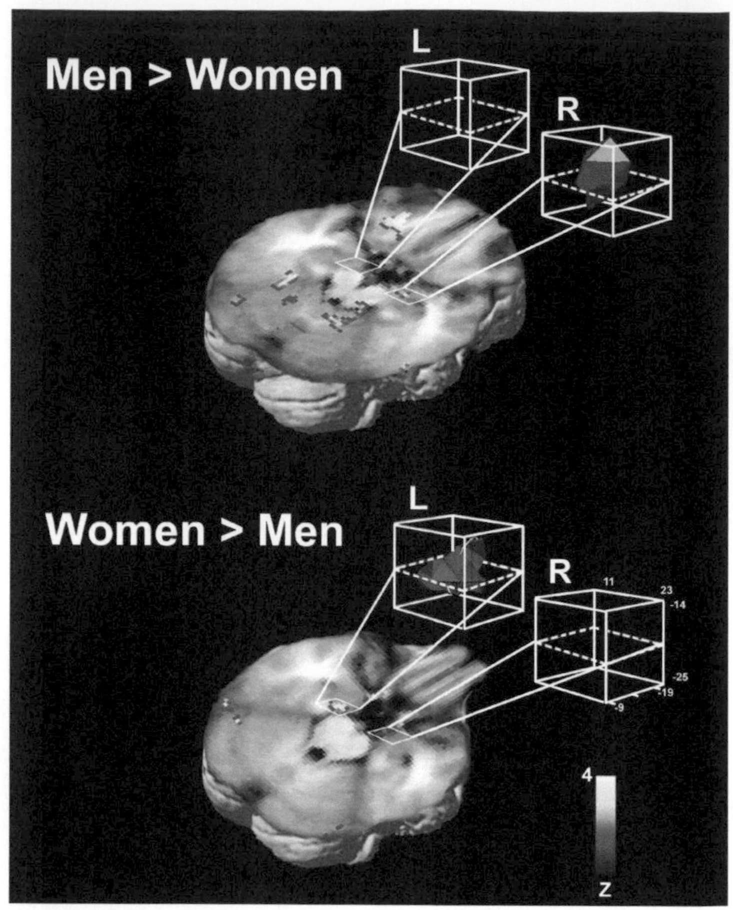

FIGURE 15.2 (See Figure caption on page 317.)

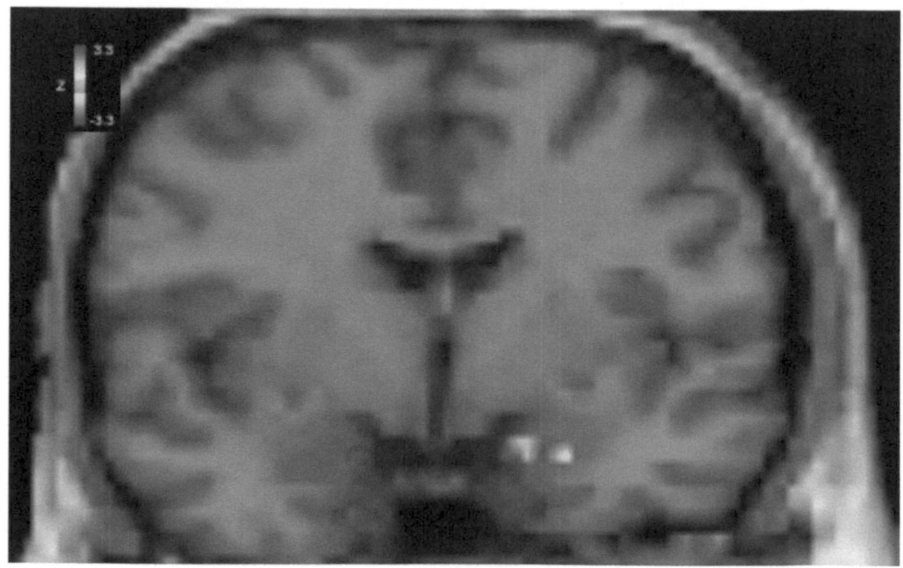

FIGURE 15.3 (See Figure caption on page 318.)

by interleukin-1 is responsible for the inhibitory effect of this protein on synaptic potentiation in the hippocampus.[61,62]

In contrast to what happens in the CA1 region of the hippocampus, NMDA receptors in the entorhinal cortex or elsewhere are not involved in STM. In the entorhinal cortex, however, again in contrast to the hippocampus, early posttraining PKC activity is necessary for STM and LTM, along with PKA activity.

The simultaneous regulation of STM and LTM by monoaminergic systems acting in the posttraining period in CA1 and in the entorhinal cortex is different and, in the case of 5HT1A receptors, opposite.[63,54] No straightforward comment can be made at this stage in terms of memory modulation by these systems related to the perception and expression of emotion and affect. They simultaneously do different things to the different memory types, and the final outcome in terms of what the subject will eventually remember in the short or in the long run very probably depends on the state of the systems at the time of training. Further, it will surely depend on the relation of the task to ongoing or previous emotions or affective states and on the impact of the cognitive content of the task on the monoaminergic systems.

It is interesting that the amygdala, which is crucial for immediate posttraining modulation of fear-motivated learning tasks such as IA[36] is almost completely unrelated both to the late modulation of LTM[63,64] and to the immediate posttraining modulation of STM and WM[50] (see next section).

10.10 PHARMACOLOGICAL ANALYSIS OF IA WORKING MEMORY

The only way to measure WM in a task such as IA, which is learned in a few seconds, is to measure immediate memory. Table 10.4 shows the effects on WM of

TABLE 10.4
Effects of Different Drugs Administered Bilaterally into CA1 Region of Dorsal Hippocampus (CA1), Entorhinal Cortex (EC), Posterior Parietal Cortex (PAR), Anterolateral Prefrontal Cortex (PrF), or Basolateral Amygdala (BLA) on IA WM Retention

Drug	CA1	EC	BLA	PAR	PrF
AP5	=	=	=	=	=
CNQX	▼	▼	=	▼	▼
SC	▼	▼	=	▼	=
MUS	▼	▼	=	▼	▼
PIC	ND	ND	=	ND	ND
STA	ND	ND	=	ND	ND
SCH	▼	=	=	▼	▼

▼ = Impairment. ▲ = Enhancement. Equal sign = no change. ND = not determined. For doses employed, see original publications.[31,46,50] See text for additional references.

several drugs known to affect STM, LTM, or both. The drugs were administered into different regions of the brain (posterior parietal, anterolateral, prefrontal or entorhinal cortex, dorsal CA1, and basolateral amygdala).

The WM retention test was carried out 3 sec after the footshock. CNQX and muscimol blocked WM when given into any of the cortical regions analyzed, indicating that AMPA receptor-mediated glutamatergic transmission may be susceptible to GABAergic inhibition which is necessary for WM processing in those areas. Scopolamine blocked WM when given into parietal or entorhinal cortex or into CA1. SCH23390 blocked WM when given into the prefrontal region, as shown previously by Goldman-Rakic and her group, but also when given into the parietal cortex or into CA1. AP5 had no effect on WM in any of the brain regions studied. None of the treatments affected WM when given into the amygdala, strongly suggesting that this nucleus plays no role in WM. In addition to the mechanisms in anterolateral prefrontal cortex described above, additional or subsidiary muscarinic and nicotinic processes in the basolateral amygdala that regulate WM have been described recently.[65]

10.11 CONCLUSIONS

The results presented above both indicate that the mechanisms involved in WM, STM, and LTM are essentially distinct and also, importantly, suggest the existence of a functional link between WM and LTM in prefrontal cortex, and between WM and STM in CA1 and in parietal and entorhinal cortex at the receptor level. Similar receptor systems appear to be involved in more than one memory type in each of those regions. Several of the results also suggest links between STM and LTM in CA1 and in the entorhinal cortex, both at the receptor level and at the post-receptor signaling level, i.e., in biochemical cascades known to be related to glutamate receptor stimulation.

The relative importance of any putative modulatory mechanism would be expected to vary with the nature of the task and with the relation of each task to other ongoing physiological events. Therefore, it may be appropriate, at least at this stage, to refrain from postulating theoretical connections or disconnections among memory types.

The popular concept that STM is only a passageway to LTM is certainly incorrect, as is the idea that WM may in any way constitute a sort of STM. At this stage, however, it is safe to say that WM, STM, and LTM pertain to and are regulated by separate subsystems of the brain that belong in some cases to the same and in others to different brain structures and involve a great variety of molecular mechanisms at the receptor and post-receptor level, some of which may be linked.

STM must rely basically on some of the nonstructural biochemical changes that occur soon after training in the synapses activated by that training. The mechanisms of STM ought to involve processes that keep recently activated synapses active while LTM slowly builds up. The phase in which STM mechanisms begin to fade away and those of LTM build up could well correspond to an intermediate type (or phase) of memory, which has not yet been demonstrated in mammals. This postulation is not really original; it merely results from a blend of the much earlier predictions of Ramón y Cajal.

REFERENCES

1. Squire, L., *Memory and Brain*, Oxford University Press, New York, 1987.
2. Markowitsch, H.J., Varieties of memory systems and structures: mechanisms of disturbance, *Neurol. Psychiatr. Brain Res.*, 2, 49, 1997.
3. McGaugh, J.L., Time-dependent processes in memory storage, *Science*, 153, 1351, 1966.
4. Cherkin, A., Kinetics of memory consolidation: role of amnesic treatment parameters, *Proc. Natl. Acad. Sci. USA*, 63, 1094, 1968.
5. Gold, P.E., The use of avoidance training in studies of modulation of memory storage, *Behav. Neural Biol.*,46, 87, 1986.
6. Da Cunha, C. et al., Memory facilitation by posttraining intraperitoneal, intracerebroventricular and intra-amygdala injection of Ro 5-4864, *Brain Res.*, 544, 133, 1991.
7. Fin, C. et al., Experiments suggesting a role for nitric oxide in the hippocampus in memory processes, *Neurobiol. Learn. Mem.*, 63, 113, 1995.
8. Izquierdo, I. and Medina, J.H., Memory formation: the sequence of biochemical events in the hippocampus and its connection to activity in other brain structures, *Neurobiol. Learn. Mem.*, 68, 285, 1997.
9. Barros, D.M. et al., Interaction between midazolam-induced anterograde amnesia and memory enhancement by treatments given hours later in hippocampus, entorrhinal cortex or posterior parietal cortex, *Behav. Pharmacol.,* 9, 163, 1998.
10. Vianna, M.R. et al., Retrieval of memory for fear-motivated training initiates extinction requiring protein synthesis in the rat hippocampus, *Proc. Natl. Acad. Sci. USA*, 98, 12251, 2001.
11. Bevilaqua, L.R. et al., Inhibition of hippocampal Jun N-terminal kinase enhances short-term memory but blocks long-term memory formation and retrieval of an inhibitory avoidance task, *Eur. J. Neurosci.*, 17, 897, 2003.
12. Cammarota, M. et al., Inhibition of mRNA and protein synthesis in the CA1 region of the dorsal hippocampus blocks reinstallment of an extinguished conditioned fear response, *J. Neurosci.*, 23, 737, 2003.
13. Luft, T. et al., Different time course for the memory facilitating effect of bicuculline in hippocampus, entorhinal cortex, and posterior parietal cortex of rats, *Neurobiol. Learn. Mem.*, 82, 52, 2004.
14. Alonso, M. et al., Endogenous BDNF is required for long-term memory formation in the rat parietal cortex, *Learn. Mem.*, 12, 504, 2005.
15. Da Silva, W.C., Histamine enhances inhibitory avoidance memory consolidation through a H2 receptor-dependent mechanism, *Neurobiol. Learn. Mem.*, 86, 100, 2006.
16. Bonini, J.S. et al., Angiotensin II disrupts inhibitory avoidance memory retrieval. *Horm. Behav.*, 50, 308, 2006.
17. Netto, C.A. and Izquierdo, I., On how passive is inhibitory avoidance, *Behav. Neural Biol.*, 43, 327, 1985.
18. Gold, P.E. and McGaugh, J.L., A single trace, two process view of memory storage processes, in *Short-Term Memory*, Deutsch & Deutsch, New York, 1975.
19. Goldman-Rakic, P.S., Regional and cellular fractionation of working memory, *Proc. Natl. Acad. Sci. USA*, 93, 13473, 1996.

20. Fuster, J.M., Distributed memory for both short and long term, *Neurobiol. Learn. Mem.*, 70, 268, 1998.
21. Wagner, A.D., Working memory contributions to human learning and remembering, *Neuron*, 22, 19, 1999.
22. James, W., *The Principles of Psychology*, New York, 1890.
23. Sara, S.J., Delayed development of amnestic behavior after hypoxia, *Physiol. Behav.*, 13, 693, 1974.
24. Bourtchuladze, R. et al., Deficient long-term memory in mice with a targeted mutation of the cAMP-responsive element-binding protein, *Cell*, 79, 59, 1994.
25. Xu, L., Anwyl, R., and Rowan, M.J., Spatial exploration induces a persistent reversal of long-term potentiation in rat hippocampus, *Nature*, 394, 891, 1998.
26. Emptage, N.J. and Carew T.J., Long-term synaptic facilitation in the absence of short-term facilitation in Aplysia neurons, *Science*, 262, 253, 1993.
27. Izquierdo, I. et al., Different molecular cascades in different sites of the brain are in charge of memory consolidation, *Trends Neurosci.*, in press, 2006.
28. Bernabeu, R. et al., Learning-specific, time-dependent increase in [^{3}H]-phorbol dibutyrate binding to protein kinase C in selected regions of the rat brain, *Brain Res.*, 685, 163, 1995.
29. Bernabeu, R. et al., Involvement of hippocampal cAMP/cAMP-dependent protein kinase signaling pathways in a late memory consolidation phase of aversively motivated learning in rats, *Proc. Natl. Acad. Sci. USA*, 94, 7041, 1997.
30. Bevilaqua, L.R. et al., Memory consolidation induces N-methyl-D-aspartic acid-receptor- and Ca2+/calmodulin-dependent protein kinase II-dependent modifications in alpha-amino-3-hydroxy-5-methylisoxazole-4-propionic acid receptor properties. *Neuroscience*, 136, 397, 2005.
31. Bianchin, M. et al., Memory of inhibitory avoidance in the rat is regulated by glutamate metabotropic receptors in the hippocampus, *Behav. Pharmacol.*, 5, 356, 1994.
32. Cammarota, M., Inhibitory avoidance training induces rapid and selective changes in [^{3}H]AMPA receptor binding in the rat hippocampal formation, *Neurobiol. Learn. Mem.*, 64, 257, 1995.
33. Cammarota, M. et al., B-50/GAP-43 phosphorylation and PKC activity are increased in rat hippocampal synaptosomal membranes after an inhibitory avoidance training, *Neurochem. Res.*, 22, 499, 1997.
34. Cammarota, M. et al., Learning-specific, time-dependent increases in hippocampal Ca2+/calmodulin-dependent protein kinase II activity and AMPA GluR1 subunit immunoreactivity, *Eur. J. Neurosci.*, 10, 2669, 1998.
35. Cammarota, M. et al., Learning-associated activation of nuclear MAPK, CREB and Elk-1, along with Fos production, in the rat hippocampus after a one-trial avoidance learning: abolition by NMDA receptor blockade, *Mol. Brain Res.*, 76, 36, 2000.
36. Jerusalinsky, D. et al., Amnesia by posttraining infusion of glutamate receptor antagonists into the amygdala, hippocampus, and entorhinal cortex, *Behav. Neural Biol.*, 58, 76, 1992.
37. Jerusalinsky, D. et al., Effect of antagonists of platelet-activating factor receptors on memory of inhibitory avoidance in rats, *Behav. Neural Biol.*, 62, 1, 1994.
38. Roesler, R. et al., Normal inhibitory avoidance learning and anxiety, but increased locomotor activity in mice devoid of PrP(C), *Mol. Brain Res.*, 71, 349, 1999.
39. Rossato, J.I. et al., Retrograde amnesia induced by drugs acting on different molecular systems, *Behav. Neurosci.*, 118, 563, 2004.

40. Walz, R. et al., Dose-dependent impairment of inhibitory avoidance retention in rats by immediate posttraining infusion of a mitogen-activated protein kinase kinase inhibitor into cortical structures, *Behav. Brain Res.*, 105, 219, 1999.
41. Wolfman, C. et al., Intrahippocampal or intraamygdala infusion of KN62, a specific inhibitor of calcium/calmodulin-dependent protein kinase II, causes retrograde amnesia in the rat, *Behav. Neural Biol.*, 61, 203, 1994.
42. Paxinos, G. and Watson, C., *The Rat Brain in Stereotaxic Coordinates*, Academic Press, San Diego, 1986.
43. Cammarota, M. et al., Relationship between short- and long-term memory and short- and long-term extinction, *Neurobiol. Learn. Mem.*, 84, 25, 2005.
44. Kamin, L.J., Retention of an incompletely learned avoidance response: some further analyses, *J. Comp. Physiol. Psychol.*, 56, 713, 1963.
45. Anisman, H., Cholinergic mechanisms and alterations in behavioral suppression as factors producing time-dependent changes in avoidance performance, *J. Comp. Physiol. Psychol.*, 83, 465, 1973.
46. Izquierdo, I. et al., Mechanisms for memory types differ, *Nature*, 393, 635, 1998.
47. Izquierdo, I. et al., Short- and long-term memory are differentially regulated by monoaminergic systems in the rat brain, *Neurobiol. Learn. Mem.*, 69, 219, 1998.
48. Izquierdo, I. et al., Differential involvement of cortical receptor mechanisms in working, short-term and long-term memory, *Behav. Pharmacol.*, 9, 421, 1998.
49. Walz, R. et al., Effects of posttraining infusions of a mitogen-activated protein kinase kinase inhibitor into the hippocampus or entorhinal cortex on short- and long-term retention of inhibitory avoidance, *Behav. Pharmacol.*, 10, 723, 1999.
50. Bianchin, M. et al., The amygdala is involved in the modulation of long-term memory, but not in working or short-term memory, *Neurobiol. Learn. Mem.*, 71, 127, 1999.
51. Vianna, M.R. et al., Intrahippocampal infusion of an inhibitor of protein kinase A separates short- from long-term memory, *Behav. Pharmacol.*, 10, 223, 1999.
52. Frey, U. and Morris, R.G., Synaptic tagging: implications for late maintenance of hippocampal long-term potentiation, *Trends Neurosci.*, 21, 181, 1998.
53. Izquierdo, I., Different forms of posttraining memory processing, *Behav. Neural. Biol.*, 51, 171, 1989.
54. Izquierdo, I. and Pereira, M.E., Posttraining memory facilitation blocks extinction but not retroactive interference, *Behav. Neural Biol.*, 51, 108, 1989.
55. Cahill, L. and McGaugh, J.L., Mechanisms of emotional arousal and lasting declarative memory, *Trends Neurosci.*, 21, 294, 1998.
56. Morris, R.G., Synaptic plasticity: down with novelty, *Nature,* 394, 834, 1998.
57. Bernabeu, R. et al., Further evidence for the involvement of a hippocampal cGMP/cGMP-dependent protein kinase cascade in memory consolidation, *Neuroreport*, 8, 2221, 1997.
58. Bhalla, U.S. and Iyengar, R., Emergent properties of networks of biological signaling pathways, *Science*, 283, 381, 1999.
59. Lisman, J.E. and Fallon, J.R., What maintains memories? *Science*, 283, 339, 1999.
60. Vogt, P.K., Jun, the oncoprotein, *Oncogene*, 20, 2365, 2001.
61. Vereker, E. et al., Evidence that interleukin-1- and reactive oxygen species production play a pivotal role in stress-induced impairment of LTP in the rat dentate gyrus, *Eur. J. Neurosci.*, 14, 1809, 2001.
62. Kelly, A. et al., The anti-inflammatory cytokine, interleukin (IL)-10, blocks the inhibitory effect of IL-1 beta on long term potentiation: a role for JNK, *J. Biol. Chem.*, 276, 45564, 2001.

63. Ardenghi, P. et al., Late and prolonged posttraining memory modulation in entorhinal and parietal cortex by drugs acting on the cAMP/protein kinase A signaling pathway. *Behav. Pharmacol.*, 8, 745, 1997.
64. Bevilaqua, L.R. et al., Drugs acting upon the cyclic adenosine monophosphate/protein kinase A signaling pathway modulate memory consolidation when given late after training into rat hippocampus but not amygdala, *Behav. Pharmacol.*, 8, 331, 1997.
65. Barros, D.M. et al., Modulation of working, short- and long-term memory by nicotinic receptors in the basolateral amygdala in rats, *Neurobiol. Learn. Mem.*, 83, 113, 2005.

11 Memory Reconsolidation or Updating Consolidation?

Carlos J. Rodriguez-Ortiz and Federico Bermúdez-Rattoni

CONTENTS

11.1 INTRODUCTION

For a long time, consolidation was seen as a process achieved only on newly acquired memories aimed to store them for the long term. However, pioneer and recent studies have demonstrated that after retrieval, long-term memories may once more undergo a consolidation-like process referred to as reconsolidation. Mainly, reconsolidation is sustained by the now widely reported observation that after a memory trace is activated by means of retrieval and is susceptible to disruption by the same treatments that disrupt memory during consolidation. However, the functional purpose of this process is still a matter of debate.

Recent evidence indicates that reconsolidation is indeed a process by which updated information is integrated through the synthesis of proteins to a memory trace. Hence, the so-called reconsolidation seems more like an updating consolidation intended to modify retrieved memory by a process that integrates updated experience into long-term memory. Through this process, previously consolidated memory is partially destabilized. By the infusion of disrupting agents, it appears as if the process is intended to consolidate memory again. In this chapter, we discuss this issue and propose that updating consolidation is a more descriptive term for this process.

11.2 CONSOLIDATION HYPOTHESIS

The classification of memories according to their duration was initiated by Hermann Ebbinghauss in his work titled "Uber das Gadachtnis" (About Memory) and formalized later by William James. From these works it appears that memory has, on the basis of its time course, at least two forms, namely short- and long-term memories. Although no fixed time span segregates these two memory forms, it is clear that information stored in long-term memory (LTM) undergoes a consolidation process that strengthens it over time into a stable memory trace.

This process does not take place for short-term memory (STM), which decays much sooner. The term *consolidation* is acknowledged to Müller and Pilzecker on their study reported in 1900. In one set of experiments, they trained subjects to memorize a list of paired syllables. On the test day, cue syllables (each one was a single syllable of a pair) were presented and the number of complementary recalled syllables was used as a measure of memory retention. A reduction in the number of retrieved syllables from the first list was observed if a second (distracting) list of syllables was presented shortly after training. Furthermore, the longer the interval between the two lists, the less the performance was affected. The researchers concluded that the second list interfered in a time-dependent manner on a physiological process that accounts for the strengthening of memories. They named this process "consolidirung."[1]

These observations were mostly ignored until Duncan reported almost 50 years later that he proved that an electroconvulsive shock (ECS) applied after training disrupted memory. Moreover, he showed that memory disruption correlated with the interval between training and ECS application. Since ECS was longer spaced in time from training, memory impairment was reduced. Since then, several other researchers have shown that interfering treatments — from ECS to intracerebral microinjections of protein synthesis inhibitors — applied after acquisition prevent LTM storage. Consistently, LTM is not affected if the intrusive treatment is applied outside the vulnerability window. This, along with the consolidation hypothesis, led to the idea that memory undergoes this time-dependent stabilization process only once. Reliability among a huge amount of related studies sustained the prominent place that this idea occupies in the current model of consolidation.[2,3]

An important transition in memory research took place after Hebb's dual-trace proposal suggesting that memory is at first in a labile state maintained by a reverberating neural ensemble. LTM arises from cellular changes in this ensemble allowing memory stabilization.[4] Although it is still matter of intense debate whether STM and LTM are serial or parallel processes, dual-trace theory stressed the weight that cellular entities have in memory processing, turning research to the cellular events underlying memory. At the cellular level, STM undergoes activation of *transduction*[*] cascades (mainly kinase pathways) after neuronal stimulation. It is proposed that

[*] *Process by which a cell converts an extracellular signal into a response.*[5]

STM remains as long as these cascades are active but for LTM, transduction signals are carried to the nucleus where *transcription** is achieved. Afterward, RNA *translation*† will ultimately lead to protein synthesis. These proteins account for cellular plastic changes that are considered the cellular correlations of stable LTM traces, i.e., they are considered the cellular counterparts of consolidation. Hence, memory consolidation requires protein synthesis. It has been extensively reported that protein synthesis inhibition disrupts LTM without affecting STM.[3,7–9]

11.3 RECONSOLIDATION ERA

As noted earlier, consolidation was seen as a process achieved only on newly acquired memories with the intent of long-term storage. However, pioneer studies indicated that consolidated memories may undergo a consolidation-like process more than once under certain conditions. In 1968, Misanin et al.[10] habituated rats to lick from a drinking bottle in a conditioning chamber, after which they were trained in a fear conditioning task in which a tone (conditioned stimulus, CS) was paired to a footshock (unconditioned stimulus, US). As a result, a conditioned response was obtained and used as a measure of memory, in this case, a reduced licking rate from the water bottle after the tone onset. They reported that an ECS applied immediately after conditioning disrupted memory consolidation (Figure 11.1b, Group 2). The interesting point arose from Group 3. Those animals were trained but without delivery of an ECS. A day later, the consolidated fear memory was reactivated by presenting the tone again. Immediately after this memory reactivation, an ECS was applied with the surprising result that memory was impaired when tested 24 hours later (Figure 11.1b, Group 3). Notably, ECS was unable to disrupt memory if the tone cue was not presented (Figure 11.1b, Group 4) and the phenomenon was referred as cue-dependent amnesia.[10]

Even though these results were at first not replicated,[11] they encouraged further (mainly unnoticed) work on the possibility that consolidated memories enter into an active stage upon retrieval. For example, Gordon showed that as occurs with newly acquired memories, retrieved memories are susceptible to disruption in a time-dependent manner.[12] Cue-dependent amnesia was further studied in the active–inactive memory model proposed by Lewis.[13] who claimed that memories become active under two conditions: when newly acquired and when reactivated by means of retrieval. Any other memory is in an inactive stable state. Recently, cue-dependent amnesia was taken up again and is now referred as reconsolidation.

Reconsolidation proposes that after a memory trace is activated by means of retrieval, it is susceptible to disruption by the same treatments that disrupt memory during consolidation.[14,15] In 1992, Bucherelli and Tassoni[16] reported that inactivation of the parabrachial nuclei by infusions of tetrodotoxin disrupted previously consolidated memories when reactivated. Similarly, Susan Sara's group reported that infusions of either NMDA or β-adrenergic antagonists (which disrupted LTM when

* *Synthesis of RNA on DNA template.*[6]

† *Synthesis of protein on mRNA template.*[6]

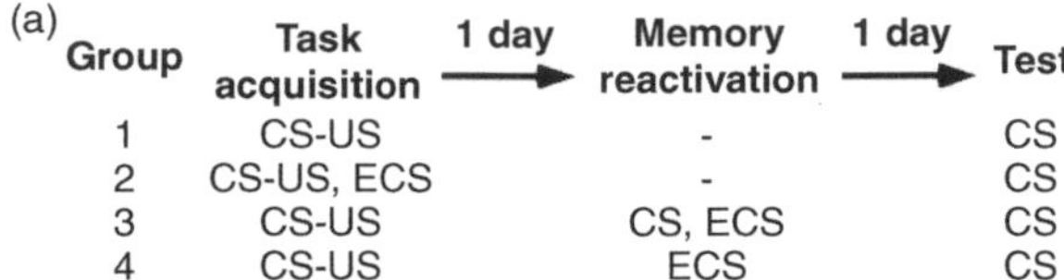

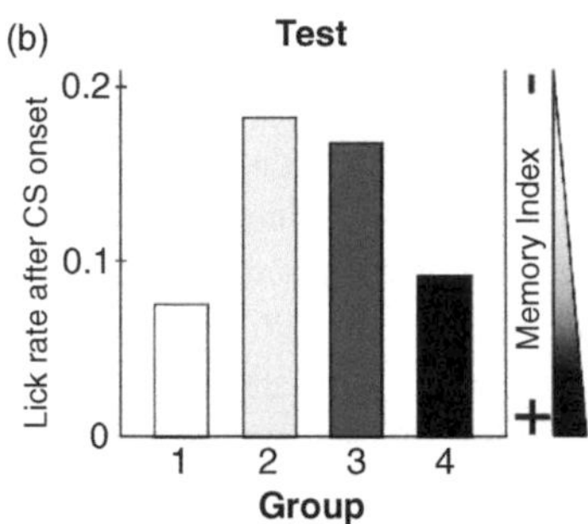

FIGURE 11.1 Data from first report on retrograde amnesia induced after memory reactivation. *(a)* Schematic representation of protocol used by Misanin et al. *(b)* Group 1 shows fear conditioning behavior displayed under this protocol, measured as reduced licking from a water tube after CS onset. ECS disrupted fear LTM either when applied after conditioning (Group 2) or after memory reactivation (Group 3). Group 4 shows that the ECS effect on Group 3 is dependent on memory reactivation. For clarity, an arbitrary memory index is shown on the right side of the graph. CS = conditioned stimulus (80-dB white noise for 10 *sec* on treatment day 1, 2 *sec* on day 2, and 10 *sec* or ten licks on test day). US = unconditioned stimulus (1.3-mA shock to floor grids for 3 *sec* simultaneously with CS offset). ECS = electroconvulsive shock (0.5-*sec*, 40-mA shock applied through earclips attached to subjects). Adapted from Misanin, J.R. et al., *Science*, 160, 554, 1968. With permission.

applied after training) disrupted a clearly established memory trace upon retrieval.[17–19] Since then, memory reconsolidation has actively been studied.

The most acknowledged study is the one carried out by Nader and coworkers in 2000.[20] This work brought general attention to the reconsolidation phenomenon because of the clean data reported and because of the use of a translational inhibitor that interfered with protein synthesis, considered to be the main cellular substrate for memory consolidation. The experiments were performed in the widely studied fear conditioning task and showed that the same treatment applied under circumstances that disrupt consolidation also impairs memory after retrieval. Similar to the report by Misanin and coworkers, Nader et al. conditioned rats in a tone-foot-shock association but memory was assessed by the percentage of the time that rats were immobile (except for movements required for breathing) to the total time the tone was presented (freezing). The day after conditioning, the protein synthesis inhibitor anisomycin was injected in the amygdala after the tone presentation.

When the subjects were tested 24 hours later, they performed poorly compared to the rats that were not anisomycin-injected (Figure 11.2b). The same treatment

(a)

Group	Task acquisition	1 day →	Memory reactivation	1 day →	Test
1	CS-US		CS, ACSF		CS
2	CS-US		CS, anisomycin		CS
3	CS-US		anisomycin		CS

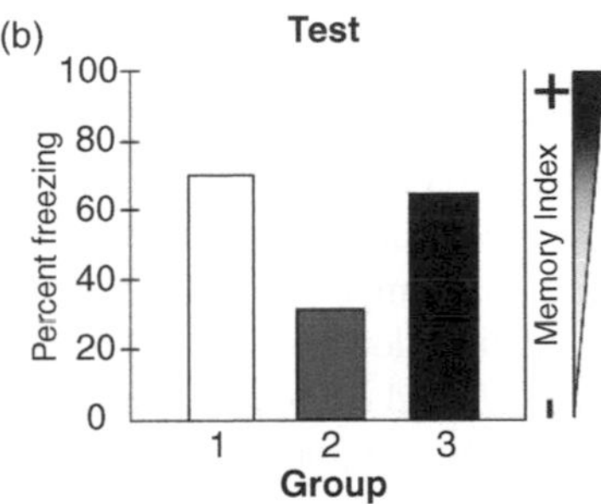

FIGURE 11.2 Intraamygdalar infusion of a protein-synthesis blocker disrupts consolidated fear memory. *(a)* Schematic representation of protocol used by Nader et al. *(b)* Group 1 shows fear conditioning behavior displayed under this protocol, measured as high percentage of time the CS is presented in immobility. Anisomycin disrupted the previously consolidated fear LTM when applied after memory reactivation (*G*roup 2). Group 3 shows that anisomycin effect on group 2 is dependent on memory reactivation. For clarity, an arbitrary memory index is shown on the right side of the graph. CS = conditioned stimulus (75-dB, 5-KHz tone for 30 *sec*). US = unconditioned stimulus (2-mA footshock for 1 *sec* simultaneously with CS offset). ACSF = artificial cerebrospinal fluid. Anisomycin = 62.5 g/0.5 L per hemisphere. Adapted from Nader K. et al., *Nature*, 406, 722, 2000. With permission.

was unable to disrupt memory if a retrieval session was not performed (Figure 11.2b, Group 3). The researchers also showed that the effects of anisomycin were time-dependent. When injected 6 hours after memory reactivation, it is unable to disrupt memory. In the years following the Nader study, a wide variety of reports have shown that reconsolidation is indeed a general process achieved in different species and different kinds of memories.[21–30]

11.4 ON RESTRAINTS OF RECONSOLIDATION HYPOTHESIS

Despite the huge body of experiments supporting reconsolidation, some did not uncover consolidated memory susceptibility to disruption after retrieval.[31–34] However, some recent reports have helped explain to an extent why a reconsolidation process is not revealed under certain protocols.[26,35,36] To address this issue, we must first look to what is called extinction and again take up the conditioning protocol on which a great number of memory tasks rely. On conditioning, a CS, like a tone, is associated to an US, like a foot shock. As a result, the CS elicits a response that is used as a measure of memory, like freezing.

However, CS presentation in the absence of US eventually leads to a response decrement; in our example, animals stopped freezing. This is extinction. On extinction, the CS is now associated to no-US. Like any other learning, extinction undergoes consolidation. To assess reconsolidation, the CS is commonly presented as a retrieval cue that may lead to extinction. During testing, treatments applied on retrieval may reflect effects over the CS-US association in which case disruption of the conditioned response is observed (reconsolidation is uncovered).

On the other hand, treatments may impair consolidation of extinction, in which case the CS-US association seems unaltered. On this latter scenario, results may be interpreted as lack of a reconsolidation process. Hence, studies like Vianna et al.[32] and Berman and Dudai[31] reported that protein synthesis inhibition disrupted extinction, leaving CS-US association unimpaired or even strengthened, and pointing at the impression that reconsolidation does not occur under these protocols.

Pedreira and Maldonado[35] offered evidence to move forward using a contextual memory task in crabs. When crabs are placed in a particular context and an object is passed overhead, they escape from the moving object, but when this stimulus is repeated several times, the crabs freeze upon presentation of the passing object. However, when the context is changed, freezing of the crabs does not take place. Thus, the context is associated to the passing object and freezing is used as a measure of memory. To induce extinction, the animals were exposed to the context in the absence of the passing object. Pedreira and Maldonado placed conditioned crabs in the training context for either 5 or 60 min as a retrieval session. During the session, they systemically applied the protein synthesis inhibitor cycloheximide and tested 24 hours later. Crabs exposed for 5 min did not undergo a clear extinction and when tested, effects over reconsolidation were found. Conversely, crabs exposed for 60 min extinguished the conditioned response and when tested, extinction was impaired.

These findings have been replicated by many others.[26,36] Eisenberg et al.[26] trained rats in a taste aversion task. Task acquisition was achieved by pairing a taste with an intraperitoneal injection of a visceral malaise-inducing agent (LiCl). Taste–malaise association produced a long-term aversive memory observed by a reduced intake of that taste in a second presentation compared to its consumption on acquisition. However, on the third presentation, intake was increased, showing that the aversive memory was extinguished. Protein synthesis inhibition disrupted extinction when applied on the second taste presentation leaving CS-US pairing unaltered, i.e., a failing to detect a reconsolidation process.

However, when rats were subjected to the taste–malaise association for two consecutive sessions, extinction was not observed on the subsequent presentations. Under these conditions, protein synthesis inhibition on the presentation following the association sessions showed aversion impairment when the animals were tested, i.e., reconsolidation was revealed. In the same study, medaka fishes were trained in a fear conditioning task. Consistent with the results obtained from rats, protein synthesis inhibition impairs consolidation on the session that led to extinction affected and, in the absence of extinction, protein synthesis inhibition impaired CS-

US reconsolidation. Thus, when consolidation of extinction memory was initiated on the retrieval session, reconsolidation of the CS-US association was not observed.

Other authors have found that pharmacological treatments disrupted LTM of recently consolidated but not older consolidated memories.[37,38] That is, when the retrieval session takes place on the days following acquisition, memory is susceptible to consolidation blockers. However, as the retrieval session is spaced in time from training, memory becomes less sensitive to these blockers. These results point to the idea that reconsolidation is a process achieved only by recently consolidated memories upon retrieval. However, Suzuki and co-workers[36] reported that stronger and older memories are susceptible to disruption upon retrieval too. They showed that stronger and older memories need of a longer retrieval trial to be disrupted by the blockade of protein synthesis than weaker and younger memories. Consistent with the reports of Pedreira and Maldonado[35] and Eisenberg et al.,[26] these effects were found as long as the retrieval trial did not lead to extinction. Therefore, it seems that the strength of the reminder is related to memory susceptibility to disruption after retrieval.

11.5 CONSOLIDATION AND RECONSOLIDATION: THE SAME PROCESS?

Probably the most important question regarding the reconsolidation process is: why and under what circumstances is reconsolidation attained? At first glance, it seems counterintuitive to carry out an already achieved process again, i.e., to consolidate once more an already consolidated memory, as is implied by the reconsolidation term. It has been reported that some of the molecular mechanisms involved in consolidation are also required for reconsolidation of the same memory trace and in the same brain region.[20,23,24,26,39–43]

For example, particular transcription factors have been proven necessary for both consolidation and reconsolidation processes in different memory tasks. Kida and colleagues[40] showed CREB involvement in contextual fear conditioning* memory in mice. Also in mice, Bozon and co-workers[41] reported a zif268 requirement in object recognition memory† and finally, Merlo et al.[42] showed NF-B participation in contextual memory using the crab model described above. In rats, Duvarci, Nader, and LeDoux[43] showed that the extracellular signal-regulated kinase (ERK) pathway must be activated in the amygdala for both consolidation and reconsolidation of fear conditioning. Furthermore Sangha et al.[24] reported that for the *Lymnaea stagnalis*

---

* *In this protocol, a context (CS) like a particular chamber is associated with a footshock (US). As with fear conditioning, the response used as a measure of memory is freezing (in this case, a reaction to the chamber, not to a tone).*

† *This kind of memory reflects the judgment of previous experience with particular stimuli. The tasks commonly rely on the natural tendency of rodents to explore new stimuli. In the first phase, animals are habituated to a novel stimulus like a light bulb. After a delay, the second phase involves presentation of a copy of the bulb along with some other stimulus like a glass jar. During this phase, the animals explore the jar over the bulb, indicating that the jar is a new stimulus and the bulb a familiar one, that is, the bulb is recognized as a familiar stimulus.*

snail, consolidation and reconsolidation occurred in the same cell. These data indicate that reconsolidation may be a remaking of the consolidation process.[15]

However, several other studies suggest that consolidation and reconsolidation are different processes. Taubenfeld and colleagues[44] reported that the transcription factor C/EBPβ is needed for consolidation but not for consolidation of a context-dependent task in the dorsal hippocampus. Tronel and Sara[45] described differential activation of several brain regions after retrieval compared to consolidation of an odor-reward task learning analyzed by c/Fos immunohistochemistry. In the same regard, Kelly and co-workers[28] demonstrated an increase in phosphorylation of ERK kinases in the dentate gyrus and the entorhinal cortex after training in an object recognition task along with increased phosphorylation in the hippocampal CA1 region and the entorhinal cortex after memory retrieval. On taste memory, it was reported that muscarinic receptor activity in the gustatory cortex is required for safe memory consolidation but not for postretrieval consolidation.[46] Similarly, protein synthesis in the central amygdala is required for consolidation but not for reconsolidation of conditioned taste aversion.[47] Finally, Lee et al.[48] reported that the growth factor BDNF is required for consolidation but not for reconsolidation, and transcription factor zif268 is needed for reconsolidation but not consolidation in the same brain region and memory task. All this evidence discards the possibility that reconsolidation is a recapitulation of consolidation but does not solve the problem. The question remains: what is the physiological purpose of reconsolidation?

11.6 RECONSOLIDATION HYPOTHESIS RECONSIDERED: UPDATING CONSOLIDATION PROPOSAL

Early and recent reviews suggest that reconsolidation may be a state for incoming information to modify established memories but experimental support is almost completely absent.[13,14,49,50] However, our group recently reported that newly acquired and retrieved taste recognition memory is susceptible to disruption by the protein synthesis inhibitor anisomycin when applied in the insular cortex (IC), a proven site for taste memory consolidation. In that work, the attenuation of neophobia (AN) task was used. Animals showed graded increases in intake after repeated presentations of the same tastant until a plateau was reached (Figure 11.3a).[51,52]

Importantly, anisomycin injections produced a partial disruption of previously consolidated memory and the observed impairment became less noticeable as a response plateau was reached (Figure 11.3b and c). On asymptotic performance, anisomycin affects no longer consolidated memory (Figure 11.3d). These results led to the proposal that a protein-synthesis-dependent process is achieved as long as updated experience capable of affecting behavior is acquired. This process is aimed to integrate updated relevant information to LTM. Consistently, part of the older consolidated memory is dependent on protein synthesis. Partial susceptibility to disruption of a previously consolidated memory trace may be the physiological substrate that allows incoming material to integrate to memory.

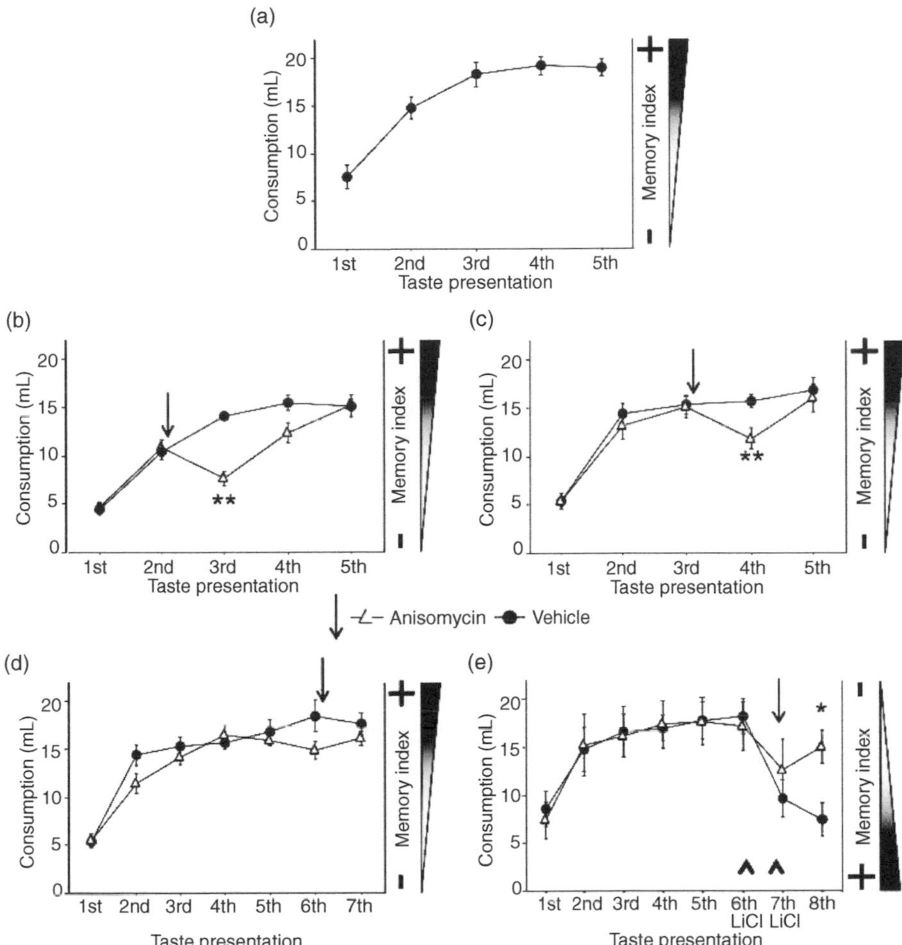

FIGURE 11.3 Attenuation of neophobia (AN) behavior and protein synthesis inhibition effect (a) Mean ± S.E.M. intake (in mL) of 0.3% saccharin solution on unoperated rats. Taste presentations were daily for 15 min. (b) and (c) Anisomycin infusion in insular cortex (IC) after the second or third taste intake partially disrupted previously consolidated memory. (d) Anisomycin infusion after sixth taste intake spared completed AN behavior. (e) Protein synthesis inhibition in IC disrupted updated aversive experience. A classical malaise agent (LiCl 0.2 M, 10 mL/Kg) injected i.p. 30 min after the sixth and seventh saccharin intake onset induced increasing aversion. Anisomycin injected before taste–malaise association impaired long-term aversive memory (eighth presentation). Solid circles = vehicle (ACSF). Open triangles = anisomycin (100 μg/μL/hemisphere). Arrows = drug infusion. Arrowheads = i.p. injections of LiCl solution. ** $p < 0.01$, * $p < 0.05$ between anisomycin-infused and corresponding vehicle groups. For clarity, an arbitrary memory index is shown on the right side of each graph. Adapted from Rodriguez-Ortiz, C.J. et al., *Learn. Mem.*, 12, 533, 2005. With permission.

Furthermore, when there is no more relevant information to be learned, i.e., after asymptotic task performance is reached, memory is no longer vulnerable to protein synthesis inhibition. Moreover, when the AN plateau has been reached and information of a different quality is provided, like aversive information, the protein-synthesis-dependent process is achieved once more (Figure 11.3e).[53]

These results were partially replicated in a widely studied hippocampus-dependent memory task, the Morris water maze (WM). In this task, animals escape from cool water by finding a hidden platform underwater. To do so, animals learn spatial cues around the room to locate the platform.[54] Rats were trained for either 3 or 5 consecutive days in the WM task. Seven days later on the memory reactivation session, rats swam for 60 sec without the platform and memory was assessed by counting the number of crossings to the platform location during training.

Clearly, the animals trained for 5 days performed much better than those trained only for 3 days. Thus, 3-day trained rats were designated middle-trained and 5-day trained rats were referred to as well-trained. When tested 7 days after the reactivation session, middle-trained subjects infused with a consolidation blocker in the dorsal hippocampus on reactivation performed poorly compared to the corresponding vehicle group. However, the same treatment did not affect consolidated memory in well-trained animals, presumably because no further updating was attained.[55] Similarly, Morris et al.[56] reported that asymptotic WM task performance was not affected by protein synthesis inhibition in the dorsal hippocampus.

Conversely, task performance was disrupted by the same treatment when updating information was continuously acquired. They trained rats for 6 days in the WM task with the platform in a constant position. On day 7, retrieval was accounted by a single trial and anisomycin was immediately injected locally. Under these conditions memory was unimpaired. Interestingly, when the platform location was changed daily during training, anisomycin injection after retrieval on day 7 disrupted previously consolidated memory. The authors concluded that acquisition of new information is required to observe consolidated memory susceptibility to protein synthesis inhibition.

Thus, the so-called reconsolidation seems more like an updating consolidation intended to modify retrieved memory by a process that integrates updated experience into long-term memory. Previously consolidated memory is partially destabilized and by the infusion of disrupting agents it appears as if the process is intended to consolidate memory again. Two important features must be stressed about the updating consolidation process: it is time- and protein-synthesis-dependent. These features again bring attention to the cellular changes that account for LTM, i.e., the stabilization of neural ensembles.[4]

Updating consolidation may be the process by means of which neural ensembles are modified and stabilized into updated memory traces. This proposal is based on the analysis of behavior, and even though it is clear that behavior is not merely a reflection of memory; we think it is possible to outline some of the changes that the updating consolidation process may produce in the memory traces based on the behavioral observations depicted above (for more on the behavior–memory dichotomy see Chapter 1). In a simple scenario, two types of information can modify behavior.

Reinforcement of previous learning — As with a learning curve, previous learning is strengthened on each trial because information of the same quality is acquired. Keeping in mind that a neuronal ensemble underlies a particular memory, reinforcing information may modify the existing consolidated trace by two means: by making the synaptic weights of the already existing ensemble stronger or by addition of cellular entities to the previously consolidated ensemble. In both cases, modifications of the synaptic weights involved in the ensemble are required.

Using artificial neural network simulation, it has been proposed that in order to preserve old memories while learning sequential new patterns, an active maintenance process is required. Otherwise, old memory is lost with incoming information. In this model, new learning is incorporated to old patterns by partially rehearsing the old ones. Importantly, modifications in synaptic weights are needed if the ensemble is to retain previously stored material while learning new information.[57]

Updating consolidation is the proposed mechanism that permits modifications of the ensemble. By protein synthesis inhibition, updating consolidation is unveiled in the limited disruption of previously acquired information that is less noticeable as plateau performance is reached. Consistently, lack of memory disruption by protein synthesis inhibitors correlates with the asymptotical level in task performance. In this regard, positive modulation of a retrieved memory was reported in crabs.[58] The study showed that through retrieval, a weak memory is strengthened by an endogenous brain mechanism mediated by angiotensin II. Although, positive modulation of retrieved memories has been reported,[14,59] this study was done to shed light upon the functional value of reconsolidation. In accordance with the updating consolidation proposal, the researchers concluded that reconsolidation is a state for modifying memory strength.

A last piece of evidence comes from memory studies in chicks. Summers et al.[60] reported that a weak memory is strengthened by means of retrieval. They suggested that memory retrieval initiates a mechanism that allows incorporation of information acquired in the retrieval session to LTM. However, memory retrieval was found to modify memory as long as consolidation was not accomplished. Thus, this mechanism in chicks seems limited to the time before memory is stored.[60,61] This is not the case in rats, where memory can be modified after consolidation is attained and even more, as noted above, limited disruption of previously consolidated memory is observed.

Shift of previous learning — Divergent information is integrated to previously consolidated memory. For example, taste aversion can be learned from a taste already tagged as a safe stimulus.[53,62] Under these conditions, taste aversion requires a protein synthesis-dependent process to be stored in the long term. One possibility for this integration to occur is that the ensemble suffers greater modifications than when strengthening information is acquired. On the other hand, a different but overlapping trace would be created for this divergent information, in which case modifications in the synaptic weights involved in the first ensemble would take place as well. Overlapping between the ensembles is supposed because they represent divergent associations between overlapping stimuli. In our taste memory example, this overlapping is uncovered on the aversion level that animals show to a taste previously tagged as safe (Figure 11.3e). Less aversion is observed when compared to the aversion shown to the same taste when novel. Reinforcement of aversive learning is required to reach similar aversion levels when the taste was previously learned as safe.

Another example has been reported in the *Manduca sexta* moth. Daly and colleagues[63] found progressive neural recruitment and changes on network activity over the course of olfactory conditioning. Their results point to the idea that olfactory memory traces are modified upon experience. Hence, memories are not separate entities; rather they overlap to some extent. Overlapping of the traces is determined by the similarities of the involved information. This idea is in line with previous theories regarding incorporation of recent experiences into long-term knowledge background.[64–66]

Extinction is another possibility in which a memory trace can be updated by divergent information. Ample evidence indicates that extinction is not forgetting nor erasing of conditioning learning, but a related learning that elicits a behavioral shift upon CS presentation.[67] This evidence is congruent with the proposed model of updating consolidation. Updating does not imply erasing of previous learning but incorporation of a related learning that takes over behavior.[53]

Eisenberg and Dudai[38] consistently reported that disrupted memory upon retrieval is recovered by presentation of an unpaired reinforcer. Similarly, contextual conditioning memory disrupted after retrieval was shown to recover spontaneously after 21 days.[68] Power et al.[69] found contextual-conditioning memory recovery 6 days after acquisition and, moreover; using the same memory task, Prado-Alcalá et al.[70] reported that repeated retrieval sessions are sufficient to fully recover memory previously affected on retrieval by tetrodotoxin injections.

These results suggest that disruption of the reconsolidation process does not abolish consolidated memory; instead, the observed memory destabilization known as reconsolidation may be related to interference with the proposed updating process aimed at the integration of related learning. The result of this process will be stable overlapping traces. The relationships of these converging (trace reinforcement) or diverging (trace shift) overlapping traces will determine behavior.

Recently, it was reported that reconsolidation and integration of new information to memory are dissociable processes. Animals were conditioned using a light and a context as CSs, and footshocks as USs. On retrieval, a new context and the same light were presented without the US. As a consequence, an association was established between the first conditioning, i.e, the first CS-US association, and the new context. When tested, animals elicited the conditioned response (freezing) when placed in the second context, that is, a new CS.

The association between a CS and a previously acquired CS-US association is called second order conditioning. Inhibition of the transcription factor C/EBPβ in the hippocampus disrupted LTM of the second conditioning. Conversely, if retrieval is assessed presenting the same stimuli as in acquisition C/EBPβ is required in the amygdala for memory to remain. Thus, it was concluded that linking new of information occurs without destabilizing the retrieved memory.[71]

Contrary to this, we found in two different memory tasks and regions that partial disruption of consolidated memory is observed by consolidation blockers upon memory updating. Moreover, protein synthesis is still required in the same region even though updated information is of different quality. It is important to note that the differences in molecular mechanisms found by Tronel et al.[71] indeed support the view that linking new information is not the same as reinforcement of previous learning (as reconsolidation is not a bona fide copy of consolidation), but do not support that reconsolidation is not intended to update memory.

The important issue is that reinforcement of previous learning is not synonymous with reconsolidation and that linking new information is different from a reconsolidation process. On their retrieval protocol, Tronel et al. used either the same (which they called reconsolidation) or different information (another context they called linking new information) compared to acquisition. Integration of information of one kind does not necessarily imply that integration of another kind requires the same mechanisms. All in all, we consider that evidence is accumulating for the hypothesis that reconsolidation is indeed an updating consolidation. In this time- and protein-synthesis-dependent process, retrieved memory seems to be modified by the integration of updated relevant experience.

ACKNOWLEDGMENTS

We thank Oreste Carbajal for technical assistance. Part of the work described in this chapter was supported by CONACYT-México 42657/A-1 and DGAPA.-UNAM IN-220706-3.

REFERENCES

1. Lechner, H.A., Squire, L.R., and Byrne, J.H., One hundred years of consolidation: remembering Muller and Pilzecker, *Learn. Mem.*, 6, 77, 1999.
2. McGaugh, J.L., Time-dependent processes in memory storage, *Science*, 153, 1351, 1966.
3. McGaugh, J.L., Memory: a century of consolidation, *Science*, 287, 248, 2000.
4. Hebb, D.O., *The Organization of Behavior*, John Wiley & Sons, New York, 1949.
5. Alberts B. et al., *Molecular Biology of the Cell, 4th ed.*, Taylor & Francis group, New York, 2002.
6. Lewin, B., *Genes VIII*, Pearson Prentice Hall, Upper Saddle River, NJ, 2004.
7. Davis, H.P. and Squire, L.R., Protein synthesis and memory: a review, *Psychol. Bull.*, 96, 518, 1984.
8. Goelet, P. et al., The long and the short of long-term memory: a molecular framework, *Nature*, 322, 419, 1986.
9. Kandel, E.R., The molecular biology of memory storage: a dialogue between genes and synapses, *Science*, 294, 1030, 2001.
10. Misanin, J.R., Miller, R.R., and Lewis, D.J., Retrograde amnesia produced by electroconvulsive shock after reactivation of a consolidated memory trace, *Science*, 160, 554, 1968.
11. Dawson, R.G. and McGaugh, J.L., Electroconvulsive shock effects on a reactivated memory trace: further examination, *Science*, 166, 525, 1969.
12. Gordon, W.C., Susceptibility of a reactivated memory to the effects of strychnine: a time-dependent phenomenon, *Physiol. Behav.*, 18, 95, 1977.

13. Lewis, D.J., Psychobiology of active and inactive memory, *Psychol. Bull.*, 86, 1054, 1979.
14. Sara, S.J., Retrieval and reconsolidation: toward a neurobiology of remembering, *Learn. Mem.*, 7, 73, 2000.
15. Nader, K., Memory traces unbound, *Trends Neurosci.*, 26, 65, 2003.
16. Bucherelli, C. and Tassoni, G., Engram activation reinstates the susceptibility of consolidated memory traces to retrograde amnesia by functional blockade of parabrachial nuclei, *Behav. Brain Res.*, 51, 61, 1992.
17. Przybyslawski, J. and Sara, S.J., Reconsolidation of memory after its reactivation, *Behav. Brain Res.*, 84, 241, 1997.
18. Roullet, P. and Sara, S., Consolidation of memory after its reactivation: involvement of beta noradrenergic receptors in the late phase, *Neural Plast.*, 6, 63, 1998.
19. Przybyslawski, J., Roullet, P., and Sara, S.J., Attenuation of emotional and nonemotional memories after their reactivation: role of beta-adrenergic receptors, *J. Neurosci.*, 19, 6623, 1999.
20. Nader, K., Schafe, G.E., and LeDoux, J.E., Fear memories require protein synthesis in the amygdala for reconsolidation after retrieval, *Nature*, 406, 722, 2000.
21. Hall, J., Thomas, K.L., and Everitt, B.J., Cellular imaging of zif268 expression in the hippocampus and amygdala during contextual and cued fear memory retrieval: selective activation of hippocampal CA1 neurons during the recall of contextual memories, *J. Neurosci.*, 21, 2186, 2001.
22. Pedreira, M.E., Perez-Cuesta, L.M., and Maldonado, H., Reactivation and reconsolidation of long-term memory in the crab Chasmagnathus: protein synthesis requirement and mediation by NMDA-type glutamatergic receptors, *J. Neurosci.*, 22, 8305, 2002.
23. Debiec, J., LeDoux, J.E., and Nader, K., Cellular and systems reconsolidation in the hippocampus, *Neuron*, 36, 527, 2002.
24. Sangha, S., Scheibenstock, A., and Lukowiak, K., Reconsolidation of a long-term memory in Lymnaea requires new protein and RNA synthesis and the soma of right pedal dorsal 1, *J. Neurosci.*, 23, 8034, 2003.
25. Child, F.M.et al., Memory reconsolidation in Hermissenda, *Biol. Bull.*, 205, 218, 2003.
26. Eisenberg, M. et al., Stability of retrieved memory: inverse correlation with trace dominance, *Science*, 301, 1102, 2003.
27. Walker, M.P. et al., Dissociable stages of human memory consolidation and reconsolidation, *Nature*, 425, 616, 2003.
28. Kelly, A., Laroche, S., and Davis, S., Activation of mitogen-activated protein kinase/extracellular signal-regulated kinase in hippocampal circuitry is required for consolidation and reconsolidation of recognition memory, *J. Neurosci.*, 23, 5354, 2003.
29. Salinska, E., Bourne, R.C., and Rose, S.P., Reminder effects: the molecular cascade following a reminder in young chicks does not recapitulate that following training on a passive avoidance task, *Eur. J. Neurosci.*, 19, 3042, 2004.
30. Wang, S.H. et al., Consolidation and reconsolidation of incentive learning in the amygdala, *J. Neurosci.*, 25, 830, 2005.
31. Berman, D.E. and Dudai, Y., Memory extinction, learning anew, and learning the new: dissociations in the molecular machinery of learning in cortex, *Science*, 291, 2417, 2001.

32. Vianna, M.R.M. et al., Retrieval of memory for fear-motivated training initiates extinction requiring protein synthesis in the rat hippocampus, *Proc. Natl. Acad. Sci. USA*, 98, 12251, 2001.
33. Cammarota, M. et al., Retrieval does not induce reconsolidation of inhibitory avoidance memory, *Learn. Mem.*, 11, 572, 2004.
34. Izquierdo, I. et al., The inhibition of acquired fear, *Neurotox. Res.*, 6, 175, 2004.
35. Pedreira, M.E. and Maldonado, H., Protein synthesis subserves reconsolidation or extinction depending on reminder duration, *Neuron*, 38, 863, 2003.
36. Suzuki, A. et al., Memory reconsolidation and extinction have distinct temporal and biochemical signatures, *J. Neurosci.*, 24, 4787, 2004.
37. Milekic, M.H. and Alberini, C.M., Temporally graded requirement for protein synthesis following memory reactivation, *Neuron*, 36, 521, 2002.
38. Eisenberg, M. and Dudai, Y., Reconsolidation of fresh, remote, and extinguished fear memory in Medaka: old fears don't die, *Eur. J. Neurosci.*, 20, 3397, 2004.
39. Hall, J., Thomas, K.L., and Everitt, B.J., Fear memory retrieval induces CREB phosphorylation and Fos expression within the amygdala, *Eur. J. Neurosci.*, 13, 1453, 2001.
40. Kida, S. et al., CREB required for the stability of new and reactivated fear memories, *Nat. Neurosci.*, 5, 348, 2002.
41. Bozon, B., Davis, S., and Laroche, S., A requirement for the immediate early gene zif268 in reconsolidation of recognition memory after retrieval, *Neuron*, 40, 695, 2003.
42. Merlo, E. et al., Activation of the transcription factor NF-kappa-B by retrieval is required for long-term memory reconsolidation, *Learn. Mem.*, 12, 23, 2005.
43. Duvarci, S., Nader, K., and LeDoux, J.E., Activation of extracellular signal-regulated kinase-mitogen-activated protein kinase cascade in the amygdala is required for memory reconsolidation of auditory fear conditioning, *Eur. J. Neurosci.*, 21, 283, 2005.
44. Taubenfeld, S.M. et al., The consolidation of new but not reactivated memory requires hippocampal C/EBP-beta, *Nat. Neurosci.*, 4, 813, 2001.
45. Tronel, S. and Sara, S.J., Mapping of olfactory memory circuits: region-specific c-fos activation after odor-reward associative learning or after its retrieval, *Learn. Mem.*, 9, 105, 2002.
46. Gutierrez, R., Tellez, L.A., and Bermúdez-Rattoni, F., Blockade of cortical muscarinic but not NMDA receptors prevents a novel taste from becoming familiar, *Eur. J. Neurosci.*, 17, 1556, 2003.
47. Bahar, A. et al., The amygdalar circuit that acquires taste aversion memory differs from the circuit that extinguishes it, *Eur. J. Neurosci.*, 17, 1527, 2003.
48. Lee, J.L.C., Everitt, B.J., and Thomas, K.L., Independent cellular processes for hippocampal memory consolidation and reconsolidation, *Science*, 304, 839, 2004.
49. Duvarci, S. and Nader, K., Characterization of fear memory reconsolidation, *J. Neurosci.*, 24, 9269, 2004.
50. Alberini, C.M., Mechanisms of memory stabilization: are consolidation and reconsolidation similar or distinct processes? *Trends Neurosci.*, 28, 51, 2005.
51. Domjan, M., Attenuation and enhancement of neophobia for edible substances, in *Learning Mechanisms in Food Selection*, Barker, L.M., Best, M.R., Domjan, M., Eds., pp 151–180. Baylor University Press. Texas, 1977.
52. Bermúdez-Rattoni, F., Molecular mechanisms of taste-recognition memory, *Nat. Rev. Neurosci.*, 5, 209, 2004.

53. Rodriguez-Ortiz, C.J. et al., Protein synthesis underlies post-retrieval memory consolidation to a restricted degree only when updated information is obtained, *Learn. Mem.*, 12, 533, 2005.
54. Morris, R.G. et al., Place navigation impaired in rats with hippocampal lesions, *Nature*, 297, 681, 1982.
55. Rodriguez-Ortiz, C.J. et al., Spatial memory undergoes post-retrieval consolidation only if updating information is acquired, presented at 35th Annual Meeting, Society for Neuroscience, Washington, D.C., November 12–16, 2005, 654.20.
56. Morris, R.G. et al., Memory reconsolidation: sensitivity of spatial memory to inhibition of protein synthesis in dorsal hippocampus during encoding and retrieval, *Neuron*, 50, 479, 2006.
57. Abraham, W.C. and Robins, A., Memory retention: the synaptic stability versus plasticity dilemma, *Trends Neurosci.*, 28, 73, 2005.
58. Frenkel, L., Maldonado, H., and Delorenzi, A., Memory strengthening by a real-life episode during reconsolidation: an outcome of water deprivation via brain angiotensin II, *Eur. J. Neurosci.*, 22, 1757, 2005.
59. Gordon, W.C. and Spear, N.E., Effect of reactivation of a previously acquired memory on the interaction between memories in the rat, *J. Exp. Psychol.*, 99, 349, 1973.
60. Summers, M.J., Crowe, S.F., and Ng, K.T., Modification of a weak learning experience by memory retrieval in the day-old chick, *Behav. Neurosci.*, 114, 713, 2000.
61. Summers, M.J., Crowe, S.F., and Ng, K.T., Memory retrieval in the day-old chick: a psychobiological approach, *Neurosci. Biobehav. Rev.*, 27, 219, 2003.
62. Bures, J., Bermúdez-Rattoni, F., and Yamamoto, T., *Conditioned Taste Aversion: Memory of a Special Kind*, Oxford University Press, Oxford, 1998.
63. Daly, K.C. et al., Learning modulates the ensemble representations for odors in primary olfactory networks, *Proc. Natl. Acad. Sci. USA*, 101, 10476, 2004.
64. Marr, D., Simple memory: a theory for archicortex, *Philos. Trans. R. Soc. Lond. B Biol. Sci.*, 262, 23, 1971.
65. Sutherland, G.R. and McNaughton, B., Memory trace reactivation in hippocampal and neocortical neuronal ensembles, *Curr. Opin. Neurobiol.*, 10, 180, 2000.
66. Frankland, P.W. and Bontempi, B., The organization of recent and remote memories, *Nat. Rev. Neurosci.*, 6, 119, 2005.
67. Bouton, M.E., Context and behavioral processes in extinction, *Learn. Mem.*, 11, 485, 2004.
68. Lattal, K.M. and Abel, T., Behavioral impairments caused by injections of the protein synthesis inhibitor anisomycin after contextual retrieval reverse with time, *Proc. Natl. Acad. Sci. USA*, 101, 4667, 2004.
69. Power, A.E. et al., Anisomycin infused into the hippocampus fails to block "reconsolidation" but impairs extinction: the role of re-exposure duration, *Learn. Mem.*, 13, 27, 2006.
70. Prado-Alcala, R.A. et al., Amygdala or hippocampus inactivation after retrieval induces temporary memory deficit, *Neurobiol. Learn. Mem.*, 2006, in press.
71. Tronel, S., Milekic, M.H., and Alberini, C.M., Linking new information to a reactivated memory requires consolidation and not reconsolidation mechanisms, PLoS, *Biology*, 3, e293, 2005.

12 Memory Impairments Associated with Stress and Aging

Carmen Sandi

CONTENTS

Memory processes can be profoundly affected by life experiences. In particular, stress has proved to be a major modulator of memory function.[1–4] However, we should bear in mind that stress is an extremely wide concept that ranges from situations that require moderate adaptations from the individual to circumstances that can be overwhelmingly adverse and persistent.

As can be expected, the impacts of such diverse stressful experiences on cognitive functions are not the same. Whereas moderate stress experienced during learning can facilitate information storage,[5–7] experiencing excessive stress acutely or severe stress chronically can be highly detrimental to memory function. Moreover, substantial evidence indicates that there are important time-windows during the lifespan when experiencing stress can exert an impact on later life including detrimental consequences for cognitive performance during aging. How the two latter stress conditions (chronic stress experienced in adulthood and the developmental effects of stress on the aging process) affect memory function will be the focus of the first part of this chapter.

The second part will deal with memory alterations that characterize the aging period. In both parts, phenomenological descriptions of cognitive alterations will be followed by sections dealing with major mechanisms that have been implicated in mediating the described effects of stress or aging.

12.1 STRESS

12.1.1 Concept of Stress

Before dealing with the different topics related to stress, aging, and memory interactions, important issues in relation to the concept of stress and stress physiology must be introduced. Stress is considered to imply any challenge to the homeostasis of an individual that requires an adaptive response of that individual.[8]

Since life is a cumulative exposure to changing and challenging situations, virtually all living organisms experience stress, more or less frequently, during their life spans.

Although stress is a loose concept that historically has meant different things for different authors, today we recognize the importance of distinguishing three components that together define every stress experience.

12.1.1.1 Stressors

Stressors are stimuli, generally aversive and potentially harmful, that exert impacts on individuals. Stressors can be classified as either exteroceptive (extreme temperatures, electric shocks, social situations) or interoceptive (ranging from health problems such as gastric disturbances to psychogenic problems such as unjustified fear).

12.1.1.2 Evaluation of Situation

The way an individual interprets a potentially stressful situation is a critical step to determine whether a specific stimulus acts as a stressor. A sudden noise can be judged as dangerous by one individual and experienced as harmless by another. Their respective reactions can depend on many factors such as previous experiences with similar noises, or may be based on the expectations that each individual generates about the potential consequences derived from that particular noise. Various psychological processes are important, with controllability or the ability to cope with the situation serving as a very important factor in determining how stressful situations are experienced.[9–11]

12.1.1.3 Response of Individual

Response includes both physiological and behavioral reactions to a stressful situation. The physiological stress reaction typically comprises central (sensory, emotional, and cognitive processing of stimuli by the central nervous system) and peripheral (activation of the sympathetic nervous system and the hypothalamus–pituitary–adrenal axis) responses (see below). The behavioral reactions include both direct responses to the specific stressors and adaptive responses that are addressed to optimize survival.[8]

12.1.2 Physiological Stress Response

The stress response involves a complex reaction in the organism that, in addition to the activation of peripheral stress systems, includes the activation of specific circuits in the brain. Most of these neural circuits have the capacity not only of processing information, but also eventually affect the degree and direction of activation of peripheral physiological systems.[12] As to the peripheral responses, the two major systems activated during stress are the sympathetic (SNS) branch of the autonomic nervous system (ANS) and the neuroendocrine system consisting of the hypothalamus–pituitary–adrenocortical (HPA) axis.

12.1.2.1 Sympathetic Nervous System

Unlike the parasympathetic branch of the ANS that mediates calm vegetative functions such as growth, digestion, and relaxing responses of the organism, the SNS is stimulated by activating and stressful situations. This system comprises a number of projections that connect with virtually every organ in the body where they secrete norepinephrine.

An important projection of the SNS is its input to the medulla of the adrenal glands, where adrenaline and noradrenaline hormones are secreted into the bloodstream. Many well-known responses to stress are caused by activation of the SNS, including increased heart rate and blood pressure, increased glucose levels, increased muscle tension, and increased sweating. In parallel, activation of the SNS delays functions that are not directly required to survive at that particular moment; typical examples are the lessening or suspension of digestion and reproduction.

12.1.2.2 Hypothalamus–Pituitary–Adrenal Axis

Most of the work examining the deleterious effects of stress on memory function has focused on the HPA axis (Figure 12.1). This neuroendocrine system involves the sequential activation of messenger molecules produced by the hypothalamus, the pituitary, and the adrenal cortex. The main hypothalamic HPA messengers, corticotrophin releasing hormone (CRH) and vasopressin (AVP), are synthesized in the paraventricular nucleus. Upon the appropriate stimulus, these peptides are released and, through the portal vein system, get access to the anterior pituitary where they stimulate the production and release of the adrenocorticotropic hormone (ACTH) into the bloodstream. Eventually, ACTH reaches the adrenal cortex where it stimulates the secretion and production of glucocorticoids (cortisol in humans; corticosterone in a variety of animals including rodents).

Glucocorticoids are steroid hormones that produce extensive effects on virtually all physiological systems. Among their many roles, they exert essential feedback actions at a variety of levels (prefrontal cortex, hippocampus, hypothalamus, and pituitary) to inhibit the activity of the axis. Such negative feedback is crucial to suppress excessive levels of these steroids, whose brief action can be highly adaptive, but their maintenance at high levels for prolonged periods can be highly detrimental to an organism.

Due to their lipophilic nature, glucocorticoids can achieve rapid access to the brain. In addition to rapid nongenomic actions through membrane receptors, glucocorticoids affect the brain by acting through two classical intracellular corticosteroid receptors that exert genomic effects.[13] They are the mineralocorticoid receptor (MR) and the glucocorticoid receptor (GR). Corticosterone binds with a 10-fold higher affinity to MRs than to GRs and therefore it is not surprising that many stress effects are mediated through GRs. The hippocampus shows the highest density of corticosteroid receptors, with some amygdala nuclei and the prefrontal cortex also showing moderate to high levels of GRs.[1]

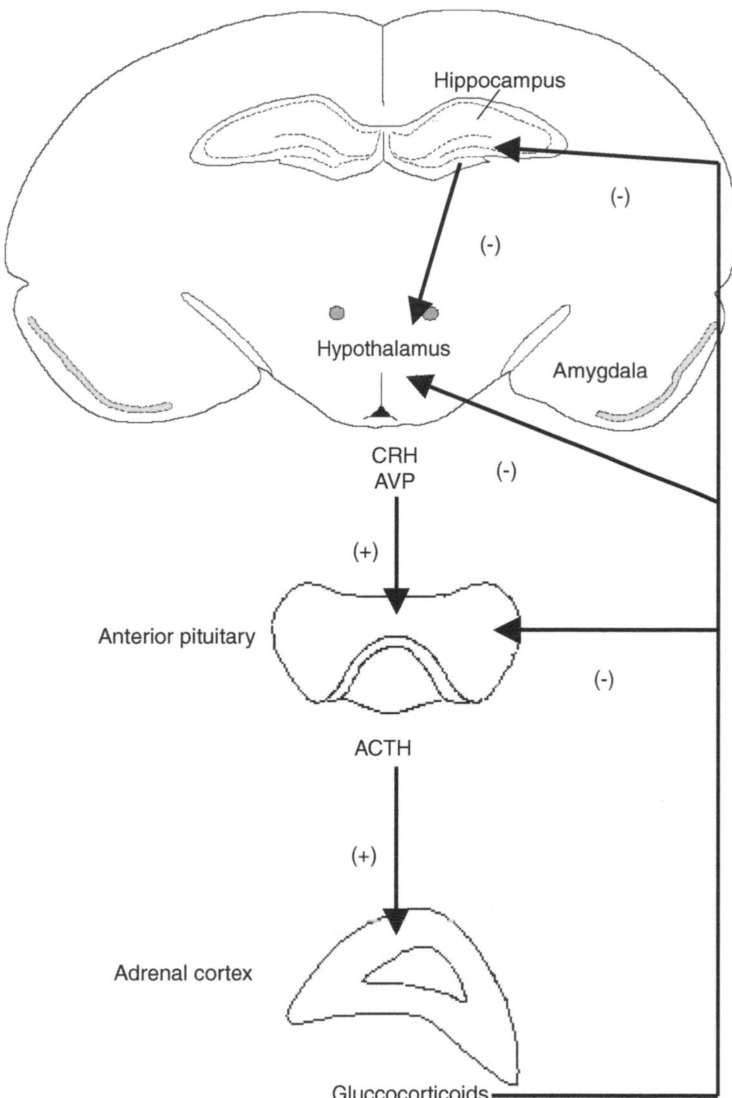

FIGURE 12.1 The hypothalamus–pituitary–adrenal axis. Activation of the hypothalamus results in a chain of events that eventually result in the release of glucocorticoids. Once in the bloodstream, these steroid hormones exert negative feedback at the different stations of this neuroendocrine axis. Importantly, glucocorticoids can also penetrate into the brain rapidly and affect different aspects of behavior and cognition.

12.1.3 Stress and Memory Function

As noted above, *stress* covers a wide spectrum of circumstances that can eventually have differential effects in the acquisition, consolidation, and retrieval of information. Based on the importance for mental health of the negative effects that highly stressful circumstances can impinge on cognitive function, the focus of this chapter is on the detrimental effects of stress on memory processes.[3,4,6,14] For reviews on the positive aspects of moderate brief stress periods on memory formation, see References 5, 7, and 15. A number of important factors related to stress and cognition must be taken into account when trying to understand how stress affects cognitive function. The following parameters are particularly important.

12.1.3.1 Stress Magnitude and Intensity

Intuitively, the impacts of extreme stressors (such as a real life threat, for example, a strong earthquake) on cognitive function are expected to differ greatly from those impinged by moderate stressors (such as exposure to novelty), and experimental evidence largely supports this view.[16,17] In any case, it is important to note the drastic individual differences in stress reactivity existing among conspecifics. Therefore, when evaluating the impact of stress intensity, it is advisable to take into account both the specific characteristics of the stressor and measure individual behavioral and physiological responses in order to determine the actual stress magnitude experienced by each experimental subject.

12.1.3.2 Stressor Timing

The time when stress is experienced with regard to the cognitive function under evaluation seems to be a crucial factor of both the types of effects observed and the mechanisms implicated.[17] Depending on whether stress is experienced before, during, or after the cognitive challenge, different processes (acquisition, consolidation, and/or retrieval of information) can be affected. Consistent evidence indicates that acute stress exerts different effects on consolidation (frequently facilitating) and retrieval (frequently impairing) of information.[5–7,17]

12.1.3.3 Stressor Duration

As we will see in the following sections, taking into account the duration of the stressor is essential, particularly when the question under analysis is related to the mechanisms whereby stress impairs cognitive function. We will review the experimental work that illustrates impaired memory function following either acute or chronic stress (see below).

12.1.3.4 Stressor Controllability

Substantial work in humans and animals indicates that an individual's perception of his or her ability to cope with a stressful experience has profound consequences on the degree of cognitive alteration induced by stress. Uncontrollable stressors gener-

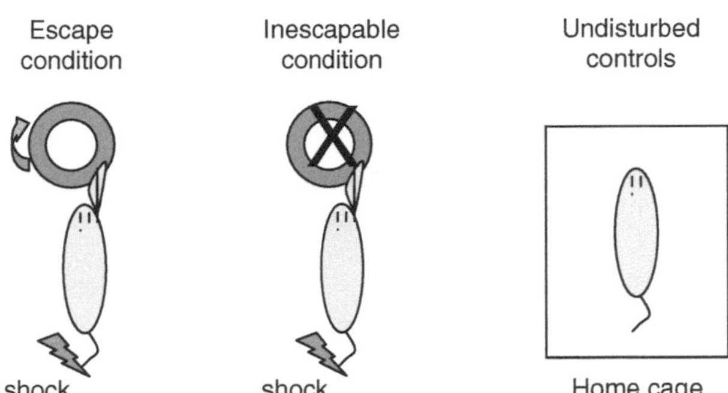

FIGURE 12.2 Cartoon representing classic triadic design used to evaluate behavioral and physiological impacts of exposure to controllable or uncontrollable stress in rats. The design involves three groups. Two were submitted to stress (electric shocks in the tail) and the third group consisted of undisturbed controls that normally remained in their home cage or were only submitted to handling on experimental days. Among the stressed groups, the one in the controllability condition was given the possibility to stop (escape) the stressor by performing a particular response (for example, by rotating a wheel or pressing a lever). The behavior displayed by the animals in the uncontrollable (inescapable) condition was not contingent on shock delivery. Each animal in the inescapable condition was "yoked" to an animal in the escapable condition, i.e., it received equal amounts of stress at the same time as the companion animal in the escapable schedule experienced.

ally provoke more behavioral impairments than controllable stressors, and many neurochemical changes ordinarily elicited by uncontrollable stressors are not observed when control is possible.[10,11,18] However, recent evidence suggests that the different impacts produced by controllable and uncontrollable stressors in the brain may not be due simply to the contribution of uncontrollability, but may in fact be affected by the ability to control. By using a triadic design (see Figure 12.2), the medial prefrontal cortex (mPFC) was proposed to inhibit stress-induced neural activity in brainstem nuclei (notably, the dorsal raphe nucleus) in individuals who exerted control over stress in contrast to the prior view that such brainstem activity was induced by the lack of control.[19]

In addition to the memory phase under study (see Section 12.1.3.2, "Stressor Timing"), other factors are also important to take into account with regard to the cognitive function under study.

12.1.3.5 Factors Related to Memory Processes

As mentioned above, not all phases in the information process related to memory function are equally susceptible to disruption by stress. It is, therefore, very important to design experiments that allow one to establish which memory phase (acquisition, consolidation, retrieval, or even reconsolidation) is affected by the stress procedure under study (Figure 12.3).

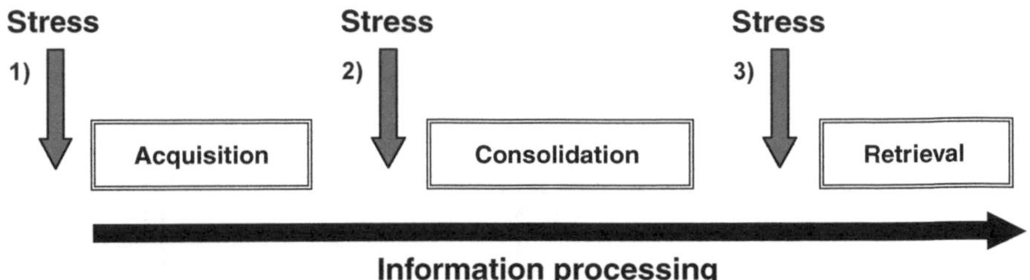

FIGURE 12.3 Depiction of the importance of the timing when stress is experienced with regard to the phase of information processing under study. If stress is given before acquisition of information (1), it can potentially affect all cognitive phases involved in memory function (learning, memory consolidation, retrieval). If stress is experienced after acquisition (2), any effect observed in retention may be due to an impact of stress on either consolidation or retrieval and any effects on acquisition can be discarded. If stress is delivered before the retention test (3), it should normally affect the retrieval processes. However, a note of caution should be mentioned, depending on how soon the retention test is applied with regard to training since consolidation mechanisms are increasingly recognized to last longer than previously hypothesized and therefore this type of manipulation may influence both consolidation and retrieval. Research should take into account this complexity and apply the necessary controls to ascertain which phases and mechanisms of information processing are affected by the stress procedure under study.

Another particularly important factor is the type of learning process evaluated (i.e., implicit/procedural explicit/ declarative, nonassociative learning, etc). Notably, implicit memory processes have been shown to be positively influenced by stress.[20,21] Both acute[20–22] and chronic[23–25] stress experiences were reported to potentiate associative types of learning such as eyeblink conditioning and fear conditioning in male (but not female[20]) rodents. On the contrary, explicit/declarative/relational types of memories are much more vulnerable to interference by stress. Since this chapter covers the detrimental effects of stress on memory, we will mainly focus on these latter types of memory that have been shown to be particularly vulnerable to alteration by stress.

12.1.4 Acute Stress and Memory Impairment

Experiencing an acute highly stressful situation can interfere with subsequent information processing. This holds true particularly for those circumstances in which a stressed individual is required to retrieve previously stored information while the acquisition of new information is shown to be particularly resistant to disruption in experimental animals. In fact, most rodent studies in which acute stress has been applied before animals were confronted to learn a hippocampus-dependent task failed to find alterations in the acquisition rate.[26,27] If any consistent effects were observed, in most cases they were not evident in the performance of animals during the training (or learning) phase, but appeared in subsequent retention tests.

For example, Baker and Kim[28] showed that exposure to uncontrollable stress can affect a nonspatial task, the object-recognition memory. In their study, rats given inescapable restraint and tail-shock stress just before exposure to a novel object recognition task showed normal memory when tested 5 min after first exposure to objects, but were impaired when tested 3 hours later. Control rats displayed a preference for a novel object (over a familiar one) when they were tested at different time delays (5 min and 3 hours). Unlike the unstressed controls, at the 3-hour posttraining test, stressed animals spent comparable time exploring novel and familiar objects.

When the impact of stress on the retrieval of previously acquired information was directly assessed, similar detrimental results on retention were reported. De Quervain et al.[29] found that exposing rats to either stress or glucocorticoids 30 min before testing impaired retention performance in the spatial task Morris water maze. Convincing evidence indicates that the level of difficulty of the task (memory load) is a critical factor in observing the detrimental effects of stress on retrieval processes. Using the radial arm water maze (RAWM; a modified Morris water maze that contains four or six arms, with a hidden platform located at the end of one of them), Diamond et al.[30] showed that exposure to a cat during a 30-min delay period between training and testing for the platform location (the platform was located in the same arm on each trial within a day and was in a different arm across days) had no effect on memory in the easiest RAWM, but stress impaired memory in more difficult versions of the RAWM. By lesioning the hippocampus, the authors also confirmed that the RAWM is a hippocampal-dependent task.

In addition to the importance of memory load (difficulty or memory demand of the task), it seems that flexible forms of memory are particularly susceptible to show disrupted retrieval by stress, as opposed to more stable ones that remain largely unaffected.[31] In humans, stress or pharmacological glucocorticoid treatments given just before retrieval have also been found to impair the recovery of information.[7,32–35] As in animals, memory load is also an important factor for stress-induced retrieval impairments in humans.[33] Interestingly, the effect of stress in memory retrieval seems to be related to the emotional content of the information. For example, psychosocial laboratory stress (as induced by the Trier Social Stress Test) was shown to particularly impair recall of emotionally arousing but not of neutral words.[36] Therefore, emotionally arousing material appears to be especially sensitive to the impairing effects of stress in retrieval.

12.1.5 Neurobiological Mechanisms Involved in Acute Effects of Stress on Memory

Cognitive and neurobiological studies have provided converging evidence that the hippocampus is critically involved in long-term memory formation[37–39] and also a primary central nervous system target of stress hormones.[2,6] The great sensitivity of the hippocampus to stress is revealed by the profound suppression of hippocampal synaptic plasticity after acute exposure to stressors[40–44] or increased glucocorticoids.[44] Moreover, adrenergic activation in the basolateral amygdala and hippocampus was shown to be critical for the impairing effects of glucocorticoids on delayed memory retrieval in spatial water maze tasks.[45]

A crucial role for the medial temporal lobe (and the hippocampus in particular) in mediating these stress-induced retrieval impairments is also supported by human neuroimaging studies.[33] Specifically, de Quervain et al.[33] used positron emission tomography (PET) to investigate the effects of pharmacologically increased glucocorticoid levels in regional cerebral blood flow during declarative memory retrieval in healthy male humans. A single stress-level dose of cortisone (25 mg) given 1 hour before testing impaired cued recall of word pairs learned 24 hours earlier but did not significantly affect performance in other tasks such as verbal recognition, semantic generation, and categorization. Simultaneously, this treatment resulted in a large decrease in regional cerebral blood flow in a number of brain areas including the right posterior medial temporal lobe, left visual cortex, and cerebellum. The decrease in the right posterior medial temporal lobe was maximal in the parahippocampal gyrus, a region associated with successful verbal memory retrieval.

In addition to the hippocampus, evidence indicates that acute stress-induced memory impairing effects can also be mediated by activation of dopaminergic[46,47] and noradrenergic[48] transmission in other structures known to be involved in high-order (including working memory and executive function) processing such as the prefrontal cortex (PFC).

Only a few studies have been reported on potential molecular mechanisms whereby stress could lead to less effective functioning of neural networks during retrieval. Recently, the potential role of the neural cell adhesion molecule (NCAM) was investigated in a rat model of stress-induced retrieval deficits in the RAWM by cat stress.[49] NCAM (see Figure 12.4) is a part of a family of cell surface glycoproteins that play key roles in neural development and in synaptic plasticity in the adult brain.[50–52] Encoded by a single gene, the three main isoforms derived by alternative splicing are NCAM-120, NCAM-140, and NCAM-180 according to their approximate molecular weights. In addition to playing roles in cell–cell recognition and synapse stabilization, NCAM also participates in neurite outgrowth, activation of signal transduction cascades, and synapse formation and elimination.[53,54] Moreover, NCAM has been implicated in the induction of hippocampal long-term potentiation (LTP; a physiological model of memory) and in memory formation.[50–52] Finally, these molecules have been shown to be sensitive to stress.[4]

In the cat stress study,[49] rats were trained to locate a hidden platform and then during a 30-min delay period they were either left undisturbed or exposed to a cat, after which all animals were given retention trials and brain samples [hippocampus, basolateral amygdala (BLA), PFC, and cerebellum] were extracted immediately afterward to assess for NCAM levels in synaptosomal preparations. Two other control groups were included: a group of undisturbed rats submitted only to handling and a swim control group that was exposed to the maze but not to spatial learning. The platform location changed from trial to trial.

NCAM expression in the hippocampus was not altered in animals with intact spatial memories that were not stressed. However, predator exposure impaired spatial memory and dramatically reduced NCAM levels in the hippocampus (particularly the NCAM-180 isoform) and PFC (although specificity of the PFC effect is questioned since reduced NCAM levels were also found in trained but unstressed animals and in the swim control group). No significant changes in NCAM levels were

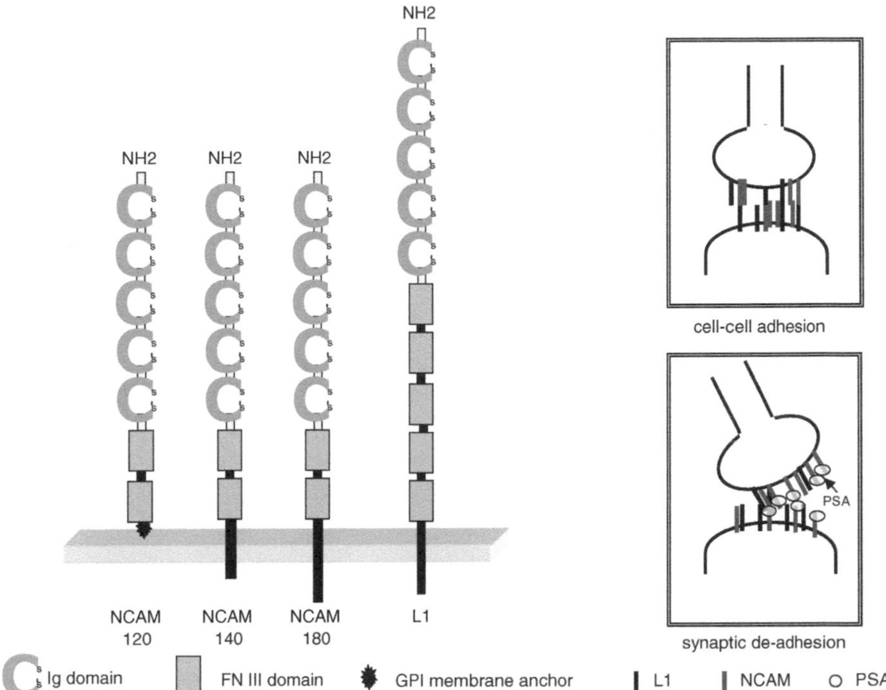

FIGURE 12.4 (See color insert following page 202.) Cell adhesion molecules of the immunoglobulin superfamily NCAM and L1. Left: the molecular structures of these molecules are represented. NCAM has three major isoforms that differ in molecular weight and type of attachment to cell membranes. Right: two of the main mechanisms whereby these molecules regulate synaptic function and plasticity are illustrated: (1) cell–cell adhesion, important for the formation and maintenance of synapses and circuits and (2) synaptic de-adhesion, a process in which NCAM polysialylation by polysialic acid (PSA) plays a key role in allowing plasticity to remodel synapses and circuits.

observed in the amygdala or cerebellum. These observations of drastic reductions of NCAM in stressed memory-impaired rats is consistent with an increasing body of data indicating that hippocampal NCAM is important for long-term memory formation.[55–58] The drastic suppression of hippocampal NCAM levels found in the hippocampus after rat stress may also contribute to impaired long-term consolidation and/or retrieval processes of spatial memory.

12.1.6 Impairing Effects of Chronic Stress on Cognitive Function

Prolonged exposure to stress is now recognized as a condition that can induce deleterious effects on brain structure and cognition[2,59,60] and increase the risks of developing neuropsychiatric disorders.[61,62] Since most of the pioneer work in the field focused on the hippocampus as a primary target of stress actions,[2,63,64] the possibility that chronic stress affects hippocampal-dependent learning has been extensively tested. Chronically stressed male rats were shown to exhibit learning and memory deficits in a variety of spatial tasks including the radial-arm maze,[65] the Y maze,[66] the radial-arm water maze,[67] and the Morris water maze.[57,68]

Evidence from the animal and human literature supports the existence of considerable variability in the vulnerability to stress among conspecific individuals.[69–72] Numerous studies have reported important individual differences in the impact exerted by stress in learning, memory, and retrieval processes.[70–73] While some individuals are particularly vulnerable, others may be resistant to the effects of stress. These differences may be due to predisposing factors, to previous life experiences or, more likely, to both. Given the devastating consequences that stress impinges in susceptible individuals, developing tools able to predict which individuals are in particular danger would be of great value for developing more effective strategies to prevent and/or reverse the effects of adverse life periods. Three types of factors have been identified as particularly important in influencing an individual's susceptibility to develop cognitive alterations under chronic stress: (1) certain personality traits; (2) gender; and (3) age.

12.1.6.1 Personality Traits

The level of locomotor activity displayed by rats in a novel environment has been identified as an accurate index to categorize individuals with relevant psychobiological profiles.[74,75] By exposing rats to novelty, it is possible to classify them in groups, one comprising those that exhibit a high locomotor activity (high-responding or HR) and another including those that present low levels of activity (low-responding or LR). See Figure 12.5. This behavioral trait of novelty reactivity in rats has been proposed to resemble some of the features of high-sensation seekers in humans.[76]

Individual differences in reactivity to novelty in adult male rats have been related to differences in susceptibility to develop cognitive alterations after exposure to chronic stress.[77] Specifically, when 4-month old LR and HR Wistar male rats were submitted to psychosocial stress for 21 days (daily cohabitation of each young adult rat with a new middle-aged rat), HR, but not LR, rats subsequently showed marked deficits in spatial learning in the water maze.

Anxiety trait is a well-known risk factor for the development of stress-related neuropsychiatric disorders, like depression in humans,[78,79] and it has been associated with degrees of cognitive impairment following chronic stress in rodents. Specifically, peripubertal anxiety levels of male rats (as evaluated using open field and elevated plus mazes at 43 days of age) were shown to be predictive of the detrimental effects of chronic restraint stress (21 days) on hippocampal-dependent spatial memory as assessed in young adulthood (75 days). Memory was tested on the spatial Y-maze using two inter-trial interval levels of difficulty (1 min or 4 hours). No differences among groups were observed in the less difficult 1-min version of the Y-maze. However, in the 4-hour version of the Y-maze, chronically stressed high anxiety rats — but not the other groups — showed impaired spatial memory. Moreover, a month after the chronic stress ended, high anxiety rats had significantly higher basal corticosterone levels than low anxiety rats (control and stress). In fact, anxiety trait in

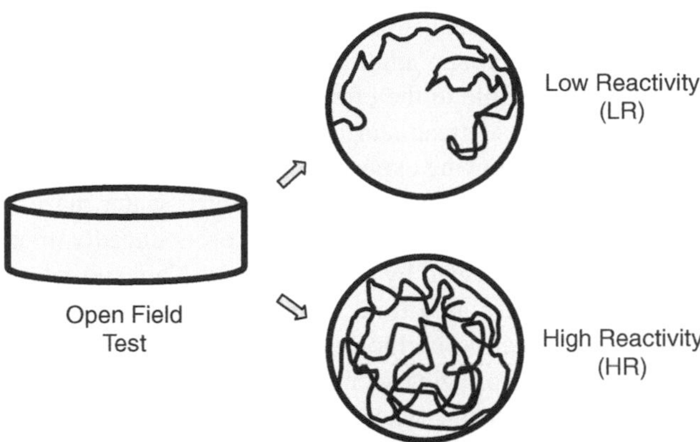

FIGURE 12.5 One of the classic experimental procedures used to characterize animals on the behavioral trait of novelty reactivity. Animals were exposed to a novel environment (open field is depicted in the figure; circular corridors are classically used) and their locomotor activity during a particular period (ranging from 5 min to 1 hour or longer) was monitored. The animals were then classified as highly reactive (HR) or low reactive (LR) by comparing their performance in relation to the sample distribution.

rats was also found to predict impaired spatial learning performance in the stressful water maze task under acute conditions[80] that highlight anxious individuals as particularly prone to show cognitive deficits under stressful conditions.

12.1.6.2 Gender

The importance of gender on the effects of stress in cognition remained elusive until recently due to the routine use of only male rodents in behavioral studies. However, intensive work over the past few years involving female rodents shows that gender is indeed a critical factor in an individual's susceptibility to chronic stress.[81,82]

When both male and female rats were submitted to chronic stress procedures (such as 21 days of chronic restraint stress), males were impaired in all tasks in which they were tested (novel object recognition and two spatial memory tasks: object placement and radial arm maze), while females were either enhanced (spatial memory tasks) or not impaired (nonspatial memory tasks).[83] As indicated below, age seems to be an important factor in the modulatory role of gender in stress and memory interactions.

12.1.6.3 Age

Age has been identified as a critical factor in the interactions between stress and cognition from two main perspectives. One is related to a differential susceptibility to stress that is manifested by some individuals at different times across the life span. The second relates to the impact that experiencing stress at a particular life period might have in future cognitive functioning.

With regard to the first perspective, aging has been clearly identified in male rats as a risk factor for developing stress-induced cognitive impairments. A pioneer study by Bodnoff et al.[84] in young adult and mid-aged male rats showed that mid-aged rats were more vulnerable to the effects of chronic corticosterone administration. Three months of steroid treatment at doses sufficient to mimic the elevated hormone levels observed following exposure to mild stress induced learning impairments in the mid-aged but not young, rats in the Morris water maze. Mid-aged rats exposed for 6 months to high social stress were also pronouncedly impaired in spatial learning. This effect was prevented by adrenalectomy. This and related findings[85,86] (see below) highlight midlife as a time of particular sensitivity to the effects of chronic stress and corticosteroid hormones.

Interestingly, the effects of aging seem to be gender-dependent. A recent review of the literature[82] pointed out that whereas the impairing effects of stress on male rodents are observed across the whole lifespan, females show more variable responses to stress. Stress-induced facilitations observed in females in young adulthood were not further observed following stress exposure at old age.[82]

The second perspective implies that exposure to stress at a particular life period may have long-term and/or delayed consequences in memory function. Early life experiences are known to exert profound influences in stress reactivity in adulthood and cognitive aging.[62,87] Much work has been done with early postnatal stress manipulations[88–91] which, in addition to affecting other behavioral and physiological aspects in later adulthood, consistently resulted in learning and memory deficits in hippocampus-dependent tasks such as the water maze.

Interestingly, a recent study has presented evidence that some consequences of early-life stressful experiences may not be manifested during young adulthood, then become apparent later during midlife. Brunson et al.[92] explored whether psychological early-life stress in rats caused an enduring deterioration of hippocampal function that worsened from young adulthood to middle age. To induce stress, environment and maternal behavior were altered by placing pups and dams in cages with limited nesting and bedding material on postnatal days 2 to 9. This resulted in abnormal nurturing behavior in the dams including reduced and fragmented nursing and grooming of pups. The selection of such procedure was based on its ability to produce substantial neuroendocrine changes early in life[93] that become fully normalized by adulthood.[92] Although the offspring showed virtually normal cognitive function during young adulthood (4 to 5 months of age), they were severely impaired in hippocampus-dependent tasks (spatial learning in the water maze and novel object recognition) at mid-age (12 months). The authors suggested that stress during periods of hippocampal development may permanently influence hippocampal systems that are particularly vulnerable during these periods.[89,94]

Substantial work indicates that lifetime exposure to stress can also affect cognitive function at aging. This is discussed in detail below, after the next section that provides a general overview on the main neurobiological mechanisms that have been implicated in the deleterious actions of chronic stress on memory function.

12.1.7 Neurobiological Mechanisms Involved in Deleterious Effects of Chronic Stress on Brain and Behavior

First, it is important to note that the mechanisms whereby chronic stress impairs cognitive function are not necessarily the same as the ones mediating acute stress effects. While neural alterations involved in acute stress effects seem to be mainly mediated by dynamic functional alterations among cellular and molecular interactions, chronic stress is now known to have a major impact on both functional aspects and neuronal structures. In this section, the main structural and functional effects of chronic stress on specific neural circuits will be discussed, followed by an overview of the molecular processes reported to contribute to such effects.

12.1.7.1 Structural Effects of Chronic Stress

Because many examples in the literature indicating impairing effects of chronic stress in memory processes were obtained in hippocampus-dependent tasks, the hippocampus is the brain region that has received the most attention. However, intensive work during the past few years is providing increasing evidence for a more integral impact of chronic stress throughout the brain that, as illustrated below, is now documented to a certain extent at the level of the prefrontal cortex and amygdala.

Hippocampus — The hippocampus plays a central role in memory processes,[39,95] particularly in spatial learning which is generally affected by stress manipulations.[96] In humans, neuroimaging studies have reported hippocampal atrophy in association with stress- and glucocorticoid-related cognitive and neuropsychiatric alterations.[97–99] In rodents, the CA3 subregion appears to be particularly vulnerable to the effects of chronic stress. In rats subjected to stress for 3 to 4 weeks, CA3 has been reported to experience the following structural alterations:

- Dendritic atrophy of apical CA3 pyramidal neurons[100,101] (Figure 12.6)
- A striking reorganization within mossy fiber terminals[102]
- Synaptic loss of excitatory glutamatergic synapses[57,103]
- A reduction in the surface area of postsynaptic densities[103]
- A marked retraction of thorny excrescences[104]

Although stress-induced alterations in CA1 morphology are not as drastic as those occurring in CA3, some changes have also been reported in this hippocampal subregion (particularly in excitatory axo-spinous synaptic connectivity in rat CA1 stratum lacunosum moleculare) after stressing rats for 3 to 4 weeks. These changes include:

- Alterations in the lengths of the terminal dendritic segments of pyramidal cells in rat CA1[103]
- Increases in postsynaptic density surface area and volume in CA1 stratum lacunosum moleculare[105]
- An overall reduction of the dorsal anterior CA1 area volume[105]

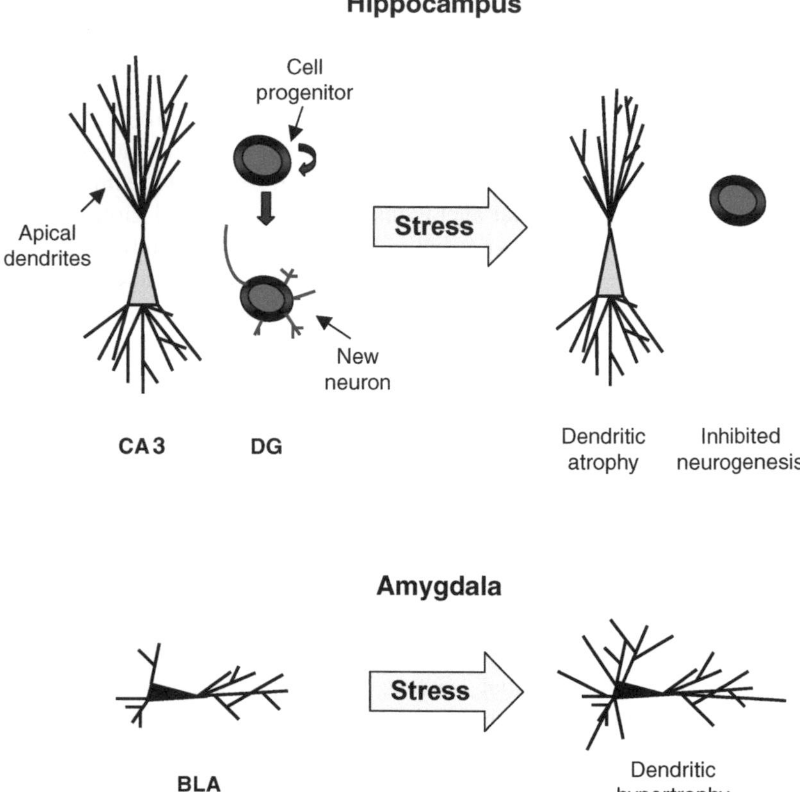

FIGURE 12.6 (See color insert following page 202.) Structural effects of chronic stress in the hippocampus and amygdala. Different hippocampal subregions can be markedly affected by exposure to chronic stress. The upper part of the figure represents the stress-induced atrophy of apical dendrites in CA3 and the inhibition of neurogenesis in the dentate gyrus (DG). The lower part shows the increased dendritic arborization described in the basolateral amygdala (BLA).

In addition, stress and high glucocorticoid levels can suppress neurogenesis in the dentate gyrus[106] (Figure 12.6). Furthermore, stress can compromise cell survival and eventually lead to overt neuronal loss by exacerbating the neurotoxicity induced by other hippocampal insults.[107]

Prefrontal cortex — The prefrontal cortex (PFC), particularly its medial part (mPFC), is critically involved in higher cognitive processes and in the integration of cognitive and emotionally relevant information.[108–110] Moreover, the PFC contains high levels of glucocorticoid receptors[111,112] and is also involved in the regulation of stress-induced hypothalamic–pituitary–adrenal (HPA) activity.[113] Clinical evidence highlights mPFC as a core alteration in a wide variety of neuropsychiatric disorders.[114,115]

Rodent studies have provided evidence that major neuronal remodeling occurs in the mPFC as a consequence of repeated exposure to chronic stress or repeated glucocorticoid treatment. Chronic stress also results in major changes in layer II/III of the PFC following 21 days of repeated stress:

- Dendritic atrophy: decrease of total length[116,117] and number[116] of apical dendrites from pyramidal neurons.
- Spine loss: a decrease in apical dendritic spine density. It is estimated that nearly one-third of all axospinous synapses on apical dendrites of pyramidal neurons in medial PFC are lost following repeated stress.[118]

Glucocorticoids seem to be major players in the remodeling induced by stress in the mPFC. Rats chronically treated (4 weeks) with either corticosterone (25 mg/kg) or dexamethasone, a synthetic glucocorticoid (300 μg/kg), showed neuronal loss and atrophy of layer II of the infralimbic, prelimbic, and cingulate cortices.[119] Moreover, morphological studies have established that chronic daily corticosterone injections (3 weeks) in rats resulted in dendritic reorganization in pyramidal neurons in layer II-III of the mPFC,[120] with major changes observed in apical arbors consisting of increased dendritic material proximal to the soma and decreased dendritic material distal to the soma.

Amygdala — The amygdala plays key role in emotional behavior and especially in fear.[121] It is not yet clear whether this structure is involved in the deleterious effects of stress in memory function since amygdala-dependent memories such as fear conditioning are potentiated by chronic stress.[23,24]

Strikingly, the structural alterations that have been observed in the amygdala contrast with the dendritic atrophy observed in the hippocampus or PFC. Repeated exposure of rats to restraint stress (10 days) induced enhanced dendritic branching of pyramidal and stellate neurons in the BLA[122] (Figure 12.6). This effect was dependent on the stressor used, since no changes were observed in these neuronal types following a chronic unpredictable stress procedure that, instead, induced atrophy only in BLA bipolar neurons.[122] Moreover, the restraint procedure also resulted in increased spine density across primary and secondary branches of spiny neurons in the BLA.[123]

Further studies are needed to confirm whether sensitization of amygdala activation occurring as a consequence of sustained stress exposure may also be an important component of the reported memory impairments in more explicit types of memories.

12.1.7.2 Effects of Chronic Stress on Synaptic Plasticity

Electrophysiological experiments have consistently shown impaired synaptic plasticity following chronic stress, indicative of functional consequences on neural circuits of the structural alterations described above. Thus, long-term potentiation (LTP) is impaired in different hippocampal areas including CA1,[124,125] the commissural/associational (but not mossy fiber) input to CA3,[126] and the dentate gyrus.[124] Likewise, treating rats chronically with corticosterone was found to impair hippocampal synaptic potentiation.[84,127] Moreover, evidence indicates stress-inducing changes in LTP in the mPFC–amygdala pathway.[128]

Interestingly, early-life stress can also result in late-onset hippocampal dysfunction. Early-life stress in rats causes a decline in a number of measures of synaptic function and plasticity (LTP in CA1 and CA3 hippocampal subregions) when evaluated at mid-age (12 months).[92]

12.1.7.3 Molecular Alterations Induced by Chronic Stress

A number of molecular mechanisms seem to participate in the deleterious effects induced by stress in brain structure and cognitive function. Certain neurotransmitters, signal transduction pathways, neurotrophic factors, and adhesion molecules have been implicated in the effects of chronic stress on the brain.[4,5,59,107,129]

Excitatory amino acids — Alterations in glutamatergic transmission have been proposed to result in an excitotoxic cascade of mechanisms finally leading to neuronal endangerment and/or neurotoxicity.[107] In line with evidence that stress and glucocorticoids increase glutamate levels in the hippocampus and other brain regions,[130–132] glutamate has been involved in the deleterious effects of stress and corticosterone on hippocampal structure.[100,101] Furthermore, increased NMDA and decreased AMPA receptor density have been reported in the hippocampus after exposure to stress.[133–135] In parallel, NMDA-mediated synaptic responses were found to be increased after chronic stress.[136]

Neurotrophic factors — Changes in neurotrophin levels have been hypothesized to play a key role in stress-induced neuronal damage. Hippocampal BDNF is reduced both by stress and glucocorticoid[137] treatments. Conversely, fibroblast growth factor-2 (FGF-2) expression was shown to be increased after both stress and glucocorticoid treatments, which might represent a neuroprotective mechanism to preserve neuronal viability in challenging situations.[129]

Moreover, stress can influence intracellular transduction pathways involved in neurotrophin receptor signaling as shown for Ras-MAP kinase cascades[138,139] that play critical roles in synaptic plasticity and neuronal survival. Chronically stressed rats also showed severe and lasting hyperphosphorylation of the extracellular signal-regulated kinases ERK1 and ERK2 involved in the Ras–MAP kinase pathway, along with a decrease in phospho-CREB expression in a number of areas including the hippocampus.[138,140] Interestingly, phosphorylated CREB modulates the transcription of several genes that code for molecules involved in neuronal plasticity including tyrosine hydroxylase, BDNF, and NCAM.

Cell adhesion molecules — Chronic stress can markedly affect the expression of cell adhesion molecules in the hippocampus. Exposure of rats to chronic stress for 21 days has been reported to result in:

- Reduced mRNA and protein expression NCAM in the hippocampus.[24,68] Although the expression of the mRNA coding for the NCAM-180 isoform was not altered,[68] chronic stress specifically reduced NCAM-140 protein expression.[77,141] Moreover, a milder but widespread decrease in NCAM mRNA levels was observed across other brain areas.[68]

- Post-translational modification of NCAM with -2,8-linked polysialic acid (PSA) is also profoundly affected by chronic stress that increases its hippocampal expression[24] in the dentate gyrus.[142] In addition to its role in cell–cell de-adhesion, PSA-NCAM has been associated with newly generated cells[143] since this post-translational modification of PSA-NCAM contributes to the migration of new progenitors and neurons. However, because chronic stress actually decreases cell proliferation in the dentate gyrus, the PSA-NCAM increase induced by stress cannot be attributed to a secondary effect on neurogenesis.[141] Interestingly, the effects of stress on NCAM polysialylation are not restricted to the hippocampus. Chronic stress was also reported to enhance PSA-NCAM expression in the piriform cortex[144] and reduce it in several amygdala nuclei.[145]
- Increased L1 mRNA and protein expression in the hippocampus[24,68]. Like NCAM, L1 is another cell adhesion molecule of the immunoglobulin superfamily that has been largely implicated in synaptic plasticity and memory formation.[50] Based on the neuroprotective effects of this molecule, a neuroprotective role has been hypothesized for the stress-induced increases of L1.[4]

Early postnatal stress was also reported to cause a profound reduction of NCAM expression in the hippocampus and cortex when the rats reached adulthood.[91]

12.1.8 Stress and Aging

Aging is a period during which individual differences in cognitive abilities become larger, both in humans[146–149] and rodents.[150–152] Lifetime exposure to stress and the corresponding increases in glucocorticoid hormones have been proposed to be critical factors contributing to variability in the aging process.[60,153–156] In particular, exposure to stress or high levels of glucocorticoids has been implicated in the acceleration and/or exacerbation of cognitive deficits in elderly subjects.[14,59,60,154,157–159] Therefore, in addition to enhancing the magnitude of cognitive disturbances observed in aged individuals, stress may also accelerate their appearance.

Aging is associated with higher basal cortisol levels[160] and reduced feedback sensitivity of the HPA axis to pharmacological challenges.[161,162] A role for stress and stress hormones in cognitive deficits at aging is also supported by the finding that rats classified as inferior (as opposed to good) learners when aged over 22 months showed both impaired memory and increased corticosterone levels.[157,163,164] Moreover, hippocampal corticosteroid receptors have been also implicated in aging-associated increased glucocorticoid levels and the accompanying alterations on negative feedback regulation of the HPA axis.[1,165]

In most rat strains, aging has been linked to decreased MR binding and/or expression, with alterations in GR function being normally mild or nonexistent.[166–169]

In addition to the hippocampus, differences in GR expression were found in aged rats (24 months), depending on their capability to learn the water maze task.[170] Specifically, old rats classified as superior learners had lower expression of GR mRNA in the parvocellular paraventricular nucleus of the hypothalamus than aged inferior learners. In parallel, aged inferior learners showed exaggerated stress-induced ACTH responses.[170]

As stated above, middle age seems to be a relevant time for stress and neuroendocrine interactions with the subsequent aging processes. Middle-aged rats (10 to 12 months old) were shown to be more vulnerable than younger rats to stress- or glucocorticoid-induced cognitive disturbances.[84,85] Also, interfering with age-associated increases in corticosterone levels by submitting rats to adrenalectomies at 12 months was found to prevent age-related cognitive impairment (in reversal learning) as well as certain alterations in hippocampal structure.[158]

The importance of individual differences in the impact of stress experienced at mid-age on accelerating cognitive decline is illustrated in a recent study.[86] Male rats were classified according to their locomotor reactivities to novelty as either highly reactive (HR) or low reactive (LR) as young adults and submitted to chronic stress (1 month) during mid-age (12 months). At early aging (18 months), their learning abilities were tested in the water maze and a number of neuroendocrine (plasma corticosterone, hippocampal corticosteroid receptors) and neurobiological (hippocampal expression of neuronal cell adhesion molecules) parameters were evaluated. Impaired learning was observed in stressed HR rats. Increased hippocampal mineralocorticoid receptors were found in stressed LR rats when compared with stressed HR and control LR groups. Moreover, mid-life stress induced an increased corticosterone response and a reduction in NCAM-180 isoform and L1 regardless of the behavioral trait of novelty reactivity. These findings support the view that stress experienced throughout life can contribute to cognitive impairment occurring during the early aging period.

Likewise, evidence in aged humans also supports such a link among increasing glucocorticoid levels, memory deficits, and hippocampal atrophy.[159] In particular, aged humans with significant prolonged cortisol elevations were found to display reduced hippocampal volumes and deficits in hippocampus-dependent memory tasks as compared to normal-cortisol controls.[159] More recently, Wolf et al.[171] reported that individuals who complain about memory impairments (in the absence of measurable impairments) have enhanced HPA axis activity as indicated by both higher basal cortisol levels and higher cortisol levels after dexamethasone.

12.2 AGING

Age-associated cognitive impairment has been described in a variety of species, including rats, macaque monkeys and humans.[172–175] In this second part of the chapter, I will review the main memory alterations that characterize cognitive decline associated with aging in humans and experimental animals (notably rodents). In each case, the neurobiological mechanisms linked to such declines will follow the phenomenological descriptions.

12.2.1 Memory Deficits in Aging Human Population

As stated above, there are considerable individual differences in the course of aging, with particularly large variation occurring in humans.[148] Establishing what represents normal cognitive decay is complicated by the difficulties of distinguishing stable mild impairments and deficits related to early symptoms of neurodegenerative diseases such as Alzheimer's disease that show progressive deteriorations of brain function and behavior.[174] In fact, most aged humans experience some form of age-related neural pathology such as Alzheimer's disease (AD), Parkinson's disease, diabetes, hypertension, and arteriosclerosis. Other difficulties for determining the cognitive alterations due to aging are the limitations intrinsic to the types of studies that can be done with human subjects. Instead of providing proper experimental evidence, studies on aged human subjects normally provide only correlational evidence and therefore cannot be considered highly conclusive. Moreover, these studies are frequently based on cross-sectional evaluations of individuals of different age groups. The limitation relates to comparing groups that may differ in the sociological impacts of living their respective life periods during different decades. However, the recent trend is to perform longitudinal studies, most of the current ones focusing on longitudinal changes occurring after the age of 60.

However, normal aging is also associated with changes in the neural basis of cognition. Regardless of individual differences, aging influences certain memory types and cognitive fields more than others. In general terms, as indicated by both cross-sectional and longitudinal studies, aging is characterized by considerable reductions in certain capacities:[176–179]

- Speed of information processing
- Working memory
- Formation of new episodic memories
- Spatial learning

Other abilities such as emotional processing, short-term memory, autobiographical memory, semantic knowledge, and priming remain relatively intact.[174–180] Cumulative knowledge suggests that the identified memory deficits are mainly the consequences of age-related changes in two types of cognitive processes:

- Disrupted executive functions that eventually exert major consequences on a variety of memory functions. The importance of executive function for memory is mainly related to the controlled processing frequently required during the encoding (particularly when strategic elaboration is required) and retrieval (when an active searching strategy is required) of information. For example, one cognitive process that is particularly dependent on executive processes that are disrupted in aging is the recall of the source of information and temporal details of past episodes.
- Decay of long-term declarative memory.[174]

Recent findings suggest that the personal appraisal of the changes that come with aging is an important factor that determines who is not greatly impaired by aging and who deteriorates rapidly. Wellbeing and a positive view of aging seem to act as major protective factors against the detrimental effects of age, not only on brain and cognitive function, but also at a more general level of the organism.[181] It seems that, at odds with older adults showing rapid declines, those who are not much impaired in their cognitive abilities may show compensation for brain decline in aging that involves increased recruitment of brain activity during cognitive performance.

12.2.2 Neurobiological Mechanisms Associated with Age-Related Cognitive Decline in Humans

There is great interest in understanding the neurobiological mechanisms that underlie memory decline occurring at aging and identifying the factors that determine differential impacts of aging on various cognitive domains and on different individuals. In agreement with the behavioral alterations observed in executive function and declarative memory, neuroimaging studies have shown that age-related cognitive deficits are linked to multiple structural and functional changes in the frontal–striatal circuits, medial temporal lobe (MTL), regions and white matter tracts.[174]

Thus, the deficits of executive function observed in the nondemented aged population have been associated with alterations in frontal–striatal circuits. A variety of pathophysiological changes that have been reported to occur in frontal–striatal areas in the aged population may account for the reported executive difficulties.[173]

At the structural level, multiple changes including atrophy of frontal grey matter and striatal volume loss have been reported. Neurotransmitter systems can also experience considerable alteration during the aging process. An age-associated decline in dopamine content, for example, appears to be associated with executive impairments.

Frontal white matter appears to be particularly susceptible to age-related damage (showing diffuse changes and small infarcts), and a link with the degree of cognitive impairment has been established in studies linking behavioral testing with structural magnetic resonance imaging (MRI) evaluating white matter lesions. This latter pathology seems to be related to problems in vascular function (mainly hypertension) that appear to have a special impact on white matter structures supporting frontal—striatal circuits.

On the other hand, the characteristic alterations of long-term declarative memory occurring during aging have been linked to age-related changes in the MTL, including the hippocampus and adjacent regions. The MTL is strongly affected in AD (from its earlier stages), with a number of pathophysiological features characterizing the damage to these structures. These include atrophy, cell loss, and cellular damage, and are consistently associated with marked memory deficits. More specifically, cellular pathology in AD is linked to abnormal extracellular deposition of amyloid protein and intracellular accumulations of tau.[182]

Substantial evidence supports a key role of deposits (plaques) and soluble forms of amyloid on the triggering of neuronal dysfunction and eventual cell death. Such deposits also lead to neurofibrillary tangles that represent a major pathology in the MTL and eventually spread to associated cortex. In AD, the symptoms progress to the eventual overall impairment as the disease advances. Recent imaging studies suggest that what may account for the memory impairment observed in this disease is the disruption of a network of connections including the MTL and other areas, notably the precuneus, extending into retrosplenial and posterior cingulate cortex.[173] In any case, it is important to note that the circuits that degenerate in AD are also vulnerable to normal aging, but the vulnerability is reflected by compromised synaptic communication rather than by neuron death.[183]

One interesting feature indicated by functional imaging studies of non-demented old individuals is that unique patterns of brain activation distinguish older individuals showing high-performance in cognitive tasks from younger adults.[184] A subset of older adults showed increased recruitment of brain areas that has been interpreted as a potential compensatory response to increasing task difficulty.[173] They may require the use of additional brain resources to guarantee a certain performance level when other physiological alterations interfere with their cognitive functions. This type of compensatory process has been proposed to play a role in individual differences in cognitive decline during the course of aging.

12.2.3 Memory Deficits in Aged Rodents

Research on experimental animals is essential for gaining insight into what is normal cognitive decline associated with aging and what is pathological. It is also necessary to our understanding of the relative involvement of different factor with age differences in cognition. Most commonly, rodents are used to characterize age-related alterations in memory processes and ascertain the neurobiological processes underlying such cognitive deficits.

Although aged rodents display a variety of cognitive deficits, a large part of the research on this topic has focused on the hippocampus and spatial learning. Before reviewing that issue, we will deal with methodological aspects that are relevant to research in this area, then present a brief discussion of the research carried out in rodents to explore the degree of alteration on frontal lobe functions in these animal species.

12.2.3.1 Methodological Aspects of Aging Research in Rodents

Given the relatively short life-spans of rodents (normally 2 to 4 years), they are particularly appropriate for longitudinal studies that are ideal for obtaining aging curves and collecting information about essential factors contributing to developmental decline. However, they are also the exceptions rather than the rules in animal research because they are both expensive and time-consuming. The most frequent approach, as in human studies, is the use of cross-sectional comparisons of groups of animals of different ages, typically including young adults and older individuals.[185]

The study of aging involves a number of difficulties that are particularly relevant when the focus of research is cognition.[186] Aging is generally associated with changes in sensorimotor abilities and motivation, factors that can impact the performances of animals in learning and memory tasks but should be distinguished from putative impairments in cognitive performance.[187] Particularly, visual competence can be highly degraded in aging rats, an aspect that should be specially controlled when studying animal performance of tasks with visual components.[188]

Another factor that requires special attention is that rodents that have been maintained undisturbed in their home cages during the course of their lives may not be appropriate subjects for cognitive testing at old age. Rodents raised in animal houses are normally not confronted with environmental challenges. Therefore, their organisms had no opportunities to adapt and to develop behavioral and physiological strategies relevant for successful performance of many learning and memory tasks.[187] One solution proposed to overcome this problem is to raise and house rats in enriched environments.

12.2.3.2 Alterations in Frontal Lobe Function in Aged Rodents

Most animal research that has addressed the behavioral alterations associated with frontal lobe dysfunction has been performed on non-human primates. The cognitive deficits observed (deficits in delayed response testing, increased perseveration, difficulties in reversal learning, etc.) were strikingly similar to those reported in aged humans and in young nonhuman primates with frontal lesions.[189] However, a more limited number of studies in old rats could also detect similar cognitive impairments that were also comparable to those induced in younger rats by specific frontal lobe lesions. Using different behavioral testing procedures (notably delayed nonmatch to sample), clear evidence was obtained that the temporal organization of memory is significantly disrupted in aged rats, in a similar way as that observed in younger rats with prefrontal cortical damage.[190,191]

Evidence for impaired cognitive flexibility mediated by prefrontal circuits in aged rats has been provided using an attentional set-shifting task. Barense et al.[192] trained young and aged male rats on two problems. The reward was always associated with the same stimulus dimension (for example, they had to link the reward to a particular odor) and a reversal of one problem (for example, they had to make a new association because the reward was predicted by an alternative odor and not by the former odor). Then, a new problem was presented in which the reward was consistently associated with the previously irrelevant stimulus dimension (extradimensional shift or EDS). For example, odors no longer predicted the reward; the digging medium in which the reward was hidden predicted it. Aged rats were significantly impaired on the EDS, although some individual aged rats performed as well as young rats on this phase. Moreover, some aged rats were impaired on the reversal. These deficits of the EDS paralleled those manifested by young rats submitted to neurotoxic lesions of medial frontal cortex. The impairment of rapid reversal learning observed in aged rats was linked to orbitofrontal cortex dysfunction.[193]

12.2.3.3 Alterations in Medial Temporal Lobe–Hippocampal Function in Aged Rodents

Due to the great interest in understanding the mechanisms underlying hippocampal dysfunction at aging, a large number of studies focused in characterizing the performance of aged rodents in spatial learning tasks. For reviews see References 194 through 196. Age-related spatial learning deficits were reported, for example, in the radial-arm maze. Aged rats were slower than younger adult rats in learning to this task,[197–199] an effect that is clearly dependent on the requirement to develop a spatial strategy since aged rats were shown to be impaired in nonspatial reference memory versions of the radial-arm maze.[200]

Consistent deficits in learning, memory, and the acquisition of new response solutions have also been found in aged rodents trained in the Barnes circular platform task,[201] in which animals learn to identify which of 18 holes distributed along the perimeter of a circular platform allows them access to a tunnel to escape eventually from exposure to light.[151,201] Similar age-related deficits have also been reported in the Morris water maze spatial learning task.[202–205] Aged rats normally take longer to learn the location of the hidden platform, while they show no signs of impairment when trained in a cued platform version.[203,206]

An assessment of hippocampal-dependent spatial learning and memory capabilities of healthy aged rodents revealed striking individual differences.[207–209] For example, the water maze task revealed the existence of important individual differences in spatial memory abilities within old rats.[152,207,210–212] While some animals show clear deficits in spatial memory, others perform similarly to younger animals and represent a very interesting tool for investigating the neurobiological substrates of cognitive aging (see below).

12.2.4 Aging and Structural and Functional Plasticity

Based on the well reported individual differences in cognitive aging, one of the most popular strategies in current research is to first characterize aged animals in a learning task to subsequently investigate neurobiological correlates of the observed learning and memory deficits.

A pioneer study showed in aged rats (22 to 24 months) a correlation between the degree of decline in performance in learning and place navigation tasks and brain energy metabolism (evaluated as regional glucose utilization) in 5 of 45 brain regions examined: dentate gyrus, medial septum-diagonal band area, hippocampal CA1, hippocampal CA3, and prefrontal cortex. Learning impairments in the aged rats were related to the extent of decrease in glucose utilization in restricted areas of the limbic system.[213]

12.2.4.1 Structural and Neurochemical Alterations

The literature contains controversy as to whether normal aging is accompanied by a loss of neurons[214,215] because the most recent findings seem not to confirm earlier reports indicating such cell death. However, consensus is greater on the view that alterations in relevant neurocircuits may underlie age-related cognitive deficits.[183]

Human and monkey studies reported regressive changes with age in dendritic arbors and spines of cortical pyramidal neurons in specific regions and layers of the frontal lobe.[216–218] Evidence of degeneration in the PFC was found both in old monkeys and humans, as indicated by drastic alterations in the morphology of terminal dendrites and reduction of synaptic and spine densities.[183]

Synaptic alterations are believed to be associated with changes in the expression levels of glutamate receptors, with available evidence indicating decreases in N-methyl-D-aspartic acid (NMDA; particularly the NR2B subunit) and -amino-5-hydroxy-3-methyl-4-isoxazole propionic acid (AMPA) receptors in older individuals.[219,220] In addition, degeneration of myelinated axons in both deep cortical layers and white matter has been reported to correlate with sensory and cognitive capabilities in old animals.[221]

At the MTL, the hippocampus is the brain area more deeply studied. Using unbiased stereological methods, Geinisman et al.[222] reported a decrease in the number of axospinous synapses in the mid-molecular layer of the dentate gyrus of aged rats (28 months) that was hypothesized to underlie reductions in the amplitude of excitatory postsynaptic potentials and the decline in functional synaptic plasticity detected in the dentate gyrus of senescent rats.

The cholinergic and monoaminergic systems that project from the basal forebrain and brainstem also displayed functional impairments in aging.[223] Interestingly, signal transduction pathways seem to be differentially regulated in the aged hippocampus and PFC. Whereas activation of the cAMP/protein kinase A (PKA) pathway has been proposed as a mechanism for improving age-related hippocampus-related cognitive deficits, agents that increase PKA activity impair — instead of improving — prefrontal cortical function in aged rats and monkeys with prefrontal cortical deficits. Conversely, PKA inhibition was shown to ameliorate prefrontal cortical cognitive deficits.[224] These findings further illustrate the complexity and difficulty in understanding the mechanisms affecting cognitive function in the aged brain.

12.2.4.2 Functional Alterations

There is controversy in the literature as to whether aged animals show deficits in hippocampal LTP.[196] In general terms, age-related LTP-induction deficits are mainly found when the induction protocols involve low-intensity stimulation, but no consistent alterations are observed when high-intensity and robust stimulation is applied.[196,201] Moreover, the threshold for LTP induction is increased in aged rats, which may be related to the greater difficulties displayed by aged rats to encode memories. As to LTP maintenance, whenever high-intensity stimulation has been used, age-related maintenance deficits appear at late recording time points,[196,201] LTP maintenance deficits have been correlated with impaired performance in hippocampus-dependent learning tasks, including the Barnes circular platform task,[151]

As to long-term depression (LTD) and depotentiation, in contrast to LTP, these are more readily produced in aged than in adult rats.[196] A recent study[224] investigated whether LTD in area CA1 is related to individual differences in learning abilities in the outbred Long-Evans rat strain. Young rats exhibited larger NMDAR-dependent

LTD (NMDAR-LTD) than the aged animals (24 months), and no differences were found between the aged unimpaired and the aged impaired groups. When an NMDAR-independent form of LTD (non-NMDAR-LTD) was examined, the aged unimpaired group showed significantly larger non-NMDAR-LTD than either the young or the aged impaired groups.

The authors also found a significant correlation between the magnitude of non-NMDAR-LTD and learning abilities in aged, but not in young, rats. This study suggests that high-performing aged rats maintain the ability to generate LTD through mechanisms different from those used by young adults, whereas aged animals that fail to make a switch to the mechanisms that mediate LTD will be impaired in learning performance.

Interestingly, variability in escape and spatial learning in the water maze in the aged unimpaired (outbred male Wistar rats 28 to 30 months old), but not in aged impaired (selected from a large pool based on water maze escape performance over a 9-day period) group was correlated with variability in short-term and long-term potentiation.[152]

12.2.4.3 Aged Hippocampus and Place Cells

Recent evidence indicates that the older hippocampus may also be slower to switch between cognitive maps and that such failure to switch between hippocampal maps in time may account for their impaired spatial performance.[225] Spatial abilities in rodents have been largely related to hippocampal neurons called place cells that encode spatial information defined by visual landmarks[226] or by self-motion cues.[227] A cognitive map of an animal's environment would be formed by a population of place cells activated by multiple cues on that particular environment.[228] Rosenzweig et al.[225] found that the ability of rats to find a reward in a particular environment is correlated with the ability of place cells to switch between two different cognitive maps, one based on self-motion cues that are unrelated to the task and another based on relevant landmark cues. Interestingly, old rats were impaired relative to young adult rats, both in switching from the irrelevant to the relevant map and in finding the reward.

12.3 CONCLUSIONS

Stress is a potent modulator of brain structure, brain function, and cognition. Although not all types of stress are deleterious to memory function, there are many instances in which stress (both acute and chronic) interferes with explicit types of memory, both in humans and animals (Figure 12.7). Stress hormones are also strong modulators of brain development, and excessive stress experienced at certain time windows of vulnerability during life can profoundly affect cognitive function at later stages, with a particular impact on cognitive aging. In fact, exposure to chronic stress seems to recapitulate cognitive deficits observed at aging, as well as accelerating the decline in memory function that characterizes senescence.

In addition to a number of neurobiological similarities (including reduced expression of NCAM or altered levels of corticosteroid receptors), both chronic

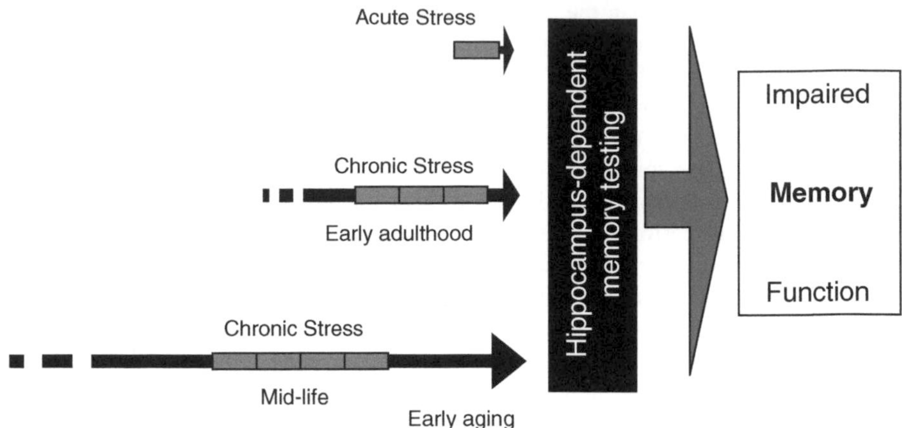

FIGURE 12.7 Exposure to stress outside the context of cognitive testing can have impairing effects on memory function. Hippocampus-dependent memory processes such as spatial learning or explicit/declarative types of learning processes are particularly vulnerable to different stress manipulations including acute and chronic stress. Moreover, stress experienced at mid-life can also accelerate cognitive decline during early aging, as reported for spatial learning in rats.[86]

stress and aging have been associated with increased basal levels of glucocorticoid hormones and impaired negative feedback causing delayed high glucocorticoid levels after their activation. In all instances, the deleterious effects of stress and aging seem to particularly impair hippocampus- and prefrontal cortex-dependent memory processes. One of the main challenges of future research will be identifying key factors that determine individual differences in vulnerability to both stress and aging.

REFERENCES

1. De Kloet, E.R. et al., Brain corticosteroid receptor balance in health and disease, *Endocr. Rev.*, 19, 269, 1998.
2. McEwen, B.S., Stress and hippocampal plasticity, *Annu. Rev. Neurosci.*, 22, 105, 1999.
3. Kim, J.J. and Diamond, D.M., The stressed hippocampus, synaptic plasticity and lost memories, *Nat. Rev. Neurosci.*, 3, 453, 2002.
4. Sandi, C., Stress, cognitive impairment and cell adhesion molecules, *Nat. Rev. Neurosci.,* 5, 917, 2004.
5. Sandi, C., The role and mechanisms of action of glucocorticoid involvement in memory storage, *Neural Plast.*, 6, 41, 1998.
6. De Kloet, E.R., Oitzl, M.S., and Joëls, M., Stress and cognition: are corticosteroids good or bad guys? *Trends Neurosci.*, 22, 422, 1999.
7. Roozendaal, B., Stress and memory: opposing effects of glucocorticoids on memory consolidation and memory retrieval, *Neurobiol. Learn. Mem.*, 78, 578, 2002.

8. Steckler, T., The neuropsychology of stress, in *Handbook of Stress and the Brain Part 1: The Neurobiology of Stress*, Steckler, T., Kalin, N.H., and Reul J.M.H.M., Eds., Elsevier, Amsterdam, 2005, p. 25.
9. Mineka, S. and Hendersen, R.W., Controllability and predictability in acquired motivation, *Annu. Rev. Psychol.*, 36, 495, 1985.
10. Maier, S.F. and Watkins, L.R., Stressor controllability and learned helplessness: the roles of the dorsal raphe nucleus, serotonin, and corticotropin-releasing factor, *Neurosci. Biobehav. Rev.*, 294, 829, 2005.
11. Maier S.F. and Watkins L.R., Stressor controllability, anxiety, and serotonin, *Cognit. Ther. Res.*, 22, 595, 1998.
12. Herman, J.P. et al., Central mechanisms of stress integration: hierarchical circuitry controlling hypothalamo–pituitary–adrenocortical responsiveness, *Front. Neuroendocrinol.*, 24, 151, 2003.
13. Yudt, M.R. and Cidlowski, J.A., The glucocorticoid receptor: coding a diversity of proteins and responses through a single gene, *Mol. Endocrinol.*, 16, 1719, 2002.
14. Lupien, S.J. and McEwen, B.S., The acute effects of corticosteroids on cognition: integration of animal and human model studies, *Brain Res. Rev.*, 24, 1–27, 1997.
15. McGaugh, J.L. and Roozendaal, B., Role of adrenal stress hormones in forming lasting memories in the brian, *Curr. Opin. Neurobiol.*, 122, 205, 2002.
16. Cordero, M.I., Merino, J.J., and Sandi, C., Correlational relationship between shock intensity and corticosterone secretion on the establishment and subsequent expression of contextual fear conditioning, *Behav. Neurosci.,* 112, 885, 1998.
17. Joëls, M. et al., Learning under stress: how does it work? *Trends Cogn. Sci.*, 10, 152, 2006.
18. Anisman, H. and Matheson, K., Stress, depression, and anhedonia: caveats concerning animal models, *Neurosci. Biobehav. Rev.*, 29, 525, 2005.
19. Amat, J. et al., Medial prefrontal cortex determines how stressor controllability affects behvior and dorsal raphe nucleus, *Nat. Neurosci.*, 8, 365, 2005.
20. Shors, T.J., Learning during stressful times, *Learn. Mem.*, 11, 137, 2004.
21. Shors, T.J., Stressful experience and learning across the lifespan, *Annu. Rev. Psychol.*, 57, 55, 2006.
22. Cordero, M.I. et al., Prior exposure to a single stress session facilitates subsequent contextual fear conditioning in rats: evidence for a role of corticosterone, *Horm. Behav.,* 444, 338, 2003.
23. Conrad, C.D. et al., Repeated restraint stress facilitates fear conditioning independently of causing hippocampal CA3 dendritic atrophy, *Behav. Neurosci.*, 113, 902, 1999.
24. Sandi, C. et al. Effects of chronic stress on contextual fear conditioning and the hippocampal expression of the neural cell adhesion molecule, its polysialylation, and L1, *Neuroscience*, 102, 329, 2001.
25. Cordero, M.I., Kruyt, N.D., and Sandi, C., Modulation of contextual fear conditioning by chronic stress in rats is related to individual differences in behavioral reactivity to novelty, *Brain Res.,* 970, 242, 2003.
26. Warren, D.A., No spatial learning impairment following exposure to inescapable shock, *Psychobiology,* 19, 127, 1991.
27. Healy, D.J. and Drugan, R.C., Escapable stress modulates retention of spatial learning in rats: preliminary evidence for involvement of neurosteroids, *Psychobiology,* 24, 110, 1996.
28. Baker, K.B. and Kim, J.J., Effects of stress and hippocampal NMDA receptor antagonism on recognition memory in rats, *Learn. Mem.* 9, 58, 2002.

29. De Quervain, D.J., Roozendaal, B., and McGaugh, J.L., Stress and glucocorticoids impair retrieval of long-term spatial memory, *Nature*, 394, 787, 1998.
30. Diamond, D.M. et al., Exposing rats to a predator impairs spatial working memory in the radial arm water maze, *Hippocampus,* 9, 542, 1999.
31. Celerier, A. et al., Contextual and serial discriminations: a new learning paradigm to assess simultaneously the effects of acute stress on retrieval of flexible or stable information in mice, *Learn. Mem.*, 112, 196, 2004.
32. De Quervain, D.J. et al., Acute cortisone administration impairs retrieval of long-term declarative memory in humans, *Nat. Neurosci.*, 3, 313, 2000.
33. De Quervain, D.J. et al., Glucocorticoid-induced impairment of declarative memory retrieval is associated with reduced blood flow in the medial temporal lobe, *Eur. J. Neurosci.*, 176, 1296, 2003.
34. Wolf, O.T. et al., Cortisol differentially affects memory in young and elderly men, *Behav. Neurosci.*, 115, 1002, 2001.
35. Buss, C. et al., Autobiographic memory impairment following acute cortisol administration, *Psychoneuroendocrinology*, 298, 1093, 2004.
36. Kuhlmann, S., Piel, M., and Wolf, O.T., Impaired memory retrieval after psychosocial stress in healthy young men, *J. Neurosci.*, 25, 2977, 2005.
37. Eichenbaum, H., A cortical–hippocampal system for declarative memory, *Nat. Rev. Neurosci.*, 11, 41, 2000.
38. Martin, S.J., Grimwood, P.D., and Morris, R.G., Synaptic plasticity and memory: an evaluation of the hypothesis, *Annu. Rev. Neurosci.*, 23, 649, 2000.
39. Squire, L.R., Stark, C.E., and Clark, R.E., The medial temporal lobe, *Annu. Rev. Neurosci.*, 27, 279, 2004.
40. Foy, M.R. et al., Behavioral stress impairs long-term potentiation in rodent hippocampus, *Behav. Neural Biol.*, 48, 138, 1987.
41. Bennett, M.C. et al., Serum corticosterone level predicts the magnitude of hippocampal primed burst potentiation and depression in urethane-anesthetized rats, *Psychobiology,* 19, 301, 1991.
42. Diamond, D.M. et al., Inverted-U relationship between the level of peripheral corticosterone and the magnitude of hippocampal primed burst potentiation. *Hippocampus*, 4, 421, 1992.
43. Mesches, M.H. et al., Exposing rats to a predator blocks primed burst potentiation in the hippocampus *in vitro*, *J. Neurosci.*, 19, C18, 1999.
44. Alfarez, D.N. et al., Corticosterone and stress reduce synaptic potentiation in mouse hippocampal slices with mild stimulation, *Neuroscience*, 115, 1119, 2002.
45. Roozendaal, B. et al., Glucocorticoid effects on memory retrieval require concurrent noradrenergic activity in the hippocampus and basolateral amygdala, *J. Neurosci.*, 24, 8161, 2004.
46. Murphy, B.L. et al., Increased dopamine turnover in the prefrontal cortex impairs spatial working memory performance in rats and monkeys, *Proc. Natl. Acad. Sci. USA*, 933, 1325, 1996.
47. Arnsten, A.F.T. and Goldman-Rakic, P.S., Noise stress impairs prefrontal cortical cognitive function in monkeys, *Arch. Gen. Psychiatr.*, 55, 362, 1998.
48. Birnbaum, S. et al., A role for norepinephrine in stress-induced cognitive deficits: alpha-1-adrenoceptor mediation in the prefrontal cortex, *Biol. Psychiatr.*, 469, 1266, 1999.
49. Sandi, C. et al., Stress-induced impairment of spatial memory is associated with decreased expression of NCAM in hippocampus and prefrontal cortex, *Biol. Psychiatr.,* 57, 856, 2005.

50. Schachner, M., Neural recognition molecules and synaptic plasticity, *Curr. Opin. Cell Biol.*, 9, 627, 1997.
51. Ronn, L.C. et al., NCAM-antibodies modulate induction of long-term potentiation in rat hippocampal CA1, *Brain Res.*, 677, 145, 1995.
52. Kiss, J.Z. et al., The role of neural cell adhesion molecules in plasticity and repair, *Brain Res. Rev.*, 36, 175, 2001.
53. Fields, R.D. and Itoh, K., Neural cell adhesion molecules in activity-dependent development and synaptic plasticity, *Trends Neurosci.*, 19, 473, 1996.
54. Kleene, R. and Schachner, M., Glycans and neural cell interactions. *Nat. Rev. Neurosci.*, 5, 195, 2004.
55. Doyle, E. et al., Intraventricular infusions of anti-neural cell adhesion molecules in a discrete posttraining period impair consolidation of a passive avoidance response in the rat., *J. Neurochem.*, 59, 1570, 1992.
56. Cambon, K. et al., Posttraining administration of a synthetic peptide ligand of the neural cell adhesion molecule, C3d, attenuates long-term expression of contextual fear conditioning, *Neuroscience,* 122, 183, 2003.
57. Sandi, C. et al., Rapid reversal of stress induced loss of synapses in CA3 of rat hippocampus following water maze training, *Eur. J. Neurosci.*, 17, 2447, 2003.
58. Venero C. et al., Hippocampal upregulation of NCAM expression and polysialylation plays a key role on spatial memory, *Eur. J. Neurosci., 23*, 1585, 2006.
59. McEwen, B.S., Stress and the aging hippocampus, *Front. Neuroendocrinol.*, 20, 49, 1999.
60. McEwen, B.S., Sex, stress and the hippocampus: allostasis, allostatic load and the aging process, *Neurobiol. Aging*, 23, 921, 2002.
61. Mazure, C.M., Does stress cause psychiatric illness? in *Progress in Psychiatry*, Spiegel, D., Ed., American Psychiatric Press, Washington, 1995, p. 270.
62. Heim, C. and Nemeroff, C.B., The impact of early adverse experiences on brain systems involved in the pathophysiology of anxiety and affective disorders, *Biol. Psychiatr.*, 46, 1509, 1999.
63. Uno, H. et al., Hippocampal damage associated with prolonged and fatal stress in primates, *J. Neurosci.*, 9, 1705, 1989.
64. Magariños, A.M. et al., Chronic psychosocial stress causes apical dendritic atrophy of hippocampal CA3 pyramidal neurons in subordinate tree shrews, *J. Neurosci.,* 16, 3534, 1996.
65. Luine, V. et al., Repeated stress causes reversible impairments of spatial memory performance, *Brain Res.*, 639, 167, 1994.
66. Conrad, C.D. et al., Chronic stress impairs rat spatial memory on the Y maze, and this effect is blocked by tianeptine pretreatment, *Behav. Neurosci.,* 110, 1321, 1996.
67. Park, C.R., Campbell, A.M., and Diamond, D.M., Chronic psychosocial stress impairs learning and memory and increases sensitivity to yohimbine in adult rats, *Biol. Psychiatr.,* 50, 994, 2001.
68. Venero, C. et al., Chronic stress induces opposite changes in the mRNA expression of the cell adhesion molecules NCAM and L1, *Neuroscience,* 115, 1211, 2002.
69. Hellhammer, D.H. and Wade, S., Endocrine correlates of stress vulnerability, *Psychother. Psychosom.*, 601, 8, 1993.
70. Rudolph, K.D. and Hammen, C., Age and gender as determinants of stress exposure, generation, and reactions in youngsters: a transactional perspective, *Child Dev.*, 703, 660, 1999.

71. Grootendorst, J. et al., Stress alleviates reduced expression of cell adhesion molecules NCAM, L1, and deficits in learning and corticosterone regulation of apolipoprotein E knockout mice, *Eur. J. Neurosci.*, 14, 1505, 2001.
72. Troisi, A., Gender differences in vulnerability to social stress: a Darwinian perspective, *Physiol. Behav.*, 733, 443, 2001.
73. Oitzl, M.S. et al., Maternal deprivation affects behavior from youth to senescence: amplification of individual differences in spatial learning and memory in senescent brown Norway rats, *Eur. J. Neurosci.*, 12, 3771, 2000.
74. Piazza, P.V. et al., Corticosterone levels determine individual vulnerability to amphetamine self-administration, *Proc. Natl. Acad. Sci. USA*, 88, 2088, 1991.
75. Kabbaj, M. et al., Neurobiological correlates of individual differences in novelty-seeking behavior in the rat: differential expression of stress-related molecules, *J. Neurosci.*, 2018, 6983, 2000.
76. Dellu, F. et al., Behavioral reactivity to novelty during youth as a predictive factor of stress-induced corticosterone secretion in the elderly: a life-span study in rats, *Psychoneuroendocrinology*, 5, 441, 1996.
77. Touyarot, K., Venero, C., and Sandi, C., Spatial learning impairment induced by chronic stress is related to individual differences in novelty reactivity: search for neurobiological correlates, *Psychoneuroendocrinology*, 29, 290, 2004.
78. Parker, B. et al., The influence of anxiety as a risk to early onset major depression, *J. Affect. Disord.*, 52, 11, 1999.
79. Gladstone G.L. and Parker, G.B., Is behavioral inhibition a risk factor for depression? *J. Affect. Disord.*, 2006, in press.
80. Herrero, A.I., Sandi C., and Venero C., Individual differences in anxiety trait are related to spatial learning abilities and hippocampal expression of mineralocorticoid receptors, *Neurobiol. Learn. Mem.*, 2006, in press.
81. Luine, V., Sex differences in chronic stress effects on memory in rats, *Stress* 5, 205, 2002.
82. Bowman, R.E., Stress-induced changes in spatial memory are sexually differentiated and vary across the lifespan, *J. Neuroendocrinol.*, 178, 526, 2005.
83. Bowman, R.E., Beck, K.D., and Luine, V.N., Chronic stress effects on memory: sex differences in performance and monoaminergic activity, *Horm. Behav.*, 43, 48, 2003.
84. Bodnoff, S.R. et al., Enduring effects of chronic corticosterone treatment on spatial learning, synaptic plasticity, and hippocampal neuropathology in young and mid-aged rats, *J. Neurosci.*, 15, 61, 1995.
85. Levy, A. et al., Aging, stress, and cognitive function, *Ann. NY Acad. Sci.*, 717, 79, 1994.
86. Sandi, C. and Touyarot, K., Mid-life stress and cognitive deficits during early aging in rats: Individual differences and hippocampal correlates, *Neurobiol. Aging*, 27, 128, 2006.
87. Meaney, M.J. et al., Effect of neonatal handling on age-related impairments associated with the hippocampus, *Science*, 239, 766, 1988.
88. Sanchez, M.M., Ladd, C.O., and Plotsky, P.M., Early adverse experience as a developmental risk factor for later psychopathology: evidence from rodent and primate models, *Dev. Psychopathol.*, 133, 419, 2001.
89. Avishai-Eliner, S. et al., Stressed-out or *in utero*? *Trends Neurosci.*, 25, 518, 2002.
90. Huot, R.L. et al., Neonatal maternal separation reduces hippocampal mossy fiber density in adult Long Evans rats, *Brain Res.*, 52, 9501, 2002.

91. Koo, J.W. et al., The postnatal environment can counteract prenatal effects on cognitive ability, cell proliferation, and synaptic protein expression, *FASEB J.*, 17, 1556, 2003.
92. Brunson, K.L. et al., Mechanisms of late-onset cognitive decline after early-life stress, *J. Neurosci.*, 25, 9328, 2005.
93. Avishai-Eliner, S. et al., Altered regulation of gene and protein expression of hypothalamic–pituitary–adrenal axis components in an immature rat model of chronic stress, *J. Neuroendocrinol.*, 139, 799, 2001.
94. Khalilov, I., Holmes, G.L., and Ben-Ari, Y., *In vitro* formation of a secondary epileptogenic mirror focus by interhippocampal propagation of seizures, *Nat. Neurosci.*, 610, 1079, 2003.
95. Kesner, R.P. and Hopkins, R.O., Mnemonic functions of the hippocampus: a comparison between animals and humans, *Biol. Psychol.*, 73, 3, 2006.
96. Kim, J.J., Song, E.Y., and Kosten, T.A., Stress effects in the hippocampus: synaptic plasticity and memory, *Stress*, 9, 1, 2006.
97. Bremner, J.D., Does stress damage the brain? *Biol. Psychiatr.,* 45, 797, 1999.
98. Sheline, Y.I. 3D MRI studies of neuroanatomic changes in unipolar major depression: the role of stress and medical comorbidity, *Biol. Psychiatr.,* 48, 791, 2000.
99. Kitayama, N. et al., Magnetic resonance imaging MRI measurement of hippocampal volume in post-traumatic stress disorder: a meta-analysis, *J. Affect. Disord.*, 88, 79, 2005.
100. Watanabe, Y. et al., Phenytoin prevents stress- and corticosterone-induced atrophy of CA3 pyramidal neurons, *Hippocampus,* 2, 431, 1992.
101. Magariños, A.M. and McEwen, B.S., Stress-induced atrophy of apical dendrites of hippocampal CA3c neurons: involvement of glucocorticoid secretion and excitatory amino acid receptors, *Neuroscience,* 69, 89, 1995.
102. Magariños, A.M., Verdugo-Garcia, J.M., and McEwen, B.S., Chronic restraint stress alters synaptic terminal structure in hippocampus, *Proc. Natl. Acad. Sci. USA,* 94, 14002, 1997.
103. Sousa, N.et al., Reorganization of the morphology of hippocampal neurites and synapses after stress-induced damage correlates with behavioral improvement, *Neuroscience,* 97, 253, 2000.
104. Stewart. M.G. et al., Stress suppresses and learning induces ultrastructural plasticity in CA3 of rat hippocampus: a three-dimensional ultrastructural study of thorny excrescences and their post-synaptic densities, *Neuroscience,* 131, 43, 2005.
105. Donohue, H.S. et al., Volume measurements show that synaptic density is unchanged in CA1 rat hippocampus after chronic restraint stress but postsynaptic density size increases, *Neuroscience,* 140, 597, 2006.
106. Gould, E. and Tanapat, P., Stress and hippocampal neurogenesis, *Biol. Psychiatr.,* 46, 1472, 1999.
107. Sapolsky, R.M., The possibility of neurotoxicity in the hippocampus in major depression: a primer on neuron death, *Biol. Psychiatr.,* 48, 755, 2000.
108. Bush, G. et al., The counting Stroop: an interference task specialized for functional neuroimaging validation study with functional MRI, *Hum. Brain Mapp.*, 6, 270, 1998.
109. MacDonald, A.W. et al., Dissociating the role of the dorsolateral prefrontal and anterior cingulate cortex in cognitive control, *Science*, 288, 1835, 2000.
110. Kerns, J.G. et al., Anterior cingulate conflict monitoring and adjustments in control, *Science*, 303,1023, 2004.

111. Ahima, R.S. and Harlan, R.E., Differential corticosteroid regulation of type II glucocorticoid receptor-like immunoreactivity in the rat central nervous system: topography and implications, *Endocrinology*, 129, 226, 1991.
112. Sanchez, M.M. et al., Distribution of corticosteroid receptors in the rhesus brain: relative absence of glucocorticoid receptors in the hippocampal formation, *J. Neurosci.*, 20, 4657, 2000.
113. Diorio, D., Viau, V., and Meaney, M.J., The role of the medial prefrontal cortex cingulate gyrus in the regulation of hypothalamic–pituitary–adrenal responses to stress, *J. Neurosci.*, 13, 3839, 1993.
114. Drevets, W.C. et al., Subgenual prefrontal cortex abnormalities in mood disorders, *Nature,* 386, 824, 1997.
115. Rauch, S.L. et al., Selectively reduced regional cortical volumes in post-traumatic stress disorder, *Neuroreport*, 14, 913, 2003.
116. Cook, S.C. and Wellman, C.L., Chronic stress alters dendritic morphology in rat medial prefrontal cortex, *J. Neurobiol.*, 60, 236, 2004.
117. Radley, J.J. et al., Chronic behavioral stress induces apical dendritic reorganization in pyramidal neurons of the medial prefrontal cortex, *Neuroscience*, 1251,1, 2004.
118. Radley, J.J. et al., Repeated stress induces dendritic spine loss in the rat medial prefrontal cortex, *Cereb. Cortex*, 16, 313, 2006.
119. Cerqueira, J.J. et al., Morphological correlates of corticosteroid-induced changes in prefrontal cortex-dependent behaviors, *J. Neurosci.*, 25, 7792, 2005.
120. Wellman, C.L. Dendritic reorganization in pyramidal neurons in medial prefrontal cortex after chronic corticosterone administration, *J. Neurobiol.*, 49, 245, 2001.
121. Phelps E.A. and LeDoux J.E., Contributions of the amygdala to emotion processing: from animal models to human behavior, *Neuron*, 48,175, 2005.
122. Vyas, A. et al., Chronic stress induces contrasting patterns of dendritic remodeling in hippocampal and amygdaloid neurons, *J. Neurosci.*, 22, 6810, 2002.
123. Mitra, R. et al., Stress duration modulates the spatiotemporal patterns of spine formation in the basolateral amygdala, *Proc. Natl. Acad. Sci. USA*, 102, 9371, 2005.
124. Alfarez, D.N., Joëls, M., and Krugers, H.J., Chronic unpredictable stress impairs long-term potentiation in rat hippocampal CA1 area and dentate gyrus *in vitro*, *Eur. J. Neurosci.*, 17, 1928, 2003.
125. Gerges, N.Z. et al., Reduced basal CaMKII levels in hippocampal CA1 region: possible cause of stress-induced impairment of LTP in chronically stressed rats, *Hippocampus,* 14, 402, 2004.
126. Pavlides, C., Nivon, L.G., and McEwen, B.S. Effects of chronic stress on hippocampal long-term potentiation, *Hippocampus,* 12, 245, 2002.
127. Pavlides, C., Watanabe, Y., and McEwen, B.S., Effects of glucocorticoids on hippocampal long-term potentiation, *Hippocampus,* 3, 183, 1993.
128. Maroun, M. and Richter-Levin, G., Exposure to acute stress blocks the induction of long-term potentiation of the amygdala-prefrontal cortex pathway *in vivo*, *J. Neurosci.*, 11, 4406, 2003.
129. Molteni, R. et al., Modulation of fibroblast growth factor-2 by stress and corticosteroids: from developmental events to adult brain plasticity, *Brain Res. Rev.*, 37, 249, 2001.
130. Lowy, M.T., Gault, L., and Yamamoto, B.K., Adrenalectomy attenuates stress-induced elevations in extracellular glutamate concentrations in the hippocampus, *J. Neurochem.*, 61, 1957, 1993.
131. Moghaddam, B. et al., Glucocorticoids mediate the stress-induced extracellular accumulation of glutamate, *Brain Res.*, 655, 251, 1994.

132. Venero, C. and Borrell, J., Rapid glucocorticoid effects on excitatory amino acid levels in the hippocampus: a microdialysis study in freely moving rats, *Eur. J. Neurosci.*, 11, 2465, 1999.
133. Krugers, H.J. et al., A single social stress-experience alters glutamate receptor-binding in rat hippocampal CA3 area, *Neurosci. Lett.*, 154, 73, 1993.
134. Bartanusz, V. et al., Stress-induced changes in messenger RNA levels of N-methyl-D-aspartate and AMPA receptor subunits in selected regions of the rat hippocampus and hypothalamus, *Neuroscience,* 66, 247, 1995.
135. Weiland, N.G., Orchinik, M., and Tanapat, P., Chronic corticosterone treatment induces parallel changes in N-methyl-D-aspartate receptor subunit messenger RNA levels and antagonist binding sites in the hippocampus, *Neuroscience,* 78, 653, 1997.
136. Kole, M.H., Swan, L., and Fuchs, E., The antidepressant tianeptine persistently modulates glutamate receptor currents of the hippocampal CA3 commissural associational synapse in chronically stressed rats, *Eur. J. Neurosci.*, 16, 807, 2002.
137. Schaaf, M.J.M. et al., Corticosterone regulates expression of BDNF and trkB but not NT-3 and trkC mRNA in the rat hippocampus, *J. Neurosci. Res.,* 48, 334, 1997.
138. Trentani, A. et al., Selective chronic stress-induced in vivo ERK1/2 hyperphosphorylation in medial prefrontocortical dendrites: implications for stress-related cortical pathology? *Eur. J. Neurosci.*, 15, 1681, 2002.
139. Meller, E. et al., Region-specific effects of acute and repeated restraint stress on the phosphorylation of mitogen-activated protein kinases, *Brain Res.*, 979, 57, 2003.
140. Kuipers, S.D. et al., Molecular correlates of impaired prefrontal plasticity in response to chronic stress, *J. Neurochem.*, 85, 1312, 2003.
141. Touyarot, K. and Sandi, C., Chronic restraint stress induces an isoform-specific regulation on the neural cell adhesion molecule in the hippocampus, *Neural Plast.*, 9, 147, 2002.
142. Pham, K. et al., Repeated restraint stress suppresses neurogenesis and induces biphasic PSA-NCAM expression in the adult rat dentate gyrus, *Eur. J. Neurosci.,* 17, 879, 2003.
143. Seki, T. and Arai, Y. Highly polysialylated neural cell adhesion molecule NCAM-H is expressed by newly generated granule cells in the gyrus dentatus of the adult rat, *J. Neurosci.*, 13, 2351, 1992.
144. Nacher, J. et al., Chronic restraint stress and chronic corticosterone treatment modulate differentially the expression of molecules related to structural plasticity in the adult rat piriform cortex, *Neuroscience,* 126, 503, 2004.
145. Cordero, M.I. et al., Chronic restraint stress down-regulates amygdaloid expression of PSA-NCAM, *Neuroscience,* 133, 903, 2005.
146. Christensen, H., What cognitive changes can be expected with normal aging? *Austrzal. N. Z. J. Psychiatr.*, 35, 768, 2001.
147. Rabbit, P. et al., Identifying and separating the effects of practice and of cognitive ageing during a large longitudinal study of elderly community residents, *Neuropsychologia*, 39, 532, 2001.
148. Nyberg, L., Persson, J., and Nilsson, L.G., Individual differences in memory enhancement by encoding enactment: relationships to adult age and biological factors, *Neurosci. Behav. Rev.*, 26,835, 2002.
149. Singer, T., Lindenberger, U., and Baltes, P.B., Plasticity of memory for new learning in very old age: a story of major loss? *Psychol. Aging*, 18, 306, 2003.
150. Rowe, W.B. et al., Reactivity to novelty in cognitively impaired and cognitively unimpaired aged rats and young rats, *Neuroscience*, 83, 669, 1998.

151. Bach, M.E. et al., Age-related defects in spatial memory are correlated with defects in the late phase of hippocampal long-term potentiation *in vitro* and are attenuated by drugs that enhance the cAMP signaling pathway, *Proc. Natl. Acad. Sci. USA*, 96, 5280, 1999.
152. Schulz, D. et al., Water maze performance, exploratory activity, inhibitory avoidance and hippocampal plasticity in aged superior and inferior learners, *Eur. J. Neurosci.*, 16, 2175, 2002.
153. Landfield, P.W., Waymire, J.C., and Lynch, G., Hippocampal aging and adrenocorticoids: quantitative correlations, *Science*, 202, 1098, 1978.
154. Porter, N.M. and Landfield, P.W., Stress hormones and brain aging: adding injury to insult? *Nat. Neurosci.*,1, 3, 1998.
155. Singer, B.H. and Ryff, C.D.E., *New Horizons in Health: An Integrative Approach*, National Research Council, National Academy Press, Washington, 2001.
156. Hibberd, C., Yau, J.L., and Seckl, J.R., Glucocorticoids and the ageing hippocampus, *J. Anat.*, 197, 553, 2000.
157. Issa, A.M. et al., Hypothalamic–pituitary–adrenal activity in aged, cognitively impaired and cognitively unimpaired rats, *J. Neurosci.*, 10, 3247, 1990.
158. Landfield, P.W., Baskin, R.K., and Pitler, T.A., Brain aging correlates: retardation by hormonal–pharmacological treatments, *Science*, 214, 581, 1981.
159. Lupien, S.J. et al., Cortisol levels during human aging predict hippocampal atrophy and memory deficits, *Nat. Neurosci.*,1, 69, 1998.
160. Van Cauter, E., Leproult, R., and Kupfer, D.J., Effects of gender and age on the levels and circadian rhythmicity of plasma cortisol, *J. Clin. Endocrinol. Metab.*, 81, 2468, 1996.
161. Wilkinson, C.W., Peskind, E.R., and Raskind M.A., Decreased hypothalamic–pituitary–adrenal axis sensitivity to cortisol feedback inhibition in human aging, *Neuroendocrinology*, 65, 79, 1997.
162. Wolf, O.T. et al., Basal hypothalamo–pituitary–adrenal axis activity and corticotropin feedback in young and older men: relationship to magnetic resonance imaging derived hippocampus and cingulate gyrus volumes, *Neuroendocrinology*, 75, 241, 2002.
163. Yau, J.L. et al., Glucocorticoids, hippocampal corticosteroid receptor gene expression and antidepressant treatment: relationship with spatial learning in young and aged rats, *Neuroscience*, 66, 571, 1995.
164. Bizon, J.L. et al., Hypothalamic-pituitary-adrenal axis function and corticosterone receptor expression in behaviourally characterized young and aged Long-Evans rats, *Eur. J. Neurosci.*, 14, 1739, 2001.
165. Nichols, N.R., Zieba, M., and Bye, N., Do glucocorticoids contribute to brain aging? *Brain Res. Rev.*, 37, 273, 2001.
166. Lorens, S. et al., Neurochemical, endocrine and immunological responses to stress in young and old Fischer 344 male tasks, *Neurobiol. Aging*, 11, 139, 1990.
167. Peiffer, A., Barden, N., and Meaney, M.J., Age-related changes in glucocorticoid receptor binding and mRNA levels in the rat brain and pituitary, *Neurobiol. Aging*, 12, 475, 1991.
168. Van Eekelen, J. et al., The effect of aging on stress responsiveness and central corticosteroid receptors in the brown Norway rat, *Neurobiol. Aging*, 13, 159, 1991.
169. Hassan, A.H. et al., Plasticity of hippocampal corticosteroid receptors during aging in the rat, *FASEB J.*, 13, 115, 1999.
170. Meijer, O.C. et al., Correlations between hypothalamus–pituitary–adrenal axis parameters depend on age and learning capacity, *Endocrinology*, 146, 1372, 2005.

171. Wolf, O.T. et al., Subjective memory complaints in aging are associated with elevated cortisol levels, *Neurobiol. Aging*, 26, 1357, 2005.
172. Peters, A. et al., Neurobiological bases of age-related cognitive decline in the rhesus monkey, *J. Neuropathol. Exp. Neurol.*, 55, 861, 1996.
173. Buckner, R.L., Memory and executive function in aging and AD: Multiple factors that cause decline and reserve factors that compensate, *Neuron*, 44, 195, 2004.
174. Hedden, T. and Gabrieli, J.D.E., Insights into the aging mind: a view from cognitive neuroscience, *Nat. Rev. Neurosci.*, 5, 87, 2004.
175. Discoll, I. and Sutherland, R.J., The aging hippocampus: navigating between rat and human experiments, *Rev. Neurosci.*, 16, 87, 2005.
176. Weber, R., Brown, L., and Weldon, J., Cognitive maps of environmental knowledge and preference in nursing home patients, *Exp. Aging Res.*, 4, 157, 1978.
177. Kirasic, K.C., Allen, G.L. and Haggerty, D., Age-related differences in adults' macrospatial cognitive processes, *Exp. Aging Res.*, 18, 33, 1992.
178. Lipman, P.D. and Caplan, L.J., Adult age differences in memory for routes: effects of instruction and spatial diagram, *Psychol. Aging*, 7, 435, 1992.
179. Moffat, S.D., Zonderman, A.B., and Resnick, S.M., Age differences in spatial memory in a virtual environment navigation task, *Neurobiol. Aging*, 22, 787, 2001.
180. Fleischman, D.A. et al., Repetition priming and recognition memory in younger and older persons: temporal stability and performance, *Neuropsychology*, 19, 750, 2005.
181. Lupien, S.J. and Wan, N., Successful ageing: from cell to self, *Philos. Trans. R. Soc. Lond. B Biol. Sci.*, 1449, 1413, 2004.
182. Dermaut, B. et al., Tau is central in the genetic Alzheimer–frontotemporal dementia spectrum, *Trends Genet.*, 2112, 664, 2005.
183. Hof, P.R. and Morrison, J.H., The aging brain: morphomolecular senescence of cortical circuits, *Trends Neurosci.*, 27, 607, 2004.
184. Cabeza, R., Hemispheric asymmetry reduction in older adults: the HAROLD model, *Psychol. Aging*, 171, 85, 2002.
185. Ingram, D.K., Brain-behavior linkages in aged rodent models: strategies for examining individual differences, *Neurobiol. Aging*, 17, 497, 1996.
186. Van der Staay, F.J., Assessment of age-associated cognitive deficits in rats: a tricky business, *Neurosci. Biobehav. Rev.*, 267, 753, 2002.
187. Van der Staay, F.J. and Blokland, A., Behavioral differences between outbred Wistar, inbred Fischer 344, brown Norway, and hybrid Fischer 344, brown Norway rats, *Physiol. Behav.*, 60, 97,1996.
188. Spencer, R.L., O'Steen, W.K., and McEwen, B.S., Water maze performance of aged Sprague-Dawley rats in relation to retinal morphologic measures, *Behav. Brain Res.*, 68, 139, 1995.
189. Gallagher, M. and Rapp, P.R., The use of animal models to study the effects of aging on cognition, *Annu. Rev. Psychol.*, 48, 339, 1997.
190. Winocur, G., Conditional learning in aged rats: evidence of hippocampal and prefrontal cortex impairment, *Neurobiol. Aging*, 13, 131, 1991.
191. Zyzak, D.R. et al., Cognitive decline associated with normal aging in rats: a neuropsychological approach, *Learn. Mem.*, 2, 1, 1995.
192. Barense, M.D., Fox, M.T., and Baxter, M.G., Aged rats are impaired on an attentional set-shifting task sensitive to medial frontal cortex damage in young rats, *Learn. Mem.*, 9, 181, 2002.
193. Schoenbaum, G. et al., Encoding changes in orbitofrontal cortex in reversal-impaired aged rats, *J. Neurophysiol.*, 95, 1509, 2006.

194. Barnes, C.A., Aging and the physiology of spatial memory, *Neurobiol. Aging*, 9, 563, 1988.
195. Gallagher, M. and Pelleymounter, M.A., Spatial learning deficits in old rats: a model for memory decline in the aged., *Neurobiol. Aging*, 9, 363, 1988.
196. Rosenzweig, E.S. and Barnes, C.A., Impact of aging on hippocampal function: plasticity, network dynamics, and cognition, *Prog. Neurobiol.*, 69, 143, 2003.
197. Barnes, C.A., Nadel, L. and Honig, W.K., Spatial memory deficit in senescent rats, *Can. J. Psychol.*, 34, 29, 1980.
198. Caprioli, A. et al.,. Spatial learning and memory in the radial maze: a longitudinal study in rats from 4 to 25 months of age, *Neurobiol. Aging*, 12, 605, 1991.
199. Mizumori, S.J.Y., Lavoie, A.M., and Kalyani, A., Redistribution of spatial representation in the hippocampus of aged rats performing a spatial memory task, *Behav. Neurosci.*, 110, 1006, 1996.
200. Barnes, C.A. et al., Behavioral and neurophysiological examples of functional sparing in senescent rat, *Can. J. Psychol.*, 41, 131, 1987.
201. Barnes, C.A., Memory deficits associated with senescence: a neurophysiological and behavioral study in the rat, *J. Comp. Physiol. Psychol.*, 93, 74, 1979.
202. Gage, F.H., Dunnett, S.B. and Björklund, A., Age-related impairments in spatial memory are independent of those in sensorimotor skills, *Neurobiol. Aging* 10, 347, 1989.
203. Rapp, P.R., Rosenberg, R.A., and Gallagher, M., An evaluation of spatial information processing in aged rats, *Behav. Neurosci.*, 101, 3, 1987.
204. Aitken, D.H. and Meaney, M.J., Temporally graded, age-related impairments in spatial memory in the rat, *Neurobiol. Aging*, 10, 273, 1989.
205. Yau, J.L., Morris, R.G., and Seckl, J.R., Hippocampal corticosteroid receptor mRNA expression and spatial learning in the aged Wistar rat, *Brain Res.*, 657, 59, 1994.
206. Rosenzweig, E.S. et al., Role of temporal summation in age-related LTP-induction deficits, *Hippocampus*, 7, 549, 1997.
207. Gallagher, M. and Nicolle, M.M., Animal models of normal aging: relationship between cognitive decline and markers in hippocampal circuitry, *Behav. Brain Res.*, 57, 155, 1993.
208. Nicholson, D.A. et al., Reduction in size of perforated postsynaptic densities in hippocampal axospinous synapses and age-related spatial learning impairments, *J. Neurosci.*, 2435, 7648, 2004.
209. Topic, B. et al., Aged and adult rats compared in acquisition and extinction of escape from the water maze: focus on individual differences, *Behav. Neurosci.*, 119, 127, 2005.
210. Markowska, A.L. et al., Individual differences in aging: behavioral and neurobiological correlates, *Neurobiol. Aging*, 10, 31, 1989.
211. Rapp, P.R. and Amaral, D.G., Individual differences in the cognitive and neurobiological consequences of normal aging, *Trends Neurosci.*, 15, 340, 1992.
212. Drapeau, E. et al., Spatial memory performances of aged rats in the water maze predict levels of hippocampal neurogenesis, *Proc. Natl. Acad. Sci. USA*, 100, 14385, 2003.
213. Gage, F.H., Kelly, P.A., and Björklund, A., Regional changes in brain glucose metabolism reflect cognitive impairments in aged rats, *J. Neurosci.*, 4, 2856, 1984.
214. Coleman, P.D. and Flood, D.G., Neuron numbers and dendritic extent in normal aging and Alzheimer's disease, *Neurobiol. Aging*, 8, 521, 1987.
215. Rapp, P.R. and Gallagher, M., Preserved neuron number in the hippocampus of aged rats with spatial learning deficits, *Proc. Natl. Acad. Sci. USA*, 93, 9926, 1996.

216. Anderson, B. and Rutledge, V., Age and hemisphere effects on dendritic structure, *Brain*, 119, 1983, 1996.
217. Jacobs, B., Driscoll, L., and Schall, M., Life-span dendritic and spine changes in areas 10 and 18 of human cortex: a quantitative Golgi study, *J. Comp. Neurol.*, 386, 661, 1997.
218. Duan, H. et al., Age-related dendritic and spine changes in corticocortically projecting neurons in macaque monkeys, *Cereb. Cortex*, 139, 950, 2003.
219. Hof, P.R. et al., Age-related changes in GluR2 and NMDAR1 glutamate receptor subunit protein immunoreactivity in corticocortically projecting neurons in macaque and patas monkeys, *Brain Res.*, 928, 175, 2002.
220. Bai, L. et al., Changes in the expression of the NR2B subunit during aging in macaque monkeys, *Neurobiol. Aging*, 25, 201, 2004.
221. Peters, A., The effects of normal aging on myelin and nerve fibers: a review, *J. Neurocytol.*, 31, 581, 2002.
222. Geinisman, Y. et al., Age-related loss of axospinous synapses formed by two afferent systems in the rat dentate gyrus as revealed by the unbiased stereological dissector technique, *Hippocampus*, 2, 437, 1992.
223. Arnsten, A.F.T., Age-related cognitive deficits and neurotransmitters — the role of catecholamine mechanisms in prefrontal cortical cognitive decline, in *Cerebral Cortex: Neurodegenerative and Age-Related Changes in Structure and Function of Cerebral Cortex*, vol. 14, Peters, A. and Morrison J.H., Eds., Elsevier, New York, 1999, p. 89.
224. Lee, H.-K. et al., NMDA receptor-independent long-term depression correlates with successful aging in rats, *Nat. Neurosci.*, 8, 1657, 2005.
224. Ramos, B.P. et al., Dysregulation of protein kinase A signaling in the aged prefrontal cortex: new strategy for treating age-related cognitive decline, *Neuron*, 40, 835, 2003.
225. Rosenzweig, E.S. et al., Hippocampal map realignment and spatial learning, *Nat. Neurosci.*, 6, 611, 2003.
226. O'Keefe, J., A review of the hippocampal place cells, *Prog. Neurobiol.*, 13, 419, 1979.
227. Gothard, K.M., Skaggs, W.E. and McNaughton, B.L., Dynamics of mismatch correction in the hippocampal ensemble code for space: interaction between path integration and environmental cues, *J. Neurosci.*, 16, 8027, 1996.
228. O'Keefe, J. and Nadel, L., *The Hippocampus as a Cognitive Map*, Oxford University Press, New York, 1978.

13 Adrenal Stress Hormones and Enhanced Memory for Emotionally Arousing Experiences

Christa K. McIntyre and Benno Roozendaal

CONTENTS

13.1 INTRODUCTION

Emotionally significant experiences tend to be well remembered.[1,2] We know this from personal experiences as well as from extensive research findings. Significant experiences such as birthdays, graduation ceremonies, or the loss of a loved one typically leave lasting and vivid memories. Findings of experimental studies indicate that people have good recollections of where they were and what they were doing when they experienced earthquakes[3] or witnessed accidents.[4] Similarly, a rat remembers the place in an apparatus where it received a footshock or the location of an escape platform in a tank filled with water.[5,6] Such memory enhancement is not limited to experiences that are unpleasant or aversive. Pleasurable events also tend to be well remembered. Our research focuses on understanding the role of emotional responses induced by such arousing experiences in enabling the significance of events to regulate their remembrance.

Extensive evidence indicates that stress hormones released from the adrenal glands are critically involved in memory consolidation of emotionally arousing experiences. Epinephrine, glucocorticoids, and specific agonists for their receptors administered after exposure to emotionally arousing experiences enhance the consolidation of long-term memories of these experiences.[7–10]

Do stress hormones also enhance memories of experiences that are not emotionally arousing? The findings of recent experiments suggest that this may not be the case. As discussed below, we recently reported that the endogenous glucocorticoid corticosterone enhanced memory consolidation of object recognition training when administered to rats that were emotionally aroused by an unfamiliar training apparatus. However, the treatment had no effect when administered to rats that had extensive prior habituation to the training context in order to reduce novelty-induced arousal.[11] In studies of human memory, epinephrine or cortisol treatment also appear to selectively enhance memory for emotionally arousing material.[12–15]

These findings thus provide some important clues concerning the neurobiological mechanism(s) underlying adrenal hormone effects on memory consolidation and suggest that at least some degree of training-associated endogenous emotional arousal is essential for enabling their effects on memory consolidation. Our findings indicate that adrenal stress hormones influence memory consolidation of emotional experiences via interactions with arousal-induced activation of noradrenergic mechanisms within the amygdala.

13.2 STRESS HORMONE EFFECTS ON MEMORY CONSOLIDATION

It is well established that hormones of the adrenal medulla (epinephrine) and adrenal cortex (corticosterone, cortisol in humans) are released during and immediately after stressful stimulation of the kind used in emotionally arousing learning tasks. The degree to which these hormonal systems are activated depends on the severity as well as type of stressor employed.[16] As removal of endogenous hormones by adrenalectomy impairs memory consolidation for emotionally arousing experiences,[5,17–19] such evidence indicates that stress hormones released by the training experience may act as endogenous modulators of memory consolidation.

In support of this view, single injections of epinephrine or glucocorticoids administered after training enhance the long-term retention of many different kinds of training experiences typically used in animal memory studies including inhibitory avoidance, active avoidance, contextual and cued fear conditioning, spatial discrimination, conditioned taste aversion, object recognition, and appetitively motivated tasks.[11,20–23] Further, antagonists of adrenoceptors or adrenal steroid receptors as well as drugs that disrupt glucocorticoid functioning (i.e., metyrapone) impair memory consolidation.[5,17,24,25] Injections of stress hormones at doses that enhance memory when administered shortly after training are generally ineffective when administered several hours after training.[26,27] Such findings indicate that the hormones affect memory by modulating the storage or "consolidation" phase. Extensive evidence also indicates that epinephrine and glucocorticoids or stressful conditions that stimulate their release enhance memory consolidation in human subjects when administered shortly before or after learning.[12,13,28,29]

Although epinephrine and glucocorticoids interact in influencing memory consolidation,[24,30,31] their effects are initiated through different mechanisms. Because epinephrine does not readily cross the blood–brain barrier, a peripheral central pathway must be involved in mediating epinephrine effects on brain activity in modulating memory consolidation. The findings of many experiments indicate that epinephrine effects on memory consolidation are initiated by activation of peripheral β-adrenoceptors located on vagal afferents that project to the nucleus of the solitary tract (NTS) in the brain stem. Noradrenergic projections originating in the NTS innervate forebrain structures involved in learning and memory, including the amygdala,[32,33] but may also influence norepinephrine release via projections to the nucleus paragigantocellularis in the lower medulla, which projects to the locus coeruleus. The locus coeruleus noradrenergic system is viewed as a broad system with projections to many areas involved in memory processing including the amygdala, hippocampus, and prefrontal cortex.[34–36]

Glucocorticoids are highly lipophilic and readily enter the brain to bind to mineralocorticoid receptors (MRs) and glucocorticoid receptors (GRs). These two receptor types differ in their affinities for corticosterone and synthetic ligands. MRs have a high affinity for the natural steroids and are almost saturated during basal levels of corticosterone and cortisol, whereas GRs have a high affinity for synthetic ligands such as dexamethasone and RU 28362.[37] In contrast to MRs, GRs become occupied only during stress and at the circadian peak. Several studies using pharmacological and genetic techniques indicate that the memory–modulatory effects of glucocorticoids selectively involve activation of GRs.[17,38–41] GRs are considered classical intra-somatic receptors that, after their activation, translocate to the nucleus and regulate gene transcription by binding of receptor homodimers to DNA or other nuclear proteins.[42–45] However, glucocorticoids or specific GR agonists also have rapid (milliseconds to minutes) effects on the brain and behavior, suggesting that they may also produce fast-acting, nongenomic effects, presumably involving an activation of membrane receptors.[46–48]

13.3 STRESS HORMONES SELECTIVELY ENHANCE MEMORY CONSOLIDATION OF EMOTIONALLY AROUSING EXPERIENCES

Stress hormone effects on memory consolidation follow an inverted-U shaped dose-response effect. Moderate doses of epinephrine or glucocorticoids enhance memory consolidation but lower or higher doses are less effective or may even impair memory consolidation.[49,50] Other variables such as gender and age may also influence the direction of the effects of stress hormones on memory consolidation due to differences in stress responses and vulnerability across populations.[51–53]

Stress hormone effects on memory consolidation depend further on the level of emotional arousal induced by the training experience. For example, posttraining injections of moderate doses of corticosterone or dexamethasone, a synthetic ligand, enhance memory consolidation in a water-maze spatial task.[54] However, the same glucocorticoid treatment impairs memory consolidation when the task becomes more aversive by lowering the water temperature.[54,55] Similarly, epinephrine and glucocorticoids, as well as drugs affecting many other neurotransmitter systems, are known to enhance memory of inhibitory avoidance training when administered after a mild, low-arousing foot shock, but to impair memory consolidation when given after a strong, highly aversive foot shock that produces robust memory in control animals.[56] Thus, these findings indicate that the efficacy and even the direction of the effects of exogenous drug administration on memory consolidation depend on the level of endogenous emotional arousal evoked by the training experience.

To address the question raised earlier in this chapter of whether stress hormone effects on memory consolidation require emotional arousal, we recently investigated the importance of emotional arousal in influencing stress hormone effects on memory consolidation in rats trained on an object recognition task.[11] Learning tasks in animal experiments are often emotionally arousing because of the punishment or reward necessary to elicit changes in behavior. It is obvious that with the use of such experimental conditions, it is not possible to determine whether emotional arousal is a prerequisite in regulating stress hormone influences on memory processes. Although no rewarding or aversive stimulation is used during object recognition training,[57] such training induces modest novelty-induced stress or arousal. However, extensive habituation of rats to the training apparatus (in the absence of any objects) prior to the training reduces the arousal level induced by object recognition training. Thus, object recognition training may be performed under two distinct conditions in which rats are either exposed to the objects while in a state of heightened arousal or in a less aroused state. We found that corticosterone administered systemically immediately after training enhanced 24-hour retention performance of rats that were not previously habituated to the experimental context (i.e., emotionally aroused rats). In contrast, corticosterone did not affect 24-hour retention of rats that received extensive prior habituation to the experimental context and thus had decreased novelty-induced emotional arousal during training.[11] Clearly, these findings indicate that at least some degree of training-associated endogenous emotional arousal is essential for enabling stress hormone effects on memory consolidation.

Recent studies of human memory have also investigated interactions of stress hormones with training-associated emotional arousal. Decreasing glucocorticoid levels below baseline with the cortisol synthesis inhibitor metyrapone impaired long-term memory for both emotionally arousing and emotionally neutral information,[58] presumably involving a reduced MR occupancy. However, cortisol administration selectively enhance long-term memory of emotionally arousing, but not emotionally neutral, pictures.[12,15] Consistent with these findings, Abercrombie and colleagues[14] reported that levels of endogenous cortisol correlated with enhanced memory consolidation only in individuals who were emotionally aroused.

The memory-enhancing effects of epinephrine administration or stress exposure immediately after learning also appear to depend on the arousal level.[13,29] For example, Cahill and Alkire[13] recorded electrodermal skin responses in human subjects as they viewed standard nonarousing slides, followed by infusions of epinephrine or saline. They reported that epinephrine-treated subjects showed enhanced memory for the first slides (i.e., primacy effect). Likewise, electrodermal skin responses to those slides were significantly greater than responses to slides shown at a later time. Therefore, the authors concluded that epinephrine effects on memory depend on the level of arousal at the time of encoding.

13.4 INVOLVEMENT OF AMYGDALA IN MEDIATING STRESS HORMONE EFFECTS ON MEMORY CONSOLIDATION

Why do stress hormones selectively enhance memory for emotionally arousing experiences? The findings described above suggest that stress hormones must interact with some other component of emotional arousal in mediating memory enhancement. Our findings indicate that stress hormone effects on memory consolidation require amygdala activity. It is well established that emotional experiences that induce the release of adrenal stress hormones also activate the amygdala.[59]

Lesions or temporary inactivation of the amygdala block the memory-modulatory effects induced by posttraining systemic injections of drugs affecting a variety of neuromodulatory systems including norepinephrine, opioid peptides, GABA, vasopressin, and ACTH.[9,60] Furthermore, as noted above, the amygdala mediates epinephrine as well as glucocorticoid effects on memory consolidation.[20,61] Selective NMDA-induced lesions of the amygdala restricted to the basolateral complex (BLA; consisting of the lateral, basal, and accessory basal nuclei) block inhibitory avoidance memory enhancement induced by posttraining systemic injections of the synthetic glucocorticoid dexamethasone.[39] In contrast, lesions of the adjacent central nucleus (CEA) do not block the dexamethasone-induced memory enhancement. Moreover, posttraining infusions of the specific GR agonist RU 28362 administered into the BLA, but not the CEA, enhanced memory consolidation in a dose-dependent fashion, whereas intra-BLA infusions of the GR antagonist RU 38486 impaired memory consolidation.[39] Corticotropin-releasing hormone (CRH) is another neurotransmitter that is released into the amygdala as well as several other brain regions in response to arousing or stressful stimulation. Blockade of endogenous CRH in the BLA with infusions of a CRH receptor antagonist impaired memory for emotionally arousing training,[62] whereas preliminary findings indicate that infusions of CRH into the BLA dose-dependently enhance memory consolidation. This evidence indicates that BLA activation by emotional arousal is a general gateway in mediating stress hormone and neurotransmitter effects on memory consolidation.

13.4.1 Amygdala Interacts with Other Brain Regions

Other evidence indicates that the BLA is not a site of permanent storage of the enhanced memory trace but rather is involved in strengthening consolidation processes in other brain regions.[9,60] The evidence that lesions of the stria terminalis, a major amygdala input–output pathway, block the memory-modulatory effects of systemic drug infusions and of drugs infused directly into the amygdala[63–65] strongly suggests that the amygdala regulates memory consolidation by influencing the storage of information in efferent brain regions. The BLA interacts with many brain regions, including the hippocampus, caudate nucleus and insular, entorhinal, and anterior cingulate cortices in regulating the consolidation of different types of information.[60] It also interacts with the hippocampus in regulating stress (hormone) effects on memory consolidation of contextual/spatial components of training. Hippocampal GRs play a role in neuroplasticity[66–69] and posttraining activation of hippocampal GRs enhances memory consolidation for both appetitive and aversive training.[40,70,71] However, BLA lesions block the memory enhancement produced by posttraining intra-hippocampal infusions of a GR agonist.[40] Similarly, electrophysiological findings indicate that BLA lesions or temporary blockade of BLA functioning impair stress- or perforant path stimulation-induced long-term potentiation in the dentate gyrus.[72,73] These findings indicate that BLA neuronal activity is required for enabling memory modulation induced by local GR activation in the hippocampus. Since the BLA is normally activated by emotional arousal, such evidence may provide an explanation for the findings that stress hormones selectively influence memory consolidation of emotionally arousing experiences.

Other findings indicate the existence of interactions between the BLA and medial prefrontal cortex (mPFC). The mPFC is implicated in higher cognitive functions such as thought, decision-making, and working memory[74,75] and also plays a role in memory consolidation.[76] The BLA interacts with the mPFC via reciprocal inhibitory connections.[77,78] In a recent study, we examined whether the BLA and mPFC interact in regulating glucocorticoid effects on memory consolidation.[79] A GR agonist infused posttraining into either the mPFC or the BLA enhanced memory consolidation of inhibitory avoidance training. The same GR agonist administered into the mPFC also increased BLA neuronal activity, as assessed by elevated phosphorylation levels of the transcription factor mitogen-activated protein kinase (MAPK) in the BLA. Importantly, the GR agonist infused into the mPFCs of animals that had not received inhibitory avoidance training did not increase MAPK levels in the BLA, supporting the hypothesis that glucocorticoid effects on memory consolidation and brain activity require training-associated emotional arousal. Because the inhibition of this MAPK activation in the BLA with infusions of a MEK inhibitor blocked the memory enhancement induced by intra-mPFC infusions of the GR agonist,[79] these findings further indicate that BLA activity is essential in regulating stress hormone effects on the consolidation of emotionally arousing memories.

13.4.2 Amygdala Involvement in Human Studies

Considerable evidence from human studies indicates that the enhancing influence of emotional arousal on memory involves activation of the amygdala. Human studies, however, have not yet investigated a possible selective involvement of the BLA. The evidence that emotionally arousing stimulation does not enhance long-term memory in human subjects with amygdala lesions supports the view that amygdala activation may be critical for emotionally enhanced memory.[80] Interestingly, the reactions of amygdala-damaged subjects to the emotional material in these studies appeared normal, suggesting that the amygdala in humans may not be as critical for the production of emotional reactions *per se*.

The involvement of amygdala activation in emotionally influenced memory has also been investigated in many studies using positron emission tomography (PET) and functional magnetic resonance imaging (fMRI) in healthy humans.[81–84] These studies reported that activity of the amygdala assessed during the presentation of emotionally arousing stimuli correlated highly with memory of the stimuli tested weeks later. Further, the relationship between amygdala activity during encoding and subsequent long-term memory was greatest for the most emotionally arousing stimuli. Human studies indicate that the enhanced memory for emotionally arousing events (versus non-arousing events) involves amygdala modulation of the hippocampal formation.[85–87] Collectively, these studies of emotionally influenced memory in human subjects are consistent with findings of animal experiments and indicate that emotional arousal-induced amygdala (BLA) activation may be a critical step in enabling stress hormone effects in modulating memory processes involving other brain regions including hippocampus-dependent explicit/declarative memory.

13.5 ROLE OF EMOTIONAL AROUSAL-INDUCED NORADRENERGIC ACTIVATION WITHIN AMYGDALA IN ENABLING EPINEPHRINE AND GLUCOCORTICOID EFFECTS ON MEMORY CONSOLIDATION

The enhancing effects of adrenal stress hormones on memory consolidation depend on the integrity of the amygdala noradrenergic system. Infusions of β-adrenoceptor antagonists administered into the amygdala block the memory-enhancing effects of peripherally administered epinephrine that, as discussed above, are known to be mediated by activation of the noradrenergic cells of the NTS and locus coeruleus.[61] Glucocorticoids also require noradrenergic activation within the amygdala to influence memory for emotionally arousing training. A β-adrenoceptor antagonist infused into the BLA blocks the memory-enhancing effect of systemically administered glucocorticoids.[88,89] Furthermore, a β-adrenoceptor antagonist infused into the BLA blocked memory enhancement induced by a GR agonist infused into the hippocampus.[90]

Studies using *in vivo* microdialysis indicate that stress induced by prolonged immobilization or tail pinch increased amygdala norepinephrine levels.[91,92] Even a single mild foot shock of the kind typically used in inhibitory avoidance training increased amygdala norepinephrine levels[93] and the increase in norepinephrine varied with footshock intensity.[94] Furthermore, as shown in Figure 13.1, amygdala norepinephrine levels assessed following inhibitory avoidance training correlated with retention latencies tested 24 hours later,[95] whereas posttraining infusions of norepinephrine or β-adrenoceptor agonists administered into the BLA enhanced memory consolidation.[96,97]

Such findings suggest that systemically administered stress hormones may influence noradrenergic function by altering the synthesis, release, and/or reuptake of norepinephrine. In accord with this hypothesis, Williams and colleagues[33] showed that epinephrine administered immediately after inhibitory avoidance training increased norepinephrine levels in the amygdala.

Brainstem noradrenergic cells in the locus coeruleus and NTS are involved not only in mediating epinephrine effects on memory consolidation but also express high levels of GRs.[98] Posttraining infusions of a GR agonist into the NTS dose-dependently enhanced memory consolidation of inhibitory avoidance training and the memory enhancement was blocked by intra-BLA infusions of the β-adrenoceptor antagonist atenolol.[50] The findings of a recent *in vivo* microdialysis experiment support the view that glucocorticoids may influence norepinephrine release in the BLA. Corticosterone administration after inhibitory avoidance training increased norepinephrine levels in the amygdala.[99] In contrast, corticosterone did not increase

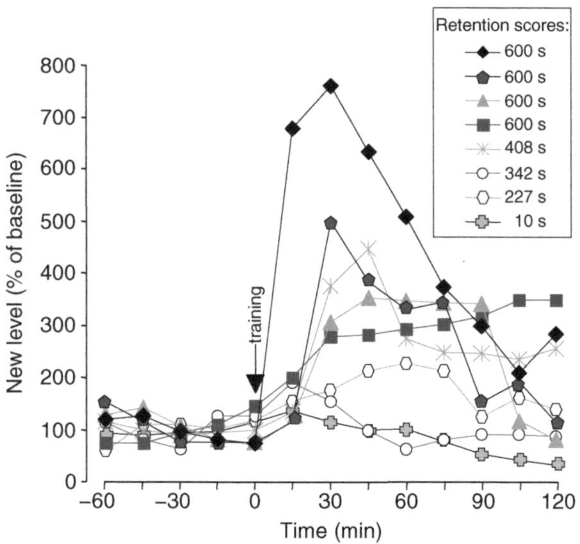

FIGURE 13.1 Norepinephrine levels in the amygdala are significantly correlated with retention latency scores. Each line represents norepinephrine levels as a percentage of baseline for an individual rat. Latency to enter the dark compartment on the retention test 24 hours after microdialysis and training is identified in the key. (From McIntyre, C.K. et al., *Eur. J. Neurosci.*, 16, 1223, 2002. With permission.)

norepinephrine levels in the amygdala when administered to naive rats that did not rcceive inhibitory avoidance training, indicating that glucocorticoids facilitate, but cannot initiate, the release of norepinephrine in the amygdala.

At a postsynaptic level, glucocorticoids may enhance memory consolidation by potentiating β-adrenoceptor-cAMP/PKA efficacy in the BLA.[100] Activation of β-adrenoceptors in the BLA enhanced memory consolidation via stimulation of the cAMP/PKA pathway.[101,102] We found that intra-BLA infusions of a GR antagonist attenuated the dose-response effects of a β-adrenoceptor agonist on retention enhancement for inhibitory avoidance training. The GR antagonist had no effect on memory enhancement induced by posttraining intra-BLA infusions of the synthetic cAMP analog 8-Br-cAMP.[100] These findings suggest that glucocorticoids facilitate the efficacy of noradrenergic stimulation in the BLA on memory consolidation via an interaction with the β-adrenoceptor-cAMP cascade. A model of this interaction is illustrated in Figure 13.2.

13.5.1 Role of Emotional Arousal-Induced Noradrenergic Activation

The findings summarized above indicate that emotional arousal induces the release of norepinephrine in the BLA and that adrenal stress hormones may facilitate this training-induced noradrenergic activation. Such findings suggest that emotional arousal-induced noradrenergic activation within the BLA may be essential in enabling stress hormone effects on memory consolidation.

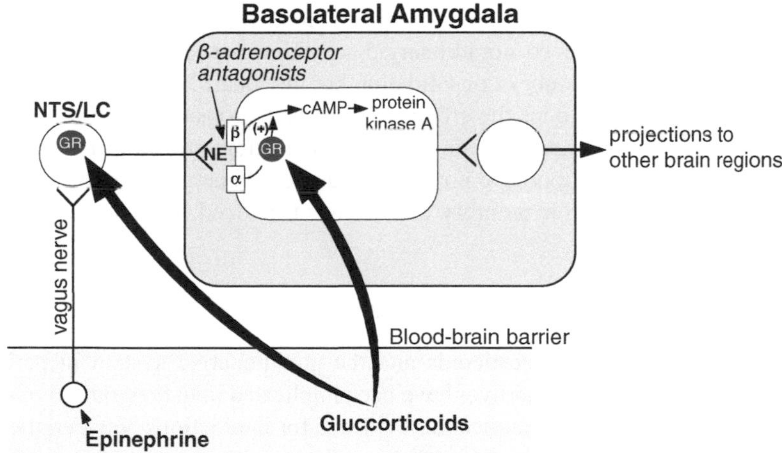

FIGURE 13.2 Summary of interactions of glucocorticoids with the noradrenergic system of the basolateral amygdala at both presynaptic and post-synaptic sites as suggested by the findings of our experiments. α_1 = α_1-adrenoceptor. β = β-adrenoceptor. GR = glucocorticoid receptor. NTS = nucleus of solitary tract. (From Roozendaal, B., *Psychoneuroendocrinology*, 25, 213, 2000. With permission.)

In a recent experiment we investigated this hypothesis.[89] As addressed above, corticosterone enhanced memory consolidation of object recognition training only in emotionally aroused rats that were not previously habituated to the context. Object recognition training in these rats also induced marked increases in noradrenergic activity within the BLA, as assessed by immunoreactivity for phosphorylated tyrosine hydroxylase (the rate-limiting enzyme in the biosynthesis of norepinephrine). As shown in Figure 13.3, a β-adrenoceptor antagonist administered either systemically or into the BLA blocked this corticosterone-induced memory enhancement. In contrast, infusion of a β-adrenoceptor antagonist into the hippocampus did not prevent the corticosterone-induced memory enhancement of object recognition training. These findings further indicate that glucocorticoids require noradrenergic activity in the BLA in regulating memory consolidation.

Importantly, training of context-habituated rats on the object recognition task did not induce significant increases in noradrenergic activation within the BLA.[89] If the failure of corticosterone to enhance memory consolidation in context-habituated rats is due selectively to insufficient arousal-induced noradrenergic activation, then posttraining pharmacological augmentation of noradrenergic activity should provide the activation normally produced by novelty stress and enable glucocorticoid enhancement of memory consolidation. To examine this implication, a low dose of the α_2-adrenoceptor antagonist yohimbine, which increases norepinephrine levels in the brain, was administered to habituated rats either alone or together with corticosterone immediately after object recognition training. Yohimbine administered alone did not affect retention performance. However, as shown in Figure 13.3, corticosterone administered concurrently with yohimbine induced dose-dependent retention enhancement. Posttraining injections of the two drugs separated by a 4-hour delay did not induce a preference for the novel object on the retention. These findings thus indicate that arousal-induced noradrenergic activation is necessary to mediate glucocorticoid effects on memory consolidation but that pharmacologically stimulated noradrenergic activity mimics the effects of emotional arousal in enabling glucocorticoid enhancement of memory consolidation under low-arousing training conditions.[89] These finding support the notion that the noradrenergic component of emotional arousal is critical for memory enhancement induced by glucocorticoids and possibly by epinephrine.

13.5.2 Interactions at Cellular Level

Synergistic effects of glucocorticoids and the noradrenergic system in peripheral tissues including the lungs and liver have been implicated in the regulation of several cellular functions.[103] Is there molecular evidence for interactions between these two systems in regulating memory consolidation? We recently reported that corticosterone interacts with emotion-induced noradrenergic activation in activating the cAMP response-element binding (CREB) pathway in the BLA.[89] Several findings have implicated CREB phosphorylation in the BLA in the modulation of memory consolidation.[104,105] We found that corticosterone administered immediately after object recognition training significantly increased the number of pCREB-positive neurons in the BLA. Corticosterone did not alter the number of pCREB-positive BLA neurons

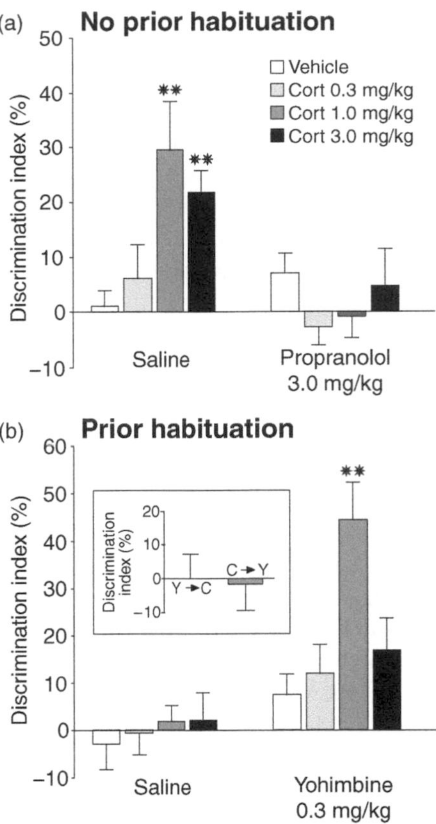

FIGURE 13.3 Glucocorticoid effects on memory consolidation for object recognition training require noradrenergic activation. Data represent discrimination index (%) on a 24-hour retention trial, expressed as mean ± SEM. (A) Effects of immediate posttraining administration of the β-adrenoceptor antagonist propranolol (3.0 mg/kg s.c.) on corticosterone-induced enhancement of object recognition memory in naïve rats. ** $P < 0.0001$ versus vehicle ($n = 8$ to 12 per group). (B) Effect of co-administration of the α_2-adrenoceptor antagonist yohimbine (0.3 mg/kg s.c.) with corticosterone on object recognition memory in habituated rats. ** $P < 0.0001$ versus vehicle ($n = 9$ to 17 per group). (B Inset) Effect of posttraining injections of yohimbine (0.3 mg/kg s.c.) and corticosterone (1.0 mg/kg s.c.) separated by a 4-hour delay. Y→C = yohimbine administered immediately after training and corticosterone 4 hours later. C→Y = corticosterone administered immediately after training and yohimbine 4 hours later. (From Roozendaal, B. et al., *Proc. Natl. Acad. Sci. USA*, 103, 6741, 2006. With permission.)

in rats that received prior habituation to the training context. Importantly, however, corticosterone administered together with the noradrenergic stimulant yohimbine after object recognition training significantly increased pCREB immunoreactivity in the BLA. Thus, these findings are in accord with behavioral studies and indicate that corticosterone activates the CREB pathway in the BLA only with training conditions that induce sufficient noradrenergic activation.

Other studies have indicated that glucocorticoids may interact with noradrenergic mechanisms in increasing the expression and enzymatic activity of the MAPK pathway, leading to an increased expression of the immediate early gene Egr1 (early growth response-1).[106] Like CREB, phosphorylation of MAPKs is considered critical for memory consolidation and long-term neuronal plasticity.[107,108] Blockade of MAPK signaling in the hippocampus abolishes the enhancing effect of systemically administered corticosterone on contextual fear conditioning.[106] Glucocorticoid effects on MAPK activation may be modulated by β-adrenoceptor activation. Activation of β-adrenoceptors by epinephrine and norepinephrine leads to the dissociation of G protein subunits β and γ. It has been demonstrated that β G protein subunits interact with phosphoinositide-3 kinase to stimulate the MAPK pathway.[109,110] Further, epinephrine and norepinephrine were found to potentiate ligand-dependent GR transactivation in cultured hippocampal cells via β_2-adrenoceptors.[111]

13.6 CONCLUSIONS

The evidence summarized in this chapter indicates that adrenal stress hormones influence memory processes in various animal and human memory tasks. Acutely administered or released epinephrine or glucocorticoids dose-dependently enhance the consolidation of long-term memory. However, the effects of stress hormones on the storage of long-term memories depend critically on the arousal state and noradrenergic activation of the BLA. These findings may help to explain why stress hormones do not uniformly modulate memory for all kinds of information but rather, preferentially influence the consolidation of emotionally arousing information. As adrenal stress hormones also play a critical role in the development of traumatic memories and posttraumatic stress disorder (PTSD),[112–114] these findings may provide some understanding of the neurobiological processes that underlie the development of PTSD as well as some possible implications for therapeutic intervention (see Reference 115) to ensure that significant events are well remembered, but do not turn into pathophysiological conditions.

ACKNOWLEDGMENT

We sincerely appreciate Gabriel Hui's assistance with the figures.

REFERENCES

1. Kleinsmith, L.J. and Kaplan, S., Paired-associate learning as a function of arousal and interpolated interval. *J. Exp. Psych.*, 65, 190, 1963.
2. Bradley, M.M., Greenwald, M.K., Petry, M.C., and Lang, P.J., Remembering pictures: pleasure and arousal in memory. *J. Exp. Psych. Learn. Mem. Cognition,* 18, 379, 1992.
3. Neisser, U., Winograd, E., Bergman, E.T., Schreiber, C.A., Palmer, S.E., and Weldon, M.S., Remembering the earthquake: direct experience vs. hearing the news. *Memory,* 4, 337, 1996.

4. Bohannon, J.N., Flashbulb memories for the space shuttle disaster: a tale of two theories. *Cognition*, 2, 179, 1988.
5. Roozendaal, B., Bohus, B., and McGaugh, J.L., Dose-dependent suppression of adreno-cortical activity with metyrapone: effects on emotion and learning. *Psychoneuroendocrinology,* 21, 681, 1996.
6. Vazdarjanova, A. and McGaugh, J.L., Basolateral amygdala is not critical for cognitive memory of contextual fear conditioning. *Proc. Nat. Acad. Sci. USA,* 95, 15003, 1998.
7. de Kloet, E.R., Oitzl, M.S., Joëls, M., Stress and cognition: are glucocorticoids good or bad guys? *Trends Neurosci.,* 22, 422, 1999.
8. McGaugh, J.L., Memory: a century of consolidation. *Science*, 287, 248, 2000.
9. McGaugh, J.L., The amygdala modulates the consolidation of memories of emotionally arousing experiences. *Annu. Rev. Neurosci.,* 27, 1, 2004.
10. Roozendaal, B., Glucocorticoids and the regulation of memory consolidation. *Psychoneuroendocrinology,* 25, 213, 2000.
11. Okuda, S., Roozendaal, B., and McGaugh, J.L., Glucocorticoid effects on object recognition memory require training-associated emotional arousal. *Proc. Natl. Acad. Sci. USA,* 101, 853, 2004.
12. Buchanan, T.W. and Lovallo, W.R., Enhanced memory for emotional material following stress-level cortisol treatment in humans. *Psychoneuroendochrinology,* 26, 307, 2001.
13. Cahill, L. and Alkire, M.T., Epinephrine enhancement of human memory consolidation: interaction with arousal at encoding. *Neurobiol. Learn. Mem.*, 79, 194, 2003.
14. Abercrombie, H.C., Speck, N.S., and Monticelli, R.M., Endogenous cortisol elevations are related to memory facilitation only in individuals who are emotionally aroused. *Psychoneuroendocrinology,* 31, 187, 2006.
15. Kuhlmann, S. and Wolf, O.T., Arousal and cortisol interact in modulating memory consolidation in healthy young men. *Behav. Neurosci.*, 120, 217, 2006.
16. Korte, S.M., Corticosteriods in relation to fear, anxiety and psychopathology. *Neurosci. Biobehav. Rev.,* 25, 117, 2001.
17. Oitzl, M.S. and de Kloet, E.R., Selective corticosteroid antagonists modulate specific aspects of spatial orientation learning. *Behav. Neurosci.,* 106, 62, 1992.
18. Beylin, A.V. and Shors, T.J., Glucocorticoids are necessary for enhancing the acquisition of associative memories after acute stressful experience. *Horm. Behav.*, 43, 124, 2003.
19. Pugh, C.R., Tremblay, D., Fleshner, M., and Rudy, J.W., A selective role for corticosterone in contextual-fear conditioning. *Behav. Neurosci.,* 111, 503, 1997.
20. Roozendaal, B. and McGaugh, J.L., Amygdaloid nuclei lesions differentially affect glucocorticoid-induced memory enhancement in an inhibitory avoidance task. *Neurobiol. Learn. Mem.,* 65, 1, 1996.
21. Cordero, M.I. and Sandi, C., A role for brain glucocorticoid receptors in contextual fear conditioning: dependence upon training intensity. *Brain Res.,* 786, 11, 1998.
22. Hui, G.K., Figueroa, I.R., Poytress, B.S., Roozendaal, B., McGaugh, J.L., and Weinberger, N.M., Memory enhancement of classical fear conditioning by posttraining injections of corticosterone in rats. *Neurobiol. Learn. Mem.*, 81, 67, 2004.
23. Smotherman, W.P., Burt, G., Kimble, D.P., Strickrod, G., BreMiller, R., and Levine, S., Behavioral and corticosterone effects in conditioned taste aversion following hippocampal lesions. *Physiol. Behav.*, 27, 569, 1981.

24. Roozendaal, B., Carmi, O., and McGaugh, J.L., Adrenocortical suppression blocks the memory-enhancing effects of amphetamine and epinephrine. *Proc. Natl. Acad. Sci. USA,* 93, 1429, 1996.
25. Cahill, L., Pham, C.A., and Setlow, B., Impaired memory consolidation in rats produced with beta-adrenergic blockade. *Neurobiol. Learn. Mem.,* 74, 259, 2000.
26. Flood, J.F., Vidal, D., Bennett, E.L., Orme, A.E., Vasquez, S., and Jarvik, M.E., Memory facilitating and anti-amnestic effects of corticosteroids. *Pharmacol. Biochem. Behav.,* 8, 81, 1978.
27. Sandi, C. and Rose, S.P.R., Training-dependent biphasic effects of corticosterone in memory formation for a passive avoidance task in chicks. *Psychopharmacology,* 133, 152, 1997.
28. Abercrombie, H.C., Kalin, N.H., Thurow, M.E., Rosenkranz, M.A., and Davidson, R.J. Cortisol variation in humans affects memory for emotionally laden and neutral information. *Behav. Neurosci.,* 117, 505, 2003.
29. Cahill, L., Gorski, L., and Le, K. Enhanced human memory consolidation with post-learning stress: Interaction with the degree of arousal at encoding. *Learn. Mem.,* 10, 270, 2003.
30. Borrell, J., de Kloet, E.R., Versteeg, D.H., and Bohus, B., Inhibitory avoidance deficit following short-term adrenalectomy in the rat: the role of adrenal catecholamines., *Behav. Neural Biol.,* 39, 241, 1983.
31. Borrell, J., de Kloet, E.R., and Bohus, B., Corticosterone decreases the efficacy of adrenaline to affect passive avoidance retention of adrenalectomized rats. *Life Sci.,* 34, 99, 1984.
32. Fallon, J.H. and Coifi, P., Distribution of monoamines within the amygdala, in *The Amygdala: Neurobiological Aspects of Emotion, Memory, and Mental Dysfunction,* Aggleton, J.P., Ed., Wiley-Liss, New York, 1992, p. 84.
33. Williams, C.L., Men, D., Clayton, E.C., and Gold, P.E., Norepinephrine release in the amygdala following systemic injection of epinephrine or escapable foot shock: contribution of the nucleus of the solitary tract. *Behav. Neurosci.,* 112, 1414, 1998.
34. Loy, R., Koziell, D.A., Lindsey, J.D., and Moore, R.Y., Noradrenergic innervation of the adult rat hippocampal formation. *J. Comp. Neurol.,* 189, 699, 1980.
35. Devoto, P., Flore, G., Saba, P., Fa, M., and Gessa, G.L., Stimulation of the locus coeruleus elicits noradrenaline and dopamine release in the medial prefrontal and parietal cortex. *J. Neurochem.,* 92, 368, 2005.
36. Petrov, T., Krukoff, T., and Jhamandas, J., Branching projections of catecholaminergic brainstem neurons to paraventricular hypothalamic nucleus and central nucleus of the amygdala in the rat. *Brain Res.,* 609, 81, 1993.
37. Reul, J.M.H.M. and de Kloet, E.R., Two receptor systems for corticosterone in the rat brain: Microdistribution and differential occupation. *Endocrinology,* 117, 2505, 1985.
38. Roozendaal, B., Portillo-Marquez, G., and McGaugh, J.L., Basolateral amygdala lesions block glucocorticoid-induced modulation of memory for spatial learning. *Behav. Neurosci.,* 110, 1074, 1996.
39. Roozendaal, B. and McGaugh, J.L., Glucocorticoid receptor agonist and antagonist administration into the basolateral but not central amygdala modulates memory storage. *Neurobiol. Learn. Mem.,* 67, 176, 1997.
40. Roozendaal, B. and McGaugh, J.L., Basolateral amygdala lesions block the memory-enhancing effect of glucocorticoid administration in the dorsal hippocampus of rats. *Eur. J. Neurosci.,* 9, 76, 1997.

41. Oitzl, M.S. and de Kloet, E.R., Selective corticosteroid antagonists modulate specific aspects of spatial orientation learning. *Behav. Neurosci.* 108, 62, 1992.
42. McEwen, B.S., Brinton, R.E., and Sapolsky, R.M., Glucocorticoid receptors and behavior: Implications for the stress response. *Adv. Exp. Med. Biol.,* 245, 35, 1988.
43. Sapolsky, R.M., Romero, L.M., Munck, A.U., How do glucocorticoids influence stress responses? Integrating permissive, suppressive, stimulatory, and preparative actions. *Endocr. Rev.,* 21, 55, 2000.
44. Beato, M., Herrlich, P., Schultz, G., Steroid hormone receptors: many actors in search of a plot. *Cell,* 83, 851, 1995.
45. Datson, N.A., van der Perk, J., de Kloet, E.R., and Vreugdenhil, E., Identification of corticosteroid-responsive genes in rat hippocampus using serial analysis of gene expression. *Eur. J. Neurosci.,* 14, 675, 2001.
46. Orchinik, M., Murray, T.F., and Moore, F.L., A corticosteroid receptor in neuronal membranes. *Science,* 252, 1848, 1991.
47. Falkenstein, E., Tillmann, H.C., Christ, M., Feuring, M., and Wehling, M., Multiple actions of steroid hormones: a focus on rapid, nongenomic effects. *Pharmacol. Rev.,* 52, 513, 2000.
48. Dallman, M.F., Fast glucocorticoid actions on brain: back to the future. *Front. Neuroendocrinol.,* 26, 103, 2005.
49. Gold, P.E. and van Buskirk, R., Facilitation of time-dependent memory processes with post-trial epinephrine injections. *Behav. Biol.,* 13, 145, 1975.
50. Roozendaal, B., Williams, C.L., and McGaugh, J.L., Glucocorticoid receptor activation in the rat nucleus of the solitary tract facilitates memory consolidation: involvement of the basolateral amygdala. *Eur. J. Neurosci.,* 11, 1317, 1999.
51. Yang, Y., Cao, J., Xiong, W., Zhang, J., Zhou, Q., Wei, H., Liang, C., Deng, J., Li, T., Yang, S., Xu, L., and Xu, L., Both stress experience and age determine the impairment or enhancement effect of stress on spatial memory retrieval. *J. Endocrinol.,* 178, 45, 2003.
52. Mabry, T.R., Gold, P.E., and McCarty, R., Age related changes in plasma catecholamine responses to acute swim stress. *Neurobiol. Learn. Mem.,* 63, 260, 1995.
53. Wolf, O.T., Dziobec, I., McHugh, P., Sweat, V., de Leon, M.J., Javier, E., and Convit, A., Selective memory complaints in aging are associated with elevated cortisol levels. *Neurobiol. Aging,* 26, 1357, 2005.
54. Sandi, C., Loscertales, M., Guaza, C., Experience-dependent facilitating effect of corticosterone on spatial memory formation in the water maze. *Eur. J. Neurosci.,* 9, 637, 1997.
55. Akirav, I., Kozenicky, M., Tal, D., Sandi, C., Venero, C., and Richter-Levin, G., A faciltative role for corticosterone in the acquisition of a spatial task under moderate stress. *Learn. Mem.,* 11, 188, 2004.
56. Gold, P.E., Hankins, L. Edwards, R.M., Chester, J., and McGaugh, J.L., Memory interference and facilitation with posttrial amygdala stimulation: effect on memory varies with footshock level. *Brain Res.,* 86, 509, 1975.
57. Ennaceur, A. and Delacour, J., A new one-trial test for neurobiological studies of memory in rats. 1: Behavioral data. *Behav. Brain Res.,* 31, 47, 1988.
58. Maheu, F.S., Joober, R., Beaulieu, S., and Lupien, S.J., Differential effects of adrenergic and corticosteroid hormonal systems on human short- and long-term declarative memory for emotionally arousing material. *Behav. Neurosci.,* 118, 420, 2004.
59. Pelletier, J.G., Likhtik, E., Filali, M., and Paré, D., Lasting increases in basolateral amygdala activity after emotional arousal: Implications for facilitated consolidation of emotional memories. *Learn. Mem.,* 12, 96, 2005.

60. McGaugh, J.L., Memory consolidation and the amygdala: A systems perspective. *Trends Neurosci.,* 25, 456, 2002.
61. Liang, J.C., Juler, R., and McGaugh, J.L., Modulating effects of posttraining epinephrine on memory: Involvement of the amygdala noradrenergic system. *Brain Res.,* 368, 125, 1986.
62. Roozendaal, B., Brunson, K.L., Holloway, B.L., McGaugh, J.L., and Baram, T.Z., Involvement of stress-released corticotropin-releasing hormone in the basolateral amygdala in regulating memory consolidation. *Proc. Natl. Acad. Sci. USA,* 99, 13908, 2002.
63. Liang, K.C. and McGaugh, J.L., Lesions of the stria terminalis attenuate the enhancing effect of posttraining epinephrine on retention of an inhibitory avoidance response. *Behav. Brain Res.,* 9, 49, 1983.
64. Roozendaal, B. and McGaugh, J.L., The memory-modulatory effects of glucocorticoids depend on an intact stria terminalis. *Brain Res.,* 709, 243, 1996.
65. Roozendaal, B., de Quervain, D.J., Ferry, B., Setlow, B., and McGaugh, J.L., Basolateral amygdala–nucleus accumbens interactions in mediating glucocorticoid enhancement of memory consolidation. *J. Neurosci.,* 21, 2518, 2001.
66. Foy, M.R., Stanton, M.E., Levine, S., Thompson, R.F., Behavioral stress impairs long-term potentiation in rodent hippocampus. *Behav. Neural Biol.,* 48, 138, 1987.
67. Diamond, D.M., Bennet, M.C., Fleshner, M., and Rose, G.M., Inverted U-relationship between the level of peripheral corticosterone and the magnitude of hippocampal primed burst potentiation. *Hippocampus*, 2, 421, 1992.
68. Palvides, C., Watanabe, Y., and McEwen, B.S., Effects of glucocorticoids on hippocampal long-term potentiation. *Hippocampus*, 3, 183, 1993.
69. Korz, V. and Frey, J.U., Stress-related modulation of hippocampal long-term potentiation in rats: Involvement of adrenal steroid receptors. *J. Neursci.,* 23, 7281, 2003.
70. Cottrell, G.A. and Nakajima, S., Effect of corticosteroids in the hippocampus on passive avoidance behavior in the rat. *Pharmacol. Biochem. Behav.,* 7, 277, 1977.
71. Micheau, J., Destrade, C., and Soumireu-Mourat, B., Time-dependent effects of posttraining intrahippocampal injections of corticosterone on retention of appetitive learning tasks in mice. *Eur. J. Pharmacol*., 106, 39, 1984.
72. Ikegaya, Y., Saito, H., and Abe, K., High-frequency stimulation of the basolateral amygdala facilitates the induction of long-term potentiation in the dentate gyrus *in vivo*. *Neurosci. Res*., 22, 203, 1995.
73. Ikegaya, Y., Nakanishi, K., Saito, H., and Abe, K., Amygdala β-noradrenergic influence on hippocampal long-term potentiation *in vivo*. *NeuroReport*, 8, 3143, 1997.
74. Arnsten, A.F.T., and Goldman-Rakic, P.S., Noise stress impairs prefrontal cortical cognitive function in monkeys: evidence for a hyperdopaminergic mechanism. *Arch. Gen. Psychiatr.*, 55, 362, 1998.
75. Bechara, A., Damasio, H., Damasio, A.R., and Lee, G.P., Different contributions of the human amygdala and ventromedial prefrontal cortex to decision-making. *J. Neurosci*., 19, 5473, 1999.
76. Runyan, J.D. and Dash, P.K., Intra-medial prefrontal administration of SCH-23390 attenuates ERK phosphorylation and long-term memory for trace fear conditioning in rats. *Neurobiol. Learn. Mem*., 82, 65, 2004.
77. Perez-Jaranay, J.M. and Vives, F., Electrophysiological study of the response of medial prefrontal cortex neurons to stimulation of the basolateral nucleus of the amygdala in the rat. *Brain Res*., 564, 97, 1991.

78. Rosenkranz, J.A. and Grace, A.A., Cellular mechanisms of infralimbic and prelimbic prefrontal cortical inhibition and dopaminergic modulation of basolateral amygdala neurons *in vivo*. *J. Neurosci.*, 22, 324, 2002.
79. McIntyre, C.K., Roozendaal, B., and McGaugh, J.L., Glucocorticoid-induced inhibition of the medial prefrontal cortex enhances memory consolidation and increases consolidation of the extracellular signal-regulated kinases I/II in the amygdala. *Soc. Neurosci. Abstr.*, 539.3 online, 2005.
80. Cahill, L., Babinsky, R., Markowitsch, H.J., and McGaugh, J.L., The amygdala and emotional memory. *Nature*, 377, 295, 1995.
81. Adolphs, R., Tranel, D., and Denburg, N., Impaired emotional declarative memory following unilateral amygdala damage. *Learn. Mem.*, 7, 180, 2000.
82. Cahill, L., Haier, R.J., Fallon, J., Alkire, M.T., Tang, C., Keator, K., Wu, J., and McGaugh, J.L., Amygdala activity at encoding correlated with long-term, free recall of emotional information. *Proc. Natl. Acad. Sci. USA*, 93, 8016, 1996.
83. Canli, T., Zhao, Z., Brewer, J., Gabrieli, J.D., and Cahill, L., Event-related activation in the human amygdala associates with later memory for individual emotional experiences. *J. Neurosci.*, 20, RC99, 2000.
84. van Stegeren, A.H., Goekoop, R., Everaerd, W., Scheltens, P., Barkhof, F., Kuijer, J.P., and Rombouts, S.A., Noradrenaline mediates amygdala activation in men and women during encoding of emotional material. *Neuroimage,* 24, 898, 2005.
85. Kilpatrick, L. and Cahill, L., Amygdala modulation of parahippocampal and frontal regions during emotionally influenced memory storage. *Neuroimage*, 20, 2091, 2003.
86. Dolcos, F., LaBar, K.S., and Cabeza, R., Remembering one year later: Role of the amygdala and the medial temporal lobe memory system in retrieving emotional memories. *Proc. Natl. Acad. Sci. USA*, 102, 2626, 2005.
87. Strange, B.A., and Dolan, R.J., β-Adrenergic modulation of emotional memory-evoked human amygdala and hippocampal responses. *Proc. Nat. Acad. Sci. USA*, 101, 11454, 2004.
88. Quirarte, G.L., Roozendaal, B., and McGaugh, J.L., Glucocorticoid enhancenemt of memory storage involves noradrenergic activation in the basolateral amygdala. *Proc. Natl. Acad. Sci. USA*, 94, 14148, 1997.
89. Roozendaal, B., Okuda, S., Van der Zee, E.A., and McGaugh, J.L., Glucocorticoid enhancement of memory requires arousal-induced noradrenergic activation in the basolateral amygdala. *Proc. Natl. Acad. Sci. USA*, 103, 6741, 2006.
90. Roozendaal, B., Nguyen, B.T., Power, A.E., and McGaugh, J.L., Basolateral amygdala noradrenergic influence enables enhancement of memory consolidation induced by hippocampal glucocorticoid receptor activation. *Proc. Natl. Acad. Sci. USA.*, 96, 11642, 1999.
91. Tanaka, T.H., Yokoo, K., Mizoguchi, et al., Noradrenaline release in the rat amygdala is increased by stress: studies with intracerebral microdialysis. *Brain Res.*, 544, 174, 1991.
92. Pacak, K., Palkovitz, M., Kvetnanasky, R., et al., Effects of single or repeated immobilization on release of norepinephrine and its metabolites in the central nucleus of the amygdala in conscious rats. *Neuroendocrinology*, 57, 626, 1993.
93. Galvez, R., Mesches, M., and McGaugh, J.L., Norepinephrine release in the amygdala in response to footshock stimulation. *Neurobiol. Learn. Mem.*, 66, 253, 1996.
94. Quirarte, G.L., Galvez, R., Roozendaal, B., and McGaugh, J.L., Norepinephrine release in the amygdala in response to foot shock and opioid peptidergic drugs. *Brain Res.*, 808, 134, 1998.

95. McIntyre, C.K., Hatfield, T., and McGaugh, J.L., Norepinephrine levels in the amygdala following inhibitory avoidance training predict retention score. *Eur. J. Neurosci.*, 16, 1223, 2002.
96. Ferry, B., Roozendaal, B., and McGaugh, J.L., Involvement of α_1-adrenoceptors in the basolateral amygdala in modulation of memory storage. *Eur. J. Pharm.*, 372, 9, 1999.
97. Hatfield, T. and McGaugh, J.L., Norepinephrine infused into the basolateral amygdala posttraining enhances retention in a spatial water maze task. *Neurobiol. Learn. Mem.*, 91, 232, 1999.
98. Härfstrand, A., Fuxe, K., Cintra, A., Agnati, L.F., Zini, I., Wikström, A.C., Okret, S., Yu, Z.Y., Goldstein, M., Steinbusch, H., Verhofstad, A., Gustafsson, J.A., Glucocorticoid receptor immunoreactivity in monoaminergic neurons of rat brain. *Proc. Natl. Acad. Sci. USA*, 84, 9779, 1987.
99. McIntyre, C.K., Roozendaal, B., McGaugh, J.L., Glucocorticoid treatment enhances training-induced norepinephrine release in the amygdala. *Soc. Neurosci. Abstr.*, 772.12 online, 2004.
100. Roozendaal, B., Quirarte, G.L., and McGaugh, J.L., Glucocorticoids interact with the basolateral amygdala β-adrenoceptor-cAMP/PKA system in influencing memory consolidation. *Eur. J. Neurosci.,* 15, 553, 2002.
101. Liang, K.C., Chen, L.L., and Huang, T.E., The role of amygala norepinephrine in memory formation: involvement in memory-enhancing effects of peripheral epinephrine. *Chin. J. Physiol.*, 38, 81, 1995.
102. Ferry, B., Roozendaal, B., and McGaugh, J.L., Basolateral amygdala noradrenergic influences on memory storage are mediated by an interaction between beta- and alpha1-adrenoceptors. *J. Neurosci.*, 19, 5119, 1999.
103. Barnes, P.J., Anti-inflammatory actions of glucocorticoids: Molecular mechanisms. *Clin. Sci.*, 94, 557, 1998.
104. Saha, S. and Datta, S., Two-way active avoidance-specific increases in phosphorylated cAMP response element binding protein in the dorsal hippocampus, amygdala, and hypothalamus. *Eur. J. Neurosci.*, 21, 3403, 2005.
105. Josselyn, S.A., Kida, S., and Silva, A.J., Inducible repression of CREB function disrupts amygdala-dependent memory. *Neurobiol. Learn. Mem.*, 82, 159, 2004.
106. Revest, R.M., Di Blasi, F., Kitchener, P., Rouge-Pont, F., Desmedt, A., Turiault, M., Tronche, F., Piazza, P.V., The MAPK pathway and Egr-1 mediated stress-related behavioral effects of glucocorticoids. *Nat. Neurosci.*, 8, 835, 2005.
107. Impey, S., Obrietan, K., Storm, D.R., Making new connections: Role of ERK/MAP kinase signaling in neuronal plasticity. *Neuron*, 23, 11, 1999.
108. Schafe, G.E., Atkins, C.M., Swank, M.W., Bauer, E.P., Sweatt, J.D., and LeDoux, J.E., Activation of ERK/MAP kinase in the amygdala is required for memory consolidation of Pavlovian fear conditioning. *J. Neurosci.*, 20, 8177, 2000.
109. Crespo, P., Xu, N., Simonds, W.F., and Gutkind, J.S., Ras-dependent activation of MAP kinase pathway mediated by G-protein beta–gamma subunits. *Nature*, 369, 418, 1994.
110. Lopez-Ilasaca, M., Crespo, P., Pellici, P.G., Gutkind, J.S., and Wetzker, R., Linkage of G protein-coupled receptors to the MAPK signaling pathway through PI 3-kinase gamma. *Science*, 275, 394, 1997.
111. Schmidt, P., Holsboer, F., and Spengler, D., Beta(2)-adrenergic receptors potentiate glucocorticoids receptor transactivation via G-protein beta gamma-subunits and the phosphoinositide 3-kinase pathway. *Mol. Endocrinol.*, 15, 553, 2005.

112. Pitman, R.K., Sanders, K.M., Zusman, R.M., Healy, A.R., Cheema, F., Lasko, N.B., Cahill, L., and Orr, S.P., Pilot study of secondary prevention of post-traumatic stress disorder with propranolol. *Biol. Psychiatr.*, 51, 189, 2002.
113. Schelling, G., Roozendaal, B., and de Quervain, D.J., Can post-traumatic stress disorder be prevented with glucocorticoids? *Ann. NY Acad. Sci.*, 1032, 158, 2004.
114. Delahanty, D.L., Nugent, N.R., Christopher, N.C., and Walsh, M., Initial urinary epinephrine and cortisol levels predict acute PTSD symptoms in child trauma victims. *Psychoneuroendocrinology*, 30, 121, 2005.
115. Southwick, S.M., Bremner, J.D., Rasmusson, A., Morgan, C.A. 3rd, Arnsten, A., and Charney, D.S., Role of norepinephrine in pathophysiology and treatment of posttraumatic stress disorder. *Biol. Psychiatr.*, 46, 1192, 1999.

14 Neuro-Immune Associative Learning

Gustavo Pacheco-López, Maj-Britt Niemi, Harald Engler, and Manfred Schedlowski

CONTENTS

14.1 INTRODUCTION

Experimental evidence demonstrates intensive and extensive interactions between the nervous and immune systems.[1–4] The central capacity of associating a certain immune response or status (allergen, toxin, antigen) with a specific stimulus (environment or flavor) seems to be of high adaptive value; this special kind of associative learning may have been acquired as an adaptive strategy during evolution in order to protect an organism and/or prepare it for danger. Furthermore, it is possible that, depending on the different environmental challenges, the species formed species-specific associations during evolution.[5]

Classical conditioning or associative learning is often described as the transfer of the response-eliciting property of a biologically significant stimulus (unconditioned stimulus; US) to another stimulus (conditioned stimulus; CS) without that property.[6–10] This transfer is thought to occur only if the CS serves as a predictor of the US.[11–13] Thus, classical conditioning can be understood as learning about the temporal or causal relationships between external and internal stimuli, to allow for the appropriate preparatory set of responses before biologically significant events occur.

Regarding neuro-immune associative learning (NIAL), an immunomodulatory stimulus (antigen, immunomodulating drug) is employed as an US and paired with a neutral stimulus. After this associative phase, the neutral stimulus becomes a CS that can modify the immune response on demand (conditioned response; CR). The influence of NIAL on immune responses has been reviewed several times.[14–32] However, in this chapter we propose an innovative approach, pointing out the biological meaning and possible clinical implications of neuro-immune associative learning. Furthermore, after analyzing the available literature, we propose a general theoretical framework for this special kind of associative learning.

14.1.1 Historical Development

S. Metalnikov and V. Chorine are generally credited with having conducted the first studies on NIAL.[33] However, V.I. Luk'ianenko cites the 1911 dissertation of I.I. Makukhin at the University of St. Petersburg and a 1925 report by A. Voronov and I. Riskin as perhaps the first researchers to demonstrate the "conditioned leukocytic reaction."[17] Metalnikov and Chorine reported a series of experiments that clearly demonstrated the possibility of associating exteroceptive stimuli with alterations in immune parameters induced for the most part by injections of bacterial and viral preparations.[33,34] Guinea pigs were given daily association trials with contingent pairing of scratching or heating of the skin as a CS and an immune challenge (i.p. injection of a small dose of tapioca, *Bacillus anthrax*, or a Staphylococcus filtrate) as an US. The CR was an increase in peritoneal leukocyte numbers that was weaker and more transitory than the UR. Follow-up experiments indicated that after the recall phase, conditioned animals survived longer after lethal injections of *Vibrio cholera* bacteria.

These initial results were rapidly replicated,[35,37] and in the following years Soviet investigators paid considerable attention to this topic.[17,38] Many of these experiments were basically similar to those performed by Metalnikov and Chorine, and apparently a controversy arose over the reproducibility of certain experiments. In parallel to the Soviet experiments, but not as well-known, were investigations performed in Romania[39–41] and Switzerland[42–47] reporting modulation of phagocytic activity and anaphylactic reaction, respectively, by evoking specific NIAL. In 1975, R. Ader and N. Cohen reported an immunosuppressive status after recalling the specific association of a taste stimulus (CS) and an immunosuppressive drug (US).[48]

Later, these researchers and other groups developed different NIAL protocols, most of them using taste and olfactory stimuli (CS) in rodents and humans. More than 30 years of clinical and experimental research have demonstrated that by evoking NIAL, the brain can suppress or enhance humoral as well as cellular immune responses (Table 14.1). These effects are biologically relevant for the organism, as they affect the course and outcome of disease and thus have possible applications in clinical settings.

TABLE 14.1
Immune Parameters Affected after Recalling Neuro-Immune Associative Learning Paradigms

Conditioned Stimulus	Unconditioned Stimulus		Conditioned Response	Relevant References
Taste/odor (e.g., saccharine, chocolate)	Immunosuppressant drug (e.g., CsA, CY)	⇓	Antibody production	Ader and Cohen 1975; Rogers et al. 1976; Wayner et al. 1978; Ader et al. 1982; Schulze et al. 1988
			Lymphocyte proliferation	Neveu et al. 1986; Kusnecov et al. 1988; Exton et al. 1998b; Goebel et al. 2002
			Hypersensitivity	Roudebush and Bryant 1991; Exton et al. 2000
			Arthritic inflammation	Klosterhalfen and Klosterhalfen 1983; Klosterhalfen and Klosterhalfen 1990
			Cytokines	Hiramoto et al. 1987; Janz et al. 1996; Exton et al. 1998b
			Allograph rejection	Grochowicz et al. 1991; Exton et al. 1998a
Taste/odor/auditory/visual/touch (e.g., saccharine, camphor, context, scratch, heat)	Immunostimulating drug/antigen (e.g., SEB, LPS, KLH, OVA, poly I:C	⇑	Skin hypersensitivity	Bovbjerg et al. 1987
			NK cell activity	Hiramoto et al. 1987; Solvason et al. 1988; Buske-Kirschbaum et al. 1992; Buske-Kirschbaum et al. 1994
			Cytotoxic T cell activity	Gorczynski et al. 1982; Hiramoto et al. 1993
			Neutrophil activity	Chao et al. 2005
			Antibody production	Jenkins et al. 1983; Ader et al. 1993; Husband et al. 1993; Alvarez-Borda et al. 1995; Chen et al. 2004
			Histamine release	Russell et al. 1984; Irie et al. 2002
			Cytokines	Pacheco-López et al. 2004
			Complement	Reidler 1956; Dolin et al. 1960
			Anaphylaxis/asthma	Noelpp and Noelpp-Eschenhagen 1951; Djuric et al. 1988; Palermo-Neto and Guimarães 2000

Source: Adapted from Pacheco-López, G. et al., in Psychoneuroimmunology, *4th ed., Ader, R., Ed., Academic Press, New York, 2006. With permission.)*

CsA = cyclosporine A. CY = cyclophosphamide. SEB = staphylococcal enterotoxin B. LPS = lipopolysaccharide. KLH = keyhole limpet hemocyanin. OVA = ovoalbumin poly I:C = polyinosinic:polycytidylic acid.

14.2 PHENOMENON: ASSOCIATION BETWEEN EXTEROCEPTIVE AND IMMUNE STIMULI

Two basic steps compose any conditioning protocol: an *association* phase in which one or more CS-US contingent pairings occur, inducing an associative learning process, and a *recall* phase in which the memory of such an association is retrieved after exposing the subject to the CS. Pioneer NIAL reports were based on the association of somatosensory stimulation (CS) and peripheral immune challenges (US). See Figure 14.1C. However, most of the recent work reporting conditioned effects on immune function has followed two basic associative protocols (Figure 14.1). The principal difference between them is the nature of the CS: taste/olfactory (Figure 14.1A) or visual/auditory (Figure 14.1B).

Although conditioned stimuli may employ any of the exteroceptive sensory modalities (touch, vision, taste, olfaction, and audition), the naturalistic relation between the CS and the US may explain the feasibility and strength of a specific association.[10]

14.2.1 Taste- and Olfactory-Immune Associative Learning

Theoretically this protocol is based on the naturalistic relation of food and drink ingestion with possible immune consequences that may also induce behavioral modifications after the experience. On the experimental bench, the association step involves the pairing of a taste (e.g., saccharin), odor (e.g., camphor), or flavor (e.g., chocolate drink) as a CS with a stimulus that has immune consequences as a US (e.g., immunomodulating drug, or antigen), usually administered intraperitoneally. At recall time, subjects are normally exposed to the CS alone (Figure 14.1A) and some protocols employ a vehicle injection as an additional component of the CS.

Conditioned ingestive avoidance and aversion are often displayed after a single association trial; however, the conditioned effects on the immune system may not be evident until several association trials are applied.[49] It is important to indicate that the behaviorally conditioned response (i.e., aversion or avoidance) has been elicited by NIAL in which T-dependent antigens such as protein antigens,[50–52] T-independent antigens such as lipopolysaccharides,[53–55] superantigens such as staphylococcal enterotoxin,[56,57] immunosuppressive drugs such as cyclophosphamide,[48,58] and cyclosporine A[59,60] have been employed (Figure 14.2). Additionally, the magnitude of the behaviorally conditioned response seems to be modulated by the intensity of the immune stimulation at association time.

For instance, a dose–response relationship between the amount of antigen used (US) and the conditioned taste aversion has been demonstrated: the higher the antigen dose, the more pronounced the conditioned taste avoidance.[51,61] Using a mild dose of antigen after an immune sensitization procedure induces a strong behaviorally conditioned avoidance response.[62] Regarding immunosuppressive drugs, it has been documented that the immunosuppressive effects of cyclosporine A (US) can be associated with the taste of saccharin (CS). After recalling such an association,

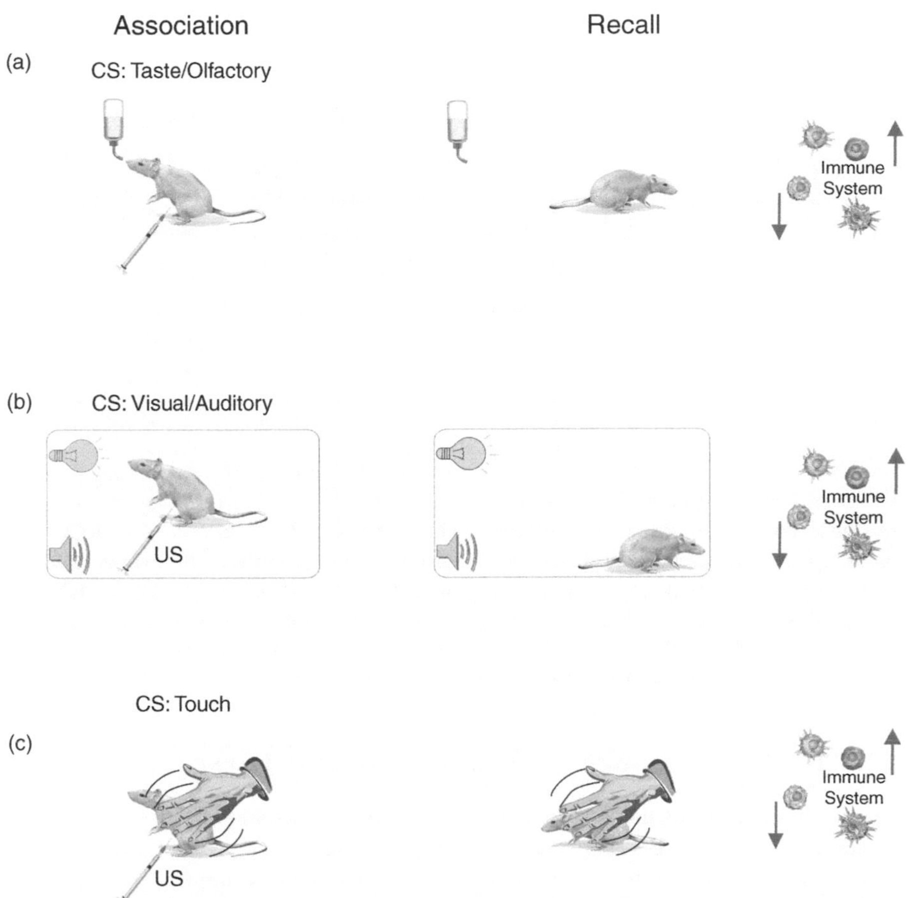

FIGURE 14.1 (See color insert following page 202). Neuro-immune associative learning. A. After water regimen consumption is established, animals are exposed to a novel taste/olfactory conditioned stimulus (CS) paired with an immunomodulating unconditioned stimulus (US) generally administered intraperitoneally (e.g., saccharin as CS, cyclosporine A as US). B. Certain contextual CS composed of visual/auditory cues are associated with exposure to an immunomodulating US (e.g., light and sound as CS; ovo-albumin in aerosol as US). C. Somatosensory stimulation is employed as CS, paired with an immunomodulating US (e.g., scratching as CS; bacterial antigen i.p. as US). Evoking such associations often results in aversive/avoidance behavior and a complex repertory of physiological responses that inclusively affects immune functions. Enhanced or suppressive immune status can be established after the recall phase.

experimental subjects displayed immunosuppressive status (CR).[30,60] However, different behaviorally conditioned responses result from such associative learning. In the case of mice, this specific taste-immune association does not result in conditioned taste avoidance behavior,[5] whereas rats display reduced appetitive behavior,[30] and for humans the palatability of the conditioned taste is affected.[63]

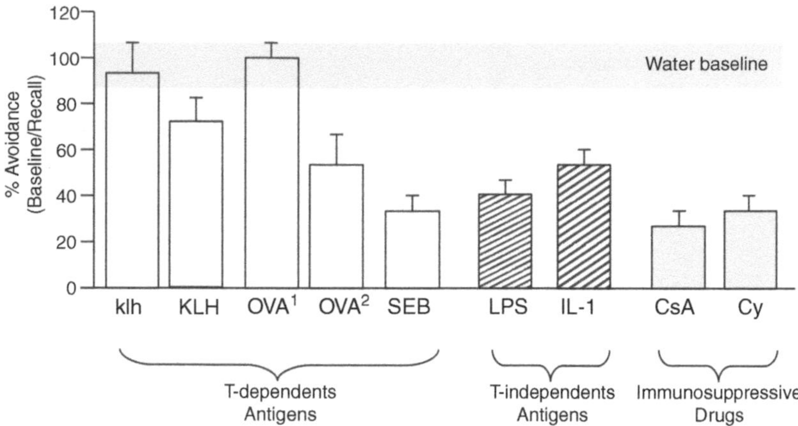

FIGURE 14.2 Neuro-immune associative learning differentially affects drinking behavior. Different immune stimuli were employed as unconditioned stimuli resulting in associative learning. klh = small dose of keyhole limpet hemocyanin. KLH = high dose of KLH (data extracted from Reference 51). OVA1 = primary immune response to ovalbumin. OVA2 = secondary immune response to ovalbumin (data extracted from References 52 and 62). LPS = lipopolysaccharide (data extracted from Reference 180). SEB = staphylococcal enterotoxin B (data extracted from Reference 56). Cy = cyclophosphamide (data extracted from Reference 106). CsA = cyclosporine A (data extracted from Reference 59).

14.2.2 Visual- and Auditory-Immune Associative Learning

This protocol induces the association of a certain context and an immune response or status (Figure 14.1B). At association time, a certain context composed of visual and/or auditory cues (CS) is paired with a stimulus that has immune consequences (US). At recall time, the subject is exposed to the same context that induces the CR (Figure 14.1B). To induce conditioned effects on the immune system, it is usually necessary to submit the experimental subject to several association trials.

Aversive behavior to the context associated with the US may also be part of the CR displayed. For instance, an immune sensitization [s.c. injection of ovalbumin (OVA), i.p. injection of *Bordetella pertussis,* and larval infection with the nematode *Nippostrongylus brasiliensis*] induced higher levels of IgE after subsequent antigen injections and increased the number of intestinal mast cells.[64] In subsequent trials, s.c. injections of OVA (US) were contingently paired with an auditory or visual cue (CS) in three association trials. One hour after a single recall trial (CS alone), rat mast cell protease (RMCP)-II levels in the serum were enhanced, suggesting that the degranulation of mucosal mast cells was behind the immune response.

Five hours after recall, serum RMCP-II levels did not significantly differ from control groups. A strong anaphylactic response in the lung as a conditioned response has recently been reported following a similar NIAL protocol.[65] In addition, these authors reported high levels of stress and anxiety postrecall and demonstrated that the audio-visual stimulus (CS) was stressful and anxiogenic *per se.*

Another set of animal studies supports the associability of environmental stimuli (CS) with anaphylactic shock reaction.[66–68] Rats sensitized with OVA were given injections of the same antigen to elicit a second anaphylactic shock in a context different from that in which the first anaphylactic shock was induced. Animals experiencing both anaphylactic shocks in the same context displayed much smaller shocks than rats subjected to the second shock in a different context. Repeated, non-reinforced presentation of the antigen in the new context prior to the CS and induction of the first anaphylactic shock prevented the increased resistance to the induction of a second anaphylactic shock reaction. These findings were ascribed to the CR that attenuated the UR (anaphylactic shock).

Accordingly, it has recently been shown that OVA-immunized mice avoid the context previously associated with presentation of the allergen against which they have been immunized.[69] In a modified classical passive avoidance test, OVA aerosol was employed as an aversive stimulus (US); although attracted by the supposedly safer, dark compartment of the apparatus (CS), OVA-immunized mice avoided entering the dark side, preferring the bright (usually aversive) side of the box.

When CNS activity was tracked using c-Fos expression as a neuronal metabolic marker, allergic animals showed enhanced c-Fos immunoreactivity in the hypothalamic paraventricular nucleus and central nucleus of the amygdala after airway OVA challenge. These brain structures are commonly linked to emotional and affective behavioral patterns that are important components in the development of learned aversive behavior such as conditioned taste aversion.[70]

14.2.3 Touch-Immune Associative Learning

With touch-immune associative learning, somatosensory stimulation (scratching, heating the skin) can be employed as a CS paired with a stimulus that has immune consequences (US). At recall time, the subject is exposed to the CS that induces the CR and affects peripheral immune functions (Figure 14.1C). To our knowledge, apart from pioneer studies in the 1920s[33,34] and their replications[35–37] (see Section 14.1.1), no further attempts have been made to develop NIAL employing somatosensory stimulation as a CS. Furthermore, it should be noted that behavioral control conditions and immunological interpretations have changed substantially since those experiments were reported.

14.3 Theoretical Framework for Neuro-Immune Associative Learning

After reviewing the existing data about NIAL, it is possible to summarize guidelines for the general mechanisms underlying these phenomena (summarized in Figure 14.3). Part of this conceptualization has already been elaborated.[28,71,72] According to this theory, in the terminology of behavioral conditioning, both the CS (changes in the external environment) and the US (changes in the internal environment) must be inputs to the CNS, which in turn processes and associates this information. Thus, at association time, only a change in the immune system sensed by the CNS can serve as a US. Furthermore, both the CR and the UR must be outputs of the CNS.

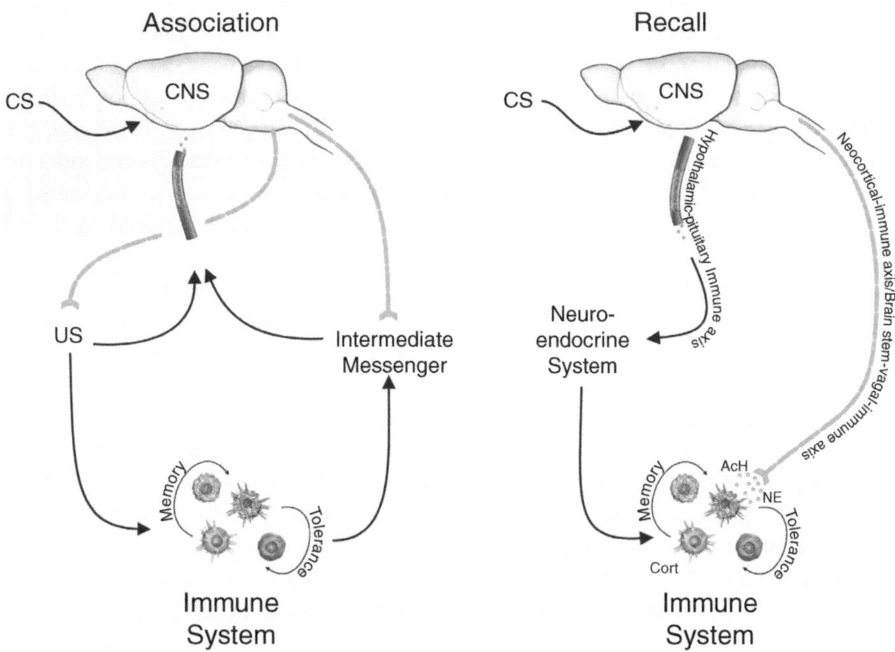

FIGURE 14.3 (See color insert following page 202.) Theoretical framework for neuro-immune associative learning. At association time two possible unconditioned stimuli (US) were associated with a conditioned stimulus (CS). The US directly detected by the CNS is defined as a *directly perceived US*. The one that needs one or more intermediary molecules released by another system in order to be detected by the CNS is called an *indirectly perceived US*. Any US, directly or indirectly perceived, has two possible afferent pathways to the CNS: a neural afferent pathway and a humoral afferent pathway. At recall time, the CNS can modulate immune functions via these two possible pathways. The humoral efferent pathway may imply changes in neuro-hormones that directly or indirectly modify the immune response. The neural efferent pathway is supported by the direct innervations of primary and secondary lymphoid organs. Features such as novelty, intensity, duration and naturalistic relation to the US may explain the feasibility of associating the CS with the US, along with the stability and strength of such an association. It is also necessary to consider that the immune history (tolerance and memory) of a subject may vary the response to the US, resulting in different associative learning at association time and/or in a different conditioned response at recall time. (Adapted from Pacheco-López, G. et al., in *Psychoneuroimmunology*, 4th ed., Ader, R., Ed., Academic Press, New York, 2006.)

Thus, only an immune parameter directed by the CNS can serve as a UR for conditioning and at recall time the CR will resemble such a UR.

14.3.1 Association Phase

Two possible kinds of US are employed to induce NIAL. The US that is directly detected by the CNS is defined as a *directly perceived US,* whereas the one that needs one or more intermediary molecules released by another system in order to be detected by the CNS is an *indirectly perceived US*. Any US perceived directly or indirectly has two possible afferent pathways to the CNS: (1) a neural afferent pathway and (2) a humoral afferent pathway. The *neural afferent pathway* may detect the US and translate this information into neural activity. This sensory process implies the interoceptive capacities, including immunoception, of the CNS.[73,74] Theoretically, this afferent pathway may also be able to codify the location of stimulation (local versus systemic).

The *humoral afferent pathway* is required for any US that is not detected locally or for molecules induced by a given US (indirectly perceived US) that reach the CNS via the blood stream. If a given US has effects on several cell types, it is reasonable to assume that several molecules are candidates to be perceived by the CNS (directly perceived US). Figure 14.3 indicates that for an indirectly perceived US, the pathway to the CNS is complex and longer than for a directly perceived US. After administration of a given US, it can be hypothesized that the CNS takes longer to respond to indirectly perceived unconditioned stimuli than to those perceived directly. This feature can be employed in experimental designs in order to elucidate the nature of the US. For instance, backward conditioning should not be possible in the case of a directly perceived US, whereas an indirectly perceived US could result in associative learning under such conditions.

For an indirectly perceived US that affects immune functions, one should consider that the immune history (tolerance and memory) of a subject may interfere with the response to such a US, resulting in a different immune reaction, and thus a different signal intensity to the CNS. For example, the immune responses to a given antigen differ completely between the first and second times because an immune memory process takes place after the first exposition. Another example is the immune tolerance phenomenon developed after repeated exposition to the same drug. Applying the same conditioning protocol to two subjects with varying immune histories may result in different associative learning processes that in turn may affect the immune system in diverse ways at recall time.

In Pavlovian conditioning, the strength of the association of the CS and the US is affected by the temporal relation (inter-stimulus interval) between these stimuli. Orthodox theory predicts that when the US precedes the presentation of the CS (backward conditioning), learning is poor. In addition, when the CS precedes the US by increasing intervals, the probability of a CR declines.[13] The specific inter-stimulus interval that yields the most pronounced CR varies with organisms and responses studied. For NIAL, this associative feature may be employed to delineate the nature of the US (directly versus indirectly perceived) by systematically varying the inter-stimulus interval between the CS and US and describing the UR kinetics.

Regarding the CS, it is important to mention that features such as novelty, intensity, duration, and naturalistic relation to the US may explain the feasibility of associating the CS with the US, as well as the stability and strength of such an association. For instance, it is well documented that gustatory or olfactory stimuli are strongly and easily associated with visceral US, in contrast to tactile, visual, or auditory stimuli.[10,75] The strength and lastingness of flavor-visceral association is reflected in several features of the CR, such as high magnitude and low forgetting rate or extinction resistance. Additionally, the neutrality of the CS toward the immune system must be assured for each experimental setting.

14.3.2 Recall Phase

The CR represents tacit and unique proof that an associative learning process has occurred at association time. In several NIAL protocols, the experimental subjects displayed complex CRs with behavioral and neuroendocrine components in addition to the effects observed in the immune system. Furthermore, it is necessary to consider that the immune system displays sensitization (memory) and habituation (tolerance) responses to specific stimuli and that many immune parameters underlie circadian rhythms. Thus, the specific time points for association and recall and the immunological history of each experimental subject may be important variables for the final immunological outcome after recalling a given NIAL. Thus, some immune parameters modulated at recall time may be the bizarre reflections of neural activities not explained by established learning and memory rules.

For example, the expression of neural activity (e.g., behavior) may follow a normal extinction process during consecutive recall trials, whereas the effects of such activity on the peripheral immune response may not display the same extinction slope or may even be enhanced. Such peculiar results may be explained in several ways. It is possible that the interval between the recall trials is not long enough for the specific immune measure to return to baseline, resulting in an additive effect on the conditioned immune response during consecutive near-recall trials. Another possibility is related to immune processes that may be modulated by neural activity; however, once such a process has started it is basically independent of neural modulation. Additionally, it has been demonstrated that a stable and sturdy memory under extinction can to a great extent be reconsolidated by contingent exposure to the US, even if it is of low intensity.[76]

Thus it is possible that, after an intensive association phase, the conditioned immune effects work as a putative US, inducing a reconsolidation process of the memory trace at each recall trial and therefore maintaining or enhancing the conditioned effects on the immune system in subsequent recall trials. In this regard, it should be indicated that some changes in the immune response after recalling NIAL cannot strictly be called CRs.[71] In summary, immune responses can be affected by NIAL, but this does not necessarily imply that such immune responses were behaviorally conditioned.

Regarding the conditioned immune response, specific features may give important clues to its nature and should be considered in an experimental design in order to differentiate the underlying mechanisms. The two possible pathways by which the CNS can modulate immune functions are (1) the humoral efferent pathway and (2) the neural efferent pathway. The *humoral efferent pathway* may imply changes in neuro-hormones that directly or indirectly modify the immune response at recall time. The peripheral effects evoked after activation of this pathway are diffuse and long-lasting like any neuroendocrine responses. The *neural efferent pathway* is supported by the direct innervations of primary and secondary lymphoid organs.[77,78]

Several immune parameters are subject to neural modulation: T cell differentiation,[79,80] hematopoiesis,[81–83] T cell activity, B cell activity,[84] natural killer (NK) cell activity,[85–87] and inflammatory responses.[3,88,89] We hypothesize that many of these neuro-immune interactions may be affected by NIAL but few have been investigated experimentally to date.

The extinction of the conditioned immune response is another feature that may give hints about the underlying mechanisms. It has been demonstrated that for behavioral conditioning in which the nervous system directly modulates the CR (e.g., nictitating membrane, gastric secretion, aversive behavior), an extinction process occurs when the CS is repeatedly presented without the US (active forgetting). However, if the CR observed is the reflection of neural activity on different types of cells, like immune cells that exhibit tolerance and memory processes, CR extinction will not necessarily be elicited in an orthodox Pavlovian manner. Moreover, if the CR observed reflects neural activity on two or more cellular types, the picture may be more abnormal (e.g., the neuroendocrine efferent pathway affecting immune functions). Further consideration is required since the life spans of immune cells are short and thus each recall trial may affect different leukocyte or lymphocyte subsets.

Several experimental approaches allow analysis of the mechanisms responsible for behavioral conditioning. For example, treatment performed before association may affect sensory and early associative processes (short-term memory). Consolidation and long-term memory can be experimentally analyzed by varying the timing of treatment after association. If the treatment is given before recall, then the memory process can be studied. This scheme seems to be applicable for short-term treatments. However, for long-lasting treatment, differentiating between the learning and the memory processes is only possible by comparing the effects of treatment given before association with those of treatment given before recall. In addition, the specific timing of a given treatment may depend on the nature of the treatment (short- versus long-term effects) and the pharmacokinetics and pharmacodynamics of the drugs applied.

14.4 NEUROBIOLOGY OF NEURO-IMMUNE ASSOCIATIVE LEARNING

The naturalistic associability of food and drink ingestion with its possible immune consequences has been experimentally appraised in rodents and humans employing the conditioned taste aversion paradigm.[90] Conditioned taste aversion or avoidance is a type of associative conditioning in which the subjects learn to associate a taste with delayed malaise.[70] This learning has been conserved across the animal kingdom[91–94] including humans[95] which reflects its high adaptive value in food selection strategies. However, reduced ingestive behavior may be only part of a complex and diverse repertory of physiological responses that the individual evokes to avoid, reject and/or prepare to counteract the unconditioned effects.[5]

One discrete neural network involved in taste-visceral associative learning has already been described, mainly including sensory and hedonic neural pathways.[96,97]

Such a neural circuit consistently includes the nucleus tractus solitary, the parabrachial nucleus, medial thalamus, amygdala, and insular cortex.[98] In particular, the insular cortex is essential for the acquisition and retention of this associative learning[99,100] and it has been postulated that the insular cortex may integrate gustatory and visceral stimuli.[101] More recently, using the neuronal activity marker c-Fos, it was possible to confirm the preponderant role of the insular cortex in conditioned antibody production[102] in agreement with a previous report.[103]

Regarding other forebrain structures, the amygdala seems to play an important role during the formation of aversive ingestive associations[104] and is also relevant for limbic–autonomic interactions.[105] A series of reports indicates that the insular cortex and amygdala are key structures in conditioned immunosuppression after evoking taste-cyclophosphamide association.[106,107]

It has also been proposed that the ventromedial hypothalamic nucleus, widely recognized as a satiety center,[108] is intimately associated with sympathetic facilitation in peripheral tissues[109] including modulation of peripheral immune reactivity.[110] In agreement with previous reports,[103,106,107] we have identified the neural substrates involved in behaviorally conditioned immunosuppression (CS: saccharin; US: cyclosporine A) in rats.[111] The conditioned effect on the immune system reducing splenocyte responsiveness and cytokine production (IL-2 and IFN-γ) was affected by brain excitotoxic lesions; this shows that the insular cortex is essential to acquiring and evoking this conditioned response. In contrast, the amygdala seems to mediate the input of visceral information necessary at acquisition time, whereas the ventromedial hypothalamic nucleus appears to participate in the output pathway to the immune system needed to evoke a behaviorally conditioned immune response.

Using a pharmacological approach, the neurochemical features of the conditioned effect enhancing NK cell activity in rodents have been described. Central catecholamines seem to be essential, and glutamate — but not GABA — is also required at the recall stage.[112,113] Furthermore, it has been demonstrated that cholinergic and serotonergic central systems are required at the association and recall stages.[114]

In addition to classical neurotransmitters, cytokines have been demonstrated to play an important role within the CNS, modulating neuronal and glial functions in non-pathological settings such as learning and memory processes.[2,115,116] Specifically, pro-inflammatory cytokines such as IL-1, IL-6, and TNF-α have been shown to modulate spatial learning tasks and long-term potentiation phenomena.[117–124] In this sense, it is plausible that cytokines are significant factors in the associative processes occurring during behavioral conditioning of immune functions.

Apart from these neuromodulatory properties, pro-inflammatory cytokines seem to play an important part in the afferent pathway between the immune system and the CNS.[2,125,126] Therefore, it can be hypothesized that central cytokines act as mediators in the brain during "immune-sensing" in the association phases of behaviorally conditioned immunomodulating paradigms. These hypotheses are supported by observations that (1) receptors for these pro-inflammatory cytokines are expressed in the CNS,[127,128] (2) peripheral immune changes affect central cytokine production and cytokine receptor expression in the brain,[129,130] and (3) cytokines can act as unconditioned stimuli to induce conditioned taste aversion or avoidance.[131–134] Apart from these reports, we know of no systematic attempts to elucidate the neural substrates underlying immunomodulating effects based on neuro-immune associative learning.

14.5 BIOLOGICAL RELEVANCE OF NEURO-IMMUNE ASSOCIATIVE LEARNING

Neuro-immune interactions appear to bring several adaptive advantages to those organisms that acquired and further developed them during ontogeny and phylogeny.[94,135,136] This complex repertoire of physiological responses including immune, endocrine, neural, and behavioral responses may be orchestrated to achieve better adaptation of the organism to a constantly challenging environment. In vertebrates, the many intricate interactions in both directions between the immune and nervous systems are well established.[137–140] It was recently shown that invertebrate biology also evolved around acquiring and developing complex neuro-immune communications.

For example, interaction between neurons and immune cells has been demonstrated in the mollusk *Aplysia californica*.[141] Furthermore, invertebrates also express neuropeptides (e.g., opioids) in the neural and immune tissues that play a key role as neuro-immune messengers during their evolution.[137] Neuro-immune complexity appears as well in the behavior of insects; for example, in the linkage between the immune and nervous systems of bees and humblebees.[142,143] Noninfected honey bees whose immune systems were challenged by a nonpathogenic immunogenic elicitor (lipopolysaccharide) displayed reduced abilities to associate an odor with sugar reward in a classical conditioning paradigm.

Classical conditioning can be understood as learning about the temporal or causal relationships between external and internal stimuli to allow for the appropriate preparatory set of responses before biologically significant events.[13,144] The capacity to associate a certain immune response or status (allergen, toxin, antigen) with a specific stimulus (environment or flavor) is of high adaptive value.

Thus, it can be hypothesized that this capacity was acquired during evolution as an adaptive strategy in order to protect organisms and/or prepare them to face danger. Furthermore, such associative learning is typically acquired under certain stressful conditions. For example, the exposure to a specific antigen (and its categorization as an allergen) may be associated (*learning*) with a specific environment or food. An adaptive response is then elicited (*memory*), consisting first of behavioral modification in order to avoid the place or food associated with the antigen.[66,69]

If this is not possible, the organism will try to reduce contact with the allergen, i.e., by coughing or sneezing.[145] At the same time, its immune system may prepare the body for interaction with the antigen by mast cell degranulation[64,65,146,147] or antibody production.[50,102,148,149] Although under experimental conditions such associative learning can be extinguished, it is likely that it will last for a long time since an organism in a natural situation will try to avoid contact with the environmental cues that signal the CS.

14.6 CLINICAL RELEVANCE OF NEURO-IMMUNE ASSOCIATIVE LEARNING

Few attempts have been undertaken to specifically investigate conditioned effects that directly modulate peripheral immune functions in human subjects. Since the 19th century, anecdotic case studies have reported the occurrence of allergic symptoms in the absence of allergens provoked simply by different cues (i.e., conditioned stimuli) such as a picture of a hay field or an artificial rose.[150] Several decades later, researchers reported conditioned dermatitis responses in adolescent male subjects (n = 4) resulting from evocation of a specific association (CS: blue solution application; US: 2% raw extract *R. Venicifera* application).[151]

In another case report, two asthmatic patients suffering from skin sensitivities to house-dust extract and grass pollen were exposed to these allergens by inhalation.[152] After a series of conditioning trials, they experienced allergic attacks after inhalation of the neutral solvent used to deliver the allergens. This work showed not only fast conditioning of the asthmatic attack (CR), but also tenacious retention, i.e., lack of extinction. This observation along with data from animal experiments resulted in the early hypothesis that asthma could be conceived of as a learned response.[153] This view was further supported by a conditioning protocol (CS: taste; US: dust mite allergen) in nine patients with allergic rhinitis.[154] After the association phase, elevated mast cell tryptase in mucosa was observed when an intranasal saline application was given simultaneously with the CS.

Another type of allergic reaction, the delayed-type hypersensitivity response, was tested in seven healthy volunteers who received five monthly tuberculin skin tests.[155] In this conditioning protocol both tuberculin (US) and saline were injected; while the latter was taken from a green vial (CS–), tuberculin was drawn from a red vial (CS+). On the test day, the color labeling of the substances was reversed. Although the saline injections did not induce skin reactions (erythema and induration), the severity of the symptoms was significantly blunted in all the subjects tested when the tuberculin was drawn from the green vial (conditioned effect). However, a similar protocol using various allergens (mite dust, fur) taken from colored vials did not result in conditioned modulation of skin reactions in the 15 subjects tested.[156]

Associative learning has been consistently reported in the context of cancer treatment, particularly chemotherapy.[28] Chemotherapy agents (e.g., cyclophosphamide) generally have immunosuppressive effects. They are typically administered in cycles, with each outpatient treatment infusion followed by a period of recovery prior to the next infusion. From a conditioning perspective, clinic treatment visits can be viewed as association trials in which the distinctive salient features of the clinic environment (CS) are contingently paired with the infusion of agents (US: cyclophosphamide) that have effects on the immune system.

Immune function was assessed in 20 cancer patients in a hospital prior to chemotherapy and compared with assessments conducted at home. Proliferative responses to T cell mitogens were lower for cells isolated from blood samples taken in the hospital (after recall) than for home samples.[157] These results were replicated in 22 ovarian patients[158] and 19 pediatric patients receiving chemotherapy.[159] However, chemotherapy patients often develop conditioned nausea,[157,160–162] anxiety,[163,164] and fatigue[165] responses to reminders of chemotherapy. These conditioned nausea and anxiety responses can also be elicited by thoughts and images of chemotherapy,[166,167] raising the possibility that conditioned effects may affect patients during the course of normal life for years after treatment.

Only a few human studies have tried to affect immune parameters on the cellular level by employing behavioral conditioning procedures. Based on the knowledge that adrenaline administration leads to the immediate mobilization of leukocytes in the periphery, especially of NK cell numbers with simultaneous augmentation of their lytic activity,[168,169] one research group assessed the conditionability of NK cell numbers and their lytic activity in healthy volunteers. Although positive results were reported after evoking a taste (CS)–adrenaline (US) association.[170,171] these effects could not be replicated by other research groups.[172]

The efficacy of a conditioning protocol was also tested in multiple sclerosis patients, for whom four monthly cyclophosphamide infusions (US) were contingently paired with the taste of anise-flavored syrup (CS).[173] Long-term treatment with cyclophosphamide decreased blood leukocyte numbers, often leading to leukopenia. Interestingly, after 6 months of administering a placebo infusion paired with the drink, 8 of 10 patients showed conditioned reductions in peripheral leukocyte numbers. In addition, by pairing s.c. interferon-γ injections (US) with a distinctively flavored drink (CS), it was possible to induce elevations of neopterin and quinolinic acid serum levels after evoking such an association in healthy volunteers (n = 10).[174]

It has been hypothesized that more than a single associative learning trial pairing a distinctive taste (CS) with interferon-β injections (US) is necessary to produce immune conditioned effects.[175] This view is supported by experimental data for healthy male volunteers (n = 18). The immunosuppressive drug cyclosporine A (US) was paired four times with a distinctively flavored and colored solution (CS),[63] inducing taste-immune associative learning. The immunopharmacological mechanism of cyclosporine A involves its binding to cyclophilins, which leads to intracellular phosphatase calcineurin inhibition, then selectively reducing the expression of interleukin-2 (IL-2) and interferon- (IFN-γ) cytokines, which finally resulted in specific suppression of T cell function.[176] After association, the mere re-exposure to the drink (CS) induced conditioned inhibition of *ex vivo* cytokine (IL-2 and IFN-γ) mRNA expression and cytokine release along with the proliferative responsiveness of human peripheral blood lymphocytes similar to the drug effect.

14.7 SUMMARY AND FUTURE PERSPECTIVE

Conceptualizing Pavlovian conditioning as a mechanism by which an organism anticipates the onset of a biologically important event (US) and initiates preparatory responses (CR) to allow the organism to deal better with US effects invites the hypothesis that one reason for the neural control of immunity lies in accommodating the adaptive value of classical conditioning.[18] In its natural environment, an animal with a cut or a scratch must build up immunological defenses against microorganisms. In the laboratory or a clinical setting, an antigen is reliably preceded by an injection. Therefore, conditioned immune effects may, in fact, be very common.

The difficulty for the investigator lies not so much in inducing such responses, but in employing the proper controls, both immunological and psychological, in order to demonstrate that these responses exist and to explore the underlying mechanisms. Due to the physiological basis of the conditioned effects, the magnitude of the conditioned immune response should not to be expected to override the homeostatic balance of the organism. However, this does not mean that conditioned effects on immune functions are not of biological and clinical significance, as reviewed here and in previous work.[27]

A very small increase in the potential of the immune system may be of great value in the fight against pathogens when a system reaches an allostatic load,[177,178] but it may increase the occurrence and severity of allergies and autoimmune disorders in other conditions. It is important to emphasize that several immune responses may be affected by NIAL protocols, but this does not necessarily imply that such immune responses are conditioned. Because of the complexity of neuro-immune interaction, such differentiation is not easy to establish.

As we have seen, the use of a US with immune consequences, such as immunomodulating drugs or antigens, is not the only requirement for *genuinely* conditioning an immune response through behavioral protocol. Experimental data reflect a dichotomy that is possibly supported by different mechanisms that may follow different rules. In our own experience and after reviewing the available literature, we conclude that the direction of the CR is a key feature of conditioning; i.e., the direction of this response should be independent of the immune, endocrine, and circadian status of the subject at association and recall time.

Before NIAL can be implemented as supportive therapy together with traditional pharmacological regimens, it is essential to describe some of its features. For example, we do not yet know how long conditioned immune responses last and how immune-specific they are. Since it may be necessary to apply reinforcement at appropriate intervals, questions arise whether reconditioning is possible. Therapy will eventually stop. What is the forgetting pattern of conditioned immune responses? How predictable is the conditioned immune response in a human population with different immune and psychological histories? What are the impacts of age and gender on immunoconditioning? When using immunomodulating drugs as the unconditioned stimuli, are some side effects conditioned?

To date, experimental evidence indicates that behavioral conditioning may have practical implications in a clinical setting and be of use as supportive therapy, with the aim of reducing undesired side effects and maximizing the effects of pharmacological therapies.[179] In summary, we have reviewed and summarized the current data indicating that both innate and adaptive immune responses are affected by evoking neuro-immune associative learning. The effect of NIAL on immune functions is just about to be understood and the possible clinical applications seem to be enormous.

In future studies it will be essential to analyze the afferent and efferent pathways in brain-to-immune communications before NIAL paradigms can be employed as beneficial tools in clinical settings. Finally, research on behavioral immunoconditioning has revealed that organisms have important adaptive psychoneuroimmunological strategies acquired to deal with constantly changing and challenging environments in a better way.

REFERENCES

1. Elmquist, J.K., Scammell, T.E., and Saper, C.B., Mechanisms of CNS response to systemic immune challenge: the febrile response, *Trends Neurosci*, 20, 565, 1997.
2. Dantzer, R., Cytokine-induced sickness behaviour: a neuroimmune response to activation of innate immunity, *Eur J Pharmacol*, 500, 399, 2004.
3. Tracey, K., The inflammatory reflex, *Nature*, 420, 853, 2002.
4. Glaser, R. and Kiecolt-Glaser, J.K., Stress-induced immune dysfunction: implications for health, *Nat Rev Immunol*, 5, 243, 2005.
5. Niemi, M.B. et al., Murine taste-immune associative learning, *Brain Behav Immun*, 20, 527, 2006.
6. Hawkins, R. et al., A cellular mechanism of classical conditioning in Aplysia: activity-dependent amplification of presynaptic facilitation, *Science*, 219, 400, 1983.
7. Pavlov, I., *Conditioned Reflexes: An Investigation of the Physiological Activity of the Cerebral Cortex*, Oxford University Press, Cambridge, 1927.
8. Fanselow, M. and Poulos, A., The neuroscience of mammalian associative learning, *Annu Rev Psychol*, 56, 207, 2005.
9. Carew, T. and Sahley, C., Invertebrate learning and memory: from behavior to molecules, *Annu Rev Neurosci*, 9, 435, 1986.
10. Domjan, M., Pavlovian conditioning: a functional perspective, *Annu Rev Psychol*, 56, 179, 2005.
11. Rescorla, R. and Wagner, A., A theory of pavlovian conditioning: variations in the efectiveness of reinforcement and nonreinforcement, in *Classical Conditioning II: Current Research and Theory*, Black A. and Prokasy W., Eds., Appleton-Century-Crofts, New York, 1972, p. 64.
12. Pearce, J., A model for stimulus generalization in Pavlovian conditioning, *Psychol Rev*, 94, 61, 1987.
13. Rescorla, R., Behavioral studies of Pavlovian conditioning, *Annu Rev Neurosci*, 11, 329, 1988.
14. Ader, R. and Cohen, N., Conditioned immunopharmacologic responses, in *Psychoneuroimmunology*, 1st ed., Ader R., Ed., Academic Press, New York, 1981, p. 185.
15. Ader, R. and Cohen, N., The influence of conditioning on immune responses, in *Pschoneuroimmunology*, 2nd ed., Ader R., Felten D., and Cohen N., Eds., Academic Press, New York, 1991, p. 611.
16. Ader, R. and Cohen, N., Conditioning and immunity, in *Psychoneuroimmunology*, 3rd ed., Ader R., Felten D., and Cohen N., Eds., Academic Press, New York, 2001, p. 3.
17. Luk'ianenko, V., The problem of conditioned reflex regulation of immunobiologic reactions, *USP Sovrem Biol*, 51, 170, 1961.
18. Brittain, R. and Wiener, N., Neural and Pavlovian influences on immunity, *Pavlov J Biol Sci*, 20, 181, 1985.
19. Spector, N., Old and new strategies in the conditioning of immune responses, *Ann NY Acad Sci*, 496, 522, 1987.
20. Kusnecov, A., King, M., and Husband, A., Immunomodulation by behavioural conditioning, *Biol Psychol*, 28, 25, 1989.

21. Markovic, B., Dimitrijevic, M., and Jankovic, B., Immunomodulation by conditioning: recent developments, *Int J Neurosci*, 71, 231, 1993.
22. Hiramoto, R. et al., The use of conditioning to probe for CNS pathways that regulate fever and NK cell activity, *Int J Neurosci*, 84, 229, 1996.
23. Spector, N., Neuroimmunomodulation: a brief review: can conditioning of natural killer cell activity reverse cancer and/or aging? *Regul Toxicol Pharmacol*, 24, S32, 1996.
24. Hiramoto, R. et al., Psychoneuroendocrine immunology: site of recognition, learning and memory in the immune system and the brain, *Int J Neurosci*, 92, 259, 1997.
25. Hiramoto, R. et al., Psychoneuroendocrine immunology: perception of stress can alter body temperature and natural killer cell activity, *Int J Neurosci*, 98, 95, 1999.
26. Spector, N., The NIM revolution, *Rom J Physiol*, 36, 127, 1999.
27. Ader, R., Conditioned immunomodulation: research needs and directions, *Brain Behav Immun*, 17, Suppl 1, S51, 2003.
28. Bovbjerg, D., Conditioning, cancer, and immune regulation, *Brain Behav Immun*, 17 Suppl 1, S58, 2003.
29. Hucklebridge, F., Behavioral conditioning of the immune system, *Int Rev Neurobiol*, 52, 325, 2002.
30. Exton, M. et al., Conditioning in the rat: an *in vivo* model to investigate the molecular mechanisms and clinical implications of brain-immune communication, *Immunol Rev*, 184, 226, 2001.
31. Exton, M. et al., Pavlovian conditioning of immune function: animal investigation and the challenge of human application, *Behav Brain Res*, 110, 129, 2000.
32. Pacheco-López, G. et al., Expectations and associations that heal: immunomodulatory placebo effects and neurobiology, *Brain Behav Immun*, 20, 430, 2006.
33. Metalnikov, S. and Chorine, V., Role des réflexes conditionnels dans l'immunité, *Ann Inst Pasteur*, 11, 893, 1926.
34. Metalnikov, S. and Chorine, V., Role des réflexes conditionnels dans la formation des anticorps, *Compt R Seances Soc Biol Ses Fil*, 99, 142, 1928.
35. Nicolau, I. and Antinescu-Dimitriu, O., Rôle des réflexes conditionnels dans la formation des anticorps, *Compt R Seances Soc Biol Ses Fil*, 102, 133, 1929.
36. Nicolau, I. and Antinescu-Dimitriu, O., L'influence des réflexes conditionnels sur l'exsudat peritonéal, *Compt R Seances Soc Biol Ses Fil*, 102, 144, 1929.
37. Ostravskaya, O., Le réflex conditionnel et les réactions de l'immunité, *Ann Inst Pasteur*, 44, 340, 1930.
38. Ader, R., A historical account of conditioned immunobiologic responses, in *Psychoneuroimmunology*, Ader R., Ed., Academic Press, New York, 1981, p. 321.
39. Baciu, I. et al., Sur les centres nerveux régulateurs de l'erythropoièse, *Rev Roum Physiol*, 2, 123, 1965.
40. Benetato, G., Central nervous mechanism of the leukocytic and phagocytic reaction, *J Physiol (Paris)*, 47, 391, 1955.
41. Benetato, G. et al., Despre rolul scoartie cerebrale in activarea sistemului fagocitar si mobilizarea anticorpilor, *Studi Cercetari Fil Acad RPR Chij*, 8, 264, 1952.
42. Noelpp, B. and Noelpp-Eschenhagen, I., Experimental bronchial asthma in guinea pigs. Part II. The role of conditioned reflexes in the pathogenesis of bronchial asthma, *Int Arch Allergy Appl Immunol*, 2, 321, 1951.
43. Noelpp, B. and Noelpp-Eschenhagen, I., Experimental bronchial asthma in guinea pigs. Part I. Methods for objective registration of asthma attacks, *Int Arch Allergy Appl Immunol*, 2, 308, 1951.

44. Noelpp, B. and Noelpp-Eschenhagen, I., Role of conditioned reflex in bronchial asthma: experimental investigation on the pathogenesis of bronchial asthma, *Helv Med Acta*, 18, 142, 1951.
45. Noelpp, B. and Noelpp-Eschenhagen, I., Experimental bronchial asthma in guinea pigs. Part III. Studies on the significance of conditioned reflexes: ability to develop conditioned reflexes and their duration under stress, *Int Arch Allergy Appl Immunol*, 3, 108, 1952.
46. Noelpp, B. and Noelpp-Eschenhagen, I., Experimental bronchial asthma in guinea pigs. Part IV. Experimental asthma in the guinea pig as an experimental model, *Int Arch Allergy Appl Immunol*, 3, 207, 1952.
47. Noelpp, B. and Noelpp-Eschenhagen, I., Experimental bronchial asthma in guinea pigs. Part V. Experimental pathophysiological studies, *Int Arch Allergy Appl Immunol*, 3, 302, 1952.
48. Ader, R. and Cohen, N., Behaviorally conditioned immunosuppression, *Psychosom Med*, 37, 333, 1975.
49. Espinosa, E. et al., Enhancement of antibody response by one-trial conditioning: contrasting results using different antigens, *Brain Behav Immun*, 18, 76, 2004.
50. Husband, A.J. et al., A conditioning model for immunostimulation: enhancement of the antibody responses to ovalbumin by behavioral conditioning in rats, in *Psychoimmunology*, Husband, A.J., Ed., CRC Press, Boca Raton, 1993, p. 139.
51. Pacheco-López, G. et al., Peripheral protein immunization induces rapid activation of the CNS, as measured by c-Fos expression, *J Neuroimmunol*, 131, 50, 2002.
52. Djuric, V. et al., Conditioned taste aversion in rats subjected to anaphylactic shock, *Ann NY Acad Sci*, 496, 561, 1987.
53. Bull, D.F. et al., Modulation of body temperature through taste aversion conditioning, *Physiol Behav*, 49, 1229, 1991.
54. Janz, L.J. et al., Pavlovian conditioning of LPS-induced responses: effects on corticosterone, splenic NE, and IL-2 production, *Physiol Behav*, 59, 1103, 1996.
55. Cross-Mellor, S.K., Kavaliers, M., and Ossenkopp, K.P., Comparing immune activation (lipopolysaccharide) and toxin (lithium chloride)-induced gustatory conditioning: lipopolysaccharide produces conditioned taste avoidance but not aversion, *Behav Brain Res*, 148, 11, 2004.
56. Pacheco-López, G. et al., Behavioral endocrine immune-conditioned response is induced by taste and superantigen pairing, *Neuroscience*, 129, 555, 2004.
57. Kusnecov, A. and Goldfarb, Y., Neural and behavioral responses to systemic immunologic stimuli: a consideration of bacterial T cell superantigens, *Curr Pharm Des*, 11, 1039, 2005.
58. Lambert, J.V. and Whitehouse, W.G., Conditioned inhibition of cyclophosphamide-induced taste aversion, *J Gen Psychol*, 129, 68, 2002.
59. Exton, M.S. et al., Conditioned taste aversion produced by cyclosporine A: concomitant reduction in lymphoid organ weight and splenocyte proliferation, *Physiol Behav*, 63, 241, 1998.
60. Klosterhalfen, S. and Klosterhalfen, W., Conditioned cyclosporine effects but not conditioned taste aversion in immunized rats, *Behav Neurosci*, 104, 716, 1990.
61. Djuric, V. et al., Anaphylactic shock-induced conditioned taste aversion. II. Correlation between taste aversion and indicators of anaphylactic shock, *Brain Behav Immun*, 2, 24, 1988.
62. Markovic, B. et al., Anaphylactic shock-induced conditioned taste aversion. I. Demonstration of the phenomenon by means of three modes of CS-US presentation, *Brain Behav Immun*, 2, 11, 1988.

63. Goebel, M.U. et al., Behavioral conditioning of immunosuppression is possible in humans, *FASEB J*, 16, 1869, 2002.
64. MacQueen, G. et al., Pavlovian conditioning of rat mucosal mast cells to secrete rat mast cell protease II, *Science*, 243, 83, 1989.
65. Palermo-Neto, J. and Guimarães, R., Pavlovian conditioning of lung anaphylactic response in rats, *Life Sci*, 68, 611, 2000.
66. Markovic, B., Dimitrijevic, M., and Jankovic, B., Anaphylactic shock in neuropsychoimmunological research, *Int J Neurosci*, 67, 271, 1992.
67. Djuric, V.J. et al., Pavlovian conditioning in rats subjected to anaphylactic shock, in *Neuroimmune Networks: Physiology and Disease*, Wiley-Liss, New York, 1989, p. 207.
68. Djuric, V.J. et al., Manifestations of repeated anaphylactic shock are context-specific, *Neuroendocrinol Lett*, 9, 215, 1987.
69. Costa-Pinto, F.A. et al., Avoidance behavior and neural correlates of allergen exposure in a murine model of asthma, *Brain Behav Immun*, 19, 52, 2005.
70. Bermúdez-Rattoni, F., Molecular mechanisms of taste-recognition memory, *Nat Rev Neurosci*, 5, 209, 2004.
71. Eikelboom, R. and Stewart, J., Conditioning of drug-induced physiological responses, *Psychol Rev*, 89, 507, 1982.
72. Pacheco-Lopez, G. et al., Behaviorally conditioned enhancement of immune responses, in *Psychoneuroimmunology*, 4th ed., Ader, R., Ed., Academic Press, New York, 631, 2006.
73. Blalock, J., The immune system as the sixth sense, *J Intern Med*, 257, 126, 2005.
74. Goehler, L. et al., Vagal immune-to-brain communication: a visceral chemosensory pathway, *Auton Neurosci*, 85, 49, 2000.
75. Domjan, M., Role of ingestion in odor-toxicosis learning in the rat, *J Comp Physiol Psychol*, 84, 507, 1973.
76. Berman, D. and Dudai, Y., Memory extinction, learning anew, and learning the new: dissociations in the molecular machinery of learning in cortex, *Science*, 291, 2417, 2001.
77. Mignini, F., Streccioni, V., and Amenta, F., Autonomic innervation of immune organs and neuroimmune modulation, *Auton Autacoid Pharmacol*, 23, 1, 2003.
78. Elenkov, I. et al., The sympathetic nerve: an integrative interface between two supersystems: the brain and the immune system, *Pharmacol Rev*, 52, 595, 2000.
79. Sanders, V. and Kohm, A., Sympathetic nervous system interaction with the immune system, *Int Rev Neurobiol*, 52, 17, 2002.
80. Sanders, V. and Straub, R., Norepinephrine, the beta-adrenergic receptor, and immunity, *Brain Behav Immun*, 16, 290, 2002.
81. Artico, M. et al., Noradrenergic and cholinergic innervation of the bone marrow, *Int J Mol Med*, 10, 77, 2002.
82. Miyan, J., Broome, C., and Whetton, A., Neural regulation of bone marrow, *Blood*, 92, 2971, 1998.
83. Maestroni, G., Catecholaminergic regulation of hematopoiesis in mice, *Blood*, 92, 2971; author reply: 2972, 1998.
84. Downing, J. and Miyan, J., Neural immunoregulation: emerging roles for nerves in immune homeostasis and disease, *Immunol Today*, 21, 281, 2000.
85. Hori, T. et al., The autonomic nervous system as a communication channel between the brain and the immune system, *Neuroimmunomodulation*, 2, 203, 1995.
86. Katafuchi, T. et al., Hypothalamic modulation of splenic natural killer cell activity in rats, *J Physiol*, 471, 209, 1993.

87. Katafuchi, T., Take, S., and Hori, T., Roles of sympathetic nervous system in the suppression of cytotoxicity of splenic natural killer cells in the rat, *J Physiol*, 465, 343, 1993.
88. Pavlov, V. and Tracey, K., The cholinergic anti-inflammatory pathway, *Brain Behav Immun*, 2005.
89. Czura, C. and Tracey, K., Autonomic neural regulation of immunity, *J Intern Med*, 257, 156, 2005.
90. Garcia, J., Kimeldorf, D.J., and Koelling, R.A., Conditioned aversion to saccharin resulting from exposure to gamma radiation, *Science*, 122, 157, 1955.
91. Kawai, R. et al., Conditioned taste aversion with sucrose and tactile stimuli in the pond snail *Lymnaea stagnalis*, *Neurobiol Learn Mem*, 82, 164, 2004.
92. Marella, S. et al., Imaging taste responses in the fly brain reveals a functional map of taste category and behavior, *Neuron*, 49, 285, 2006.
93. Paradis, S. and Cabanac, M., Flavor aversion learning induced by lithium chloride in reptiles but not in amphibians, *Behav Proc*, 67, 11, 2004.
94. Schedlowski, M., Insecta immune-cognitive interactions, *Brain Behav Immun*, 20, 133, 2006.
95. Garb, J.L. and Stunkard, A.J., Taste aversions in man, *Am J Psychiatry*, 131, 1204, 1974.
96. Sewards, T.V., Dual separate pathways for sensory and hedonic aspects of taste, *Brain Res Bull*, 62, 271, 2004.
97. Sewards, T.V. and Sewards, M., Separate, parallel sensory and hedonic pathways in the mammalian somatosensory system, *Brain Res Bull*, 58, 243, 2002.
98. Yamamoto, T. et al., Neural substrates for conditioned taste aversion in the rat, *Behav Brain Res*, 65, 123, 1994.
99. Bermudez-Rattoni, F. and McGaugh, J.L., Insular cortex and amygdala lesions differentially affect acquisition on inhibitory avoidance and conditioned taste aversion, *Brain Res*, 549, 165, 1991.
100. Cubero, I., Thiele, T.E., and Bernstein, I.L., Insular cortex lesions and taste aversion learning: effects of conditioning method and timing of lesion, *Brain Res*, 839, 323, 1999.
101. Sewards, T.V. and Sewards, M.A., Cortical association areas in the gustatory system, *Neurosci Biobehav Rev*, 25, 395, 2001.
102. Chen, J. et al., Enhancement of antibody production and expression of c-Fos in the insular cortex in response to a conditioned stimulus after a single-trial learning paradigm, *Behav Brain Res*, 154, 557, 2004.
103. Ramírez-Amaya, V. and Bermúdez-Rattoni, F., Conditioned enhancement of antibody production is disrupted by insular cortex and amygdala but not hippocampal lesions, *Brain Behav Immun*, 13, 46, 1999.
104. Reilly, S. and Bornovalova, M.A., Conditioned taste aversion and amygdala lesions in the rat: a critical review, *Neurosci Biobehav Rev*, 29, 1067, 2005.
105. Swanson, L.W. and Petrovich, G.D., What is the amygdala? *Trends Neurosci*, 21, 323, 1998.
106. Ramírez-Amaya, V. et al., Insular cortex lesions impair the acquisition of conditioned immunosuppression, *Brain Behav Immun*, 10, 103, 1996.
107. Ramírez-Amaya, V., Alvarez-Borda, B., and Bermúdez-Rattoni, F., Differential effects of NMDA-induced lesions into the insular cortex and amygdala on the acquisition and evocation of conditioned immunosuppression, *Brain Behav Immun*, 12, 149, 1998.

108. Vettor, R. et al., Neuroendocrine regulation of eating behavior, *J Endocrinol Invest*, 25, 836, 2002.
109. Saito, M., Minokoshi, Y., and Shimazu, T., Accelerated norepinephrine turnover in peripheral tissues after ventromedial hypothalamic stimulation in rats, *Brain Res*, 481, 298, 1989.
110. Okamoto, S. et al., Ventromedial hypothalamus suppresses splenic lymphocyte activity through sympathetic innervation, *Brain Res*, 739, 308, 1996.
111. Pacheco-López, G. et al., Neural substrates for behaviorally conditioned immunosuppression in the rat, *J Neurosci*, 25, 2330, 2005.
112. Hsueh, C. et al., Involvement of catecholamines in recall of the conditioned NK cell response, *J Neuroimmunol*, 94, 172, 1999.
113. Kuo, J. et al., The involvement of glutamate in recall of the conditioned NK cell response, *J Neuroimmunol*, 118, 245, 2001.
114. Hsueh, C. et al., Cholinergic and serotonergic activities are required in triggering conditioned NK cell response, *J Neuroimmunol*, 123, 102, 2002.
115. Balschun, D. et al., Interleukin-6: a cytokine to forget, *FASEB J*, 18, 1788, 2004.
116. Tonelli, L.H., Postolache, T.T., and Sternberg, E.M., Inflammatory genes and neural activity: involvement of immune genes in synaptic function and behavior, *Front Biosci*, 10, 675, 2005.
117. Gibertini, M., IL1 beta impairs relational but not procedural rodent learning in a water maze task, *Adv Exp Med Biol*, 402, 207, 1996.
118. Schneider, H. et al., A neuromodulatory role of interleukin-1-beta in the hippocampus, *Proc Natl Acad Sci USA*, 95, 7778, 1998.
119. Fiore, M. et al., Learning performances, brain NGF distribution and NPY levels in transgenic mice expressing TNF-alpha, *Behav Brain Res*, 112, 165, 2000.
120. Banks, W.A. et al., Intravenous human interleukin-1alpha impairs memory processing in mice: dependence on blood-brain barrier transport into posterior division of the septum, *J Pharmacol Exp Ther*, 299, 536, 2001.
121. Matsumoto, Y. et al., Effects of intrahippocampal CT105, a carboxyl terminal fragment of beta-amyloid precursor protein, alone/with inflammatory cytokines on working memory in rats, *J Neurochem*, 82, 234, 2002.
122. Matsumoto, Y. et al., Involvement of cholinergic and glutamatergic functions in working memory impairment induced by interleukin-1-beta in rats, *Eur J Pharmacol*, 430, 283, 2001.
123. Rachal Pugh, C. et al., The immune system and memory consolidation: a role for the cytokine IL-1-beta, *Neurosci Biobehav Rev*, 25, 29, 2001.
124. Lynch, M.A., Interleukin-1 beta exerts a myriad of effects in the brain and in particular in the hippocampus: analysis of some of these actions, *Vitam Horm*, 64, 185, 2002.
125. Besedovsky, H.O. and del Rey, A., Immune-neuro-endocrine interactions: facts and hypotheses, *Endocr Rev*, 17, 64, 1996.
126. Turnbull, A.V. and Rivier, C.L., Regulation of the hypothalamic–pituitary–adrenal axis by cytokines: actions and mechanisms of action, *Physiol Rev*, 79, 1, 1999.
127. Sredni-Kenigsbuch, D., TH1/TH2 cytokines in the central nervous system, *Int J Neurosci*, 112, 665, 2002.
128. Szelényi, J., Cytokines and the central nervous system, *Brain Res Bull*, 54, 329, 2001.
129. Del Rey, A. et al., Not all peripheral immune stimuli that activate the HPA axis induce proinflammatory cytokine gene expression in the hypothalamus, *Ann NY Acad Sci*, 917, 169, 2000.

130. Pitossi, F. et al., Induction of cytokine transcripts in the central nervous system and pituitary following peripheral administration of endotoxin to mice, *J Neurosci Res*, 48, 287, 1997.
131. Tazi, A. et al., Interleukin-1 induces conditioned taste aversion in rats: a possible explanation for its pituitary-adrenal stimulating activity, *Brain Res*, 473, 369, 1988.
132. Dyck, D.G. et al., The Pavlovian conditioning of IL-1-induced glucocorticoid secretion, *Brain Behav Immun*, 4, 93, 1990.
133. Janz, L.J. et al., Conditioned taste aversion but not adrenal activity develops to ICV administration of interleukin-1 in rats, *Physiol Behav*, 49, 691, 1991.
134. Hiramoto, R. et al., Identification of specific pathways of communication between the CNS and NK cell system, *Life Sci*, 53, 527, 1993.
135. Tada, T., The immune system as a supersystem, *Annu Rev Immunol*, 15, 1, 1997.
136. Ottaviani, E., Valensin, S., and Franceschi, C., The neuro-immunological interface in an evolutionary perspective: the dynamic relationship between effector and recognition systems, *Front Biosci*, 3, 431, 1998.
137. Salzet, M., Vieau, D., and Day, R., Cross-talk between nervous and immune systems through the animal kingdom: focus on opioids, *Trends Neurosci*, 23, 550, 2000.
138. Vishwanath, R., The psychoneuroimmunological system: a recently evolved networking organ system, *Med Hypotheses*, 47, 265, 1996.
139. Ottaviani, E. and Franceschi, C., The neuroimmunology of stress from invertebrates to man, *Prog Neurobiol*, 48, 421, 1996.
140. Straub, R. and Besedovsky, H., Integrated evolutionary, immunological, and neuroendocrine framework for the pathogenesis of chronic disabling inflammatory diseases, *FASEB J*, 17, 2176, 2003.
141. Clatworthy, A., Neural-immune interactions: an evolutionary perspective, *Neuroimmunomodulation*, 5, 136, 1998.
142. Mallon, E., Brockmann, A., and Schmid-Hempel, P., Immune response inhibits associative learning in insects, *Proc Biol Sci*, 270, 2471, 2003.
143. Riddell, C.E. and Mallon, E.B., Insect psychoneuroimmunology: immune response reduces learning in protein-starved bumblebees (*Bombus terrestris*), *Brain Behav Immun*, 20, 135, 2006.
144. Rescorla, R., Contemporary study of Pavlovian conditioning, *Span J Psychol*, 6, 185, 2003.
145. Pinto, A. et al., Conditioned enhancement of cough response in awake guinea pigs, *Int Arch Allergy Immunol*, 108, 95, 1995.
146. Russell, M. et al., Learned histamine release, *Science*, 225, 733, 1984.
147. Irie, M., Maeda, M., and Nagata, S., Can conditioned histamine release occur under urethane anesthesia in guinea pigs? *Physiol Behav*, 72, 567, 2001.
148. Ader, R. et al., Conditioned enhancement of antibody production using antigen as the unconditioned stimulus, *Brain Behav Immun*, 7, 334, 1993.
149. Alvarez-Borda, B. et al., Enhancement of antibody production by a learning paradigm, *Neurobiol Learn Mem*, 64, 103, 1995.
150. MacKenzie, J., The production of the so-called rose effect by means of an artificial rose, with remarks and historical notes, *Am J Med Sci*, 91, 45, 1886.
151. Ikemi, Y. and Nakagawa, S., A psychosomatic study of contagious dermatitis, *Kyushu J Med Sci*, 13, 335, 1962.
152. Dekker, E., Pelser, H., and Groen, J., Conditioning as a cause of asthmatic attacks: a laboratory study, *J Psychosom Res*, 2, 97, 1957.
153. Turnbull, J., Asthma conceived as a learned response, *J Psychosom Res*, 6, 59, 1962.

154. Gauci, M. et al., Pavlovian conditioning of nasal tryptase release in human subjects with allergic rhinitis, *Physiol Behav*, 55, 823, 1994.
155. Smith, G.R. and McDaniel, S.M., Psychologically mediated effect on the delayed hypersensitivity reaction to tuberculin in humans, *Psychosom Med*, 45, 65, 1983.
156. Booth, R.J., Petrie, K.J., and Brook, R.J., Conditioning allergic skin responses in humans: a controlled trial, *Psychosom Med*, 57, 492, 1995.
157. Bovbjerg, D.H. et al., Anticipatory immune suppression and nausea in women receiving cyclic chemotherapy for ovarian cancer, *J Consult Clin Psychol*, 58, 153, 1990.
158. Lekander, M. et al., Anticipatory immune changes in women treated with chemotherapy for ovarian cancer, *Int J Behav Med*, 2, 1, 1995.
159. Stockhorst, U. et al., Anticipatory symptoms and anticipatory immune responses in pediatric cancer patients receiving chemotherapy: features of a classically conditioned response? *Brain Behav Immun*, 14, 198, 2000.
160. Andrykowski, M.A., Defining anticipatory nausea and vomiting: differences among cancer chemotherapy patients who report pretreatment nausea, *J Behav Med*, 11, 59, 1988.
161. Matteson, S. et al., The role of behavioral conditioning in the development of nausea, *Am J Obstet Gynecol*, 186, S239, 2002.
162. Morrow, G.R., Lindke, J., and Black, P.M., Anticipatory nausea development in cancer patients: replication and extension of a learning model, *Br J Psychol*, 82 (Pt 1), 61, 1991.
163. DiLorenzo, T.A. et al., Sources of anticipatory emotional distress in women receiving chemotherapy for breast cancer, *Ann Oncol*, 6, 705, 1995.
164. Jacobsen, P.B., Bovbjerg, D.H., and Redd, W.H., Anticipatory anxiety in women receiving chemotherapy for breast cancer, *Health Psychol*, 12, 469, 1993.
165. Bovbjerg, D.H., Montgomery, G.H., and Raptis, G., Evidence for classically conditioned fatigue responses in patients receiving chemotherapy treatment for breast cancer, *J Behav Med*, 28, 231, 2005.
166. Redd, W.H. et al., Nausea induced by mental images of chemotherapy, *Cancer*, 72, 629, 1993.
167. Dadds, M.R. et al., Imagery in human classical conditioning, *Psychol Bull*, 122, 89, 1997.
168. Benschop, R.J., Rodriguez-Feuerhahn, M., and Schedlowski, M., Catecholamine-induced leukocytosis: early observations, current research, and future directions, *Brain Behav Immun*, 10, 77, 1996.
169. Schedlowski, M. et al., Catecholamines modulate human NK cell circulation and function via spleen-independent beta 2-adrenergic mechanisms, *J Immunol*, 156, 93, 1996.
170. Buske-Kirschbaum, A. et al., Conditioned increase of natural killer cell activity (NKCA) in humans, *Psychosom Med*, 54, 123, 1992.
171. Buske-Kirschbaum, A. et al., Conditioned manipulation of natural killer (NK) cells in humans using a discriminative learning protocol, *Biol Psychol*, 38, 143, 1994.
172. Kirschbaum, C. et al., Conditioning of drug-induced immunomodulation in human volunteers: a European collaborative study, *Br J Clin Psychol*, 31 (Pt 4), 459, 1992.
173. Giang, D.W. et al., Conditioning of cyclophosphamide-induced leukopenia in humans, *J Neuropsychiatr Clin Neurosci*, 8, 194, 1996.
174. Longo, D.L. et al., Conditioned immune response to interferon-[gamma] in humans, *Clin Immunol*, 90, 173, 1999.
175. Goebel, M. et al., Behavioral conditioning with interferon beta-1a in humans, *Physiol Behav*, 84, 807, 2005.

176. Bukrinsky, M., Cyclophilins: unexpected messengers in intercellular communications, *Trends Immunol*, 23, 323, 2002.
177. McEwen, B. and Lasley, E., Allostatic load: when protection gives way to damage, *Adv Mind Body Med*, 19, 28, 2003.
178. McEwen, B., Stress, adaptation, and disease: allostasis and allostatic load, *Ann NY Acad Sci*, 840, 33, 1998.
179. Ader, R., The role of conditioning in pharmacotherapy, in *The Placebo Effect: An Interdisciplinary Exploration*, Harrington A., Ed., Harvard University Press, Cambridge, 1997, p. 138.
180. Pacheco-López, G., Niemi, M.B., and Schedlowski, M., unpublished data, 2006.

15 Human Brain Imaging Studies of Emotional Memory: Uncovering Influences of Sex and Hemisphere

Larry Cahill

CONTENTS

ABSTRACT

The advent of human brain imaging techniques (PET, fMRI) has allowed previously unimaginable examination of human brain functions including studies of the mechanisms underlying memory for emotional events. Many of these studies have been guided by findings from animal research that identified the amygdala as a key candidate brain region crucial to emotional memory. Evidence from human brain imaging studies has robustly confirmed this conclusion. At the same time, it has expanded our understanding of emotional memory in unsuspected directions. For example, it is now evident that males and females on average do not process memories of the same emotional events in identical ways. This fact is most clear at present regarding the amygdala, for which a sex by hemisphere interaction in its relation to memory has been documented. Whether and how these sex differences influence what is retained in memories of men and women from emotional events is now an important area of research. The evidence to date also makes clear that the long standing and still widespread assumption that subject sex matters little if at all in studies of the neurobiology of emotional memory is no longer tenable and should be abandoned.

15.1 INTRODUCTION

For most of human history, those interested in understanding how brains work possessed few methods to interrogate a healthy human brain without damaging it. This situation changed dramatically about 20 years ago with the advent of imaging techniques such as positron emission tomography (PET) and functional magnetic resonance imaging (fMRI). With these new methods, we are now able to ask questions of the intact, healthy human brain with ever-increasing spatial and temporal resolution. Indeed, so rapid are the advances that those working with these methods struggle to understand how best to utilize this new-found power.

Not surprisingly, scientists interested in the neural mechanisms underlying the influence or emotion on memory (emotional memory) were eager to apply the power of PET and fMRI to their questions. The primary focus of this chapter is on this work. I will also address related work uncovering sex-related influences on other aspects of brain mechanisms of emotional memory storage. A major conclusion from this work is that studies of emotional memory (at least involving human subjects) can no longer safely assume that subject sex will not significantly influence experimental findings and hence conclusions about brain mechanisms.

15.2 THE AMYGDALA: BUILT TO MODULATE

Before discussing this work, it is helpful to appreciate some of the evidence on which the “memory modulation” view of amygdala function rests. Consider first the anatomical connectivity of the primate amygdala. Figure 15.1 comes from a meta-analysis of cortico–cortical connectivity in the monkey by Young and Scannell.[1] The analysis conducted by these investigators was agnostic to any particular brain region including the amygdala. Still, they uncovered a striking and unique aspect of the amygdala. Alone among the cortical brain regions examined, the amygdala is possessed of extremely wide connectivity. Furthermore, the vast majority of its connections with the cortex are amygdalofugal — from the amygdala to other brain regions. From this anatomical fact alone, it appears that the amygdala is elegantly and uniquely situated to widely influence cortical function.

This anatomical structure of the amygdala’s connectivity dovetails nicely with a well supported concept of amygdala function, namely that it modulates memory

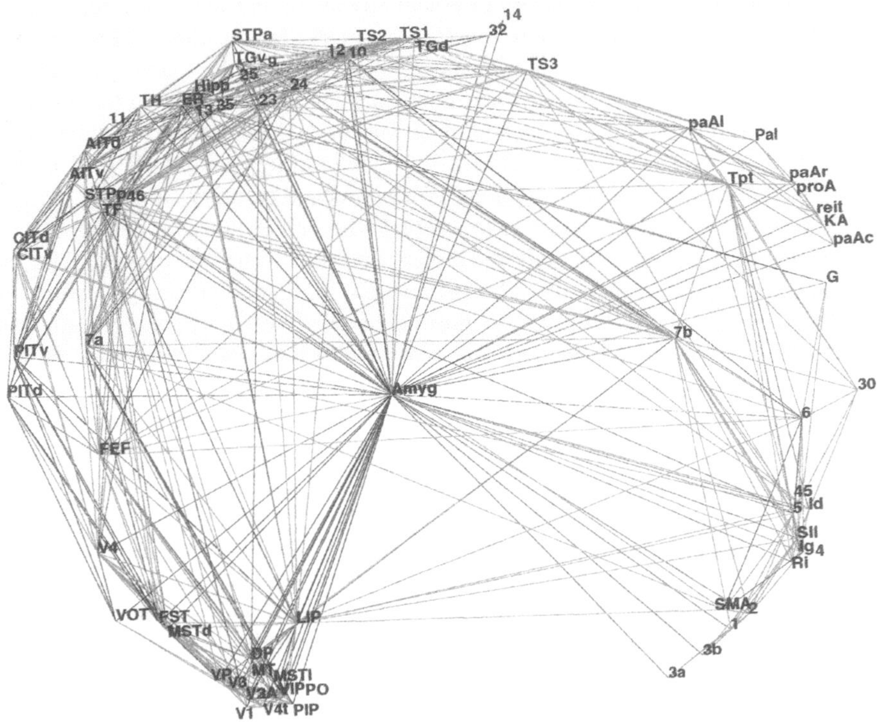

FIGURE 15.1 Meta-analysis of cortico–cortico connectivity in the primate brain. Note that the vast majority of amygdala connections are amygdalofugal, suggesting that the amygdala is well positioned to widely influence brain function. (From Young, M.P. and Scannell, J.W., *Rev Neurosci*, 5, 227, 1994. With permission.)

storage processes for emotionally arousing events in other brain regions.[2] A very large, diverse, yet cohesive body of evidence indicates that a major amygdala function is to modulate memory storage processes during and after an emotionally arousing event via interactions with endogenous stress hormones released by the events. Across many species, learning tasks, and laboratories, stimulation of the amygdala (and in particular its basolateral complex) potently modulates —enhances or impairs — memory storage processes. Most often, stimulation has been given immediately after learning, allowing the conclusion that the effects of the stimulation on memory resulted from an influence on consolidation processes.[2]

Extensive and remarkably consistent evidence also indicates that the amygdala's ability to modulate memory consolidation depends crucially on endogenous stress hormones. Indeed, the same amygdala stimulation may either enhance or impair memory storage, depending on the state of the adrenal glands.[2] So strong is the evidence for an interaction between stress hormones and the amygdala in memory that one may fairly conclude that concepts of amygdala function in memory that fail to actively incorporate influences of the body's hormonal milieu can be considered incomplete at best.

Amygdala function is necessary in essentially all circumstances for peripherally administered drugs and hormones to affect memory. For example, lesions of the amygdala or its key circuitry (e.g., stria terminalis) block the memory-enhancing and -impairing effects of all drugs and hormones tested to date. Even the amnestic effect of general anesthetics is blocked by lesions of the basolateral amygdala.[3] Thus the amygdala appears to be a necessary "door" through which all peripherally administered drugs and hormones must go to influence memory storage.

If a major amygdala function is to interact with endogenous stress hormones to influence memory, then we should find a disproportionate effect of amygdala lesions in learning situations that are relatively stress hormone-activating. Cahill and McGaugh[4] tested this possibility by examining in rats the effects of amygdala lesions on learning in a series of arousing and presumably hormone-activating tests with their effects on a series of closely matched but relatively non-arousing learning tests. Amygdala lesions impaired memory only in the relatively arousing circumstances. Cahill and McGaugh concluded that "the degree of arousal produced by the unconditioned stimulus, and not the aversive nature per se, determines the level of amygdala involvement (in a learning situation). The amygdala appears to participate in learning especially when the reinforcement is of a highly arousing nature." The amygdala then is not particularly involved with any particular emotion such as fear, but with arousing learning situations, whether pleasant or unpleasant.

This conclusion is sharply reinforced by four recent human brain imaging studies from four different laboratories, each of which compared the response of the human amygdala to stimuli that varied across the arousing dimension (arousing–calming) and across the valence dimension (pleasant–unpleasant).[5–8] All four studies reported that the amygdala responded to the arousing qualities of the stimuli, and not to their valence. As one example, Lewis et al.[8] used fMRI to examine the responses of the human amygdala to words that varied according to either their valence or arousal-inducing qualities. Amygdala activity did not correlate with ratings of valence, but correlated significantly with ratings of arousal.

15.3 HUMAN SUBJECT STUDIES RELATING AMYGDALA ACTIVITY TO EMOTIONAL MEMORY

Several studies utilizing human brain imaging examined the amygdala's role in memory for arousing material. The consistent conclusion from these studies fits very well with the memory modulation view of amygdala function derived from animal research (described above). Amygdala activity while subjects experienced emotional stimuli related significantly to subsequent (usually long-term) memory for the stimuli. However, amygdala activity in the same subjects failed to correlate with subsequent memory for relatively non-arousing stimuli.

In the first of these studies, Cahill et al.[9] scanned healthy male subjects with PET for regional cerebral glucose while they viewed either a series of relatively emotionally arousing (negative) films or a matched but much more emotionally neutral set of films. Memory for the films was assessed in an incidental free recall test given 3 weeks later. We found that activity of the right amygdala while viewing a series of emotional films correlated very highly (r = 0.93) with long-term recall of the films but did not relate to recall of the emotionally neutral films.[9]

This basic finding was subsequently confirmed in three studies from two additional laboratories.[10–12] However, unexplained hemispheric asymmetries in the amygdala were evident in each study. We observed that those studies reporting amygdala effects predominantly or exclusively on the right side of the brain involved only male subjects, whereas studies reporting amygdala effects predominantly or exclusively on the left side of the brain involved only female subjects, raising the possibility that subject sex determined, at least in part, the hemispheric lateralization of amygdala function. This conclusion could not, however, be made with confidence on the basis of these studies because they differed along many other dimensions (e.g., type of scanning, type of to-be-remembered material).

15.4 AN ASIDE ON SEX DIFFERENCES IN THE BRAIN

Sex (that is, being male or female) influences brain function to a far greater extent than neuroscience has recognized to date.[13] Increasingly we see demonstrations of pronounced neurobiological differences between males and females outside the traditional domain of reproduction in which they are to be expected. Clear sex differences exist in every brain lobe,[14] even in "cognitive" brain regions such as the neocortex and hippocampus.

Studies employing human brain imaging techniques report functional sex-related differences in brain correlates of emotional processing,[15] facial processing,[16,17] working memory,[18] auditory processing,[19–21] language processing,[22,23] and even in visual cortex responsiveness to specific light wavelengths.[24] Even cellular mechanisms of neuronal death in cell cultures differ, depending on whether the cells were derived from male or female brains.[25] Sex-related differences were also reported in stress hormone responses. For example, Wolf and colleagues recently reported a sex-related difference in the relationship of cortisol to short-term memory.[26] They found a negative correlation between the cortisol response to a stressor and memory in their subjects as a whole (men and women considered together), but this effect resulted from a highly significant correlation in men and no such correlation in women.

Finally, sex appears to affect the emotional consequences of amygdala damage in primates. Indications that female monkeys often displayed heightened aggressive behavior following amygdala damage have been in the literature for some time[27] — findings in direct opposition to typical effects following amygdala damage in males. Kling[28] directly compared the effects of amygdala damage on aggressivity in a group of three female and three male monkeys. He observed that in both his experiment and in the extant literature, "paradoxical" heightened aggressivity after amygdala damage was present only in females. Had potential influences of subject sex been examined starting with the original investigation by Kluver and Bucy,[29] we might now have a very different conceptualization of the behavioral consequences of amygdala damage. Within this context, it is clear that studies examining sex-related influences on the amygdala and its relation to memory acquire heightened importance.

15.5 SEX-RELATED INFLUENCES ON AMYGDALA RELATION TO MEMORY FOR EMOTIONAL EVENTS

Given this context, my colleagues and I examined whether subject sex influenced lateralization of the amygdala relationship to long-term memory for emotional material by directly comparing activities in the brains of men and women within a single study.[30] Healthy adult subjects (11 women, 11 men) were scanned for regional cerebral glucose utilization while watching a series of emotionally arousing film clips and again while watching a series of matched but more emotionally neutral clips. Memory for the films was assessed in a surprise free recall test three weeks later.

The results showed that a large area of right but not left hemisphere amygdala activity was significantly related to enhanced memory for the emotional film clips in men. An identical analysis in women revealed a large area of left and not right hemisphere amygdala activity related to enhanced memory for the emotional films. The general finding of Cahill et al.[30] was confirmed in a separate study of amygdala function employing fMRI.31 Subjects were scanned while viewing a series of emotionally arousing or neutral slides. As reported by Cahill et al.,[30] activity of the right and not left amygdala in males related significantly to memory for the most emotional slides. Conversely, activity of the left and not right amygdala related significantly to memory for the most emotional slides in women. Canli et al.[31] noted that "both correlations were so robust that they were present even with multiple comparisons across the brain and without selecting the amygdala as a region of interest."

The single most compelling demonstration of a sex-related hemispheric lateralization to date comes from an fMRI study by Cahill et al.[32] Like Canli et al.,[31] they used fMRI to examine the relationship of amygdala activity at encoding and subsequent memory for a series of images of varying emotional content. Consistent with the previous studies, activity of the right hemisphere amygdala was significantly more related to subsequent memory for emotional images in men than in women, but activity of the left hemisphere amygdala was significantly more related to subsequent memory for emotional images in women than in men. These findings are shown in Figure 15.2. Crucially, Cahill et al.[32] documented a significant interaction between sex and hemisphere in the amygdala relation to memory for emotional material.

A simple, but very important conclusion emerges from these studies. No matter what this sex-related lateralization of amygdala function in emotional memory ultimately proves to mean for memory of emotional events in men versus women, these results indicate the studies of the amygdala role in memory (at least for humans) risk conclusions that are incomplete at best and wrong at worst if they fail to account for influences of sex and hemisphere.

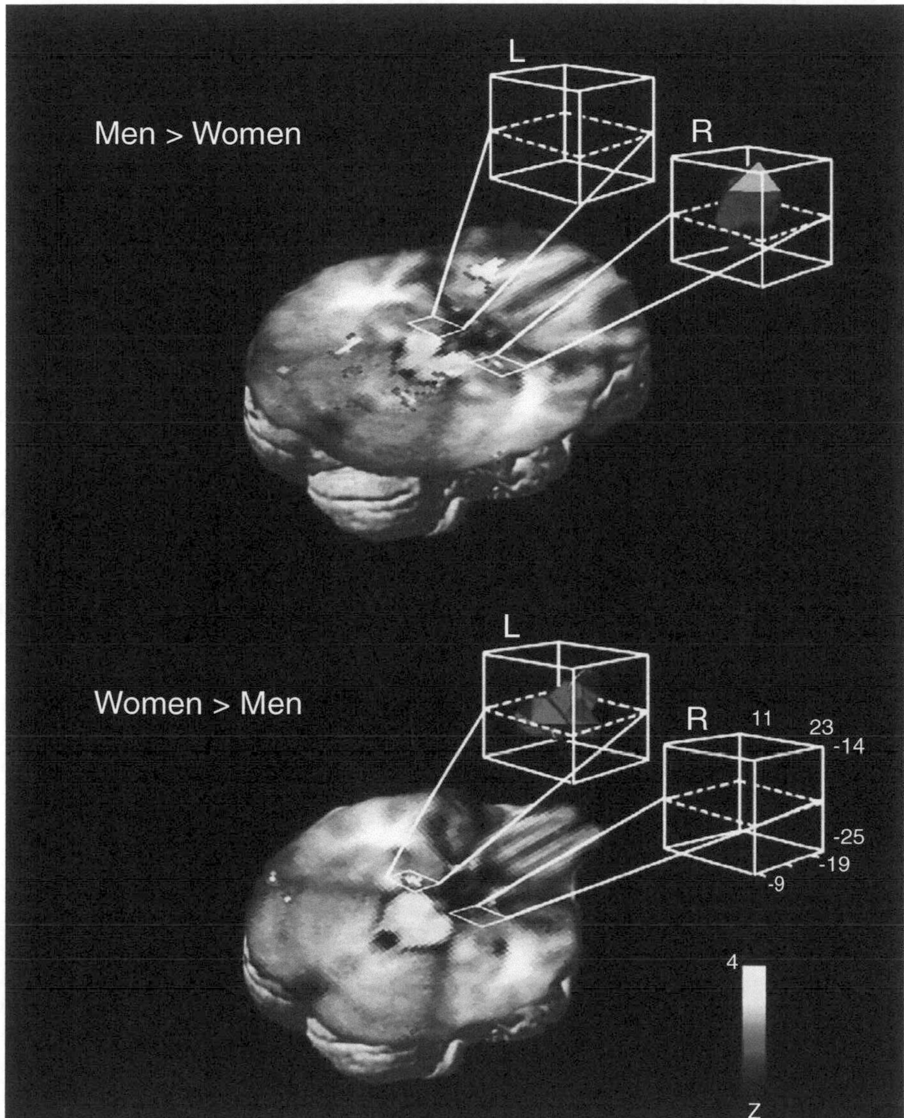

FIGURE 15.2 (See color insert following page 202.) Sex-related hemispheric lateralization of amygdala function in long-term memory for emotionally arousing films. Activity of the right and not left amygdala in males while viewing emotionally arousing films related significantly to memory of the films two weeks later. Activity of the left and not right amygdala in women related significantly to memory of the films. (From Cahill, L. et al., *Learn Mem*, 11, 261, 2004. With permission.)

15.6 SEX DIFFERENCES IN HUMAN AMYGDALA FUNCTIONAL CONNECTIVITY AT REST

We next examined whether the sex-related hemispheric lateralization of amygdala function in its relation to memory for emotional material might result from differential amygdala connectivity at rest in the absence of emotional stimulation. To do so, we examined the patterns of covariance between the left and right hemisphere amygdalae and the rest of the brain in a large sample of men and women (36 of each sex) who received PET scans while simply resting with their eyes closed.[33]

The results revealed far wider patterns of covariance between the right hemisphere amygdala and the rest of the brain in men than in women, but far wider patterns of covariance between the left hemisphere and the rest of the brain in women than in men. The key result is shown in Figure 15.3. Although only one slice through the amygdala in the rostral/caudal plane is shown, the pattern was evident throughout the entire extent of the amygdala. All voxels in the right hemisphere displayed significantly greater correlations with the rest of the brain in men than in women, while all voxels in the left hemisphere displayed significantly greater correlations with the rest of the brain in women than in men.

An additional, and unsuspected, result concerned the regions in which the amygdalae covaried in the two sexes. In men but not women, the amygdala (right side) covaried with several brain regions (such as the caudate nucleus and visual

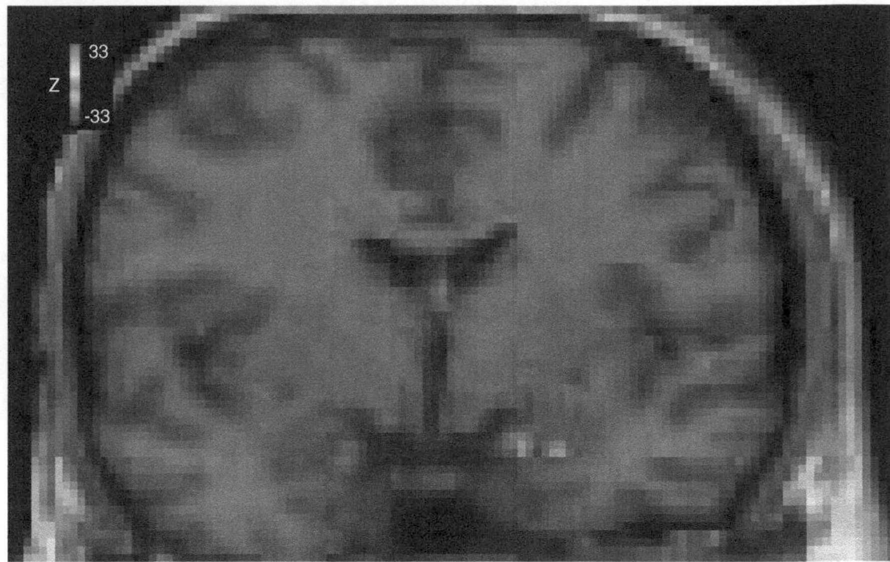

FIGURE 15.3 (See color insert following page 202.) Location of amygdala seed voxels displaying significant sex-related differences in amygdala functional connectivity during resting conditions. Red areas are associated with greater functional connectivity in women than in men. Blue areas are associated with greater functional connectivity in men than in women. (From Kilpatrick, L.A. et al., *Neuroimage*, 30, 452, 2006. With permission.)

cortex) important for interactions with the external environment. In women but not men, the amygdala (left side) covaried with several regions (such as the hypothalamus, insular cortex, and cingulate cortex) strongly associated with sensations from the internal milieu. This result raises the intriguing possibility that prior to any overt stimulation there exists in the amygdala at rest a differential "tilt" of its functions toward the external environment in men and toward the internal environment in women.[33] This possibility would seem to warrant future investigation.

15.7 POTENTIAL RELATIONSHIP OF SEX-RELATED AMYGDALA HEMISPHERIC SPECIALIZATION TO HEMISPHERIC GLOBAL AND LOCAL PROCESSING BIAS

To better understand implications of the sex-related hemispheric lateralization of amygdala function in relation to explicit memory of emotional events, we integrated it with an already well investigated framework of hemispheric functional specialization positing that the cerebral hemispheres possess differential biases in the processing of relatively global, diffuse versus local, precise aspects of a stimulus or scene.

Substantial evidence from studies of both brain damaged and healthy subjects indicates that the right hemisphere is biased toward the processing of more global holistic aspects of a stimulus or scene, while the left hemisphere is biased towards more local, finer detail processing of the same stimulus or scene.[34–40]

Considering the evidence of a gender-related hemispheric asymmetry of amygdala function in memory for emotional material described above (males right, females left) and the evidence of hemispheric biases in processing global versus local information (holistic right, detail left), we created a specific hypothesis about a sex-related difference in the effects of a ß-adrenergic blockade on emotional memory. Combining these two lines of evidence with two additional assumptions, namely that amygdala modulatory influences on brain function are predominantly ipsilateral (because amygdalo-cortical projections are almost exclusively ipsilateral[41,42] and the amygdala's modulatory ability requires ß-adrenergic receptor activation[43]), we predicted that propranolol should impair long-term memory for relatively global (central, gist) aspects of an emotionally arousing story in men, but not memory for relatively local (peripheral detail) aspects of the story. In women, propranolol should produce the opposite effect: impairing memory for peripheral story details but not memory for central story information.

We tested this hypothesis through a re-analysis of published data from two studies demonstrating an impairing effect of ß-adrenergic blockade on memory for an emotionally arousing story.[44] Data from the retention tests from these two studies were pooled to increase statistical power and re-analyzed with respect to (1) whether subjects were male or female and (2) whether the questions pertained to central story information or peripheral story detail. Central information was defined as "any information that cannot be changed or removed without changing the fundamental story line," as determined by consensus of three fourths of independent judges. Figure 15.4 shows the results of this analysis.[44]

Note in particular the results for story phase 2 (P2 on the x-axis) in which the emotional story elements were introduced (concerning severe injuries to a small boy in an accident while his mother watched) and for which the hypothesis at issue most clearly holds. The P2 results reveal a double dissociation of gender and type of to-be-remembered information (central versus peripheral) on propranolol's impairing effect on memory: Propranolol significantly impaired P2 memory of central information in men but not women, yet impaired P2 memory of peripheral detail in women but not men.

These results are consistent with the hypothesis that, under emotionally arousing conditions, activation of right amygdala/hemisphere function produces a relative enhancement of memory for central information in males. Activation of left amygdala/hemisphere function in females produces a relative enhancement of memory for peripheral details in women.

15.8 SOME IMPLICATIONS FOR DISEASE STATES

Sex differences exist in the incidence and/or nature of a host of brain-related disorders such as Alzheimer's disease, schizophrenia, and autism, to name only three.[13] More relevant to the present discussion, sex differences also exist in the incidence of emotion-related disorders such as anxiety disorders, post-traumatic stress disorder (PTSD), and clinical depression.

It is well known that PTSD incidence is approximately twice as high in women compared to men.[45] Despite this fact, basic science investigations of emotion and memory have left the issue of sex-related influences virtually unexplored. Thus at present we have very little insight into why men and women differ in their susceptibility to PTSD; consequently we know virtually nothing about how we might tailor PTSD treatments to optimally benefit women versus men. Investigations of sex-related influences on emotion and memory should be crucial in helping to fill these important gaps.

This research is also relevant to our understanding of clinical depression, another major disorder about twice as likely to occur in women as in men.[46] Interestingly, depression is associated with enhanced activity of the left amygdala in studies predominantly involving women.[47] Thus interesting parallels involving amygdala function already exist between mechanisms of emotionally influenced memory in healthy women and clinical depression. It seems likely that studies of the influences of sex on basic mechanisms of emotion and memory will help elucidate neural mechanisms underlying sex differences in depression incidence and potential treatments for depression. Logically, we cannot fully understand disorders with clear sex differences in their incidence and/or nature without careful attention to the influence of sex in our basic science investigations relevant to the disorders.

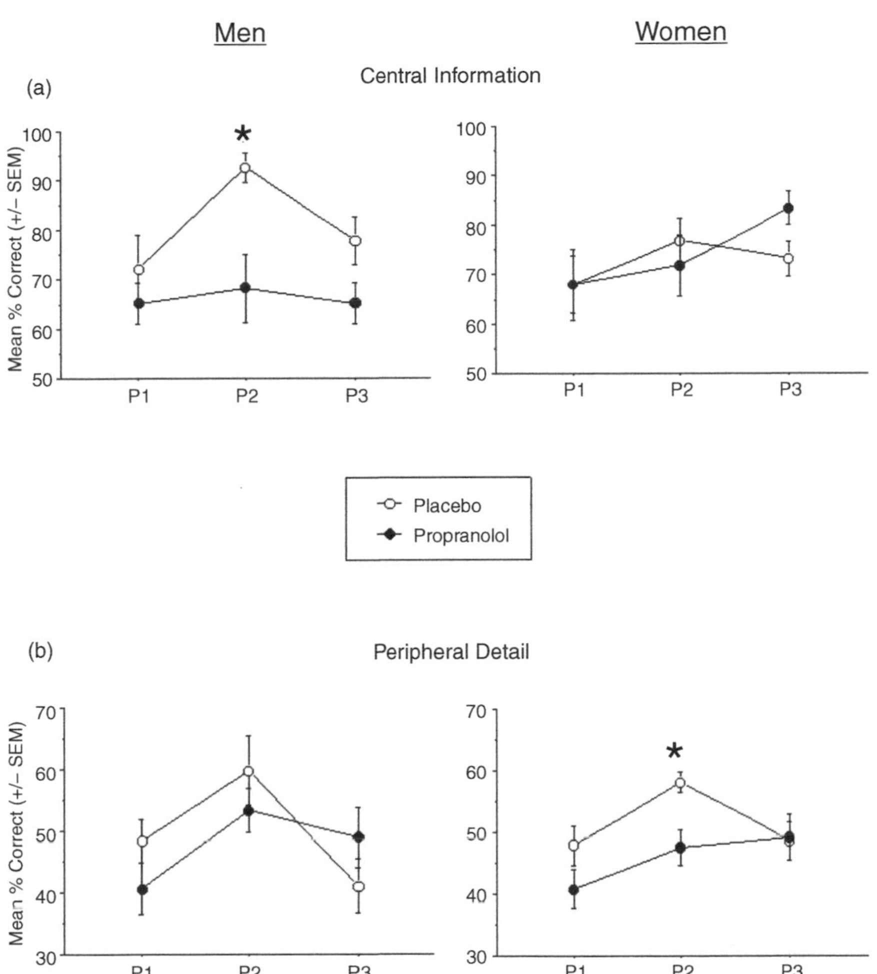

FIGURE 15.4 Recognition test scores for three-phase emotional story. (A) Values for questions defined as pertaining to central information. (B) Values for questions defined as pertaining to peripheral detail. Values represent mean percent correct (± SEM) on recognition test in each experimental group. P1, P2, and P3 indicate story phases 1, 2, 3, respectively. Emotional story elements were introduced in P2. * = $p < 0.01$ placebo compared with corresponding P2 propranolol group (post-hoc, two-tailed, unpaired t-test comparison). (From Cahill, L. and van Stegeren, A., *Neurobiol Learn Mem*, 79, 81, 2003. With permission.)

15.9 SUMMARY

Substantial evidence from animal studies indicates that endogenous stress hormones and the amygdala interact to modulate memory consolidation for emotional events.[2] Evidence from human subject studies has clearly reinforced this view. At the same time, it revealed previously unsuspected influences of subject sex on these memory-modulating mechanisms. This evidence combined with a growing number of indications that sex powerfully influences memory-related brain processes[13] suggests that future studies of the neurobiology of emotional memory must actively account for the influences of sex. In so doing, the field will be better positioned to understand and treat clinical disorders with sex differences in their incidences and nature.

ACKNOWLEDGMENT

This study was supported by National Institute of Mental Health Grant NIMH RO1 57508.

REFERENCES

1. Young, M.P. and Scannell, J.W. Analysis of connectivity: neural systems in the cerebral cortex. *Rev Neurosci*, 5, 227, 1994.
2. McGaugh, J.L. The amygdala modulates the consolidation of memories of emotionally arousing experiences. *Annu Rev Neurosci*, 27, 1, 2004.
3. Alkire, M., Vazdarjanova, A., Dickinson-Anson, H., White, N.S., and Cahill, L. Selective basolateral amygdala lesions block propofol-induced amnesia. *Anesthesiology,* 95, 708, 2001.
4. Cahill, L. and McGaugh, J.L. Amygdaloid complex lesions differentially affect retention of tasks using appetitive and aversive reinforcement. *Behav Neurosci*, 104, 532, 1990.
5. Small, D.M. et al. Dissociation of neural representation of intensity and affective valuation in human gustation. *Neuron*, 39, 701, 2003.
6. Anderson, A.K. et al. Dissociated neural representations of intensity and valence in human olfaction. *Nat Neurosci*, 6, 96, 2003.
7. Kensinger, E.A. and Corkin, S. Two routes to emotional memory: distinct neural processes for valence and arousal. *Proc Natl Acad Sci USA,* 101, 3310, 2004.
8. Lewis, P.A., Critchley, H.D., Rothstein, P., and Dolan, R.J. Neural correlates of processing valence and arousal in affective words. *Cereb Cortex*, May 22, 2006 (Epub preceded print).
9. Cahill, L. et al. Amygdala activity at encoding correlated with long-term, free recall of emotional information. *Proc Natl Acad Sci USA*, 93, 8016, 1996.
10. Canli, T., Desmond, J.E., Zhao, Z., Glover, G., and Gabrieli, J.D. Hemispheric asymmetry for emotional stimuli detected with fMRI. *Neuroreport,* 9, 3233, 1998.
11. Canli, T., Zhao, Z., Brewer, J., Gabrieli, J.D., and Cahill, L. Event-related activation in the human amygdala associates with later memory for individual emotional experience. *J Neurosci*, 20, RC99, 2000.
12. Hamann, S.B., Ely, T.D., Grafton, S.T., and Kilts, C.D. Amygdala activity related to enhanced memory for pleasant and aversive stimuli. *Nat Neurosci,* 2, 289, 2001.

13. Cahill, L. Why sex matters for neuroscience. *Nat Rev Neurosci*, 7, 477, 2006.
14. Goldstein, J.M. et al. Normal sexual dimorphism of the adult human brain assessed by *in vivo* magnetic resonance imaging. *Cereb Cortex*, 11, 490.
15. George, M.S., Ketter, T.A., Parekh, P.I., Herscovitch, P., and Post, R.M. Gender differences in regional cerebral blood flow during transient self-induced sadness or happiness. *Biol Psychiatry*, 40, 859, 1996.
16. Killgore, W.D., Oki, M., and Yurgelun-Todd, D.A. Sex-specific developmental changes in amygdala responses to affective faces. *Neuroreport*, 12, 427, 2001.
17. Killgore, W.D. and Yurgelun-Todd, D.A. Sex differences in amygdala activation during the perception of facial affect. *Neuroreport*, 12, 2543, 2001.
18. Speck, O., Ernst, T., Braun, J., Koch, C., Miller, E., and Chang, L. Gender differences in the functional organization of the brain for working memory. *Neuroreport*, 11, 2581, 2000.
19. Baumann, S.B., Rogers, R.L., Guinto, F.C., Saydjari, C.L., Papanicolaou, A.C., and Eisenberg, H.M. Gender differences in source location for the N100 auditory evoked magnetic field. *Electroencephalogr Clin Neurophysiol*, 80, 53, 1991.
20. Reite, M., Sheeder, J., Teale, P., Richardson, D., Adams, M., and Simon, J. MEG based brain laterality: sex differences in normal adults. *Neuropsychologia*, 33, 1607, 1995.
21. Salmelin, R. et al. Native language, gender, and functional organization of the auditory cortex. *Proc Natl Acad Sci USA*, 96, 10460, 1999.
22. Pugh, K.R. et al. Cerebral organization of component processes in reading. *Brain*, 119, 1221, 1996.
23. Shaywitz, B.A. et al. Sex differences in the functional organization of the brain for language. *Nature*, 373, 607, 1995.
24. Cowan, R.L. et al. Sex differences in response to red and blue light in human primary visual cortex: a bold fMRI study. *Psychiatry Res*, 100, 129, 2000.
25. Li, H. et al. Sex differences in cell death. *Ann Neurol*, 58, 317, 2005.
26. Wolf, O.T., Schommer, N.C., Hellhammer, D.H., McEwen, B.S., and Kirschbaum, C. The relationship between stress induced cortisol levels and memory differs between men and women. *Psychoneuroendocrinology*, 26, 711, 2001.
27. Rosvold, H., Mirsky, A., and Pribram, K. Influence of amygdalectomy on social behavior in monkeys. *J Comp Physiol Psychol*, 47, 173, 1954.
28. Kling, A. Differential effects of amygdalectomy in male and female nonhuman primates. *Arch Sex Behav*, 3, 129, 1974.
29. Kluver, H. and Bucy, P.C. Preliminary analysis of functions of the temporal lobes in monkeys. *J Neuropsychiatr Clin Neuros*ci, 9, 606, 1937.
30. Cahill, L. et al. Sex-related difference in amygdala activity during emotionally influenced memory storage. *Neurobiol Learn Mem*, 75, 1, 2001.
31. Canli, T., Desmond, J.E., Zhao, Z., and Gabrieli, J.D. Sex differences in the neural basis of emotional memories. *Proc Natl Acad Sci USA* , 99, 10789, 2002.
32. Cahill, L. et al. Sex-related hemispheric lateralization of amygdala function in emotionally influenced memory: an fMRI investigation. *Learn Mem*, 11, 261, 2004.
33. Kilpatrick, L.A., Zald, D.H., Pardo, J.V., and Cahill, L.F. Sex-related differences in amygdala functional connectivity during resting conditions. *Neuroimage*, 30, 452, 2006.
34. Beeman, M.J. and Bowden, E.M. The right hemisphere maintains solution-related activation for yet-to-be-solved problems. *Mem Cognit*, 28, 1231, 2000.
35. Delis, D.C., Robertson, L.C., and Efron, R. Hemispheric specialization of memory for visual hierarchical stimuli. *Neuropsychologia*, 24, 205, 1986.

36. Fink, G.R. et al. Where in the brain does visual attention select the forest and the trees? *Nature,* 382, 626, 1996.
37. Fink, G.R. et al. Neural mechanisms involved in the processing of global and local aspects of hierarchically organized visual stimuli. *Brain*, 120, 1779, 1997.
38. Fink, G.R., Marshall, J.C., Halligan, P.W., and Dolan, R.J. Hemispheric asymmetries in global/local processing are modulated by perceptual salience. *Neuropsychologia,* 37, 31, 1999.
39. Ivry, R.B. and Robertson, L.C. *The Two Sides of Perception*, Bradford, London, 1998.
40. Sergent, J. The cerebral balance of power: confrontation or cooperation? *J Exp Psychol Hum Percept Perform*, 8, 253, 1982.
41. Amaral, D.G. and Price, J.L. Amygdalo-cortical projections in the monkey (*Macaca fascicularis*). *J Comp Neurol*, 230, 465, 1984.
42. Porrino, L.J., Crane, A.M., and Goldman-Rakic, P.S. Direct and indirect pathways from the amygdala to the frontal lobe in rhesus monkeys. *J Comp Neurol*, 198, 121, 1981.
43. McGaugh, J.L., Cahill, L., and Roozendaal, B. Involvement of the amygdala in memory storage: interaction with other brain systems. *Proc Natl Acad Sci USA*, 93, 13508, 1996.
44. Cahill, L. and van Stegeren, A. Sex-related impairment of memory for emotional events with ß-adrenergic blockade. *Neurobiol Learn Mem*, 79, 81, 2003.
45. Breslau, N. et al. Sex differences in post-traumatic stress disorder. *Arch Gen Psychiatr*, 54, 1044, 1997.
46. Kendler, K. S., Thornton, L.M., and Prescott, C.A. Gender differences in the rates of exposure to stressful life events and sensitivity to their depressogenic effects. *Am J Psychiatr*, 158, 587, 2001.
47. Drevets, W.C. et al. Glucose metabolism in the amygdala in depression: relationship to diagnostic subtype and plasma cortisol levels. *Pharmacol Biochem Behav,* 71, 431, 2002.

Index

B

F

M

N

Q

R

S

T

U

V

W

X

Y

Z

T - #0363 - 071024 - C4 - 234/156/16 - PB - 9780367389222 - Gloss Lamination